Born *to* Rule

Born *to* Rule

Five Reigning Consorts,
Granddaughters of Queen Victoria

JULIA P. GELARDI

St. Martin's Press
New York

www.stmartins.com

Library of Congress Cataloging-in-Publication Data

Gelardi, P. Julia.
    Born to rule : five reigning consorts, granddaughters of Queen Victoria / Julie P. Gelardi.—1st ed.
        p.   cm.
    Includes bibliographical references (p. 427) and index (p. 441).
    ISBN 0-312-32423-5
    EAN 978-0312-32423-0
        1. Queens—Europe—Biography.   2. Queens—Russia—Biography.
3. Victoria, Queen of Great Britain, 1819–1901—Family.   I. Title.

D352.3.G46   2005
940.2'8'0922—dc22
[B]

                                                                2004057021

First Edition: March 2005

10   9   8   7   6   5   4   3   2   1

For my children, Victoria and Gabriella,
whose patience with their busy mother
and curiosity about this project never abated,
I happily dedicate this book to them both.

CONTENTS

ACKNOWLEDGMENTS

In the course of researching and writing this book, I have been fortunate in receiving help from many individuals. Without them, it would never have come to fruition. I therefore wish to express my debt of gratitude to the following who have helped me through the years.

I acknowledge and thank Her Majesty, Queen Elizabeth II, for granting permission to quote from unpublished material and to reproduce photographs from the Royal Photographic Collection. The collection's curator, Frances Dimond, was cordial and helpful during my visit to Windsor Castle. I also wish to thank the Registrar of the Royal Archives, Pamela Clark, for her assistance.

For inviting me to his home near Geneva where he shared his impressions of his two grandmothers, Queen Marie of Romania and Queen Sophie of Greece, I am deeply indebted to His Majesty, King Michael of Romania. The king and his wife, Queen Anne, were most gracious and accommodating. King Michael's secretary, Constanza Iorga, was unfailing in assisting me as well.

I wish to express my gratitude to H.R.H. Crown Prince Alexander of Yugoslavia for taking the time to discuss his two great-grandmothers, Queen Marie of Romania and Queen Sophie of Greece, during a visit I made to London.

For graciously inviting me to her home in Buckinghamshire to give her reminiscences, I would like to thank Queen Sophie's daughter, Lady Katherine Brandram. Her kindness and generosity in sharing her memories of her mother were invaluable. I also wish to thank Lady Katherine's son, Paul Brandram, for his help.

To the staff of the numerous archives and university libraries, a sincere thank-you. These include in the United Kingdom: the Bodleian Library and Nuffield

College at the University of Oxford; the British Library; the National Archives of Great Britain (formerly the Public Record Office); G. M. C. Bott of the University of Reading; the Hartley Library at the University of Southampton; Cambridge University Library, Department of Manuscripts and University Archives; the Cumbria Record Office; the Public Record Office of Northern Ireland; the Hampshire Record Office; the House of Lords Record Office; and the Isle of Wight Record Office. In the United States: the Hoover Institution at Stanford University and in particular R. Bulatoff; Nancy Birk at Kent State University; Colleen Schaforth and Betty Long of the Maryhill Museum; the New York Public Library and Western Washington University Library. In Canada: Simon Fraser University Library and the University of British Columbia Library.

The following individuals have also kindly helped with my queries: H.R.H. the Duke of Edinburgh, H.R.H. Princess Alexandra, Sir Brian McGrath, and Jean Mazaré. A special thank-you is extended to Hugo Vickers and Marlene Eilers Koenig; also to Ian Shapiro and J. Hanson of Argyll Etkin.

Friends and acquaintances who have shown interest and given help include: Leo de Adrian, Art Beeche, Paul Gilbert, Jan Hill, Dee Ann Hoff, Cedric Jeffery, Greg King, Linda Obermeier, Roy Stephenson, and John Stubbs. Thanks as well to my translators: Dan Manarovici, Mette Drager, and Hans R.W. Goksøyr. To all the many others who have been helpful and supportive, a sincere thank-you.

My agent, Julie Castiglia, of the Castiglia Literary Agency, was encouraging and ever ready to answer my queries and offer sound advice. I greatly appreciate the enthusiasm and support of my editor, Charles Spicer, whose knowledge and expertise were equally matched by his kindness. I am also indebted to Michael Homler and the hardworking staff at St. Martin's Press who steered this book through the process of publication.

Lastly, I wish to thank my family: my parents for their help in a variety of ways and my husband, Alec, for his unwavering support, be it in evaluating the numerous drafts of the text or in accompanying me to half a dozen countries and numerous libraries and archives during my research.

DRAMATIS PERSONAE

Alexandra (1872–1918)—Tsarina of Russia, consort of Nicholas II, Tsar of Russia (1868–1918). Born at Darmstadt on 6 June 1872, she was the sixth child and fourth daughter of Princess Alice of Great Britain and Louis, Grand Duke of Hesse. Christened Alix Victoria Helena Louise Beatrice, upon converting to the Russian Orthodox faith in 1894, Alix took the name of Alexandra Feodorovna. Formal title until marriage: H.G.D.H. Princess Alix of Hesse and By Rhine. Married H.I.M. Tsar Nicholas II of Russia on 14 November 1894 (o.s.) at the Chapel of the Winter Palace in St. Petersburg.

Children:

1. Olga Nikolaevna (1895–1918), Grand Duchess of Russia
2. Tatiana Nikolaevna (1897–1918), Grand Duchess of Russia
3. Marie Nikolaevna (1899–1918), Grand Duchess of Russia
4. Anastasia Nikolaevna (1901–1918), Grand Duchess of Russia
5. Alexei Nikolaevitch (1904–1918), Tsarevitch of Russia

Alexandra was brutally murdered along with her family on the night of 16/17 July 1918 at Ekaterinburg. Eighty years later she was buried at the imperial mausoleum in the Fortress of St. Peter and Paul, St. Petersburg. See *Nicholas II.*

Alfonso XIII (1886–1941)—King of Spain, 1886–1931, third child and only son of King Alfonso XII and his wife, the Archduchess Maria Cristina of Habsburg-Lorraine. As the posthumous son of Alfonso XII, Alfonso XIII was king at birth. Born on 17 May 1886 at Madrid, he married H.R.H. Princess

Victoria Eugenie of Battenberg on 31 May 1906 at the Church of San Jerónimo. Alfonso left Spain without abdicating for a life in exile on 14 April 1931, never to return. He died in Rome on 28 February 1941 and is buried at El Escorial in Spain. His grandson, Juan Carlos I, is the present King of Spain. See *Victoria Eugenie.*

Constantine I (1868–1923)—King of the Hellenes (or of Greece), 1913–17 and again 1920–22. Constantine was born on 2 August 1868 in Athens. He was the eldest son of King George I of the Hellenes and the Grand Duchess Olga Constantinovna of Russia. On 27 October 1889, in Athens, he married H.R.H. Princess Sophie of Prussia, daughter of the Emperor Frederick III and Victoria (referred to after her widowhood as the Empress Frederick). Constantine succeeded his assassinated father as king on 6 March 1913. Forced to flee into exile on 11 June 1917, Constantine's second son, Alexander, became king in his absence. Constantine was recalled to the throne by a plebiscite in 1920. However, a military revolt forced him to flee for a second time in 1922. He was then succeeded by his eldest son, George II. Constantine died on 11 January 1923 at Palermo, Sicily. See *Sophie.*

Ferdinand I (1865–1927)—King of Romania, 1914–27. The second son of Prince Leopold of Hohenzollern-Sigmaringen and the Infanta Antonia of Portugal, Ferdinand was born on 24 August 1865 at Sigmaringen, Prussia. In 1889 Ferdinand was adopted by his childless uncle King Carol I of Romania and designated crown prince and heir presumptive. Ferdinand married H.R.H. Princess Marie of Edinburgh on 10 January 1892 at Sigmaringen. He became king 11 October 1914 and died 20 July 1927 at Sinaia. Ferdinand was succeeded by his grandson, the five-year-old Michael I. See *Marie.*

Haakon VII (1872–1957)—first King of Norway, 1905–57. Born on 3 August 1872 at Charlottenlund, Denmark, H.R.H. Prince Christian Frederik Carl Georg Valdemar Axel was the second son of Frederick VIII of Denmark and his consort, Louise of Sweden-Norway. Known until his accession as Prince Charles of Denmark, he married H.R.H. Princess Maud of Wales on 22 July 1896. Haakon died on 21 September 1957 at Oslo, where he is buried. See *Maud.*

Marie (1875–1938)—Queen Consort, 1914–27, of King Ferdinand I of Romania. Born at Eastwell Park, Kent, on 29 October 1875 and christened Marie Alexandra Victoria (she was also known as "Missy"), Marie was the eldest daughter and second child of Alfred, Duke of Edinburgh, and Grand Duchess

Marie of Russia. She married H.R.H. Crown Prince Ferdinand of Romania on 10 January 1892 at Castle Sigmaringen in Germany.
Children:

1. Carol II (1893–1953), King of Romania (1930–40); married [1] Joana Marie Valentina Lambrino (1898–1953), annulled in 1919; and [2] Princess Helen of Greece (1896–1982)

2. Elisabeth (1894–1956), Queen Consort of King George II of Greece (1890–1947)

3. Marie (1900–61), Queen Consort of King Alexander I of Yugoslavia (1888–1934)

4. Nicolas (1903–78), Prince of Romania; married [1] Joana Doletti (1902–63); and [2] Thereza de Mello (1913–70)

5. Ileana (1909–91), Princess of Romania; married [1] Archduke Anton of Austria-Tuscany (1901–87), divorced 1954; and [2] Stephen Issarescu (1906–2002), divorced 1965; Ileana took religious vows and became Mother Alexandra of the Monastery of the Transfiguration in Pennsylvania

6. Mircea (1913–16), Prince of Romania

Marie died on 18 July 1938 at Peles Castle, Sinaia, and is buried at Curtea de Arges; her heart was for a time interred at Balcic. See *Ferdinand I.*

Maud (1869–1938)—Queen Consort, 1905–38, of King Haakon VII of Norway. Born at Marlborough House, London, on 26 November 1869 and christened Maud Charlotte Mary Victoria, Maud was the youngest daughter and last surviving child of Edward VII of Great Britain and Alexandra of Denmark. She married H.R.H. Prince Charles of Denmark (later King Haakon VII of Norway) on 22 July 1896 at the Chapel Royal, Buckingham Palace.
Children:
Olav V (1903–91), King of Norway (1957–91), born Prince Alexander Edward Christian Frederick of Denmark.

Maud died at London on 20 November 1938 and is buried in Norway. See *Haakon VII.*

Nicholas II (1868–1918)—Tsar of Russia, 1894–1918. Nicholas Alexandrovitch was born on 6 May 1868 (o.s.) at Tsarskoe Selo. Nicholas was the eldest son of the Tsarevitch Alexander (Tsar Alexander III from 1881) and Maria Feodorovna, the former Princess Dagmar of Denmark. He succeeded his father as tsar on 20 October 1894 (o.s.). On 14 November 1894 (o.s.) he married Princess Alix of Hesse-Darmstadt at St. Petersburg. See *Alexandra.*

Sophie (1870–1932)—Queen Consort of Constantine I of the Hellenes, 1913–17, and again in 1920–22. Born at the Neues Palais, Potsdam, on 14 June 1870 to Victoria, Princess Royal of Great Britain and Crown Prince Frederick (later Emperor Frederick III of Germany), she was christened Sophia Dorothea Ulrica Alice. On 27 October 1889, she married Crown Prince Constantine of Greece at the Metropolitan Cathedral, Athens.

Children:

1. George II (1890–1947), King of the Hellenes (1922–24; 1935–47); married Elisabeth of Romania (1894–1956)

2. Alexander I (1893–1920), King of the Hellenes (1917–20); married Aspasia Manos (1896–1972)

3. Helen (1896–1982), Crown Princess and later Queen Mother of Romania; married Crown Prince Carol of Romania (1893–1953), later King Carol II; divorced 1928

4. Paul I (1901–64), King of the Hellenes (1947–64); married Frederike of Hanover (1917–81)

5. Irene (1904–74), Duchess of Aosta; married Aimone, Duke of Aosta (1900–48)

6. Katherine (1913–); married Richard Brandram (1911–94)

Sophie died on 13 January 1932 at Frankfurt-am-Main, Germany, and is buried at Tatoi in Greece. See *Constantine I.*

Victoria Eugenie (1887–1969)—Queen Consort, 1906–31, of King Alfonso XIII of Spain. Born at Balmoral, Scotland, on 24 October 1887, the second child and only daughter of Princess Beatrice of Great Britain and Prince Henry of Battenberg. Christened Victoria Eugenie Julia Ena, she was known as Ena. Princess Victoria Eugenie was created a royal highness by King Edward VII before her mariage. She married King Alfonso XIII of Spain on 31 May 1906 at the Church of San Jerónimo in Madrid.

Children:

1. Alfonso, Prince of the Asturias (1907–38); married [1] Edelmira Sampedro (1906–94), divorced 1938; and [2] Marta Rocafort (1913–93)

2. Jaime, Duke of Segovia (1908–75); married Emanuela de Dampierre (1913–)

3. Beatriz, Princess of Civitella-Cesi (1909–2002); married Alessandro Torlonia, Prince of Civitella-Cesi (1911–86)

4. Maria Cristina, Countess Marone (1911–96); married Enrico Cinzano, Count Marone (1895–1968)

5. Juan, Count of Barcelona (1913–93); married Maria de las Mercedes of Bourbon Two-Sicilies (1910–2000)

6. Gonzalo, Infante of Spain (1914–34)

Queen Victoria Eugenie died on 15 April 1969 at Lausanne, Switzerland. She is buried at El Escorial in Spain. See *Alfonso XIII*.

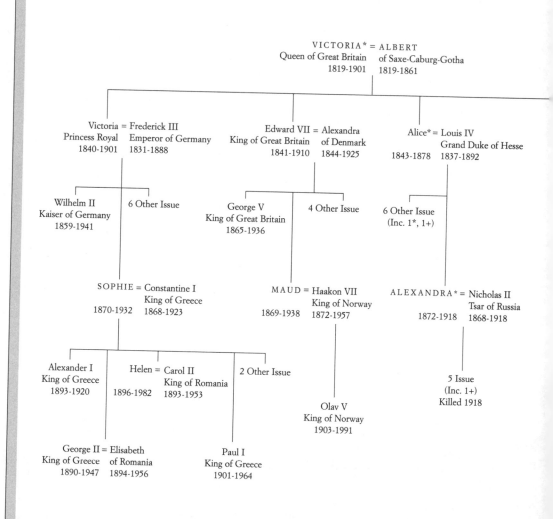

VICTORIA* = ALBERT
Queen of Great Britain   of Saxe-Caburg-Gotha
1819-1901   1819-1861

Victoria = Frederick III
Princess Royal   Emperor of Germany
1840-1901   1831-1888

Edward VII = Alexandra
King of Great Britain   of Denmark
1841-1910   1844-1925

Alice* = Louis IV
Grand Duke of Hesse
1843-1878   1837-1892

Wilhelm II
Kaiser of Germany
1859-1941

6 Other Issue

George V
King of Great Britain
1865-1936

4 Other Issue

6 Other Issue
(Inc. 1*, 1+)

SOPHIE = Constantine I
King of Greece
1870-1932   1868-1923

MAUD = Haakon VII
King of Norway
1869-1938   1872-1957

ALEXANDRA* = Nicholas II
Tsar of Russia
1872-1918   1868-1918

Alexander I
King of Greece
1893-1920

Helen = Carol II
King of Romania
1896-1982   1893-1953

2 Other Issue

5 Issue
(Inc. 1+)
Killed 1918

Olav V
King of Norway
1903-1991

George II = Elisabeth
King of Greece   of Romania
1890-1947   1894-1956

Paul I
King of Greece
1901-1964

SIMPLIFIED GENEALOGICAL TABLE

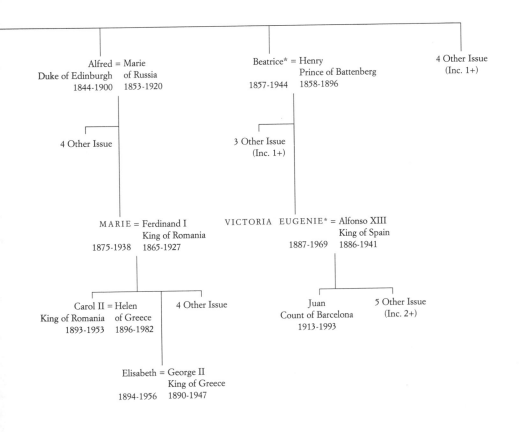

Alfred = Marie
Duke of Edinburgh of Russia
1844-1900 1853-1920

Beatrice* = Henry
Prince of Battenberg
1857-1944 1858-1896

4 Other Issue
(Inc. 1+)

4 Other Issue

3 Other Issue
(Inc. 1+)

MARIE = Ferdinand I
King of Romania
1875-1938 1865-1927

VICTORIA EUGENIE* = Alfonso XIII
King of Spain
1887-1969 1886-1941

Carol II = Helen
King of Romania of Greece
1893-1953 1896-1982

4 Other Issue

Juan
Count of Barcelona
1913-1993

5 Other Issue
(Inc. 2+)

Elisabeth = George II
King of Greece
1894-1956 1890-1947

HEMOPHILIA: * = Carrier, + = Sufferer

INTRODUCTION

ON 31 MAY 1906, MADRID WAS IN A FESTIVE MOOD. IT WAS THE wedding day of the King of Spain, Alfonso XIII. His bride was the beautiful eighteen-year-old Princess Victoria Eugenie of Battenberg ("Ena"), a favorite granddaughter of England's Queen Victoria. Ena could not know that on the day she became Alfonso's wife and Queen of Spain, her life would nearly end in spectacular fashion.

Within an hour after the brilliant religious ceremony, as the couple rode in the royal carriage to their reception, someone threw a powerful bomb at them. Pandemonium broke out. Numerous spectators were killed or seriously injured. After regaining her composure, Ena noticed that her white gown was spattered with blood. At first she thought she and Alfonso had been hurt. The blood on her wedding gown, however, was not hers or Alfonso's but that of a guardsman who was riding close to the carriage. The man was decapitated the instant the bomb exploded. His blood had spilled into the royal carriage, soaking Ena's magnificent satin wedding gown. In place of anticipated joy, those first few hours as the new Queen of Spain were for Ena moments of unimaginable terror. Without a doubt, it was the most dramatic wedding day for any of Queen Victoria's granddaughters.

Queen Ena was the last of a unique group of Victoria's descendants to marry. They consisted of five royal cousins who were all granddaughters of the queen. But what sets them apart from the queen's seventeen other granddaughters is the illustrious destiny each of these five cousins came to share—for all five became consorts of reigning European monarchs. The royal cousins who are the subject of this book are Queen Maud of Norway (1869–1938); Queen Sophie of

Greece (1870–1932); Tsarina Alexandra of Russia (1872–1918) ("Alix"); Queen Marie of Romania (1875–1938) ("Missy"); and Queen Victoria Eugenie of Spain (1887–1969) ("Ena"). Some remarkable stories will unfold as we follow their lives from childhoods often spent with their grandmother at her homes in Windsor, Osborne, and Balmoral to married life in the courts of Christiania, Athens, St. Petersburg, Bucharest, and Madrid.

Though these five women shared the same destiny in that all became consorts of a reigning monarch, each was to experience a vastly differing life. Happiness and sadness, triumphs and tragedies of great magnitude awaited them in faraway lands. Born in the Victorian era, these royal women came to experience such tumultuous political events as World War I and the Russian Revolution. Three would come to relish their popularity, whereas two came to be reviled. And although three of the royal cousins would be spared the trauma of living with the dreaded bleeding disease hemophilia, inherited from Queen Victoria, two would not.

This is the absorbing true story of five women who coped as best they could in their adopted countries and who were, above all, profoundly shaped by their ties to England and the strong influence exerted by their formidable grandmother, Queen Victoria.

Two of the royal cousins were descended from Victoria's sons. Maud of Norway was the daughter of King Edward VII and Queen Alexandra. Marie of Romania was the daughter of Victoria's second son, Alfred, Duke of Edinburgh, and his wife, the Grand Duchess Marie of Russia. The other three cousins were descended from Queen Victoria's eldest, second eldest, and youngest daughters: Victoria, Alice, and Beatrice. Sophie of Greece was the daughter of Victoria, the Princess Royal, and her husband, Emperor Frederick III of Germany; Alexandra of Russia was the daughter of Alice and her husband, Louis, Grand Duke of Hesse-Darmstadt; Princess Beatrice and Prince Henry of Battenberg were the parents of Victoria Eugenie of Spain.

Each of these cousins would come to occupy the thrones of countries in the four corners of Europe—in the Northwest (Norway), in the Northeast (Russia), in the Southeast (Greece and Romania), and in the Southwest (Spain). The countries and courts into which these princesses married were as varied as the women themselves. Romania, for instance, was created in 1878, while Norway became independent from Sweden in 1905. Both nations—and Greece for that matter, which was declared independent in 1830—were relatively young in comparison to Russia and Spain.

The one person who links these women, Queen Victoria, was a beloved grandmother to all of the royal cousins. Not only had their grandmother's dictums become almost law to them; Grandmama's prestige as the reigning monarch of a respected kingdom and burgeoning empire ensured that they would, as they matured into beautiful young women, become desirable commodities in the royal marriage market. Without a doubt, their descent from Queen Victoria was an important consideration when it came time to choosing these women as royal brides. As we shall see, Cupid's arrow also played its part in uniting them with their respective husbands.

This book is the first to focus on these five royal cousins as a group. It builds upon the work of previous biographers and historians who, for the most part, have done an admirable job of bringing to life the descendants of Queen Victoria. It is not an exhaustive biography, nor could it be—such an undertaking would have amounted to five volumes. Rather, this book is a portrait of the women as they relate to their grandmother, and to one another. It takes the reader into the lives of a very special group.

For the most part, this is a chronicle of the personal lives of Maud, Sophie, Alexandra, Marie, and Victoria Eugenie. But those lives were very much entwined with the politics of their countries. No work could be complete without some details about the political maelstrom that was as much a part of these women's lives as their own personal triumphs and tragedies. Furthermore, since the main factor that binds these women together is their grandmother, one of modern history's most famous figures, Queen Victoria, it naturally follows that their relationship with the queen, and her influence on how they lived their lives and faced the challenges that came their way, is relevant.

The stories of these granddaughters of Queen Victoria whose shared destinies as reigning consorts were to end so differently make for compelling reading. All were born into a world of privilege, luxury, and power, yet some would come to know destitution, loneliness, and exile. Their lives, covering the one hundred years from Maud's birth in 1869 to Victoria Eugenie's death in 1969, have encompassed many important historical events. Several, including Alexandra of Russia, were pivotal players in their country's histories.

In the following pages, we find the fascinating stories of five very special royal women, who took their sadness, betrayals, and defeats in the spirit of Queen Victoria's motto, "Still endure."[1] In so doing, their tales of redemption and inspiration highlight the special legacy of their grandmother.

Queen Marie of Romania once wrote of "the sadness we Princesses endure in having to marry into foreign countries."[2] Readers are invited to enter the world of these five princesses and see for themselves what Marie of Romania might have meant by those intriguing words.

PART ONE

Sovereigns in the Making:

THE FORMATIVE YEARS (1869–1901)

One

MORE MOTHER THAN
GRANDMOTHER

THE STORY OF QUEEN VICTORIA'S FIVE SPECIAL GRANDDAUGHTERS begins with the birth of the eldest of the group, the future Queen Maud of Norway. As the third daughter and youngest surviving child of Edward, Prince of Wales, and his wife, Alexandra of Denmark, Maud was not expected to occupy the same vaulted position as her eldest brother, Albert Victor ("Eddy"). But like her other brother, George, Maud came to occupy a throne unexpectedly, becoming in 1905 the first Queen Consort of a newly independent Norway. Maude was born on 26 November 1869 in Marlborough House, her parents' palatial London home; her siblings included Eddy (b. 1864), George (b. 1865), Louise (b. 1867), and Victoria ("Toria," b. 1868).

When Maud was christened (Maud Charlotte Mary Victoria) in the inner hall of Marlborough House, her aunt and godmother, Vicky (the Crown Princess of Prussia), was not in attendance as she was already *enceinte* with her seventh child. A little more than six months after Maud's birth, on 14 June 1870, Vicky presented her mother, Queen Victoria, with another grandchild, Princess Sophie Dorothea Ulrike Alice of Prussia. Vicky gave birth amidst the marble splendor of the Neues Palais, her Potsdam home. The newborn Sophie was to bring much joy to the her parents, Crown Prince Frederick of Germany ("Fritz") and his wife, Victoria, the Princess Royal. At the age of seventeen, the highly intelligent and forthright Vicky had married Fritz and made a new life for herself in the vapid and antagonistic Berlin court. Surrounded by suspicious and reactionary relations of the ruling House of Hohenzollern, the liberal-leaning Fritz and Vicky sought valiantly to raise their children in a loving atmosphere.

At Sophie's christening in July 1870, Prussia had just declared war against

France in what became known as the Franco-Prussian War of 1870–71, a conflict that had great ramifications for Prussian and German history. Most of the men present at Sophie's christening were dressed in their uniforms, prepared to go to the front, including Fritz. Describing the occasion to her mother, Vicky noted that "the Christening went off well, but was sad and serious; anxious faces and tearful eyes, and a gloom and foreshadowing of all the misery in store spread a cloud over the ceremony, which should have been one of gladness and thanksgiving."[1] Among those present was the chancellor, Otto von Bismarck, largely responsible for the upcoming conflict with France, who was dressed as a major of the dragoons.

The crown prince returned home from war in 1871 after Paris had surrendered to the victorious Germans. As Bismarck predicted, the South German states united with the North German confederation, led by Prussia. Bismarck's dream of a Prussian-dominated Germany was born. To cement this major accomplishment, Bismarck engineered an impressive ceremony to take place at Versailles, the former palace of France's Louis XIV. There, amid a sea of military uniforms resplendent with shining medals, Princess Sophie's paternal grandfather, King Wilhelm I of Prussia, was solemnly proclaimed Kaiser Wilhelm I of Germany in the Hall of Mirrors. The House of Hohenzollern became the preeminent power of continental Europe.

The English environment in which the young Princess Maud of Wales thrived was far less constricting and certainly far less militaristic than the one in which her cousin, Sophie, was immersed. Nevertheless, all was not bliss in the Wales household. The marriage of Maud's parents was far from ideal. For all her famed beauty and feminine charms, Princess Alexandra found herself unable to compete for her husband's undivided attention. The Princess of Wales had to tolerate an unending string of mistresses who streamed in and out of her husband's bedroom. But while she endured the pain of her husband's constant infidelities in private, there were never any acrimonious fits of jealous outrage from Alexandra in public, for she knew that duty came above all else. Decorum must be maintained.

Princess Alexandra was not without her faults. In order to compensate for her unhappy marriage, she lavished affection on her offspring, prompting the Prince of Wales to admit to Queen Victoria that his wife's "whole life is wrapt up in her children."[2] The Princess of Wales, in turn, expected her children to reciprocate her love unequivocally. "Motherdear," as she was affectionately called by them throughout their lives, saw to it that her own children were raised to be as dependent on her as possible. And to enforce this dependency, Alexandra

treated all of them as if they had never left the nursery. The princess also encouraged her daughters' insularity. Outside of an intimate circle of friends and
family, no one knew how fun-loving and unpretentious the Wales girls could be.
At seventeen, for instance, Maud wrote to a childhood friend in a distinctly ju-
venile, jocular, and self-deprecating tone: "my darling little Evie, how dare you
call me 'dear Madam' you nasty little monkey . . . I am sending you a horrible
little photograph of myself which I thought you might like. Ever your loving little friend, Maud."[3]

For Maud, growing up with her brothers and sisters in the 1870s meant fun,
interspersed with schoolwork, amidst a variety of homes. In London, home was
a massive redbrick pile, Marlborough House. Located near Buckingham Palace,
Marlborough House proved a suitable setting for a future queen. Whenever
Princess Maud and her parents were in residence there, no less than eighty-five
servants attended them; in addition, at the stables, which held forty-five stalls,
some forty individuals worked full-time maintaining the horses and paddocks.

In the autumn, the family went off to their well-loved Norfolk estate at Sandringham. Of all her homes, Sandringham was to hold a special place in Maud's
heart. Like her brother George, Maud would come to love Sandringham and
the surrounding flat landscape which the children knew so well. They also enjoyed playing with the many animals that roamed the grounds, including an ele-
phant, a bear, and a favorite miniature Indian pony.

⬦

Since her marriage in 1862 to Prince Louis of Hesse, Princess Alice (Queen Victoria's second eldest daughter) had given birth to a succession of children: Victoria in 1863, Elizabeth ("Ella") in 1864, Irene (1866), Ernst ("Ernie," 1868),
and Friedrich ("Frittie," 1870). On 6 June 1872, another girl—Victoria Alix Helena Louise Beatrice—was born, named after all of Queen Victoria's daughters.
But this princess would always be Alix. So cheerful was young Alix's disposition
that she was known too as "Sunny" and "Alicky."

Alicky's home centered on the cobblestoned medieval city of Darmstadt, its
buildings decorated with elaborate wood carvings. There, the Hesse family had
possession of the New Palace, where Alice ensured that they were surrounded
by reminders of England. Alice was very proud to have inserted touches of her
native land; she boasted to Queen Victoria that "the decoration and domestic
arrangements were so English that it was hard to realise one was in Germany."[4]

Alix's childhood was not too dissimilar from that of her cousins Maud of
Wales and Sophie of Prussia; all three enjoyed playing outdoors, amusing themselves with a menagerie of animals. Alix's congenial childhood did not last long,

however, for in 1873 tragedy intruded. While playing with his brother, Ernie, two-and-a-half-year-old Frittie fell out of a second-story window. Frittie, who suffered from hemophilia passed on to him by his mother, died soon afterwards. This bitter loss resigned Alice to the fact that "all is in God's hands, not in ours."[5] Hemophilia, the painful bleeding disease that strikes males but is passed to them by their mothers, was marked by its high mortality rate. The defective gene made its appearance in Queen Victoria, who passed on the disease to her son, Leopold, who died in his early thirties in 1884. Victoria also passed the deadly gene to two of her daughters, who became carriers.

When Maud of Wales was almost six, Sophie of Prussia five, and Alix of Hesse three, another child joined the rarefied circle of Queen Victoria's granddaughters. This time, a beautiful baby girl had been born on 29 October 1875 to Victoria's second eldest son, Alfred, Duke of Edinburgh, and his wife, the formidable Grand Duchess Marie Alexandrovna, daughter of Tsar Alexander II of Russia. The baby, born at her parents' home, Eastwell Manor in Kent, was given the names Marie Alexandra Victoria. But this fair-haired baby would be known to her intimates all her life as "Missy," while to the rest of the world she would come to gain fame as Queen Marie of Romania.

Upon arriving at Queen Victoria's court in 1874, after her marriage, Marie Alexandrovna found to her horror that as Duchess of Edinburgh, she ranked low in precedence among the immediate family. Because of her husband's position as the second son in the British royal family, Marie had to give way to other more senior members. The duchess despised what she perceived to be a humiliating position. Proud of being the powerful Tsar of Russia's daughter, Marie never forgave the British court, and in time this perceived snub developed into a lifelong antipathy toward all things English. Her own marriage to Prince Alfred degenerated into an unhappy union, and the Duchess of Edinburgh soon yearned to flee from England. Because she refused to hide her true feelings, Marie gained a reputation for being haughty and difficult. But Marie, a strong and forceful character, did not care what anyone thought, including her mother-in-law.

Curiously, though the Edinburgh marriage turned sour, it nevertheless produced a healthy number of children. Besides Missy, there were four others: Alfred (b. 1874) and the Princesses Victoria Melita ("Ducky," 1876), Alexandra ("Sandra," 1878), and Beatrice ("Bea," 1884).

Missy's arrival did not cause much discomfort for the duchess. Her husband told a family friend, two weeks after the happy event, that "The confinement itself was of the shortest possible duration barely over an hour in all, although warnings about three hours before. The baby was born in the most natural and easy manner without any sort of assistance and nobody was with Marie but Mrs. Johnson and myself; we had not even time to call the Doctor from the other room. Dr. Farre did not arrive from London till half an hour after it was over." As for Missy, the proud father added that his new daughter "promises to be as fine a child as her brother and gives every evidence of finely developed lungs and did so before she was fairly in the world."[6]

The Duchess of Edinburgh also described Missy's birth. "Everything has happily ended," she reported to her former governess. Writing in French, the proud mother continued: *"La gentille petite j'ai produit, avec de grands yeux et un grand nez, et une petite bouche, et beaucoup de cheveux et un appetit monstre. En un mot, je suis très fière de ma production et une fille, après tout et surtout après toutes ces predictions!"* And she added, in a tender tone, *"la petite faisant un concert épouvantable et messant ses dix doigts dans la bouches, car elle avait déja faim. J'étais stupefaite et ne voulais pas croir à mes oreilles!"* [7]

When Princess Alix of Hesse was five, her paternal grandfather died, making her parents the new reigning Grand Duke and Grand Duchess of Hesse. This thrust Alix's mother into the much more visible position of first lady of the land. Even though she derived some satisfaction from implementing improvements in the health and welfare of her subjects, Princess Alice did not really enjoy the role of *Landsmutter*. Like Vicky, her sister in Berlin, who always pined for England, Alice never could feel completely at home in Darmstadt—a place she found to be dotted with "narrow-minded . . . intolerant interfering people."[8]

Though comfortably off, the grand ducal family was never extravagantly wealthy, and economizing was high on the agenda. The children's holidays inevitably took them annually to their grandmother in England. In time, Victoria's homes became familiar places for Alix. The princess grew up moving between the sweet-smelling roses and sea breezes of Osborne House on the Isle of Wight, the thick walls and towers of Windsor Castle, and the heather-clad hills and gray baronial castle of Balmoral in Scotland.

These visits gave Alix the chance to get to know her English cousins. She became fast friends with the Wales family, including Maud. "Do you like little Alix?" Maud wrote to her cousin, Tsarevitch Nicholas, in 1884 about her friend and relative from Hesse who was then visiting Russia. "She is my best friend, we always go for walks together when we meet. They say I am very much like her, but I do not think I am like her at all."[9]

Presiding over the everyday rearing of Alix, who grew up on a staple of rice puddings and baked apples, was the inevitable English governess. Princess Alice brought other English traditions to Darmstadt, such as the consumption of mince pies and plum puddings at Christmas. Sadly, the family was rent asunder in November 1878 when a virulent strain of diphtheria struck. Nearly everyone in the family, including Alicky, came down with the illness, which killed Alix's three-year-old sister, May. When Alice broke the news of his sister's death to Ernie, she was so overcome by his grief that contrary to doctor's orders, she clasped the little boy in her arms as any loving mother would be moved to do. It was literally a fatal move. Within a fortnight, Princess Alice was dead.

The deaths in quick succession of her youngest sister and mother shattered Alix. The distraught girl could not even take comfort from her favorite toys: to prevent the disease from spreading, they were burnt. In one fell swoop, everything that had been familiar and comforting to the six-year-old Alix was suddenly and permanently wrenched from her. Alicky withdrew into herself—setting a pattern that would mark her propensity to withdraw and brood. From then on she was always cautious with her affections. Alicky would find comfort solely among a small and select group of family members and friends; only then would she show any semblance of that once cheerful girl who had earned the nickname "Sunny."

In England, Princess Maud and her siblings thrived. Their parents sparkled as the leaders of society, while the children settled into a routine, receiving an adequate but unspectacular education at home. Thanks to Princess Alexandra's influence, paramount in the Wales household was a strong sense of merriment, which suited the boisterous Maud. Her fearlessness earned the tomboyish Maud the nickname "Harry," after her father's friend, Admiral Sir Henry Keppel.

Visitors to Sandringham were startled to find the Wales brood on the warpath, sliding on tea trays downstairs and ringing bells to call the servants needlessly. Invited to a formal dinner at their Norfolk home, Benjamin Disraeli was surprised to feel one of the princesses pinching his legs under the table. These shenanigans were sedate when compared to the time when astonished visitors were greeted by ponies inside Sandringham. It was a prank very much to Princess Alexandra's liking. After all, "I was just as bad myself," exclaimed their amused and indulgent mother.[10]

To the queen, Maud and her siblings seemed too unruly. A much more disciplined atmosphere reigned for the Wales children when it came time to visit their grandmother; in fact, Maud once refused to visit Queen Victoria. Princess Alexandra related how just before her daughters were due to set off for Balmoral, "they all cried floods." "Little Harry," noted Alexandra, "declared at the last minute 'I won't go,' with a stamp of her foot."[11]

Maud's fearlessness among her young relations and her tomboyish ways did not abate as she grew older. Though sickly, the sports-mad princess delighted in riding horses every day, and cycling became another favorite sport. When she insisted on riding out in public—the first British princess to be seen doing so—Queen Victoria was unamused. The queen reprimanded her granddaughter for such a daring move. Maud replied simply, "But grandmother, everyone knows that I have legs!"[12]

Maud's intransigence was never allowed to get the better of her. For despite their unruliness, Princess Alexandra had also instilled good qualities into her children, as Queen Victoria acknowledged and praised, saying there is "one thing, however she [Alexandra] does insist on, and that is great simplicity and an absence of all pride, and in that respect she has my fullest support."[13]

As a child and young woman, Maud regularly visited her mother's native Denmark and so became close friends with her first cousins, the Tsarevitch Nicholas and his younger brother, Grand Duke George, sons of Alexandra's sister, Empress Marie of Russia. As teenagers, Nicholas and George corresponded with Maud. She addressed Nicholas as "Mr. Toad" or "Darling little Nicky" (often underlining the "little").[14] George took on the more lyrical nickname of "Musie," while Maud often signed off as "Stumpy."

During her teenage years, Princess Maud did not hold her Danish relations in high esteem, fun-loving though they were. She especially thought her first cousin, Prince Charles of Denmark, immature. When he went off to sea in 1886, seventeen-year-old Maud was convinced this would do the fourteen-year-old prince much good. Writing to "my little darling Musie," Maud did not mince words about Charles: "I am sure it will be good for him since he used to be so daft."[15]

⁂

It was much to the Crown Prince and Princess of Prussia's credit that their daughter, Sophie, had a contented childhood. Her paternal grandparents, Emperor Wilhelm I and Empress Augusta, who were always at loggerheads with each other, largely ignored Sophie and her sisters, Viktoria ("Moretta," b. 1866) and Margrete ("Mossy," b. 1872). The emperor and empress were interested only in Sophie's older siblings—Wilhelm ("Willy," b. 1859), Charlotte ("Charly," b. 1860), and Henry (b. 1862).

Almost from the moment she set foot in Germany as a teenage bride, Vicky saw how gossip, intrigue, and perpetual family rows were the norm at the Berlin court. Sophie's paternal grandparents were particularly notorious for their bitter and loud rows. These unremitting squabbles and intrigues only served to reinforce in the Princess Royal her undying belief in the superiority of nearly all things English. As soon as Vicky and Fritz were blessed with the arrival of children, the new mother saw to it that their nurseries were modeled on those in which Vicky grew up in England. In no time, the Prussian princes and princess were being raised by their mother with a great love for her native country and things associated with it. Vicky accomplished this most successfully with the youngest in her brood—Sophie, Moretta, and Mossy.

Trips to England reinforced this bond. During these visits, the Prussian royal family stayed in many of the homes that had been dear to Vicky, a special favorite being Osborne House. Here, her children immersed themselves in the island's charms, often collecting shells from the nearby beaches. Years later, Kaiser Wilhelm II, Queen Victoria's eldest grandchild, recalled how when he and his siblings visited their grandmother, "we were treated as children of the house." As for Queen Victoria, Willy noted that "we looked up to our grandmother . . . with affectionate awe,"[16] a compliment seconded by Moretta, who fondly remembered their English grandmama as being "always so gracious and kind, and so full of understanding of us children."[17]

Vicky was grateful to see the bond that developed between her children and her mother. During one of the family's frequent visits, Vicky told Queen Victoria that "the children are so full of dear Grandmama and all her kindness that it does my heart good." Young Sophie was particularly taken with the old queen. "She is so nice to kiss you cannot think," exclaimed the eleven-year-old happily.[18] So comfortable was Princess Sophie in her grandmother's presence that Vicky was pleased to leave her in England for long stays. Since she was bereft of much contact with her paternal grandparents, Sophie's formative years were therefore largely shaped by her parents and Queen Victoria.

Sophie's childhood was divided chiefly between her parents' two homes: the Kronprinzenpalais on the Unter den Linden, in Berlin, and the Neues Palais in Potsdam. The Neues Palais, built by Frederick the Great in the eighteenth century, was a magnificent three-story edifice, redolent of rococo splendor, rising amidst verdant parkland. Visitors to the palace were instantly attracted by the large central cupola. Topping it were three classical female figures holding aloft an intricate crown. Inside, it was an enchanting place, where Sophie could wander and let her imagination transport her to another world. Among the two hundred rooms was the *Marmorsaal*—a huge ballroom, dotted with inlaid marble, with a gilded ceiling and crystal chandeliers. Just as richly ornate was the Silver Salon, with its sumptuous and intricate rococo decor on walls and ceiling. Most spectacular of all was the *Muschelsaal* or Shell Hall, decorated with nearly twenty thousand semiprecious stones, shells, and corals.

Like her sister, Alice, at Darmstadt, Vicky insisted that touches of Britain be introduced into her home. Vicky's attempts to inculcate an enduring love for England in her children worked. Not everybody, however, was pleased with the way the Prussian princes and princesses were being so heavily exposed to British influences. The German royal family and the chancellor, Otto von Bismarck, were among the crown princess's harshest critics. To them, Vicky soon became "*Die Engländerin* [the Englishwoman]," a term of abuse that would come to haunt Queen Victoria's eldest child.[19]

In 1879, when Sophie was nine, her brother, Waldemar ("Waldie"), died unexpectedly at the age of eleven from diphtheria. With her two favorite sons, Sigi and Waldie, gone, Vicky grew closer to her youngest daughters—Moretta, Sophie, and Mossy. The crown princess proudly boasted of "my three sweet girls" as "my trio" and "my Kleeblatt."[20]

Like Maud of Wales, Missy of Edinburgh's early years were largely spent in England. The family divided their time between their London home, Clarence House; Osborne Cottage on the Isle of Wight; and a rambling gray Jacobean manor house, Eastwell Manor, near Ashford, in Kent. It was during summers spent at Osborne and the occasional visit to Windsor that Missy recalled seeing her grandmother, Queen Victoria. To Missy, Victoria was always "Grandmamma Queen" in order to differentiate her from Missy's namesake and maternal grandmother, the Empress of Russia, who was "Grandmamma Empress."[21]

Missy's impressions of "Grandmamma Queen" were those of a cherished grandmother who nevertheless inspired "reverential fear" in many. The *grande dame* held interviews with her grandchildren, and high on the agenda were inquiries about behavior and morals. To Missy, these audiences at Windsor were intimidating. Trudging gingerly down the corridors of the ancient castle, a wellgroomed Missy would be led silently until she arrived at the hallowed Queen's Apartments. The hushed tone and reverential atmosphere surrounding the lady herself was so "awe-inspiring," recalled Missy, that "it was like approaching the mystery of some sanctuary." But when Missy did come face to face with her grandmother—"the final mystery to which only the initiated had access"—she was confronted not by some fearful ogre but by her "wonderful little old Grandmamma," who was swathed in black silk but had a "shy little laugh."[22]

These interviews at Windsor were not the only memories Missy had of her early youth in England. She remembered summers at Osborne, with Queen Victoria sitting placidly under a large green tent in the gardens, breakfasting or working diligently on government business. Inevitably, she was surrounded by innumerable dogs, not to mention exotic Indian attendants, and her Highlanders.

With a father whose duties at sea often took him away from home, it was the Duchess of Edinburgh who grew closer to the children and became the central figure in their lives. Though demanding and oftentimes a hard taskmaster, Marie was also a caring mother, who loved her children. The duchess was pleased with her brood, singing their praises, as when she said of seven-year-old Missy: *"son caractère est toujours délicieux."*[23]

In 1886, a new life began for Missy. Prince Alfred took up his command of the Royal Navy's Mediterranean Squadron and settled his family in Malta, where Missy lived for several years. Lessons and picnics to places of interest throughout the island filled her days. It was during these picnics that Missy and Ducky indulged in what became a great passion for them: horse riding. Missy's riding skills may have been acquired in London but they were honed during her teenage years in Malta. Missy and Ducky earned the disapproval of English matrons who found the Edinburgh princesses wild creatures, allowed too much free rein.

⚬︎

With her Hessian grandchildren bereft of their mother, the redoubtable Queen Victoria took charge, renewing Victoria's zest for life, which had been seriously sapped when she suddenly found herself a widow at forty-two. A grateful Grand Duke of Hesse acquiesced to Victoria's dominant role in the rearing of his children. Who better to supervise their education than a loving grandmother who also happened to be the Queen of England? Indeed, Victoria virtually usurped the Grand Duke of Hesse in matters pertaining to his children, so that she "never for a minute relaxed her watch" on their education.[24] Instructions and memoranda flew from England to Darmstadt charting the children's upbringing. No detail was too minute for Queen Victoria's eye. Solicited or not, the queen's endless advice covered every conceivable topic in the education of Princess Alix. Detailed daily and monthly summaries were sent by Alix's English governesses in Darmstadt to England for Queen Victoria's examination. When in England, the introspective princess also absorbed, both consciously and subconsciously, much of her grandmama's ways, including "the emotional atmosphere"[25] that had pervaded Victoria's life since the death of her husband, the Prince Consort.

The motherless grandchildren from Hesse touched a chord in Queen Victoria. Their visits to England served to bind her and the grandchildren closer. The queen missed them dreadfully when they were not around. She admitted as much, writing, "how I often wish to see you dear children. How long it seems since we parted & till we can meet again."[26] Five years after she wrote those words, Queen Victoria's love for these grandchildren had not abated. She continued to give unsolicited advice, reiterating her role as their primary counsellor and substitute mother figure. Victoria emphasized this to Alix's eldest sister, imploring her to look upon her as "a loving *Mother* (for I feel I *am that* to you beloved Children far *more* than a Grandmother)."[27]

Two

"MAD. NEVER MIND."

AFTER THREE IDYLLIC YEARS IN MALTA, THE EDINBURGH FAMILY found themselves on the move again, this time to Coburg in Germany, where Alfred and Marie were destined to reign as the Duke and Duchess of Saxe-Coburg-Gotha upon the death of Alfred's childless uncle. Here, as in Malta, Missy's mother was in her element. She thoroughly enjoyed being her own mistress in a land where she could indulge in simple, unsophisticated tastes. For all her exposure to the magnificence of the Russian court, Marie was never able to attain an air of elegance and was therefore happiest in her little kingdom, where no one dared express any negative opinions they might have of her. Missy's years in Coburg would never match the happiness of her time in England or Malta, thanks in large part to two members of the Edinburgh household, an odious German governess, *"Fraulein,"* and her equally loathsome fiancé, whom Missy referred to in her memoirs as a certain "Dr. X." Dr. Rolfs, his real name, and the Fraulein took a perverse pleasure in wreaking havoc among the Edinburgh children.

These two characters continually sought to incite jealousies and rivalries among the girls. This battle royal between Missy and members of her mother's household was an experience she shared with her grandmother. Like Missy, Victoria had had her own version of Dr. X in the form of Sir John Conroy, the comptroller of her mother's household. To Victoria he was, above all, a "monster and demon incarnate."[1] And just as the Duchess of Edinburgh trusted Rolfs, so too was the Duchess of Kent (Victoria's mother) under the sway of Conroy. Both Dr. X and Conroy sought to ingratiate themselves with persons of consequence in order to further their own power or agenda. Taking advantage of women whose lives were largely devoid of a close male companion, both men came to be seen by these women as indispensable to their respective households.

Dr. X's and Conroy's methods were similar—they were cunningly charming to the women who employed them but ruthless with the women's children. When the future Queen Victoria was sixteen years old and desperately ill, Conroy attempted to browbeat the weak patient into agreeing in writing to have him become Victoria's secretary. She refused. Victoria admitted that "I resisted in spite of my illness."[2] Fortunately for Missy, the same degree of dogged determination did not desert her when her time came to do battle with her nemesis.

Dr. X, in Missy's opinion, represented "German *'kultur'* at its worst, full of tyrannical arrogance and ridicule." Her brother, Alfred, suffered mercilessly because Dr. X "liked to ridicule him before others, seeming to delight in making him . . . feel a fool."[3] Not content with trying to destroy Alfred's soul, Rolfs also targeted the girls, ruthlessly attempting to Germanicize them. The girls, who were thoroughly English, were made of sterner stuff. And it was this, the preservation of their English identity, that spurred them to fight. As Missy recalled: "His object was to uproot in us the love of England and to turn us into Germans. We resisted this with all our might, pitting our wills against his with that magnificent fighting courage of children when their gods are attacked."[4]

Queen Victoria possessed the same strong sense of place, and she successfully transmitted it to many of her descendants. When Vicky, her eldest daughter, was betrothed to marry Prince Frederick of Prussia (the future Emperor Frederick III), the queen refused Berlin's demand that Vicky should marry in Germany. The idea was simply "too absurd." After all, proclaimed Victoria proudly, "it is not *every* day that one marries the eldest daughter of the Queen of England."[5]

Like Queen Victoria, Missy and her sisters possessed a keen English identity. So strong was this bond, that despite the love the Edinburgh girls had for their mother, they never came to share her own dislike of England. As it turned out, by the time Rolfs unleashed his attack, the girls were so devoted to one another and, just as important, so thoroughly English that they fought off Dr. X's enormous efforts at getting them to become German. Missy and her sisters were infuriated by the devious methods employed by this destructive duo. But the two were so adept at their twisted games that the Duchess of Edinburgh was blind to their behavior. This was particularly hurtful to the sisters, who hated to see their mother so taken in.

Fraulein and Dr. X used honeyed words aimed at the duchess, for instance, to wangle their way into her favor while spewing venomous attacks on the children behind her back. Missy remembered how the governess would "lead us on by equivocal conversation to ask questions about the hidden mysteries of life and would then show us up to Mamma as nasty little girls with unhealthy minds, whilst it was *she* who was trying to stir us up out of the somewhat torpid but paradisiacal innocence in which Mamma desired to keep us."[6] Fortunately, Missy and her sisters saw through this destructive charade and would have none of it. Then the duo married and left for their honeymoon. The new Frau Rolfs had brought in her younger sister, Louiserowitch, as a substitute. With Louiserowitch's help and the Duchess of Edinburgh away, the girls seized the chance to be rid of their nemeses, explaining their predicament to their father.

The duke exploded in anger—not at his children but at their intended target, Rolfs and his wife. A bitter fight broke out between Missy's parents. In the end, Dr. and Mrs. X stayed on but were never able to exercise the same earlier tyrannical behavior. Fortunately, a much more amiable governess joined the household, bringing further harmony into the girls' lives. Queen Victoria would have been proud of Missy and her sisters' defense of their English heritage and their commendable struggles to be rid of such a repugnant pair.

In her mid-teens, the increasingly attractive Missy began gathering more attention from admiring young men, who hovered around her like bees around a honey pot. To Missy, attentions from the opposite sex were always to her liking— whether from the young gardener to whom Missy once gave a small decorated egg at Easter or from the dashing officers who gallantly presented her with flowers and keepsakes. Missy's many admirers, it seems, were never far off. Not surprisingly, romance was soon in the air for this outgoing and pretty granddaughter of Queen Victoria.

☙

To outsiders, the "whispering Wales girls" appeared painfully shy. "Her Royal Shyness" was how people referred to Maud, Louise, or Toria, who spoke "in a minor key, *en sourdine,*" as Missy recalled of them. This timidity was a trait Maud shared with her cousin, Alix of Hesse-Darmstadt, and with their grandmother. Even as late as 1867, Queen Victoria admitted that "I am terribly shy and nervous and *always so.*"[7]

Missy noted that her shy Wales cousins also spoke in an almost patronizing manner, saying, "dear little" or "poor little" so-and-so. The future Queen Marie of Romania was sometimes on the receiving end of this annoying habit, often called "dear little Missy," with a whiff of condescension. Years later, she recalled how "the three cousins were very kind, but they too treated us as the young things we were then, which made us feel cruelly the inferiority of our five to ten years less."[8]

By her teens, Maud had inherited a little of her mother's famed beauty, but did not outshine her. Another of Queen Victoria's granddaughters, however—

Princess Alix of Hesse—had already become an acknowledged beauty, whose at-
tributes did not go unnoticed. Never one to mince words where looks were concerned, even when they involved her own family, Queen Victoria was thoroughly
pleased with Alix, exclaiming that Alicky was "the handsomest child I ever
saw."[9]

At twelve years of age, Alicky's good looks made their first memorable impression on a young man of sixteen. It was a meeting that changed the course of
history: in 1884, the future Tsar Nicholas II and Tsarina Alexandra encountered
each other for the first time when Alix attended the wedding of her sister, Ella,
to Nicky's uncle, Serge. Alix's arrival in Russia for her sister's wedding opened
the young girl's eyes to the splendors of the Russian imperial court. In wealth and
spectacle, this court was still unsurpassed in all of Europe. But even more fascinating than the surroundings and ceremonials was the sixteen-year-old tsarevitch himself. If Nicky was the object of a preadolescent crush on Alix's part,
she proved equally intriguing to the future tsar. Eventually, using a diamond, the
pair carved their names on a windowpane, and the tsarevitch recorded that "we
love each other."[10]

⌀︎⌀

It was the norm for many Victorian widows to have a daughter designated to
spend her life by her mother's side. Queen Victoria was no exception—and the
one on whom this onerous burden fell was none other than the baby of the family, Princess Beatrice, Victoria's fifth daughter. As her mother's anointed lifelong
companion, it was Beatrice's role to be at Victoria's beck and call. Years later,
Beatrice's daughter, Ena, said of her mother's life: "She had to be in perpetual
attendance on her formidable mother. Her devotion and submission were complete."[11]

A husband for Beatrice was not conducive to this arrangement, so when Beatrice wished to marry Prince Henry ("Liko") of Battenberg, her mother was furious. Beatrice eventually won—but at a price. In this battle of wills, the queen was
the undeniable winner because Beatrice and Liko capitulated, agreeing to live
with Queen Victoria all year round. By the wedding day, Queen Victoria had not
only reconciled herself to Liko but, according to the Duchess of Edinburgh, "has
found in him true perfection."[12] Among Beatrice's wedding attendants were
fifteen-year-old Maud of Wales, thirteen-year-old Alix of Hesse-Darmstadt, and
nine-year-old Missy of Edinburgh. Queen Victoria had specifically written to
Missy's parents telling them of her desire to have Missy and Ducky as part of the
bridal entourage. The girls were thrilled. As their mother noted, "they are very
flattered and very proud" to be able to play such an important role in their aunt

Beatrice's wedding.[13] Never had the parish church of Whippingham in the Isle of Wight seen such a gathering of royalty as that of 23 July 1885. The bride, who was to become the mother of a future Queen of Spain, was married in the simplest of ceremonies, attended by three nieces who were to grace the thrones of Norway, Romania, and Russia.

The next major celebration was Queen Victoria's Golden Jubilee. For one granddaughter, the Jubilee in the summer of 1887 was more than a chance to celebrate her grandmother's fifty-year reign. Sophie of Prussia's prolonged stay in England meant that she became better acquainted with a tall, handsome prince from Greece, Constantine ("Tino"), heir to his father, George I, King of the Hellenes. Queen Victoria watched the budding romance, even venturing to ask Sophie's mother: "Is there a chance of Sophie's marrying Tino? It would be very nice for her, for he is very good."[14]

Months after the queen's celebrations, Princess Beatrice, already the mother of a son, Alexander ("Drino"), gave birth at Balmoral on 24 October 1887 to a girl whom Queen Victoria referred to as "my little Jubilee grandchild."[15] At her christening at Balmoral, the baby was given the names Victoria Eugenie Julia Ena. Victoria was for the queen; Eugenie was for the baby's godmother, the Empress Eugénie; Julia was for her paternal grandmother, the Countess Julia von Hawke; and Ena was a Gaelic Highland name given in tribute to her birthplace. The little girl came to be known as Ena, the most unusual of all these names.

Officially, Princess Ena was referred to as Victoria Eugenie. They were illustrious names, fit for a future queen since they were the names of two empresses, one of India and one of France. Because Princess Beatrice was so close to her mother, the choice of Victoria for her only daughter was inevitable. Eugenie was less obvious. It came as a result of the friendship between Beatrice and the Empress Eugénie of France, who along with her husband, Emperor Napoleon III, had settled into a life of exile in England in 1871 after the French defeat in the Franco-Prussian War.

Little did anyone guess at the time of her birth that little Ena would one day become queen of her godmother Eugénie's native country, Spain. The Empress Eugénie took an interest in Ena as she grew up, never forgetting to send her gifts. Years later, Ena remembered how the empress had shown an "unfailing kindness and interest in me, since I was a tiny child."[16]

Queen Victoria's close relationship with her Battenberg family intensified as the family was augmented with the arrival of more children—Leopold in 1889 and Maurice in 1891. Sadly, it was discovered that Leopold was a hemophiliac.

Nowhere was the contrast between the closeness Queen Victoria felt toward the Battenbergs living with her and the distant relationship with the Waleses more evident than in March 1888, when the Prince and Princess of Wales celebrated their silver wedding anniversary. A formal family dinner at Marlborough House, with Queen Victoria as the guest of honor, was to be the highlight of the celebrations. The queen's presence was special, for it marked the first time that Maud's grandmother had ever dined at the London home of the Prince and Princess of Wales, located within walking distance of Buckingham Palace.

During this time, Princess Maud became infatuated with one of her childhood playmates, Prince Frank of the Teck, a handsome young man with jet black hair and blue eyes. At eighteen years of age, the shy, tomboyish "Harry" had become a young woman. With her dark hair and tiny waist, and her illustrious pedigree, Maud was bound to become the object of attention from suitors. However, during this period Maud found herself in the position of pursuer as her infatuation with Frank grew.

Princess Sophie of Prussia, in the meantime, was coping with a family tragedy, as she watched her father slowly dying from throat cancer. Fritz soldiered on, bravely putting up with the painful and humiliating effects of his disease. Waiting in the wings was Sophie's brother, Willy, who made no secret of his desire to mount the throne and inaugurate a grandiose era.

Willy stepped up his bitter quarrel with his mother, knowing that people were inclined to side with him. Backing up Willy against Vicky were the Berlin elite, who disliked the English princess, chief among them Otto von Bismarck. Contemptuous and jealous of this brilliant daughter of Queen Victoria, enemies of Fritz and Vicky were poised to throw in their lot with Willy, who became heir when his father succeeded Wilhelm I on the death of the ninety-year-old monarch on 9 March 1888.

Within the space of three short months, Germany witnessed the succession of two highly divergent monarchs in the form of the emperors Frederick III and his son, Wilhelm II. In Berlin, the new emperor, weak and dying, was a pitiful sight. Unable to talk, he was reduced to scribbling messages to get himself understood. The dying emperor spent his last days in his beloved Neues Palais. There, Sophie and her family began their vigil. Fritz fought long enough to live to see Sophie turn eighteen. On the morning of her birthday, it was clear that Fritz's death was imminent. Nevertheless, the emperor found the strength to wish her a happy birthday. In a letter to Queen Victoria, Vicky described the unfolding drama: "With a pleasant smile he asked after her at once and wanted us to do something to amuse her. What a birthday for the poor child! What a recollection for the whole of her life! At nine she came over with her sisters, he embraced her and gave her the bouquet, looked at her so kindly and did not appear sad or depressed, he had no idea how seriously ill he was."[17] It was one of the most heart-wrenching ways a daughter could celebrate such a special occasion.

Within twenty-four hours, Fritz's agonies ended. Having just celebrated her eighteenth birthday some hours before, Sophie now witnessed the poignant last good-bye between her parents. After lapsing into unconsciousness, Frederick III died. Scarcely had the corpse grown cold, however, when Willy's unsavory character emerged in spectacular manner. With great disrespect, he ordered his soldiers to ransack the Neues Palais for "incriminating" evidence of "liberal plots." In his delusion, the new Kaiser was sure he could find something to accuse his mother and father of. His newly widowed mother was horrified that "William's first act as Ruler was to have our house, our sanctuary, our quiet house of mourning where death had set up his throne, cordoned off by a regiment of Hussars who appeared unmounted with rifles in their hands from behind every tree and every statue!"[18] Wilhelm's soldiers found nothing—despite literally turning the contents of the entire palace upside down, leaving papers and other objects strewn everywhere. Anticipating this, Fritz had had his papers sent to England, where Wilhelm could not get his hands on them.

With the death of Frederick III, Willy's latest and cruelest plundering became too much to bear for Vicky, Sophie, Moretta, and Mossy. Vicky knew that her three youngest daughters, without a father, were now more dependant than ever on her for emotional support. They had stood together throughout the ordeal of Fritz's illness and death; they would now stand by to face whatever else the future held for them. The four women clung to one another as if to avoid sinking further into despairing grief. Vicky recognized this, and on the night of Fritz's death, told her mother so: "I have my three sweet girls—he loved so much—that are my consolation."[19]

As a girl, Sophie of Prussia already exuded a regal bearing. Sophie's youngest daughter, Lady Katherine Brandram, remembered her mother as being "dignified" but also "quiet, not stern, a lovely personality."[20] Sophie's sister, Moretta, recalled how Sophie "was always dignified and queenly." Even Sophie's nurse confidently predicted: "Sophie will be a queen one day."[21] This prediction proved prescient, for just as Queen Victoria had hoped, Sophie did marry Crown Prince Constantine of Greece.

Fair-haired, with deep blue eyes, and towering at just over six feet, Tino had been born on 2 August 1868 at Athens, a birth heralded throughout Greece. Since his parents were Danish and Russian, Tino's birth on Greek soil meant that the next King of the Hellenes was to be a native Greek.

Thanks to intermarriages among the royal houses of Europe, Tino was a first cousin of Maud of Wales on his father's side, while another cousin was the Tsarevitch Nicholas, and yet others the future kings Frederick VIII of Denmark and Haakon VII of Norway. By the time Tino was twenty, his good looks and joie de vivre proved intoxicating to the impressionable young Sophie, hardly a surprising development considering the funereal atmosphere that prevailed at the home of her widowed mother. Esme Howard, a young secretary at the British Embassy in Berlin who was visiting Sophie and her mother at the time, wrote of "the terrific atmosphere of mourning which pervaded the whole place after the death of the Emperor Frederick. The Empress herself, the three Princesses, were dressed in crape from head to foot. The long room in which we sat was scarcely lighted, with the exception of one large picture of the Emperor Frederick, the frame of which was draped in crape. This dominated the entire scene and made it almost impossible to forget his tragic death."[22] Little wonder that Tino, and Greece, proved alluring to Sophie or that she accepted Tino's proposal.

The Athens of the late 1880s to which Sophie went to live was a small city set in a landscape that Sophie's mother, the Empress Frederick, called "very bare, arid and sandy"; yet the hills made for "a most striking and interesting panorama." There was no doubt that Athens was "certainly more eastern than European."[23] The city's Royal Palace, an unassuming building, lacked artistic inspiration but housed a huge ballroom, reputedly the largest in Europe. The rooms were decorated with marble statues and ceiling frescos depicting Greek wars. Bloodied flags from past conflicts hung in parts of the palace.

Earlier in the year, Princess Maud of Wales had expressed her excitement at the thought of going to Greece for Sophie's wedding, as it might provide a chance to see her favorite cousin, Grand Duke George. Maud wrote an effusive letter to George about the visit: "It would be lovely if we all went to Athens for Tino and Sophie's wedding." Maud imagined the British royal and Russian imperial yachts sailing side by side in Greece and added, "we could see each other the whole way. It would be extremely amusing."[24] That nineteen-year-old Maud was smitten with George was evident in one letter in which she ordered George to "let no one see this [letter]. You wrote such *lovely* things. I miss *you* sweet Musie. It is terrible without you now that everything reminds me so of you."[25]

On 27 October 1889, in a ceremony that united two reigning houses, Sophie became the first of Queen Victoria's five special granddaughters to marry. Bearded bishops performed the solemn Greek Orthodox service as Sophie and Constantine, holding tapered candles, walked three times around a table draped in gold cloth and bearing a Bible. According to one witness, the "elaborate ritual" turned out to be "impressive but very long." It was exhausting, but the bridal couple acquitted themselves well as they stood "for upwards of an hour without swerving."[26] This was all the more impressive as Tsarevitch Nicholas wrote to his mother that "everyone was suffocating from the heat." Nevertheless, Nicky was glad to report that "everything went off very well" and the bride and groom "were both calm."[27]

Sophie's marriage was a sign to the Greeks that Greece was set to see greatness again, for there was an old prophecy which said that when Constantine and Sophia reigned, Constantinople would again fall into Greek hands. It had "seemed to me," noted Sophie's brother-in-law, Prince Nicholas, "that the Greek people felt at last, that they were nearing the realisation of their lifelong dream— the dream that lasted throughout the dark centuries of slavery, the dream that had saved their souls from despair."[28] It came then as no surprise that when Sophie appeared outside the cathedral on the arm of her new husband, "the enthusiasm of the people was unprecedented."[29]

After the Orthodox ceremony, in deference to the bride's religion, a Protestant service was performed in the Royal Palace, conducted by the king's own chaplain. The day ended with a spectacular fireworks display, which bathed the Parthenon in blazing reds and greens. When Kaiser Wilhelm prepared to depart Athens, he took leave of everyone "most affectionately." "The only one he forgot to say good-by to," according to a witness, "was his own sister, the bride!"[30] It was a far different kind of good-bye, however, where the Empress Frederick was concerned. To Queen Victoria, the empress wrote, "my trio . . . is broken up now and I feel it bitterly." Though Vicky "felt dreadfully upset" because it was difficult "having to part with her," she was nevertheless proud of "my darling Sophie [who] looked so sweet and grave and calm, my little lamb."[31]

The parting was just as wrenching for Sophie as it was for her mother. Searching for words for emotions too difficult to put on paper, Sophie wrote: "I also miss you dreadfully, it seems too odd not to have you anywhere. . . . It was too disgustingly awful, that saying goodbye the other day, and I never thanked you half enough for all your trouble and care for me. I am so touched by all you have done, and hope you know how grateful I am and always will be." The letter was signed: "your loving and obedient little child, Sophie."[32]

This was the start of a voluminous correspondence, written in English, between mother and daughter, which came to two thousand letters and a million words, beginning in 1889 and ending in 1901, when the Empress Frederick died. No small detail was too trivial to chronicle. The empress often began her letters with endearments such as "Sophie love," "My own Sophie darling," or, "My precious child." Sophie's letters to her mother began and ended just as affectionately.

Princess Maud may have harbored fond feelings for Grand Duke George of Russia, but she was increasingly drawn toward Prince Frank, though he was not in the least bit interested in her. Maud's letters were left unanswered. In one letter to Frank's sister, May (the future Queen Mary, consort of King George V of England), Maud tried to enlist May's help to push her brother to answer. "Frank promised to write to me," lamented Maud, "but he has not done so: if you ever write [to] him, you may remind him of that promise."[33]

By 1893, Maud's siblings, Louise and George, were already married off; Louise to the Duke of Fife and George to none other than May of Teck. This meant that "Motherdear"'s possessive hold over Maud and Toria grew even tighter, prompting Queen Victoria to complain: "If any one *has* a right to be *offended* it is I—who am *never allowed* to have Victoria & Maud to visit me, when *all* my *other* Grand Children come & stay with me. I call it unkind & especially very selfish; but that is not *Uncle's* fault."[34]

The fate of her unmarried Wales granddaughters preyed on Queen Victoria's mind and that of their aunt, Vicky, who exclaimed, "I cannot understand their not being married, they would make such charming wives."[35] Queen Victoria had written to their father, expressing her concern about the girls' unmarried situation, but the Prince of Wales indicated to his mother "that Alix found them such companions that she wld not encourage their marrying & that they themselves had no inclination for it." "I think he is mistaken as regards Maud,"[36] noted the queen presciently. "He said," wrote Victoria to Vicky, that "he was 'powerless' [in the matter] wh. I cannot understand."[37]

At twenty-five, Maud had blossomed into an attractive young woman. Her aunt, Vicky, found "dear Maudie . . . very much en beuté [*sic*]." Moreover, Vicky also saw the Wales girls in a better light than their Hesse cousins, whose unrivaled beauty was universally acknowledged. Vicky's praises were high, as she told Crown Princess Sophie: "I cannot help admiring them [Maud and Victoria of Wales] more than Ella or Alicky. They are more graceful and more natural, and so much more agreeable and bright. I think they are more clever too."[38]

Maud had certainly caught the attention of one admiring young man in the form of her first cousin, Prince Nicholas of Greece, but he was unsuccessful in getting her to marry him. Nevertheless, he took Maud's rejection in stride. At one point Queen Victoria had hoped to see Maud married to Ernie, who succeeded his father as Grand Duke of Hesse. But hemophilia in his family plus Maud's weak constitution scuttled that idea. Victoria, instead, focused on getting Ernie and Ducky married.

Maud at the Hessian court would have been too much for her mother—not that Maud would have wanted to live in Darmstadt. When she was a guest at the wedding of Ernie and Ducky in 1894, Maud launched a verbal attack on Princess Alix's hometown and Ducky's mother. "Thank God I am not her daughter," exclaimed Maud of her aunt Marie. "*No one* would make *me* marry these German vandals. Imagine, having to live in Darmstadt one's whole life!"[39] The Princess of Wales had succeeded in raising Maud to share in her aversion for Germany. When Maud was in Germany in 1886, she disdainfully described her opinions of Germans to her friend, Evie Forbes: "You never saw such frights (just like Germans always are!) I hate every sort of German and I must say they are such vulgar people I think."[40] These words sounded almost as if they had been dictated by Princess Alexandra; evidence, no doubt, of Motherdear's strong influence in the life of Maud and her sisters. Despite Alexandra's widely known antipathy to all things German, Queen Victoria and Vicky were still trying to pair Maud off as late as 1894 to another German; this time, the young man in question was Prince Maximilian of Baden.[41] But nothing came of it. An exasperated Empress Frederick wrote how "it really is *not* wise—to leave the fate of these dear girls—'*dans le vague.*'"[42]

The ongoing guessing game as to whom Maud would marry was not to be resolved until 1895. By then, she was already struck by the fact that life was passing her by. She wrote to Princess May how "it seems *so* funny that *all* these *younger* cousins are getting married and nothing is happening with us, the older ones!"[43]

⟳

In February 1980, Sophie excitedly told her mother that a baby was on the way. Since, as the Empress Frederick later explained, "accidents happen very easily," Vicky wisely thought that Sophie might need some help in a medically primitive Athens. She accordingly smuggled into Sophie's entourage a midwife from Germany, a certain Frau von E. Displaying a characteristically Victorian approach to sexuality, Vicky went on to explain to Sophie why there was a need to keep Frau von E.'s true purpose a secret: "Of course I could not tell you what her real profession was when you were a young girl, so I have to invent the name and function of housekeeper, so that you might have her always near at hand . . . you married, so she went with you; but I could not tell you why."[44]

Had it not been for her mother's foresight, Sophie's life and that of her baby might not have been saved. The birth, on 19 July 1890, was dangerous—at one point the umbilical cord was wrapped around the baby's neck. The doctor in attendance was at a loss what to do, but thanks to the German midwife's skill,

Sophie's life and that of her baby, George, were saved. In England, Queen Victoria followed events in Greece with a close eye. The queen was taken aback with the speed at which little George arrived—not quite nine months after his parents' wedding, prompting the queen to write to the Empress Frederick: "What shall I say at this most unfortunate and yet fortunate event happening so soon?" The queen calculated that "it must be a week at least too soon, for she won't have been married nine months till the 27th."[45]

During the first year in Greece, Sophie found herself drawn to the religion of her adopted country. George's birth spurred her to adopt the Greek Orthodox faith. After all, as she admitted, "a mother's church should be that of her children; a wife's fatherland that of her husband."[46] The news was welcomed by the Greek royals and accepted calmly by Sophie's own family, including her mother and grandmother. Sophie's planned conversion, however, earned Wilhelm II's ire. The fact that Sophie was willing to stick by her convictions and openly defy her brother speaks volumes to the strength of her character and the depths of her conversion. After all, Sophie knew just how unpredictable and unreasonable Willy could be. If there was one thing Wilhelm II could not stand it was disobedience; and a very public act of disobedience from one of his family was tantamount to treason. Here "was a man out of the ordinary run," an acquaintance once said of the Kaiser. "There was something abnormal, almost unhealthy about him which kept me perpetually asking myself what he would ultimately do."[47]

Sophie announced her intentions to the Kaiser during a visit she and Tino made to Germany in November 1890 for the wedding of Moretta to Prince Adolf zu Schaumburg-Lippe. When Wilhelm's wife, Empress Auguste Viktoria ("Dona"), heard about Sophie's plans, she worked herself into a frenzy. Narrow-minded and simple, with few interests apart from her husband, Dona was the perfect fawning wife for Willy. She was also once described by her mother-in-law as possessing "religious prejudices [which were] quite exaggerated and ridiculous!"[48]

In the course of the wedding festivities, Dona summoned Sophie to her suite. The heavily pregnant empress immediately confronted Sophie, firing off a venomous attack. Was it true, asked Dona, that Sophie was planning to change her religion? It was indeed, answered Sophie defiantly. But Willy would never hear of it, argued the empress. As head of the church in Germany, it simply would be unforgivable for his own sister to leave the religion she was raised in. Dona shrieked that if Sophie persisted, she would never hear the end of it from Wilhelm, and above all, she would end up in hell. With that, an equally indignant Sophie retorted, "That does not concern anyone here and I do not need to ask anyone." As for Wilhelm, Sophie continued, "I know him better than that, he has absolutely no religion. If he had, he would never have behaved as he did." Moreover, "whether I go to hell or not is my own affair." The heated exchange continued but Sophie dug in her heels, not caring what Willy or Dona thought. "Does Dona imagine that I am going to be ordered about?" said a disgusted Sophie.[49]

After their argument, Dona was so agitated that doctors were called in to calm the hysterical empress. Infuriated, Wilhelm II exploded. He fired off an arrogant telegram to King George of Greece: "Should she persist in her intention, I shall no longer regard her as a member of my family and will never again receive her."[50] King George wisely kept a cool head and replied that he did not feel it right to try to sway Sophie in either direction. The Kaiser's pompous attitude was in keeping with his character. Count Robert Zedlitz-Trützschler, marshal of the Kaiser's court, described his master as having "the arrogant conviction that he was called on to play the judge over everybody and everything."[51]

Caught between the warring siblings was their ever-suffering mother, Vicky, who vented her frustration on Queen Victoria. The queen was aghast at Willy's outbursts. Vicky went on to tell Sophie how the queen felt that Wilhelm's behavior was "so entirely unnecessary and uncalled for . . . I myself do not understand such narrowmindedness." Pleased to find her mother siding with Sophie, Vicky then went on to reassure her daughter, "you see, dear Grandmama thinks just as we do."[52] The Empress Frederick nevertheless grew increasingly anxious that Sophie and Willy's bitter feud would irreparably damage their already fragile relationship. With this in mind, Vicky urged her daughter to write a conciliatory letter to her brother. In doing so, Sophie tried to explain calmly the reasons for her decision to convert. She sent a copy of her letter to her mother, and it met with Vicky's approval. However, Vicky knew her son's character and she warned Sophie what to expect:

> your letter to Wilhelm—I am afraid your kind and nice words will be lost on him, as he has absolutely *no heart*. . . . There is no sentiment in his nature, so I fear he will not answer your letter lovingly and sensibly as he should. . . . With Wilhelm it is *not religion* that vexes him, it is his silly vanity and pride of being "head of the family," and *their* being obliged to bend to his will.[53]

The empress was right. Sophie's conciliatory letter met with Willy's usual arrogant rebuff. Sophie telegraphed her mother with her brother's reply: "Received answer. Keeps to what he said in Berlin. Fixes it to three years. Mad. Never mind. Sophie."[54]

Sophie may not have minded, but Vicky did. "It is really *too* unheard of," wrote the empress. "It is a piece of *tyranny* and *injustice* which fills me with *contempt,* indignation and disgust . . . you are *quite* at liberty to do as you like, you are not his subject, but King George's."[55]

Willy's anger did not subside straightaway. Dona and Wilhelm characteristically laid the blame for the premature birth in December 1890 of a son on Sophie. Even five months later, when it was obvious to all that the baby was flourishing, Wilhelm continued to send outrageous comments to Queen Victoria about Sophie's conversion. One of them reached ridiculous proportions, Willy exploding to his grandmother that "if my poor baby dies it is solely Sophie's fault and she has murdered it."[56]

Wilhelm's threat to banish Sophie never materialized. A wise Queen Victoria knew her grandson and predicted that nothing would happen if Sophie decided to visit Germany, provided that Tino accompanied her. The queen proved correct. Nevertheless, irreparable damage had been done. Willy and Sophie, who had not been close as siblings, would never again find themselves truly at ease in each other's company.

By 1892, Sophie was settling in Greece and earnestly learning the language, a fact that won the approval of the Empress Fredrick. By the next year, the crown princess could proudly boast to her mother that she was able to speak Greek to the new ministers who came to a reception at the palace. In time, Sophie was to master the language completely. Her youngest daughter, Lady Katherine Brandram, recalls her mother speaking "beautiful Greek."[57]

Aside from the rupture between Sophie and Wilhelm, overall Sophie's life since her marriage had run a fairly smooth course. By 1893, Prince George was joined by a baby brother, Alexander, also born at Tatoi—the Greek royal family's summer estate near Athens. Salutes fired from Russian and British warships at the port of Piraeus greeted Alexander's arrival. No one could have known that the crown princess had given birth to another future King of the Hellenes, one whose tragic destiny was to leave a painful mark on his mother.

Three

"GANGAN"

WITH PRINCESS BEATRICE AND HER HUSBAND, LIKO, FIRMLY AN-
chored to the aging and dependent Queen Victoria, the monarch indulged the
youngest brood in her immediate family, the boisterous Princess Ena and her
brothers. Compared with her older grandchildren, the dynamics in the relationship between Queen Victoria and these, her youngest grandchildren, were nearly
as opposite as night and day. It was a metamorphosis on the queen's part that was
nothing short of astonishing. Whereas the queen's older granddaughters had an
almost reverential admiration for their grandmother, young Ena and her brothers
possessed a much more easygoing approach toward the elderly Victoria, whom
they affectionately called "Gangan." Unlike decades before, when she would
have balked at the ruckus created by young grandchildren, Queen Victoria put up
with the shenanigans of her Battenberg brood. Led by the tomboyish Ena,
chirpy voices were heard all day in a never-ending round of " 'Gangan this' and
'Gangan that' from rising to bedtime."[1] That the queen adored these grandchildren there is no doubt; on how she herself commented "little Drino & Ena are
quite delightful—so amusing."[2]

All was not boisterous fun and games, however. The queen still insisted on
discipline and decorum. Ena remembered that "having been born and brought
up in her home she was like a second mother to us. She was very kind but very
strict with old fashioned ideas of how children must be brought up; the one she
most insisted upon was that children must be seen and not heard."[3] By Queen
Victoria's side, Ena learned early how royalty should act. Once, when an older
cousin spoke out in the presence of the queen and Ena by saying quite inno-

cently, "I think it is time for us to go to bed," the queen shot back: "Young woman, a princess should say, 'I think it is time for me to retire.' "[4]

Living year-round with Queen Victoria meant that the princess was influenced a good deal by the queen. It also came as no surprise that Princess Ena grew to love animals, a predilection she shared with Maud of Norway, Sophie of Greece, Alexandra of Russia, and Marie of Romania. These women, throughout their lives, were surrounded by a menagerie of animals—though dogs were a particular favorite. For Ena, a cherished pet nearly put an abrupt end to her life. In 1894, six-and-a-half-year-old Ena was thrown off her pony at Osborne and hit her head on the ground, causing a severe concussion. The queen recorded being "much distressed. Of course the anxiety we were in was terrible. I love these darling children so, almost as much as their own parent."[5] For Queen Victoria, the next several weeks were tinged with great concern, as "the little treasure" slipped in and out of danger.

The queen's physician noticed "dangerous symptoms" appearing and recorded "evident signs of brain pressure, probably a haemorrhage."[6] Ena's Aunt Vicky, then at Osborne, related to Sophie of Greece the anxiety they all went through during the uncertain hours after Ena had suffered a concussion. "Grandmama . . . much tormented, and we are all so distressed . . . it is so grievous that she [Ena] cannot take notice or open her eyes." And in another letter from her mother, Sophie read that "the whole day yesterday was one of great anxiety about dear little Ena. She is still in great danger."[7]

After some terrible days, Queen Victoria was finally able to write, "Thank God! she is out of danger today." The queen added: "We have gone thro' terrible anxiety since Saturday evg. Tho' she began to get a *little better* that very night & she has gone *on steadily* improving ever since."[8] Even Kaiser Wilhelm was apprised of his English cousin's health by their grandmother; at the end of February he sent back a telegram: "so glad to hear Ena better."[9] By the beginning of March, the little patient was out of bed. During tea one day, the queen was pleased to see her granddaughter, noting how "sweet little Ena came in. She looks very white and speaks so quietly, but is quite well, only still rather weak."[10] Within a month of the frightening accident, all was well, much to the queen's relief. She recorded in her journal: "Four weeks since sweet little Ena met with that dreadful accident, and how thankful we must be that she is so wonderfully recovered!"[11]

Aside from her fall, Ena continued to enjoy an idyllic life at Windsor, Balmoral, and Osborne. Her placid world, though, was shattered in January 1896, when her father died unexpectedly while serving with the British in the Ashanti Expedition. Liko was felled by typhoid fever on his way to Africa. His body was brought back to England to a distraught Queen Victoria and Beatrice. Ena, like

Alix of Hesse, was orphaned at a young age, another factor they shared with Queen Victoria, whose father died before she was a year old.

⟨✦⟩

In a faraway land a young man reigned over a historic kingdom. On 17 May 1886, a collective sigh of relief was let out in Spain when it was officially announced that Queen Maria Cristina had given birth to a boy, whose titles were lengthy and impressive, a reminder of the glories of old. The newborn Alfonso XIII was:

> King of Spain, Castille, León, Aragon, the Two Sicilies, Jerusalem, Navarre, Granada, Toledo, Valencia, Galicia, Majorca, Minorca, Seville, Sardinia, Cordova, Corsica, Murcia, Jaen, Algarve, Algeciras, Gibraltar, the Canary Islands, East and West Indies, India and the Oceanic Continent: Archduke of Austria; Duke of Burgundy, Brabant, and Milan; Count of Habsburg, Flanders, the Tyrol, and Barcelona; Seigneur of Biscay and Molina; Catholic Majesty.[12]

The fact that the child was a male was all the more reassuring to the nation because just six months before, the child's father, King Alfonso XII, had died suddenly, leaving a widow and two daughters. The birth of a posthumous son also meant that Spain might more than likely be spared the violence that had marred the country for much of the earlier part of the nineteenth century. Then, a series of wars centering on the Spanish succession pitted the Carlists against supporters of the reigning Queen, Isabella II.[13]

The young boy-king grew into a lively and spirited individual, in whose veins coursed the blood of two great dynasties, the Habsburgs and the Bourbons. Alfonso's unbridled energy was evident from an early age. Maria Cristina noted that "he is good, but so eager, so turbulent, so eager for liberty."[14] In raising her son, Queen Maria Cristina struggled with an unenviable task. Well aware of the need to create a sense of balance in the king, she trod a careful path in ensuring that Alfonso not only understood his station in life and his responsibilities but also kept his feet firmly on the ground. She appeared to have succeeded early on, for Alfonso blurted out to a courtier at the tender age of three: "For mother I am Bubi [the German equivalent of "boysey"]: for you I am the King."[15] Alfonso XIII may have enjoyed an affectionate relationship with his mother, but he always gave her the respect accorded to a sovereign of Spain.

In this, Alfonso was not alone. One of Maria Cristina's contemporaries said that she "never lets you forget that she is Queen."[16] The widowed regent also gained the nickname "Doña Virtudes, meant as a compliment by some, a sneer by others."[17] What, then, would Maria Cristina be like as a mother-in-law? Would she prove as caring to her daughter-in-law as she had been to her own children, or was there to be more of the unsympathetic demeanor so visible to the public?

⚮

As the pretty Missy of Edinburgh grew into a lovely young woman, her admirers multiplied. One turned out to be none other than Princess Maud's brother, Missy's highly eligible and favorite cousin, Prince George of Wales. The future King George V's infatuation with the adolescent Marie grew from the time spent with his Edinburgh cousins while he was stationed at Malta with the Royal Navy during the 1880s.

Always a welcome guest at the Maltese home of his uncle and aunt, the Duke and Duchess of Edinburgh, George of Wales spent many hours by Missy's side. A mutual attraction took hold. George, then in his early twenties, was smitten with the attractive teenager, ten years his junior. Though a frequent companion to both Missy and her sister, Ducky, George did not hide his preference for the fair-haired elder sister. Whenever they went for rides to watch the spectacular sunsets over the island, it was Missy, not Ducky, who sat next to George in the carriage. It was not long before Missy sensed her older cousin's feelings.

On one occasion, after being scolded for some minor offense, the teenaged Missy, sobbing her eyes out, sought the consoling arms of Prince George. George gently embraced his young cousin and offered her his sympathy. "Poor dear little Missy," he whispered in her ear as her mass of golden hair cascaded about his arms. "Poor dear little Miss," murmured George tenderly. Never averse to being the center of attention, the teenager savored the encounter. It was at that moment that poor little Missy learned "how very sweet the big, grown-up cousin could be!"[18]

Far from dimming, as time and distance might normally have been expected to do, George's infatuation grew as Missy neared marriageable age. Her sparkling blue eyes and silky fair hair, framing delicate features, haunted his thoughts as the prince sailed the seas. Because of his duties, George was away at sea for months, meaning that the only way he could let Missy know of his feelings was through letters. Early in 1891, the lovesick George penned his devotion to his "darling Missy," explaining that "it is nearly 9 months since I have seen you now, but you are constantly in my thoughts." It ended with the prince beseeching Missy not to "forget your most loving and devoted old Georgie."[19]

This was a union very much to the liking of George's father, the Prince of Wales, as well as Missy's father, the Duke of Edinburgh. George's hopes, however, were cruelly dashed. Hampered in his pursuit by major obstacles—his physical absence and the implacable opposition of two stubborn mothers—George was saddened to find that he could not fight two formidable opponents to the marriage.

As George's love letters arrived, the Duchess of Edinburgh watched her daughter like a hawk. Her fierce opposition to the match doomed any plans for marriage between the two infatuated cousins. Like the Princess of Wales, who refused to countenance any of her daughters marrying Germans, Marie prevented her daughters from marrying British princes. Thus did the duchess destroy all chance of her daughter becoming the wife of the future King George V.

Unhappy with the sentimental letters her nephew was penning to Missy, Marie convinced the dutiful Missy to tell George that a marriage between them was impossible. As instructed, Missy then wrote to tell George that instead of becoming her husband, he must remain her "beloved chum."[20] It was a bitter blow to Prince George, who had waited patiently for years for his Missy to grow up. His reward was within reach when it was cruelly snatched from his arms.

Though their relationship did not end in engagement and marriage, Missy and George remained on very good terms. Well into the 1920s Missy still kept a crystal ball given to her by George from his courting days. And whenever she handled it, an enigmatic smile lit up her face. In fact, some of Missy's fondest memories were of the times she spent with Prince George in Malta. After living in Romania for several years, she wrote to George in 1901, confessing that "the brightest times I ever had were these Malta days."[21]

Had Missy accepted George, she might well have been Queen Consort of England instead of Queen Consort of Romania. The thought undoubtedly haunted George and Missy's grandmother when she admitted, not long after Missy's marriage, that "Georgie lost Missy by waiting & waiting."[22]

This episode galvanized the Duchess of Edinburgh into action. With a beautiful daughter on the brink of womanhood, Marie knew that she had to act quickly in order to avert another unsuitable romance. Ever the ambitious mother, Marie had her sights set on a glittering future for her eldest daughter. Though the British throne was not to Marie's liking, the Romanian throne was another matter. Fortunately for the ambitious mother, King Carol I of Romania was also on the prowl for an ideal wife for his nephew and heir, Crown Prince Ferdinand of Romania, who was nursing a broken heart after an unsuitable romance. Before Missy realized it, and before Ferdinand embroiled himself in another objectional romance, the machinations of King Carol and the Duchess of Edinburgh would work to unite the destinies of these two young people.

Romania's current ruler was the former Prince Karl of Hohenzollern-Sigmaringen, who had been chosen to take over the reins of power in 1866. The senior branch of this dynasty had provided rulers for Prussia. And now a strong, united Germany was ruled by the same Hohenzollern family with Missy's pompous and bombastic cousin, Kaiser Wilhelm II, at its head. A lifelong admirer of his own dynasty and Teutonic heritage, Karl nevertheless threw himself wholeheartedly into his role as leader of Romania. After successfully leading a combined Romanian and Russian contingent to victory against the Turks at Plevna in the Russo-Turkish War of 1877–78, Prince Karl became Romania's first king in 1881, taking the name Carol I.

Like his uncle, King Carol, Prince Ferdinand ("Nando") belonged to the same junior, Catholic branch of the Hohenzollern family, the Sigmaringens. As his marriage was childless, Carol chose a nephew, Ferdinand, as his heir in 1889. All was calm in Bucharest until Ferdinand embroiled himself in an unsuitable romance. This scandal was the catalyst that sent Nando in Missy's direction. King Carol and the Duchess of Edinburgh arranged for the couple to meet in Germany.

Dressed in a mauve gown adorned with an orchid, Missy sat next to Nando at a gala dinner. They conversed in German and Missy found him shy but amiable. Their next meeting in Munich was just as agreeable. Masking his shyness again through laughter, Nando aroused in Missy a desire to put him at ease, while her beauty and feminine charms worked their wonders on the young prince.

At twenty-six, Ferdinand was ten years older than Missy. Bookish, mild-mannered, inclined toward intellectual pursuits, Nando, who had dark brown hair and eyes, might have been considered handsome except for large ears that tended to protrude and a long, straight nose, characteristic of the House of Hohenzollern. In character, they differed tremendously. Where she was outgoing, Ferdinand was introverted. Missy admitted that during these days it was "his extraordinary timidity . . . [that] gave you a longing to put him at his ease, to make him comfortable; it aroused your motherly feelings, in fact you wanted to help him." These were not exactly words of passion, but for the innocent sixteen-year-old it was enough to prompt her to accept his marriage proposal—a proposal prompted by the Kaiser, Missy's mother, and Charly, Kaiser Wilhelm and Sophie of Greece's sister. As a close friend of the Duchess of Edinburgh, Charly became a frequent visitor to Coburg. Missy was at first a great admirer, but that soon changed to disappointment and anger. Charly, recalled Missy, was "capable of lifelong friendships, of generosity and even of abnegation, [yet] she was for all that, one of the most fickle and changeable women I have ever had to deal with."[23]

Taken aback by news of the betrothal, Queen Victoria admitted that "the *Verlobung* [engagement] of Ferdinand has given her [Queen Elisabeth of Romania] a shock but she is not ill-disposed towards poor little Missy."[24] Queen Elisabeth's acceptance of Missy was surprising, considering the part she played in inflaming passions between Ferdinand and an unsuitable commoner. Ever the romantic, Carol's wife Elisabeth—or Carmen Sylva, as the poetess Queen of

Romania was known—had been instrumental in promoting Nando's romance with one of the ladies of the Romanian court, a certain Helene Vacarescu. But the Romanian elite and the king, for that matter, disapproved of the match. To them, for any member of the royal family to marry a Romanian was simply out of the question for political reasons. King Carol ordered Ferdinand to choose between the throne or his love. Ever obedient, the crown prince chose duty. Enraged by his wife's part in encouraging the couple, King Carol I banished his queen from Romania for two years: Elisabeth was sent packing to her mother in Germany. Not surprisingly, Missy's knowledge of the Vacarescu affair was non-existent at the time of her engagement. Missy and her sisters had been sheltered all their lives; so much so, in fact, that Missy years later admitted she and her sisters "had been kept in glorious, but . . . dangerous and almost cruel, ignorance of realities," so that their upbringing was "based upon nothing but illusions . . . and a completely false conception of life."[25]

Stories about the affair spread beyond Bucharest. This, combined with the news of Missy's betrothal, was too much for one member of the British royal family, the Duke of Cambridge, and his confidante, Lady Geraldine Somerset, who wrote: "disgusted to see the announcement of the marriage of poor pretty nice P. Marie of Edinburgh to the *Prince of Roumania*!!! It does seem too cruel a shame to cart that nice pretty girl off to semi-barbaric Roumania and a man to the knowledge of all Europe desperately in love with another woman."[26] Queen Victoria took a similar view of the situation. When the queen realized that her daughter-in-law, Marie, had engineered the match, she felt sorry for her grand-daughter, calling Missy "a great victim . . . to be enormously pitied."[27]

The queen also could not help expressing her misgivings about the engagement. For a start, the country itself and the society in general were, in the queen's eyes, valid reasons for being wary about the marriage. The queen was also perplexed that Missy would be married at so tender an age, obviously forgetting that her own daughter, Vicky, the Princess Royal, was engaged at fourteen and married at seventeen. The queen confided to Victoria of Hesse herself that "We have been much startled lately to hear of *Missy's Engagement* to *Ferdinand of Rumania*. He is nice I believe & the Parents are charming—but the Country is very insecure & the immorality of the Society at Bucharest *quite awful*. Of course the marriage would be delayed some time as Missy won't be 17 till the end of Oct!"[28]

Moved by the plight of her grandson, George, who had waited so long for Missy and now had suddenly lost her, the queen admired his stoic response to the engagement, "Poor Georgie . . . is not bitter."[29] Despite her initial misgivings, Queen Victoria gave her approval to the marriage. But it was done with some concerns on her part. Her eldest daughter, the Empress Frederick, confided to Sophie of Greece the British royal family's uneasiness over the engagement:

Aunt Beatrice [Ena's mother] is not at all delighted at Missy of Edinburgh's engagement, and thinks about Ferdinand as we all do. Neither my Mama nor Uncle Alfred seem much pleased. It seems Marie was perplexed and did not know what to do. There were different suitors, and this was thought the best way to solve the question. Still my family regret it. Missy is till now quite delighted, but the poor child is so young, how can she guess what is before her?[30]

Queen Victoria was active in the ensuing negotiations over the marriage contract between Missy and Nando. The fact that Missy was marrying a Roman Catholic meant she was automatically forfeiting her place in the line of succession to the English throne. Nevertheless, the queen gave her views on the matter to her prime minister, Lord Rosebery, who duly passed them on the British Foreign Office, stating: "Her Majesty considers that there should be a treaty of marriage, as the union is one between a British Princess and the heir to a foreign crown . . . she thinks that the Princess's renunciation of her British rights should appear as an article in the treaty, though it is in fact involuntary."[31]

After careful analysis, the Foreign Office concluded that Missy need not undergo any sort of formal renunciation at all because she would be "disabled *'ipso facto'* by her marriage" and thus "any renunciation in a treaty is, strictly speaking, unnecessary and superfluous."[32] Queen Victoria disagreed. Lord Rosebery issued a memorandum stating that "the Queen is of the opinion that something must be mentioned in the treaty with regard to the renunciation."[33] Victoria's preoccupation with this issue was best summed up by her private secretary, who told Rosebery, "I return the Roumanian Treaty with the Queen's corrections. . . . The Queen thinks . . . it could be more graceful if Princess Marie were voluntarily to renounce the Crown of Great Britain and Ireland instead of being ruled out of it."[34] In the end, Queen Victoria won, as the "renunciation would be by separate instrument of which note would be taken in the treaty."[35] No stone was left unturned in the marriage negotiations; what seemed a pedantic exercise was in Queen Victoria's eyes a necessity. Thanks to her intervention, Missy was spared the "humiliation" of being automatically "struck off" the English line of succession for her forthcoming marriage to a Catholic prince.

Not content with this small triumph, Queen Victoria was still giving her views to the Foreign Office on how Missy should be addressed. Just a month before the wedding day, the Foreign Office instructed the British chargé d'affaires at Bucharest, Charles Hardinge, that Queen Victoria "thinks that the Princess should also be styled granddaughter of the Sovereign, giving the Queen's full title."[36]

The wedding, on 10 January 1893, was held at Sigmaringen Castle, a fairy-tale edifice perched high above a mighty cliff overlooking the Danube River. Missy was dressed in a a voluminous gown in keeping with the tastes of the day. When the time came to affirm before the world their intention to marry, the bride and groom's responses were almost a reflection of how they viewed their marriage. Nando's *"ja"* was "heard distinctly over the church, but the answer of Princess Marie was quite inaudible."[37]

If Missy was overcome by the thought of her new life and position, she betrayed nothing to the throngs of guests who watched her carefully. In reporting to Lord Rosebery, Lord Malet, Britain's minister in Berlin, who had been specifically asked by Queen Victoria to witness Missy's wedding, praised the princess:

> I cannot close this Despatch without mentioning the effect which the great beauty of the Bride, and the charm of her manner produced upon all who saw her. Her Royal Highness took the hearts of her future countrymen by storm. The Ministers and the ladies who had come with the King of Roumania spoke to me in the most rapturous terms of Her Royal Highness and said they were completely under her fascination.[38]

Though Queen Victoria was unable to get to her granddaughter's wedding, she did not forget to honor Missy. On the wedding day itself, salutes were fired from forts and ships at Portsmouth. At Osborne, the queen held a dinner party which included the Romanian minister to London and Lord Rosebery, the prime minister. In her toast to the newlyweds, Queen Victoria raised her glass with the words: "I wish to propose the health of my dear grandchildren Prince and Princess Ferdinand of Romania, with every wish for their happiness."[39]

The Empress Frederick gave her opinion to Sophie of Greece, "I think it very hard upon her, that she should be married off so young, and go so far away."[40] How right she proved to be.

Missy's honeymoon lasted only a few days, but the experience left the young woman in a daze. Completely unprepared for what was in store for her, Missy became suddenly bewildered with married life. The almost brusque fashion in which Nando exercised his conjugal rights left the more mystical and unworldly bride in shock. "He was," recalled Missy, "terribly, almost cruelly in love. In my immature way I tried to respond to his passion, but I hungered and thirsted for something more."[41] Despite the romantic setting of her honeymoon cottage and the obvious pleasure Nando was deriving from their time alone together, the young bride felt disappointed if not deceived by her experiences.

Already within a few days of their marriage, Missy sensed a mental gulf. Her new husband, a man of few words, found it difficult to communicate with his wife in the way she wanted to be understood. A bit of imagination and patience on Nando's part, with some bantering and wooing during their first days of marriage, might have gone a long way in easing Missy's transition to married life. Queen Victoria was right when she had noted upon hearing of Missy and Nando's engagement: "she is a mere Child, & quite inexperienced!"[42]

The day after Missy's wedding, Queen Victoria wrote to the Empress Frederick of her concern for the newly married bride:

> Yesterday poor little Missy was married—the irrevocable step taken "for better, for worse." I ought not to tell you now, who have this so soon before you, what I feel about a daughter's marrying, but to me there is something so dreadful, so repulsive in that one has to give one's beloved and innocent child, whom one has watched over and guarded from the breath of anything indelicate [that she] should be given over to a man, a stranger to a great extent, body and soul to do with what he likes. No experience in [life (?)] will ever help me over that.[43]

In another letter to Vicky in 1860, Queen Victoria expanded her view of marriage: "All marriage is such a lottery—the happiness is always an exchange—though it may be a very happy one—still the poor woman is bodily and morally the husband's slave. That always sticks in my throat. When I think of a merry, happy, free young girl—and look at the ailing, aching state a young wife generally is doomed to—which you can't deny is the penalty of marriage."[44] Mercifully for Queen Victoria, she was unaware just how closely these thoughts mirrored the conjugal experience of her innocent granddaughter.

Within days of the marriage, the unsophisticated Missy boarded a train and began her journey to Bucharest and a new life in an exotic land in the East—a land over which she would one day be queen. Waiting to greet her in Bucharest was *"der Onkel,"* the imposing King Carol I, soon to be joined from exile by his wife, the outrageously bizarre Carmen Sylva. A strange and arduous stage in Missy's life was set to begin. And, as we shall see, the seventeen-year-old Missy would need to draw upon all her resources to keep her wits about her in a new and hostile court.

Four

IN PURSUIT OF ALIX

TIME HAD NOT DIMINISHED THE AFFECTION TSAREVITCH NICHOLAS
had for Alix of Hesse-Darmstadt. The adolescent princess had grown into a
highly attractive young woman, so that when she became of marriageable age,
the tsarevitch was determined to make Alix his wife.

For the twenty-five-year-old Tsarevitch Nicholas, the day of reckoning was fast
approaching. Consumed by a conflicting mass of emotions, Nicky, heir to his father, Emperor Alexander III, boarded the imperial train bound for an unsched-
uled visit to Germany. Just days before, Nicholas had had no intention of joining
his uncle, Grand Duke Vladimir, and other members of the imperial family for the
long journey. Now, he was a member of the party, uncertain as to what lay ahead,
counting the hours as the train lumbered its way out of Russia and headed east-
ward. Confidence and doubt consumed the tsarevitch. He was both elated and
troubled—elated at the thought that he was soon to be reunited with the young
woman he loved but troubled that this longed-for reunion might easily turn into
disaster.

For a day and a half, Nicholas pondered, read, and endured an uncomfortable journey, punctuated by excessive heat as the train sped toward its destination, the picturesque town of Coburg in Germany. Ostensibly, Nicky was on his
way to the small duchy to attend the wedding of Ernie, the Grand Duke of Hesse,
to Ducky, Missy of Romania's favorite sister. In reality, Nicholas had seized
upon the chance to leave for Coburg in order to confront the groom's youngest
sister, Alix. For the Tsarevitch Nicholas was intent on one purpose: to extract
from Alix the much-coveted "yes" to his quest to make her his wife.

When the tsarevitch left Russia, all indications pointed to a daunting task ahead. Already he had been told by Princess Alix that all was over between them; Nicholas must look elsewhere for a bride. Yet for a man who throughout his life was hampered by irresoluteness, Nicky's single-minded determination where Alix was concerned was astonishing. Although various members of the Romanov family were already set to represent the imperial family at the wedding of Ernie and Ducky, Nicholas suddenly announced to his father two days before the departure date that he too would leave for Coburg. Granted permission by his ailing father to go and propose to Alix, Nicholas's abrupt change in plans sent the royals gathered in Coburg for the nuptials into a twitter. But none was more affected by Nicky's sudden appearance than the object of his visit, Alix herself. Almost from the moment the tsarevitch stepped off the imperial train, there was not to be a moment's peace for Princess Alix of Hesse-Darmstadt.

For the next four days—tense days full of high drama—the twenty-one-year-old Alix set the future Tsar of All the Russias on an emotional roller-coaster ride. So resolute was she in refusing to accept Nicky's proposal, yet so insistent was the tsarevitch, that the outcome was in question right to the very end. A sense of urgency hung heavily in the air. And so immersed were the guests in the high-stakes drama that the wedding of Ernie and Ducky, instead of being the centerpiece, was turning into a sideshow.

Princess Alix of Hesse-Darmstadt had long occupied the thoughts of the Tsarevitch Nicholas; the two met as adolescents in the 1880s and again at the end of the decade. By 1891, Nicky's feelings had increased in intensity. It was easy to understand why he felt this way. At eighteen years of age, the object of his desire had blossomed into a stunningly beautiful woman. Tall and slender, with lustrous gray eyes and near-perfect features framed by masses of rich golden-red hair, Alix bewitched many.

Some observers, however, were put off by a decidedly melancholy air that already hung about the princess. This, coupled with her intense timidity, made her appear gauche and cold. But where others might view this as a strike against Alix, the Tsarevitch Nicholas was enchanted. To him, nothing marred his impressions of the princess from Hesse: Alix was perfection.

In his diary, Nicholas wrote toward the end of 1891 that his dream was "one day to marry Alix H[esse]. I have loved her for a long time, but more deeply and strongly since 1889. . . . For a long time I resisted my feelings, and tried to deceive myself about the impossibility of achieving my most cherished wish! But now that Eddy has withdrawn or been rejected, the only obstacle or gulf between us—is the question of religion!"[1]

The "Eddy" Nicholas was referring to was none other than Princess Maud's brother. Efforts to educate this young man who was expected to become King of England came to naught. One glance at Eddy said it all: he was a sorry specimen. Not only did he lack any sort of intellectual prowess; Eddy also possessed a short attention span.

Even into young adulthood, Eddy did not impress, as the Duchess of Edinburgh discovered when she and her family visited Sandringham in January 1885 in order to celebrate her nephew's twenty-first birthday. When the time came for Eddy to receive his birthday gifts and congratulations, the duchess found him "pale" and "horribly timid." "In a word," wrote his aunt, Eddy "is still a real child in spite of his twenty-one years."[2] In time, Eddy also grew increasingly debauched. In fact, so bizarre was his scandalous behavior that years later the theory that he was Jack the Ripper was seriously bandied about. In the eyes of his family, the only answer was to marry him off to a suitable and sensible woman. Such, then, was the peculiar creature that Queen Victoria was foisting on her dearest of granddaughters. Eddy did not take much persuading to warm to the idea of having Alix as his wife. Just as everyone thought, he could not resist the lovely princess, duly fell in love, and proposed.

Alix, however, was not interested in marrying the most unprepossessing of Queen Victoria's grandsons, prompting the queen to ask, "what fancy has she got in her head?"[3] That "fancy" was none other than the Tsarevitch of Russia, with whom Alix was already in love. This scuttled any plans for fulfilling Queen Victoria's great wish.

By the autumn of 1889, Queen Victoria had resigned herself to the fact that there was little hope of seeing her two grandchildren united in matrimony. Yet however much Alix loathed Eddy, and despite the fact that she was in love with Nicky, she was also imbued with a strong sense of duty, a result of Queen Victoria's hands-on "mothering." So, despite her professed dislike of Eddy, Alicky was not obstinate enough to defy orders. But Queen Victoria did not wish to force Eddy on Alix and regretfully accepted the princess's refusal.

Alix's decision, in May 1890, was "a real sorrow" to Queen Victoria. However, the girl's boldness in speaking her mind touched a chord of admiration in a woman long accustomed to getting her way. It was commendable that her darling Alicky was not swayed in her decision by the glittering prospect of the crown of England. Alix's refusal was, in her grandmother's eyes, evidence of courage and integrity. "This shows great strength of character" was how the queen summed up her granddaughter's obstinacy.[4]

As for Eddy, soon after Alix's rejection, he set his heart on the twenty-one-year-old Princess Hélène d'Orléans. But as a Roman Catholic, Hélène was debarred by English law from marrying an heir to the British throne. Even though she was willing to convert to Protestantism, her father and the Pope forbade it, putting an end to that romance.

The choice of a wife for Eddy finally fell on the unfortunate Princess May of Teck. But weeks before the wedding, May and and members of the Wales family watched in disbelief at Sandringham by his bedside as Eddy struggled for his life. By the morning of 14 January 1982, he was dead from influenza. Maud had joined her family to bid her brother farewell, his last hours shrouded in delirium. Eddy was just twenty-eight years old.

Once Alix rejected Eddy, Tsarevitch Nicholas redoubled his efforts at making Alix of Hesse-Darmstadt his wife, much to Queen Victoria's horror. She loathed the Romanovs, whom she viewed as morally corrupt as well as "false and arrogant." Moreover, Russian expansionist aims concerning Turkey and Afghanistan, which directly challenged Britain's interests in both regions, served to inflame further Queen Victoria's views against the tsarist empire. Neither did memories of the Crimean War help to alleviate the British monarch's entrenched Russophobia. As the queen once put it succinctly: "Russia is *our real* enemy & totally antagonistic to *England*."[5]

Since Alix's sister, Ella, had done the unforgivable by marrying Grand Duke Serge and hence gone over to the enemy camp, Queen Victoria watched Alix carefully. When the queen found out that Ella was doing all she could to promote the match between Alix and Nicky, she fumed with indignation, telling Ella and Alix's sister, Victoria: "Behind *all* your backs, Ella & S. [Serge] do *all* they can to bring it about, encouraging & even urging the Boy [Nicky] to do it! . . . *this* must not be *allowed to go on*. Papa *must* put his foot down & there *must* be no more visits of Alicky to Russia—"[6]

The strength of Nicky's love for Alix can be seen in his open defiance of his parents' opposition to the match. For just as Alexandra, the Princess of Wales, was an ardent anti-German, so too was her sister, Empress Marie Feodorovna of Russia. As Danish princesses, the sisters' anger with Prussian attempts to swallow up their father's duchies of Schleswig-Holstein turned them into rabid Germanophobes.

Alix's German blood was not the only strike against her in the eyes of Empress Marie. She also knew the young woman was excruciatingly shy and more than likely ill-equipped to play her part as tsarina at the court of St. Petersburg. The demanding public role of an empress required adroit skills, which Marie was certain Alix did not possess. The princess's aloofness and cold demeanor were bound go down badly in the Russian capital. Better that Nicky find himself a more gregarious wife than the beautiful but introverted Alix.

Like a caged animal awaiting its release, the tsarevitch bided his time, hoping that he would be permitted to marry Alix. But more worrisome to Nicholas was the object of all this expended energy, his adored Alicky, for it became evident that the greatest opposition to the match came from Alix herself! And this was all because of her steadfast refusal to forsake her religion. It was beginning to appear as if the anguished lovers were destined never to marry.

Well aware that any future tsarina needed to belong to the Russian Orthodox faith, Alix, to whom her religion was a sincerely and deeply felt spiritual commitment, was too attached to her Protestant faith to contemplate converting. Like her mother before her, Alix had imbibed deeply the teachings reinforced by her own strong sense of faith—one honed skillfully by her spiritual mentor, Dr. Sell. Sell advised the princess that her refusal to forsake Lutheranism for Orthodoxy was truly the only option. To do otherwise was to commit apostasy, which was equivalent to spiritual suicide. The princess from Darmstadt who had already said no to the throne of England was set on rejecting the throne of Russia as well, surrendering to Dr. Sell's admonition that "when heart and conscience are at war, it is God's will that conscience should win."[7]

Marie Feodorovna's own misgivings over Princess Alix as a future daughter-in-law colored the views of her husband. With his wife so implacably against Alix of Hesse as a wife for Nicky, it was not surprising to find Emperor Alexander III in agreement about his son's choice. But even if his wife had not been so opposed, it was likely Alexander III would have found the Hessian princess too German for his taste as well, for the highly Slavophile emperor himself harbored strong anti-German sentiments, which were further exacerbated when Kaiser Wilhelm II ascended the throne in 1888. The Russian emperor found Willy excessively loud and nothing but "an ill-mannered, dishonest rogue,"[8] further fueling his own suspicions about Germany. Undeterred by his failure to charm the tsar, Wilhelm II nevertheless proceeded to woo Russia in an attempt to keep the empire allied to his. Securing a German wife for the future Nicholas II inevitably became part of the Kaiser's plan to contain imperial Russia.

As the suspicions between Wilhelm II and Alexander III grew through the early 1890s, so too did relations between their two countries rapidly sour. Not wishing to be isolated, and in need of the foreign currency that France offered, Alexander III and his ministers set about aligning Russia with the French Republic. In no time, the unthinkable had emerged: a rapprochement between autocratic Russia and republican France, an alliance that was cemented in January 1894 by a military agreement. The Kaiser smelled danger. Germany was suddenly flanked by two powerful countries allied to each other with little sympathy for Berlin. Thus did Wilhelm pounce on the chance to play Cupid to Nicholas and Alix in an effort to secure some influence in Russo-German relations. But before that could happen, Emperor Alexander urged Nicky to divest himself of his obsession with Alix and set his heart instead on another princess in the interest of cementing the Russo-French entente. This princess proved to be none other than Princess Hélène d'Orléans—the very same Hélène who had briefly been Prince Eddy's fiancée. For the emperor and Empress of Russia, a marriage between the tsarevitch and the French princess was a political match made in heaven, a perfect culmination of years of friendship between France and Russia.

Thus, where Alexander III and Wilhelm II were concerned, the question of Nicholas's choice of a bride took on added urgency. For Nicky's wife, whoever she may be, was to become a potential weapon in the ongoing diplomatic battle brewing between the two empires. Yet there was never any doubt where Nicky's heart lay—Hélène never stood a chance against Alix.

Not all the pleadings of his mother or the gruff pronouncements from his huge, bearlike father intimidated the slightly built tsarevitch one bit. All their arguments fell on deaf ears. Always the dutiful son, this good-natured and God-fearing young man had never truly caused his parents much concern. However, his open defiance of them over his choice of a bride startled Alexander and Marie. For the first time, and in the most important issue of all for their son, and for Russia—the choice of a wife and future empress—Nicholas was adamant.

Emperor Alexander grew impatient, telling his stubborn son, "She won't have you. She's a confirmed Lutheran." Then, wondering what Nicholas found attractive in the intensely shy and awkward princess besides her looks, Alexander asked, "And what in the world do you see in her?" The tsarevitch shot back, "Everything."[9]

Nicholas received the same kind of comments from his mother. "Alix of Hesse," insisted Empress Marie, "does not wish to have you. You are the heir. It is your duty to marry." "And I shall," replied an exasperated Nicky. "And she'll have me yet," he added defiantly.[10] Nicky declared: "It's Alicky of Hesse—or nobody—for me!"[11]

But so inflexible was Alix on the religious question that her aunt, Empress Frederick, wrote to Sophie of Greece: "I hear (and only tell you in confidence) that Alix of Hesse has now decided not to entertain the idea of marrying Nicky of Russia, though he wished it deeply, and Ella took great pains to bring it about. Alicky likes him very much, but will not change her religion on any account . . . I am sorry for the poor girl, and I am sorry for Nicky, as I fear he had set his heart upon it."[12]

Amidst all this, Nicky was dallying with a young ballerina, Mathilde

Kschessinksa. Yet he was moved to confess, "What a surprising thing our heart is!" How was it that he could carry on with Kschessinksa and long for Alix at the same time? The affair with the ballerina was just that—an affair—but it was not true love. In reality, Nicky's heart was firmly fixed in Darmstadt. No matter how much he tried to amuse himself in order to temper his thoughts about the beautiful Hessian princess who had captured his heart, he could not succeed in eradicating thoughts of his Alicky—nor did he want to. Finally admitting defeat, he confessed: "I never stop thinking of Alix!"[13]

Queen Victoria was winning this game of tug-of-war, but only just, and only because of Alix's strong affinity to Lutheranism. Thanks to Alix's religious convictions, there appeared little hope that this Hessian granddaughter would be sacrificed to Russia. When Ella converted to Russian Orthodoxy after several years of marriage, Alix could not understand her sister's actions. "I'll live and die a Lutheran," she told Ella. "Religion," said Alix, "isn't a pair of gloves to pull on and off."[14] Her abiding commitment to her Lutheran faith was unshakable. If this meant that marriage to Nicky was impossible, so be it.

But Nicky would not give up. Displaying a tenacity that surprised those who knew him intimately, he refused to countenance a future without Alix. He plied her with letters pledging his love and devotion. By November 1893, Alix was still not budging on the religious issue. She even went so far as to send Nicky's sister, Grand Duchess Xenia, a letter explaining that all this wishing for marriage had to come to an end. "I cannot become untrue to my own confession," Alix explained. And because this was so, "I don't want him to go on hoping."[15]

As for Nicky, Alix begged him to realize that they must end this fruitless quest for happiness because she could not bring herself to convert. Better to end this tortuous situation once and for all. Nicholas had to understand her point of view, because "I have tried to look at it in every light . . . but I always return to one thing. I cannot do it against my conscience." To do so would be "a sin . . . and I should be miserable all the days of my life, knowing that I had done a wrongful thing." Therefore, "what happiness can come from a marriage which begins without the real blessing of God?"[16]

If she changed religions out of convenience, Alix explained in a final letter, "I should never find my peace of mind again, and like that I should never be your real companion who should help you on in life; for there always should be something between us two, in my not having the real conviction of the belief I had taken, and in the regret for the one I *had* left." Alix ended her letter by pointing out that it was useless for Nicky to go on hoping, because "I can *never* change my confession."[17] Those six words combined to cut Nicky's heart with razor-sharp precision.

Devastated by the news, he wrote in his diary: "It is impossible for her to change religion, and all my hopes are shattered by this implacable obstacle."[18] A month passed before Nicholas found the courage to take up a pen and reply. When he did so, he was full of tender sympathy for the anguish his Alix was going through. He also admired her for the depth of her commitment to God. But Nicholas wrote too of his own desolation, of feeling "so lonely and so beaten down!!" He would place his trust in God and pray that "He will guide my darling along the path." Then Nicky's gentleness turned to defiance.

> Oh! do not say "no" directly, my dearest Alix, do not ruin my life already! Do you think there can be any happiness in the whole world without you! After having *involuntarily*! kept me waiting and hoping, can this end in such a way?[19]

The tsarevitch was still hoping against all hope for a miracle. His chance came four months later, during the fateful visit to Coburg in April 1894.

Once he was in Coburg, Alix's presence spurred Nicholas into action. Left alone together, Nicholas chipped away at her defenses. In an experience emotionally draining for them both, Nicky argued and cajoled for two interminable hours. Alix cried the whole time, whispering, "No! I cannot."[20] But little did Nicky know that despite her refusal, the ground beneath her was already giving way.

Kaiser Wilhelm II, ever the busybody, was just as caught up as everyone else by the drama. Anxious to see a Russo-German alliance come true—a union that might come in politically handy for Germany—Willy proceeded to convince Alix to convert. It was an ironic move on the Kaiser's part in view of Wilhelm's fight with his sister, Sophie, over her conversion to Orthodoxy.

At Coburg, Wilhelm used all his skills of persuasion to convince Alix of Hesse that she must forsake her Protestant faith and become a Russian Orthodox. Consumed by her own conflicting emotions, Alix was unaware that she was being used by the Kaiser as a pawn in his game of political chess. Wilhelm's matchmaking was an attempt at countering growing Russian animosity toward Germany, a disturbing trend that had begun after Willy ascended the throne in 1888.

Ever since he visited Russia in 1886, Wilhelm II—as one historian puts it—"considered himself to be a specialist in Russian affairs, in which he took a conspicuous interest." Moreover, the Kaiser "regarded Russia as a special preserve for his alleged diplomatic expertise."[21] Sensing a diplomatic coup in the offing for Germany if he could get Alix of Hesse-Darmstadt to walk down the aisle in St. Petersburg, Willy set about pushing the lovebirds to commit themselves. In so doing, Willy fancied himself playing not so much Cupid as Bismarck. So grateful would Nicky and Alix be for his help in getting them together that Germany and the Kaiser would soon assert themselves on the Russian stage and, even more important, on the European scene. But however much playing the diplomat tickled the Kaiser's inflated ego, the fact was that Wilhelm II had for years feared Russia. His frenetic attentions at Coburg were therefore more than mere exercises to amuse his own self-worth. They were, in fact, calculated maneuvering on the Kaiser's part to shape the destiny of Germany. This was, after all, "the heyday of 'personal rule'" where Kaiser Wilhelm was concerned.[22] And the period during which the tsarevitch seriously pursued Princess Alix fell squarely during the era when Wilhelm II exercised dominance over German affairs.

While Wilhelm II was cajoling Alix into making her fateful decision, also working in the wings was her sister, Ella. But in meddling in the affair at Coburg, the bombastic Kaiser Wilhelm was careful as much as possible not to cross paths with the still-ravishing Ella, for years before he had been hopelessly in love with her but was spurned when he offered her marriage. Ella's rejection hurt Willy deeply. And seeing and talking to her now brought back painful memories to a Kaiser who was so accustomed to being obeyed.

The Empress Frederick, also in Coburg for the wedding, kept Sophie abreast of what was happening with her cousins. After telling her daughter that "little Missy of Roumania was looking pale and thin, and is expecting No. II!" Vicky went on to add her bit about the drama: "I wish I could tell you that everything is settled about him and Alicky, they both much wish it, but the religious question still seems the obstacle."[23]

⚬〰〰〰〰⚬

With the kind of maddening existence Crown Princess Marie of Romania was leading since her arrival at Bucharest, it was not surprising that Empress Frederick found Missy looking pale and thin. The Romania that the sheltered seventeen-year-old princess was set to call home was a bewildering place. As one biographer has written:

> In the nineteenth century it was called "the kingdom at the edge of the Western World." Born from the ashes of the Ottoman Empire, breathtakingly beautiful, wrapped in mystery and age-old legends, it is a land of towering mountains and rich pastures, powerful rivers and fertile plains that merge into the eastern steppes. It was said to have been the habitat of mythical-sounding princes—Michael the Brave, Mircea the Old, Vlad the Impaler, Brancovan the Good, whose names now belong to the pantheon of local folklore.[24]

Upon her arrival in Bucharest, Missy was seized with fear. The new crown princess, very much the unseasoned performer on public occasions, could feel thousands of eyes scrutinizing her every move. Missy suffered through her ordeals, feeling "small, foolish insignificant and 'exceedingly lonely amidst the multitude.'" Throughout all the welcoming events, the one thing that touched her was the sight of Union Jacks flying next to the Romanian flags all over Bucharest. Upon seeing "the beloved old flag!" recalled Missy, "tears came into my eyes, [for] that flag meant home!" So new to the country, the yellow, red, and blue Romanian colors meant nothing yet to this very British princess.

Once she began to settle down, Missy's irrepressible high spirits were quickly quashed. Home was the imposing Royal Palace, a regal but cold and forbidding abode, more suited to the taste of Romania's King Carol I than to a teenage girl accustomed to comfortable surroundings. Instead of chintzes and an airy milieu, the new crown princess was consigned to spend endless hours cooped up in a palace resembling a marble sarcophagus. Much to Missy's chagrin, the apartments that were now her home were in her view "a disaster." Done up in what she derided as *"Altdeutsch,"* a heavy and garish style of "bad rococo," the furnishing and living arrangements only served to depress the new bride so that her heart sank "lower and lower" until she "wondered if it would ever end sinking."[25]

Even more depressing than her gloomy surroundings was the fact that she and her new husband were expected to live under the same roof as King Carol. From the start, Carol I made no concessions to the new arrival. As a member of the Romanian royal family, Missy was expected to fit in—seamlessly. All of the king's demands were to be assumed without question. *Der Onkel* brooked no opposition to his highly attuned sense of discipline and duty. And no one was more aware of this than *der Onkel's* nephew and heir, Crown Prince Ferdinand. Both men, so thoroughly at home in the strict military Prussian world, had no idea how to deal with a lonely seventeen-year-old girl whose high-spirited personality was now undergoing a profound change.

In time Carol I was to find to his exasperation that he had to reckon with a spitfire. But in the early days, the new crown princess had little energy to fight back. Shocked at her new role as a wife, depressed at living in a new country, disappointed that her husband was completely subservient to the king, Missy's first year in Bucharest became an absolute nightmare. She chafed at the restrictions—not even the carefully screened Madame Grecianu, her lady-in-waiting, was allowed to be chummy with her.

The choice of Missy's lady-in-waiting had been made with the utmost care by King Carol. Thanks to Queen Victoria's strict dictums, the king had to tread carefully here. The queen, who had described "the immorality of the Society at

Bucharest [as being] *quite awful*," wanted her granddaughter's lady-in-waiting to be beyond reproach. The British chargé d'affaires at Bucharest, Charles Hardinge, was of the same opinion. "Owing to the laxity of morals and the looseness of their divorce laws," noted Hardinge, "Roumanian society was hopelessly complicated and involved due to the number of people divorced, married to others who had been divorced and with sometimes families of more than one previous marriage on either side." Because of this, "the King experienced considerable difficulty in finding a lady to act as Mistress of the Princess's Household unconnected with any scandal." But, when finally "the lady was found," Hardinge recalled that Sir Henry Ponsonby wrote to him on behalf of Queen Victoria, saying, "we were glad to learn the name of the pure Madame Greciano."[26]

Missy might have been less miserable if Nando had taken her side and been more understanding. Unfortunately, he was too frightened of his uncle to do anything other than the old man's bidding. Soon enough, Missy found that her gallant knight was nothing more than a shadow of *der Onkel*. He was, after all, "uncle's nephew, a man of duty, trained to do uncle's bidding, trained to see with uncle's eyes, almost to use uncle's words."[27] This was a far cry from the reassuring words Missy wrote to Queen Victoria not long before the wedding, when she assured her concerned grandmother that all would be well. "My dear Grand Mama," wrote Missy, "though my task may at first seem difficult, I am sure that both Ferdinand and the King will do all they can to make it easy for me."[28] How those words must have haunted Crown Princess Marie as she languished in the gilded cage of the Royal Palace at Bucharest.

To make matters worse, Missy found that her normally healthy constitution was failing her. She was at a loss as to the reason for her lethargy and queasiness. But it was soon apparent what was behind these unnerving changes. Within a few months of her arrival, Missy learned that she was pregnant. It was a bewildering jolt to the innocent young bride. She was still trying to cope with the demands of being Nando's wife while at the same time battling her deepening homesickness and increasing unhappiness with her living arrangements, and the news of impending motherhood hit her like a bolt of lightning.

It was the motherly Lady Monson, an Englishwoman who had been of some help to Missy in her early days in Bucharest, who broke the news to the seventeen-year-old princess. Just before leaving for England, Lady Monson found a pale, sullen Missy languishing in her "disastrous rococo room." Usually energetic and eager for exercise, the newlywed was bewildered by her sudden attacks of queasiness. "I feel giddy," confessed Missy, "food disgusts me. . . . Everything makes me feel sick; smells, noises, faces, even colours. I'm altogether changed, I don't recognize my own self!" Lady Monson knew exactly what was the matter.

She told Missy that everyone would be delighted. But when Missy showed signs of confusion and seemed about to burst out crying, Lady Monson asked her, "You don't mean to say no one ever told you?" Nearly panicking, Missy replied frantically, "Told me what?"[29] It was at that moment that the new crown princess was told about the birds and the bees. It also then dawned on Missy that her primary role was to provide heirs to the throne—and she took the news badly.

As for Nando and King Carol, the news that a new Romanian prince or princess was soon to be born was a welcome one. If his plan in providing a docile and malleable wife for Nando was not materializing right away, at least King Carol was satisfied to see that his wish for dynastic heirs was quickly coming to fruition.

With an heir on the way, the noose around Missy tightened. Concerned for her health and that of the baby growing inside her, the mother-to-be was cosseted even further. Feeling trapped, constantly sick, and missing her mother and Ducky terribly, Missy's deep depression knew no bounds. Finally, on 15 October 1893, Missy's firstborn—a boy—came into the world at Peles Castle, the picturesque castle constructed by King Carol on the foothills of the Carpathian Mountains at the summer resort of Sinaia. Romanian doctors and clergymen had been adamant that the birth be free of chloroform, for in their eyes, "women must pay in agony for the sins of Eve."[30] They and King Carol, however, had not reckoned with Missy's mother who, like the autocratic Romanov that she was, insisted that chloroform was necessary for the birth. Also fighting for Missy was her grandmother, Queen Victoria. One of the first women to have used chloroform to ease labor pains, Victoria knew firsthand of its benefits. King Carol received many missives from his formidable British counterpart, who insisted that Missy be given chloroform. The king gave in.

Queen Victoria was soon reporting the birth of her latest great-grandchild to the Empress Frederick, noting that "Missy's baby arrived a fortnight before they expected it." The eagle-eyed queen betrayed the same sense of propriety she exhibited with Sophie of Greece over the arrival date of *her* first baby. Missy's baby came at the appropriate time because the queen added that its appearance was "not too soon really."[31] The infant was the queen's seventeenth great-grandchild. Not surprisingly, in deference to the new baby's great-uncle, Missy's firstborn child was given the name Carol.

It came as a welcome break for Missy to flee to the more amenable atmosphere of Coburg in 1894 for the marriage of Ducky to Ernie. Once there, just like the rest of the "royal mob," Missy was gripped by the unfolding drama of Nicky and Alix, which threatened to overshadow the wedding of Missy's sister to Alix's brother.

At Coburg, the Kaiser finally took matters into his own hands. Willy went after the dithering Alix himself and lectured her. It worked. Alix came to a decision that would seal her fate. Willy had convinced her that her place was by Nicky's side as his wife. Determined to see this marriage alliance secured once and for all, Willy forced a still doubting Nicky to confront Alix. Nicky then found to his amazement that the tantalizing fruit so far out of reach suddenly and miraculously fell into his hands. The tsarevitch's description of the scene speaks for itself: "The first thing she said was . . . that she agreed! Oh God, what happened to me then! I started to cry like a child, and so did she, only her expression immediately changed; her face brightened and took on an aura of peace."[32] Nicholas was ecstatic: "A wonderful, unforgettable day in my life—the day of my betrothal to my dear beloved Alix. . . . God what a mountain has fallen from my shoulders."[33]

If much of the tsarevitch's reaction revealed a sense of utter relief that everything finally fell into place, Alix's reaction was one of sheer joy. Her cousin and close friend, Princess Marie Louise of Schleswig-Holstein, recalled how "Alix stormed into the room, threw her arms round my neck, and said, 'I am going to marry Nicky.' "[34] And to her former governess, Alix wrote, "I am more happy than words can express; at last after these 5 sad years!"[35]

How was it that Alix finally relented after all these years—years filled with her own intractable brand of obstinacy, a trait that would manifest itself to her detriment in times to come? Ducky's role, for one, as the new Grand Duchess of Hesse meant that there was not much point in Alix staying on in Darmstadt, where she would simply be in the way. Besides, much as they tried to appreciate each other, Ducky and Alix were never to be friends, thanks in large part to their differing personalities. Living in the same small principality as the self-assured Ducky was bound to make the more gauche Alix feel out of place.

There was also Ella's painless religious conversion, which undoubtedly helped settle her younger sister's mind. But in the end, Alix's unbounded love for Nicholas was the strongest factor in her decision to agree to his proposal. His undiminished devotion through the stormiest objections was more than enough to move any woman in love. Yet there was one more element in the saga that made Alix want to dedicate her life to Nicky and to Russia. For despite the fact that she was as devoted to him as he was to her, the twenty-one-year-old princess was not blind to the tsarevitch's shortcomings. Nicholas's fiancée understood that her gentle and loving Nicky lacked the backbone necessary to rule the vast and unruly empire that was his destiny. Even Mathilde Kschessinska sensed this, admitting that though Nicholas had the "character and will-power" to be a tsar, he definitely "did not have the gift of making his opinion prevail, and he often gave in to others though his first impulses had been right."[36] And Nicholas himself confessed his weakness to his uncle, Grand Duke Vladimir, soon after he had become emperor: "I always give in and in the end am made the fool, without will, and without character."[37] Because Princess Alix was aware of this fault, she concluded that in becoming Nicky's wife, she could best serve God by helping Nicholas become a better tsar. Not surprisingly for the serious-minded Alix,

> She accepted him in the end because it came to her that she and she alone could make him envisage duty from the only possible point of view; that her very passion for him was strong enough to evoke qualities she considered dormant; that in marrying him she would be able to guide and to counsel; that in their joint happiness they would fulfil their high duty to the utmost. And, as she reflected on those points, she came to see that she would not violate her conscience . . . it was her true vocation to love and to serve him. Therein lay God's will for her.[38]

Thus, in reconciling herself to her conversion to Orthodoxy, Alix welded this irrevocable decision to a greater calling. She was to be an instrument of God, sent to transform the future Nicholas II and the Russian Empire. In tandem, she and Nicky would work for the greater good of Russia.

Once Alix's engagement was announced to the family, the Empress Frederick rushed off a letter to Athens, telling Sophie, "Alicky is quite radiant and beaming with joy. The moment Nicky arrived I saw by her face that she *would*— though it was so strange to refuse him first, and to swear to everyone that though she was very fond of him, she would never take him." The empress went on to add, "even my dear Mama thought she [Alix] would not accept him, she was so positive about it . . . I could not help chuckling to myself that William did not think Alicky so very sinful to accept Nicky, and with him the necessity of conforming to the Orthodox Church. Of course, I made no remarks!"[39] This, no doubt, was an allusion to the irony in Willy's actions in Coburg.

As Alix had loved Queen Victoria as her own mother, it came as no surprise that the queen was the first person to hear news of the engagement. And from none other than Nicky and Alix themselves. After breakfast, they eagerly sought the queen's blessing and burst into her room, brimming with excitement. "I was quite thunderstruck," noted the bewildered queen. "Though I knew Nicky much wished it, I thought Alicky was not sure of her mind. Saw them both. Alicky had tears in her eyes, but looked very bright, and I kissed them both." The queen added: "Nicky said, 'She is much too good for me.' I told him he must make the religious difficulties as easy as he could for her, which he promised to do. People generally seem pleased at the engagement, which has the drawback that Russia is so far away, the position a difficult one, as well as the question of religion. But, as her brother is married now, and they are really attached to one another, it is perhaps better so."[40]

Nicholas secured a promise from his parents that like Ella, Alix would not have to abjure her old faith upon formally embracing Orthodoxy. Nicholas knew how much this meant to his fiancée, telling her soon after his return to Russia that he was "only too glad to be the first one who may comfort" her with this news.[41] Alix was most fortunate not to have had to renounce her old faith. No such accommodation was to accompany Princess Victoria Eugenie's religious conversion a decade later. In stark contrast to Alix, the ceremony itself for Ena was to take on a much harsher and painful tone.

As for Kaiser Wilhelm, he had deluded himself into thinking that he had pulled off a diplomatic coup. One contemporary account noted that the Kaiser was so thrilled at news of the engagement, his "beaming face" made him look "as if he had suddenly succeeded in adding another party to the Triple Alliance."[42]

Well aware of her granddaughter's emotional state, Queen Victoria wisely invited Alix to stay with her at Windsor right after the engagement at Coburg. Here, Victoria could keep the girl away from prying eyes. Now, without the distraction of others about them, the queen questioned Alicky avidly about every detail of how the engagement came about. Alix told her grandmama so much that she confessed to Nicky, "I no longer knew what to say."[43]

In one of her letters to Nicholas, Alix commented on her cousins Maud of Wales and Sophie of Greece. Comparing her lot with theirs, it seemed to Alix as if good fortune had shone upon her while Maud had yet to reap the benefits of finding a soul mate and Sophie was suffering along with fellow Greeks as the country was jolted by numerous devastating earthquakes—"poor thing it must be too terrible in Greece, these incessant shocks." Reading about Sophie's concerns for Greece and her countrymen's suffering had moved Alix to tell Nicholas of her own view of God and of man's lot on earth. "What sorrows this life does bring, what great trials and how difficult to bear them patiently. . . . Suffering always draws one nearer to God, does it not, and when we think what Jesus Christ had to bear for us, how little and small our sorrows seem in comparison, and yet we fret and grumble and are not patient as He was." But the focus was not solely on suffering and religious introspection. Grateful for the happiness she had been blessed with, Alix could not help but wish the same kind of blessing for

Toria and Maud of Wales. "May He some day make her [Victoria] very happy, she deserves it the dear Child, and little Maudy too. When one is so happy, one longs to see others also joyous and grieves one cannot do anything for them—don't you too?"[44]

During this time, letters between the two lovers flew every day between St. Petersburg and Windsor. Beneath Alix and Nicky's reserved Victorian exteriors lay deep passions that spilled forth from their pens. From Alix to Nicky came the tender words: "Oh, if you only knew how I adore you and the years have made my affection for you grow stronger and deeper; I wish only I were worthier of your love and tenderness."[45]

And from Nicky to Alix many messages like this one:

> You have got me entirely and for ever, soul and spirit, body and heart, everything is *yours,* yours; I would like to scream it out loud for the world to hear it. It is me who am proud to belong to such a sweet angel as you are and to venture to claim for your love to be returned.[46]

Interspersed between the lines of love was Alix's keen interest in learning about Nicky's faith. She asked him to send her religious books. She also revealed her fears about converting, telling him: "You must understand how nervous it makes me, but God will help me, you too, my love, won't you, so that I may always get a better Christian and serve my God as truly as hitherto and more."[47]

In preparation for her future role, Alix began learning about the Orthodox faith in earnest. In order to help her granddaughter come to terms with her conversion, Queen Victoria had passed on this delicate task of easing Alix's transition from Protestantism to Orthodoxy to a favored clergyman, William Boyd Carpenter, the Bishop of Ripon. He duly came to Windsor, where he spoke to Alix at length, taking pains to point out the similarities in both the Protestant and Orthodox faiths. It was a topic of great interest to the future tsarina and one to which she paid close attention.

Upon celebrating her twenty-second birthday, Alix wrote to thank Queen Victoria for her good wishes and birthday present, and tried to reassure the queen:

> Yes, darling Grandmama, the new position I am sure will be full of trials and difficulties, but with God's help and that of a loving husband it will be easier than we now picture it to ourselves. The distance is great, but yet in three days one can get to England. I am sure his parents will often allow us to come over to You. Why I could not bear the idea of not seeing You again, after the kind Angel You have been to me, ever since dear Mama died, and I cling to You

more than ever, now that I am quite an Orphan. God bless You for all Your kindness to me, beloved Grandmama dear. I have no words to thank you enough for all. Please do not think that my marrying will make a difference in my love to You—*certainly it will not,* and when I am far away, I shall long to think that there is One, the dearest and kindest Woman alive, who loves me a little bit.[48]

After months of declining health, by October 1894, to everyone's surprise, the once burly and Herculean-like Emperor Alexander III lay dying in the Crimea. Fearing the worst, Nicky summoned Alix to the imperial family's retreat, Livadia, near Yalta. Hurriedly, the future Empress of Russia traveled to the Crimea, with a minimum of fuss. Once there, her presence was barely acknowledged. So preoccupied was the imperial court with the dying tsar that they were unable to prepare anything special for Alix's entry to Russia.

Upon her arrival at Livadia, a ten-day drama began to unfold. It would end in the accession to the throne of her beloved Nicky. During this trying time, the future tsarina noticed how her fiancé was overshadowed by others. She wrote in Nicholas's diary, urging him to assert himself. "Your Sunny is praying for you. . . . Be firm and make the doctors . . . come alone to you every day . . . so that you are the first to know. . . . Don't let others be put first and you left out. . . . Show your own mind and don't let others forget who you are."[49] It was the beginning of Alix's many exhortations to Nicholas to be strong. And in a theme that was to play itself out until their dying days, Alix, like any devoted spouse, also added, "let her, who will soon be your own little wife, share all with you."[50] "Tell me everything my soul. You can fully trust me, look upon me as a bit of yourself. Let your joys and sorrows be mine, so that we may ever draw nearer together."[51]

Despite all the doctors' efforts, Alexander III died on 20 October 1894, aged only forty-nine. A wave of sadness and foreboding swept over Nicky, sustaining as he did the double blow of losing his father and ascending the throne with little practical preparation. Recalling that fateful moment, Grand Duke Alexander, Nicky's brother-in-law, wrote that "the weight of this terrifying fact crushed him." A sobbing Nicholas II asked: "Sandro, what am I going to do. . . . What is going to happen to me . . . to Alix, to mother, to all of Russia? I am not prepared to be a Tsar. I never wanted to become one. I know nothing of the business of ruling. I have no idea of even how to talk to the ministers."[52]

Yet there was one thing Nicky was absolutely certain about and that was the consolation that Alix brought to him in this time of distress. He proudly wrote to Queen Victoria that "the one great comfort I have got in my utter misery—is my darling Alicky's deep love, that I return her fully."[53]

Writing to her aunt, the newly widowed Empress Marie, Princess Maud of

Wales, expressed her hope that Alix would bring Nicholas all the help he would need in his new role as tsar: "I do *so* feel for dear Nicky in this anxious and difficult position he now is finding himself, and I only hope that Alicky will help and support him in every way."[54]

Events had moved so rapidly and so profoundly. Wishing to become a member of the Romanov family right away, Alix was adamant that her conversion take place as soon as possible. Her wish was granted. On the day after Alexander III's death, Alix was received into the Russian Orthodox Church and took the names of Alexandra Feodorovna. Ella described the ceremony to their grandmother as being "so beautiful and touching." And despite all the soul-searching and hand-wringing that had accompanied her decision, when the time came for Alix to embrace her new faith, she did so wholeheartedly. Ella made it a point to reassure Queen Victoria that the ceremony had not been an ordeal. Alix, proclaimed her sister proudly, was "very calm."[55]

When the queen finally received the dreaded news that Alexander III had died, she feared for the couple. "Poor dear Nicky and darling Alicky," she noted in her diary. "What a terrible load of responsibility and anxiety has been laid upon the poor children!" Then, perceptively, the queen added: "I had hoped and trusted they would have many years of comparative quiet and happiness before ascending to this thorny throne."[56] The queen expressed the same worries to Vicky, decrying: "What a horrible tragedy this is! And what a position for these dear young people. God help them! And now I hear that poor little Alicky goes with them to St. Petersburg and that the wedding is to take place soon after the funeral. I am quite miserable not to see my darling child again before, here. *Where* shall I *ever* see her again?"[57]

Determined to have Alix by his side from now on, Nicky intended his marriage to take place immediately at Livadia, and not in the spring. His mother approved of the idea. However, Nicky's uncles (the imposing brothers of Alexander III) would hear none of it. They urged him to marry in state at St. Petersburg after the funeral. It was the only way, they insisted, for an emperor to marry. And so St. Petersburg it was.

On the eve of the wedding, Queen Victoria, in a resigned tone, wrote to Vicky: "Tomorrow morning poor dear Alicky's fate will be sealed. No two people were ever more devoted as she and he are and that is the *one* consolation I have, for otherwise the dangers and responsibilities fill me with anxiety and I shall constantly be thinking of them with anxiety . . . I daily pray for them."[58]

Charlotte Knollys, a close friend of the Wales family, who was in attendance to the Princess of Wales in Russia, wrote of her impressions. Of the Empress Marie, Alix's new mother-in-law, Charlotte noted: "The poor Empress is so dreading the wedding tomorrow fancy having to . . . [face] the Ordeal of seeing herself superseded by a young girl of whom she knows but little & of having to step down into the 2nd place when she has so long held the 1st."[59]

As for the Empress Frederick, she told her daughter: "I am glad and thankful my Sophie does not live there, but in the free air of sunny Hellas. I would not change your position with hers, not for all the state and grandeur, the splendour, riches and jewels which hide the other dark side from view."[60] Little did Vicky know that one day, her own Sophie would find more than her fair share of agonizing problems in "sunny Hellas."

Seven days after Alexander III was buried, one of history's greatest love stories was officially sealed as Nicholas and Alexandra were united in matrimony on 14 November 1894. Queen Victoria lamented to Alix's sister, "*cela me revolte* to feel she has been taken *possession* of & carried away as it were by these Russians. I wish she had *not* gone to Livadia & *yet* that was also impossible!"[61]

On her wedding day, in the spectacular green Malachite Hall of the immense Winter Palace, Alix dressed in her bridal finery. An ermine-lined mantle of gold tissue was attached to her dress of cloth of silver by her ladies-in-waiting. Resting on Alix's head was a small circlet of diamonds, along with fragrant orange blossoms brought especially from the imperial conservatories in Poland. And on one of her fingers the bride wore a ring given to her by her grandmother, Queen Victoria. Together with Nicholas, who was dressed in the uniform of the Red Hussars, Alix made her way to the chapel for the wedding service.

Outside, large crowds had gathered to wish their emperor and his bride much happiness. Despite the cold gray day, the streets of St. Petersburg were packed. Having to make her way under the watchful gaze of the throng was painful for Alix, but she managed to thrill nearly everyone. Excited murmurs of admiration followed her, for Alix looked stunning in her bridal attire. Two of Queen Victoria's daughters-in-law—the Princess of Wales and the Duchess of Saxe-Coburg-Gotha—who both witnessed the wedding, sent glowing reports to the queen, saying how she looked "too wonderfully lovely." This elicited a sigh from the bride's grandmother, who admitted forlornly: "Oh! How I do wish I had been there!"[62]

On the wedding day, Queen Victoria confessed that her thoughts were "constantly with dear Alicky, whose wedding takes place to-day. I prayed most earnestly for her, and felt so sad I could not be with her." But despite being preoccupied with Alix and her wedding, the queen was also thinking about another granddaughter, one whom she would not live to see become Queen of Norway. "This was also dear little Maud's birthday," remarked Victoria, "and I had a table with presents for her in my room."[63] It was Maud's twenty-fifth birthday. Of that day, Maud later wrote, "I received many nice presents from *my* many admirers, but from *the one, nothing,* how sad for poor, poor *me!*" Prince Frank, *"the one,"* had forgotten Maud on her birthday, which prompted the dejected princess to confess to May, Frank's sister, "I nearly shed a tear, but thought no—that might spoil my birthday look! Please laugh; it sounds *too* funny!"[64]

That Alix should be elevated to such a vaunted position filled Queen Victoria with a sense of awe. "How I thought of darling Alicky, and how impossible it seemed that gentle little simple Alicky should be the great Empress of Russia!"[65] Charlotte Knollys was of the same mind, though she took a more biting tone. In describing the change Alix underwent as she watched the bride enter the room where she was to be dressed, Charlotte recorded how Alix appeared "in a dress of cloth of silver without a single ornament . . . & then half an hour after she came out with 2 crowns on her head. . . . What a change! A little scrubby Hessian Princess—not even a Royal Highness & now the Empress of the largest Empire in Europe!"[66]

For all the magnificence of the wedding ceremony, Nicholas II confessed to his younger brother, Grand Duke George, that it was "absolute torture both for her and for me."[67] As for superstitious Russians, they had harsher opinions. Whispers were murmured that Alexandra was becoming Empress of Russia in the most inauspicious way. She was coming to them behind a coffin, and for those who disapproved of this, a foreboding swept through them not only for the imperial couple but for Russia itself. When masses of Russians first caught a glimpse of their future tsarina, it was at the funeral procession for the Emperor Alexander. Alix's arrival at the imperial capital amidst the somber pall of death could not have made a worse impact. Far from being joyous and resplendent, her entry into St. Petersburg was shrouded in dismal shades of black, lending an undeniably sepulchral tone that would cling to her until the end of her life.

Yet, despite the superstitious whispers and the heavy weight of mourning surrounding her wedding, many Russians greeted their new tsarina and the new reign with excitement. Queen Victoria must have been gratified to hear from Ella that when Nicky and Alix visited the tomb of Alexander III the day after their wedding, people were "kissing Alix's hands, nearly pulling off her cloak." And on the wedding day itself, when the bride and groom left the Winter Palace, the crowd who saw the couple went "mad with joy."[68]

The days following the wedding were busy ones; often the newlyweds were overwhelmed by the many messages of congratulations that had to be answered. Not until a week after their wedding were Nicholas and Alexandra able to escape for four days to the imperial village of Tsarskoe Selo outside St. Petersburg. Alix, overcome with happiness, wrote in Nicky's diary: "Never did I believe that there could be such utter happiness in this world, such a feeling of unity between two mortal beings. I LOVE YOU—those three words have my life in them."[69]

Tsarina Alexandra did not forget Queen Victoria. Alix wrote to tell her how Nicky's love for the queen "touches me so deeply, for have You not been as a Mother to me, since beloved Mama died." Then she added a word about her Wales cousins, saying, "how nice for dear Toria and Maud that they stayed with You at Windsor, as they so seldom really see You."[70]

As the momentous year drew to a close, Tsar Nicholas reflected on the incredible changes of the recent past. What undoubtedly stood out in his mind was the fact that his choice of Alix as a wife had been a wise one. "Every hour that passes I bless the Lord from the bottom of my soul for the happiness which he has granted me. My love and admiration for Alix continually grow." An equally enraptured Alix filled Nicky's diary with her own passionate responses:

> Ever more and more, stronger and deeper, grow my love and devotion, and my longing for you. Never can I thank God enough for the treasure He has given me for my VERY OWN—and to be called yours, darling, what happiness can be greater? . . . No more separations. At last united, bound for life, and when this life is ended we meet again in the other world to remain together for all eternity. Yours, yours![71]

At the end of 1894, Nicholas reflected on the momentous events that had passed so unexpectedly and so quickly. In his diary, the young tsar wrote tellingly of the burden of being an autocrat that weighed so heavily on his shoulders— that "the worst has already happened, that which I feared all my life!" But to help him cope with his appointed destiny was his new wife, whom "the Lord has rewarded me with a happiness I could never have imagined. He has given me Alix."[72]

As for Alix, she confessed to the Bishop of Ripon that so much had happened to her, "it all seems like a dream."[73] Writing to her brother-in-law, Prince Louis of Battenberg, the newlywed happily confessed: "I can assure you that I never thought one could be as happy as I am now, life is so different to what it was in the past—though there are many difficulties, and all is not easy when one comes first into a new country and has to speak another language yet in time I hope I shall be of some help and use."[74]

Unbeknownst to Alix, she would find to her dismay that those many difficulties were soon to emerge and multiply with great rapidity. Just as Queen Victoria had feared, the life of Russia's beautiful young tsarina was about to become one dreadful trial after another. And Alix need look no further than home to see where one battle was already brewing. Her new mother-in-law was not about to concede her position as first lady in the land. Despite showering Alix with lavish gifts, Empress Marie, ever majestic and confident, could not and would not bring herself to retire gracefully into the shadows. Not long after Nicky and Alix became officially engaged, Empress Marie's own mother, Queen Louise of Denmark, urged Marie to work at being a good mother-in-law toward Alix:

> For yours and Nicky's sake start treating her like your own child, without fear, right away. I have done wrong by Louise [the queen's daughter-in-law and wife of Crown Prince Frederick] and therefore spoiled Freddy's life, and she is pulling him away from me, this is where I am afraid for you: and therefore I am warning you.—Pull her [Alix] towards you, then you will keep him and pull her towards you with love! God help you if you lose Nicky's trust and love, it will be the death of you.[75]

Unfortunately, the empress did not heed her mother's wise counsel, and instead showed herself, early on, to be a domineering mother-in-law. Alix, naturally timid and painfully self-conscious, was understandably slighted by such insensitivity. And caught in the middle of two increasingly stubborn women was Nicholas II. The gloves were now off—which of the two dueling tsarinas would win?

Five

"MAUD COULD NOT HAVE DONE BETTER"

SHORTLY BEFORE THE BIRTH OF MISSY AND NANDO'S SECOND baby, Elísabetta, Carmen Sylva was allowed back into Romania by King Carol after a three-year exile. Descending on the Bucharest court with characteristic melodrama, the queen took her rightful place as first lady of the land. Queen Elisabeth continued to be a perplexing creature, whose behavior could be described as unpredictable at best. *Der Onkel*, King Carol, was an overbearing, unbending, predictable, and colorless man, whose devotion to duty knew no bounds. His wife, on the other hand, was capricious and eccentric, with a propensity for overacting. The only thing this mismatched couple had in common temperamentally was an imperious streak that left many quaking. Crown Prince Ferdinand was one such individual. Missy, though, was made of sterner stuff and slowly stood her ground. She was not the Duchess of Coburg's[1] daughter for nothing and from that end Missy received every encouragement to fight back. "If you give way," wrote Missy's mother, "you are lost and they regularly trample upon you and stamp every bit of life and pleasure out of you."[2]

With Carmen Sylva's arrival, Missy's dull days in Bucharest took on more color. Visits to the poetess queen's artistic salons were among the best places to see Elisabeth in action. At times, these gatherings provided quality entertainment. Carmen Sylva was not completely without her merits as a connoisseur of talent, becoming an enthusiastic patron of the legendary Romanian violinist and composer George Enescu. But oftentimes, the queen could not resist extolling the artistic "virtues" of second-rate performers. To Missy's amazement, these salons frequently took on overdramatic airs. Basking in the glory of an adoring audience, many of whom were unable to distinguish between a talented artist and a charlatan, Carmen Sylva was in her element. Playing the patroness and surrounded by sycophants, Elisabeth liked having Missy "learn" by her side. At these gatherings, the queen would beckon her over and with an overblown wave of her hands order Missy to "sit down here at my feet and listen, darling." Though barely twenty at the time, and herself imbued with a strong streak of romanticism, Missy nevertheless found Carmen Sylva and her hangers-on absurd— "nothing was ever taken calmly, everything had to be rapturous, tragic, excessive or extravagantly comic." Because the queen loved to have a "continual audience," this motley crew "was trained to hang on her every word, to follow her every mood, they had to laugh or weep, praise or deplore according to the keynote given."[3] Missy never felt at home in these gatherings, nor did she feel at ease among many of Carmen Sylva's "friends." They, in turn, harbored suspicions about Missy, finding too much of the foreigner about her.

If Missy shrank from Carmen Sylva's outlandish theatricality at these salons, the same could be said when Elisabeth set her sights on dispensing charity. For she excelled at presenting herself here too in the most absurd light. It was not out of character to find the queen sitting dramatically on a palace windowsill in plain view of the public below her, ready to mete out help to those who approached their benevolent sovereign. Crown Princess Marie often cringed at the spectacle, sensing that many of Elisabeth's audience laughed behind her back. Carried away by her own monologues, the poetess queen would "speak of her soul, of her most sacred and intimate belief . . . of the real and imaginary slights . . . of the non-comprehension . . . of her husband."[4]

It was pointedly obvious that thanks to Carmen Sylva's outrageous theatricality, the court of King Carol and Queen Elisabeth took on a decidedly bizarre atmosphere. With two such highly disparate personalities to please, Marie of Romania often found herself at her wit's end trying to juggle *der Onkel* and Aunty, both of whom had her and Ferdinand at their beck and call. But Missy also felt pity for the royal couple. The king, with his excessive obsession to duty, made his life and that of those surrounding him dull and burdensome; while the queen's high-flown flights of fantasy made her prey to ridicule. Missy also had to cope with an indifferent and cowed husband. The crown princess could hardly be blamed for taking the opportunity, when she could, to escape from it all. But such opportunities were few and far between in the early days. Missy had to bide her time in Romania amid a motley cast. Another curious character at court who made life unpleasant was none other than Kaiser Wilhelm and Crown Princess Sophie's sister, Charly.

In Romania, Charly, the arch intriguer, set about destroying Missy's reputation before the king and queen, who readily agreed with her pronouncements. Cleverly, Charly hid her ammunition against Missy through honeyed words.

Unfortunately for Missy, Charly's position at court was unassailable. She had enjoyed the king's ear for years, poisoning whatever good views he had of the errant young princess.

In order to escape from her weighted existence, Missy found that the best antidote during these early years in Romania was to rely on the support of her mother and Ducky. She also took refuge in riding, her favorite sport. Unafraid of daring jumps, fearless of riding fast and hard, Missy was a superb horsewoman. But even in this, her finest accomplishment, she could not escape the scrutiny and disapproval of her exacting masters. To them, Missy's daredevil escapades were yet more reasons to keep a close eye on her. This, of course, did nothing to lift up Missy's spirits.

Queen Victoria was not ignorant of Missy's predicament in this far corner of Europe and tried her best to ameliorate her granddaughter's situation. The queen enlisted the help of the British chargé d'affaires at Bucharest, Charles Hardinge. He recalled how "Queen Victoria had heard from the Crown Princess of Romania that she felt very lonely in Bucharest and needed the society of an English lady."[5] What Missy wanted more than anything at this stage, besides the company of her mother or sisters, was a British friend—a touch of home in a sea of Teutonic personalities at the Bucharest court. The plan, however, never materialized. But despite all the outlandish goings-on between Queen Elisabeth and King Carol, Missy was able to acquire something positive from the royal couple, which she would put to good use years later. From Queen Elisabeth, Missy acquired something of her spirit of charity. Moreover, Missy's tutelage under Carol I would come to the fore many years later. But during the first few years of her life in Bucharest, Missy—young, beautiful, impetuous, and impulsive—sought only to be happy and carefree. She could not yet grasp why old Carol's creed was centered on work, on "iron duty."[6] Nor could she grasp King Carol's exasperation with her unwillingness to make Romania "her entire *raison d'être.*"[7] That would come only with time.

⌒⌒⌒⌒⌒

News that they were expecting their first child thrilled Tsar Nicholas and Tsarina Alexandra. Two months before her due date, the tsarina had the satisfaction of moving into her newly furnished quarters at the Alexander Palace in Tsarskoe Selo, where they savored their new surroundings. It was here, just shy of their first wedding anniversary, that Nicholas and Alexandra became the proud parents of a hefty ten-pound baby girl, Olga, after an agonizing birth.

A girl instead of a male heir did not bother Nicky and Alix. Like all new parents, they doted on their firstborn. "You can imagine our intense happiness now that we have such a precious little being of our own to care for and look after," wrote Alix to a sister.[8] Queen Victoria noted happily: "Darling Alicky is entirely wrapt up in her splendid Baby."[9] Princess Maud wrote, "Nicky is now a happy father, but it is a pity it was not a boy!"[10] Only twenty-three at the time of Olga's birth, there would be plenty of time for Alix to give Nicky and Russia the all-important male heir.

By September 1895, any hopes of Princess Maud marrying Prince Francis of Teck had been virtually abandoned by the lovelorn princess. "Imagine I wrote to F.[rank] and he has never answered," she lamented to her sister-in-law, May. "And also right before we travelled abroad and still no answer, *dreadful* I call it! When you write to him, tell him that I think it is *extremely* unfriendly: I am genuinely *hurt!*"[11]

Besides Frank's obvious lack of interest in Maud, there were even more worrisome aspects that put him out of the running. Frank, for one, was an inveterate gambler whose gaming habits had reached alarming proportions. The last straw occurred when Frank rashly bet £10,000 on the horses—money which he did not have. This irresponsible behavior earned him exile to India, where it was hoped he would come to his senses.

Those privy to the prolonged attachment were in total sympathy with the princess. *"Pauvre petite elle l'a bien aimé,"* wrote Mme Bricka, Princess May's former governess. Indignant at Frank's behavior, Mme Bricka did not mince words, castigating Frank: *"sa conduite envers cette petite [Maud] était cruelle; il ne répondait à ses lettres, et vous savez qu'on ne peut toujours jouer avec le coeur d'une femme."*[12] What sparked these candid remarks was the news of Maud's engagement to Prince Carl of Denmark in the autumn of 1895.

Soon after the engagement was announced, Maud's father wrote to a friend about Carl, noting that "in her cousin she has made an excellent choice, as he is both charming and good-looking."[13] Some misgivings, however, were expressed about the match. The Duchess of Teck, Frank's mother, thought that Carl "looks *fully 3 years younger* than Maud, has *no money,* [and] they are not going either to give him a *house*." The duchess then bluntly opined: "My feeling is, Maud does not care for him enough to leave England for his sake & live in Denmark & I dread her finding this out when too late."[14]

As cousins, Maud and Charles (who was born on 3 August 1872) knew each other well, but Maud never thought much of him in romantic terms. Besides, she disliked his family—"the Swan family," as they were known—and never felt completely at ease among them. When Prince Carl left for prolonged periods with the Danish Navy, Maud did not think much of his behavior and instead immersed herself in keeping up with two other young men in whom she was interested, Grand Duke George, in Russia, and the hapless Prince Frank.

Carl had admired Maud since 1892. By the autumn of 1895, he was prepared to take the risk of proposing, though scared he might be rejected. Family cycling trips throughout the Danish countryside had the effect of lightening the mood for one and all, including Maud.

"I will tell you that I am honestly suffering from a terrible disease," Prince Carl confessed in October 1895 in a letter to a friend. "I am very much in love, you know that I for many years have highly esteemed one of my English cousins, and now she is more charming than ever." Two weeks later, he reported happily: "I proposed to my cousin Maud and she was so sweet and charming and said yes." This made him the "happiest individual who exists on this earth."[15]

Unlike Alix of Hesse, who kept Nicholas of Russia in agonies over her steadfast refusal to his proposal of marriage, Maud of Wales accepted Carl on the spot. What most appealed to Maud, besides the fact that Carl was obviously devoted to her, was that since her fiancé had very little chance of ascending the Danish throne, or any throne for that matter, Maud could lead a quiet life. The engagement surprised many. "It was like a bolt from the blue," wrote Carl's brother, Christian. "No one had any notion that this was a result from our cycling tours."[16]

Maud recorded her happiness in her prayer book, noting on 22 October 1895: "engaged to my dearest C(h)arl(es). May God's blessing always be with us and our love never change."[17] Maud's insistence that "Carl" be changed to "Charles" exemplified her desire to let the English aspect prevail over all else. By transforming her future husband's name into an English one, Maud was in effect Anglicizing her Danish prince.

But her happiness was evident in a letter to Prince Frank's brother: "Everything happened very suddenly; my cousin Charles has really liked me for 3 years, but I never thought it would last and that he would forget me when he went back to sea; instead the opposite happened: when he met me again this autumn, it got *stronger,* and in the end it had this happy ending!" Maud also admitted, "it will be awful to have to leave my dear home and my family and go back to Denmark." Then, in a telling remark, she added: "but I will never stay there *long*; I plan to return home as *often* as possible." And when Princess Maud reported on a five-day visit that Charles made to England, she was thrilled, and busy fomenting plans for her future husband: "He managed so well and loves England so much; I actually have plans to make him completely English."[18]

Maud also wrote to Queen Victoria about her newfound happiness: "I thought you would like to hear from me myself dear Grandmama, as you have always been so very kind to me and I wanted to tell you how happy I am and I hope you approve of my choice." She explained that Charles was expected to be away on a trip to the West Indies. "But after his journey he means to come here and thus I hope he may see you dear Grandmama as he has never seen you yet."[19] Queen Victoria noted with some relief that "she seems to be very happy and I am much pleased."[20]

In the spring of 1896, Queen Victoria recorded with satisfaction her opinion of her future grandson-in-law. "Maud's fiancé Charles came for lunch. He seems to be a pleasant young man." Always an admirer of handsome men, the queen also noted, "He is very tall and good-looking."[21] Charles was indeed tall, towering over his bride to be, who, at five-feet-two, always wore heels so as not to appear too small next to her handsome prince.

⌒∭⌒

The happiness that Nicholas and Alexandra enjoyed was overshadowed by the friction that increasingly took hold between the two women he was most devoted to: his bride and his mother. In a clash involving two strong-willed women, Empress Marie let it be known that she intended to maintain her position as the leading lady of the land; protocol, after all, allowed a dowager empress to take precedence over a reigning one. It was a situation that seemed perfectly satisfactory to the new tsarina's mother-in-law. Though Alix did not exhibit any jealousy, this order of precedence must have seemed strange.

Since both Marie and Alexandra were anxious to claim the tsar's undivided attention, the ingredients were all there for an unhappy family situation that none could escape. Thus, day in and day out, was Nicky torn between being the loyal son and the adoring husband.

"I still believed that they had tried to understand each other and failed," recalled Nicky's sister, the Grand Duchess Olga, years later; "they were utterly different in character, habits, and outlook."[22] The fractious relationship was based upon a clash of personalities. Where Marie Feodorovna sparkled and socialized, Alexandra glowered and withdrew. Though Alix was beautiful, tall and stately, she never came to be considered an elegant dresser and appeared cold and stiff when on show. Marie on the other hand was a petite brunette whose love of dressing and good clothes was just what the Russian court sought in a tsarina. Attired in her magnificent accoutrements, Marie had a commanding presence. She "instinctively understood that to the Russian people the appearance of greatness was as important as greatness itself."[23] According to a niece, Marie "held herself in such a way that she could never have been taken for anything but an Empress." But above all, the dowager empress possessed an undeniable "personal charm that captivated everyone she met."[24]

Thus, where Tsarina Alexandra failed and where the Empress Marie Feodorovna succeeded was in the ability to project themselves to the people. This exercise in projection, an element so necessary to the popularity of a monarchy, was
something that eluded Alexandra throughout her life as a tsarina. Curiously, it
was one quality that Alix had never acquired throughout all the years spent by
Queen Victoria's side. For Britain's queen was a seasoned professional when it
came to projecting an aura of grandeur. Indeed, it was once said that "whenever
the Queen withdrew, the effect was 'like an ascension to heaven,' those left behind stared after her, transfigured."[25]

Tsarina Alexandra may have had a natural inability to project herself on the
public stage, but even more alarming was the fact that after her few feeble attempts at being pleasant backfired, Alix practically ceased trying to please people. For no matter how hard she tried to be engaging and disarming during
public appearances, one invariably came up against her glacial facade. This resulted in nearly everyone mistaking the tsarina's fears and shyness for arrogance
and boredom.

As the relationship between the two tsarinas soured, so too did Alexandra's
standing with St. Petersburg society. To the capital's elite, Alexandra could never
be the empress that Marie was. Even more grating, however, was the young tsarina's judgmental attitude. Reflecting Queen Victoria's views of exacting standards of behavior, Alix felt nothing but contempt for the immorality she saw all
around her and for those who pursued a licentious lifestyle, including a number
of Romanovs. Queen Victoria had once pronounced a woman who painted her
lips and colored her cheeks a "Jezebel."[26] Raised to respect traditional Victorian
values toward matrimony and decorum, in this respect, Alexandra was very
much a product of her grandmother's teachings.[27]

Many of St. Petersburg's elite believed that their unsympathetic tsarina derived
her puritanical tastes from her grandmother. In their criticism of Alexandra, there
was a distinct emphasis of blame on Victoria for turning this granddaughter into a
haughty and judgmental prude. "What else could we expect from Victoria's
grand-daughter?" crowed the tsarina's critics. "Hemming red-flannel petticoats
on weekdays and reading the Bible on Sundays—there's an Englishwoman for
you!" went one saying. Alexandra Feodorovna was mocked in the capital unmer-
cifully. It was said that "the young Empress outshone even her mother's countrymen, because they were gloomy on one day in the week and she kept gloomy on
seven."[28]

That Queen Victoria had influenced Alexandra's upright views on morality,
there can be little doubt. One of the tsarina's closest friends, Lili Dehn, concluded that "the intimacy with her grandmother unconsciously brought out the
Early Victorian strain in the Empress's character. She undoubtedly possessed

this strain, as in many ways she was a typical Victorian; she shared her grandmother's love of law and order, her faithful adherence to family, duty, her dislike
of modernity."[29] These ideals may have been suited to the almost bourgeois court
cultivated by Queen Victoria and Prince Albert, but they were certainly not suited
to the more hedonistic and ostentatious court of St. Petersburg.

Alexandra's disdain toward Russia's aristocrats can also partly be ascribed to
the fact that she always gravitated toward those who lacked pretenses. Alexandra Feodorovna was a woman who intensely disliked play-acting. Those who
could penetrate the tsarina's protective exterior found a down-to-earth person,
who delighted in domesticity filled with familiar and unpretentious individuals.
This partly explains why she eventually found firm friends in such simple-minded
and unambitious individuals as Anna Viroubova and Lili Dehn. Lili once ventured to ask Alexandra "why she preferred 'homely' friends to the more brilliant
variety." The tsarina answered that though she was "painfully shy" with strangers,
she remained true to those who were her true confidantes. Displaying a lack of
snobbery, something Alexandra "detested," she told Lili: "I don't mind whether
a person is rich or poor. Once my friend, always my friend."[30] Alexandra's affinity for people who appeared devoid of pretension goes far in explaining why she
also disliked the Russian elite. They were simply too artificial and too full of intrigue for her taste. Sadly for Alix, the group wholly reciprocated her feelings.

Every misstep acted like a lead weight, dragging the tsarina deeper into an
abyss from which she could never escape. By the early 1900s, the tsarina had all
but abandoned hope of ever feeling free. A contemporary of Alexandra's, General
Alexander Kireev, pitied the wife of Nicholas II, noting how, in the following exchange, Alexandra Feodorovna's dismay was all too evident: " 'Poor unfortunate
Tsaritsa! Naryshkin says that the young Empress commented that she and the
Tsar saw few people.' [Naryshkin replied,] 'Then you both need to see a few
more people.' Alix answered, 'Why? So as to hear still more lies?' "[31]

Tsar Nicholas II was no less immune from his own set of deeply distressing
problems. His lack of training for becoming tsar, for one, gnawed at Nicky. The
fact that he was not adequately prepared for the monumental task before him
was "by no means his fault." These were the words of Grand Duchess Olga,
Nicky's sister, who admitted that though her brother "had intelligence . . . he was
wholly ignorant about governmental matters." Olga was correct when she
pointed out: "Nicky had been trained as a soldier. He should have been taught
statesmanship, and he was not."[32] Added to his unpreparedness for the task
ahead was the fact that Nicky was surrounded by intimidating uncles, brothers
of his father, all attuned to their nephew's deficiencies.

Since he was browbeaten, harangued by his own flesh and blood, and lacking
any strongly identifiable group of loyal supporters and friends who could be of

any real help to him, it came as no surprise that Nicholas fell under the influence of his beloved Alix. Increasingly at odds with the court's elite, Alexandra dug in her heels and decided once and for all to shut out everything and everyone who did not please her. She did so by fleeing to Tsarskoe Selo, some fifteen miles from the capital.

Tsarskoe Selo was an imperial village consisting of an assortment of spectacular buildings and enchanting gardens. The imperial compound has been described as an "isolated, miniature, world, as artificial and fantastic as a precisely ordered mechanical toy."³³ The park itself was eighteen miles in circumference, interspersed with oaks and limes, and ornamental lakes, one of which contained "a collection of boats of all nations, varying from a Chinese sampan to an English light four-oar; from a Venetian gondola to a Brazilian catamaran."³⁴ Elsewhere were hanging gardens, grottoes, fountains, statues, and arches interspersed with a Dutch dairy, an English Gothic castle, and a Chinese theater and village. For all its delights, this playground of the tsars was, above all, "a magnificent symbol, a supreme gesture, of the Russian autocracy."³⁵

But the crowning glories of Tsarskoe Selo were two large edifices standing next to each other: the flamboyant Catherine Palace, commissioned in 1752 by the Empress Elizabeth and designed by the Italian architect Rastrelli; and the smaller, more sedate Alexander Palace, commissioned in 1792 by Catherine the Great. It was at the Alexander Palace that Alix was to know her greatest happiness and greatest sorrow for the next twenty-plus years.

For Alix, 1896 proved to be an unforgettable year. In May, she and Nicholas traveled to the quintessential Russian city, Moscow, for their coronation. This event may have been dreaded by the perennially shy tsarina, as she had to be on public display for hours on end. But where the outgoing Crown Princess Marie of Romania was concerned, Alix's coronation was an event she eagerly anticipated, for it would give the twenty-year-old Missy—suffering from the claustrophobic court of Carol I—the chance to breathe and enjoy life again.

For Nicholas and Alexandra, this magnificent affair in Moscow was far more than a mere outward display or just another monarchical ceremony. As they were both deeply religious, the coronation was, in fact, a sacred event for the imperial couple. This was the moment when Alexandra, "along with her husband, would be consecrated, crowned, and revered as God's chosen to rule Russia."³⁶ The venue itself reinforced this uniting of the couple to their office and their people. Instead of the sophisticated "European" capital, St. Petersburg, forced into existence by its Western-oriented founder, Peter the Great, the crowning of the tsar and tsarina took place in "the city of Russia's past" whose onion domes shaped

Moscow's identity, "and even the Kremlin reflected the power of the Church, not that of the State." "Moscow stood for Orthodox piety, for the old way of doing things, and for the time when Russians had bowed to the Church that had dominated their lives."[37] This most sacred and Russian of cities proved to be the ideal venue for Nicholas and Alexandra's coronation.

The ceremony took place on 26 May 1896. Alix, dressed in an elegant silver brocade gown in the Russian court style, endured the lengthy coronation, lasting well over four hours, at the Cathedral of the Assumption. Inside the cathedral, laden with jewel-studded icons, were dozens of bearded churchmen and a stirring Orthodox choir. One witness described the magnificent voices glowingly: "I have heard Russian music hundreds of times, but never, not even on Easter morning in the chapel of the Winter Palace, have I heard anything so thrilling as this."[38]

After the Mass, the investing of regalia was followed by the anointing of Nicholas and the proclamation of him as autocrat of all the Russias. Having first crowned himself with the diamond- and ruby-encrusted crown made for Catherine the Great, the tsar then placed that same crown on the head of Alexandra.

Of the granddaughters of Queen Victoria who were to reign, only Marie of Romania witnessed Alexandra's coronation and noted that Alexandra "was beautiful." And whereas Nicholas II seemed to have been overwhelmed by his heavy robes and crown, Alix, "his young wife, stood steadily upright, her crown did not appear to crush her." But "even at this supreme hour no joy seemed to uplift her, not even pride; aloof, enigmatic, she was all dignity but she shed about her no warmth. It was almost a relief to tear one's gaze from her."[39] Another witness thought that "the Czarina was easily the most beautiful woman to be seen"; her face "upon her coronation day was charged with profound emotion. . . . It was like the face of a martyr walking with measured steps to her funeral pyre."[40]

But the coronation, like so much of the reign of the tsar and tsarina, was to be overshadowed by tragedy. Three days later, a vast crowd gathered at Khodynka field to celebrate. Anxious to partake of the free drinks and receive mugs emblazoned with the imperial cipher, an estimated one million people assembled. Suddenly, panic set in when rumors circulated that there might not be enough drink and mugs for all. In no time, men, women, and children were screaming helplessly as they toppled over one another. Some one thousand four hundred souls perished, leaving the tsar and tsarina horrified.

The imperial couple lost no time in visiting the hundreds of injured. They went to hospitals, consoling people and assuring them of their desire to compensate families for their terrible losses. True to his word, the tsar paid for individual coffins out of his own pocket so that the victims would not be buried together in one mass grave, while thousands of rubles were also given to the victims' families. But numerous unclaimed bodies had to be buried in a mass grave. There were so many victims that it took six hundred men, digging all night, to create eleven trenches, fifty yards long, to serve as the burial ground.

Moved by what had befallen his subjects, Nicholas II was inclined to cancel further festivities and retire in prayer. Alix agreed. Years later, Marie of Romania wrote of this moment: "I remember that the poor Empress did all in her power to try and have it [a ball] put off, begged to be allowed to abstain from any festivity that night, but in vain." However, the tsar's formidable uncles pressured him to go to the most extravagant gala of all, the ball to be held in their honor by the French ambassador. To cancel their appearance would offend Russia's ally, who had taken great pains and spent vast sums. Nicky reluctantly bowed to their wishes and took Alix to the ball. But their hearts were not in it. Missy, privy to the drama behind the scenes and no great fan of her cousin Alix, nevertheless wrote for posterity: "No doubt many that night considered the Empress heartless because she went to a ball on the evening of the great disaster, yet God alone knows how much rather she would have stayed at home to pray for the dead!"[41] The British ambassador supported this view when he described Alexandra to Queen Victoria as appearing "in great distress, her eyes reddened by tears."[42]

After their coronation, Nicholas and Alexandra accepted an invitation to stay for ten days with Nicky's uncle and Alix's sister, Serge and Ella, at their country home, Ilinskoe. Also invited were the Crown Prince and Princess of Romania. It must have been striking to see Queen Victoria's beautiful granddaughters together—Ella, Alix, and Missy—still glowing in the flush of youth. Observers would have noted the startling contrast between the last two cousins. Marie of Romania's social skills already far exceeded those of Tsarina Alexandra. A born flirt, Missy thought nothing of galloping away on an officer of the Imperial Guards' horse to show off her excellent riding, in spite of Nando's protestations. It is hard to imagine Alexandra Feodorovna doing anything similar.

Giddy with delight, Missy relished the lavish Russian hospitality. But more intoxicating was the attention she elicited everywhere she went. Together with Ducky, whose marriage was already unraveling, they were the toast of Moscow. "I was enjoying myself with all my heart," Missy wrote years later. "In fact, the joy of it all, the glamour, the beauty, the atmosphere of constant admiration which surrounded me, had slightly gone to my head. My suppressed youth and spirits were responding almost dangerously to all this spoiling and adulation. . . . This was indeed an inebriating contrast to the life I led at Uncle Carol's court."[43] Heading the list of Missy's many admirers, which ranged from her pageboy to the hot-blooded Russian officers, was the handsome Grand Duke Boris, whose own brother, Kyril, was carrying on with Ducky. Two years Missy's junior, Boris was not shy in letting his feelings be known to his married cousin. Missy, in turn, did nothing to discourage Boris's attentions.

By the middle of 1896, much to Queen Victoria's satisfaction, preparations were well in place for a much-anticipated event, the marriage of Princess Maud of Wales to her cousin, Prince Charles of Denmark. This wedding helped lift the somber mood at court that had prevailed since the death of Princess Ena's father.

At her wedding, held in the Private Chapel at Buckingham Palace, Maud looked composed as she took her vows. Maud's bridal gown of white satin was noted for its simplicity, something which she specifically desired. As befitted a British princess, the silk for the gown came from Spitalfields Market.

Among the guests present were Constantine and Sophie of Greece. The bride's grandmother watched the wedding from a privileged position, just behind the bridal couple. When the service ended, Maud and Charles knelt before the queen to receive her blessing, which she bestowed with a warm embrace and kiss for them both.

The newlyweds then made their way to Appleton House on the Sandringham estate. Of all the presents Maud received for her wedding, Appleton—given by her father—was the one that was to grant her many years of happiness. Maud recounted to her comptroller, Sir Henry Knollys, how Appleton came into her possession:

> I was talking alone with my Father, and he suddenly said to me "My wedding present to you is—Appleton." I scarcely realized all that he might mean. I was quite silent, I believe white, with surprise & pleasure. He laughed & said to me again quite plainly: "Yes. I give to you Appleton." I went as fast as possible to find Charles, and I said to him: "Oh, is it not kind of Papa; he has given to us Appleton as a wedding present." So you see, Appleton is really mine. Of course we both thanked him at the time.[44]

Not long after her marriage, Maud was in raptures about her husband, writing how "sometimes I actually think I am dreaming and can not understand that I am married and have a *husband,* and even one that is *so* good-looking." Not far behind in her affections was Appleton itself: "I am going to hate leaving this *heavenly* little place and get depressed just thinking about it. We are happy and my C. behaves like a *real* Angel to me, *so* nice and selfless, we have not had *one* quarrel *so far*!, only small discussions once in a while."[45]

It was to Appleton that Maud would find herself gravitating. In some respects, she would come to view Appleton House as her one true home, as it was located in the country she loved most and in the county—Norfolk—she liked best. In fact, the new Princess Charles of Denmark was so fond of Sandringham—and England—that she managed to postpone her departure for Denmark time and time again.

Crown Princess Sophie of Greece also relished her visits to England. Part of the thrill stemmed from Sophie's delight at visiting English department stores, famed for their marvelous stocks. As Sophie was in the midst of building a bigger home in Athens as well as a cottage in the English style on the grounds of Tatoi, the trip to London gave her a chance to look at possible ideas for her two new homes. "We spent I don't know how many hours at Maple & Liberty!" she exclaimed from England to her mother. "I screamed at the things to Tino's horror, but they were too lovely! *No* those shops I go mad in them! I would be ruined if I lived here longer!—Divine shops!"[46]

Maud, still nicely ensconced at Sandringham in August, showed little sign of moving. But by December, things had come to a head. Maud conceded at last and left with Charles for Copenhagen.

When Princess Maud finally arrived in Copenhagen, the welcome from the Danish people and the royal family was a hearty one. Maud wrote to her grandmother about how she was settling into her new home: "It has been great trouble in finding and arranging all our things, but now at last we have got our rooms tidy and comfortable and we like the house very much, though it is rather damp just now as the days are so short and the weather is abominable, so raw and damp and dreadful cold winds."[47] Already, at this very early stage, Maud was finding the cold Danish winters intensely unpalatable. She would never change her mind. And as she settled into a routine in her new country, she was to find very little in charming Copenhagen to match the serene and bucolic life she had left behind so reluctantly at Sandringham.

⟨⟩

In the autumn of 1896, Nicholas, Alexandra, and baby Olga paid an official visit to Queen Victoria at Balmoral. From the end of September to the beginning of October, the sleepy Scots hideaway was inundated with security forces and the tsar and tsarina's entourage. So many people accompanied the couple that an entire village had to be erected for the overflow of guests.

From Ballater station, Nicholas and Alexandra were escorted by a squadron of uniformed Scots Greys, complete with bearskin hats, whose honorary colonel-in-chief was none other than the tsar. Despite the unrelenting rain, Nicky and Alix arrived at Balmoral to a warm welcome. Tenderly embracing her grandmother, Alix of Russia had come home again.

During this special visit, a historic milestone was attained. As one contemporary aptly put it, "today the dear old Queen has reigned longer than any British Sovereign. What a day of emotions for her. The young Emperor of Russia, Nicholas II, & the Empress, our Princess Alix, came to her at Balmoral & she sat waiting to receive them in a room full of trophies from Sebastopol! It was the anniversary of the fall of Sebastopol."[48] Not surprisingly, Victoria received many messages on the occasion of achieving such a lengthy reign. Alix was at hand to help her grandmother answer them. Victoria seemed impressed that despite having been tsarina of Russia for two years, Alexandra had not let her position go to her head. The queen wrote to tell her daughter, the Empress Frederick, that "Dear Nicky and Alicky are quite unspoilt and unchanged and as dear and simple as ever and as kind as ever. He is looking rather thin and pale and careworn, but sweet Alicky is in great beauty and very blooming. The baby is magnificent, bigger than she and Ella ever were, and a lovely, lively [great-] grandchild."[49]

During their stay at Balmoral, Nicky and Alix had the pleasure of seeing a number of relations. Nicky wrote to tell his mother that "we met Maud and Carl—it seems rather strange for them to be husband and wife."[50] The imperial visitors also took part in a historic moment involving a novel technological wonder. For the first time, Queen Victoria and members of her family were filmed with a ciné camera. Soon afterwards, Nicholas and Alexandra planted a tree on the grounds to commemorate their visit. Then, as Queen Victoria recorded: "in the afternoon drove out with them, alas! for the last time."[51] The visit ended after a quiet day passed in the company of the aging queen. Nicholas, in the uniform of the Scots Greys, and Alexandra, swathed in a pink gown adorned with white fur, said their farewells amid kilted attendants holding blazing torches to illuminate the darkness. "It has been such a very short stay and I leave dear kind Grandmama with a heavy heart," wrote Alix from Balmoral to her English governess on the day of her departure. And in a poignant sentence, she added: "Who knows when we may meet again and where?"[52]

⁋

The void left by the death of Ena's father was difficult for Queen Victoria and Princess Beatrice to fill. As for Ena, she was resilient and coped well. But she also had to contend with the emotional havoc that swept over her mother during the early stages of her long widowhood—an unanticipated fate that Beatrice did not accept lightly.

Nearly a year after Prince Henry died, his desolate widow still found it difficult to come to terms with her profound loss. This elicited pity from the Duchess of Coburg. Missy's mother noted that "poor Beatrice is very sad." But Marie was also baffled by Beatrice's behavior which, in her eyes, bordered on the un-stable. Ena's mother, noted a stupefied Marie, would be crying one moment, raging at a picture of her dead husband the next. After this, the despondent young widow went out to ride her bicycle in heavy mourning. Then she read a book on piety or talked for hours about the small economies being made on all the candles in her homes. Such were her mood swings and peculiar behav-ior. "This bizarre mourning," as the no-nonsense Marie called it, was simply "incomprehensible."[53]

Queen Victoria's attention to her Battenberg grandchildren was therefore dou-bly important while their mother, the widowed Princess Henry, was immersed in her grief. But within a few years, Beatrice and Ena would find themselves in mourning again—this time for none other than Victoria herself.

Six

"TOO PAINFUL TO BEAR"

AFTER NEARLY HALF A DOZEN YEARS IN ROMANIA, MISSY FOUND to her surprise that King Carol I began loosening his tight rein on her and Nando. Carol granted them a new home, Cotroceni Palace, on the outskirts of Bucharest, and allowed the couple to attend parties with certain members of the Bucharest aristocracy. The elite society of late nineteenth-century Bucharest in which Missy began mixing was high-flying, almost hedonistic in nature. This explains in part King Carol's hesitancy in allowing such an attractive, vivacious, and impressionable young woman into their midst. A cultured group, often educated abroad, especially in Paris, the men and women were so full of life that one visitor to the city during the era described it as a "riotous place." Morals were loose and divorce was easy. An elderly French diplomat who spent twelve years there was heard to exclaim that "in all Bucharest . . . I don't believe there is a single honest woman."[1] So untamed was life among the elite that one British minister sent his wife and daughter to live in England, then closed his legation and lived in a hotel in the city to spare his family the vices of Bucharest. Carmen Sylva was equally forthright about the Romanians' lax attitude when it came to morals. After spending several decades in the country, the queen candidly admitted in a sheepish tone to an American that Romania was "a country where one was not even ashamed, but rather proud, of one's immorality!"[2]

In contrast to Tsarina Alexandra at St. Petersburg, Marie at Bucharest enjoyed rubbing shoulders with her country's aristocracy. Rivaling the Russian nobility's lackadaisical attitude toward morality and excesses, the Romanian upper classes' hedonistic behavior did not shock Missy to the point that she felt repulsed, unlike her cousin, whose disdain for the Russian elite's decadence knew no bounds. To the high-minded and idealistic Alix, her bond with the Russian people seemed to extend only to the simple peasants and the clergy, whereas Missy's emerging attachment to her new country, gradual as it was, extended to Romanians of all walks of life. To her, the true spirit of Romania was not to be found exclusively in the country's peasants. Rich and poor alike were appreciated by their crown princess. And in this time of her life, Missy's discovery of the country's fun-loving elite held much appeal for one so naturally inclined to loving life.

Missy was still looked upon by King Carol and Queen Elisabeth as being "too English, too free and easy, too frivolous . . . too fond of dress, of riding, of outdoor life . . . too outspoken . . . not enough respect for conventions or etiquette."[3] This, plus her frightfully wild riding habits (which entailed galloping at full speed in all types of weather and riding astride in Sinaia), were used by the king, and especially the queen, to reinforce the point that Missy was simply too young and too irresponsible to watch over her own children. This was the excuse employed by Queen Elisabeth to physically remove Missy's children. Deprived of any children of her own, Carmen Sylva bullied the young mother into handing over little Carol and Elisabetta—with devastating consequences.

〇〰〰〇

For Princess Maud, her task as a newly married woman was to try to fit in comfortably with her husband's family, as well as identifying with her new country. But this was proving to be a case of easier said than done. Once Charles took up his duties as a Danish naval officer, Maud felt out of place in her new homeland. As she wrote in 1898 to her family in England: "I think of *all* of you almost *constantly* and sometimes I feel *so* depressed and full of homesickness, and when he is away, it is *terrible*."[4]

For Maud, meeting up with Charles's family once or twice a year was bearable, but living in their vicinity for longer periods grated on her nerves. This, combined with the very cold winters in Copenhagen, plus cramped living quarters for one accustomed to such expansive houses as Marlborough House and Sandringham, got the better of Maud. In a letter to one friend, Lady Charles Scott, whose husband had been transferred from the British Legation in Copenhagen to St. Petersburg, Maud expressed astonishment that Lady Scott could miss Denmark, saying: "I can't get over that you are homesick for Copenhagen!" Part of Maud's amazement centered on the bleak Danish winter. As she endured her second winter in Denmark, she complained: "The weather is *so* terrible *always* rain & wind & so gloomy & dark, that we are obliged to have light all day!"[5]

Letters to her mother began to take on a note of loneliness interspersed with complaints. But if Maud thought she could get sympathy from there, she was wrong. The Princess of Wales herself had long suffered the humiliation of her husband's infidelities, choosing to face them with admirable calm and dignity. Alexandra was in a position to understand her daughter's feelings, for though Alexandra loved her native Denmark, her first loyalty was to England. And so it had to be with her Maud: Denmark must supersede England if not in her affections, then certainly in her loyalty and sense of duty. So Princess Alexandra expressed very little patience. "She must on *no* account," wrote the princess firmly, "forget that she married a *Danish* Prince and a *naval* man and *he owes* his first duty both to *his country* and his profession."[6]

As befitting an unassuming young couple, life in Copenhagen was relatively modest. Despite their distinguished pedigree, neither Maud nor Charles had a taste for the extravagant life. It was just as well. Charles's income would not have supported such a life, since the couple was denied an allowance by the Danish government. His earnings as a naval officer had to suffice.

In Copenhagen, Maud's new home consisted of a ten-room apartment in a large house located at 48 Bredgade, not far from the Amalienborg Palace, home to Denmark's kings. Much as she tried to personalize the place, Maud never came to see Bredgade as a true home. For one thing, with over a dozen live-in servants, the home was crowded and lacked privacy. Even more disconcerting was the fact that during the winter months some of Copenhagen's homeless could be found huddling in the building to ward off the cold.

Life at Bredgade was certainly a far cry from Alix's grand surroundings in Russia, Missy's new palace in Bucharest, or Sophie's home in Athens. Maud's much more modest abode was not only small but uncomfortable in comparison. Moreover, Maud continued to suffer from shyness. Within just weeks of arriving in Copenhagen in 1897, she confessed to Lady Charles Scott: "I feel *very* shy, as I hardly know any one. I am dreading the dinner on Friday . . . but I hope you will come & *help* me as you are *always* so kind to me."[7]

Increasingly, Maud's thoughts focused on the life she had left behind in England, as Charles returned to his full-time duties as a naval officer. She yearned for Appleton. During a visit to England in 1898, Maud wrote from Sandringham to Lady Scott: "I am having a delightful time here in my own beloved Country . . . I have become quite fat & sun-burnt & you will never know me again . . . all the trees & flowers out, so delightful & makes it very hard leaving again so soon."[8]

Without children to occupy her attentions, Maud's homesickness reinforced her closeness to her mother and sister, Toria. Maud wasted no time in showing her eagerness to visit England at every opportunity. But her visits were also made for the sake of the unmarried Toria, who badly needed a break from being at her mother's constant beck and call. Maud sympathized and admitted minding leaving Toria "*alone* again as her life is not an easy one."⁹ George, the sole surviving male offspring of the Princess of Wales, concurred. Years later, he came to admit that Alexandra was one of the most selfish women he had ever known. Though the Wales children loved their mother dearly, they were not blind to her faults.

⊙⊙⊙

Owing to their differing temperaments, Missy and Nando's marriage continued to remain rocky. In 1897, Nando was struck by typhoid fever. For a while, the prince's life hung in the balance. Double pneumonia set in, leaving Missy very anxious. To make matters worse, the drama held a strange appeal for Carmen Sylva's disordered personality. She almost gloated at every detail of Nando's declining condition. Understandably, the crown princess was horrified to find the queen standing by the palace windows, "with tragic face and finger on lip pantomming the news to those waiting below."¹⁰ So close to death was Nando that Missy was summoned to his bedside, where she held his perspiring hands as she knelt to say her last good-bye. Fortunately, however, Nando rallied. But his convalescence was long and slow. Missy stayed close to her husband so that a degree of intimacy, lacking for some time, now entered their marriage.

This brief interlude was soon broken, for Missy began to chafe. With boredom at her heels, she embarked on a liaison with a Romanian officer, Lieutenant Zizi Catacuzene, a member of her own Hussar regiment. This scandal played nicely into the hands of Queen Elisabeth. It did not take much for Elisabeth to convince King Carol to impose her latest plan for Missy's household—one that would ensure that the crown princess had even less control over her son and daughter.

The ongoing campaign she fought with Queen Elisabeth over the issue of raising the children was truly shaping into a battle royal, and one that continually exasperated Missy, for there was no letup in the queen's hold over Carol and Elisabetta. Much to Missy's consternation, the childless queen tightened her hold over both children's minds with the connivance of her own set of servants, who sympathized completely with the queen's agenda.

⊙⊙⊙

The celebrations surrounding the birth of the modern Olympic Games in Athens in 1896 were followed by a more personal one when, on 2 May 1896, Sophie and

Tino were blessed with the arrival of their third child, Princess Helen. Sophie's happiness was, however, soon marred by talk of war.

The island of Crete proved to be the flashpoint that sent Greece's fortunes (and the royal family's) plummeting in 1897. The island was then under the rule of the Ottoman Empire, a sore point that rankled with many of King George's subjects, who viewed Crete as unredeemed land. Since most of the island population consisted of Greeks, it took very little provocation to inflame the hearts and minds of Greeks to want Crete dislodged from its Turkish masters and united with the mainland.

Caught in the middle was the Greek royal family. Events moved beyond the control of the family's patriarch, the cautious and realistic King George. His daughter-in-law knew this, and so did not mince words in a letter to her mother:

> I am dying to go to Grandmama's Jubilee but there will be many things to prevent it. I fear fighting in Macedonia and Crete; there is no possibility or hope of preventing people here; they were *poussés à bout* [exasperated]; they make their preparations secretly. Do not speak about it in general. It will be known soon enough. This is, alas, the result of the Powers doing nothing decided enough and letting matters drift.[11]

Full of exasperation at deteriorating events, Sophie wrote frantically: "You can imagine how this torments me! The Sultan is an impossible creature, and does not keep a single promise! He is so false, sly, and mad, and such awfully untrustworthy people about him."[12] Queen Victoria and the British prime minister, Lord Salisbury, read the dire warnings. Salisbury reported that in his view, to allow the Cretans to unite with Greece would send Macedonia rising against the Ottomans, leading to "a bloody struggle between the Moslems and the Christians throughout the Empire."[13]

Since King George I of the Hellenes, as Queen Victoria noted, "can no longer keep his people back,"[14] Crown Prince Constantine had the unenviable task of taking over command of unprepared Greek forces.

Faced with impending war, an anxious Sophie confessed to her mother: "I think with fright and horror of the future. It makes one mad to think of all the misery that may yet come! . . . Even if the Powers do *not* give us Crete, they must know that never, never will the Cretans rest or the island have peace until they are Greek."[15] After reading Sophie's letter, the Empress Frederick told her mother, "how one longs for this nightmare to be removed, and to be able to sleep and breathe again."[16] If Sophie thought she could find some comfort during this political crisis in her ties with Kaiser Wilhelm II, she was sadly mistaken. The fact that Crown Princess Sophie was in Greece mattered not at all to her brother when he sided unequivocally with the Turks during the entire crisis.

To exacerbate matters, Wilhelm's support of the Turks was utterly transparent. So anti-Greek was Willy that Queen Victoria reprimanded him on the tone he took toward Sophie. The queen asked Lord Salisbury to pass on her disgust at her grandson's behavior. "I wish you would desire Sir F. Lascelles, to tell the German Emperor from me, that I was astonished and shocked at his violent language against the country where his sister lives. He could surely have abstained from such language."[17]

In reply to Vicky's pleas to help Sophie, Queen Victoria wrote: "I do feel so deeply for you . . . and for darling Sophie and all. We are doing what we can but it is very difficult."[18]

Reluctantly, King George finally went to war against the Ottoman Empire. According to the Duke of York, if the king had "not declared war—and he did so much against his will,—he would have been assassinated."[19] The Greek military forces, defective and insufficient in many areas, were no match against a numerically superior and well-trained Turkish army, which had benefitted from improvements introduced by German officers. Sophie and Tino were aware of the stakes riding on his military campaign. At Larissa, Constantine implored his troops to be firm and disciplined. The men, spoiling for war, greeted their commander with shouts of "Hurray for war" and "Long live the Crown Prince."[20]

In Athens, decorated with Greek flags and crowded with citizens cheering lustily for their royal family, a *Te Deum* was said in the Metropolitan Cathedral with Sophie and the royal family attending. Those same crowds were far less enthusiastic when members of the diplomatic corps made their way to the cathedral. Instead of cheers, they were met by an eerie silence or mocked with chants of "Down with the Europeans!" The blockade which the Great Powers had imposed upon Greece to keep weapons and supplies flowing freely from the mainland to Crete was met with derision by the Greeks. Only the royal family received loud and approving cheers that day, cheers that echoed the country's mood—"Long live the King" and the ever ominous "Hurray for War."[21]

War between the Greeks and Turks broke out in April 1897, prompting a frantic Vicky to confess to Queen Victoria that "what Tino and Sophie are going through makes me quite miserable." Moreover, "William's personal hatred to Greece and enmity to the King and whole Royal family is well known everywhere and does not improve matters."[22] One British diplomat in Berlin noted how "the Government papers urge the extinction of the 'miserable country—people, dynasty and all.' "[23] Sophie was indignant that her brother could be so callous. Her mother sympathized completely: "oh my Sophie how well I understand the state you are in! . . . Pray do not think I suffer less because I am William's mother."[24]

Constantine failed to meet his military objectives and was forced to retreat into Thessaly. Toward the end of April, all was over for the Greeks. Prince Nicholas recalled how his brother, Tino, "though aware from the very first of the many deficiencies of the Army, had never let personal consideration interfere with the fulfilling of his duty." Therefore, "how far more bitter were the feelings of the Crown Prince, who suffered not only as a Greek, but even more in his capacity of soldier, and Commander-in-Chief."[25]

Angered by being trounced so soundly, the Greek people turned on their leaders. "Not being able to understand the true cause of the disaster, they began to accuse of treason" those in high places.[26] As it turned out, King George, Crown Prince Constantine, and the royal family bore the brunt of the accusations. Edward Egerton, the British minister in Athens, reported to London that crowds were gathering in Athens with the avowed intention of attacking the Royal Palace. "It is difficult to imagine anything more painful and humiliating than the position of the King and Royal Family. . . . Today in Church the prayer for the Royal Family could not be said by the Metropolitan owing to the cries and hisses of the congregation." There was not much sympathy from the local media, either. "The language of the press," noted Egerton, "was most insulting to the king."[27]

Vicky implored Sophie to be careful: "Your safety and that of darling Tino and the children . . . is now my first care and anxiety. Is it wise for you all to remain in the town? Would you not be safer where there is no mob? Have you ever thought of having your valuables and jewels and papers packed up and sent on board a German or English ship?"[28]

Queen Victoria was equally sick with worry, telling Vicky "how my heart bleeds for our darling Sophie and you as well. And to think of William's shameful behavior, for he it is who has urged this on!"[29] The queen also sent Sophie a message of support. Edward Egerton replied, saying that "H.R.H. the Crown Princess is deeply touched by your Majesty's loving sympathy. She is terribly worried and anxious, and tries to keep up, though low-spirited."[30]

The Empress Frederick tried to encourage Sophie, stressing that "it is *no use* to spend one's energies in only complaining, one must try to get out of the mess. You are Papa's daughter, so I know you will be courageous and patient, as he was, and do your duty as he did. . . . I have written a long letter to William to do what he can to help, and I bombard my dear Mama with letters and telegrams."[31]

On 9 May, Queen Victoria conceded in her journal: "Had another urgent appeal from poor little Sophy, and answered that nothing could be done by us alone, that Greece must yield to the conditions of the Powers."[32] Earlier that day, the queen instructed Egerton to pass on the following message to Sophie's father-in-law, King George: "You know how deeply I feel for you, your children, and your country. I have done all in my power to obtain easier terms for you but without success. . . . For the sake of humanity I now urge you to yield. I grieve for you all."[33]

Wilhelm II reveled in the discomfiture felt by his sister in Athens. Nor did he have much sympathy for Tino. The Kaiser saw to it that his sister and brother-in-law would not find help from Germany easily. Willy ordered his ambassador in Athens to hold back from cooperating fully with his counterparts, insisting that Greece suffer further humiliations.

Then, envisioning himself as the saviour of Greece and harbinger of peace, he responded to Queen Victoria's request to intervene: "I am happy to be able to communicate to you that, after the King and Government had begged for my intervention through Sophy, and after having officially notified to my Minister and again through Sophy to me personally that they unconditionally accepted the conditions I had proposed, I have ordered Baron v. Plessen to take the necessary steps to restore peace in conjunction with the representatives of the other Powers."[34]

Hostilities ceased on 17 May 1897. Unfortunately, the Greek royal family's woes continued to escalate. So unpopular were Sophie and Constantine that "they were jeered at and spat on in the streets and there were demands for him to be court-martialled."[35] Sadly for Sophie, her dedication to the wounded soldiers through her ministrations in the Red Cross hospitals was ignored or forgotten.

The Empress Frederick and Queen Olga had both been active patrons in the nursing field; Sophie followed their examples and improved nursing care in Greece. Sophie's youngest daughter, Katherine, later recalled that her mother "brought English nurses over from England, which was very difficult in those days . . . to teach the Greek nurses."[36]

In addition, the crown princess advanced other social initiatives in the fields of childhood education and feeding the destitute. The Union of Greek Women "owed much to her inspiration and encouragement."[37] When the organization was a year old in 1897, it already had its hands full. The fledgling institution was busy preparing for a worst-case scenario. With war on the horizon, the Union directed "refugee work, purchasing medical supplies, outfitting a hospital, and giving lectures on care of the wounded."[38]

Crown Princess Sophie did not focus her energies solely in Athens. She visited Larissa, where she supervised hospitals for the wounded and dying, going about her exhausting work amid the deafening boom of artillery fire. "Sophie converted an immense building which had just been finished as a military school into a hospital," noted her sister-in-law, Marie, "and worked there for the greater part of every day."[39] When she was not making her rounds caring for the sick and injured, Sophie (along with Queen Olga) sat in on final examinations of the Red Cross nurses.

The sights that greeted Crown Princess Sophie during her hospital visits were often heart-wrenching. At a military hospital at Lamia, Sophie prayed at the bedside of a dying Greek soldier. While a priest dipped the bread in wine and gave the dying man the sacraments, Sophie, Queen Olga, and some Greek officers "followed the service reverently, crossing themselves as the poor, weak fellow made his devotions."[40]

The sight of this dying man receiving the sacraments made a strong impression on Sophie. Not long afterwards, when several of the Red Cross nurses were invited to dine with the royal family on board their yacht, the *Sphacteria,* Sophie spoke at length to one of them, Harriet Boyd Hawes. An American volunteer, Harriet found Sophie extremely likable and devoted to the Greek people. Harriet often saw the crown princess in Athens attending first aid courses. And that evening on the yacht, Sophie's first words upon meeting with Harriet "were to ask after the soldier . . . who had received the last rites while she stood near his bedside. Then she wanted to know at length about hospitals in the States, particularly Johns Hopkins."[41]

Even after war's end, Sophie continued to make her hospital rounds, comforting the wounded and encouraging the overworked nurses and doctors in such places as the English hospital at Chalcis, which was recognized for its efficiency. These attempts on Sophie's part did not go unnoticed. When the Empress Eugénie visited Athens in August 1897, she was impressed, and told Queen Victoria so. The queen in turn passed on the empress's firsthand account to Vicky: "Today I saw the Empress Eugénie who, as you know, has been to Athens and seen Olga and darling Sophie who, she said, did not *look* ill and who she spoke of in the highest terms, her anxiety, her devotion. You would have been pleased to hear her."[42]

Queen Victoria was among those who wanted to see Sophie credited for her tireless efforts on behalf of the Greek people. The queen asked Vicky if she might not send a red enamel cross for those "who had helped the Red Cross Societies or done independent work for the sick and wounded." The queen noted of Queen Olga and Princess Sophie, "you know they nursed Turks also in their hospitals."[43]

Victoria wanted Sophie and Queen Olga to be officially recognized for the services they rendered, ordering her private secretary, Sir Arthur Bigge, to look into the matter. Bigge concluded that a royal Order of the Red Cross could not be granted to either woman because of their nationality, unless "the Crown Princess received it as a British Princess."[44] Since this was impossible, Queen Victoria then asked "whether it would not be possible to alter the statutes of the order so as to enable the Sovereign to bestow it upon any Royal person independent of their nationality."[45] No objections were raised to this request. And so in December 1897, Queen Olga and Crown Princess Sophie duly received the Royal Order of the Red Cross.

By year's end, the Empress Frederick admitted to the Bishop of Ripon that the year had been a "most trying and harassing" one. And above all, "the anxiety and sorrows about poor Greece were terrible."[46] Queen Olga of the Hellenes called it "the never to be forgotten year. . . ."[47]

The family's fortunes changed dramatically in February 1898, when King George and his daughter, Princess Marie, were nearly shot to death by would-be assassins. Instantly, the tide turned in the Greek royal family's favor. The would-be assassins had accomplished what they surely had not set out to do. Hostility turned into sympathy for the royals. But this interlude of peace and popularity was not to last. A pattern had begun in Greece, one that was to appear with perplexing regularity. In the ensuing years the royal family was to find itself riding a pendulum that would swing wildly in both extremes. And much to her chagrin, Sophie would find herself playing no small part in the royal family's misfortunes.

⟨⟩

On the sixtieth anniversary of Queen Victoria's ascension to the throne, 22 June 1897, the queen rode in state to St. Paul's Cathedral. In the procession were a number of her relations. One youngster in particular reveled in the attention and panoply around her. She was none other than ten-year-old Ena of Battenberg. Her cousin and companion in the carriage, Princess Alice of Albany, recalled how "very excited" Ena was, and that her "pretty looks attracted the attention of the crowds."[48]

One happy event that occurred in the midst of Queen Victoria's Diamond Jubilee celebrations was the birth of the Grand Duchess Tatiana to Tsarina Alexandra. Though both baby and mother were healthy, Tatiana's arrival was nevertheless greeted with disappointment. According to one account, the appearance of the tsarina's second baby met with silence. Awakening from the effects of the chloroform, Alix saw around her "anxious and troubled faces." The new mother took this to mean that she had failed to give birth to a son. The anguished mother "burst into loud hysterics," crying out: "My God, it is again a daughter. What will the nation say, what will the nation say?"[49]

Back in Greece, meanwhile, Sophie tried not to dwell on the problems that had plagued her family in the wake of her country's losses, but it was difficult at times, as Maurice de Bunsen, then first secretary at the British Embassy in Constantinople (later to become British ambassador in Madrid, 1906–13), noted. De Bunsen met the crown princess in Athens in November 1898, and recorded his impressions, noting: "She was very agreeable, and we had a long *tête à tête*. Life at Athens is evidently a great trial to her."[50]

A bright spot in all the turmoil surrounding Crown Princess Sophie's life were her children. The Empress Frederick proudly told Queen Victoria of the queen's Greek great-grandchildren: "I wish indeed you could see Sophie's children. The elder is a most interesting child. The second a really splendid child—enormous blue eyes with dark eyelashes, a steep forehead with wavy dark hair, a lovely mouth and a little turned-up nose and dimples in his pink cheeks. . . . Little Ellena (Sitta as they call her) is so sweet and pretty but very shy and a little fretful at times, which will wear off when she gets older."[51]

As the nineteenth century drew to a close, Sophie, Missy, and Alix were the mothers of a rapidly growing brood of children. But of the three, only Alexandra still yearned for a firstborn son. To her dismay, the tsarina was still not very popular, especially among the smart set of St. Petersburg. Relations with her mother-in-law, the Dowager Empress Marie, remained frosty, and though Nicholas and Alexandra were happily married, there was no denying the fact that her inability to provide the much-desired male heir for the Romanov dynasty was proving a great disappointment to many, not least Alix herself.

Alexandra was never well during her pregnancies, nor did she have an easy time giving birth. This was true again in June 1899, when she gave birth for the third time, but both mother and child pulled through. Hopes, though, were dashed when it became known that the tsarina had produced a third girl, Marie Nicolaevna. The baby's aunt, Grand Duchess Xenia, summed up people's feelings: "What a disappointment that it isn't a son. Poor Alix!"[52] Even Nicholas II felt let down by the birth of a third daughter. Unable to face his wife and fearful of showing his disappointment, the tsar took a long walk in the park to collect himself before greeting Alix immediately after the birth.

Queen Victoria, too, could not help but express her disappointment to Nicholas, telling him: "I regret the 3rd girl for the country. I know that an Heir would be more welcome than a daughter."[53] Nicky's sadness in no way diminished his love for his wife. In a letter to Alix less than a month after Marie's birth, he expressed his devotion by saying: "I dare complain the least, having *such happiness* on earth, having a treasure like you my beloved Alix, and already the three little cherubs. From the depth of my heart do I thank God for all His blessings, in giving me you He gave me paradise and has made my life an easy and happy one. Labour and passing troubles are nothing to me once I have got you by my side."[54]

During her final years on the throne, contemporary events prevented Queen Victoria from ruling peacefully. Instead, the queen was absorbed by a war that demanded all her courage, resilience, and optimism, particularly when word from the battlefront brought bad news.

The Boer War was raging in South Africa, inflicting heavy casualties on British troops. By the time the conflict ended, nearly 450,000 men had come to fight, and of that number, over 20,000 were to die. Yet when the queen had to comment on the staggering setbacks inflicted by the Boers on her troops, she projected a confident, even defiant mood. Despite one week (known as Black Week) in December 1899 in which three British generals and the men fighting under their command were vanquished in quick succession, the queen revealed an indomitable spirit. "Please understand that there is no one depressed in this house," Victoria declared. "We are not interested in the possibilities of defeat; they do not exist." It was not mere grandstanding on the queen's part. Even in her own private journal, in which she confided her innermost thoughts, she did not let slip any signs of doubt or fear. On the contrary, ever since Black Week, as Lady Longford has remarked, her entries had been nothing but "a model of vigorous courage—no complaints, no self pity."[55]

Though in frail health, the queen did her utmost to rally her soldiers' spirits in times of darkness. She visited hospitals, not minding if her soldiers saw their sovereign in physical decline as she made her rounds. And in her spare time, Victoria, now nearly blind, worked in helping to create such useful items as caps, socks, cholera belts, waistcoats, and khaki comforters for the British troops still fighting. This kind of unselfish devotion to duty would later reappear in her reigning granddaughters.

As Crown Princess Sophie kept abreast of the conflict in South Africa, her thoughts went out to her grandmother at this time of trial. In one letter to the queen, in February 1900, Vicky reported that "Sophie writes to me as follows: 'How is dearest Grandmama bearing all this; it is so trying for her.' "[56] Sophie did what she could for the fighting men of the British Army, despatching personal items. Queen Victoria did not forget this kind gesture and told the Empress Frederick, "I telegraphed to dear Sophie 'thank you' for so kindly sending things to our brave soldiers."[57] The tide eventually turned in favor of the British later in the year with the relief of Mafeking. In the end, Queen Victoria's faith in her troops in their darkest hour was vindicated.

⊙⊙⊙⊙

Envious of Missy's position as the boy's mother, the childless Queen Elisabeth of Romania continued to isolate young Carol, imposing a disagreeable governess who turned the boy further against his mother. Missy's problems did not go unnoticed by her numerous relations. Empress Frederick told Sophie firmly what she thought of it all: "I think Missy of Roumania is more to be pitied than you. The King is a great tyrant in his family, & has crushed the independence in Ferdinand so that no one cares about him, & his beautiful & gifted little wife, I fear, gets into scrapes, & like a butterfly, instead of hovering over the flowers, burns her pretty wings by going rather near the fire!"[58]

Just as Sophie of Greece's mother was there for her daughter, so was the Duchess of Coburg looking out for the interests of her daughter. The duchess, however, never hesitated to show her disapproval of her daughter's wayward life and always gave Missy a piece of her mind. Missy may come to her mother for sympathy and help, but in the Duchess of Coburg's eyes, she had to do so on her mother's terms, which meant listening and acting upon the duchess's reprimands and sage advice.

Though the Duchess of Coburg had raised Missy to be ignorant of marital life, once married, Missy managed to share her marital woes with her mother. "All intimate life with a man is difficult for me," she once confessed. "My husband sees me cry . . . he is awfully sorry, he wants to console me, he has every intention to do so, his heart is full of love, he begins to kiss me then he forgets that, and tries to console me by giving way to just that, that I dread most on earth." When she wanted Nando to read to her, Missy complained, "he hurries it over only to get to bed for other amusements which he does not perhaps think is a one-sided amusement."

Later, the duchess vented her rage at King Carol when the scandal over Lieutenant Cantacuzene swirled. In 1897, Missy embroiled herself in a romance involving a lieutenant Zizi Cantacuzene, a member of her household. The scandal became widely known and was ended by King Carol. While Missy's mother admitted that there was no excuse for Missy's lapse of judgment, the duchess nevertheless took a swipe at her son-in-law. The "worst of all" of Nando's faults was "his sensual passion for Missy [which] finished by . . . repulsing her. . . . Nando will himself avow," fumed Marie, "that he treated his wife like a mistress, caring little for her emotional well-being in order to constantly assuage his physical passions." And to top it off, Missy had to contend with Nando's own extramarital escapades which were, according to the duchess, "a positive fact."[59]

When, in the fall of 1897, Missy found herself pregnant, it was to her mother that she fled for refuge. As this was at the height of her affair with Cantacuzene, the uproar caused by the pregnancy prompted Missy to leave Romania. Nothing was ever known of the child born at Coburg. One historian has suggested that it may have either been sent to an orphanage or was stillborn at birth. Whatever happened, the story of this mysterious child of Marie of Romania was one secret "she apparently took with her to the grave."[60]

A precedent had been set when Missy fled to Coburg and to the protection of her mother in 1897. That was why, when Missy found herself pregnant again late in 1899, the duchess did not hesitate. Her instructions were set out with precision: "My plan is to take you immediately to Coburg, where we can wait until you give birth . . . I will take care of the rest." True to her word, the duchess, like the Romanov that she was, fired off a warning to King Carol, telling him "she would not allow Missy to have a miscarriage at Cotroceni [Palace in Bucharest]."[61]

When King Carol held his ground and still refused to allow the crown princess to leave for Coburg, Missy pleaded with him to let her go. Already exhibiting a dynamism that was to distinguish her from her other royal cousins, Missy defiantly confronted King Carol and told the king "right to his face" that "she wanted a divorce, and that the child she was carrying was Boris's."[62] The romance that had been kindled in May 1896 while Missy and Nando were in Moscow had continued on and off its erratic course. Missy's threat worked. The king was aghast. For once, this grizzled veteran of Balkan political intrigue and bizarre behavior was thrown off course—and by a sprightly young woman who was clearly his subordinate. To have such a scandal tainting the House of Hohenzollern was unthinkable for the old king.

In the end, King Carol met his match in the combined onslaught of the Crown Princess of Romania and her mother. So, Missy gave birth in the more tranquil surroundings of Coburg to her second daughter in January 1900— named Marie, though all her life she would be known as Mignon. In the weeks before the birth, Missy's attitude toward her husband and her need to follow her duties as a wife and princess had undergone a transformation.

Just as Missy was willing to make a go of her marriage, Crown Prince Ferdinand was also overcome by a desire to make amends. Well aware that he had not been an imaginative or understanding husband to his young wife, and conscious of the need to deflect any more scandal on his royal house, Nando swallowed his pride. Where Mignon was concerned, "in the end, Ferdinand reluctantly agreed to accept the child as his own."[63]

Queen Victoria was not deaf to the scurrilous stories sweeping Europe concerning Marie of Romania. As Marie wrote: "In these days she was following my career with grandmotherly affection, but also with the anxious severity of one who wished that those of her House should do it every honour, no matter where they were placed."[64]

⊙∭⊙

A sad pall hung over Missy's life when in 1899 her brother, Alfred, died in tragic circumstances after a botched suicide attempt. Then, in July 1900, Marie's father died of cancer. By the fall of 1900, there was little doubt that Queen Victoria was declining rapidly, and in mid-January 1901, it became obvious that the end was at hand. The Kaiser hastened from Germany to her bedside at Osborne House. Of the five granddaughters, only the eldest, thirty-one-year-old Maud, and the youngest, thirteen-year-old Ena, could be present at Osborne for the death vigil. On the morning of 22 January 1901, the final curtain descended on the life of Queen Victoria. Family and close retainers gathered in hushed reverence by the bedside. When the queen died, Kaiser Wilhelm, exhausted from holding up his grandmother for the last two hours, turned his attention to his cousin, Princess Victoria Eugenie. Moved by what he had just witnessed, and wishing to seize the moment, forty-three-year-old Wilhelm solemnly told the somber-faced thirteen-year-old girl that "I am the eldest grandchild and you are the youngest."[65] He then sat Ena on his knee and they both contemplated their dead grandmother—the longest reigning monarch in English history.

The draped coffin containing the queen's body was laid in the dining room, which contained an altar and religious paintings. On top of it lay Victoria's famous diamond encrusted crown, and surrounding it were six massive candlesticks. At each corner of the bier stood a tall grenadier guardsman, "looking as though [they were] marble statues, their gloved hands crossed over rifle butts, the weapons' muzzles on the toe of each man's left boot." There was an overpowering scent from the funeral wreaths—white lilies from Princess Louise, blue hyacinths from Princess Beatrice, and an enormous one of white laurel from Kaiser Wilhelm. With the "red velvet hangings covering the walls and the sparkle of the Imperial and Garter jewels twinkling" from the queen's coffin, "the gloomy old Dining Room took on an other worldliness."[66] Princess Ena's memory was seared by this magnificent display, which mixed death, obeisance, patriotism, and grandeur. "For me," she recalled years later, "it was one of the most awesome sights of my childhood."[67]

From the Isle of Wight, Queen Victoria's body was then taken to London, where a million souls paid their last respects to the sovereign who had reigned for nearly sixty-four years. Yet despite the huge crush of humanity, complete silence prevailed. Princess Maud thought it all "terribly sad and impressive, the crowds of people . . . and not a single sound and all in black, and mauve the houses."[68]

The emotional funeral was held at Windsor Castle on a bitingly cold February day. The thirteen-year-old Ena naturally found the funeral procession "extremely impressive."[69]

All over the British Empire and Europe, services were held to commemorate the passing of such a significant contemporary figure. In Athens, a requiem service was held at the English Church of St. Paul's, attended by members of the Greek royal family. A remembrance service was also conducted on the day of the funeral in St. Petersburg, attended by the tsar, tsarina, and Ella. By the end, Alix and Ella were emotionally drained; a witness noted how the sisters were "visibly much affected on leaving the church."[70]

When the tsarina received condolences from the Metropolitan of St. Petersburg, his words touched a chord in her heart. She cabled her reply: "Your kind words of comfort in my great sorrow have sunk into my heart, and I am deeply affected by your true appreciation of my love for my grandmother, who was as a mother to me.—Alexandra."[71] In a letter to her sister Victoria, Alexandra poured out her sorrow: "How I envy you being able to see beloved Grandmama being taken to her last rest. I cannot believe she is really gone, that we shall never see her any more. It seems impossible. Since one can remember, she was in our life, and a dearer kinder being never was."[72]

"In a way she was the arbiter of our different fates," wrote Marie of Romania. "For all members of her family her 'yes' and her 'no' counted tremendously. She was not averse from interfering in the most private questions. She was the central power directing things. . . . She was a tremendous presence . . . and her places, whilst she breathed within their walls, had something of shrines about them, which were approached with awe not unmixed with anxiety."[73]

Alexandra echoed these sentiments, admitting to a confidante that her grandmother "was very forceful."[74] Maud, the eldest of the five cousins, was the one who perhaps felt most awed by the queen's character. Maud's son, King Olav V, later described the relationship by saying, "I had the impression that my mother and her sisters were somewhat afraid of her."[75]

As for the youngest of Queen Victoria's granddaughters, Ena of Battenberg was so accustomed to living by the side of the woman she called "Gangan" that she admitted years later to feeling as if the queen were some sort of deity, for "it seemed that my grandmother was not destined to die, that she belonged to those immortal beings who follow to the other side of time."[76] But perhaps Marie of Romania best summed up what Queen Victoria had meant in the lives of her granddaughters when she wrote: "what a wonderful, unforgettable little lady she was."[77]

PART TWO

Trials and Tribulations (1901–1914)

Seven

SPLENDID ISOLATION

WITH THE DEATH OF QUEEN VICTORIA, A NEW AGE WAS USHERED in. But where her five special granddaughters were concerned, a loving, reliable, and oftentimes wise influence had gone from their lives. Nowhere was this loss of wise counsel more profoundly felt than in faraway St. Petersburg, where Alexandra, Russia's increasingly isolated empress, had yet to endear herself to her country.

Queen Victoria had once written to Princess May of Teck that "the trials of life *begin* with marriage."[1] And to the Tsarina Alexandra's sister, she wrote similarly in 1887: "I never *can* look but with gt. Anxiety upon marriage. Life becomes so full of trials & difficulties in the *happiest* marriage."[2] For Tsarina Alexandra, who was fortunate in having the happiest of marriages, her immediate anxiety centered on the fact that with each passing year, she had yet to fulfill her dynastic obligation by providing Russia with the much-anticipated male heir. It was said that she could be found sobbing "for hours at a stretch," murmuring to herself, "Why, *why* will God not grant me a son?"[3]

Tsarina Alexandra's latest pregnancy ended successfully with the birth of a hefty eleven-and-a-half pound baby. But again, it was a daughter. "What a disappointment!" noted Grand Duchess Xenia. "A fourth girl! They have named her Anastasia."[4]

The Romanovs were not the only ones let down, for Anastasia's birth was greeted with equal consternation in England, where the *Daily Mail* boldly underscored the news with the headline: ILLUMINATIONS, BUT DISAPPOINTMENT. "There is much rejoicing," noted the newspaper, "although there is a popular undercurrent of disappointment, for a son had been most keenly hoped for." And where

Nicholas and Alexandra were concerned, "the legitimate hopes of the Czar and Czarina have so far been cruelly frustrated, whatever may be their private parental feelings towards their four little daughters . . . [who] had been born into an expectant world with distressing regularity."[5] This was not to say that her daughters did not bring Alexandra happiness. On the contrary, she doted on them. In a letter to the Bishop of Ripon, she wrote of her pride in them, telling him that she would "be so happy" to "show you our little four leaved clover. Our girlies are our joy & happiness, each so different in face & character. May God help us to give them a good & sound education & make them above all brave little Christian soldiers fighting for our Savoiur."[6]

But the nagging void left Alix prone to the influence of two of the most colorful members of the Romanov clan: Militza and Anastasia ("Stana"), daughters of King Nicholas of Montenegro. Not content with the conventional practices and beliefs offered by Orthodoxy, Militza and Stana were easily deceived by a parade of charlatans and "holy men" who appealed to their bizarre sense of the supernatural. Alexandra was drawn to the pair at a time when she was at her lowest ebb over her inability to produce a son, allowing her to believe in quacks introduced or recommended by the two grand duchesses. This included a certain Philippe Nazier-Vachot, a one-time butcher from France, said to have the ability to manipulate an unborn child's sex. He was dismissed in 1903 after being unmasked as a charlatan.

In 1903 the two women urged the tsarina to seek the intercession of a certain Seraphim, a holy man who had been dead for seventy years. It was imperative, insisted Militza, that Seraphim be declared a saint in order for Alexandra to benefit from his prayers. Never mind that it was too soon for Seraphim to be made a saint, never mind that there was opposition from the church against such a move. Undeterred, Alexandra convinced her husband to press for Seraphim's case.

When told by Constantin Pobedonostsev, Chief Procurator of the Holy Synod and one-time tutor to the tsar, that Seraphim's canonization was premature, according to one contemporary, "the Empress responded that the Emperor could do anything."[7] Where Seraphim's canonization was concerned, Alexandra was right. She succeeded in having Seraphim made an Orthodox saint in an impressive ceremony at Sarov in the summer of 1903, and later bathed in the waters of the Sarov River in hopes that she would at last conceive a male child. These efforts seemed to have reaped their intended reward, for within months of Seraphim becoming a saint Alexandra Feodorovna found to her satisfaction that she was again with child.

For Sophie, the year 1901 was a tragic one. Quick on the heels of Queen Victoria's death came the agonizing decline of the Empress Frederick. Sophie lived out again the tragic long good-bye to a much-loved parent as she watched her mother slowly succumb to the painful ravages of the same disease that had claimed her father's life in 1888. Vicky's tortures increased, compelling her to write: "My own Sophie . . . the *terrible* nights of agony are worse than ever, no rest, no peace. The tears rush down my cheeks when I am not shouting with pain. . . . It is fearful to endure. My courage is quite exhausted, and this morning I cried for an hour without ceasing."[8]

In spite of her intense suffering, the Empress Frederick never ceased to help and bring comfort to her daughter in Athens in a barrage of letters, for Sophie's own letters were sometimes tinged with a sense of frustration over a variety of subjects. Mother urged daughter to think of her accomplishments and to be patient in expecting change: "Do not forget darling that you have many a nice success to be thankful for. In 10 years, much has been done. . . . Changes can only come gradually, and slowly. . . . In Greece you are still suffering from the effects of the Turkish rule. Countries and states are not made in a day, and *long* and *many* are the struggles they have to go through . . . you must not lose heart." As for Sophie's country and future subjects, the empress continued, "The Greek people are splendid, I admire them more than I can say . . . Greece is worth fighting and suffering for."[9] The empress's words did not go unheeded. Many years later, after Sophie did indeed suffer much as Greece's queen and had to live out her final years in exile, the one thing she missed the most living away from her adopted country was the Greek people themselves, whom she had come to cherish. "She adored the people," recalled her daughter, Katherine.[10]

The final death struggle of the Empress Frederick was heart-breaking. The morphine given by the doctors barely eased her suffering. Sophie was at her mother's side that summer of 1901, knowing full well that the end was at hand. It was not an easy vigil. Despite the beautiful gardens and view surrounding the Friedrichshof, nothing could blunt the agonized wait as the empress drifted off to her final rest. Even the guards stationed outside were so affected by the cries they heard that they pleaded to be moved farther off.

On 5 August 1901, the Empress Frederick was finally released from her earthly torment. Sophie had just stepped outside with her sister, Mossy, for a breath of fresh air. They were called back to their mother's room. But by the time they returned, it was too late. The empress had wished to have the words of the English burial service said over her and in this her son, the Kaiser, agreed.

He, along with the rest of the family, gathered around her coffin to hear the Bishop of Ripon read the service.

If Sophie thought that all was to be calm in the aftermath of her mother's death, she was mistaken. Unbelievably, once again she had to endure the callous treatment of the Kaiser. Just as he had done in 1888 immediately after his father died, Willy ordered soldiers to ransack his mother's home for her papers. The empress, however, had had her papers spirited away to England right under the Kaiser's nose in an episode worthy of any cloak and dagger mystery.

The weeks and months prior to her mother's death had been physically and emotionally exhausting for Sophie of Greece. Moreover, the fact that when the empress died, Sophie was five months pregnant with her fourth child made it all the more important that the trauma did not overwhelm her. Nevertheless, Sophie made sure not to forget individuals who had been kind to her mother and the family. One of those who expressed her sympathy at the death of the empress was an old governess of Sophie's. Typical of the compassionate manner in which Sophie had been raised, the crown princess wrote a touching reply, notable for its wrenching honesty, in which she spoke of "my terrible grief!"

> You can feel & understand what we have been through during all this sad time, it was frightful to see beloved Mama suffer like a martyr & not be able to help her, & one thankful that God released her of all pain & that she has peace & rest at last! But oh! the blank she leaves behind is too terrible & you know what we have lost in her; it seems all like a dream, not possible to be true! . . . all the details . . . are too long & painful to write.[11]

"With the death of the Empress Frederick there passed from the European stage one of the most tragic figures in nineteenth-century history," wrote her godson, Sir Frederick Ponsonby.[12] But as Princess Sophie so poignantly said in her letter, the loss of her mother was profoundly more personal in nature, leaving a deep void in her life.

In the space of only seven months, Princess Sophie had lost a cherished grandmother and mother. She would have seconded Tsarina Alexandra's cry: "Oh this dreadful 1901, I am truly thankful it lies behind us . . . the sorrows and the troubles it brought."[13]

⚬⚬⚬

The court into which Tsarina Alexandra had married was the most splendid in all Europe. Even in the rarefied world of contemporary European royalty, few, if any, could surpass the gilt-encrusted fairy-tale kingdom of imperial Russia, where luxury and opulence were the bywords of the Romanov dynasty.

Peter the Great's ambitious plan in taming acres of marshland in a corner of the Gulf of Finland to become St. Petersburg had garnered impressive results. By the nineteenth century, grandiose buildings designed by some of the leading architects of the day imparted their special stamp on the imperial city on the Neva. Aristocratic mansions in the Neo-classical and Baroque styles, owned by the princely families of the land, added a magnificent sheen. Canals, like shimmering silver ribbons, cut swatches into this, the grandest city in the Russian Empire. And in this majestic city, there was nothing grander than the imposing Winter Palace. Among its one thousand five hundred rooms and acres of glass stood out marvels of elaborate design such as the massive Jordan staircase with its extensive expanse of gleaming white marble; the Malachite Hall, which awed visitors with its tons of vivid green malachite; and the Gold Drawing Room, layered in gilt from floor to ceiling.

Marie of Romania, who was no stranger to Russia and visited her Romanov relations in her youth, described imperial Russia as "the most aristocratic of courts, the splendour of which had to be seen to be realized."[14] Sadly for Alexandra, it was not enough for her to be a part of this magnificent court. As the Empress of Russia, she was expected—indeed, it was assumed automatically—to take on the leading role that every wife of a ruling aristocrat must carry out. But her shy and diffident nature prevented her from doing so. Moreover, multiple pregnancies kept Alexandra indisposed; and as time passed, her ill health, ranging from sciatica to weak legs and painful headaches, contributed to the tsarina's disappearing acts.

By the early 1900s, Nicholas and Alexandra had practically ceased to entertain those that mattered and, instead, firmly ensconced themselves at Tsarskoe Selo. Alix delighted in decorating her home. Unlike many a royal couple, the tsar and tsarina shared the same bed and so had one bedroom. Decorated in a riot of pink and green, recalling an English garden, this room also gave evidence of the tsarina's increasing religious conviction and her total immersion in Russia's Orthodox Church. On one wall of her bedroom were innumerable religious icons and nearby was a prayer center, which Alexandra often used. Next to the imperial bedroom was the very nerve center of the private quarters and the most famous of all the rooms in the Alexander Palace: the tsarina's Mauve Room, or Mauve Boudoir, so named for the color scheme—Alexandra's favorite—which completely dominated the room. From the expensive silks covering the walls down to the chintzes and even the vases of perfumed lilac and other flowers placed all over the room, mauve and yet more mauve cascaded. The Mauve

Boudoir also contained not one but two pianos, as this enabled Alexandra to participate in duets. Her skill at the piano was something Alix shared with Ena of Battenberg. The Mauve Boudoir was to remain Alix's favorite room, especially when her health gave way through the years. In this refuge, the tsarina increasingly rested on a plump, comfortable couch propped up with embroidered cushions and pillows, where she would write, sew, or embroider.

As the years passed, the tsarina cherished what friendships she could find, particularly those with a connection to her English past. One such friend was William Boyd Carpenter, the Bishop of Ripon. His kindly disposition had endeared him to Alexandra when she was newly engaged and visiting Queen Victoria at Windsor Castle. It was Boyd Carpenter who tried to ease the future tsarina's conversion from Lutheranism to Russian Orthodoxy by pointing out the similarities between both religions.

After nearly a decade as Empress of Russia, Alexandra never forgot Boyd Carpenter and told him so: "For me it is indeed a great happiness to find old friends have not forgotten me, tho' I live so far away." In this letter, written at the turn of 1902–03, Alexandra reveals much about herself. Uppermost in her mind was Queen Victoria's death, as the tsarina was still coming to terms with the fact that her grandmother was gone. Alix told the bishop: "I cannot imagine England without beloved Grandmama. How well I remember sitting by her side, listening to your beautiful sermon—one you kindly gave me at Windsor." This was nearly two years after Victoria's death and sheds light on how Alix's thoughts were still very much with the grandmother who had meant so much to her. Alexandra also permitted herself to ruminate about man's place on earth, saying, "we have so much to do in our short sojourn on this earth; such manifold tasks for all of us to accomplish. What joy if in any small way we can help another wanderer bear his heavy cross or give him courage to battle bravely on! How many faults we have to try and master—the hours seem too scarce in which to fulfil all our tasks."[15] These were not shallow thoughts or empty words but an expression of the tsarina's sincere and deeply held religious convictions, which permeated so much of her life. The Reverend William Boyd Carpenter was one of the few individuals whom Alexandra allowed an intimate glimpse of her religious views, which had only increased in profundity.

When not at Tsarskoe Selo, the imperial family moved in the summer to Peterhof, Russia's answer to Versailles. From Peterhof, which is on the Baltic, the tsar and tsarina and their family embarked on leisurely cruises. On board the gleaming-hulled imperial yacht *Standart,* Nicholas and Alexandra, their children and retinue, relaxed as they sailed the waters, often disembarking for picnics on the many islands dotting the gulf.

After a stay at Peterhof and the *Standart* cruises, the family would go off again, this time to their retreats in Russian Poland, where the tsar went hunting. The village of Bialowieza contained a comfortable hunting lodge and stables, along with a nearby Russian Orthodox church. The forest of age-old oaks was famous for its huge bison, which roamed freely. These creatures often towered over six feet tall and made for spectacular hunting trophies. A second imperial hunting ground in Poland was located at Spala. Years later, the very word "Spala" was to bring back bitter memories for the tsarina.

No such unhappy memories clouded Alexandra's views of the Palace of Livadia, in the Crimea. The family's journey to this southern part of the empire began by boarding the imperial train. It was a much-anticipated holiday, for the Crimea was a veritable paradise, with its picturesque views and balmy climate. As the years passed, the Livadia Palace, near Yalta, was transformed into a large and impressive white limestone building. With its proximity to the Black Sea, its location in the temperate South, and its Italianate style, Livadia could easily be cast as the Russian equivalent of Osborne House. Just as Queen Victoria loved escaping to her Isle of Wight retreat, so too did Tsarina Alexandra delight in going south to Livadia for some much-needed rest and relaxation amidst the scent of oleanders, acacias, and cypresses.

Ever since she had decided to join herself in holy matrimony to Tsar Nicholas II, the former Princess Alix of Hesse-Darmstadt threw herself into absorbing as much of Russia as she could. And though years after her arrival Tsarina Alexandra continued to harbor misgivings about the country's elite, the same could not be said where the country's peasants were concerned. In Alexandra's eyes, it was these, the ordinary people—whom she referred to as the "simple minded"[16]—who truly reflected the Russian character and soul. What increasingly drew the tsarina to Russia's illiterate and poverty-stricken masses was the fact that they seemed to lack the artifice found among the educated and wealthy classes. This was most appealing to a woman who valued honesty. Even more important, in the eyes of Alexandra, the Russian peasants took their religion to heart, and in so doing, welded the tsar, their father figure, with faith in the Almighty.

In many ways, the rich traditions, dogmas, and practices of the Russian Orthodox Church were more in tune with Tsarina Alexandra's passionate and intensely serious nature than the less flamboyant characteristics of German Lutheranism. Once she had embraced Orthodoxy, the form and beliefs offered by her new religion struck a deep chord in Alexandra's heart. She was certainly not the first to come under the spell of Russia's brand of Christianity. Even those who were not of the Orthodox faith could not help but express great admiration for the religion of Russia. One foreign observer who lived in Tsarist Russia wrote of the church's music in exalted terms: "I know no country except Russia where church music attains such heights of mystery and majesty by vocal polyphony alone . . . I could stay for hours listening to these anthems, responses, chants, psalms, and free passages."[17] Above all, "what is so particularly splendid in these works is the deep religious feeling; their appeal is to the mysterious recesses of the soul, and they touch the most secret places of the heart." Little wonder then, that once she embraced Orthodoxy, Tsarina Alexandra was overcome by the music, services, and doctrines of her new religion. Here was faith so rich it helped Alix face her increasingly frail and disordered world. As a result of the music alone, Alexandra found herself transported into a deeper, more spiritual communion with God.

For the tsarina, the heady effects of Orthodoxy, coupled with an almost naive understanding of Russia's peasants, would make her ripe for the complete acceptance of a new figure in her life, who seemed the very embodiment of a Russian soul touched through God's mercy.

Alix was drawn even closer to the Russian soul by her own marriage to a man who himself so readily identified with the country over which he was tsar. Although it has been calculated that "Tsar Nicholas II was only 1/128 Russian,"[18] this did not in any way prevent him from feeling Russian to the core. Here was a man who easily cleaved to the traditions and culture of his country. Above all, Tsar Nicholas's devotion to the Russian Church was genuine and strong, and here his wife readily found a supportive soul mate, who encouraged her growing devotion to the church he loved.

By the time she had been in Russia for a decade, Alexandra Feodorovna had become an exotic hybrid, combining characteristics derived from her Western childhood and adolescence with Eastern traits from her adopted land. This was certainly the conclusion arrived at by two of the tsarina's close friends, who believed that although Alexandra still on the surface continued to be "a practical Englishwoman," underneath, she had been transformed into a "mystical Russian."[19]

For all the comfort and luxury surrounding the tsarina, her world was essentially a hermetically sealed environment that few could penetrate. Away from the prying eyes and wagging tongues of St. Petersburg and those meddlesome Romanovs, Nicholas and Alexandra had succeeded in creating a retreat that kept them in splendid isolation. Considering the tsarina's excessive timidity, profound dislike of society, and now her increasing frailty, this desire to hide away at the Alexander Palace was understandable. But it ultimately led to tragic consequences. Splendid isolation might do for a country squire, a role much better suited to Nicky's character than that of the autocrat demanded of him; splendid isolation might do as well for the squire's wife or the leading lady of a small and far less significant principality such as Alexandra Feodorovna's native Darmstadt.

But mighty and vast Russia was neither a squire's fiefdom nor some small principality. The empire and the court demanded that the first couple of the land be on show in a manner befitting their exalted station in life.

In many respects, the tsarina's decision to shut herself away gradually from the public gaze was much like that of Queen Victoria soon after she was left a widow in 1861. The death of the Prince Consort was an earth-shattering event for the queen. The only way she could cope with this sudden widowhood was to retreat from public life for years, which naturally did not sit well with certain elements of the government and society. As Victoria's biographer, Lady Longford, has described this episode in the life of the queen: "She was not an hysteric in search of a sharp slap but someone disabled by a fearful wound."[20] Those same words could just as easily be applied to the tsarina, for her intense shyness, like some fearful wound, had a serious debilitating effect upon her.

The tsarina's spells of depression, brought about by her timidity and struggle at conversing with strangers, were characteristics that Queen Victoria had herself experienced. Even after over twenty years on the throne, the queen could still be seized with attacks of nerves while making a speech. At one point, she told her eldest daughter, Vicky, "I often wonder how I shall ever be able to go on. Everything upsets me. Talking especially tries me."[21] Yet Queen Victoria did go on. Like her grandmother, Alexandra had a strong sense of self that alternated with bouts of self-doubt. She also had the same sort of steeliness. This granitelike aspect in her personality was to harden and become even clearer as a debilitating illness in one of the tsarina's children transformed her life into a bitter struggle with death.

Eight

EMBATTLED BUT
NOT DEFEATED

AFTER YEARS OF SOMBER DIGNITY UNDER QUEEN VICTORIA, THE English court burst forth in full bloom under the stylish and gregarious new monarchs, King Edward VII and his still-youthful-looking queen, Alexandra. Poised to cut a blazing trail in the realms of fashion, entertainment, and social egalitarianism, and to some extent also relaxing rigid moral principles at court, the new King of England lent his name to a more sophisticated era. The coronation of such a charismatic couple became an eagerly anticipated event.

When it took place at Westminster Abbey on 9 August 1902, an impressive array of royals were in attendance. Riding in state that day to the abbey in a splendid line of carriages were the king's daughter, thirty-two-year-old Princess Maud, and the king's three nieces: twenty-six-year-old Crown Princess Marie of Romania; thirty-two-year-old Crown Princess Sophie of Greece; and fourteen-year-old Princess Ena of Battenberg.

With her parents on the throne of England, Princess Maud continued her regular visits to her native land. Appleton, of course, became her favorite destination. Her cozy two-story English-style home on the Sandringham estate had everything she could hope for. King Edward VII could not have done better in giving this country house to his daughter as a wedding present.

These visits to Appleton, however, were not only meant to soothe Maud's very English soul; from a physical standpoint, they proved to be a necessity. Without such visits, Maud's bronchitis and neuralgia would have aggravated her already delicate constitution. The princess waited out the winter months in a climate more amenable to her health.

When the welcome news came that Maud, married for over six years, was at last expecting a child, her doctors encouraged the princess to go to England for the birth. Since the child was not destined to reign in Denmark, or anywhere else for that matter, an accouchement in England seemed perfectly acceptable at the time. On 2 July 1903, a son—Alexander—was born to Maud at Appleton. When Alexander was two days old, the bells of St. George's Chapel, Windsor, were rung in honor of this infant prince. No one realized he would one day become King of Norway.

ᘛ••••ᘚ

For Crown Princess Marie of Romania, life continued its erratic course. But at Cotroceni, her three-story Bucharest palace, she decorated zealously. Already a budding artist, with an eye for flamboyance and theatricality, Missy set about imprinting her own unique style on the many rooms, a project that would keep her occupied through the years. Visitors gaped at the fantastic decor: intricate Byzantine artwork in gold, evoking true Oriental splendor, vied with the sleeker, more modern lines of Art Nouveau in a riot of styles. Flowers overflowed from vases—especially lilies, Missy's favorite.

For Missy, her memories of that English summer of 1902 when she was in England for Edward VII's coronation were forever etched in her mind thanks in large part to two newfound friends, Pauline Astor and her brother, Waldorf, whose father, the immensely wealthy William Waldorf Astor, a transplanted American, made his home in England but had been, at one time, the richest man in the United States. For Missy, wealth was not the overriding factor that drew her to the Astor siblings, though. She simply found like-minded individuals, kindred spirits who became fast friends. So attached did she become to Waldorf and Pauline that in her memoirs, she unequivocally told the world: "my dearest friends of all were the Astors."[1]

The crown princess first met Waldorf and Pauline when she accepted an invitation to Sunday lunch with the Astor family at Cliveden, their spectacular home in the Buckinghamshire countryside overlooking the Thames. There, Missy found to her delight that she had a close affinity with the brother and sister, who like her, led lonely lives. Just as the crown princess suffered under an oppressive taskmaster, King Carol I of Romania, Waldorf and Pauline were subjected to an equally difficult and diffident father.

By the end of the visit, the trio had bonded to such an extent that Marie became a fixture at Cliveden for the rest of the summer. Years later, she was to write that "those few weeks at beautiful Cliveden belong to the most perfect memories of my life. It was pure bliss."[2] A large part of this bliss undoubtedly came from Missy's growing attachment to Waldorf Astor.

Thereafter, Pauline and Waldorf paid Missy an annual visit in Romania. Their enthusiasm for Romania helped to cement Missy's growing appreciation for her adopted country. But as attached as she was to both siblings, there can be no doubt that Marie's feminine nature naturally gravitated to Waldorf, who did not hide his admiration for the woman who became a cherished friend.

Those watching Waldorf and Missy closely during this time could have easily concluded that the crown princess was falling for the rich Astor and putting her marriage in peril. But however distant Ferdinand and Marie had become, the fact was that separation was not an option for the couple. Such a move would have been far too damaging to the Hohenzollern dynasty in Romania. Carmen Sylva was convinced that Missy herself did not want to leave Nando. She wrote to a friend about the crown prince and princess that "They are not going to divorce and [she] wants to be a Queen! She feels young and strong and daring!"[3]

Being unhappy in her marriage had certainly left Missy vulnerable. But if Carmen Sylva is to be believed, it would appear that by the time she met Waldorf, she had already determined to stay with Nando and work alongside him for Romania.

Waldorf and Missy opened their hearts to each other during many an intimate ride through the pine-clad forests of Sinaia, the summer resort at the foot of the Carpathian Mountains. But despite their shared love of horses and riding, this was not the only thing Missy found attractive about Waldorf. In fact, what seems to have drawn her to the Astor heir was that there was an air of sadness about him; and though he had, in Missy's own words, "large velvety brown eyes and a charming smile," the "tall and exceedingly slim" Waldorf also possessed "a certain shyness of manner which added to his charm."[4]

Marriage being out of the question, Waldorf inevitably looked elsewhere for someone to marry. He found a flame-haired American divorcée, Nancy Shaw, whose vitriolic and mercurial temper would cause her to run afoul of friend and foe alike. As one of the five celebrated Langhorne sisters of Virginia, Nancy was to make a name for herself as the first female member of the British House of Commons. As Nancy Astor, she was also to become famous for her acerbic tongue.[5]

Missy, though overcome with a sense of sadness at the thought that she and Waldorf could never be as close as when he was single, nevertheless graciously accepted the woman Waldorf chose to be his wife. In fact, she gave Nancy a nudge in Waldorf's direction when the former Langhorne belle could not make up her mind whom to marry, as Waldorf was not the only one interested in becoming Nancy's second husband. In an act of magnanimity that was devoid of jealousy—one that illustrated the depth of Missy's feelings for Waldorf—the princess took it upon herself to try to win Waldorf's happiness. Marie boldly took pen in hand and wrote to Nancy, addressing her in her early letters as Mrs. Shaw.

In 1906, she wrote to present Waldorf's case. In this long and candid letter to a stranger, the crown princess told the dithering Nancy that "I feel as if I could not but help him to fight for his happiness." Even Marie admitted her tactic was "an unconventional step," and she hoped Mrs. Shaw would accept it in the spirit intended. "I quite realise that you may find it impertinent of me to seem to mix up with what hardly seems my business, but knowing Waldorf in the middle of the struggle for his happiness, I felt as if even if you could not help you would listen to me." Marie then launched her case for Waldorf, explaining, "I long for his happiness . . . I think you will have understood that there are not many like him, and that one may go far before one meets his like."[6]

Marie of Romania's unconventional letter might have helped to propel Nancy Shaw. Not long after it was written, Nancy Shaw became officially engaged, to the relief of Marie, who felt free to call Waldorf's fiancée Nancy.

Soon Nancy was on the receiving end of full-blown accounts from Missy of her embattled existence in Romania, one in which the princess depicted herself as a caged butterfly, emphasizing how much the Astor friendship meant to her. Eager to latch on to anyone closely associated with Waldorf, the crown princess wrote as if Nancy had been a lifelong friend. She did not hide the travails of being crown princess but also admitted that her exuberance and desires needed to be tempered:

> we solitary royalties have a heart like other human beings and need love and affection like others, but we seldom get it as we are supposed to be happy enough in our so cold grandeur . . .

> I *am rather* an unconventional person, that I have realised, but being so lonely and so apart from the rest of the world, has made me a bit of an original. . . .

> I have felt lately, that life is so much stronger than I am . . . my endeavours to make myself useful or popular or to help others, all has seemed to crumble away from me, and only leave me more tired and older. My one pride is, that outwardly no one could ever realise how sad all my inward self is, I always look . . . pleased and energetic.[7]

Nancy Astor accepted Marie's offer to become friends. However, they would never be close. Missy did not quite realize what she was contending with when she had urged Nancy Shaw to become Waldorf's wife. Once married, Nancy wished to keep the effusive Marie at arm's length. The new Mrs. Astor saw to it that letters between Waldorf and Marie ceased. It was reported that Nancy Astor said, "Marie of Rumania used to write to Waldorf every day at the time I first met him. I thought this too much on our honeymoon and I said I'd go home if it went on."[8] The domineering Nancy, it seemed, was uncomfortable with an expansive crown princess playing such an important role in Waldorf's life. Nancy quickly let Waldorf know in no uncertain terms that she was not going to share him with Romania's future queen. But Waldorf did not give in that easily.

When the issue of godparents came up for Waldorf and Nancy's first child, Waldorf understandably wanted Missy to be one of them. But Nancy refused, causing one of their earliest marital rows. Nancy complained to her sister that her husband wanted "that lunatic Princess" as a godmother. In the end, Waldorf refused to budge and Nancy conceded. "I hate it but I gave in to Waldorf," she admitted. She also could not resist a dig at Princess Marie, telling her sister, "I hear her hair is v. yellow these days and her cheeks v. pink."[9]

The one thing Marie of Romania learned gradually during these years, and wrote about in 1926, was the necessity of forbearance for someone in her position:

> One of the great lessons royalty has learned through the ages is PATIENCE—a huge, never-ending, all comprehending, all forgiving patience. Without it their task would overpower and crush them. If that patience fails them, then they will crumble. And royalty has to stand being hedged in, limited in their rights, limited in their freedom, cramped by their traditions which become a form of servitude. But their traditions are also their armour. If they rid themselves of their traditions, they take off that which defends them not only against others, but also against their own passions, desires and urge toward greater liberties.[10]

These were hard-won lessons that Marie had learned so many years before, when she was still a young princess in a strange and distant land among unforgiving taskmasters.

⟨∽∿∽⟩

By the early years of the twentieth century, paralyzing strikes, demonstrations, and mutinies were engulfing Russia. Workers in the cities became increasingly militant while peasants in the countryside agitated against injustices. Driving the metropolitan workers was fury at an absence of political rights; the peasantry for their part were roused by their enduring poverty. Into this potent mix came war in the Far East, a conflict that erupted after years of escalating tensions in Asia between the Russian and Japanese empires. From 1904 to 1905, Russia was embroiled in what became known as the Russo-Japanese War.

Many Russians greeted the war with confidence, including Tsarina Alexandra.

Alexandra, Princess of Wales ("Motherdear"), with her children: the princes Albert Victor (Eddy) and George; the princesses Louise, Victoria (Toria), and Maud *(at the top)*, 1874.

Balmoral, 1884. *Standing, back row, left to right:* Prince Albert Victor of Wales; Princess Beatrice; Princess Victoria of Wales; Duchess of Edinburgh (mother of the future Queen Marie of Romania); Victoria (Vicky), Crown Princess of Germany (mother of the future Queen Sophie of Greece); and Princess Louise of Wales. *Seated, left to right:* Princess Victoria of Prussia; Princess Alexandra of Edinburgh *(standing)*; Queen Victoria; Princess Maud of Wales; Princess Victoria Melita ("Ducky") of Edinburgh *(standing behind Maud)*; Princess of Wales; and Princess Marie of Edinburgh.

The three cousins (and three
future queens)—Princess
Maud of Wales *(far left, second
row)*, Princess Alix of Hesse
(right, next to Maud), and
Princess Marie of Edinburgh
(second from left, front row)—
as bridesmaids at the wedding
of their aunt, Princess Beatrice
(youngest daughter of Queen
Victoria), to Prince Henry of
Battenberg, at Whippingham
Church on the Isle of Wight
on 23 July 1885. Beatrice and
Henry's only daughter, Victoria
Eugenie, was to become
Queen of Spain in 1906.

A future Tsarina of Russia (Alix)
and a future Queen of Spain
(Ena) with their grandmother,
Queen Victoria, 1891.
Standing, left to right: Princess
Alix of Hesse; unidentified servant;
Prince Henry of Battenberg (Ena's
father); and Victoria, Princess Louis
of Battenberg (Alix's sister). *Seated,
left to right:* Beatrice and her son,
Prince Alexander of Battenberg
(Ena's mother and brother);
Queen Victoria and Prince Leopold
of Battenberg (Ena's youngest
brother); Louis IV, Grand Duke
of Hesse (Alix's father), with
Princess Victoria Eugenie of
Battenberg (Ena).

Princess Victoria Eugenie (Ena) of Battenberg with her grandmother, Queen Victoria, 1897. A favorite granddaughter of the queen, Ena, along with her three brothers, lived year-round with their grandmother, enlivening Victoria's last years.

Princess Alix of Hesse and Tsarevitch Nicholas of Russia, 1894. The engaged couple's stiff demeanor for the camera belies the underlying passion they had for each other in private.

Tsarina Alexandra of Russia in 1895, at the height of her beauty, in a photo inscribed in her own hand to her beloved grandmother, Queen Victoria.

Princess Maud at her favorite home, Appleton House, on the Sandringham estate in Norfolk, 1899. The photo is signed "Harry," Maude's nickname.

An engagement photograph of Princess Maud of Wales and Prince Charles of Denmark, 1896.

Crown Princess Marie of Romania, 1902. Renowned for her beauty, men easily succumbed to the vivacious Marie's charms.

M.S. Regele Ferdinand

Queen Marie's husband, King Ferdinand of Romania (c. early 1900s). Though Ferdinand and Marie's marriage proved rocky, they stayed together and were united in their devotion to Romania.

King George V (Queen Maud's brother), c. early 1900s, cherished a desire to marry Marie in their younger days.

The immensely wealthy Waldorf Astor (c. early 1900s) and Crown Princess Marie were drawn to each other in the early 1900s and remained lifelong friends.

Princess Ena of Battenberg and
King Alfonso XIII. Behind Ena is
her mother, Princess Beatrice, and
behind Alfonso is his mother, Queen
Maria Cristina of Spain, 1906.

The bomb blast in Madrid that nearly killed Queen Victoria Eugenie and King Alfonso XIII on
their wedding day, 31 May 1906.

Queen Ena of Spain
with Alfonso, her eldest child,
c. 1907. The robust-looking baby
turned out to be a hemophiliac,
shattering Ena's marriage to
King Alfonso XIII.

Queen Maud and King Haakon VII of Norway in their coronation robes, 1906. Maud remained
unswervingly British throughout her life.

Crown Princess Sophie of Greece, c. 1912.

Crown Princess Marie of Romania, c. 1909.

Russia, in their minds, would handily defeat its Asian enemy. Writing to her brother, Ernie, Alix explained how "we did everything to avoid it [war], but it seems it had to be, & it has done our country good."[11] The tsarina's naive assessment was to prove devastatingly wrong.

In the meantime, in the empire's capital, an act of civil disobedience brought about by frustration with their daily existence set a large group of the tsar's subjects on a march to plead their case. What began as a peaceful demonstration, however, ended in a brutal bloodbath.

January 1905 was characteristically freezing cold in St. Petersburg. This, though, did not prevent a large group of people from assembling outdoors. Animated by a desire to present the tsar with a list of their grievances in hopes he would listen to them and implement change, a large gathering of workers, mothers, and children (some 200,000), led by a priest, Father Gapon, began an unarmed march toward the Winter Palace. They advanced in a manner that was not aggressive, driven by a belief that the tsar would listen to their demands, such as calls for an eight-hour work day and a constituent assembly. Evidence of the marchers' loyalty to their sovereigns was visible in the portraits of the tsar and tsarina seen among the crowd. But waiting soldiers were ordered to suppress the crowd. Armed infantrymen repeatedly shouted orders for people to disperse, but were ignored. The infantrymen then fired indiscriminately, killing and wounding hundreds, whose mangled bodies scattered in front of the palace, blood staining the snow on the ground. That tragic day would forever be known as "Bloody Sunday." The government's brutal response to Father Gapon's march was a disaster. In fact, it was nothing short of a massacre.

Tsarina Alexandra, who was at Tsarskoe Selo with Nicholas, was aghast at the bloodshed. "It is a time full of trials indeed," she wrote one sister. Alexandra also explained her views on domestic politics, showing she was not averse to the idea that reforms had to be introduced. But she added that

Reforms can only be made gently with the greatest care and forethought. . . . Things are in a bad state and it's abominably unpatriotic at the time when we are plunged into war to break forth with revolutionary ideas. The poor workmen, who had been utterly misled, had to suffer, and the organisers have hidden as usual behind them. Don't believe all the horrors the foreign papers say. They make one's hair stand on end—foul exaggeration. Yes, the troops, alas, were obliged to fire. Repeatedly the crowd was told to retreat and that Nicky was not in town . . . and that one would be forced to shoot, but they would not heed and so blood was shed. . . . It is a ghastly thing, but had one not done it the crowd would have grown colossal and 1000 would have been crushed.[12]

The violent demonstration outside the Winter Palace brought home to the tsarina the burdens carried by her husband: "My poor Nicky's cross is a heavy one to bear, all the more as he has nobody on whom he can thoroughly rely and who can be a real help to him." Alix felt it her duty as wife and empress to serve and aid her husband as best she could. "On my knees I pray to God to give me wisdom to help him in his heavy task." But she viewed what was happening through the prism of the dichotomy that she felt divided the capital from the rest of Russia: "Petersburg is a rotten town, not an atom Russian. The Russian people are deeply and truly devoted to their Sovereign and the revolutionaries use his name for provoking them against landlords, etc., but I don't know how." Since Nicholas II needed help, Alix was overwhelmed with an urge to do something practical. "How I wish I were clever and could be of real use!" she sighed. "I love my new country. It's so young, powerful, and has so much good in it, only utterly unbalanced and childlike."[13]

Alix was right to worry about her beloved country. She needed only to look nearer home for a grim reminder that the forces of nihilism were still set on destroying the ruling dynasty. For decades, assassinations had dotted the Russian political landscape; there had been no letup on this method of intimidation used by the enemies of the tsarist government. Tsarina Alexandra's fears of instability could only have been exacerbated when Serge, Ella's husband, was murdered. In a scene reminiscent of the 1881 brutal assassination of Tsar Alexander II in St. Petersburg, his son met the same fate seventeen years later in Moscow. But whereas Alexander II, the "Tsar-Liberator," had his admirers, Grand Duke Serge was almost universally loathed. Long hated for his reactionary views and policies, Nicholas II's uncle was blown to bits by a bomb as he rode away from the Kremlin in a carriage. Serge's murder was another reminder for Alix that the throne of Russia, and her husband's fate, hung by the thinnest of margins. Little did she know just how dangerously thin that margin would be in the years to come.

In 1901, Alexandra's brother Ernie, the Grand Duke of Hesse, and his wife, Ducky, were divorced, angering Alix. When Ducky married Grand Duke Kyril, a cousin of Nicholas II, in 1905, the tsarina was appalled that the Romanovs had admitted a divorcée into the family. Unlike Alix, Missy sympathized with Ducky. In the midst of this scandal involving Crown Princess Marie of Romania's sister, Missy gave birth to her fourth child and second son, Nicolas. The baby was named after the tsar in the hope that this might soften his stand against Ducky and Kyril.

The birth of Missy's latest child in August 1903 offered yet more fodder for the gossips. Speculation was rife that baby Nicky's father was not Crown Prince Ferdinand. The gossip was further fanned when Waldorf's sister, Pauline, and an Astor family friend, Dr. Madge, returned to Romania in July to assist at the birth. Whatever the truth of Nicolas's paternity, Ferdinand accepted the child as his. And as time passed, Prince Nicolas did not appear to look like the Astors but, instead, came to resemble the Hohenzollern side of the family, with their protruding ears, piercing eyes, and hawkish noses.

If Missy thought her problems in Romania were overwhelming, she need only look to neighboring Russia to see that despite the power her cousin Alix could wield as tsarina, there was no doubt that Alexandra struggled at being the empress. Though Missy was still a step away from the throne itself, her increasing confidence and forceful personality were making headway. The tsarina had yet to make the same kind of impact in Russia as Marie was already starting to do in Romania.

Why was Missy's star in the ascendant while Alix's was still awaiting a jump start? Part of the reason stems from the fact that Marie of Romania undoubtedly had a great sense of charm and a joie de vivre that were so lacking in Alexandra of Russia. Though both women were undeniably beautiful, Missy's ability to charm people placed her far ahead of the dour and introverted Alix. And in an era gradually marked by a newfound elegance and sophistication, coupled with an increasingly public acceptance of permissiveness, the extrovert Marie was bound to reap more admirers than the intransigent and unforgiving Alexandra.

Two factors beyond the control of both women also made this possible. The first one lay in the very nature of the courts themselves and the high society of Bucharest and St. Petersburg, both of which were permeated by a degree of licentiousness and intrigue that would have been unacceptable at Queen Victoria's court. Victoria's court was rightly described at the time of her death as one in which the queen saw to it that "princes and courtiers should put levity far from them" and where the "Victorian ideal of simplicity and high seriousness" was admired and promoted.[14] At the opposite end of the spectrum in Eastern Europe, and the very antithesis of "simplicity and high seriousness," were the Romanian and Russian capitals over which Marie and Alexandra presided.

Bucharest was more than once mentioned by firsthand observers, both homegrown and foreign, as a place where there was a distinct "laxity of morals."[15] According to a well-placed Romanian of the time, "morality has never been a strong point with my compatriots" and "passionate, violent, and usually short-lived affairs are so numerous and intricate that, unless you live on the spot, it is difficult to keep track of the unending intrigues of one's friends."[16] St. Petersburg was equally decadent. In the season prior to the austere Lenten observations, "there was no livelier place in all Europe than the capital of imperial Russia, 'cosmopolitan in its leanings but thoroughly Russian in its recklessness.' "[17] Missy's dabbling in the odd flirtation with handsome admirers was very much in keeping with the way many of Romania's elite carried on. After all, as one contemporary put it, "Roumania gossips, but rarely blames."[18]

For the more upstanding but luckless Alexandra, her opinionated dealings with the hedonistic elite of Russia served to drive a wedge between the tsarina and the large supporting cast of the imperial court. To the tsarina, numerous members of the upper echelons of society were outright moral frauds, since they paid mere lip service to the religion into which they were born; Alexandra, on the other hand, had embraced Russian Orthodoxy and practiced her religion with fervor and devotion. To accept these religious hypocrites was simply antithetical to the tsarina's own truthful nature. That was partly why she had taken such a dislike to the haute monde of Russia. Sadly, Alexandra's contempt was heartily reciprocated. Thus, it was to the tsarina's misfortune that her high moral principles, derived from a genuine and profound approach to religion, were more scorned at Russia's capital than admired.

The increasingly divergent paths taken by these two royal consorts were also reflected in stark differences that arose in the leading royal court of the day— that of Edward VII. For just as the English court emerged from the strait-laced authoritarian atmosphere that permeated Queen Victoria's reign and plunged head-on into a more permissive one presided over by the gregarious King Edward VII, so too did Marie and Alexandra personify the differences between the old world and the new. Whereas the prim and proper Alix continued to value the Victorian ideals promoted by her late grandmother, Missy embraced the liberal social mores espoused by her uncle.

The ascension to the throne of the pleasure-loving Edward VII was, of course, another factor that was beyond Missy and Alix's control. And on the surface, it would appear that the king's presence on the international stage had no effect whatsoever on the way in which his nieces were perceived in Romania and Russia. Nevertheless, Edward VII's accession did have some impact on the acceptance or ostracization of Marie and Alexandra in their respective capitals. Edward was the undisputed leader of society both in England and on the European continent. The king's ability to maintain his acknowledged social standing, despite personal shortcomings in the area of marital fidelity, had the unintended side effect of helping Marie of Romania and hurting Alexandra of Russia.

Gossip had shadowed the gregarious monarch from his days as Prince of Wales, leaving as he did an endless trail of mistresses in his wake, "for he was the very model of genial but remorseless infidelity."[19] But herein lay the success with which Edward was able to deflect criticism on this front. Through a potent combination of bonhomie and refusal to indulge in hypocrisy where his matrimonial dalliances were concerned, Edward for the most part overcame criticism for being unfaithful to his ever patient wife. This continued well into the king's reign as his marital dalliances did not abate with the passage of time.

Edward VII's ability to transcend such rooted disapproval was largely due to his openness about his transgressions. Because he was "intensely human" and because "he never attempted to hide his weaknesses,"[20] Edward succeeded in winning over most of his critics. He managed to tinge his extramarital exploits with a lustrous sheen to the point where, instead of being condemned, Edward's infidelities became legendary. After he succeeded Victoria to the throne, society was more accepting of such conduct since the very arbiter of taste and behavior was none other than "Edward the Caresser" himself. And nowhere was this more evident than in the new feminine ideal that emerged with the new reign. For the arrival of the new king meant that the Victorian feminine ideal was usurped. In its place came a new, Edwardian woman: confident, audacious, and itching to practice a moral relativism denied her under the strictures of the Victorian era.

Thus, in tandem with the change in reigns, a shift of subtle but discernable proportions in the code of moral probity also emerged. Such high ideals as marital fidelity, so publicly prized in the Victorian era, were now shunted aside to make room for a greater acceptance of permissive behavior, epitomized by King Edward himself.

No longer was it enough for the Edwardian woman to accept benignly the marital infidelities of her husband while embarking on an affair at her own social peril. This was already evident toward the end of the Victorian era and gained momentum with the dawn of the Edwardian era and the emergence of a set of women known as "the Souls." According to Barbara Tuchman, this restricted group of society people—"self-consciously clever and endlessly self-admiring"— had chosen, "in conscious reaction to the Victorian feminine ideal," to allow themselves "a new freedom of private morality." It became a kind of desiderata for people who subscribed to this "new freedom of private morality" to "depart from Victorian morality without deserting propriety."[21] Marie of Romania exemplified this new Edwardian woman. The crown princess, with her male friends, had far more in common with these women who rebelled against the Victorian feminine ideal than with her strait-laced cousin. The Tsarina of Russia was more like the "Incorruptibles"—that "strict, reactionary" group of individuals who had found the loose-living Marlborough House set presided over by Edward VII when he was Prince of Wales so "vulgar."[22]

As the Edwardian era unfolded, Tsarina Alexandra still clung tenaciously to her principled Victorian ideals. After nearly a dozen years in Russia, she refused to tolerate the shenanigans of the elite. Instead of allowing St. Petersburg society to guide her—the outsider—the tsarina remained intractable and refused to be dictated to. This stubborn streak was driven by personal characteristics that were downright disastrous. When combined with her transparent honesty, the tsarina's notorious insecurity transformed Alexandria into a defensive wounded animal in retreat.

In comparison to Marie of Romania and their uncle, Edward VII, neither of whom was afraid to show their flawed but very human side, Tsarina Alexandra appeared thoroughly out of touch, out of date, and unsympathetic to all but a narrow circle of intimates. Tragically for Alix, this only led to her descending deeper and deeper into misunderstanding and vilification from which she was never to emerge.

But in analyzing the factors that contributed to the acceptance of Marie in Romania and the growing criticisms of Alexandra in Russia, there was one more reason why Missy's trajectory veered toward success and promise of great potential whereas Alix's was still aimlessly adrift. Marie succeeded where Alix had failed in the one area that counted the most: their role as mothers of a dynasty. Alexandra had yet to complete the all-important task of providing the coveted male heir. For Marie, the fact that she had given birth to a second son in 1903 meant that she had certainly done her duty where the dynasty was concerned. Such an achievement was something Alix could only dream of, and the presence of four lovely daughters could not make up for the lack of that precious son. Married for nearly ten years at the dawn of the Edwardian era, Alix was beginning to wonder if she was ever going to give birth to the much-longed-for tsarevitch.

☙

By 1904, Princess Victoria Eugenie of Battenberg had blossomed. One London newspaper was in raptures, describing Ena as "tall and slender without being too thin . . . [with] golden hair . . . large luminous blue eyes, a straight nose, well outlined lips, a rosy complection; in sum, a grand beauty."[23]

The princess had already garnered the attention of one of Europe's most eligible bachelors. During a visit to England, Grand Duke Boris met the teenaged, blue-eyed princess and took a fancy to her. When they met again in the South of France early in 1905, the grand duke courted the seventeen-year-old princess. However, nothing came of Boris's attentions. Soon after her debut, Ena was so busy enjoying herself in a round of parties that she all but forgot her Russian suitor.

It was just as well, for this was the very same Boris who had, a decade before, unashamedly pursued Marie of Romania while she was in Moscow for the coronation of Nicholas II and Alexandra. Ena's admirer was thus none other than the infamous Boris whom Missy so brazenly used to taunt King Carol of Romania, with the startling news that Boris was the father of her third child. Ena's decision not to marry Boris was a wise one; the grand duke has been rightly described as "a world class womanizer . . . the terror of jealous husbands as well as of watchful mothers."[24]

Despite having morganatic blood in her veins on her father's side, the fact that Ena had been a favored granddaughter of Queen Victoria and was born and raised in the English court made her an eligible princess in the highly contested matrimonial stakes. And Ena's obvious physical attractions garnered her a fair share of admirers. As Princess Ena launched into society, settling into a round of official engagements and entertainments, London was gearing up for the visit of Spain's King Alfonso XIII. The niece of King Edward VII and Queen Alexandra, like her other female English cousins living in and around London, would be expected to take part in the festivities surrounding the king's visit. But their presence was to be as more than mere adornments in the sparkling court of Edward VII. For these eligible princesses of the realm were to be discreetly paraded before Alfonso in an exercise intended to secure a potential English queen for Spain.

Nine

THE FACADE CRUMBLES

AFTER SUCCESSFULLY PUSHING FOR THE CANONIZATION OF SERA-
phim, the tsarina found to her satisfaction that she was again *enceinte*. The arrival of a male heir would help lift the empire's spirits, with Russia enmeshed in
a devastating war in the Pacific against Japan. Russia found to its consternation
that the Japanese Empire was proving to be more than an equal foe.

Tsarina Alexandra wasted little time in throwing herself wholeheartedly into
the war effort, organizing workshops in the Winter Palace where ladies of different classes met to prepare supplies and sew clothes for Russia's soldiers. The
tsarina often joined the ladies in their tasks, being careful not to monopolize
any one group. All in all, she managed to secure the aid of some five thousand
women in the war effort.

The tsarina encouraged her daughters to do their part for the empire's troops
by having them knit scarves and caps. One of the more effective ideas the tsarina came up with was to send parcels to the troops for Easter. Inside were such
much-needed items as soap, bandages, a shirt, a handkerchief, sugar, notepaper
and a stamped envelope. These thoughtful gifts elicited much gratitude from
the troops. Later in the war, Alexandra also created her own hospital in the
grounds of Tsarskoe Selo, where she paid visits every day to the wounded. And
in a gesture toward those soldiers who were wounded, the tsarina created an in-
valids' home for a number of them.

Alexandra's dedication to her country's soldiers was in abundant evidence
during this crisis, and though she was pregnant again, she did not slow down until just two months short of her confinement. By then, wracked by tremendous

pain when standing or walking, the tsarina had no other recourse but to spend the remaining weeks prostrate in bed or on a sofa.

It became apparent that Russia was faring badly in the war. Hampered by geography, Russia could not replenish its supplies and aid its troops fast enough. Neither were the Russian military leaders up to par. At the Battle of Mukden alone, which took place in February–March 1905, 330,000 Russian soldiers fought and nearly 90,000 fell in battle. To place this in perspective, one historian has noted that "Mukden was, in terms of the numbers involved, the biggest battle until then recorded. . . . Over six hundred thousand men, more than were ever engaged in any nineteenth-century battle, fought desperately for over two weeks instead of for a day."[1]

Like most Russians, the tsarina was anxious about the war, but through sheer willpower, she managed to keep herself from succumbing to anxiety, exhaustion, and illness. On a hot summer's day in August 1904, the miracle Alexandra had been fervently praying for finally took place: A beautiful baby, weighing in at eleven pounds, was born to Nicholas and Alexandra at Peterhof.

When the tsarina awoke from the effects of the chloroform, she saw from her husband's radiant face that their most cherished wish had come true. "Oh, it cannot be true; it cannot be true," exclaimed the incredulous mother. "Is it really a boy?" she asked.[2] The ecstatic parents named their precious son Alexei, in honor of Nicholas II's favorite tsar, Alexei I, the father of Peter the Great.

Nicholas and Alexandra's happiness proved short-lived, for anxiety over their son's health soon tinged the parents' waking hours. Within weeks of the baby's birth, Nicholas confided to his diary a disquieting episode: "Alix and I are very disturbed at the constant bleeding in little Alexei. It continued at intervals from his navel until evening."[3] From that moment on, neither parent would know a moment's peace. Their precious bundle of joy, the boy destined to be Emperor of Russia, was already showing signs of that most dreaded disease—hemophilia.

When Port Arthur fell to the Japanese at the end of 1904, the loss came as a bitter blow for the Russians. More than ever, the need to secure victory became an absolute imperative for the country's leaders. Much hope, therefore, lay in the performance of their Baltic Fleet, which had been sent on a nine-month, 30,000-kilometer voyage to Japan in order to inflict great damage on the Japanese. What the Russians got instead was total defeat. Soon after its arrival in Japanese waters at the end of May 1905, the fleet was unexpectedly annihilated by the enemy at what became known as the Battle of Tsushima. In a destructive and decisive battle lasting an incredibly brief forty-five minutes, the empire of Japan defeated the empire of Russia. The barrage of Japanese firepower resulted in the mind-boggling loss for Russia of six destroyers, twelve cruisers, eight battleships, and thousands of men. It was an ignominious end for Russia's Baltic Fleet.

According to the Grand Duchess Olga, Tsarina Alexandra's sister-in-law, who was with Nicholas II and Alix at the moment they received news of the disaster at Tsushima, the tsar "turned ashen pale . . . and clutched at a chair for support," while "Alicky broke down and sobbed."[4]

Vanquished, Russia had no alternative but to make peace with Japan. The Treaty of Portsmouth was signed, ending the Russo-Japanese War, which had brought nothing but humiliation for the empire of Nicholas II. Of the 2 million men who fought in that conflict, the country lost 125,000, and all, it seemed, had died in vain.

The stunning outcome of the Battle of Tsushima had a detrimental impact on the prestige of the tsar and the government. It is not an exaggeration to state that this crushing defeat led in some direct measure to the revolutionary fever that engulfed Russia in 1905. The overwhelming defeat in war plus the Bloody Sunday riots combined to make 1904–05 one of the most harrowing years for the tsar and tsarina. Events of such magnitude peeled away the facade of near impregnability associated with the Romanov dynasty. Though the imperial family had been dogged by assassinations and instability, by the end of 1905 an ever greater sense of vulnerability emanated from Tsarskoe Selo. From then on, every misstep taken by the tsar, and especially the tsarina, was not only to have the effect of stripping away further the illusion of stability and affection; the blunders were to provide the imperial couple's enemies with the ammunition to destroy them.

Ever since Bloody Sunday, growing mass unrest and a string of endless actions directed against the government had made for greater instability. Strikes, revolts, and demonstrations in many parts of the country were commonplace, so much so that "between Bloody Sunday and the late fall, Nicholas and his military advisers assigned 15,297 companies of infantry and 3,665 squadrons of cavalry, with 224 cannon and 124 machine guns, to suppress strikes and peasant riots."[5]

In Odessa, two thousand deaths resulted after eight hundred men mutinied on the battleship *Potemkin*. By the first week of October 1905, a massive railway strike involving three quarters of a million railroad employees snowballed, causing others to join in, so that millions of workers brought the empire to a virtual standstill. Mob violence erupted and ominous swathes of revolutionary red were unfurled in cities and towns as workers sang the *Marseillaise* and loudly proclaimed: "Long Live the Revolution!" and "Down with Autocracy!"[6]

In St. Petersburg that October, striking workers cut off all electricity. The capital's university teemed with revolutionaries consisting of the soon to be familiar Bolsheviks and Mensheviks. The stage was set for civil war as the tsar ordered troops to crush the agitators.

Faced with anarchy, there were only two options left to Tsar Nicholas II and the government: Either answer the insurrections with violence or institute some kind of major reform such as the granting of a constitution. In the end, the chairman of the Committee of Ministers, Sergei Witte, one of the ablest members of the Russian government, convinced his master that the latter was the way to go, though Nicholas himself was more inclined toward some form of military dictatorship.

Throughout this time, Alexandra was never far from her husband's side. When Count Witte went to Peterhof for a meeting with the tsar during these torturous days of decision making, he was astonished to find that not a single Romanov grand duke had joined the tsar for the meeting. Instead, an incredulous Witte found only Tsarina Alexandra with her husband. During the course of his audience with the tsar, in which discussions over changes to autocracy were explained, Witte noticed how uncomfortable and angry Alexandra seemed to be. "The Empress," Count Witte recalled, "sat stiff as a ramrod, her face lobster-red, and did not utter a single word."[7] Tsarina Alexandra was finally making her mark with Nicholas II. Having been married to him for over a decade and having provided the son they so fervently prayed for, Alexandra had at last superseded the Dowager Empress Marie in gaining the tsar's confidence when it came to giving him political advice.

Some who knew the tsarina were full of misgivings about her increased influence over the tsar. Count Witte himself concluded that "it is fatal for the Russian Empire that a person such as this should be adviser to its Autocratic Master, able to affect the fate of tens of millions of human beings."[8] Kaiser Wilhelm II was no less damning of Alexandra's meddling. In March 1905, Wilhelm maintained that Tsar Nicholas was "in great danger" if he did not soon end his wife's increasing influence. Writing in reply to a report which told the Kaiser that Alexandra now wielded influence with Nicholas, Wilhelm exploded: "The little Hessian Princess, who never heard anything about politics, is giving political advice!?" And in English, he added, "fools rush in where angels fear to tread!"[9]

When the time came to make his final decision, Nicholas II prevaricated. The tsar's cousin, the tall and imposing Grand Duke Nicholas ("Nikolasha"), was so furious about plans to proceed with a military dictatorship that he stormed into

Peterhof and exclaimed: "I'm going now to the Czar and I will beg him to sign the manifesto and the Witte program. Either he signs or in his presence I will put a bullet through my head with this revolver."[10]

On 17 October 1905, Tsar Nicholas II put an end to three hundred years of Romanov autocracy. After making the sign of the Cross, the tsar affixed his signature to a manifesto granting Russia a constitution, thus paving the way for the creation of a parliamentary body known as the Duma. In so doing, with the stroke of a pen, the tsar had succumbed to the latest assault against autocracy.

The tsarina never forgave Nikolasha for his histrionics or his bullying tactics. From then on, Alexandra was to regard the grand duke with disdain and suspicion. Nor did Count Sergei Witte come out of the episode in anything but a negative light for Alexandra. Witte himself recorded, "I heard that the Empress herself took the liberty of saying that I had forced the manifesto on her husband."[11]

Other Romanovs also despised the manifesto. "That was the end," concluded Sandro, Alix's brother-in-law. To him, the October Manifesto meant "the end of the dynasty and the end of the empire. A brave jump from the precipice would have spared us the agony of the remaining twelve years."[12]

The tsar himself found it hard to stomach his decision to end autocracy, which was tantamount to signing his own abdication. Nicholas described his action as a "terrible decision." His "only consolation," wrote a distraught Nicholas, was that "this grave decision will lead my dear Russia out of the intolerable chaos she has been in for nearly a year."[13] To a friend, the tsar was more blunt. With tears in his eyes, Nicholas II murmured: "I am too depressed. I feel that in signing this act I have lost the crown. Now all is finished."[14]

For Tsarina Alexandra, far from being an enlightened act designed to move Russia toward more democratic and liberal principles for the benefit of the people, the manifesto was nothing but an act of appeasement that rewarded the enemies of autocracy. She knew that this concession granted by her husband shook the Romanov dynasty to its very foundations, for here was a classic example of what Barbara Tuchman has called "the bitter truth of history: that progress and gain by one group is never accomplished without loss of some permanent value of another."[15] As a witness to the torturous days of negotiations and soul-searching her husband went through, Alexandra remarked that "these days had been like a very difficult labor."[16] The tumultuous events of the recent past were more than enough to try the nerves of even the most patient and fatalistic of rulers. For the tsar, one thing was certain: especially where the disastrous Russo-Japanese War was concerned, had it not been for the support Nicholas received from Alexandra, he could not have survived the incredible stress of that fateful year. In essence, the tsar owed his sanity to his wife. "Without her," he confessed to one of the family's close friends, Anna Viroubova, "I could never have endured the strain."[17]

Tsarina Alexandra and the Dowager Empress Marie accompanied Nicholas II to the opening in April 1906 of the Duma (Parliament). The mere fact that the tsar was opening what in theory was a consultative legislative body was itself a significant blow to autocracy.

Princess Galitzine, a member of one of Russia's aristocratic families, who watched the tsar that day, was overcome by the feeling that "something great was crashing—as if all Russian tradition had been annihilated by a single blow."[18] Even more frightening was the fact that most of the Duma's members watching the proceedings did not hide their contempt for the tsar and his supporters. "They looked at us as upon their enemies, and I could not make myself stop looking at certain faces, so much did they seem to reflect an incomprehensible hatred for all of us," admitted the Dowager Empress Marie.[19] Sandro echoed these sentiments, recalling, "I saw burning hatred in the faces of some of the parliamentarians."[20] His wife, Xenia, was even more critical: "The Duma is such filth, such a nest of revolutionaries, that it's disgusting and shaming for the rest of Russia in front of the whole world."[21] Xenia had every right to feel anxious. As one contemporary account had it: "out of the nearly 493 members, 380 have been elected. Of these, the Government can count on the support of 20."[22]

The situation in Russia continued to be so chaotic that "murder, armed robbery, and bomb-throwing" remained "as common as ever." The October Manifesto and the Duma's opening had done nothing to calm the agitated masses. Added to this was the government's inability to deal with such crises as the widespread famine that gripped the country. So unstable and violent had the nation become that the fact that "no important personage has been killed during the past fortnight" was thought significant news warranting inclusion by the British Embassy in its report to London.[23] Such was the crumbling empire over which Nicholas and Alexandra still ruled.

⟨∞⟩

Instability was not confined solely to Russia. Even in the relatively tranquil calm of Scandinavia, disputes that had been simmering for some time finally erupted. A bitter separation was set to wrench apart the two countries which, until 1905, had constituted the Kingdom of Sweden-Norway.

Ever since 1811, Norway and Sweden had been joined in union, with the kings of Sweden as head of state. It was an unequal partnership, for Norway had long been dominated by Sweden. Since the middle of the nineteenth century, Norwegians had made their unhappiness known, viewing the kings of Sweden-Norway as not being Norwegian enough. In order to placate their junior partners, the Swedes introduced concessions; but by 1905, matters had come to a head. The final issue prompting the Norwegians to seek full independence centered on the seemingly benign issue of Norway's right to consular representation. When King Oscar II of Sweden refused his consent to this latest disagreement, a row broke out.

As the months dragged by, it became evident that Norway would split from Sweden. The question then arose as to what type of government Norway would decide upon—a republic or a kingdom. For those wishing to set up a kingdom, the candidature of Prince Charles of Denmark looked ideal. When first approached by British diplomats about accepting the throne of Norway, Charles had brought up the fact that "he would find it a great personal sacrifice." Furthermore, "he knew nothing of the Norwegian people and their form of society." Charles was deeply immersed in his work at the Danish Navy; "would he not be happier in such a career, or possibly in the British navy?"[24] Charles obviously enjoyed his life in the navy, while Maud, who preferred to stay away from the limelight, feared that becoming a queen might end the kind of privacy she craved.

The year 1905 was to prove memorable for Tsarina Alexandra in other ways. Two individuals who were to become close made their mark. Anna Taneeva (later Viroubova) entered the hallowed halls of the Alexander Palace early that year. The other individual who came into the tsarina's life that year and who was to have a more profound impact on Alexandra and, by extension, on Russia itself, was a mysterious peasant from the Siberian village of Pokrovskoie by the name of Grigory Rasputin. The tsar recorded the couple's fateful meeting with Rasputin in his diary, stating simply, "We've made the acquaintance of a man of God, Grigory from the Tobolsk Guberniya."[25]

Rasputin entered the tsarina's life at a propitious time for him. Though some might have found this peasant too unseemly, with his straggly looks and disturbing eyes that penetrated through anyone he stared at, to the tsarina he was a God-fearing man from the hinterland—the very embodiment of the holy and simple Russian peasant who unquestioningly loved his sovereigns.

Rasputin was to play a prominent role in Alexandra's life as a tragedy of huge proportions began unfolding. Ever since the day Alexei began to bleed at the navel, she had been tormented over her son's health. Confirmation that her precious boy was a hemophiliac hit the child's mother with savage force. The fact that she had transmitted the disease added to her mortification.

This never-ending cycle of fear for her son's life led to the rapid collapse of Alexandra's already fragile health. For days on end, she could be found in the Mauve Boudoir lying on her sofa, suffering from very real and acute pains in the head, back, legs, or heart.

From the time the diagnosis was pronounced, anxiety over Alexei's welfare was to consume the tsarina until the day she died. And so, to her sciatica and other ailments was added nervous exhaustion. Only those in closest contact could see the toll her ill health was taking on her. In 1907, one of the tsarina's ladies found her mistress "looking miserable." Asked how she was feeling, the tsarina replied, "Oh, I am so ill, I don't know why, but I am miserable."[26]

It was one of the few times Alexandra openly complained about her health. For as with nearly every misfortune that befell her, the tsarina accepted her latest tribulation without complaining, telling her sister, Victoria: "Don't think my ill health depresses me personally. I don't care, except to see my dear ones suffer on my account, and that I cannot fulfil my duties. But once God sends such a cross, it must be borne." And though burdened by bad health, Alix still found much to be grateful for. "I have had so much, that, willingly, I give up any pleasures—they mean so little to me, and my family life is such an ideal one, that it is a recompense for anything I cannot take part in."[27]

As Alexei grew into a lively and enchanting child, Nicholas and Alexandra continued to keep their son's affliction to themselves. Even the grand duchesses' tutor, Pierre Gilliard, did not know the true nature of Alexei's illness until he had been employed for eight long years. Yet when he was first introduced by the tsarina to Alexei, Gilliard instantly detected that there was something about her son that preoccupied Alexandra. "I could see," he recalled of that day, that the tsarina was "transfused by the delirious joy of a mother who at last has seen her dearest wish fulfilled. She was proud and happy in the beauty of her child"—a child who was "certainly one of the handsomest babies one could imagine, with his lovely fair curls and his great blue-grey eyes under their fringe of long curling lashes." But at that first meeting, continued Gilliard, "I saw the Czarina press the little boy to her with the convulsive movement of a mother who always seems in fear of her child's life." There was in Alexandra's face a look of "secret apprehension so marked and poignant, that I was struck at once."[28]

Anna Viroubova was also kept in the dark about Alexei's illness until one day, by chance, she witnessed the tsarina's near hysteria when her son became entangled with a chair. When Alexandra saw Alexei screaming "like a wounded animal," she ran toward him and shouted at Anna: "Leave him, stop, his leg's caught in the chair!" Anna was perplexed at what seemed an overreaction. Sensing her friend's confusion, Alexandra said, "I'll explain in a minute." Then, as the tsarina carefully extricated Alexei's leg and calmed him down, Anna noticed that the boy's leg was "bruised and swollen." Only then did Alexandra break down; in tears, she finally told Anna of her son's "dreadful disease."[29] The disease that afflicted Alexei was to have a devastating impact not only on the boy but on his mother, and, ultimately, the Russian Empire itself.

Ten

DESTINY BECKONS

KING ALFONSO XIII'S KINGDOM HAD ARRIVED AT A CROSSROADS AS tensions within society contributed to a long-drawn-out battle for Spain's soul. For decades, the country had endured problems that undermined its internal stability and the dynasty. When in 1898 Spain suffered the humiliating losses of Cuba, Puerto Rico, and the Philippines—among the last vestiges of what had once been a huge empire—it was obvious that Alfonso XIII's kingdom had become a spent power. In addition, a bankrupt treasury, rampant corruption, unproductive farms, rigged elections, and lackluster trade figures beset what had once been a mighty imperial power.

Unenviable, then, was King Alfonso's task when he came of age in 1902 and assumed the reins of power. Alfonso was never to know a moment's peace ruling his kingdom. In the first four years after reaching his majority, he had to deal with "no less than fourteen ministerial crises, and with eight different Prime Ministers."[1] The rest of Alfonso's reign would prove no less volatile. Just as in Russia, Spain's hothouse politics would wreak havoc on the country's dynasty—in the process bringing down the happiness of Queen Victoria's youngest granddaughter.

In 1905, Spain's king toured Europe and earnestly embarked on a search for a bride. At nineteen years of age, King Alfonso was still a young man with plenty of time left before settling down. However, as head of the Spanish House of Bourbon, and as a reigning king without any direct descendants, the pressure to marry quickly and start a family was strong. The king's hunt for a wife prompted fevered speculation in the Spanish and European press. Alfonso found it all so amusing that he would arrive at breakfast saying, "to which princess are the newspapers marrying me today."[2] There were certainly many eligible ones, but the idea of having a British princess as Queen of Spain took hold, especially among those of a liberal inclination in Spain. Before heading home, Alfonso stopped in London for a hectic seven-day visit. Princess Ena's cousin, Patricia ("Patsy") of Connaught, was already deemed the most likely to catch Alfonso's attention. His London trip would determine whether the dark-haired Patsy, now eighteen, just might be the next Queen of Spain.

Confident in his powers of seduction, Alfonso duly laid siege to his intended target. But before he could exercise his charms on the Connaught princess, a bevy of other princesses were demurely paraded during a dinner at Buckingham Palace, all granddaughters of Queen Victoria. The young ladies were well aware they stood a good chance of becoming the next Queen of Spain—all, that is, except a certain Battenberg princess. Only Ena thought that she would go unnoticed. She behaved with far less affectation than her eligible cousins and seemed all the more natural. Seated next to Alfonso was Princess Helena, one of Queen Victoria's daughters, who answered the king's questions about each of the guests he scrutinized during the elegant formal dinner. When Alfonso's attention fell on Ena, his eyes followed the mysterious princess's graceful movements. Intrigued, Alfonso asked Princess Helena: "And who is that young lady with the nearly white hair?" Helena replied that she was none other than Ena of Battenberg. When the hot-blooded Spanish king laid eyes on Ena, the effect was intoxicating—and disconcerting. She immediately succumbed. Even years later, the memory of that moment stayed fresh in Ena's mind. She recalled being seized by a sudden sense of embarrassment, so that the thought that went through her mind was: "Oh God, he's taken me for an Albino!" Alfonso's penetrating gaze made a strong impact and she "blushed shamelessly."[3]

Patsy, however, proved uncooperative. She had already made up her mind before King Alfonso's visit that marriage to him was out of the question, so she ignored the king's attentions. Alfonso soon got the message: he would have to look elsewhere for a wife. Undaunted, his roving eye attached itself to another of Queen Victoria's attractive granddaughters.

During a second evening reception, this time at the palatial Londonderry House, Alfonso caught sight of Ena again. Tall, blond, dignified, she stood out as a beauty. Other eligible princesses were out in force too, but it was Ena who made an impact on the Spanish king. Unable to remember her name, Alfonso referred to her as the fair-haired one. This time, his attentions paid off. His feelings were reciprocated. Any bruises Alfonso may have nursed because of Patsy's rejection were suddenly banished by thoughts of Ena. Alfonso and Ena's final evening meeting took place during a ball at Buckingham Palace. It was only during this time that the two of them could converse freely. Since Alfonso's English was barely passable and Ena's Spanish nonexistent, the couple spoke French.

As they twirled on the dance floor, Alfonso asked Ena if she enjoyed collecting postcards, a hobby then in vogue with wellborn ladies. Surprised by the question, Ena answered, "Yes, yes, I collect postcards," even though she hardly did. "Well," answered Alfonso, "I shall send you some on condition that you reply." By the end of the ball, Alfonso daringly asked Ena, "I hope you will not forget me." Unsophisticated and naturally reserved, the princess replied, "It is very difficult to forget the visit of a foreign sovereign."[4] Her unromantic reply revealed Victoria Eugenie's reserved and uncoquettish nature. Though she was already fond of him, Ena was much too timid to give him the fiery, passionate answer he might have expected. It was the first indication that Alfonso and Ena were, in temperament, a mismatched couple.

Glimpses of Alfonso at this time make it difficult to fathom what might have attracted Ena to the spindly youth of nineteen. No doubt chivalrous attentions from a king were irresistible to most young women; yet physically, there was still much to be desired in the young Alfonso. Only years later, with maturity, did the king's slight frame fill out completely. One of the things Ena must have found irresistible was his smile, for which Alfonso became famous. This well-known smile, when "accompanied by a slight twinkling in the eyes, transformed his face" so that one felt totally dazzled.[5]

As eligible as she was as a royal bride, an elusive but sinister shadow nevertheless hovered over Princess Ena of Battenberg. That shadow was the possibility that she might be a carrier of hemophilia. Ena's own brother, after all, was a hemophiliac.

The issue did not escape the notice of Alfonso's Spanish advisers. Once his intentions toward the Battenberg princess became obvious, a whispering campaign broke out in order to try and dissuade the eager king from marrying a descendant of Queen Victoria with a brother who was a hemophiliac. So besotted was he with Ena that he carelessly ignored these warnings. In his eyes, such a beautiful and obviously healthy-looking creature could not possibly carry that dreaded disease. But if she was a carrier, Alfonso was prepared to take the risk. He was, after all, one who never flinched from peril. All his adult life, the king gravitated toward danger. He clearly did not seek out the numerous assassination attempts against him, but when they threatened, Alfonso met them courageously. His hobbies included driving cars at fast speeds and playing a hard game of polo, in which he punished his horses and risked breaking his own bones. If he seriously heeded the rumors that Ena might be a hemophilia carrier, then surely here was the ultimate risk in subconsciously toying with the future of his dynasty.

Over the next few months, King Alfonso and Princess Ena exchanged letters. Alfonso, not forgetting the promise made on the dance floor at Buckingham

Palace, regularly sent her postcards, to which Victoria Eugenie responded. The correspondence would last almost until the couple married in May 1906. Both wrote mostly in French; in this distant fashion, the serious business of courtship unfolded.

Upon Alfonso's return to Madrid from London, the king admitted his infatuation with Princess Ena of Battenberg to his mother. For the intensely Catholic queen Maria Cristina, the prospect of gaining a daughter-in-law who was born a Protestant did not sit well. Nor did Ena's morganatic blood on her Battenberg side. Maria Cristina insisted that her son look elsewhere for a bride. But Alfonso's choice never faltered.

In the meantime, the exchange of postcards continued apace. Ena's choice of cards revealed an eclectic taste. Modestly, the princess sent very few depicting herself; most consisted of scenes of London, the English countryside, and paintings by such prominent British artists as Romney, Gainsborough, and Landseer, and much later on, as she traveled in France, scenes of Paris and Biarritz.

Exchanges of news and increasing declarations of devotion flew back and forth. At first, Princess Victoria Eugenie's cards contained straightforward news of herself, interspersed with the occasional humorous comment. One of the earliest, for instance, was a photograph of her as a bridesmaid. Ena tells Alfonso how "we [the wedding party] have an air of fright, as if we were about to cry. It will amuse you!"[6]

As the months passed and she became increasingly confident of King Alfonso's devotion, the tone of Ena's messages grew friendlier and bolder. Recounting how a man at a function in her house was Alfonso's veritable double, Ena took the opportunity of assuring the real Alfonso, "But for me [the double] was *not so nice as the original.*"[7]

As their planned reunion in the South of France drew nearer, Ena grew excited. But in one card, she reveals her suspicions that she is more fond of Alfonso than he is of her, telling him: "I am convinced that [my friendship for you] is stronger on my part than yours is for me. I will fight with you if you feel the contrary!"[8]

During this time, Ena took it upon herself to begin learning Spanish, but she found the task difficult. She confessed to Alfonso, "I have no Spanish teacher whatsoever, what little I know, I have learned myself in books."[9] In December 1905, Ena wrote how determined she was to tackle this challenge: "I intend to do everything that I can to learn your language. But oh! the difficulties that I have with the grammar."[10] She eventually employed the services of a Spanish tutor, but her struggles with the language continued.

At the end of the year, the love-struck princess wrote a final message on the last day: "I am very sad at writing to you for the last time this year, [one] that has been so happy for me. Always one remembers with nostalgia a happy stage which now will never return. I hope the new year will be happier still."[11] As their reunion neared, Ena confessed that "it is too heavenly to think of meeting so soon now. God bless you darling and think of E. who loves you."[12]

Princess Ena and King Alfonso met again in January 1906 in Biarritz. There, the besotted couple became unofficially engaged. After they parted, the correspondence continued. This time, evidence of Ena's growing attachment to her admirer became more pronounced. In one postcard to Alfonso, Ena opened with "Mon cher Alfonso" and ended her message with the words, "mille et mille 000000 de ton Ena," meaning she sent him thousands of kisses.[13]

Six days after she wrote those words, Princess Ena stepped onto Spanish soil for the first time. Accompanied by King Alfonso and her mother, the trio motored from Biarritz into Spain. One of Alfonso XIII's courtiers, the Marquis of Villalobar, proclaimed to the princess, "Señora, we have set foot on Spanish territory," to which Ena replied, "I am delighted that this moment has arrived; it fills me with joy and never shall I forget the first day on which I trod the soil of Spain."[14] The party continued on to the Miramar Palace in San Sebastian, where they were welcomed by Queen Maria Cristina. The residents of San Sebastian were ecstatic about their future queen, one journalist writing lyrically of Ena: "An enchanting face . . . an exquisite grace and a sweetness rarely frequent in women of the North." Moreover, "her character is angelic . . . her blonde hair, graciously coiffed, her round face, with fine skin, a fine body and her dreamy eyes."[15] In sum, Ena was perfection personified.

Not everyone, however, was thrilled with the prospective marriage, largely due to the fact that Ena was not of the Catholic faith. As a Protestant, she would have to convert to Roman Catholicism in order to marry Alfonso. Just as it was unacceptable in Russia to have a tsarina who did not profess the Orthodox faith, so a queen in Spain could not be anything other than a Catholic.

Some in Spain grumbled about Ena's Protestant background. But even more vociferous criticism came from Ena's fellow Englishmen, once serious rumors about an engagement took root. A public campaign of indignation in England swept the press. Protestants voiced their disapproval of Ena's march toward Rome. Groups such as the Protestant Alliance and the Church Association appealed to King Edward to forbid the marriage. The upper echelons of the Church of England (of which her uncle, the king, was head) were not immune from denouncing Ena's probable repudiation of Protestantism. Both the Bishop

of London and the Archbishop of Canterbury took it upon themselves to in-
form King Edward that the signs of "public disapproval" were very real.[16]

To understand this fervent hostility toward Ena's planned conversion, one
needs to recall that anti-Catholicism had been a prominent feature of English
society for centuries. England, a Protestant country since the Reformation, had
long sought to subjugate its Catholic minority. The Catholic Emancipation Act
was passed—with dissenting voices heard—only in 1829. Anti-Catholicism in
the Victorian era was widespread and, as one historian describes it, "quite
unique. It was peculiarly related to popularly subscribed precepts about the
ends and nature of the British state; it was chauvanistic and almost general."[17]
Queen Victoria herself was not among those fired with a hatred for Catholicism;
on the contrary, she had a streak of tolerance toward the faith and had stated: "I
cannot bear to hear the violent abuse of the Catholic religion, which is so
painful and so cruel towards the many innocent and good Roman Catholics."[18]

Nevertheless, an anti-Papist atmosphere was still very much part of English
political life, even after Victoria's death. Thus, for staunch Protestants to see a
granddaughter of Queen Victoria, whom they had seen grow up by the queen's
side and had long viewed as a British princess, choose to renounce her Protestant faith for Catholicism, was something tantamount to treason. Privately,
King Edward was said to be unsympathetic, even hostile to Ena's religious conversion. He, after all, had made a declaration in Parliament during the first year
of his reign that was a blatant objection to, and renunciation of, the Roman
Catholic faith. To Ena, however, King Edward tried to gloss over his disappointment, telling her: "I do not deny that your change of religion gives me a
pang, but I am very liberal when it comes to religions and I believe it [the con-
version] to be inevitable."[19]

Not long after completing her Biarritz visit, Princess Ena embarked on a spiritual journey which was necessary in her position as the next Queen of Catholic
Spain, undergoing religious instruction in her future faith from Monsignor
Robert Brindle, the Bishop of Nottingham, who had been an esteemed and popular army chaplain during his service in Egypt.

Ena's love for Alfonso was certainly a major factor in her decision to embrace
Roman Catholicism. Nevertheless, her spiritual journey was not done simply in
exchange for a crown. The teenage Ena took her religious guidance from Monsignor Brindle seriously; and her correspondence with King Alfonso at this time
shows a princess clearly preoccupied by her lessons and by the impending ceremony itself. Alfonso told Ena of his wish to be present at her conversion. Ena
thought otherwise. "I ask only one favor of you," she wrote in February 1906,
"that you do not come to the conversion ceremony, as I have already done so
much for love of you. . . . *Viens après.* But, my darling, don't come till after my

conversion. Your presence would distract me."[20] The next day, Ena was again insistent: "*Mon vieux cher ami,* I see your strong reasons for coming to my conversion. But if you come my thoughts will be distracted." And in a not so subtle hint that betrayed both the inner turmoil she was going through in renouncing her faith and the pressure she felt from rabid English Protestants and Spanish Catholics alike, Ena added: "When I am older and have sons and daughters I will advise them not to marry a monarch of another religion."[21]

Clearly, Ena was not immune to the negativity, bordering on abuse, that was being hurled at her for her decision to convert. These objections sent her into fits of depression. Because Alfonso could never really empathize with what she was experiencing, Ena felt completely alone. It was all so novel and frightening. Accustomed all her life to being protected and loved, Ena now found to her dismay that what she was doing did not please everyone. Attacked by intolerant and bigoted Protestants and Catholics alike, who accused her simultaneously of being a traitor to her faith and an insincere convert, Ena it seemed, was in a no-win situation. "I find myself in an insupportable and cruel position," wrote a dejected Ena to Alfonso; "the English criticize me for becoming Catholic and the Spanish believe that I am not sincere." Then, in a moment of apprehension, Ena confessed: "It seems to me that I should not live my life in a country in which I am not loved. Upon giving you my heart, I gave you my life and I hopelessly see from your letters that you believe I have no wish to see you."[22]

Like Alix of Hesse before her, who suffered much in her decision to convert for the future Nicholas II, Ena of Battenberg too endured much personal turmoil in her journey of conversion for Alfonso XIII. In the end, Princess Victoria Eugenie's reception into the Roman Catholic Church took place at the Spanish royal family's home, the Miramar Palace, at San Sebastian, on 7 March 1906. Contrary to Ena's wish, King Alfonso was present to witness his fiancée become a Catholic.

The ceremony itself, presided over by the Bishop of Nottingham and also by the Bishop of Vitoria and Sion, was simple but daunting, leaving a strong impact on the eighteen-year-old. Not only did Ena have to be re-baptized; she also abjured in the strongest manner her Protestant faith. Moreover, not a single member of her family attended the ceremony. The princess in this case was supported by Queen Maria Cristina and King Alfonso. Before a small gathering, Ena, dressed entirely in white, with a mantilla, professed her new faith. Behind her stood Alfonso XIII, who after the ceremony gave his fiancée a diamond-and-sapphire bracelet. Especially treasured by Ena was another of Alfonso's gifts: a jewel-encrusted medal of the Blessed Virgin Mary.

In his official report of the ceremony to the Spanish government, the prime minister and president of the Council of Ministers, Segismundo Moret, described what he witnessed: "the act, although extremely simple, has been solemn and very meaningful. . . . The Princess was pale from emotion, and in attitude withdrawn and humble, giving off an angelic appearance."²³ The ceremony made an impact, even on Moret, a "liberal and mason,"²⁴ who was moved to compose the following passage: "The religious silence, the absence of all music, the sun . . . which penetrated the windows of the room and flooded the nearby hills already covered in green, all contributed to touching our spirit, making more intense the emotion which this [ceremony] produced, unique in the annals of Spain." Moreover, "in spite of our [the attendees] differences in ages, education and sentiments, we have been left profoundly impressed."²⁵ If someone as anti-religious as Moret was touched by this ceremony, one can only imagine what Victoria Eugenie must have felt. King Alfonso was clearly moved as he watched his intended bride take such a monumental step. Moret noted how "the King could not hide, during the reading of the rites of conversion, the emotion which overwhelmed him."²⁶

In comparing Ena's conversion to that of Alexandra of Russia, it is interesting to note that Ena did not undergo a tremendous amount of inner turmoil over her decision to leave the Anglican Church. The pain that Ena endured stemmed mainly from the criticism heaped against her for her decision. In confronting the need to switch allegiance, Victoria Eugenie was not wracked by the same degree of doubt as Alexandra had been. It took years, after all, for Nicholas II to beat down Alexandra's defenses when it came to exchanging Lutheranism for Orthodoxy. But where Ena was concerned, it did not take much prodding from anyone to get her to embrace Catholicism. In this case, Ena seems to have mirrored Sophie of Greece's journey of faith.

Because her conversion was such a special moment, and because she had been vilified for choosing to take this step, Ena wished for the ceremony to be as private as possible. Nothing and no one was to distract her attentions at the time. Sadly for Ena, her wishes were rejected. Not only King Alfonso but other less familiar figures also witnessed the event. And because her conversion was publicly announced by the newspapers before she could explain to others—especially those in England—about her change of faith, Ena felt betrayed. Years later she recalled how "I would have wanted [the ceremony] to have been something intimate, but all the newspapers published it. The *Daily News* did so in a harsh manner. Because of this, when I returned to England many turned their backs on me. . . . It was very difficult."²⁷

According to Gerard Noel, Victoria Eugenie's English biographer, Ena reacted to her own easy renunciation of faith by remaining "more Protestant than Catholic" in her religious leanings. When her life began to unravel, it was said that memories of her forceful repudiation of Protestantism had made Ena wonder whether she was cursed for such an action. Perhaps the anguish which came her way meant that "this curse was indeed operative and that such tragedies had come as a punishment for her apostasy."[28]

The religious conversions of Queen Victoria's granddaughters, Sophie of Greece, Alexandra of Russia, and Ena of Spain, all had distressing elements. For Sophie, her conversion caused a very public break with her brother, Kaiser Wilhelm II. For Alexandra, her conversion took place only after a protracted inner struggle; while Ena's conversion caused consternation in England and Spain. Moreover, Ena's re-baptism and strong denunciation of Protestantism at the actual ceremony made for a difficult experience. Even many years later, according to Noel, Ena was always hesitant to discuss this particular aspect of her life. But toward the end, she did talk about the conversion ceremony. She remembered her entrance into the Catholic Church as having been "hard, very hard. They made it as unpleasant as they could . . . it was public enough to make one suffer." The re-baptism was particularly difficult for her to understand. Yet after the difficulties involved in the ceremony and the ensuing controversy, which prompted some of her friends to turn their backs on her, Ena did confess that "afterwards, I have been very happy in the Catholic faith."[29]

With her conversion completed, Ena was set to marry Alfonso XIII. Ena's mother, Princess Beatrice, was overcome with emotion at the thought of her daughter's upcoming wedding:

> Please God the young people may [be] very happy, as they are absolutely devoted to one another, and I have every confidence in the King making her the best of husbands. He has such a charming nature, that to know him is to love him, and though the thought of my child going so far from me, is a real trial, I feel I have really gained a son, who does everything to make things easy.[30]

Anxious at the thought that she was soon to leave the Isle of Wight, Ena confessed to a friend: "I am very sad at leaving my dear Island home where I have so many friends."[31] Within weeks, she left England for her new home in Spain. There, she was set to marry Alfonso XIII in a spectacular ceremony and settle into what Ena hoped would be a happy life with the man she loved.

With Norway and Sweden slowly but surely taking the inexorable steps toward dissolving their union, the question was, should Norway become a republic or a monarchy? Among those who favored a monarchy, the candidature of Prince Charles of Denmark as Norway's king increasingly took hold. At only thirty-three years of age, Charles was still a relatively young man. He already had a son and heir aged three, who could easily grow up into a true Norwegian. Charles's consort, Maud, was also a Protestant; more important, as a daughter of Edward VII, she would bring added prestige to the Norwegian throne and royal family. Norway's future kings would then be descended from England's own Queen Victoria, who elicited widespread respect in all corners of the globe.

Destiny, it seemed, was closing in on Charles and Maud. Like it or not, they were being drawn ever closer to sharing their fate with the Norwegian people. Charged with the delicate task of negotiating and convincing Charles to accept the offer of the crown was the Norwegian minister to Denmark, Baron Fritz Wedel. In a conversation with the baron, Prince Charles emphasized that "the Norwegians would have to take me for who I am."[32] But the prince was also well aware that in choosing him as their king, Norwegians would receive Maud as their queen. Thus did Prince Charles wisely bring up his concerns about his wife. Charles stressed that because of Maud's delicate health, it was necessary for her to make prolonged visits to England, whose temperate climate suited her better than the harsh Scandinavian winters. This naturally meant that Maud would have to live for months at a time away from Norway.

Officially, the British government took a neutral stand in the proceedings. But Edward VII was not about to let a once in a lifetime opportunity pass Charles and Maud by. Wherever he could, the king took an active role in pushing for Charles's candidature. Supported in this stand by the British minister in Copenhagen, Alan Johnstone, Edward stepped up the campaign to see his son-in-law become Norway's new king. In June 1905, Edward VII wrote to the British Embassy in Copenhagen to say that he could allow his ministers to tell the Danish crown prince that the King of England "would gladly see Prince Charles of Denmark accept the throne of Norway (in which Queen Alexandra concurs) should the King of Sweden not wish any of his (Bernadotte) family to ascend the Throne."[33]

There was no denying the fact that Edward VII saw the possible accession of Charles and Maud to the Norwegian throne as another prestigious connection to add luster to an already burnished crown. With a niece as the Tsarina of Russia and others poised to become queens of Greece and Romania, why not see one of his own daughters become Queen of Norway? On the other hand, there were also the diplomatic stakes, which had to be taken into account. Astute observers were well aware that if the ever meddlesome Kaiser Wilhelm got his way, he would have gladly installed one of his numerous sons, certainly a candidate more amenable to him than the King of England's son-in-law as Norway's new king.

Edward VII assumed that his nephew, Willy, was conniving against Charles. The Kaiser's machinations plus pleas from Britain's minister in Copenhagen urging Edward to promote his son-in-law's candidature helped seal Charles and

Maud's fate. Edward VII then "made strenuous efforts to persuade Prince Charles to take up the throne and to secure British recognition for him."[34] Like it or not, there was really little Charles or Maud could do in the matter. More and more it looked as if events were moving beyond their grasp and the crown of Norway would be theirs to lose. In July 1905, Maud's father was anxious to resolve the question of Prince Charles's candidature, telling him in no uncertain terms: "I strongly urge that you should go to Norway as soon as possible to prevent someone else taking your place."[35]

This period of uncertainty provided Maud with plenty to think about. Though personally unambitious, the prospect of becoming Queen of Norway was certainly not something to scoff at. But if she and Charles had no other choice but to accept the offer of the Norwegian throne, how would this new life affect Maud's prolonged visits to England? The thought that these might have to be drastically curtailed could hardly sit well with Maud. By this time, her fixation for England was no secret. One English magazine published an article on her in 1903, noting, "Princess Charles loves her Norfolk home, which is unpretentious, but is thoroughly comfortable." It went on to describe how life at Maud's Copenhagen home, where her privacy was limited, had the effect of jarring her sensibilities. But Maud's complaining of such awkward living arrangements to her mother-in-law, "the stalwart Crown Princess of Denmark," was "useless," because she was immune from understanding "such feelings. Prince Charles was her favourite son, and his marriage with his cousin failed to please his mother, but . . . she bowed to the inevitable." Though Maud's mother-in-law was "just and kind" toward her, the crown princess "could not understand" and therefore had "no sympathy with her [Maud's] love of England and her feelings on that point."[36]

Despite her father's strenuous efforts to get Charles to commit himself to Norway, Maud was still reluctant for her husband to accept the offer of a crown. According to Germany's chancellor, Prince Bernhard von Bülow, Maud's response to the idea of becoming Queen of Norway remained tepid. At one point she was so hesitant at the thought of moving to Norway that she supposedly told her father, King Edward, she would much rather live in England or Ireland in the smallest farm than go off to Christiania. The king did not sympathize with his favorite daughter. Instead, he dismissed Maud's musings. "Princesses have duties and not hobbies," was Edward VII's tart reminder.[37]

In August, Edward VII tried again to prod his reluctant son-in-law by saying:

The moment has now come for you to act or lose the Crown of Norway. On good authority I am informed your sister in Sweden [Ingeborg, Crown Princess of Sweden] is intriguing against you. I urge you to go at once to Norway, with or without the consent of the Danish Government, and help in negotiations between the two countries. Maud and Baby would do well to follow a little later. The Queen is of the same opinion.[38]

The months of uncertainty as to her future and that of her immediate family worried Princess Maud. Writing from Copenhagen in September 1905, she explained the predicament she and Charles were in:

> *Here* we have to wait and *see* what is happening and *if* they *really* want us in Norway—the uncertainty [of] *all* the waiting has been an *enormous* strain *all* summer, but we hear that *now, finally,* the whole matter might be decided in October. . . . The whole thing seems *very* strange to *me,* and everything will naturally be different from what we are used to. My only hope is that *they* will like *us,* for that makes everything so much easier.[39]

That same month, a settlement was reached whereby the union between the two countries was formally dissolved and the Swedish parliament acknowledged the separation of the two countries. This was followed by King Oscar II of Sweden's long-awaited renouncement of the Norwegian throne and his recognition of an independent Norway. It had been an acrimonious but non-violent revolution by the Norwegians against the dominant partner of the union.

A canny Prince Charles, however, had one request before accepting the offer of the crown. Well aware how strong republican feelings were among certain segments of the population in Norway, Charles insisted that a plebiscite be held. The results were more than satisfying for Charles and his fellow monarchists. Of those eligible, 75.3 percent voted. The final result was just over 69,000 votes for a republic, while nearly 260,000 voted for a monarchy. It was a resounding victory for the monarchists. Officially accepting the blessing of the Norwegian people, Charles and Maud were now King and Queen of Norway.

The plebiscite was enough to send one particular die-hard royal into paroxysms of incredulity. The idea that a monarch was elected to ascend the throne of Norway did not sit well with Princess Augusta, Grand Duchess of Mecklenburg-Strelitz, who was a granddaughter of King George III. Writing to her niece, Princess May, in 1906, Augusta said she thought it simply "too horrible for an English Princess to sit upon a Revolutionary Throne!" In another letter, Augusta's thoughts turned to the new Norwegian queen: "So Maud is sitting on her very unsafe throne—to say the least of it." As for Charles, "he [is] making speeches, poor fellow, thanking the revolutionary Norwegians for having *elected* him! No really, it is all too odd!" Augusta also threw in her opinions on Maud's mother and son, telling May, " 'Motherdear' will not like it either, besides they have but that one *peaky* Boy."[40]

Writing from Copenhagen while on a visit to her native Denmark, the Empress Marie of Russia also told her son that a conclusion was at hand on the simmering question of Norway:

The Norwegian question seems to be settled definitely, and on Monday next a deputation is expected here to offer the throne of Norway to Charles. This time of indecision has also been very painful and annoying for Charles and Maud, but I think, since the decision has been taken, they are quite pleased though the parting is sure to be very sad.[41]

Within days of this letter being written, Prince Charles of Denmark accepted the offer of the crown. Upon receiving news that the *Storting*—Norway's Parliament—had elected him as king, Charles sent off a reply by telegram: "My wife and I call down on the Norwegian people God's richest blessing, and will consecrate our future life to its glory and prosperity."[42]

At a ceremony in the throne room of Copenhagen's Amalienborg Palace, a delegation from the *Storting* watched as Prince Charles of Denmark officially accepted the invitation to become their king. Standing beneath the opulent gold and red canopy above the throne, Maud, dressed simply in white, stood with her hands folded as she and Charles assumed the throne of Norway.

For King Edward VII, the news that all ended as he hoped was more than satisfying. When the Norwegian government sent a telegram congratulating him on Maud's new position, the king's reply, though simply stated, resonated with pride:

I thank you for your kind telegram. I am enchanted to learn that my dear daughter will be the Queen of your magnificent and interesting country. Edward R. & I.[43]

In order to identify himself with his Norwegian subjects, Charles embraced as his motto "*Alt for Norge!* (All for Norway)" and took the name of Haakon VII, in deference to the country's previous kings. Prince Alexander accordingly became Prince Olav. But Maud refused to change her name to something Norwegian-sounding. True to her English roots, Maud felt that since her name had been good enough for a British princess, then surely it was good enough for a Queen of Norway.

For generations, a kind of religious extravaganza had long permeated Russia's Orthodox Church, adding an exotic dimension to the faith that was part and parcel

of Russian life. Like so many aspects of life in Russia, Orthodoxy could lay claim
to more than its fair share of the mysterious, the contradictory, and the inexplicable. And nowhere did this phenomenon appear more clearly than in the person of
Rasputin. One historian maintains that "the rise of Gregory Rasputin would have
been impossible in any country other than Russia."[44]

In addition to a hierarchical church composed of priests and bishops, there
existed a whole other realm of "holy men" who attracted large and loyal follow-
ings. Among these holy men were those known as the *staretz,* who wandered the
countryside, often on religious pilgrimages. Adding to their aura of holiness was
the fact the *staretz* voluntarily renounced earthly goods and could impress others with their recitation of the Holy Scriptures. They provided additional spiritual ministrations to a people ever thirsty for ways to get closer to God. A mixture
of "superstition and awe, reverence and respect, by almost all levels in Russian
society" was invested in the *staretz.*[45] Thus, when Alexandra Feodorovna found
herself drawn to one supposed *staretz* called Gregory Rasputin, there was nothing particularly unusual about her belief in a holy man from Siberia. Even as the
tsarina's reliance on Rasputin descended into an all-consuming obsession, there
was still an element of believability in her stance, for the *staretz* figured promi-
nently in Russia's soul. One of Russia's greatest writers, Fyodor Dostoyevsky,
captured this most vividly in a passage in *The Brothers Karamazov,* which has
rightly been brought up by those writing about Tsarina Alexandra and Rasputin:
"The *staretz* is he who takes your soul and will and makes them his. When you
select your *staretz* you surrender your will, you give it him in utter submission,
in full renunciation."[46] The tragedy of course where Alexandra and Russia were
concerned was that Rasputin would turn out to be not a genuinely saintly man
but a fraud, whose debauchery far exceeded his good actions. Instead of renouncing things of this world, including family and possessions, Rasputin—who
was married, with three children—continued to maintain his home in Siberia.
And unlike a genuine *staretz,* Rasputin was never able to let go of sensual pleasures where women were concerned. This so-called *staretz,* notorious for his past
exploits involving the opposite sex, retained the moniker "Rasputin," meaning
"Dissolute."

Rasputin's unsavory past was not unknown to the tsar and tsarina, but it did
not prevent them from accepting Rasputin for what he purportedly claimed to
be—a repentant sinner and, more important, a healer. Nicholas II's sister, Olga,
maintained that "to Nicky and Alix he remained what he was—a peasant with a
profound faith in God and gift of healing."[47] Even leading churchmen of St. Petersburg such as John of Kronstadt and Archimandrite Theophanes were taken
in by Rasputin's seemingly penitent and religious demeanor.

It is difficult to fathom how so many individuals could find themselves so drawn to Rasputin. But some of those who encountered him attested to the fact that the mysterious "holy man" from Siberia had an undeniable ability to attract people through the hypnotic quality of his eyes. A friend of the tsarina's remembered being struck by "those shining steel-like eyes which seemed to read one's inmost thoughts."[48]

Maurice Paléologue, then French ambassador to Russia and no fan of Rasputin, had a similar story. Like many who had personally taken stock of Rasputin, Paléologue found the *staretz* possessed something that may have drawn the tsarina and others to him. This was the fact that when confronting Rasputin in person, one could not help but be mesmerized by his face. And according to Paléologue, "the whole expression of the face was concentrated in the eyes—light-blue eyes with a curious sparkle, depth, and fascination. His gaze was at once penetrating and caressing, naive and cunning, direct and yet remote."[49]

Yet to ascribe Tsarina Alexandra's fascination with Rasputin merely to his mesmerizing eyes is to miss the point completely. What truly drove Alexandra to place so much faith in this odd creature was Rasputin's ability to help keep her son alive. And once the tsarina became convinced of Rasputin's power to act as a conduit to God on behalf of Alexei, there was nothing anyone could tell her that would convince her otherwise.

Eleven

BAPTISM OF FIRE

MAY, THE PRINCESS OF WALES, THOUGHT ENA'S DEPARTURE FROM England for Spain was tinged with sadness. It was "a trying moment for the poor child," wrote May to her aunt Augusta Strelitz. "And I felt so sorry for Aunt Beatrice—I do hope Ena will get on well in Spain, I think she is a sensible girl & may do good there, anyhow she is full of good intentions—but I don't know whether she realises what a difficult future lies before her." Indeed, her aunt Augusta concurred. Writing back about Ena's future, Augusta prophetically noted that "I am sure Ena has no idea of her *real* future, now is all flowers and cheers! how long will this last in such a Country as Spain?"[1]

Fully aware that there was no turning back, Ena left home with a heavy heart. Finally abandoning England—the land where she was raised and which she so loved—for a new, unchartered life in unfamiliar Spain, the downcast princess felt overwhelmed. As she boarded the train for Dover, accompanied by her brothers, Leopold and Maurice, and her mother, Ena was choked with emotion. When she landed in Calais, a friend remarked how sad she looked. Ena bravely replied: "It is nothing—I cannot help feeling moved when I think that I am leaving the country where I have spent so many happy days to go toward the unknown."[2] And to the Lord Mayor of London, Ena sent a reply to his message of congratulations by saying, "I shall always preserve in my heart love and affection for the country of my birth."[3]

Princess Victoria Eugenie's arrival at Madrid was met with extreme exuberance by the populace. Lady de Bunsen, wife of the British ambassador there, noted the enthusiasm: "big bunches of flowers were thrown with such violence, that neither Queen Cristina, Princess Beatrice nor Princess Ena, who was sitting with her back to the horses, could even look up" for fear of being hurt by the avalanche of flowers.[4]

A sense of feverish excitement gripped Spain's capital on 31 May 1906, a day gloriously bathed in sunlight. Alfonso drove to the Pardo Palace where Ena was staying. From there, they proceeded to the Ministry of Marine, where Ena was dressed in her magnificent bridal gown, which by tradition was donated by the groom. It was a sumptuous confection, fit for a queen. The product of forty top seamstresses, who labored for fifty-six days, it was "one of the most elaborate and exquisitely embroidered gowns ever seen at the Spanish Court." Alfonso spared no expense in seeing that Ena was clothed in splendor. Rumor had it that the king paid no less than $20,000 ($400,000 in today's money) for the all-white satin gown, cut in Louis XVI style. "It was bordered with dull silver, slightly burnished and shaded at intervals and trimmed with exquisite rose-point lace, which was festooned over a background of cloth of silver. The lace flounce was eighteen inches in width and the whole gown was relieved with loops of orange blossoms."[5] The lace-bordered train in silver cloth was no less splendid. Falling from the shoulders, it measured 4.5 yards and was decorated with fleurs-de-lis, the emblem of the House of Bourbon.

Alfonso and Ena's marriage was significant in that it was the first time in nearly four hundred years that a Spanish monarch married a member of the English royal family. As the young couple seemed very much in love, many hoped this new Anglo-Spanish alliance would fare better than that of Philip II of Spain and England's Mary I.

Once inside the Church of San Jeronimo, King Alfonso started to show signs of nervousness. He was well aware of the possibility that violence could mar his wedding day. With a sigh of relief, he greeted the arrival of Ena's brothers at the cathedral signalling the beginning of the bridal procession. At the sight of the bride, guests gasped in awe.

William Miller Collier, the American minister to Madrid, who had a good view of the Spanish couple in the cathedral, thought the bride "a vision of loveliness and a perfect beauty." Collier wrote admiringly: "To say that the bride was radiantly, superbly beautiful is not flattery. One could not say less and speak the truth."[6]

After the Archbishop of Toledo declared the couple married, a nuptial Mass followed. Then came the signing of the register. Once outside, Ena and Alfonso boarded the state carriage, pulled by eight plumed horses, which drove them through the crowded streets toward the Royal Palace. There was no doubt the Spaniards had taken the couple to heart. Everywhere were shouts of *"Viva el Rey!"* and *"Viva la Reina!"* Happy to be Alfonso's wife at last, a resplendent Ena smiled and waved to the enthusiastic Spaniards, who cheered the lovely young bride. But within minutes, Victoria Eugenie's subjects would see if their queen was made of sterner stuff than the delicate image she projected.

Nearly everything had appeared to go off as planned. The excited throng packed along the wedding route, in the region of 300,000 people, was loudly cheering but well behaved. As the procession arrived at the Calle Mayor, some two hundred yards from the Royal Palace, the king and queen's coach stopped. Curious about the delay, Ena asked Alfonso what was wrong. He told her not to worry, "in five minutes we shall be home."[7] At that moment, a huge floral bouquet was thrown from a nearby balcony, falling just to the right of their carriage. In an instant, a bright red and orange flash blinded everyone in its path. And then, just as suddenly, a loud explosion sent hundreds scurrying for cover. Hidden amongst the flowers was a powerful bomb, which exploded with tremendous ferocity. In that split second, thirty-seven people were killed and over a hundred injured, many seriously. So potent was the bomb that "all that was found of one of the footmen on the royal carriage was his boots."[8]

Startled by the powerful explosion, Ena instinctively closed her eyes as she lurched forward. Unable to see Alfonso in the thick black smoke enveloping the carriage, Ena thought her husband had been killed by the blast. But miraculously, Alfonso escaped, and so did she. Their carriage was so damaged it could not move farther. Several of the eight white horses pulling it were killed. An eyewitness recorded that he saw one horse "on the ground with its legs off and stomach ripped open. His great plumes lying in a mass of blood."[9] Ena had come very close to death.

As luck would have it, at the moment of the explosion, Alfonso had drawn Ena's attention to the Church of Santa Maria, visible from his side of the carriage. Because she turned toward her husband, the queen escaped serious injury. But the effects of the explosion around them were horrifying. When the black, acrid smoke cleared, Alfonso and Ena were shocked to see that her magnificent bridal gown was soaked in blood. One of the guards riding beside the queen had been decapitated and his blood had spilled into the carriage. The magnificent silver and white confection was tainted with shades of crimson.

As if to assure himself that his new wife was unhurt, Alfonso clasped her face gently in his hands and asked in an anxious voice, "Are you wounded?" Quickly, Ena answered, "No, no, I am not hurt. I swear it." Alfonso then said, "A bomb has been thrown," to which Ena answered, "So I had thought, but it does not matter. I will show you that I know how to be Queen."[10]

Demonstrating great courage, Alfonso took charge almost immediately. He ordered up an empty carriage—the "carriage of respect" that always accompanied the royal one. When Alfonso and Ena alighted to change carriages, they met with a scene straight out of a battlefield: mangled bodies everywhere. With the stench of blood and death in the air, the impact of the attack began to sink in. In front of Ena were "disembowelled men and horses. As she made her way to the other coach she had to step aside to avoid the headless body of a bugler. Not far away lay a civil guard, his legs severed and bleeding freely."[11] The newly married queen could have been forgiven had she fainted, for her stomach must have churned wildly. But to her credit, the shaken Ena remained calm. She was also concerned for the safety and well-being of others, telling an equerry, "Please take care of yourself, you're wounded. Don't bother about us."[12]

The bomb did not deter the crowds from cheering their young sovereigns. On the contrary, as one eyewitness related: "You should have heard the ovation they got, all of us yelling ourselves hoarse, & balancing on window-ledges . . . in their Court trains, tiaras, & mantillas waving wildly."[13]

Once in the new carriage, Alfonso turned his attention back to Ena, asking: "Tell me the truth, tell it without tears; are you wounded?" His wife replied, "No, I am not wounded, I was thinking only of thee."[14] From the nearby British Embassy, some of the staff and guests who were being entertained there emerged; officers of the 16th Lancers, along with Colonel and Lady Cochrane, who were close friends of Ena's mother, and the British ambassador, Sir Maurice de Bunsen. Mrs. George Young, wife of the second secretary at the embassy, who witnessed the bombing, related how "before the poor girl [Ena] had time to faint or realise, she was surrounded by her own countrymen & they made a bodyguard of scarlet & gold close round the carriage."[15] In this manner, Ena's countrymen bravely escorted her carriage on foot toward the Royal Palace.

By the time she arrived, Ena was nearly hysterical, though outwardly she still appeared calm. She was heard to utter repeatedly: "I saw a man without any legs! I saw a man without any legs!"[16] It was an unbelievably horrific day. The shocking news made headlines all over the world.

The man who attempted the assassination was a deranged Spaniard by the name of Mateo Morral. Foiled in his first attempt in church, Morral instead aimed for the king and queen along the Calle Mayor. After being captured, Morral shot dead the policeman who arrested him, then put the gun to his own heart and pulled the trigger. He died instantly.

After her initial hysteria, Ena's training came into play. As a product of the court of Queen Victoria, where restraint and decorum were prized and encouraged, Ena very quickly gained her composure. Now a queen, she knew that she must act with the requisite dignity and bearing. After all, Queen Victoria had shown the way when she greeted the attacks upon her in the course of her long reign with courage and calmness. Ena instinctively put into action the words Queen Victoria had repeatedly uttered to her: "Young woman, when one is born a Princess, one cannot behave like others."[17]

Determined to cause as little commotion as possible amidst all the confusion, and above all, wanting Alfonso to be proud of his new wife and queen, Ena took charge. To the admiration of the bewildered guests assembled in the Royal Palace for the wedding reception, Ena's dignity and Alfonso's courage had shone through. Princess May noted that "Nothing could have been braver than the young couple were, but what a beginning for her."[18] A French diplomat concurred: "Poor little King, poor little Queen . . . there has been no massacre parallel to this in the history of assassination attempts against monarchs . . . and the Queen will always keep the horrible impression of death and of the dead as a remembrance of her wedding day."[19] Ena herself admitted to being stunned. In reply to a message from the Bishop of Ripon, she telegraphed back: "So grateful for kind sympathy in the cruel shock at the beginning of our happiness. May we further be preserved."[20]

When Sir Maurice de Bunsen, who had escorted the carriage into the Royal Palace, came upon the royal guests assembled there, he was besieged with questions. After giving details to the Prince of Wales, he also spoke to Archduke Franz Ferdinand. Amidst the excited guests assembled, one showed absolute sang-froid: Marie, Duchess of Coburg, mother of the future Queen Marie of Romania. Born a Grand Duchess of Russia, Ena's aunt Marie was a formidable woman whose own father, Tsar Alexander II, was blown to bits by an anarchist's bomb. Her brother, Grand Duke Serge, met the same gruesome fate just over a year before Ena's wedding. Now, while everyone was reeling from the shock, Marie shrugged it off by saying censoriously to anyone who cared to hear: *"Moi, je suis tellement accoutumée à ces sortes de choses."*[21]

Throughout the wedding meal, people strained to bring some semblance of normality to the proceedings. But it was difficult. Nevertheless, Ena's composure was exceptional. Ironically, a number of individuals already were reacting to the queen's calmness with suspicion and misunderstanding. Some remained unimpressed by Victoria Eugenie's lack of hysterics. They would now watch her every move with great care. Unluckily for her, she was being labeled as "distant." And in a nation of people who prized exuberance and great demonstrations of emotion, Ena began to be suspected "of being all the things most Spaniards least admired: cold, aloof, insensitive, Anglo-Saxon, Protestant at heart and (in upper-class eyes) 'liberal.' "[22]

Princess Beatrice's concern centered on the bride and groom. Writing to the Bishop of Ripon of the "painfully eventful moments we have been through, the memories of which can never be effaced," Beatrice went on:

It does seem so sad, that a day which had begun so brightly for the young couple, and where they were just returning with such thankful happiness, at belonging at last entirely to one another, should have been overclouded by such a fearful disaster. God has indeed [been] merciful to have preserved them so miraculously, and this has only if possible deepened their love for one another, and rendered the devotion of their people still more marked.[23]

The day after their wedding, Ena and Alfonso drove unattended through Madrid's streets in an open car, to the delight of their subjects. The queen remained dignified in her demeanor. Still reeling from all that had happened, a smiling Ena could not shake off her natural reserve and "visibly shrank back" when the crowds came close to her. Ena's biographer has noted, "She thus failed to gain, then or ever, a deep rapport with the Spanish masses."[24] It was an understandable reaction considering that the drive with Alfonso nearly frightened Ena out of her wits. People fought to be near her, and "the Queen's dress was actually torn to shreds by the multitude who sought to kiss the hem of her garment."[25] She was better able to cope with more sedate crowds, such as those at the Royal Palace.

There, Ena could face the deferential courtiers and guests who greeted her in a flurry of bows and curtsies. Yet some of these same people would come to judge their queen in much harsher terms than Ena could ever have imagined. Before Ena left for her new life, Princess Beatrice wrote to a friend about her thoughts on the wedding and her daughter's future: "I am glad to say Ena has now quite recovered from the shock, and looks fresh and well, and beamingly happy. That such a thing could happen, makes the parting naturally still harder for me, but we must trust in God to protect her still further, and I have the satisfaction of knowing that she is already beloved in her new country."[26]

Alfonso and Ena were more than happy to escape Madrid for a tranquil six-week honeymoon at the Palace of La Granja at San Idelfonso. Away from the busy capital, residing in a magnificent palace surrounded by beautifully laid out parks high up in the Castilian Mountains, Ena could finally relax and have her husband to herself. With time on her hands, the young bride reflected on the unforgettable day that saw her become Alfonso's wife and Spain's queen while escaping an assassination attempt. Ena described the bombing and her reaction to it to a friend in England:

My wedding day is a perfect nightmare to me & I positively shudder when I look back on it now. The bomb was so utterly unexpected that until it was all over I did not realise what had happened, then even I was not frightened. It was only when I got into the other carriage that I saw such fearful horrors & then I knew what an awful danger we had gone through. My poor husband saw his best friend, a young officer, fall down dead beside our coach fearfully mutilated & that upset him very much.—We are spending now a delicious time together in this lovely old Palace in the mountains & it all seems like a bad dream to us now.[27]

Alfonso's attentiveness helped to ease the memory of her horrible wedding day. Above all, Alfonso was obviously very much in love with her. In his eyes, Ena could do no wrong. Content in that knowledge, Ena faced her future with hope. Within a year, however, the eighteen-year-old queen's world would explode again. This time, there would be no crowds to cheer her on, and more ominously, cracks would begin to appear in Alfonso's love for his lovely young wife.

Twelve

NORWAY'S ENGLISH QUEEN

FOUR DAYS AFTER MAUD STOOD AT HER HUSBAND'S SIDE AT AMA-lienborg Palace to assume the crown of Norway, she and Haakon boarded the Danish royal yacht, *Dannebrog,* bound for their new kingdom. Not far from Christiania, the capital of their new kingdom, King Haakon VII and Queen Maud were welcomed to Norway by Christian Michelsen, the prime minister, who had spearheaded the country's move toward independence. Wealthy, confident, witty, physically large and imposing, Michelsen gave the formal welcoming speech:

> To-day a King of Norway comes to make his home in the Norwegian capital, elected by a free people to occupy, conjointly with free men, the first place in the land. The Norwegian people love their liberty, their independence, and their autonomous government, which they themselves have won. It will be the glory of the King and his highest pleasure to protect this sentiment, finding his support in the people themselves. This is why the Norwegian people hail you to-day with profound joy and cry, "Long live the King and Queen of Norway!"[1]

In some ways this was an extraordinarily bold speech, which appeared at once both threatening and welcoming. Michelsen underscored that Haakon and Maud were ascending the throne not by the grace of God but by the grace of the people themselves; should they forget this in the future, Michelsen's speech made it appear as if the people would not hesitate to make their displeasure known.

The Times correspondent who witnessed the royal welcome was struck not so much by the brightly decorated streets as by the excitement of the Norwegian people themselves, for "none who heard the cheering which greeted King Haakon and his Queen, and in particular, little Prince Olaf, and saw the faces of those who cheered could fail to realize that they were indeed the chosen of the people."[2] Maud's mother, Queen Alexandra, wrote proudly of the welcome given to her daughter, son-in-law, and grandson at Christiania, saying: "Maud and Charles were received with open arms." Even more glowing words were reserved for Maud's son: "the success of Christiania is little Olaf (my little Hamlet) who took them all by storm."[3] The couple's arrival in Norway was immediately followed by Queen Maud's own thirty-sixth birthday. In her honor, salutes were fired from the fort of Akershus and from battleships in the harbor.

In the middle of December 1905, Maud wrote to her sister-in-law, May. Retiring and modest woman that she was, Maud revealed her incredulity at her new position: "Behold! I am a *Queen*!!! *Who* would have thought it! And *I* am the very *last* person to be stuck on a *throne*! I am actually getting accustomed to be called 'Your Majesty!' and yet often pinch myself to *feel* if I am not dreaming!"[4] Based on her own family background and the precedent of inviting royals to assume thrones in foreign lands, these were rather surprising words. Maud was, after all, a daughter of the King and Queen of England, who could boast as her paternal grandmother and maternal grandfather Queen Victoria and King Christian IX of Denmark.

One problem that had to be addressed, and quickly, was the question of accommodations. Though Maud settled her family into the Royal Palace at Christiania, this cavernous building of over 150 rooms left a lot to be desired. However much the Royal Palace was meant to impress, it somehow failed to do so. One contemporary wrote that although the *Kongens Slot,* as it is called in Norwegian, "looks well at the end of a vista, especially in the enchanting glow of the long northern twilight, it is actually one of the meanest palaces in Europe." If one could find an apt quote for the *Slot* and the hill on which it is perched, wrote this same visitor, one could say that here was "the finest site in Europe and nothing to show on it!"[5] A showpiece rather than an inhabited home, years of inactivity had turned the Royal Palace into a neglected pile since its completion in the middle of the nineteenth century. When the family moved in, it could not have seemed more daunting: with no lavatory, only a few baths, running water nonexistent, and little furniture. Maud had her work cut out for her.

Now that a new king and queen were established in Norway's capital, all that was needed was a coronation. It was the sort of event that Maud always dreaded. The thought that she was to play a very public part in this spectacle was already sending the timid queen into fits of anxiety as early as March 1906, still three months away from the ceremony. "It all haunts me like an *awful* nightmare this

Coronation and that it is *just* to be ours of all people," she wrote to Princess May. "Think of me *alone* on my throne, having a crown to be shoved on my head which is very small and heavy by the aged Bishop, and a Minister and also has to be put on by them before the *whole* crowd!! and oil to put on my head, hands and *bosom*!! Gracious, it will be awful!"[6]

When the time came, Queen Maud and King Haakon set off for the city of Trondheim, the site of past coronations of the ancient monarchs of Denmark-Norway, founded in A.D. 997 by a Viking king and set just five hundred kilometers below the Arctic Circle.

First to be crowned on 22 June 1906 at Nidaros Cathedral was the king. After receiving the orb and scepter, Haakon VII made his way back to the throne and awaited the crowning of his queen. When the moment came, Maud acquitted herself with dignity and grace, though her nerves were certainly tested. One witness thought she looked pale "as she walked up the long choir, returning the salutations on each side of her." After being anointed, Maud was crowned and handed the orb and scepter. Kneeling, she received a blessing from the bishop. Thereupon, deafening salutes were fired from the warships anchored outside. As the "anointed and crowned Queen of Norway," Maud "slowly and gracefully" returned to her throne to cries of: "Long live the King and Queen" echoing from all sides of the cathedral.[7]

The election and coronation proved too much for the elderly Augusta, Grand Duchess of Mecklenburg-Strelitz, who bluntly told May, her niece: "A *revolutionary* Coronation! such a *farce,* I don't like your being there for it, it looks like *sanctioning* all that nasty Revolution. . . . How can a future K. & Q. of E. go to witness a Coronation *'par la grace du Peuple et de la Révolution!!!'* makes me sick and I should say, *you too.*" May tried to make the best of it, answering that "the whole thing seems curious, but we live in *very* modern days."[8]

From the time she set foot in Norway, Maud tried as best she could to become a conscientious queen. Far from being solely preoccupied during these early years with the modernization and redecoration of the Royal Palace, Maud took it upon herself to support causes she felt needed her imprimatur. One involved the plight of unmarried mothers in Norway—a cause that was certainly ahead of its time. Not only did the queen support this cause; she actually took "a leading role in subscribing to a home" for such women and, even more daring, attended "a public meeting on its behalf." It was a brave move that "flew in the face of 'respectable' opinion among those who considered such good works to be beneath them."[9]

Maud also learned the language and even took up skiing lessons in order to share the Norwegians' love of this sport. Kongsseteren—a log chalet that was a gift from the Norwegian people—located on Holmenkollen Mountain (within present-day Oslo) became a favorite home for Maud. The chalet epitomized the rustic indigenous style. A far cry from the formal Royal Palace, Kongsseteren was homey and informal, truly suited to the domestic queen.

Another equally appealing home awaited Maud at the Bygdøy estate. Originally on an island and part of a medieval monastery, Bygdøy was not far from Christiania and commanded a lovely view of the city. Maud and Haakon settled there soon after their coronation. In time, it became Maud's favorite home next to Appleton. Here she could lead the carefree country life she so ardently craved; and it was here that Maud could truly indulge in her desire to re-create a corner of England in her Norwegian kingdom. The house consisted of a low-lying eighteenth-century building; surrounding it were gardens that Maud created in the English style.

Haakon was to be known as *"Herre Konge"* or plain "Mr. King" instead of the more normal "Your Majesty"—evidence of the highly democratic character of the Norwegian monarchy. This was a result, noted one contemporary, of the fact that Norway at the time of the accession was republican "to the backbone."[10] When Sir Frederick Ponsonby, equerry to Edward VII, visited Christiania in 1908, he admitted that the place was "so socialistic that a King and Queen seemed out of place."[11]

The democratic nature of the monarchy and the easygoing manner of the new king and queen proved to be complementary. Had Haakon and Maud not possessed down-to-earth personalities and instead exhibited imperious ways, more than likely their time on the Norwegian throne would have been far less stable. Whenever Haakon referred in public to Maud, for instance, he spoke of her not as "the Queen" or "Her Majesty" but simply as "my wife."[12] This was in keeping with the kind of court both sovereigns preferred at Christiania.

Although she agreed completely with her husband's desire for a democratic and informal court, Queen Maud nevertheless did not escape some form of criticism, however minor, during her first year in Norway. What irritated some was that Maud seemed to be taking her role as "bourgeoisie Queen" too far. A contemporary noted that "she has been stigmatized in some quarters as a 'mere court personage.'"[13] Maud's shyness, though, did not harm her reputation to the same degree as Alexandra's did in St. Petersburg. Maud, after all, tried harder at playing the queen, and she also lacked the disdainful ways that Alexandra seemed to affect so much of the time when on show.

By early 1907, Ena found herself settling into her new country. "We have had the most splendid autumn & early winter," she wrote at the start of the new year, "& I much prefer Spain when it is like this to the fearful heat we get in the summer."[14] In the autumn of 1906, Ena had been excited to learn that she was expecting a child. The pregnancy progressed well, and unlike Tsarina Alexandra of Russia, who retreated during her pregnancies, Ena was seen in public even a few weeks before her scheduled confinement. Among many public events, Victoria Eugenie made numerous visits to churches around Madrid. In intensely Catholic Spain, Ena, Alfonso, and Queen Maria Cristina all prayed for a safe delivery and the health of the unborn child—as was the custom in the Spanish court—at various churches dedicated to the Blessed Virgin Mary. These visits taxed the queen, who had to struggle in and out of carriages at a late stage in her pregnancy.

When one of Ena's childhood friends from the Isle of Wight, Joan Kennard, visited her a month before the birth, she saw how immersed in excitement and anxiety the Spanish court was as the confinement drew near. "She was so nice and evidently so pleased to see us," Joan noted in a letter to her father about Ena. Then, mentioning King Edward VII's upcoming visit to Spain (Cartagena was chosen over Madrid because the Spanish capital was deemed too unsafe), Joan described the scene:

> There is great perturbation in the Court owing to King Edward's visit to Cartagena. This, of course, means that King Alfonso has to leave Madrid tomorrow night, and they are all terrified that the infant will arrive, while he is away. This would be the most awful affair in Spain, the baby is kept in the dark until the King has seen it. . . . The Queen is very amusing, but also very pathetic. She says she could bear anything, if only they would not fuss her so much! . . . the Queen said "Alfonso is so worried, he cannot even eat!!"[15]

Joan Kennard's father in turn told his wife: "I am glad poor little 'Ena' is to have English [people] about her at her time of trouble . . . I daresay she will have many children—even if next month does not produce a son & heir for Spain. She will have to take care not to offend the Spaniard by having too many English about her."[16]

A little over a month after that letter was written, the waiting ended. Just twenty-one days shy of her first wedding anniversary, nineteen-year-old Queen Victoria Eugenie of Spain was set to give birth to her first child at the Royal Palace in as public a manner as was decently acceptable. As soon as the signal was given, the king's halberdiers dashed off to summon the country's ministers and members of the diplomatic corps accredited to Madrid. Modern automobiles jostled with traditional horse-drawn carriages to convey brilliantly dressed notables to the gates of the Royal Palace.

The queen's labor pains began in the early morning of 10 May; they were intense and lasted twelve hours. Like her cousin Missy in Romania before her, Ena was encouraged to get on with it and bear the excruciating pain. Her well-meaning but overbearing mother-in-law was not much help, urging: "We Spaniards do not cry out when we bring a King into the world." Exasperated, Ena could only murmur to herself, "and now they will see what an Englishwoman is like!"[17]

The queen's chief physician at the birth, Eugenio Gutiérrez, was a Spaniard, but he was assisted by a British doctor by the lyrical name of Bryden Glendinning, as well as a nurse, Miss Greene. The presence of a British physician mirrored the experience of Marie of Romania's first confinement, when she was attended by Dr. Playfair.

Every care was taken to ensure the safe delivery of Ena's child and the life of both mother and baby. Sacred relics were delivered from different parts of Spain and placed in the queen's room, in accordance with a centuries-old custom. Ena most certainly had not experienced anything quite like it: according to one historian, the relics consisted of "the arm of John the Baptist and the girdle of the Virgin from Tolosa." The latter "is handed to the Queen at certain critical moments, and a prayer, while it is held in the hands or being kissed, insures a safe and happy delivery."[18]

At this crucial moment, the queen was still a slave to Spanish court etiquette and subjected to giving birth almost in public. Just outside her room, in various ornate salons, were some 150 people, all of them men, with the exception of six of Ena's ladies. Dressed in full military uniforms (complete with decorations), diplomatic attire, or full evening dress, statesmen, diplomats, prelates, representatives of civic organizations, and court officials awaited the birth of the queen's first child. True to its reputation as the most rigidly formal court in Europe, these waiting diplomats and ministers were grouped by rank and seniority; those holding the most senior positions were placed in the salon closest to the laboring queen's room.

Suddenly, the massive double doors swung open. All eyes turned to the man stepping through them, Antonio Maura, the prime minister. Queen Ena's ordeal ended at twenty minutes to one in the afternoon. Maura, moved by the occasion, announced to the dignitaries: "Gentlemen, it is a Prince." The jubilation was genuine as the crowd shouted, *"Viva la Reina! Viva el Príncipe! Viva el Rey!"*[19] "Veteran generals, former ambassadors, Ministers of the Crown, were actually hugging each other with delight." The American minister to Spain recalled how "servants were running through the corridors shouting: *'Es niño!* ('It is a boy!')"

while "outside the palace thousands—perhaps more than ten thousand people" greeted the news with joy.[20]

Within a quarter of an hour of the birth, a beaming King Alfonso emerged from Ena's room. Dressed in the uniform of a captain general of the army, with the Charles III chain and medal around his neck, the king presented his first-born child to the assembled crowd, resting naked in a golden cradle and placed on a silver tray.

The new father's pride was understandable. Ena had given him an heir who showed every promise of being a fine, healthy son. According to one eyewitness, the baby prince, who had "an abundance of fair hair, was beyond question an unusually strong and healthy-appearing infant." Another, describing the presentation ceremony, reported "the almost phenomenal physical strength of this baby, looking as if strong enough, like the infant Hercules, to strangle serpents in his cradle."[21]

Eight days after his vigorous debut, the baby was baptized in an imposing ceremony in the chapel of the Royal Palace. The baptismal font was the same one used by St. Dominic, the twelfth-century founder of the Order of the Dominicans. The child's godfather was none other than Pope Pius X (later St. Pius X). As water from the Jordan River was poured over the newborn prince's forehead, he was given the names Alfonso Pius Cristino Eduardo Francisco Guillermo Carlos Enrique Eugenio Fernando Antonio y Venancio de Todos los Santos. For years, Ena's oldest child was known as Prince of the Asturias, a title granted to Spanish heirs to the throne. But to his family he would always be "Alfonsito."

Ena had done her duty. She had given birth to a boy—the coveted heir—within a year of her wedding to Spain's reigning monarch. It was an achievement that took her cousin, the Tsarina Alexandra, ten long years to fulfill. In recounting the couple's feelings as well as her own, Princess Beatrice, the doting grandmother, wrote from Madrid to the British royal family's confidant, the Bishop of Ripon:

> No words can say the intense joy that this happy event causes the dear young Parents, & all classes in the country here. My dear daughter passed through her hours of great suffering most bravely & is a very tender mother, hardly liking to have the child out of her arms. He is a splendid strong boy & thank God both he & my daughter are doing as well as possible. I shall find it hard to tear myself away from them . . . I have had such a delightfully undisturbed 3 months, with my dear child, & it is such a comfort to feel how happy & contented she is in her new house & how this additional joy has come to complete all.[22]

After cheating death on her wedding day, the birth of Alfonsito certainly seemed to presage a better life for Victoria Eugenie; perhaps everything might now go well after all. She had come out of her ordeal successfully; King Alfonso was a proud father and loving husband; their beautiful baby boy was the very picture of health; and Ena, the young beautiful queen, commanded the admiration of a majority of Spaniards. Yet within a short space of time, Ena's world was to be shattered.

Thirteen

REVOLUTIONARY FEVER

"THE YEAR 1907 WILL BE A MEMORABLE ONE IN THE ANNALS OF Roumania, in consequence of the outbreak in the early spring of the most formidable insurrection which the country has ever seen." So began a narrative of events sent by Sir Conyngham Greene, the British minister at Bucharest, to his superior in London, the foreign secretary, Sir Edward Grey. As the movement gained momentum, upon reaching Wallachia "it changed its character and became anarchistic, wholesale destruction rather than plunder being its leading feature. The rebellion was accompanied by murders, mutilations, and crimes of the most atrocious description, committed not so much by the peasants as by organized bands of criminals from Bucharest. . . . So threatening did the outbreak become towards the end of the month that it was feared the rebels might effect a concentration and march upon Bucharest itself."[1] Thousands of protestors did march upon the capital, frightening many. In order to protect his family, the crown prince sent his wife and children to the mountain resort of Sinaia. Many aristocratic families fled there too, waiting until things cooled before returning to Bucharest. Among them was Nadèje Stirbey, the wife of Prince Barbo Stirbey.

While she stayed at Sinaia, Crown Princess Marie visited her friend Nadèje. Barbo, like many male members of the aristocracy, and the crown prince, stayed put in Bucharest. Nevertheless, Barbo also visited his family at Sinaia, and it was during these visits that he and Missy came to know each other well.

Barbo did not originally set out to conquer the crown princess, but when circumstances threw them together, the two found themselves irresistibly drawn to each other. Besides Barbo's obvious charms, title, wealth, political influence, and intelligence (he read law at the University of Paris), it perhaps might have been to Stirbey's advantage that he bore a slight physical resemblance to Waldorf Astor. As for the crown princess, "still recuperating from Waldorf Astor, Marie was not an easy conquest." But "Barbo demanded what Waldorf had not, an adult relationship. In return he offered total commitment."[2] This set the stage for a long-lasting and devoted friendship between Marie of Romania and Prince Barbo Stirbey that would survive the most trying tests in the years to come.

After Waldorf Astor married his Nancy, Missy gravitated to the next male admirer to come her way. Never in want of attention from the opposite sex, the crown princess had easily conquered the heart of the new man in her life, the popular and desirable Prince Barbo. In the eyes of a Romanian aristocrat of the time, Princess Callimachi, there was hardly a man who could offer "so intensely attractive a specimen of virile masculinity as Barbo Stirbey. Extremely personable, elegant, dark without Oriental exaggeration, some strange hypnotic quality lingered in his beautifully expressive eyes." Nor did Princess Callimachi's admiration stop there. "His manner was unassuming, yet full of charm; he spoke little, but a gift of persuasion and instinctive psychological insight made him rarely miss his aim whenever he set himself one. Extraordinary was the way he always struck the right note."[3]

Barbo was part of the smart set in Bucharest. As scion of one of Romania's wealthiest families, he easily crossed paths with the rich and powerful. In the maddeningly complex intertwining that marked Romania's aristocracy, Barbo Stirbey provides a perfect example of how members of his class could easily find themselves related to one another. Stirbey's wife, Nadèje, was a member of the Bibesco clan, of whom the most famous, Princess Marthe Bibesco, was known internationally for her writing. Barbo's sister, Elise, became the second wife of Ion Bratianu, son of the man of the same name who was instrumental in bringing King Carol I to Romania. The younger Bratianu also took an active role in politics, eventually becoming head of the Liberal Party and premier of Romania. Bratianu and Stirbey saw in Missy the makings of someone who might easily be an asset to their country. Ion had never taken Missy for granted ever since she arrived in Romania, always treating her without condescension. As Missy matured and Bratianu's political star rose, the crown princess would find her interest in politics rising in tandem. This was thanks in no small measure to Barbo Stirbey. While their personal relationship blossomed, so did Barbo's mentoring of the politically inexperienced Marie.

For a man who "relished pulling strings behind the scenes," Marie became an "ideal pupil." Whatever Barbo had to offer in the field of politics, she eagerly embraced. The crown princess came to see Stirbey's guiding hand as indispensable. Barbo was what no man had ever been to her, a mentor. And "with his careful analytical mind and her rapid powers of comprehension," Prince Barbo

Stirbey and Crown Princess Marie of Romania soon developed into "a formidable team."[4] This friendship, which blossomed into love and took on the added dimension of mentoring, was officially cemented when Prince Stirbey was appointed by King Carol in 1913 to become Superintendent of the Crown Estates. Fortuitously for Missy and Barbo, the post provided them with a cover for their relationship. His new position meant that he and Marie were thrown together every day. But more important, in giving his imprimatur to the affair, King Carol I had shown keen foresight. Realizing the potential, as yet untapped, in the future queen, and the significant role the "tactful and efficiently influential" Stirbey[5] was playing where Missy was concerned, King Carol decided to foster the couple's devotion. He understood full well that the intelligent but indecisive Crown Prince Ferdinand would need strong support once he ascended the throne. Who better to buttress and guide him than Missy, Barbo, and Bratianu? Carol I's instincts would prove correct. His hopes were to bear great fruit in the years ahead.

Missy and Barbo's close relationship was destined to bring dividends for Romania. At thirty-one years of age, not only was Marie at the height of her beauty, she had also reached a greater sense of maturity. The interest in her adopted country planted by Waldorf Astor had taken root, nurtured by Stirbey. Under Prince Barbo's careful tutelage, Marie found herself fascinated not only by her new mentor but also by the intricacies of Balkan politics upon which her country's success rested. Romania's future queen had entered a new and significant phase of her life. Moreover, the ever astute Stirbey had not only fallen in love with the princess, he had seen in her a potent force for Romania; for here was a woman who was bound to be of immense help to the more self-effacing Ferdinand when he became king. Stirbey was determined that an opportunity not be lost. He counseled King Carol that Marie must be molded to play a strong political role for the sake of Romania. It did not take much for Barbo to convince the king.

"It's essential not to break her will," Barbo told King Carol. "But if we can persuade her to take herself and her duties more seriously, her natural intelligence will do the rest."[6] Barbo Stirbey was not the only one to notice the potential in Marie of Romania. Sir Conyngham Greene told Sir Edward Grey in January 1907: "It is often said that when Prince Ferdinand comes to the Throne it will be the Princess who will be the true Ruler, but I feel sure that Her Royal Highness will be far to [sic] clever to step outside her own rôle, and that she will know how to supplement any possible deficiencies of her husband by the *savoir-faire* and tact which she has inherited from her father and the Royal Family of England."[7]

Just before the outbreak of World War I, Count Ottokar Czernin, then the Austro-Hungarian minister to Romania, was so struck by Marie that he predicted "in the near future Roumanian policy might well come to depend not so much upon Ferdinand as upon his versatile wife. Her character and mentality," wrote Czernin, "is one of the most important reasons for putting relations with Roumania on quite another basis."[8]

All of these astute observers would have to wait until Marie became queen before their opinions were put to the test. For the time being, however, it was left to King Carol to see to it that the Peasants' Revolt of 1907 was quelled forcefully and swiftly if the dynasty was to remain on the throne of Romania. The price for bringing back order was exceptionally high: It is thought that at least ten thousand peasants lost their lives in the uprising. According to Italian diplomats serving in Bucharest at the time, the revolt was very serious, particularly in Wallachia, where the rioting "equaled the Russian uprising of 1905–1906 in ferocity."[9] There is little doubt that the chaos that engulfed the Russian Empire in 1905–06 had infected the neighboring kingdom of Romania. Though the uprising was successfully stopped, the Romanian royal family and the country's elite were thoroughly shaken by events that had erupted so suddenly and so violently. Writing afterwards to Nancy Astor, Marie admitted just how frightening the whole episode was:

> We have passed through a dreadful panic and in a small country where Royalties are so initimitely [sic] mixed up with all that goes on one seems to carry all the burdens on one's own shoulders. . . . You see it had all come so unexpectedly and spread with such horrible rapidity taking such proportions that at one moment one was not sure that all the country was not lost. And we lived through it all with them all, sharing all the fears and panic and anxieties. I assure you I felt as if in some way I had suddenly got into a night-mare.[10]

Crown Princess Marie and the Tsarina Alexandra were not the only ones to experience a close brush with violent revolutionary agitations in the early part of the twentieth century, for similar movements were set to explode in Greece and Spain. Crown Princess Sophie and Queen Ena would soon learn what it must have been like for their cousins to face the winds of revolution.

〜

In Greece, reports of unrest were received in February 1909 by the British Legation at Athens. Increases in taxation helped trigger turmoil amongst all classes. This left the political landscape ripe for all manner of intrigue. By May, signs that the military might be playing a major role in instigating unrest emerged when non-commissioned officers staged a mutiny. "There is a general feeling that something may happen, no one knows exactly what," wrote one diplomat in Athens, who blamed "bad trade, scarcity of money, unemployment . . . a deplorable lack of public security" and the ongoing Cretan issue for the troubles.[11]

The government assembly of Crete had recently proclaimed that its island should be joined in union with Greece. Seeing an opportunity to gain more prominence, a Cretan lawyer named Eleutherios Venizelos quickly switched his long-standing view that Crete should be independent. Instead, he joined in the chorus of voices seeking a Greater Greece through the island's unification with the mainland. But when the Great Powers failed to favor the move, plans to unite Crete with Greece fizzled, leading to much disaffection. This disaffection played into the hands of a number of embittered military officers, paving the way for a takeover of power by the country's military.

None of this boded well for Crown Princess Sophie and her husband. At the top of the list demanded by the military was Prince Constantine's resignation from his army command, along with that of his brothers. The crown prince was commander in chief and responsible for reorganizing this branch of the military, but his efforts met with dissatisfaction. Such an onerous task meant that Constantine inevitably made enemies within the army, who saw their opportunities for advancement dashed by the prince's efforts to shake up the status quo. The crown prince was laid open to charges of favoritism among the disgruntled, which made him vulnerable to attacks.

What amounted to a military dictatorship emerged when the Military League, a group comprised of junior officers, came into being in the summer of 1909. In order to deflect criticism, the Military League tried to cast its calls for military and government reforms in patriotic terms. Those individuals who clamored for changes also voiced grave disappointment in King George and the princes of the royal house.

Things had reached such a low point that King George admitted to the British ambassador in Athens, Sir Francis Elliot, that he was "no longer able to place confidence in any one in Greece, where he could be of no further use; that he absolutely refused to be the puppet of a military junta, and that he would take his departure the next time he came into conflict with them; he had made all his preparations and was ready to leave at a moment's notice."[12] Elliot's reports to the Foreign Office were so dismal that at the end of 1909, a London official commented: "the King of Greece is between the devil and the deep sea."[13] London deemed the situation serious enough to order Royal Navy ships that happened to be near the Athenian port of Piraeus on standby in case they were needed to rescue members of the Greek royal family. Rumors were soon rampant that King George was ready to abdicate and abandon Greece, along with his family.

Relations between the royal family and the military did not improve as the months passed. It soon became all too evident that in the battle between the royal family and the Military League, the royal family was losing. In 1909, the crown prince and his brothers were told that they must be relieved of their army commissions. In order to spare their father the indignity of signing a decree stripping them of their military commands, they resigned their positions. Sadly for Constantine, this move did not prevent his popularity from sliding further. Nor did the princes' resignations ease tensions. By December "the general situation of the country appeared to be rapidly approaching a state of chaos."[14] Crown Princess Sophie was not in Greece to see this chaotic situation firsthand. She and Tino were compelled to flee the country in September that year.

As he made his way out of Greece toward Brindisi, Constantine was greeted by emotional crowds who did not want him to leave. Sophie must have been gratified that her husband met with such demonstrations of loyalty from the Greek people. While she awaited better news in Germany, Sophie received reports from the German minister to Athens, Baron von Wangenheim, which also reinforced the crown princess's critical view "of her father-in-law's moderate, compromising tactics" toward the Military League—a view understandably shared by the banished Tino.[15]

Much as she was disappointed by the king's compromising stance, Sophie was troubled by French military plans to reorganize the Greek Army. To Sophie and Tino, this creeping French influence in the military posed a real potential threat because "radical, republican influences" would more than likely "spread within the ranks of an army which had already exerted anti-dynastic pressures." This prompted Sophie to cry out in desperation to her husband while they were in Greece, "There is no longer any place for us in this country. Let us pack our suitcases and depart."[16]

By 1910, the leaders of the Military League had not met with the degree of success they had hoped. King George, though he tried to compromise and was willing to enact some of the reforms demanded, was not going to let the rebellious officers run roughshod over him. He was determined to maintain his position as a constitutional monarch and, true to his word, would not countenance being their puppet king. Finally, the Military League and King George saw an opportunity to resolve the political impasse. Eleutherios Venizelos became the prime minister in September 1910 and the Military League dissolved itself. Crown Prince Constantine was then given back his position as commander of the army. The Greek royal family had ridden out the storm.

When the time came for Sophie to part from her sister, Mossy, in Germany, it proved very difficult. "The parting," noted Mossy, "was harder than I can say. We have been together almost a year and a half, & to what uncertainty & unsettled state of affairs is she returning! It was too sad to see her trying to fight down her feelings."[17] Toward the end of the year, Mossy received word that Sophie was unhappy, her letters not sounding at all cheerful. Mossy identified the main problem: "the political out look [is] anything but bright."[18]

Returning to Greece had not changed Sophie's opinion about the troublesome officers who had sought to foment trouble. In his annual report to the Foreign Office, Sir Francis Elliot surmised that the crown princess possessed an "irreconcilable attitude towards the party of reform, whom she identifies with the leaders of the military movement of 1909, which she cannot forgive." Then, in a statement which, had it been made public, could have been seized upon and exploited by those unsympathetic to the royal family, Elliot pointed out: "Neither she nor apparently her Imperial Brother [Kaiser Wilhelm] realize the necessity for the reigning dynasty here of passing the sponge over the distasteful events of that year."[19] It was an easy statement for an observer to make, as Elliot obviously was not a member of the royal family, nor did he personally experience all that Sophie went through. Nevertheless, it is an interesting one since it foreshadowed the future to some degree by making Sophie appear to be an unmalleable character, with pro-German leanings.

Even months later, Sophie was said by the British still to be harboring some animosity toward those who wreaked havoc in Greece in 1909–10. According to a report from the British minister in Athens: "The memories of 1909 are gradually fading from the minds of the members of the Royal Family" and "the Crown Prince has shown signs of realising the necessities of his situation and of allowing bygones to be bygones; but the Crown Princess maintains an uncompromising attitude, which is unfortunately encouraged by the German Minister and his wife."[20] But this was not to say that Sophie had not forgotten how her brother, Wilhelm II, had acted toward Greece more than a decade before. If a contemporary publication is to be believed, even after over a decade had passed since Wilhelm sided against Greece in the Greco-Turkish War, "the Crown Princess of Greece has a special grievance against her brother because, when Greece last made war on Turkey in 1897, the Kaiser gave his sympathy entirely to the Turks."[21]

By the end of 1912, there was no doubt that Sophie and her family had survived the serious assault on the dynasty brought about by the Military League. In fact, the dynasty had rallied to the service of Greece to such an extent that in spite of the troubles of 1909–10, Sir Francis Elliot was moved to conclude that, as a military leader, Crown Prince Constantine "has won the confidence and affection of his men." Queen Olga, meanwhile, "always foremost in good works, has been indefatigable in the organisation of hospitals and the relief of refugees. The Crown Princess has directed her activities along similar lines."[22]

Sadly for Sophie, war, an assassination, and yet more war were looming over the horizon, so that there would be virtually no respite from tragedy.

Just like Russia in 1904–06, Romania in 1907, and Greece in 1909, Spain in 1909 was in the throes of fighting off revolutionaries. The outbreak of violence centered on the Catalonian city of Barcelona, where a combination of socialists, republicans, anarchists, and labor rebels wreaked havoc on Spain's second largest city. As one historian puts it, "terrorism was the order of the day, and the Government accordingly took extraordinary precautions" to deal with the violence. "The constitutional guarantees were suspended, the Press was muzzled, and a measure was proposed by which anarchist outrages could be repressed."[23]

To exacerbate matters, Spain at this time also had troops stationed in Morocco, where it was hoped that the humiliation suffered in the Spanish-American War could be redeemed by a new adventure in this part of Africa. Reservists from Catalonia were ordered to quell the Riff mountain tribesmen in northern Morocco. Many of these soldiers came from poor working families and their absence meant loss of income for their families back home. Many also interpreted the order to war as an order to protect the interests of the Spanish mine owners in the Riff Mountains. The opposition to the government thus took on the tone of class exploitation. A surge of anti-government feeling swept through Barcelona, Catalonia's largest city. This triggered an outbreak of violence known as "*la Semana Trágica* (the Tragic Week)" in which thirty thousand revolutionaries fought against six thousand police and troops in a ferocious battle.

According to a report sent by the British minister at Madrid, "the outburst was entirely unexpected," though it later became clear that "it was carefully and secretly prepared some time before." For a week, "a state of unveiled insurrection prevailed," claiming the life of hundreds. Since anti-clericalism was a major feature of these revolutionaries, it came as no surprise that the perpetrators of the insurrection went on an orgy of violence against anyone and anything associated with the Church. Some forty religious houses were "more or less completely destroyed by fire. . . . Communication with the outside by rail and telegraph was for a time completely cut off. Continuous heavy firing rendered the streets impassable."[24]

In his despatches from Barcelona, *The Times* reporter noted that "there has been much street fighting, and many churches and convents have been destroyed . . . it is feared that the loss of life and damage to property have been very heavy." This, plus the fact that communication with Barcelona had been cut off, led the reporter to conclude that "the situation is grave."[25]

With the outbreak of violence in Barcelona, concerns about the safety of the Spanish royal family grew. The numerous attempts on King Alfonso's life—the wedding-day bombing still fresh in people's minds—were vivid reminders of just how dangerous it was to be a monarch of a country in the Iberian Peninsula. After all, only a little over a year had passed since King Carlos I of Portugal and his son, the crown prince, were shot to death in their own country. These double assassinations involving a neighboring king and his heir undoubtedly made an impact on Ena, who had come so close to death on her own wedding day. The Empress Eugénie felt as much, writing in 1909: "I imagine that the King and my beloved Ena will be moved by the crime against Carlos I of Portugal."[26] Fears of being overthrown and assassinated no doubt crossed Ena's mind more than once in the summer of 1909. Fortunately, officials in Madrid acted quickly to head off the spread of Catalonian violence that might easily have overtaken the capital.

Though Madrid escaped the violence that wracked Barcelona, by the end of 1909, Queen Ena and King Alfonso had every right to be concerned about their country. In municipal elections, for example, the votes showed a victory for the left. And in Madrid, "not a single candidate of the Right was elected." This meant that of those occupying the capital's town council, "the majority will be antimonarchical." As Sir Maurice de Bunsen wrote to Sir Edward Grey in December 1909, "in these surroundings the throne is in a difficult and delicate position."[27] The question was, how long were King Alfonso and Queen Victoria Eugenie going to be able to fend off those who envisaged a radical move toward a republican Spain?

As the winds of revolutionary change picked up force in the twentieth century, a fight pitting royalists and radicals against each other took hold in farflung corners of Europe. The stage was set in Spain, Russia, and Greece for a showdown of ideologies; and caught right in the middle were three of Queen Victoria's granddaughters—Ena, Alix, and Sophie.

Fourteen

"LA REINA HERMOSA"

QUEEN ENA'S HAPPINESS IN HER BABY SON AND KING ALFONSO'S pride in his heir was dealt a tremendous blow when court doctors carried out a circumcision on the Prince of the Asturias and it was discovered that the baby's bleeding would not stop. Shock and consternation set in.

From the day of her marriage to King Alfonso XIII, Queen Victoria Eugenie's life careened from one tragedy to another. Like Tsarina Alexandra, who lived in a country marked by its instability and the shadow of assassination, Queen Ena faced a similar situation in Spain. But a second, more personal tragedy dogged these two women, one that had profound consequences for their lives. This tragedy—hemophilia—they shared with their grandmother, Queen Victoria. But of all three women, it was arguably Queen Ena who suffered the most; for unlike Queen Victoria and Tsarina Alexandra, whose marriages were unaffected by the appearance of the disease in their sons, Ena's transmission of the deadly gene into the House of Bourbon sent her marriage hurtling toward dangerous waters.

In 1907 there was still little, if any, hint of trouble in Ena's paradise, at least where her mother, Princess Beatrice, was concerned. Indeed, Beatrice took great pride in her daughter's happiness, telling the Bishop of Ripon: "I am so thankful for my dear child's thorough contentment in her married life with her kind excellent husband, & precious little boy. She is quite unchanged, simple & still childlike, & it reconciles one to the pain of having her so far, to know how much she is beloved in her new country, & her upright straight character appreciated." As for Alfonso XIII, "if he is only spared to do one half of what he wishes for his country he will indeed be a blessing. To me he is a most affectionate thoughtful son, & he fits so well into our little family circle."[1]

Within six months of writing this letter, Princess Beatrice became a grand-mother for the second time when Ena gave birth at La Granja to a healthy baby boy, who was named Jaime. Despite the arrival in quick succession of two sons, cracks in the marriage began to appear as early as the summer of 1908. Ena awoke one morning to find that her husband had unexpectedly left her. Writing to Al-fonso from Miramar, the queen expressed her bewilderment, confessing "I was sad yesterday upon going to bed at the knowledge that we would not see each other for a week. You left as if you did not say good-bye. . . . Your loving wife, Ena." The wounded wife, still a newlywed in some respects, added a postscript that displayed her heartache: "Our good-bye was so terribly hurried and I did not have the faintest idea why you walked by way of the garden like you did [so] that I could not reach the front to see you until finally someone came to tell me that you had left much earlier."[2] King Alfonso's unexpected absence amounted to the first real sign that he was prone to fits of depression. It would appear that the mercurial Alfonso preferred the company found in Santander to that of his beautiful young wife.

The next day, in a bid to tug at her husband's heartstrings, Ena sent a mes-sage, telling him about their sons and her busy schedule: "I saw the boys and have found that poor little Jaime has had a bad night because of stomach pains. I have many audiences." When she received a reply the following day, she was thrilled and wrote back immediately:

> My dear Alfonso: I was pleased to receive your letter. Jaime is now better but still quite pale. After the pains the poor boy suffered. Alfonso is much better and quite fun. While you are away, I spend a great deal of my time with the boys and that is how it seems I console myself from your absence. Last night was very cold and the bed seemed terribly large and vacant. I longed to have you next to me so I can rock you [to sleep] and have you warm me . . . I kiss you with all my affection, I remain your long devoted wife, Ena.[3]

Even as Alfonso began to show signs of being his old self by writing back to his wife, Ena—still only twenty at the time—showed every sign of being in love with her husband. Her replies (this time from England, where she went to visit her family) continued in an effort to keep alive the passion in their marriage. "God bless you, Alfonso," went one of them. "You cannot imagine how I miss you. Many kisses from your wife who loves you with her whole soul, Ena."[4] The situation seemed all the more tragic since in Alfonso's search for a bride, the king had been determined above all to let his heart rule. He made no secret of this and repeatedly said, "I shall marry a princess who takes my fancy, and nobody else.

I want to love my wife."[5] Yet in just a few short years, the young couple already had to weather a mini-crisis in their marriage.

Queen Victoria Eugenie's early years in Spain were nothing short of turbulent. Her introduction into the Spanish court proved daunting. Not much energy was spent initiating the perplexed queen into the intricacies of life in Madrid. Everything and everyone was foreign to her. Queen Maria Cristina may have been a more well-meaning mother-in-law to Ena than the Dowager Empress Marie was to Alix, but Maria Cristina possessed a frigid personality that was hard to penetrate. Her face, though far from frightening, rarely looked relaxed. The Queen Mother perennially swathed herself in dark, somber colors. This was a far cry from her Russian counterpart, Marie Feodorovna, who charmed everyone with her wit and effervescence, even into her widowhood. In her desire to extend her mourning for her dead husband, Queen Maria Cristina infused court life in Spain with a strong sense of the morose, long after her husband, King Alfonso XII, had died.

With time, Maria Cristina ceded some ground to her daughter-in-law, but ever so slowly. Ena also endured the added difficulty of having the dowager queen living in close proximity. At least where Alix was concerned, Empress Marie lived on her own in separate establishments. But for Ena, it was a different matter. The former Queen Regent became something of an appendage to the ever patient Ena. Whenever Ena dined, for instance, in the early years of her marriage, Maria Cristina presided over the meals, often taking charge completely, leaving Ena with very little to say.

Maintaining dominance at court proved easy for King Alfonso's mother. Not only was Ena the newcomer, she also battled one of the most difficult challenges any new bride or queen could face in a foreign land: her inability to understand and speak the local tongue. Incredibly, no one taught Queen Ena the language. Ena had tried to teach herself while she was being courted by King Alfonso, but once in Spain, she was on her own. Left to her own devices, Ena valiantly struggled to pick up as much Spanish as she could. Years later she recalled her difficulties: "You have no idea of the terrible loneliness in the soul of not understanding a language . . . It is as if one is by oneself in a country! And so I took upon the work of learning [the language]. Those whom [I] could understand best were the King and the Infanta Maria Teresa [his sister], because they spoke pure Castilian. . . ." It took Ena only six months to understand Spanish and a year and a half to tackle a conversation. Her success came from her conversations with the palace help. One of the first phrases she uttered was to a coachman, telling him to "find me a place where the wind does not blow." "That seemed to take such tremendous effort," recalled Ena; that even in her old age she noted proudly, "I have not forgotten my first phrase!"[6]

The queen's ability quickly earned her respect from one of Alfonso's relatives, the Infanta Eulalia, who admitted that "besides beauty, Ena possessed brains." Eulalia, one of the most colorful members of the Bourbon family, quickly came to admire Ena. "Brought up at the English Court," wrote the infanta years later, "she was serious and reserved in public, in spite of her friendly manner, but in private life she was a delightful woman of the world, gifted with great charm and artistic tastes, sympathetic to a degree, and affectionate to all around her."[7] Not everyone, however, was as gracious. Among those who harbored suspicions and jealousies toward the queen were the ladies surrounding Maria Cristina, whose entourage proved to be relics of a bygone age.

Yet of all the bewildering array of personalities and customs, none was more exasperating and confusing to Ena than Alfonso XIII. The blushing bride was caught completely unawares when it came to her husband's personality. Far from being her champion, the more Ena came to know Alfonso, the more Spain's king appeared to be an enigma—a complex individual whose temperament ran hot and cold. Nor could she grasp the reasons behind this behavior. Ena's confusion over her husband's sudden desire to get away from her and their little boys in 1908, just two years into their marriage, threw her off. Unsophisticated and lost, the love-struck queen responded in the only manner she knew—taking on the tone of supplicant. Her pleas, interspersed with declarations of passion for Alfonso, nevertheless betrayed her bewilderment.

Despite their reconciliation, the marriage fell into deep trouble. Sadly, King Alfonso could never reconcile himself to the fact that the dreaded hemophilia had entered his family via Ena. The proud and volatile Alfonso found it hard to forgive his wife for something over which she had no control. Not only did he blame Ena for the curse that beset their family; Alfonso looked at her with increasing disdain. Henri Valloton, a Swiss lawyer who was a confidant of both, was certain who was at fault for the collapse of the marriage: "Alfonso XIII threw the blame at his wife for the illness. . . . He could not resign himself [to the fact that] his heir could have contracted an ailment which her family had, and not his. It was unjust, he himself recognized it, but he could not think in any other manner."[8]

During Ena's early years in Spain, many found her to be the very embodiment of "*la reina hermosa* (the beautiful queen)." Members of the press vied in their rapturous descriptions of the blond-haired, blue-eyed Victoria Eugenie, who looked every inch a queen. Much to Ena's credit, she did not let such compliments go to her head. On the contrary, a mischievous streak occasionally surfaced. She once asked Alfonso if he had read the newspaper she was holding. When he answered, "No, is it anything of importance?" Ena quipped back,

"Certainly. I demand the instant execution of editor; he has omitted to hint that I am the most beautiful woman in the world!"[9]

Considering how effusive the Spanish were in the early years, Ena's remark was not without basis. In Seville, for instance, the young Queen Ena was met with shouts of *"Viva!"* Flattering phrases poured forth—"What colouring!" *Per dios,* what colouring!" *"Santa Maria,* gold is poor beside her hair!" Trying to keep her composure, Ena accepted these compliments. Only when someone loudly proclaimed, "you are not only Queen of Spain; you are Queen of all beautiful women," did she burst out laughing.[10]

As Ena slowly gained confidence, she began introducing her own touches into a court that had long stagnated under the perpetual mourning of the widowed Maria Cristina. These touches were invariably tinged with a predilection for things fresh and sparkling and, of course, for things British. Her introduction of a wedding cake was but one of several customs Victoria Eugenie brought with her to Spain. The queen was proud of her British heritage and did not hide it. Seven months after becoming queen, she wrote to thank the ladies of Monmouthshire for the gift of a screen. "The screen," noted a proud Ena, "stands in my drawing-room & is the admiration of everyone. Of course," she added, "I am very proud to be able to say that the work was done by English ladies & it makes a great impression."[11]

Being queen of Spain nevertheless proved daunting. The difficulties of adjusting to life in a foreign court, coupled with the realization that she and Alfonso were not completely compatible, disquieted Ena. In a letter to the future Queen Mary, Ena highlighted the contrast between her simple life in England and her more rigid existence in Spain:

We now are living in Madrid for some weeks, in this grand palace in which I feel like a guest of honour, although little by little I struggle to make a place for myself. I cannot leave my rooms without causing a real commotion and the racket of the famous guards, stationed in the passageways and steps of the monumental stairs. When I go close [to the guards] it makes them stand to attention, hit the marble floor with their halberds and shout: Long live the Queen!

I long [for] the far off days of Osborne where I was simply a young woman full of life who wanted to ride and have fun and also I wish to return to the months when Alfonso and I were in the palace of La Granja, a dreamy place where I hope to meet up with you not too far off one day.

In Madrid I see much less of my beloved husband, naturally, but the days they make for me are eternal. I pass the afternoons like the old ladies of [the Isle of]

Wight embroidering or dedicated to my favourite pastime which is reading, something which Alfonso does not share and which surprisingly, I am grateful for, because when he is with me there is never a book which we can both find appealing between ourselves. I miss the solitary walks with him, when we would speak of simple things that . . . for others would be trivial. Our lengthy moments of intimacy, here, are spent in the afternoon when alone together, we take tea.

Here the atmosphere amounts to an inhospitable one.[12]

One of the Spanish court's most daunting and curious rituals occurred during Ena's first year in Spain. As the consort of His Most Catholic Majesty, the King of Spain, Queen Victoria Eugenie was expected to participate fully in the Spanish court's most important ceremonies, which often meant religious observances. Probably the most difficult was one that took place on Holy Thursday: the *Lavatorio* or washing of the feet. A Spanish contemporary of Ena's captured its importance at the time: "The ceremony is profoundly significant, unbelievably poignant: it is Spain. In no other country could it take on such a living value and meaning."[13]

The *Lavatorio* was one of the highlights of the Easter ceremonies during Holy Week. King Alfonso and Queen Victoria Eugenie had to re-enact Christ's washing of the disciples' feet at the Last Supper; in so doing, the couple relived this humble act of service. Participation in the ceremony was meant to "personify the spirit of Christ." In a ritual that had not deviated from its original version dating to the thirteenth century, the king and queen donned aprons and knelt before twelve elderly men and twelve elderly women, to wash, then kiss their feet. The task was always more difficult for Ena: "She takes longer because before each one she must kneel and rise again, her long dress making the King's more expeditious method impossible."[14]

"It must have been something of an ordeal, specially for the Queen, to go through that process," recalled the Marqués de Villavieja, who witnessed Ena doing her part the year after she married. The marqués wrote admiringly of Ena's first *Lavatorio*:

I shall never forget the first time she had to do it. She was only nineteen years old then, and unaccustomed as she was to Spanish life and the many foreign habits at Court, it must have been difficult to her English mind to carry out this ceremony in all its detail. But she did it with much sweetness and grace, and one felt how deeply desirous she was of doing her duty.[15]

Of all the challenges Ena faced in Spain, the most painful was Alfonso's infidelities. In order to compensate for his frustration with Ena, and in keeping with his own restless nature, Alfonso had no compunction in betraying his marital vows with numerous women. But as unhappy as her marriage was turning out to be, Ena continued to give birth to a succession of children: Beatriz (b. 1909), Maria Cristina (b. 1911), and Juan (b. 1913).

With the possible exception of the Russian imperial family, the homes where Ena raised her children were unsurpassed in opulence. Madrid's Royal Palace was but one of several superb homes at the disposal of Ena and the Bourbons. Inside the palace, visitors marveled at the beautifully executed tapestries lining the walls. Fine-cut crystal chandeliers like huge snowflakes hung from the ceilings; Roman busts stared back menacingly. If Ena ever wanted to brush up on Spain's past, she had only to visit the Royal Library. Housed in two dozen rooms, lined with mahogany bookcases, the collection included thousands of rare manuscripts, maps, drawings, and books. The Gala Dining Room was another wonder: gold, marble, more than a dozen large crystal chandeliers, giant Sèvres porcelain and bronze jars, along with beautiful paintings depicting *The Surrender of Granada, Christopher Columbus Before Ferdinand and Isabella* ("the Catholic Kings"), and representations of what was once Spain's vast empire—Peru, the Philippines, Mexico, and Chile. The massive room contained an enormous table that could seat up to 145 guests for dinner.

In her other homes—the palaces of Miramar, La Granja, Aranjuez, El Pardo, and La Magdalena—Ena gained more privacy and the rigid court etiquette was less pervasive. But even in some of these, she could not completely escape the formality of the Spanish court. Whether through lack of opportunity or inclination, Ena's private rooms were not dotted with furnishings from London. Nor were her apartments swathed in yards of chintz, as could be found in Athens, Tsarskoe Selo, or Christiania. Ena's bedroom in her Madrid palace, for instance, would have befitted Marie Antoinette at Versailles. Surmounting the gold and white bed with its ornate headboard was an ostentatious canopy in gold swathed in sumptuous silk.

When it came to manifestations of her own Christian faith, evidence was to be found in Ena's most private quarters—her bedroom. Ena's bedroom at the Aranjuez Palace had a strongly religious tone. Hanging above the royal headboard was a huge, life-like painting of Christ crucified, while a large crucifix stood next to the sleigh bed.

For all her attempts to immerse herself in Spanish ways, there was always to be an element of suspicion and a lack of acceptance among Ena's subjects. There were, for one, too few instances of spontaneity from Ena. As the years passed, the novelty of having a lovely young English princess descend upon them like some goddess from the North—complete with fair hair, a peaches and cream complexion, and a pedigree that linked her directly to Queen Victoria—began to wane with some segments of the people. For a populace long accustomed to the art of frenzied melodrama in everyday life, Ena was turning out to be too glacial, and thus too English for their tastes.

These critics had been given ammunition in the very early days when Queen Ena made her first appearance at a bullfight in celebration of her wedding. Fresh-faced, young, and poised, the queen looked exquisite in her white mantilla, seated in the royal box with King Alfonso and Queen Maria Cristina. In front of thirteen thousand people, Ena had to dig deep within herself to show her subjects that she was different from most of her nation, who were known to be revolted by the gory spectacle of Spain's quintessential sport. Ena, who loved animals, tried to mask her disgust, but this only served to disappoint some subjects, particularly as her first bullfight turned out to be relatively unexciting. In order not to offend the queen's sensibilities and those of the foreign guests, the bulls were reputedly drugged, and lost their violent edge. Victoria Eugenie was never to overcome her intense dislike of bullfighting. She took up her brother's suggestion by having special shaded field glasses made. The queen would raise the glasses to her eyes at critical moments; the crowds, in turn, believed she was taking a closer look when in fact she was shielding her eyes.

Ena was also not immune from criticism from the arch enemies of the Bourbons: the Carlists. And their leader, Don Jaime de Bourbon, was not shy in airing in public his views of the queen. In August 1909, at the time of the insurrection in Barcelona, the Carlist pretender to the throne issued a dramatic proclamation to his followers in which he repudiated any active role as leader of the Carlist cause, so fraught with violence in the past. That may have come as a relief to Alfonso XIII. But Don Jaime also made it known that he believed King Alfonso's popularity was on the decline. As for the queen, Don Jaime noted bluntly that she "is not liked."[16] The question for Ena, of course, was how much of Don Jaime's pronouncement was false, stemming as it did from the enemy camp, and how much was true?

In May 1910, Edward VII died. Maud and King Haakon made haste for London in order to be present at the funeral and to comfort the grieving Queen Alexandra. Maud's father had always been known for his gregariousness and his joy of living. When he suddenly was taken ill at the age of sixty-eight and died, there was a genuine sense of dismay.

From Russia, Tsarina Alexandra sent her cousin, George V, Edward VII's successor, a touching letter of sympathy:

Only a few words to tell you how very much we think of you in your great grief. Besides your heart being full of sorrow after the great loss you have entertained, now come the new & heavy responsibilities crowding upon you. From all my heart I pray that God may give you strength & wisdom to govern your country. . . . I think so much of you, as Nicky & I began our married life under similar trying circumstances.

Thank God we saw yr. dear Pap still last summer—one cannot realise that he is gone.[17]

In one of the last great displays of royal pomp before the outbreak of World War I, Great Britain bid farewell to King Edward VII. As a daughter of the late king, comforting daughter of a grieving widow, and Queen Consort of Norway, Maud played a key role in the ceremonies, staying by her mother's side during the funeral; both women looked somber and dignified in black. The crowds that packed London that day to watch the funeral cortège make its way from Westminster Hall to Paddington Station for the journey to Windsor amounted to a staggering 2 million souls. Yet the silence among the massive throng—a sign of deep respect—was awesome. The crowds witnessed a panoply of historical proportions:

In scarlet and blue and green and purple, three by three the sovereigns rode through the palace gates, with plumed helmets, gold braid, crimson sashes, and jeweled orders flashing in the sun. After them came five heirs apparent, forty more imperial or royal highnesses, seven queens—four dowager and three regnant—and a scattering of special ambassadors from uncrowned countries. Together they represented seventy nations in the greatest assemblage of royalty and rank ever gathered in one place and, of its kind, the last.[18]

Among the mourners that day were an impressive array of Europe's reigning monarchs: the new king, George V, Maud's brother; Kaiser Wilhelm II of Germany; and Kings Haakon VII of Norway, George I of Greece, Ferdinand of Bulgaria, Manoel of Portugal, Albert I of the Belgians, Frederick VII of Denmark, and Alfonso XIII of Spain. It was a magnificent and dazzling display, one that gave the impression of enduring solidity. As one historian has put it, "who, seeing this self-confident parade of royalty through the streets of the world's greatest metropolis on the occasion of Edward VII's funeral, could imagine that their future was anything but assured?"[19]

At the time of Edward VII's funeral, Queen Ena was living through an exceptionally bleak period. She was again expecting a child, but weeks before her accouchement, Ena, with three pregnancies behind her, sensed something was seriously wrong. It soon became clear that her unborn baby had died. Ena was advised to complete her pregnancy so as not to hamper her ability to bear more children. In May 1910, she delivered a dead baby boy, who was named Fernando. Queen Maria Cristina sent a telegram to her son in London, advising him of the latest family tragedy:

> With profound sorrow I am letting you know that at one thirty Ena gave birth to a dead son, though very sad, thanks to God the labor and delivery lasted only four hours. . . . Ena sends her best love and all her thoughts are with you[,] you can be completely calm over Ena's state of health . . . tell every-thing to your mother-in-law[,] I embrace you affectionately[,] Mama.[20]

The day after the dead Infante Fernando was born, his body was taken by train to King Philip II's sprawling and austere creation, the forbidding compound known as El Escorial. There, Ena's dead son was laid to rest amongst his ancestors, while his distraught mother recuperated from her heartbreaking ordeal back in Madrid. None of Ena's other royal cousins had to endure the trauma of carrying to term and then giving birth to a stillborn child. That grievous distinction belonged solely to Ena. But like some curse harassing her at intervals, another misfortune struck unexpectedly within two years of Fernando's birth. This time it fell on Ena's healthy four-year-old son, Jaime.

The Infante Jaime was a normal child who came to be a close companion of his older brother. Together, Jaime and Alfonsito were a delightful pair, with the blond Alfonsito so obviously taking after his mother while the dark-haired Jaime resembled his father. In health, Jaime was everything his brother was not—the dreaded hemophilia being absent. If the heir was sickly, then at least "the spare" was robust.

However, tragedy struck. The boy was felled with acute pain in his ears. The diagnosis was double mastoiditis, requiring an immediate operation. The procedure went badly, and the auditory bones broke, causing Ena's second son to become a deaf-mute.

⁂

Missy's life in Bucharest—after weathering the Peasants' Revolt of 1907 and finding in Prince Barbo Stirbey a man to admire and love—settled down to a degree of peace she had not known in years. In 1909, the crown princess gave birth to another daughter, Princess Ileana. This child, who would come to be Marie's favorite, had none of the characteristics of her older children. So different was

Ileana from her siblings that it almost seemed as if the dark-haired girl had been sired by someone other than the crown prince. And the only man who might fall into this category was none other than Prince Barbo Stirbey.

One of Queen Marie's biographers, Hannah Pakula, has concluded that this was more fantasy than fact. In his correspondence with Marie, Stirbey's tone toward Ileana never differed from that toward her siblings. But when he refers to Prince Mircea, the last of Marie's children (b. 1913), Pakula believes that "there is a marked difference in tone" in Barbo's letters; and so concludes that Mircea was Barbo's child.[21]

⌒◍⌒

As he grew older, Alexei's mischievous personality continued to endear him to many who came into contact with the boy. But despite the ebullience and the handsome features, which on a good day made the tsarevich appear the picture of health, his was a body that could—and did—malfunction badly. The Grim Reaper kept a covetous watch on Alexei Nicolaevitch, and the uncertainty kept the boy's mother on tenterhooks.

In order to prevent the young tsarevich from getting into serious harm, two burly sailors of the Imperial Navy, Derevenko and Nagorny, were assigned to keep watch. And not far off was the omnipresent family physician, kindly and solicitous Dr. Eugene Botkin. But for all the precautions Nicholas and Alexandra took to protect their son, they did little to calm a mother's frazzled nerves. The extent of Alexandra Feodorovna's all-consuming preoccupation was best summed up by a family friend who recorded that "She could never feel for an hour that he was safe.[22]

Of all the burdens she had had to endure since her arrival in Russia, the fate of her son—"that Child of many Prayers,"[23] "the Empress's favourite child"[24]— hung heaviest on Alix. To her great credit, she accepted her son's incurable illness without venting her rage at God. Instead, she found from God the strength to face Alexei's hemophilia. "Life brings us sorrows and trials without end," confessed the tsarina to a friend once, "but all is for the best, and God gives one strength to bear one's heavy cross, and go on fighting."[25]

Increasingly, however, Alix's attentions and actions became shaped by her son's hemophilia. And owing to the nature of the illness, it was only a matter of time before a frightening incident erupted.

Fifteen

"MAMMA, HELP ME!"

PIERRE GILLIARD CAPTURED WHAT IT MUST HAVE BEEN LIKE FOR the helpless tsarina to watch as her son suffered through a life-threatening hemophilia attack:

> Think of the tortures of that mother, an impotent witness of her son's martyrdom in those hours of mortal anguish—a mother who knew that *she herself* was the cause of his sufferings, that *she* had transmitted to him the terrible disease against which human science was powerless! *Now* I understood the secret tragedy of her life! How easy it was to reconstruct the stages of that long Calvary.[1]

Gilliard found the boy to be "sensitive to suffering in others just because he had already suffered so much himself."[2] The tsarina shared this characteristic, once writing that it was her "daily prayer, for years already, that God should just send me the sorrowing, and give me the possibility to be a help to them through His infinite mercy."[3] This mutual sympathy served to create an even closer bond between mother and son.

With doctors and medical science proving little help to eight-year-old Alexei, the tsarina turned to Rasputin. Confident in his position with the tsarina, the "monk" from Siberia grew emboldened in his carnal pursuits with women, leading to louder criticisms of Alexandra. In her desperate mind, these accusations against Rasputin amounted to the vilification of a saint. She once told Dr. Botkin that "saints have always been caluminated [*sic*]."[4] For their meddling when it came to Rasputin, Alexandra froze out those who had been close to her.

The Montenegrin grand duchesses were henceforth ignored; and the tsarina's one-time confessor was summarily exiled to the Crimea. The saddest estrangement involved Alix's own sister, Ella. They would never enjoy the same closeness, thanks to Alexandra's stubborn refusal to be rid of Rasputin.

Emboldened by the hold he had over the imperial couple, Rasputin made no secret of his high standing at Tsarskoe Selo. He boasted that he enjoyed the sexual favors of countless women and even boldly embellished his stories by bragging how he kissed the tsarina. As for Alexandra, she remained completely faithful to Tsar Nicholas.

Anxiety over the growing influence of Rasputin at court grew quickly after 1910. Peter Stolypin, the prime minister and interior minister, ordered an investigation of the notorious womanizing *staretz*. Stolypin presented the damning results to the tsar, who then asked Stolypin to meet Rasputin personally. Stolypin duly met with the *staretz,* who promptly tried to hypnotize the prime minister. Stolypin recorded how "I began to feel an indescribable loathing for this vermin sitting opposite me. Still, I did realize that the man possessed great hypnotic power, which was beginning to produce a fairly strong moral impression on me, though certainly one of repulsion. I pulled myself together and addressing him roughly, told him that on the strength of the evidence in my possession I could annihilate him by prosecuting him as a sectarian."[5]

But in spite of mounting evidence against Rasputin, the tsar knew his hands were tied. When, in 1911, Stolypin warned Nicholas II of the destructive impact Rasputin was having on the imperial couple as far as people's conceptions were concerned, the tsar replied: "Perhaps everything you say is true. But I must ask you never to speak to me again about Rasputin. In any case, I can do nothing at all about it."[6] Well aware how dependent his wife was on Rasputin, Nicholas understood that it was inconceivable to remove the man. The tsar once let it slip, "Better one Rasputin than ten fits of hysterics a day."[7]

In the course of the heated debates swirling about Rasputin, another one of those violent spasms in Russia's history erupted. The victim this time was none other than Peter Stolypin. While attending a performance of the *Tale of Tsar Sultan* by Rimsky-Korsakov at the Kiev Opera House, Stolypin was shot in the presence of the tsar and his daughters, Olga and Tatiana. The wounded man, blood oozing out of his uniform, turned toward the tsar in the royal box and made the sign of the Cross. Stolypin died four days later.

The minister's death had rid Rasputin of one of his enemies. But Stolypin's replacement, Count Vladimir Kokovtsov, was equally against Tsarina Alexandra's favorite, as were the members of the Duma. Summoning Kokovtsov for an audience, the dowager empress questioned him about Rasputin. Kokovtsov recalled how Empress Marie "wept bitterly and promised to speak to the Tsar." But then she added, "my poor daughter-in-law does not perceive that she is ruining both the dynasty and herself. She sincerely believes in the holiness of an adventurer, and we are powerless to ward off the misfortune which is sure to come."[8]

Empress Marie was right. By the end of 1912, no one could persuade Alexandra that Rasputin was anything short of a miracleworker; for a terrifying drama unfolded which, by its conclusion, convinced Alexandra Feodorovna that Rasputin was the sole effective conduit between Alexei and God.

Spala, the imperial hunting lodge set amid forests in Poland, was a tranquil place. But in the autumn of 1912, it became one of anguished nightmare for Alix. The tsarevitch fell seriously ill as the result of a fall. Soon enough, a large swelling emerged on Alexei's left thigh and groin; doctors also found a tumor that was turning septic. An operation was necessary, but because of Alexei's hemophilia, this life-saving procedure was considered too dangerous. In no time, a life and death struggle unfolded. The dreaded hemophilia was claiming the life of Alexandra's only son.

By 21 October, all seemed hopeless. The tsarevitch's temperature had reached nearly 40 degrees Celsius. Inside the hunting lodge, blood-curdling screams could be heard. The boy, wracked by excruciating pain, pleaded to be freed from his misery. Everyone at Spala during those terrifying days was haunted by his anguished cries. Workers went about the large house with their ears muffled. But no such respite was allowed his horrified mother.

As Alexei's abdomen filled up with blood, the boy's agony multiplied. So moved were the workers and soldiers on the estate that they begged to hold a daily *Te Deum* in the open, where they were joined by local peasants. Alexandra sat for hours on end by her son's side; his face was "absolutely bloodless, drawn and seamed with suffering, while his almost expressionless eyes rolled back in his head." When the tsar came into the room, "seeing his boy in this agony and hearing his faint screams of pain, the poor father's courage completely gave way and he rushed, weeping bitterly, to his study."[9]

Nicholas admitted to his mother: "I was hardly able to stay in the room, but had of course to take turns with Alix for she was exhausted by spending whole nights by his bed." For four agonizing days, Alexei's condition worsened. His father recalled how "the poor darling suffered intensely, the pains came in spasms and recurred every quarter of an hour." As his temperature shot up, the tsarevitch fell into a delirium. Exhausted by lack of sleep, Alexei, according to his father, had only enough strength to moan repeatedly: "O Lord, have mercy upon me."[10] "In one of his rare moments of consciousness, [he] said to his mother: 'When I am dead build me a little monument of stones in the wood.' "[11]

Pierre Gilliard, who saw the "distracted and terror-stricken look"[12] on Alix's face, understood what the tsarina was undergoing during those tragic days at

Spala. When her son, in the rare times of lucidity, begged her: "Mamma, help me!" the tsarina felt completely helpless, knowing all she could do was wipe his brow, whisper comforting words, and pray. Worse was when Alexei asked his helpless mother: "When I am dead, it will not hurt anymore, will it?"[13]

Twice at Spala, the end seemed imminent. Yet Alexei fought on. Resigned to their son's fate, the tsar and tsarina agreed that their subjects should be forewarned of the boy's imminent death. Two bulletins were issued, a day apart, preparing all of Russia for the news that the tsarevitch had died. In the meantime, the last rites were performed.

Alexandra made one last desperate attempt to save her son's life. This time she turned to Rasputin, hoping that he might be able to effect a miracle. The exhausted tsarina asked Anna Viroubova to send a telegram to Rasputin, who was then at his village in western Siberia. It was an act of sheer desperation; Viroubova said that "Rasputin was in disfavor with the imperial couple at the time, so they did not turn immediately to the peasant for a cure, as they had for earlier hemophiliac episodes."[14]

When the reply arrived, it was all the tsarina could have hoped for. Looking "pale and emaciated," but wearing a smile, Alexandra announced "in a calm voice" to a number of individuals, including Sergei Sazanov, Russia's foreign minister: "I received a telegram from Father Grigory and it has reassured me completely." Rasputin had told her, "God has seen your tears and heard your prayers. Grieve no more! Your son will live."[15] "The little one will not die. Do not allow the doctors to bother him too much."[16] Sure enough, as if on cue, Alexei began to show signs of recovery. It was almost immediate. Grand Duchess Olga, who was no fan of Rasputin, recalled how, incredibly, "within an hour my nephew was out of danger."[17]

Tsarina Alexandra was not the only one who found Rasputin's powers astonishing. Even the tsarevitch's doctors were at a loss as to how their patient could recover so remarkably after the "intervention" of the *staretz*. The morning after the telegram arrived from Pokrovskoie, the first words the doctors assembled at Spala uttered to A. A. Mossolov, head of the Court Chancellery, were: "The haemorrhage has stopped."[18] The most preeminent physician in Russia, Dr. S. P. Fedorov, was among the professionals attending Alexei. He too was at a loss as to what happened. When Grand Duchess Olga recalled a conversation she had later that year with Professor Fedorov, Olga remembered his admitting that "the recovery was wholly inexplicable from a medical point of view."[19] Fedorov, who, had studied "all the available research material on the disease . . . was convinced that medical science was helpless." He once admitted that the tsarina could not be blamed if she saw Rasputin as some sort of miracle man; for as Fedorov said, "Rasputin would come in, walk up to the patient, look at him and spit. The bleeding would stop in no time. . . . How could the empress not trust Rasputin after that?"[20]

The secret or source of Rasputin's ability to "cure" the tsarevitch has been examined relentlessly. There appears to be no real consensus as to how he came about his "miracles." Explanations range from coincidence at Rasputin's timing to mysterious Tibetan herbs used on the imperial family to palace accomplices effecting his work, and also to his ability to calm the tsarina and so, by extension, Alexei. Then there is the theory that some sort of hypnotic ability might have been the root of his "powers." Rasputin's magnetic eyes play a major role in promoting this idea. But there is little doubt that people privy to the imperial family's troubles were mostly at a loss to explain how the monk from Siberia managed to pull off his conjuring tricks.

For the tsarina, the more she saw what Rasputin was capable of doing where her son's life was concerned, the more she could not shake off the thought that here surely was a man sent by God to help her precious boy. Olga stated simply that "never did my brother or Alicky believe that the man was endowed with any supernatural powers. They saw him as a peasant whose deep faith turned him into an instrument for God to use—but only in the case of Alexis." As Olga tartly pointed out, "Alicky suffered terribly from neuralgia and sciatica, but I never heard that the Siberiak helped her."[21] The imperial couple's acceptance of Rasputin's abilities was not based on a hysterical or excessive mystical obsession but precisely on what Olga said—that he was an instrument of God. This was very much in keeping with the framework of the Russian Orthodox Church, which taught that "certain men had been blessed by God with an ability to heal others." As one biographer notes, "Both Nicholas and Alexandra believed that this was possible, and their acceptance of Rasputin's apparent miracles was merely an extension of official church teaching."[22] And another points out that Rasputin "must be given credit for the consistency of his success, while the occasion on which he saved the boy's life, when Aleksey was lying in a Polish hunting lodge and Rasputin was in Siberia, poses a powerful challenge to rational belief."[23] As for the tsarina, Alexandra's relief was intermingled with wonder: "It is not the first time that the Staretz has saved his life."[24]

After Spala, Tsarina Alexandra wrote one of her most poignant and revealing letters, to her old friend, the Bishop of Ripon:

> I have been so ill again with my heart—the months of phisical [sic] & moral strain during our Boy's illness brought on a collapse—for some years I suffer from the heart & lead the life [of] an invalid most of the time. Thank God our Darling is getting on so well he has grown very much & looks so strong, & we trust before long to see him on his legs again running about.

It was a terrible time we went through, & to see his fearful suffering was heartrending—but he was of an angelical patience & never complaining at being ill, he would only make the sign of the cross & beg God to help him, groaning & moaning from pain. In the Orthodox Church one gives children Holy Communion, so twice we let him have that joy, & the poor thin little face with its big suffering eyes, lit up with blessed happiness as the Priest approached him with the Holy Sacrement [*sic*]. It was such a comfort to us all & we too had the same joy,—*without* trust & faith implicit in God Almighty's great wisdom & ineffable love, one could not bear the heavy crosses sent one.[25]

Alexandra appreciated her ties to the bishop, whose religious faith and link with England endeared him to her. She was moved to add: "God bless you for your loving Christian friendship, deeply valued as coming as an echo out of the past.—Well do I remember your talks to me in Windsor." By this time, Alexandra had certainly had her share of blessings and misfortune; yet she remained unequivocal in her belief in the Christian doctrine of eternal life, telling Boyd Carpenter that

The school of life indeed is a difficult one, but when one tries to live by helping others along the steep & thorny path ones [*sic*] love for Christ grows yet stronger, always suffering & being almost an invalid, one has so much time for thinking & reading & one realises always more & more that this life is but the preparation to yonder real life where all will be made clear to us.[26]

In Greece, after the royal family's close encounter with insurrection during the Military League's tenure in power, the family's fortunes took a turn for the better. By this time, Crown Princess Sophie was the mother of five children: George, Alexander, Helen, Paul, and Irene, now twenty-two, nineteen, sixteen, eleven, and eight, respectively. It seemed as if the family was finally complete. In addition, it looked as if the upheaval in Balkan politics was behind them. On both scores, however, changes were in store.

Although it still possessed a large swath of territory stretching to the Adriatic, the Ottoman Empire was vulnerable to attack from its Balkan neighbors. These countries were consequently driven to liberate their brothers from the oppressive policies carried out by the empire. Scores were ready to be settled by Turkey's ambitious—or, more accurately, ravenous—neighbors. Eager to cement their hold once and for all at the expense of Constantinople, the Balkan countries saw an opportunity to do just that when Italy launched a war against

Turkey in 1911 over the possession of Tripoli, then in the hands of Ottoman Libya. In October 1912, the Balkan League, which comprised Serbia, Bulgaria, Greece, and Montenegro, launched an offensive against the Ottoman Empire.

Greece had been spoiling for war. Ever since their humiliating defeat in 1897 at the hands of the Turks, many in Greece pined for the day when they could avenge themselves. By 1912, a golden opportunity emerged. Eager to see the dreams of a greater Greece—the *megali* idea—come to fruition (an idea fostered since the country's independence in 1830, one that advocated the reunification of Greeks at the Ottoman Empire's expense); Eleutherios Venizelos deemed the time had come for Greece to assert itself.

Venizelos, the white-haired, bearded prime minister, appeared as a benign academic to the casual observer. But in reality, he was ambitious—both for himself and his country—and had shown a streak of fearlessness and stubbornness that would come to the fore again. Prince Christopher of Greece described him as "the born political adventurer, piratical and opportunist."[27]

It was understandable that Crown Princess Sophie felt more than a hint of trepidation over this latest deadly round of Greco-Turkish conflict. But unlike the 1897 clash with Turkey, Greece's army in 1912 was much better prepared to do battle.

All the training and hard work Prince Constantine had undertaken to improve his country's forces paid off. Before the year was out, the army had made advances in a war noted for its challenges. Under Constantine's command, the Greek soldiers battled enemy forces as well as foul weather, mountainous terrain, swollen rivers, and swamps. By the end of a campaign lasting two exhausting months, in which fighting took place every day, Constantine's army had "fought 30 battles . . . crossed three great rivers and countless small ones, took 45,000 prisoners and captured 120 guns, 75,000 rifles and a vast quantity of war matériel of every kind."[28]

In November 1912, the crown prince and his troops won a major victory. The Turks showed the white flag, surrendering the ancient city of Salonika to the prince. After centuries under Turkish suzereinity, Salonika—named for Alexander the Great's sister—was again in Greek hands. In writing of this moment to Paola, Princess of Saxe-Weimar, Constantine could not contain his relief and gratitude for such a victory:

> We are here! Praise to God for His blessing! The city has surrendered to me with almost 20,000 prisoners, so some of our historical ideals have been realized. Yesterday, while making my solemn entry . . . among the frantic applause of the Greeks whom we had liberated, and who kissed my boots and

the edge of my great-coat . . . I thought to myself: "The moment to die has now arrived! Never again shall we experience a moment of such great joy!"[29]

The spectacular capture of Salonika naturally increased the good fortunes of the Greek royal family, who came to be viewed much more positively by their countrymen. No less pleased was Venizelos, who also benefitted from the victories. On 12 November 1912, King George, Crown Prince Constantine, and Eleutherios Venizelos—the three "protagonists of the national drama of renascence"—rode triumphantly through the cheering crowds in Salonika.[30]

The outbreak of the First Balkan War galvanized the women of the Greek royal household into aiding the wounded. Queen Olga and Crown Princess Sophie took the lead; both "opened subscriptions for the establishment of hospitals in the capital, and in the towns adjacent to the theatre of war."[31] In so doing, they set an example to fashionable ladies of Athens to follow suit. Sophie and her mother-in-law also ventured out into the countryside to give aid to wounded soldiers. In one excursion from Larissa to Elassona, *The Times* correspondent who accompanied the queen and crown princess noted that "the inhabitants showed great enthusiasm" for Sophie and Olga.[32]

Another member of the royal family, Princess Alice, wife of Prince Andrew, and hence sister-in-law to Sophie, displayed much courage and "manic energy"[33] during the First Balkan War, often going to the front lines to nurse the wounded and organize field hospitals. It would appear that Alice's zealousness ruffled Sophie's feathers, especially when it came to sending nurses to the front.

Early in 1913, Crown Prince Constantine led another victory against the Turks, capturing Janina in northern Epirus. Princess Alice, active as ever, wanted to organize firsthand the field hospitals there. This time, however, Sophie's husband stepped in. Mindful of the row that had erupted over Sophie's nurses being diverted by Alice to Salonika, the crown prince "suddenly entrusted all the military hospitals in Epirus" to Princess Marie, the wife of Tino's brother, George. Constantine reportedly was overheard by "the entire staff of the hospital in Philippiada" to exclaim: "Why the devil is Alice coming here to mix up everything as she did in Saloniki?"[34]

Fittingly, the capture of Salonika capped King George I's nearly fifty-year reign. King George had told his sons that the time had come for him to abdicate in the latter half of 1913, once he reached his golden anniversary. When they tried to deter him, he brushed them off, saying: "I think I'm entitled to a little rest in my old age. Besides, Tino will be able to do far more with the country than ever I could. He has been born and bred here, while I am always a foreigner."[35]

Constantine and Sophie did eventually come to the throne in the year King George intended, but not in the manner he envisioned.

Like his father before him, who allowed himself much latitude when it came to his marital vows, Crown Prince Constantine permitted himself a certain relaxation. Though King George and Queen Olga enjoyed a happy marriage overall, this did not prevent the king from letting his eye wander when it came to the opposite sex. When Sophie once asked her father-in-law what she could do about her husband's wandering eye, King George merely shrugged and told her to ask Queen Olga for advice.

Although in public the prince maintained the aura of "a stony, cold figure," in private, when he chose, Constantine could be charming. Crown Princess Sophie's husband towered over most men. His height, coupled with his athletic build, blue eyes, and illustrious position, made him irresistible to many women, particularly as Constantine could, according to one captivated lady, "charm the socks off you."[36]

One who came to be captivated by Constantine was a divorcée, Paola, Countess von Ostheim (once married to Prince Herman of Saxe-Weimar, later Count von Ostheim). She met the future king in 1912 and soon embarked on an affair with him. But for the most part the king and queen's domestic life "was happy enough," and Constantine's liaison was "accepted tacitly" by his wife.[37]

When King George savored the triumphs of his heir and the battlefield victories of Greece, there was little indication that trouble was brewing. On 13 March 1913, George went for a stroll through Salonika's streets, accompanied only by an aide. As the two walked toward the city center, a man who had been sitting alone on a low-lying stone wall took aim at the king, shooting him in the back. In an instant, George I of the Hellenes was dead, shot through the lungs and heart. The assassin turned out to be a Macedonian lunatic who later threw himself out of a prison window to his death.

The Greek people were stunned. At the height of their victories, their king, who had devoted fifty years to their service, was brutally murdered. Attention naturally shifted to the new monarch. At the time of George I's assassination, his eldest son was in command of Greek troops at Janina. He immediately returned to Athens, where he met Sophie.

At the outbreak of hostilities in October, Sophie had actively participated in helping the wounded, both in the capital and the countryside. But at the time of her husband's accession, Sophie could not do much traveling. At forty-two years old, she was seven months pregnant with her sixth child. A marshal of the court came to Sophie, who was resting, to tell her that "His Majesty has met with serious injury."[38] Together with her daughter, sixteen-year-old Princess Helen, Sophie, now Queen of the Hellenes, flew to Queen Olga's side.

Although the accession of King Constantine I and Queen Sophie of the Hellenes occurred under the most tragic circumstances, rarely had monarchs ascended the throne with such high expectations. With a Constantine and Sophie reigning once again, the much-vaunted new Byzantium was about to be realized. The hope and anticipation that Greece would finally come into glory and see the much-cherished *megali* idea materialize was widespread. King Constantine's battlefield exploits and the fall of Turkish territory into Greek hands were seen as indicators of even greater things to come.

In London, *The Times* trumpeted its verdict. Greece's king was "a thorough soldier and devoted to his profession"; moreover, "his brilliant conduct of the recent campaigns is fresh in the memory of all. History, perhaps, has never shown so complete a rehabilitation. . . . King Constantine will live in history as a soldier monarch and as the first military leader of rejuvenated Greece."[39] The British minister at Athens who reported to London on King Constantine, reached the same conclusion. "He ascended the throne at a moment when his victories had already made him a popular idol, and the successful Bulgarian campaign completed his apotheosis." And British officials in Athens were convinced that the Greek royal family was secure on the throne, as a report despatched to London in May 1914 stressed: "the rest of the Royal Family have entirely recovered the respect and affection of the people."[40]

Pregnant at time of her accession to the Greek throne, the sudden and shocking circumstances of her ascendancy were certainly more than enough to affect her pregnancy at the age of forty-two. Until the day the new queen gave birth, Mossy was never completely at ease about her sister's condition. "I cannot help feeling frightfully worried," she wrote to a friend in April 1913, "as she has been at death's door with every baby. Thank God she has kept well till now, & is frightfully busy, taking every thing into hand." But Mossy thought that things were looking up in Greece: "I also think that in many a way the country may become more prosperous, & her [Sophie's] life more satisfactory."[41]

Mossy's concerns were finally put to rest a month later. In what turned out to be a particularly harrowing year, Queen Sophie was blessed with a girl, Katherine, born in May. The baby princess was christened in June and had an illustrious set of godparents: Queen Olga of the Hellenes, King George V, Queen Alexandra, and Kaiser Wilhelm II. In honor of the armed forces, the king and queen also invited the Greek Navy and Army to act as godparents. It was an appropriate and moving gesture during a time of war.

The peace that reigned after the First Balkan War did not last long. Less than two months after Queen Sophie gave birth to Princess Katherine, Greece was at war again. This time, the victors aimed their guns against each other in an undignified scramble over the spoils of war, centering upon the distribution of Macedonia. Serbia and Greece, angered by Bulgaria's unhappiness over its portion of Macedonia, decided to fight together against Bulgaria. In June 1913 Bulgaria's ruler, King Ferdinand, ordered an attack on the Greek and Serbian soldiers already in Macedonia, marking the opening salvos of the Second Balkan War. Fortunately for Greece, King Constantine's abilities as a military commander shone forth yet again.

At the Battle of Kilkis, Constantine commanded the army, routing the Bulgarians in the process. The Greeks suffered over eight thousand casualties, while the Bulgarians incurred seven thousand, with another six thousand men taken prisoner. Kilkis marked the high point for Greece in the Second Balkan War. By August 1913, an armistice was agreed upon and the Treaty of Bucharest was signed. Greece emerged victorious, nearly doubling in size by gaining huge chunks of territory that included Kavalla, Salonika, Drama and Serres, southern Epirus and southern Macedonia. Venizelos, who represented Greece in the treaty negotiation, was congratulated by his king, who sent a telegraphed message: "The country is grateful to you." Moved by these words, Venizelos showed the telegram to his Greek colleagues, murmuring through tears, "Constantine is good."[42]

King Constantine's victories sent his countrymen into paroxysms of elation. Upon his return to Athens in early August accompanied by Crown Prince George, the returning hero and the eldest son were greeted by a proud Queen Sophie at Phaleron. Together in state carriages, the royal family made their way through crowds of excited Athenians. So full of "fervent emotionalism" was the tumultuous greeting that eyewitnesses described the procession "as seeming to be some great Greek religious ceremony."[43] Never in its eighty-year history as an independent state had Greece enjoyed such "a degree of unity and internal peace."[44]

Everything seemed to augur well for Constantine and Sophie. After all, was there not a prophecy that said when a Constantine and a Sophie reigned, Greece would again rise to new heights of glory? The hope for a new Byzantium thus rested on the shoulders of Tino and Sophie. But would expectations prove to be too high?

Sophie of Greece was not the only Balkan royal who took it upon herself to help care for the injured during the battles that raged through the region. Romania's own crown princess set another example of selfless devotion to her people. When Romanian soldiers marched into Bulgaria, they found more prosperous counterparts whose land was better utilized than those in Romania; but they also found cholera raging in their midst.

During a visit to Red Cross hospitals along the Danube, Missy was struck by the inadequate care being received by the sick and dying soldiers, prompting her to write, "I saw sights which made my blood run cold." Some villages were so short of help that men died needlessly. "This was," she noted, "my first contact with a horrible and deadly reality. The effect it had on me was galvanizing." Dismayed by such needless suffering, the princess was driven to improve conditions. Possessing what she herself described as "nerves of steel,"[45] Marie set about making her own significant contribution to Romania in the battle against the deadly cholera outbreak.

Marie rightly assessed the need for a cool-headed leader, who could rally round the disheartened. She obtained King Carol's permission to help at Zimnicea, aided by Marie's son, Carol, and by Sister Pucci, a heroic nun from the Order of St. Vincent de Paul. For two long weeks, under the most oppressive conditions in which the intense heat was broken only by torrential rain that turned the ground into muddy trenches, Marie made her rounds from one wooden barrack to another. Oblivious of the danger, the crown princess ignored the strong possibility that she might contract the highly contagious disease. Marie brought gifts, encouragement, and cheer to all—whether the sick or the volunteer doctors and nurses.

Moved by the plight of her soldiers, in awe of the inspiring work done by the volunteers, especially Sister Pucci and her fellow nuns, whom Missy affectionately called *"mes Soeurs Cyclamen"*[46] because their white wimples reminded her of the flowers, the princess came to share in the daily deprivations endured by all. Marie, who had lived a pampered life in the palaces of kings, nibbled rations in the middle of a muddy field surrounded by men dying in horrendous conditions. The experience was a turning point, prompting her to admit that "my life & interests have changed . . . I don't feel myself at all, I am a changed person."[47]

Marie of Romania's valiant efforts in alleviating the suffering of cholera victims at the time of the Second Balkan War were a taste of things to come. In the ensuing conflagration soon to engulf Europe, Marie would again rise to the challenge, and in the process emerge as Romania's warrior queen.

Sixteen

BEFORE THE STORM

THE YEAR 1913 MARKED THE THREE HUNDREDTH ANNIVERSARY OF the reign of the Romanov dynasty in Russia, an occasion that called for special celebrations. But ominous signs emanated from the people during the tsar's tours around the country. Count Kokovtsov saw this, and admitted that "I was impressed by the lack of enthusiasm and smallness of the crowds." Kokovtsov noticed that this happened "everywhere" the tsar went. Only at Kostroma, on the Volga, was there "anything approaching enthusiasm at the sight of the Tsar and his family."[1]

At this time, Tsarina Alexandra reflected on her life and was unhappy with what she found—at forty-one, her childbearing days just about over, her physical strength taxed, and above all, worried to death about her hemophiliac son. Alix was also deeply unpopular in the country she loved. Little wonder then that the tsarina confessed in one of her heart-to-heart talks with Anna Viroubova, comparing her newly married life to her current situation, "I was so happy then, so well and strong. Now I am a wreck."[2] This was not to say that Alix was unhappy with Nicholas or their family. On the contrary, her family remained the one bright spot in a difficult life.

Having spent so much time at their mother's side, by the time they grew into young women, the grand duchesses had inherited a great deal of their mother's generosity of spirit. Alexandra Feodorovna may have gained notoriety for her obsessive belief in Rasputin, her domineering influence over Nicholas II, and her haughtiness, but among the good qualities she possessed which remain largely unknown or ignored was her own sense of giving, seen clearly in her nursing of Russia's wounded and dying soldiers.

Alexandra was not someone who demanded complete undivided attention from everyone around her. She was generous to those she befriended and almost always touched by those who suffered. Like any mother, she wished only to protect, comfort, and nurture those in need. "I like the *internal being,*" she once told a friend, "and that attracts me with great force. As you know, I am of the preacher type. I want to help others in life, to help them to fight their battles and bear their crosses."[3]

Alexandra Feodorovna also reached out to people in need on whom she could exercise Christian charity. Anna Viroubova was one such individual; Alexandra saw her more as a child in need of guidance. Another was Sonia Oberliani, a lady of the court, who though only in her twenties, died after a long and painful illness. The tsarina cared for Sonia for years, even closing her eyes when the young woman died. Alexandra saw these people, who became her friends, not as burdens to be endured but as gifts from the Lord, who had answered her prayers. "That is my daily prayer," she once wrote to a friend, "that God should just send me the sorrowing, and give me the possibility to be a help to them, through His infinite mercy."[4]

Her daughters followed in the tsarina's footsteps. The grand duchesses Olga, Tatiana, Marie, and Anastasia, who collectively gave gifts and signed themselves "OTMA," grew into attractive young women. Often dressed alike, the girls were largely raised by Alexandra herself, with the help of Russian and English nurses. Alexandra chose to keep her girls cloistered from much of the pernicious influence of other members of the Romanov clan, and so they naturally grew to be close to their parents and brother, Alexei. A. A. Mossolov, the head of the Court Chancellery for sixteen years, concluded that the children seemed "entirely satisfied with their life; it hardly occurred to them that they might agitate for other distractions."[5]

Intimates of the imperial family pronounced the girls simple and unaffected beings, who delighted in one another's presence and in making their brother and parents happy. "It is not possible to imagine more charming, pure and high-minded girls," concluded one family friend, the Baroness Sophie Buxhoeveden. "The Empress really brought up her daughters herself, and her work was well done."[6] The two eldest shared one bedroom and the two youngest another. They slept on spartan camp beds in unpretentious rooms decorated in white and green. In time, all four became the best of friends.

As they emerged from adolescence into young adulthood, their own personalities came to the fore. The eldest, Olga Nicolaevna, closest to her father, was one who "took life seriously" and possessed "unusual strength of character."[7] Of medium height, with chestnut-blond hair and blue eyes, Olga had a pleasant face and was "said to be 'incapable of hiding her soul.'"[8]

Tatiana, the second eldest and the tsarina's favorite daughter, taller than Olga, exhibited a more refined, dignified bearing and had "a highly developed sense of her position as the daughter of the Tsar."[9] Sometimes referred to by her siblings as "the Governess" because of her ability to make decisions, Tatiana was "very reserved and quiet, and difficult to govern."[10] She also stood out as the family beauty. Hers was an exotic, almost Eurasian kind of beauty, with her dark hair, pale skin, and alluring gray eyes. For all her reserve, Tatiana Nicolaevna was self-assured and confident, allowing her to relish the attention aroused by her stunning looks.

Marie, the third daughter, was an artist with an inborn talent for drawing. Of the four girls, Marie outdid them all when it came to one outstanding physical trait: her eyes, which were so "magnificent" that they were called "Marie's saucers" by her admiring cousins.[11] A strong and energetic girl, she was also bright, but "the least studious" of the sisters.[12]

The last daughter, brown-haired Anastasia, was the family clown. Forever in the shadow of her more glamorous sisters, constantly battling to shed her baby fat and reach her sisters' height, Anastasia came into her own through her gift of mimicry. Never shy, always game for a good joke, Tsarina Alexandra's youngest daughter was the very antithesis of her reserved mother. An independent spirit, Anastasia "more than her sisters . . . chafed under the narrowness of her environment and used her comic sense in revolt against it."[13]

In temperament, Anastasia most resembled her brother, Alexei. Anastasia's irrepressible high spirits caused ripples of laugher from her audience. Mugging for the camera by pulling outrageous faces was not unusual for this young girl whose name would one day be famous the world over. Years after her death, millions would wonder if a mysterious stranger known as Anna Anderson was, in fact, the Grand Duchess Anastasia. Anderson's case would become a cause célèbre until, after her own death, DNA tests revealed she was not the dead grand duchess after all.

The Tsarevitch Alexei, the sickly heir and only son, quickly became his mother's favorite. For Alexandra, Alexei symbolized everything that was good, since he represented "the direct result of prayer, the Divine condescension of God, the crowning joy of her marriage."[14] Without ignoring her daughters, who remained close to her, Alexandra lavished attention and affection upon the son who was always shadowed by disease and death. And her devotion was reciprocated, as her old friend Lili Dehn saw firsthand when she accompanied the tsarina to Alexei's room to say his bedtime prayers and wish him good night. As Lili, her husband, and Alexandra were preparing to leave the room, Alexei turned off the light over his bed, leaving them all in darkness.

"Why have you done this, Baby?" asked the puzzled tsarina.

"Oh," answered Alexei, "it's only light for me, Mama, when you are here. It's always quite dark when you have gone."[15]

Tsarina Alexandra's family was her pride and joy. With the passage of time, she came to appreciate more fully their presence and the help they increasingly lent to their reclusive and sick mother. Alexandra stressed this in a letter written in 1913: "My children are growing up so fast & are such real little comforters to us—the older ones often replace me at functions & go about a great deal with their father—they are all 5 touching in their care for me—my family life is one blessed ray of sunshine excepting the anxiety for our Boy."[16]

With their eldest children of marriageable age, Tsarina Alexandra of Russia and Crown Princess Marie of Romania found themselves contemplating the possibility that their families might be united through the marriage of Prince Carol and Grand Duchess Olga. Far from merely an attempt to see two reigning houses united through marriage, the hoped-for nuptials were meant to further Russian-Romanian relations.

The scheme to get the young couple to notice each other began in earnest in late 1913, when Nando, Missy, and their son journeyed to Tsarkoe Selo. Prince Carol had already caused his parents anxiety. The boy was deeply scarred by a childhood spent under the watchful eye of King Carol I and Queen Elisabeth, who had succeeded in cunningly transferring his loyalties from his parents and, in particular, from his mother, to the king and queen. This laid the groundwork for Carol's future behavior. Moreover, because Carol was "overcontrolled by the King and overindulged by Carmen Sylva, he received no discipline at all during the brief intervals he spent uninterruptedly with his mother."[17]

Though well meaning, because he truly cared about his namesake, King Carol I failed abysmally as a surrogate parent to his great-nephew. His cruelty in wrenching the boy from his mother was followed by the appointment of a spiteful and malevolent governess. Even more disastrous was the choice of a disturbed male tutor, who appears to have harbored an obsessive desire for the boy. To lure young Carol away from his mother further, the tutor stoked the prince's hatred of Barbo Stirbey, the man who was his mother's great love. The tutor then craftily turned Carol's intense personal animosity for Stirbey toward the political arena as well, "lapping over to include Stirbey's brother-in-law and intimate, the Liberal Prime Minister Ion Bratianu."[18]

It took the concerted efforts of Marie, Ferdinand, and two court doctors to convince King Carol to dismiss the young man's tutor. By the time the king agreed, the damage was already done. The future King of Romania was a deeply flawed human being, who would never be able to escape his sordid upbringing. Ferdinand and Marie had hoped that a proper military training in Germany would help cure their son. The side trip to Russia arose during Carol's military studies.

When the Romanian royal family stayed in Russia, Carol and Olga proved indifferent to each other. As for Missy, she found a subdued imperial family holding court. The crown princess saw that "Tsarkoye Selo was looked upon as a sick man refusing every doctor and every help. And it was always Alix's name which was mentioned as the chief stumbling-block."[19]

It was clear that the two cousins, polar opposites in temperament and views, would not hit it off. According to Missy, Alix

> managed to put an insuperable distance between her world and yours. . . . She made you, in fact, feel an intruding outsider, which is of all sensations the most chilling and uncomfortable.

> When she talked, it was almost in a whisper and hardly moving her lips as though it were too much trouble to pronounce a word aloud. Although there is little difference in age between us, she had a way of making me feel as though I were not even grown up![20]

Nevertheless, when it came time to consider the all-important issue of their children's possible marriage, even Marie conceded that Alexandra proved gracious. After lunch, the two women discussed their children's future. "In all fairness towards Alix," said Marie, "she did not make conversation difficult and talked very quietly, like a reasonable mother." Keeping the interests of their children at heart, both concluded that Carol and Olga "must decide for themselves." Marie was glad that the audience was over. "At that hour we were simply two mothers, mutually relieved that 'we had it out.' I felt that I had done my duty, the rest was in the hands of Fate."[21]

When the time came to take leave of her cousin, Missy found it a relief. "To part from Alix was not difficult, she made leave-taking quite easy," she recalled. "Her life was like a closed chamber, peopled with strange imaginations and still stranger individuals, into which no outsider had entry. No fiery sword at the gates of the Garden of Eden could have been more forbidding than her tight-lipped smile which brought two unwilling dimples to her cheeks, dimples completely out of place in so austere a face. No, it was no grief to leave Alix."[22]

In the end of their stay at Tsarskoe Selo, Carol and Olga had not "discovered" each other. The much-hoped-for attraction between them never materialized. A second opportunity was arranged so that the young people could meet once again. In June 1914, the Russian imperial family paid a courtesy visit to the Romanian royal family at the port of Constanza on the Black Sea. It was a lightning visit, lasting but a day. The hope was that at the end of that fateful day, Carol and Olga might become engaged and, through their marriage, cement Russian-Romanian relations.

꩜

Before setting off for their Romanian visit, the imperial family had settled on a leisurely holiday in the Crimea through April and May. The Crimea, home of the Tartars, had long been a favorite vacation destination for the Romanovs. Located eleven hundred miles south of St. Petersburg, surrounded by the Black Sea, the Crimean peninsula provided a lush paradise for those fortunate enough to spend part of the year in this remote Russian hideaway.

Though instability had raged through their empire for years, though their hold on the throne remained tenuous, the fact that the tsar and tsarina built a large, expensive palace at Livadia, far from the capital, indicates that they had not lost all hope their reign might last for some time. The finished confection, incorporating elements of Byzantine and Gothic styles, took only seventeen months to build. So enchanted were they with Livadia, and so happy were the four girls with their Black Sea retreat, that one family friend said they "spoke of it as their real home."[23] But the time at Livadia would be short-lived, lasting only through the "the autumns of 1911 and 1913 and the springs of 1912 and 1914."[24]

The highlight of the family's stay centered upon the Easter celebrations, which marked the high point in the Orthodox calendar. In celebration of Christ's resurrection, the imperial family were out in force to greet the household, soldiers, and local schoolchildren, often exchanging Easter kisses and eggs.

Alexandra's Easter eggs came from the famed shop of Peter Carl Fabergé. Every year, in a gesture of love, Tsar Nicholas presented his wife with some of the most spectacular works of art ever created by Fabergé. Among the most dazzling was the Imperial Fifteenth-Anniversary Egg (1911), which depicted major events in the tsar's reign and contained portraits of the couple's children, all framed in green enamel; gold and diamonds bordered each portrait.

Despite the relaxing holiday spirit that pervaded their visits to Livadia, duty called. Moved by the need to modernize and improve conditions in the Crimean tubercular facilities, Tsarina Alexandra and her children actively participated in large bazaars and events set up to raise money for the region's patients. One such popular and festive occasion was known as White Flower Day. The grand duchesses, dressed alike in simple white outfits with matching summer hats, along with Alexei in his sailor suit, sold white flowers to the enthusiastic townspeople.

These events afforded a rare opportunity for the people to come close to their imperial family.

Crowds of ordinary Russians flocked to the table where their tsarina presided. Before them were flowers or needlework for sale, often embroidered by Alexandra herself, which were eagerly snatched up. Rarely had Tsarina Alexandra come face to face with so many adoring Russians. Excitement reached fever pitch when the tsarevitch joined his mother at these bazaars. During one held at Yalta, the tsarevitch's impishness made a strong impression on another little boy. Decades later, as an old man of eighty-nine, Dmitri Likhachev delighted in retelling his encounter with Alexei. With a glint in his eye, Likhachev recounted:

> There were round white marquees with stalls and literally two steps away from me was [the] heir. He turned out to be a very jolly boy, a very mischievous boy. He was pulling presents out of large sacks . . . and presenting them to the winners.

> "Oh, I can't find anything, I can't find anything," [said Alexei] searching for [a] gift. But of course, they [the sacks] were filled with gifts. And then he said, "Oh this one is heavy, so heavy. I can't lift it." He wanted to tease an elderly gentleman standing there. And then he pulled out a bottle of champagne![25]

This rare firsthand account from an outsider is a powerful reminder of the joy the tsarevitch must have brought his mother, father, and sisters. All the more wrenching, then, to imagine the tsarina's emotions as she sat by helpless during those agonizing times when Alexei suffered intensely from the hemophilia she had transmitted to him.

On 13 June 1914, Nicholas and Alexandra, with their children in tow, boarded the *Standart* at Yalta, arriving next morning at the Black Sea port of Constanza. Grand Duchess Olga, well aware of the real reason for their trip, confronted Pierre Gilliard. When he indirectly confirmed her suspicions, Olga blurted: "All right! But if I don't wish it, it won't happen. Papa has promised not to make me . . . and I don't want to leave Russia."

"But you could come back as often as you like," Gilliard pointed out.

"I should still be a foreigner in my own country. I'm a Russian, and mean to remain a Russian!"[26] With those words, Olga Nicolaevna sealed her fate. She was indeed to remain a Russian to the bitter end.

At the first sight of the impressive Russian ships gliding majestically on the

Black Sea toward them, Romanians at Constanza were convulsed with excite-ment. The grand duchesses, meanwhile, had taken it upon themselves to ensure that none of them would capture Prince Carol's attentions. During their holiday in the Crimea, the girls had soaked up the sun so that, far from showing off pale creamy complexions, they were, as Marie of Romania noted, "exceedingly sun-burnt." And because they were not dressed in the height of fashion, "the Rou-manians, very critical as to looks and clothes, did not much admire them."[27]

From the moment they arrived at Constanza, the Romanovs were subjected to an intense round of activities. Marie had noticed that Alix was not finding the visit easy. The crown princess saw that the tsarina made "brave efforts to be as gracious as possible, but it did not come easily to her and her face was very flushed."[28]

Marie, on the other hand, relished the imperial visit, as it gave her a chance to play a leading public role, from which she did not shy away, unlike her more re-tiring and dour cousin. Eugene de Schelking, a member of the Russian imperial family's entourage that day, recalled how the crown princess dazzled her way through the visit, impressing him with her immense popularity with the Roman-ian people. "Wherever she appeared," noted an admiring de Schelking, "driv-ing, riding or walking, beautiful . . . smiling and waving her handkerchief in response to the cheers of the people, the enthusiasm of the crowd for their princess was immense."[29]

During the evening banquet, Gilliard noticed that Tatiana, Marie, and Anas-tasia found their sister's predicament highly amusing. The grand duchesses "lost no chances of leaning towards me and indicating their sister with a sly wink."[30]

After the banquet and fireworks display, which the exhausted tsarina did not attend, the *Standart* set sail for Odessa. The trip had been a dismal failure. Carol and Olga did not become engaged. The day after they left, Gilliard heard that there was to be no marriage, correctly concluding: "Olga Nicolaevna had won."[31]

The one-day visit to Romania had taken such a toll on the tsarina that it was "enough to make [her] collapse entirely."[32] Nevertheless, she must have been relieved that Olga did not become engaged. "I think with terror," Alexandra once told Sergei Sazanov, Russia's foreign minister, "that the time draws near when I shall have to part with my daughters," adding, "I could desire nothing better than they should remain in Russia after their marriage." She went on to explain the predicament royal families so often found themselves in: "You know how difficult marriages are in reigning families. I know it by experience, al-though I was never in the position my daughters occupy."[33]

Then Alexandra's mind wandered back to the time when Queen Victoria nearly ordered her to marry Prince Eddy of Wales. "Still, I was once threatened with the danger of marrying without love or even affection, and I vividly remember the torments I endured."³⁴ The tsarina did not want her daughters to undergo the same sort of unpleasantness. Instead, like any loving mother, Alexandra wanted her daughters to enjoy the loving relationship she herself had enjoyed as the cherished wife of Nicholas II. Alexandra had once exclaimed to her husband: "Oh, if only our children could be as happy in their married life."³⁵ All the more reason for her to feel it was her duty "to leave my daughters free to marry according to their inclination. The Emperor will have to decide whether he considers this or that marriage suitable for his daughters, but parental authority must not extend beyond that."³⁶

As Queen of the Hellenes, Sophie continued to take a special interest in promoting one of her favorite causes, replacing the vulnerable forests around Athens and the Greek countryside, always under threat from summer fires and wild animals. Sophie's daughter, Lady Katherine Brandram, later recalled that because the queen "adored trees, she did all the plantations around Athens." But this was not the only major project undertaken by Queen Sophie. "She started the [Society for the] Prevention of Cruelty to Animals in Greece. She was the first foundress." "Very many" soup kitchens were also opened at Sophie's initiative. All these good works—reforestation, soup kitchens, orphanages, hospitals, the training of Greek nurses, animal welfare—were done because quite simply, "she loved the people."³⁷

Sadly for Queen Sophie, as one historian points out, "notwithstanding the good omen of her name, the Greeks would never trust her since she was the Kaiser's sister; they refused to accept that her relations with the Kaiser were often strained and ignored her professions of total loyalty to Greece."³⁸ Queen Sophie also remained loyal to her second home, England. Like her mother before her, Sophie was an ardent admirer of things English, and this admiration extended to the realm of education. Once her marriage was blessed with children, it was not long before Sophie wanted them to have an English education. Lady Katherine remembered that "she talked Greek very well . . . perfectly," in fact, but with her children, the language spoken was "always English."³⁹

Queen Sophie's two younger sons, Alexander and Paul, as well as her daughters Helen and Irene, attended school in England in the summers. So for years, a portion of the crown princess's summers were spent at Eastbourne in Sussex, on the south coast, often with her children in tow. Sophie usually spent her Sundays visiting them. She would come from Windsor and stay the night at the Grand Hotel, Eastbourne's large Victorian hotel, noted for its commanding views of the sea. Soon, however, these visits were set to end.

For Queen Maud, life in Norway before the outbreak of World War I remained relatively calm. Untouched by major internal upheavals, untainted by intrigues or scandal, Maud could count her good fortune in comparison to her other cousins. Only one dispute marred an otherwise tranquil existence. It centered on an ongoing and lingering difference of opinion over Maud's marriage settlement. Queen Maud's trustees, among them Colonel Sir Henry Knollys, her comptroller, worked endlessly for several years on her behalf at the behest of King Haakon. Knollys was an exemplary protector of Maud's interests, never relaxing his role and forever diligently informing King Haakon of the details and fight for the queen's cause.

The dispute concerned sums of money owed to Maud from King Edward VII's marriage settlement for her. The amount of £39,000 was settled on Maud during the king's lifetime; but the sum was later reduced by £9,000, and it was not to be touched until Edward VII died. Maud, however, was to receive interest on the £30,000. After the king died, an additional sum was to be added from the king's estate, all in all amounting to £80,000. There were further details, but it was agreed that the dispute arose over monies owed to Maud because of a badly worded settlement. This legal wrangling lasted for years, stretching into the reign of Maud's brother, George V.

Maud was aware of the negotiations, but was not involved in the dealings on her behalf. In 1907, Haakon admitted that "Maud has nothing to do with the whole matter as she does not know sufficiently [about] business matters to understand. I have explained to her from my point of view, so naturally she thought that was right."[40] Haakon wanted to ensure that Maud was getting her fair share of the marriage settlement, along with the money owed to her from King Edward's will, which in turn would eventually pass on to Crown Prince Olav. When discussions reached uncomfortable levels, King Haakon, in the interest of keeping peace in the family, advised Henry Knollys to "drop the subject."[41]

Knollys was incensed at accusations that Maud might have been a money grubber; in one letter on 5 October 1907 he told King Haakon that "any attempt to suggest that innocent Queen Maud is grasping Queen Maud should invoke the action of the 'Society for the Protection of Women.'" Sir Dighton Probyn, Edward VII's equerry, was among those who sided against Maud in the dispute, earning the enmity of Knollys. Knollys ended his letter to King Haakon with a flourishing devotion to Maud's cause: "I do not think, however, you will object to my holding on silently, but fast as grim death, to my own opinion. If within, say a week hence, I were gasping onto the dregs of my ill spent existence by a bullet from Probyn, to the byestanders [*sic*] curiously scrutinizing my expiring struggles, I would gurgle forth: 'Nine thousand Pounds for Q.Q.Q..u.een M-a-u-d.' "[42]

Knollys's continuing activities on the King and Queen of Norway's behalf elicited the couple's gratitude. As he told King Haakon, "I have been spurred to further and heated energy by the . . . injustice perpetrated against Your Majesties and against Prince Olav whom I have known since he was six days old."[43] At one point, things reached such an acrimonious low that both parties agreed to arbitration. But again, the opposing side threw up obstacles, prompting an exasperated Henry Knollys to record in a memorandum: "To reject a Tribunal of three is to refuse Queen Maud the privilege which the ordinary citizen has as a matter of right."[44] In a précis of a draft letter from King Haakon to King George, the following points, which encapsulate key areas in the long-standing dispute, emerged.

—Case unpleasant to him [King Haakon] & even more to Queen Maud.
—Queen Maud ignorant of business leaves it to him.
—King Haakon deals with the case as his own to prevent ill feeling between King George & Queen Maud. Hopes King George will accept it in most friendly manner.[45]

On 28 June 1914, the Archduke Franz Ferdinand, heir to the Austro-Hungarian throne, and his wife were shot to death at Sarajevo. The impact of the murders ranged from sadness to indifference. In England, King George V and Queen Mary wrote of the "terrible shock" and "horrible tragedy."[46]

Elsewhere, news of the murders was met with a real sense of foreboding. King Constantine of the Hellenes received word of the assassination while at the Olympic Stadium in Athens, where he was watching a sports exhibition. Crumpling the telegram after reading it in disbelief, the king turned to his eldest daughter, Princess Helen. Speaking slowly, he uttered only five words: "Now, we can expect trouble."[47]

PART THREE

On the Throne:

DISASTER AND TRIUMPH (1914–1920)

Seventeen

BALKAN CAULDRON

As soon as Austria-Hungary set its sights on punishing Serbia for the murder of the Archduke Franz Ferdinand and his wife, the diplomatic and military alliances that bound the various monarchical powers to aid one another kicked into effect. With astonishing rapidity, the powers of Europe found themselves ready to wage war. Vienna's determination to make Serbia pay compelled Serbia's ally, Russia, to aid its Slavic neighbor. Imperial Germany bore down upon the Russian Empire for aiming its sights on Austria-Hungary. With Russia under threat from Germany, England and France were not far behind in finding themselves in lockstep with their faraway ally, Russia. It was a fast-moving, complicated chess game involving the Great Powers for the highest stakes.

A flurry of last-minute attempts by King George V, Kaiser Wilhelm II, and Tsar Nicholas II to avert the oncoming onslaught failed. On 1 August 1914, orders for general mobilization were issued in France and Germany. By the next day, the point of no return had been reached, leaving the tsar no choice but to declare war on the Central Powers. In a long telegram to his cousin, George V, Nicholas II wrote with a heavy heart: "In this solemn hour I wish to assure you once more that I have done all in my power to avert war."[1] Three days later, German troops swooped down on Belgium, violating that country's neutrality. Great Britain, a guarantor of Belgium's neutrality, served Germany an ultimatum. The deadline for Germany to answer it passed, as many had expected, in complete silence. George V knew what lay ahead. He held a council on 4 August to declare war against Germany. "It is a terrible catastrophe," recorded the king, "but it is not our fault."[2]

The flames of war had been ignited just six weeks before, at Sarajevo. Now, in the waning weeks of the summer of 1914, the first volleys in a conflict of titanic proportions were fired.

⟨∞∞⟩

The royal families of Europe were to find themselves no less immune than their subjects from the impact of the Great War. This cataclysmic event, which brought devastation to the lives of so many, was to take an especially hard toll on the continent's crowned heads. A veritable Pandora's box had been opened, culminating in the dethronement, in just four years, of the three most illustrious dynasties in Europe: the Habsburgs, the Hohenzollerns, and the Romanovs.

It was the Russian Empire that felt directly and immediately the impact of the war. The other four kingdoms—Norway, Greece, Romania, and Spain—opted to stay neutral when war broke out. Russia could not.

Pierre Gilliard recalled that the tsarina was profoundly affected by the gravity of what was about to erupt. He noted Alexandra's "careworn face," the same "look of suffering" he had often seen when she was at Alexei's bedside. On the day that war broke out, Gilliard observed how during a service at church, the tsarina prayed "fervently . . . as if she wished to banish an evil dream."[3]

When the imperial family returned home after prayers, the tsar met with his foreign minister. Then Nicholas faced his anxious family, "looking very pale," and in a voice "which betrayed his agitation" informed them war was declared. "On learning the news the Czarina began to weep, and the Grand-Duchesses likewise dissolved into tears on seeing their mother's distress."[4]

That day, "a burst of patriotic enthusiasm shook the whole country to its very foundation." Attention naturally focused on St. Petersburg. There, huge crowds thronged to the Winter Palace, where the tsar, tsarina, and their children attended a *Te Deum*. Afterwards, the royal couple made their way past the thousands who had assembled inside the palace. The enthusiasm of those inside matched that of those massed outside. Many "threw themselves on their knees, kissing the hands of their Sovereigns with tears and fervent expressions of loyalty."[5]

When the imperial family made their appearance on the balcony of the Winter Palace, a scene of almost mythic proportions unfolded, as one eyewitness recorded. In a spontaneous gesture of loyalty and affection, "at the foot of the Alexander Column facing the Palace windows all the processionists fell on their knees singing 'Boje Tsaria Khrani' (God save the Tsar) and shouting 'Hurrah!' "[6] And another noted that "To those thousands of men on their knees at that moment, the Tsar was really the autocrat appointed of God, the military, political and religious leader of his people."[7] A reporter covering the event recorded that "it was a sight destined to live long in Russian history."[8] It was a remarkable show of unity, considering Russia in the first six months of 1914 had been wracked by over four thousand strikes involving nearly 1.5 million workers.

Alexandra was well aware of the titanic battle that lay ahead: "It will be a terrible, monstrous struggle; humanity is about to pass through ghastly sufferings." As to the cause, the tsarina was in no doubt. It was all due to Germany; "a changed country," as she described it, "a country I did not know and had never known."[9] She echoed these sentiments to Pierre Gilliard, saying: "I have never liked the Emperor William, if only because he is not sincere. He is vain and has always played the comedian. He was always reproaching me with doing nothing for Germany . . . He will never forgive me this war!"[10]

The tsarina was just as candid with her friend, Anna Viroubova, Looking as if a weight had fallen on her shoulders, the tsarina fell onto a sofa and murmured: "War! And I knew nothing of it. This is the end of everything."[11]

In facing the challenges imposed by the outbreak of a European war, the smaller nations of Norway, Greece, Romania, and Spain embraced neutrality as their best option. But nowhere did this elicit more difficulty and controversy than in Greece. The country's geographic position, coupled with its strategic importance to the opposing sides in what had initially been an Austro-Serbian dispute, meant that the oncoming war was bound to wreak havoc on this part of the Balkans. Moreover, Greece's desire to fulfill its dream of a Greater Greece through territorial aggrandizement—so tantalizingly near to completion with the recent victories in the Balkans—placed an added strain. Together, these internal and external pressures would serve to place the country's king in an unenviable and ultimately untenable position.

At the earliest moments of the unfolding crisis, even before hostilities broke out, the tug-of-war that was to place King Constantine I in the midst of the tussle between the Triple Entente and Central Powers had already begun. The opening salvo was fired by none other than his brother-in-law, Kaiser Wilhelm II. In a telegram despatched to Athens on 31 July 1914, Willy unambiguously threatened Tino: "If contrary to my expectations, you range yourself with our opponents, Greece will be exposed to simultaneous attack by Italy, Bulgaria, and Turkey; and our personal relations will suffer for all time. I have spoken frankly, and I beg you to communicate your decision without delay in the same perfectly frank spirit."[12]

On 2 August, Tino replied: "It seems to me that the interests of Greece demand that she should observe absolute neutrality and the maintenance of the *status quo* in the Balkans as created by the treaty of Bucarest. If we abandoned this point of view Bulgaria would . . . constitute for us an enormous danger." The Kaiser was furious. On the margin of Tino's reply, Willy scribbled ominously: "I shall treat Greece as an enemy if she does not join this alliance immediately." Reading Tino's explanation that Greece should remain neutral, Willy wrote next to it in his characteristic flourishing bold hand: "Impossible."[13]

When it came to King Constantine's determination to keep Bulgaria from pursuing a policy of aggrandizement because this would inevitably lead to greater Russian influence in the Balkans—a view "shared by the whole of my people," according to Constantine—Wilhelm II exploded again in anger at Queen Sophie's husband. In the margin of the despatch, Willy noted simply: "Rubbish."[14]

King Constantine was very angry with the Kaiser, and complained to his brother, Nicholas:

> It is extraordinary. Does he take me for a German? . . . Besides, he seems to forget his geography and that Greece, twenty-four hours after she had declared herself Germany's ally, would be reduced to cinders by the Allied fleets. What folly! Whoever heard of such a thing! No. We are Greeks, and the interest of Greece must come first. For the present, at any rate, it is imperative that we should remain neutral. But as to joining Germany, such an eventuality *is and always will be* an impossibility."[15]

Feeling that neutrality was Greece's only option, the King of the Hellenes chose a path that would incur the wrath of all the powers. Constantine would have to be on his best guard if he was to survive this very complicated and dangerous high-wire act; and accompanying him every step of the way was his wife, Sophie, the Kaiser's own sister.

◦✐✐✐◦

Romania faced the daunting task of having to decide whether to remain neutral or to side openly with either the Allied or the Central Powers. Hemmed in by Russia and Austria-Hungary, and a menacing but as yet uncommitted Bulgaria, should Romania side with the Allies, especially since France, long a country to which many of Romania's elite felt a kinship, was a major partner? This might seem the logical thing to do as the French and Russians were also formally allied to each other. However, Romania and Russia had not been on easy terms ever since the Russo-Turkish War of 1876–1877 ended and Russia was awarded Bessarabia, populated with many Romanians. If Romania threw in its lot with the Central Powers, there was the tantalizing possibility of wrestling Bessarabia from Russia and bringing that rich province under the Romanian yoke. Besides, the strength and efficiency of the German forces seemed invincible, so some thought it was better to ally themselves with the stronger side.

If Romanians were dithering as to which side to take, their king was not. The seventy-five-year-old Carol I may have devoted most of his life to Romania, but his roots were firmly German. For Carol I, aligning Romania with the Central Powers was a given. He could not think otherwise. But there were drawbacks to this alliance. Just as Romania was greedily eyeing Bessarabia, the Romanians of Transylvania lusted for a Greater Romania, which would have to be done at the expense of Austria-Hungary. This presented King Carol with a dilemma because for three decades, the monarch had adhered to a secret treaty aligning Romania with the Triple Alliance (Austria-Hungary, Germany, and Italy). A thorough Hohenzollern, King Carol did everything in his power to ensure that Romania would side with Germany and Austria-Hungary.

Crown Princess Marie, who was raised partly in Coburg, and spoke German, might easily have chosen to side with *der Onkel*'s view about the Central Powers. Her real inclinations, however, lay unequivocally with Great Britain. Not long after war was declared, she became a vocal proponent of the Allied (or Entente) cause consisting of Great Britain, France, and Russia. It was an unpopular stance, given the fact that King Carol and Queen Elisabeth were both Germans and Crown Prince Ferdinand was himself a proud member of the House of Hohenzollern, who saw no reason to deny that Germany was bound to be victorious in the end. A weaker mortal than Marie could have easily felt like a pariah amid blustering German sympathizers; but this granddaughter of Queen Victoria stood her ground.

Thus, within the Romanian royal family, daily life was highly charged. In an instant, rival camps arose. On the one side was King Carol and Queen Elisabeth, both pro-German. To Missy, Uncle Carol's stand was not surprising. But Aunt Elisabeth was something of a revelation. For years, the queen had rarely displayed much affinity for things German and even regularly championed most things English and French. Now Crown Princess Marie found her ever eccentric aunty rediscovering her Germanic heritage "with a vengeance." Queen Elisabeth in her flowing robes told anyone within earshot dramatically that she was *die Rheintochter,* a daughter of the Rhine. For Missy, it was almost comical; for Aunty Elisabeth, "it was all the time *Deutschland über Alles.*"[16]

According to the queen, this dawning of a new Teutonic world order was inevitable. The Germans, insisted Elisabeth, "*must* become lords of the world for the good of humanity." As if that were not enough, she insisted to Missy that "England *had* to fall because her women had become immoral!" That, Marie admitted, was "difficult . . . to swallow."[17] Over and over Missy listened to Elisabeth's litany of outrageous claims. Romania's crown princess found herself biting her tongue in order to prevent a quarrel between herself and the deluded queen.

After war erupted, Romania was compelled to make its stand known to the world. On 3 August 1914, a Crown Council was called by King Carol at Peles Castle, which he himself had built and infused with so many Germanic influences. At the meeting, the king pronounced that he was ready to adhere to Romania's secret alliance with the Central Powers; his ministers, though, were not. The king was devastated. Something died inside him the day his ministers sided against him.

Queen Elisabeth interpreted the ministers' action as a slap in the face and was appalled. She proceeded to harangue Missy and Nando constantly. This certainly grated on Marie's nerves, but she felt particular pity for Carol I. The poor king, already reeling from Romania's rejection of his desire to side with Germany, shriveled under the verbal assaults from his wife. Carmen Sylva challenged the king to pack his bags and leave an ungrateful country.

Marie was also sincerely saddened by the new gulf reemerging between herself and King Carol. After two decades spent deciphering Carol I, the crown princess had finally come to understand him. And he, in turn, had come to appreciate Missy's growing maturity and the fact that the popular princess was an asset to the royal family. Now, in the twilight of his life, the war threatened to wreck the peaceful co-existence both had come to appreciate.

As for Crown Prince Ferdinand, though he remained characteristically mute on the subject, even to his wife, there was little doubt that like his uncle and aunt, he too was more naturally inclined to side with their pro-German views. Thus Missy found herself alone among the royal family in espousing the Entente cause.

As for the flighty Queen Elisabeth, overcome by the death and violence engulfing Europe, she announced at lunch one day that maybe it would be best if the whole family were to hold hands and "in a mighty circle sail up to Heaven, away from the miseries of this darkened sphere." King Carol, long accustomed to his wife's unstable tirades, thought that even for her this was going too far. *"Das ist Unsinn, Elisabeth,"*[18] he answered sharply ("That is nonsense"). As far as he was concerned, King Carol wanted to stay on earth and see the war's outcome. But the king would not get his wish.

Ill from kidney disease, the battered king was soon at death's door. The final breaking point occurred when he heard of the outcome of the Battle of the Marne. A German victory on the Western Front had been dramatically halted by the French. The defeat surprised the king, this most die-hard of supporters of German omnipotence. Not long afterwards, on 9 October, King Carol I died in his sleep at Peles Castle, clasped in his wife's arms.

That night, Marie and Ferdinand were away from the castle. Nando was at their home, Cotroceni, near Bucharest, while Missy was spending the night at Mogosoaia, the sprawling home of her friend, the author Marthe Bibesco. Early on the morning of 10 October, Marie was awakened to take an urgent telephone call. Prince Barbo Stirbey was calling to tell his beloved Missy that King Carol had died. Nando automatically ascended the throne, making Missy Queen of Romania.

When this new chapter in her life opened, Marie of Romania was not inhibited by any sense of foreboding. On the contrary, as she watched her husband swear an oath before Parliament on the morning of his accession, she was strengthened in her resolve when she heard the people shout out: *"Regina Maria!"* They were voices raised in hope in this hour of darkness for Romania. Their new queen represented their future. In her memoirs, Marie wrote of that moment: "I knew that I had won, that the stranger, the girl who had come from over the seas, was a stranger no more; I was theirs with every drop of my blood!"[19]

The Tsarina Alexandra of Russia, equally devoted to her adopted country, redoubled her quest to bolster up Nicholas II, who was more than ever burdened with responsibilities as Russia began enduring setbacks in the battlefield. By April 1915, the tsarist armies were retreating on the Eastern Front. Soon, they were forced to evacuate Warsaw, and by August, Russia had ceded all of its Polish territories and incurred the staggering loss of 3 million men. Russia's ill-prepared war machine was in large part to blame for the losses. When Russia went to war in 1914, as one historian has noted, there were "a million fewer rifles in her arsenals than the number of men who were mobilized, and the same arsenals proved to be almost 600 million rounds of rifle ammunition short. There was only about one machine gun for every six hundred infantry . . . [and] the entire Russian army had only 60 batteries of heavy artillery with which to face the Austrians and Germans, while the Germans alone had 381 to direct against the Russians."[20]

Rasputin was among those against war. He sent the tsar a warning: "Let Papa not plan war for with war will come the end of Russia and yourselves and you will lose to the last man."[21] Anna Viroubova delivered the message. So incensed was the tsar at Rasputin's insolence that he tore up the telegram in front of her.

Once Rasputin was back in the capital, his reputation with the tsarina was soon permanently sealed. For another one of those astonishing "miracles" took place, and the recipient this time of the *staretz*'s incredible power would be none other than the tsarina's faithful friend, Anna. Early in 1915, Anna was severely injured in a train crash not far from Tsarskoe Selo. Trapped under hunks of bent metal, Anna's legs were damaged, her spine seriously injured, her head nearly crushed by the impact, compelling doctors to leave her for dead. They obviously had not reckoned with Rasputin the miracleworker. He flew to Anna's side, finding the tsar and tsarina already there. The unkempt *staretz* then cried out: "Annushka! Look at me!" As she opened her eyes, Anna recognized Rasputin, her saviour, praying for her life, and answered: "Grigory. Thank God. It's you." His deed done, Rasputin "staggered from the room and fell into a faint."[22] The miracle man had predicted that Anna would recover but become a cripple. Rasputin was proven correct; after her recovery, Anna relied on crutches and a wheelchair to get around.

Witnessing another of Rasputin's amazing "miracles" was the last straw for the tsarina. In no time, Alexandra became consumed with a need to seek Rasputin's counsel on numerous matters. The "mad monk" had managed to convince Alexandra of his indispensability to her, her son, the tsar, and Russia.

In truth, Rasputin dabbled in a form of emotional blackmail. Well aware of the hold he had over the tsarina because of his inexplicable ability to "cure" her precious son, Rasputin had found a foolproof way of keeping himself in Alexandra Feodorovna's good favors. The *staretz* once said to a Russian diplomat: "Many tales are told of the Empress and me. I know this. It is infamous. Yesterday I went to see her. The poor little thing; she too is in need of being able to speak frankly with some one. She suffers much. I console her. I talk to her of God, and of us peasants and she becomes calm. Ah! It is but yesterday she went to sleep on my shoulder."[23] Always astute in his dealings with the tsarina, Rasputin played on her fears when he pronounced: "Remember that I need neither the Emperor nor yourself. If you abandon me to my enemies it will not worry me. I'm quite able to cope with them. The demons themselves are helpless against me. . . . But neither the Emperor nor you can do without *me*. If I am not there to protect you, your son will come to harm!"[24]

Seeing that Rasputin was rarely wrong, Alexandra urged the tsar to trust their friend completely. So convinced was she that Rasputin was truly special that Alix even gave Nicky the *staretz*'s comb, urging him to comb his hair with it before making difficult decisions.

Because of the fighting, Nicholas II had to visit his troops and Army Headquarters. This meant that more and more Alexandra found herself governing in her husband's absence. The tsarina never hid her opinions from Nicholas about government—or anything else for that matter. With each passing month, whenever the couple was separated, she plied him with letters full of news, loving endearments, encouraging words, and, of course, opinions on the ever-changing ministry. For a mad game of Musical Chairs had set in, ministers in the upper echelons of government coming and going with astonishing rapidity. The staggering losses in men at the front, the instability in the government with Alexandra at the helm, and the fact that Rasputin still held sway, all added up to one thing: Russia's descent into chaos had begun in earnest.

∽‴⁋

The issue of Romania's neutrality was uppermost in people's minds at the accession of the new sovereigns. The nation's politicians sensed that Romanians were tilting toward joining the Allied cause. This was based primarily on the people's desire to unite with their fellow Romanians in Transylvania, creating a Greater Romania. The thought of crossing the snow-capped Carpathian Mountains and seizing that coveted land from the Hungarians was proving more and more tempting. No one understood this aspiration better than the country's prime minister, Ion Bratianu, head of the country's Liberal Party.

Bratianu was a leading proponent of the concept of a Greater Romania. If war war declared against the Habsburg Empire, this cherished dream just might come true. With his mind made up, the prime minister set about convincing King Ferdinand that the sole alternative for Romania was to side with the Entente cause and to pit its weapons against Germany and Austria-Hungary. It was a task easier said than done. Nando's greatest nightmare had actually come to pass: at the very moment of his accession, the king was being pressured to bring his country into war against his own fatherland.

∽‴⁋

Queen Sophie's husband was faced with an equally daunting dilemma in Athens. The Triple Entente Powers were no less determined to see to it that Greece sided with them. And in total agreement with the powers was Eleutherios Venizelos, the prime minister.

The ambitious and wily politician, long fired with the idea of forging a Greater Greece through territorial aggrandizement, now saw an opportunity for his country to rise to new heights. What Venizelos did not realize was that he would have to reckon with his king's more realistic assessment of Greece's position in the increasingly complex and volatile Balkans. A great schism was set to erupt in Greece.

France now became the ringleader in an ugly campaign to get Greece to throw in its lot with the Entente Powers, ignoring the dangers around it. Russia, meanwhile, was struggling with its own set of problems, and in desperate need of help from its allies. So a plan was created whereby the Entente would come to the aid of the far-flung empire.

The Allies proceeded to put into action a plan to fight in Asia Minor and so open up communications with Russia. At the same time, in attacking the Central Powers in Asia Minor, it was hoped to deal them a blow by opening up another front and forcing Turkey to do battle. King Constantine was respectful of Germany's military might, but he also knew that if Greece threw in its lot with Germany, it would be destroyed by the Allied navies in the Mediterranean. Even Queen Marie of Romania, the most consistent and staunchest of pro-Entente supporters, understood the reality of German military strength and respected Germany's war machine. During an audience with the queen in the middle of World War I, a Russian diplomat heard her opinion. " 'They are very strong,' she said again and again, in speaking of the Central Powers."[25] Thus, King Constantine, the professional soldier, above all a realist, refused to fall for the dangerous dreams of territorial aggrandizement that kept Venizelos spellbound and affected his pursuit of Greek foreign policy.

Constantine denied Greek help to an Allied venture he saw as doomed to fail. The king feared too that if he committed Greek troops to the campaign, it would tempt Bulgaria to attack Greece. But above all, Constantine was well aware that the Allies' plans for an attack in the Dardanelles was too risky because of their refusal to contemplate committing to a massive attack by land as well as by sea. The king was right. Before the largely naval campaign was over, the Allies sent matériel and half a million soldiers to Gallipoli, of which nearly 150,000 would become casualties. This disaster became known as the infamous Dardanelles or Gallipoli Campaign and would serve as a blot on the military operations of the Entente Powers.

Constantine not only incurred the anger of the Allies for his lack of support in the Gallipoli invasion; he also incurred the wrath of Venizelos. The furious prime minister resigned in March 1915. He was later reelected in June of that year but was dismissed four months afterwards by Constantine when Allied troops began pouring into Salonika.

⚬〜〜〜⚬

The acute internal struggle that Nando was waging, which pitted his natural inclination to side with his Teutonic brothers versus his duty toward Romania, had a devastating effect on the king. Queen Marie was attuned to her husband's plight and her heart went out to him. Like King Carol before him, Ferdinand's loyalty to the House of Hohenzollern was sincere and strong. Now he was being asked to forget his roots, his membership in a proud dynasty, and to strike out alone for Romania's sake. If Ferdinand made the wrong call, the consequences for himself and the country were incalculable. Marie was well aware of the stakes involved and understood that her husband was now having to make the most agonizing decision of his life.

Ferdinand, though long browbeaten by King Carol, was by no means a fool. On the contrary, he was a man of splendid intelligence, whose tragedy lay in the fact that he was hampered by his own timidity and an excessive sense of humility. An accomplished linguist, he was easily at home in German, English, Romanian, French, Russian, Greek, and Hebrew. This fluency in languages allowed the king to keep his ministers guessing when, during those all-important meetings on foreign policy, he wrote the points "in German, using the old Cyrillic alphabet, and spoke them in French or Romanian."[26] Ferdinand's interests ranged from archeology to literature and history. Botany was a particular passion, with the king surpassing any professor's knowledge on the subject. But many people were unaware just how intelligent Ferdinand was. The antithesis of the blustering Kaiser Wilhelm, King Ferdinand never wanted to flaunt his far-reaching knowledge. Even after he ascended the throne, he continued to assume a humble, sometimes even bumbling facade. It was up to his wife, Missy, to see to it that Ferdinand played the king and was not consumed by his own timidity. Soon after their ascension to the throne, the queen gave Ferdinand a golden bowl with the inscription: "Tomorrow may be thine if thy hand be strong enough to grasp it."[27]

Many of Ferdinand and Marie's subjects already sensed that much of their hope lay with their new queen. And Marie, instinctively attuned to the pulse of her countrymen, knew this. Romania's leading politicians were ready to exploit the obvious advantage they had in the queen. Like a gift from the gods, Marie, it seemed, had been sent to help bolster her husband and secure the nation's path to victory. The groundwork was laid for a campaign to get Ferdinand to place his country firmly in the Entente's camp. And the person largely responsible for this onerous task was none other than the woman on whom the king leaned so heavily for support.

With the queen eager to get her country to side with the Entente, Prime Minister Bratianu and a second important leader of Romania's Liberal Party were prepared to assist Marie in pleading their case before the king. By a curious twist of fate that second Liberal leader was none other than Missy's longtime flame, Prince Barbo Stirbey, Bratianu's brother-in-law. Slowly, the trio chipped away at King Ferdinand's defenses, carefully explaining the necessity for Romania to abandon neutrality and side with Britain, France, and Russia. Ferdinand listened, quietly weighing in his analytical mind all the arguments placed before him.

As the war progressed, the pressure exerted on Greece by the Allied and Central Powers grew in intensity, making Constantine and Sophie's predicament more treacherous. Constantine I's refusal to join the Allied cause by keeping Greece neutral immediately elicited whispers that he was pro-German. Afer all, had he not been caught wearing a German field marshal's uniform, complete with baton, when visiting his wife's brother, the Kaiser, not that long ago? And what of the queen herself? She was even more pro-German, so the rumors went, than King Constantine. The vicious rumors surrounding Queen Sophie became uglier right around the time that Venizelos and the king came to blows over the prime minister's insistence on joining the Dardanelles Campaign.

Exhausted by the unrelenting pressure, Tino fell ill in the summer of 1915. In no time, pneumonia set in. For the next several weeks, the king's condition worsened. Two of his ribs were removed. But no sooner had this occurred than blood poisoning seeped through his body. The king was near death. In the meantime, stories were flying about that what had actually happened to Constantine was not pneumonia or pleurisy compounded by blood poisoning; instead, the queen had stabbed her husband in the back in the middle of a violent argument because he could not be persuaded to get Greece to side with Germany. It was a cruel and false story. Sophie nursed the king with devotion. What these stories did mean, however, was that Sophie was eyed with deep suspicion by some. The cruel rumors also meant that Sophie was seen by the dynasty's enemies as a perfect target in their quest to bring Greece's House of Glucksburg to its knees.

When Constantine's condition became critical, a miraculous icon bearing the image of the Madonna and Child was requested to be brought before him. When the icon arrived at the palace, hoards of people outside knelt in silence, asking God to heal their king. Inside, Constantine prayed before the holy image and then lapsed into unconsciousness. Within a week, the crisis passed. King Constantine had been spared. Queen Sophie was so moved by the apparent miracle that she chose to donate a superb sapphire for the icon.

After this brush with death, Sophie's husband was never the same vigorous man. In order to let the poison out of his body, a small incision was made in the king's chest, from which fluid could escape. The wound always needed constant attention. But the king's serious illness did not lead to a cessation in the ugly rumors spread about the couple's supposed pro-German sympathies.

For those who cared to believe that the king and queen were anti-Entente and pro-German, alleged proof came by way of the fact that a number of their staff—men such as Ioannis Metaxas, the king's chief of staff—received their training and education in Germany. Then there was Constantine himself, who had received his education at the Military Academy in Berlin.

As for Queen Sophie, her chamberlain, John Theotokis, and his brother, Nicholas (the Greek minister in Berlin), were supposed to be in league with the queen, along with Baron Schenk (responsible for German intelligence in Athens), in trying to deliver Greece to Germany. One thing was certain: within Greece, the Germans were busy setting up a network to cultivate (usually by means of bribery) a pro-German press and propaganda machine. Athens at the time was described by Prince Nicholas as being "a hotbed of political intrigue, of international espionage and counter-espionage."[28]

Abroad, the foreign press were soon united in leveling accusations against the Greek monarchs. Again, the French led the way. One French newspaper "swore that a workshop at Phalerum, the pleasure beach of Athens and the constant resort of strollers, had set up a diabolical subterranean and sub-aqueous contrivance by which submarines could arrive in full daylight and, while submerged, attach themselves, 500 metres from the shore, to a pipe which yielded them huge quantities of oil. . . . Queen Sophia (it was gravely added) often came to Phalerum 'about teatime' to watch this operation." And as for Kaiser Wilhelm's villa at Corfu, the Achilleion, that was "no better than a formidable submarine base, which had been laid out in time of peace."[29] Such was some of the more outlandish slander to which Sophie was subjected abroad. Conveniently forgotten were her uneasy relations with the Kaiser, who had so publicly humiliated her and banned her from setting foot in Germany when Sophie defied him and converted to Orthodoxy.

It was Queen Sophie's great tragedy that she was "swept away" in what has been described as a "flood of vituperation." The parallels between Sophie and Tsarina Alexandra of Russia were not hard to miss. For these two German-born consorts, their close connection to Queen Victoria and their personal inclinations toward Great Britain were completely forgotten. It has been written that Queen Sophie "was presented as a fanatically pro-German, hard-hearted virago, determined to force her weak-willed husband into fighting for the Kaiser."[30] Those same words could just as easily describe how Tsarina Alexandra was being depicted by her enemies during World War I.

ᕗᴍᴍᴐ

In Romania, Queen Elisabeth had moved to the bishop's residence at Curtea de Arges in order to be near the burial site of Carol I. It was a logical move for a woman who believed in communicating with the dead. Though she continued to exasperate Queen Marie because of her staunch German sympathies and her peculiar rants about frequent talks with the Archangel Raphael, Marie treated the widowed Carmen Sylva with kindness and understanding. In a gesture of peace and magnanimity, she sought to heal the wounds that had set the two women at loggerheads with each other—wounds that were largely of Carmen Sylva's making. Queen Elisabeth's peaceful widowhood was short-lived. She died in early March 1916 from pneumonia caught while taking in the freezing cold air, a habit of the old queen because she feared being suffocated. She was buried next to Carol I.

⁍

Of the Entente Powers, France was the ringleader in the campaign to bring Constantine and his dynasty to its knees. For October 1915 marked "the beginning of French preeminence in Greek affairs."[31] By this time, stories of Constantine and Sophie's alleged pro-German stance had become well established. When M. Denys Cochin, a French minister of state, visited the king, Constantine declared his position emphatically: "I am not a German . . . I am Greek and nothing but Greek; I have no other care but for the interests of my people, and I wish to spare them, as far as possible, the evils of war. That is the whole secret of my policy."[32] The king was also beside himself over French policy in Greece, warning the British to watch out for them in this part of Europe. The British military attaché in Athens informed London of the king's "fluent tirade against the French notably against the French Minister," and that he had declared that "they were leading us [the British] by the nose."[33] But no amount of protestation on King Constantine's part seemed to have the desired effect.

As ardent Anglophiles, it must have brought some measure of comfort to Sophie and Constantine to find that they had among their staunchest supporters two British military men, one in the Royal Navy and the other in the British Army. Admiral Mark Kerr had lived for some time in Greece and was naval adviser to King Constantine and commander in chief of the Royal Hellenic Navy, thus giving Kerr ample opportunity to come to know the Greek royal family, whom he viewed with admiration. An affable-looking man, with a receding hairline and an engaging smile, Kerr came to champion King Constantine, never deviating despite the pummeling the king's reputation was to take in the ensuing years.

Admiral Kerr concluded that "the characters of King Constantine and Mr. Venizelos were 'as far as the poles asunder.'" Although the king had "a great strategic and tactical brain for war" and was also "truthful to the last degree and loathed intrigue," his main weakness lay in the fact that he was "no diplomat."[34] Venizelos, on the other hand, though "a great orator with a great deal of personal magnetism," failed Kerr's character test because he was "a born intriguer and gave one the impression that he preferred to get his way by adroitness rather than by the open methods which his King invariably used." Though to his credit the Cretan lawyer "was not to be bribed by money," he suffered from a "jealousy that almost amounted to madness"; his "weakness lay in his overweening vanity. He wished to go down in history as the re-creator of the old Greek empire, and no one should be associated with his great work but himself." Admiral Kerr also found Venizelos to lack any sympathy for the rank and file, while Constantine thought much about them, "perhaps even more, than he did about the upper classes."[35]

The other great supporter of the beleaguered king was none other than the distinguished Lord Kitchener, famed for his battlefield exploits in Africa. As secretary of state for war, Kitchener visited Athens in the fall of 1915 to assess the deteriorating situation there. The tall, commanding soldier quickly sympathized with King Constantine. The two men, both professional soldiers, took to each other instinctively. The king liked Kitchener's honest and open approach to Greece's predicament, which came as a refreshing change from the duplicity of the diplomats and politicians in Athens. When Constantine asked Kitchener "if he did not agree with me that Greece's condition was extremely precarious with nearly a million Germans waiting to fall upon us if we took the field against them," Kitchener acquiesced, telling the king that "under the circumstances neutrality was the attitude best suited" to Greece's interests, "while those of the Allied Powers would be well served by the continuance of Greece's benevolent neutrality."[36]

Sadly for Constantine and Sophie, Kitchener died within months of his visit to Athens. As one historian points out, "Had Kitchener not been lost at sea in July 1916, and had there been another point of view to counter that of David Lloyd George, an ardent admirer of Venizelos and Kitchener's successor as War Minister, the King's fate might have been a happier one"[37]—and by extension, Queen Sophie's, too. But thanks to Lloyd George's antipathy for Constantine, and France's lead in the campaign to vilify the Greek royal family and their supporters, Constantine and Sophie's fate now assumed the dimensions of a Greek tragedy.

൦ⱳⱳ൦

"I am an English woman. When Roumania comes into this war, there is but one side to choose," declared Marie of Romania.[38] Marie's steady and unrelenting call to place their country firmly on the Allied side was making an impact on Ferdinand. He had already warned the Kaiser that he was bound, as King of Romania, to put his country's interests before any personal inclinations he might have for the German fatherland. Undeterred by his Hohenzollern cousin's musings about duty and sacrifice, the Kaiser proceeded to send "snorting telegrams," as Queen Marie described them, to Bucharest. His messages, which were uncoded and therefore open for all to see, bristled with threats designed to intimidate both his Romanian and Greek cousins. Among those telegrams going through Bucharest was one addressed to Willy's sister, Sophie. According to Queen Marie, it "contained loud threats against any who would dare oppose his victorious armies and his *Deutscher Gott.*"[39] The Kaiser was clearly getting in over his head in the tug-of-war with the Allies over the Balkans. At the Berlin court, eyebrows were raised. Despite being long accustomed to their blustering sovereign, members of his entourage were shocked to find that the Kaiser "even wondered whether Romania's hesitation in joining the Central Powers was due to the fact that he had not been pleasanter to Queen Marie during her pre-war visit to Berlin."[40] Wilhelm had obviously recognized Marie's preeminent role in getting King Ferdinand to tilt toward the Entente side. The Kaiser's annoyance with the Romanian queen had prompted him in 1915 to complain that his cousin Missy in Bucharest was nothing but a "meddlesome little flirt."[41]

Marie's "unshakable belief in England," plus her embrace of "the national ideal of unity of all the Roumanians," combined to strengthen her resolve. When Count Ottokar Czernin, the Austro-Hungarian minister to Romania, pressured her to get Romania to side with the Central Powers, Marie surprised him. In spite of an audience in which Marie said Czernin was "making me go through hell," she stood firm. "I should die of grief if Roumania were to go to war against England," snapped the defiant queen.[42]

For some time, Marie had carefully handled her husband, coaxing him gently toward the Allied cause. They went for drives through the beautiful Romanian countryside, to places that had special meaning to them when first discovered as a young couple. Missy's efforts paid off when, at the end of August 1916, the moment of truth arrived. King Ferdinand summoned the Crown Council and stated his desire to have Romania enter the war on the side of the Triple Entente. An overwhelming majority of the ministers sided with their sovereign. The country had abandoned neutrality and was now at war against Germany and Austria-Hungary.

The queen, who had been waiting anxiously outside the room, sought out her husband at the end of the momentous meeting. She needed only to glance at Ferdinand's face to see the agony he had just endured. Slipping her hand into his in a gesture of love and support, Queen Marie announced to the assembled ministers: "Gentlemen, no one of you realizes so well as I what this has cost him. I am proud of him. And Roumania should be."[43] To George V, Marie wrote in detail of the tense moment: "I always knew that it would end like that. Indeed I was confident that it would not end otherwise, but the struggles were hard and poor Nando has made a tremendous sacrifice—the greatest that can be asked of a King and a man, to go against his own brothers, again [*sic*] the country he was born in, that he loved." Then, on a bittersweet note, mingled with hope, Missy continued to her beloved cousin, "we are separated from England by the whole of Europe, yet we feel that England can be our great support and it is England that we trust. I never imagined that it would be the lot of our generation, we who are children together, to see this great war and in a way to have to remodel the face of Europe."[44]

The House of Hohenzollern exacted its revenge on Ferdinand for what it saw as his traitorous action. Princess Marthe Bibesco wrote that "They killed him genealogically. His name was erased from the great book of the Hohenzollerns. At Sigmaringen they went into mourning for him as if he were dead. The head of his house, William II, King of Prussia, Emperor of Germany, annihilated him by telegraph. He took from him the order of the House of the Hohenzollerns which was equivalent to civil death."[45]

Eighteen

"HOLD MY HAND THAT I MAY HAVE COURAGE"

RESUPPLYING RUSSIA PROVED DIFFICULT, ESPECIALLY FROM THE South, owing to the fact that Turkey and Bulgaria joined the Central Powers, thus making them enemies of Russia. The Allies' failure to secure the Dardanelles plus the German blockade of the Baltic Sea meant that Russia was further cut off from help from the West, resulting in the virtual isolation of the empire. Hampered by insufficient weapons and supplies and poor food rations, Russia's armies fought on, but the losses sustained by the empire were enormous. By August 1915, a staggering 450,000 Russians a month were dying at the front. This brought the total loss of life since the previous year to 1.5 million men. For the year 1915 alone, an astounding 2 million men were captured, wounded, or killed, and the whole Russian front had for all intents and purposes crumbled.

With 15 million mobilized to fight, the strain on the Russian economy was huge. Workers for the farms and factories were syphoned off to march to war. This resulted in a decrease in production, and shortages of goods, food, and fuel. Money became scarce. Soon, troubles came simmering to the surface. Beside problems with the outcome of the war itself, there were internal economic problems that spelled political trouble. With Russian fathers, brothers, and sons dying in the slaughter at the Eastern Front, their families back home faced all kinds of hardships as they struggled to find food for the table.

Writing in early 1915, Tsarina Alexandra expressed her conflicting emotions about the war to the Bishop of Ripon: "We can only trust & pray that this terrible war may soon come to an end—The suffering around is too intense. You, who know all the members of our family so very well, can understand what we go through—relations on all sides, one against the other." Alexandra left her most scathing words for the country she felt most responsible for the war: "And the gross disappointment of seeing a country morally sinking with such depths, as Germany has—is bitter to behold."[1]

For Nicholas II, the dramatic setbacks on the front were uppermost in his mind. The losses spurred the tsar to dismiss the Grand Duke Nicholas (Nikolasha) as the Russian Army's supreme commander. In his stead, Nicholas II unwisely took personal command of his armies—a huge gamble and one he could ill afford to lose. For a tsar whose hold on the throne was precarious, taking over as generalissimo was the ultimate risk. But the tsarina greeted Nikolasha's dismissal with relief. For months she had been haranguing her husband to sack the general whose hatred of Rasputin knew no bounds.

Taking over as commander in chief meant that Nicholas needed to be at Army Headquarters (*Stavka*) at Mogilev, far from St. Petersburg. This would literally cut the tsar off from his capital, thus virtually ensuring that he became even more out of touch with his ministers.

The tsar proved ineffectual in running a Russia in crisis, and with each passing day he and his government bore the brunt of an increasingly discontented people. But where the tsarina was concerned, the anger against her grew by leaps and bounds. Because Alexandra was increasingly looked upon as a traitorous foreigner, ever ready to deliver Russia into enemy hands with the connivance of her camarilla, headed by the hated Rasputin, she reaped the ill will of a growing number of Russians. Like a slow-growing bacillus that thrives undetected, the people's hatred of Alexandra Feodorovna festered unchecked. So unhappy were people with their tsarina that rumors of plots against her were rampant. One of Nicholas II's uncles, the Grand Duke Paul, admitted to Maurice Paléologue that there was talk of locking away Tsarina Alexandra in a convent in Siberia or the Urals—a favorite method in the past for dealing with traitorous or overambitious female royals. Paléologue replied that the tsar would never allow it. And, the ambassador continued, if things indeed had degenerated to such an extent, then the only alternative was revolution—though what kind of new government might take the place of tsarism was inconceivable since ignorance, corruption, and anarchism were rampant in Russia. After pacing the room with "eyes flashing horror," the grand duke responded presciently: "If revolution breaks out, its barbarity will exceed anything ever known. . . . It will be hellish. . . . Russia won't survive it!"[2]

Tsarina Alexandra reluctantly agreed with Nicholas to let Alexei stay with him at *Stavka* in order to learn about command. Her fears proved correct when, in 1915, Alexei suffered a serious hemophiliac attack and was near death. But the frantic tsarina was reassured when she heard from Rasputin; for the *staretz* had uttered the most comforting words Alix could have hoped for: "Thanks be to God! He has given me your son's life once more."[3] Alexei did indeed survive this latest dance with death. For the tsarina, Rasputin had delivered yet another miracle.

⌒◦⌒

Having entered the war, Romania found that the cost of siding with the Allies was dear. Bearing down on the country was a quadruple onslaught from the German and Austro-Hungarian armies along with Bulgarians and Turks. When the Romanian troops tried to make headway into Transylvania, they fell back after two weeks of fighting. Dreams of a Greater Romania were shattered. Russia was not keen on coming to the aid of its ally once the pro-German Boris Stürmer ran the Russian Foreign Ministry; and neither were the French much help. Queen Marie was moved to make desperate pleas to George V and Nicholas II for help as the German forces tightened their grip: to the north were Erich von Falkenhayn's troops and to the south were those of Field Marshal August von Mackensen. In the end, the much-hoped-for rescue through the famed Brusilov offensive did not materialize. The Germans managed to check the Russian advance through their superior tactical skill and weaponry.

On the first day alone of a daylight bombing raid on Bucharest, some four hundred people were killed or wounded. One resident marveled at the audacity of the enemy fighters, describing how "the planes fly very low—they have no fear of the guns here, evidently."[4] Another depicted the brutal German onslaught as a horrifying experience, describing "puddles or streams of blood on the streets."[5] The royal family—with the exception of the king and crown prince, who went to Army Headquarters—were sequestered at Buftea, Prince Stirbey's home an hour away from Bucharest.

From there, Marie ventured off to hospitals to tend to the wounded and dying. Everywhere she went, she was touched by the uncomplaining soldiers, ordinary Romanians. Charles Vopicka, the American ambassador to Romania, accompanied the queen during a tour of one hospital set up in the Royal Palace. He followed Queen Marie from room to room, watching her as she handed out cigarettes, candy, or cigars from a tray carried by her younger son, Nicolas. To Vopicka, she seemed "utterly downcast, and the tears continually rolled down her cheeks." A good deal of this sadness came from the terrifying thought, as she said, that "if the Germans captured Bucharest, these wounded soldiers; who would be unable to leave, would meet their death."[6]

Besides trying to keep herself from falling into depression, Marie was worried that King Ferdinand might falter. The thought that Nando might not live up to his role as king exasperated Missy, who confided to her diary that "the King needs to throw off certain old bonds, old habits, all those restrictions which stifle free action. Oh! Sometimes I do mind being a woman."[7]

The one person throughout these harrowing times she could rely on completely was Barbo Stirbey, who tutored the queen in the intricacies of international relations and war strategy. Every day, they met at Buftea, often going off for rides on Stirbey's sprawling estate. King Ferdinand and Nadèje Stirbey made no move to break up the closeness of their respective spouses. Perhaps they realized that Marie and Barbo made a formidable team for Romania, and in a time of war, self-preservation mattered more than any jealousies over their relationship.

For the queen, already immersed in fear and uncertainty, October 1916 proved a particularly devastating month. Her youngest child, three-year-old Prince Mircea, fell ill at Buftea with typhoid fever. This precocious bundle of joy, so full of life, had suddenly become desperately ill. Within days, death was imminent. On 29 October, Marie's forty-first birthday, Mircea's final struggle began. The tiny youngster screamed and gnashed his teeth. But in this, her darkest hour, Marie never forgot others or her duties as Queen of Romania. On All Souls Day, Mircea's suffering ended. Marie held his small hand in hers as her boy breathed his last. The devastated mother placed him in a little coffin, with a rich cloth of gold and red brocade, and saw him buried in the chapel at Cotroceni Palace.

Barbo Stirbey had shared Marie's unbearable grief at Mircea's death. Together, they had fought to persuade Ferdinand to fight against Germany; together, they continued to fight for Romania; and now they were united in their mutual sorrow over the passing of the young prince, who was perhaps fathered by Barbo. Barbo's "constant presence" in the sickroom and the fact that Marie "often spoke with pride of [the child's] dark-brown eyes" while "all the other children were blue-eyed, like Ferdinand and herself," makes it seem likely that Barbo was indeed the father.[8]

No sooner had Marie buried her son than the Germans were on Bucharest's doorstep. The situation was so serious that at the end of November, "the panic," according to one resident, "was indescribable."[9] Prince Stirbey advised Marie to evacuate to Jassy, the capital of the province of Moldavia, less than a dozen miles from the border with Russia.

Marie and her five children were left with no choice. One of the last things Marie did was to say farewell to Mircea's grave. There she wept by herself, consumed with grief for her dead son and for the fate of Romania. But she soon overcame her sorrow: "there was no time to cry over a personal grief, in the hour of disaster so much depends upon the leaders not losing their heads."[10]

The king and the government followed, leaving Bucharest in the beginning of December 1916 to join the queen in Jassy. They left in the nick of time as the capital fell to the Germans on 6 December. The strain on Jassy, a university town of some seventy thousand, now became acute. Refugees flooded in, swelling the population to over 1 million. Hospitals overflowed with desperate patients. Doctors were few and medical supplies woefully inadequate. As the Russian troops marched through, so did the fleas they brought with them, infected with the dreaded typhus. During a bitterly cold winter—the worst in half a century—where temperatures dropped to minus 30 degrees Celsius, everyone in Jassy found themselves seeking food, shelter, and medical help. Carcasses of emaciated horses, frozen solid, lined the streets. One eyewitness was struck by the tragic scenes at Jassy—the "shocking sight" of "poor unfortunates sink down upon the snow in the broad daylight—never to rise again! It is common to see old men, dragging their feet wrapped in sacking padded with straw over the icy pavements, search (very often in vain) for crusts and bones thrown away by someone more fortunate that they. . . . It is," concluded this witness, "despairing to be surrounded with such suffering without the means of alleviating it."[11]

Members of the Romanian royal family were not immune from the hardships at Jassy, as they found themselves subsisting on small rations of bad-tasting beans, interspersed with whatever could be scraped together from the earth and unpalatable animals. The same tragic scene played itself out in Bucharest as the city's residents struggled with pitiful supplies of fuel and food.

The fuel shortage was particularly poignant because Romania possessed rich deposits of petroleum fuel, which the country had been exporting. But when it became evident that Germans were advancing into the country, the Romanians were determined not to let the oil-rich fields of Ploesti fall into enemy hands. A mad dash to beat the Germans unfolded as the scorched-earth policy took effect. With the Germans right on their heels, a group of dedicated workers destroyed everything they could get their hands on in the fields of Ploesti. Sir John Norton Griffiths, a wealthy engineering contractor, was assigned to supervise this unenviable task in the autumn of 1916. When the Romanians realized he was in their country to destroy its riches, including the corn that might end up feeding the advancing Germans, they tried to delay Griffiths. He then "went straight to Queen Marie, got her backing, and more or less did the job single-handed."[12]

In scenes worthy of the pages of Dante, tens of thousands of cubic meters of gasoline were set on fire, creating infernos that blackened the skies with asphyxiating gases. Griffiths—a strong, muscular man—personally destroyed oil pipes, swinging a heavy sledgehammer, striking blow after blow. Together with his valiant team, many of whom suffered burns from inflammable clouds of gas, they torched their way through miles of territory, ignoring exhaustion and danger. The work itself was incredibly perilous, but added to this was a sense of urgency as the Germans were nipping at the workers' heels. The price Romania paid was high as rivers of burning oil, roaring explosions from huge fuel tanks, and clouds of burning, poisonous gas suffocated every living thing in their path. According to one account, "the tortured leaping flames, the towering columns of dense black smoke . . . the flames rising like great leaping tongues nearly four hundred feet high" all amounted to "a panorama of magnificent horror!" In the end, "more than seventy refineries . . . were destroyed and more than 80,000 wagon-loads of petrol were burnt in the reservoirs."[13] All in all, the losses Romania sustained in the exercise amounted to a staggering 1 billion French francs. Griffiths and his men, now a largely forgotten set of heroes, had risked life and limb for Romania. But the Romanians succeeded in destroying their nation's wealth in a bid to beat the Germans.

⟨⟩

In Russia, wounded soldiers coming home from the front poured in. Many large buildings, including several palaces in and around St. Petersburg, were turned into working hospitals. The large Catherine Palace at Tsarskoe Selo became a hospital for Russian officers. When war broke out, Alexandra was energized to do everything in her power to help Russia's soldiers. Filled with a renewed sense of purpose, the tsarina plunged into war work, and for a while—at least while Alexei enjoyed good health—her thoughts were rarely consumed by the need to have Rasputin at her disposal. The tsarina and her two eldest daughters, Olga and Tatiana, along with the ever present Anna Viroubova, volunteered to become qualified nurses. They assiduously attended courses in medicine and were proud of having earned their Red Cross nursing certificates after passing their exams, along with dozens of other women volunteers. It was a most satisfying accomplishment where the tsarina was concerned. Viroubova, who knew Alexandra well and saw her nearly every day, recalled: "I think I never saw her happier than on the day, at the end of our two months' intensive training, she marched at the head of the procession of nurses to receive the red cross and the diploma of a certificated war nurse."[14]

Once Tsarina Alexandra earned her credentials, she set about devoting every possible moment to ministering to the sick and dying. Hers was a truly hands-on approach, for Alexandra never shuddered from helping in the most heart-wrenching cases. One moment she could be found in the operating theater, handing out instruments; another would find her making bedside rounds. Here, she made no distinction between classes. Many an officer and soldier alike were cared for by their very own tsarina.

Anna Viroubova spoke highly of Alexandra's efforts during the Great War. "I have seen the Empress of Russia in the operating room of a hospital holding ether cones, handling sterilized instruments, assisting in the most difficult operations, taking from the hands of the busy surgeons amputated legs and arms, removing bloody and even vermin-infected dressings, enduring all the sights and smells and agonies of that most dreadful of all places, a military hospital in the midst of war." Overall, "the Empress was spared nothing, nor did she wish to be."[15] Evidently Alexandra of Russia surpassed even the valiant efforts of Marie of Romania. Whereas Marie dutifully visited and comforted the wounded in hospitals, Alexandra went a step further, actually participating in the often gruesome task of assisting in the operating rooms.

Alexandra was almost always on her feet for hours on end, and often she did not get to bed until midnight. The majority of her working hours were spent visiting injured and dying soldiers in the hospitals. As the tsarina went from one soldier to another in the wards, she became a beacon of hope for the unfortunate men. Some would even call for their tsarina before they went for an amputation. Alexandra never refused these requests. More than once were the words heard: "Tsaritsa! Stand near me. Hold my hand that I may have courage."[16]

Alexandra devoted as much time and energy as possible to her nursing. She confessed to Nicholas: "My consolation when I feel very down & wretched is to go to the very ill & try & bring them a ray of light & love—"[17] And again, "Our work in the hospital is my consolation & the visiting the specially suffering ones in the Big Palace."[18]

Sadly for Alexandra Feodorovna, only a very small portion of the population was aware of her work. Never one to show her emotions, and certainly not one to show off her accomplishments, the tsarina inevitably was bound to be seen in a negative light by the many who were unaware of her contributions to the war effort. Major General Sir John Hanbury-Williams (chief of the British military mission in Russia from 1914–17) concluded that "the Empress through shyness and a nervous nature is but rarely seen, though she has worked splendidly for the sick and wounded, and has a really kind and sympathetic nature, which unfortunately no one experiences except those who are very near her, or who happen to have seen a good deal of her, as I have done."[19] Nevertheless, as the historian Dominic Lieven has rightly pointed out, the tsarina, "like her husband . . . hated self-advertisement"; but a certain amount of self-advertisement, like it or not, "is an essential feature of modern politics."[20] And as events in Russia had shown of late, the country and the rest of Europe were moving quickly toward modernity.

What Alexandra failed to realize but her counterpart, Marie of Romania, grasped intuitively, was the fact that Marie knew that she had to put a public face on her nursing role, and she benefitted tremendously from the very exposed way she went about nurturing the injured and dying. Alexandra may have succeeded in keeping her work in the background, but in the process, ironically, she lost a golden opportunity to get closer to many of her subjects.

With her ill health, Alexandra found herself exhausted by her duties. In time, much to her regret, she had to cut back on personal care of the sick. "I overtired my heart again," she admitted to the Bishop of Ripon, "so I had to give up my hospital work for some time. I miss it sorely." She went on: "It does one no end of good being with those brave fellows—how resignedly they bear all pain & loss of limbs."[21]

Alexandra's efforts to help Russia's suffering were not limited to nursing. When she had the time, she went over petitions sent for her attention. She also saw to the organization of numerous hospitals and sanitary trains used for disinfection purposes. All these charitable endeavors cost money, and the tsarina gave large sums. These efforts reaped dividends. She wrote of them to Nicholas, telling him, for instance, that "we have got masses of cribs in these three last months all over Russia for our Society for Mothers & Babies—its [sic] a great joy to me to see how all have taken to it so quickly & have realised the gravity of the question, now especially every Baby must be cared for, as the losses are so heavy at the war."[22] Toward the end of 1914, thanks to the tsarina, eighty-five hospitals were operating "under her patronage in the Petrograd area alone." This was "but one example of Alexandra's ability as an administrator."[23] The tsar himself was impressed with his wife's success. He told her so in February 1916: "the sums received & spent by yr. [Red Cross] depot are enormous—I would have never expected them to reach such a size."[24] Alexandra's selfless devotion to those in need, juxtaposed with her ever-increasing but misguided involvement in politics, underscore a complex character. On the one hand, she was humble and self-effacing; on the other, when it came to autocracy and Rasputin, she was as haughty and domineering as one could get.

For the normally indefatigable Marie of Romania, the task of rallying those around her proved daunting. In mid-December 1916, she confessed in her diary that many were coming to her, pleading for help; overwhelmed by it all, she wanted to cry out: "It is enough, it is enough!"[25] But Marie forged on. She went about her hospital rounds, in her familiar nurse's uniform, bravely facing the stench and gore that awaited her. These daily rounds were complicated by deadly outbreaks of typhoid. Spreading quickly, typhoid did not discriminate among its victims. Marie continued her visits knowing she could be struck down at any moment by the dreaded disease that had nearly killed her husband and oldest son and had already claimed the life of her youngest child. She placed her trust in God, hoping fervently that she would escape. Eschewing rubber gloves, even in the most serious cases, so as to bring as much humanity as she could when touching the infectious patients, the queen could easily have succumbed. But she was not completely careless; one historian notes that "every night she stepped fully-dressed into a tub of boiling water, only her riding boots saving her from serious burns. Then she shed her clothes into the scalding liquid to kill the typhus-carrying lice that clung to them like a gray powder."[26]

Only rarely did Queen Marie let her guard down in front of others. One foreigner, Ethel Pantazzi, encountered the queen at such a moment when, dressed in her Red Cross uniform, Marie went to the Cathedral of Jassy for a service of intercession to help Romania. "She seemed to me," recalled Pantazzi, "the symbolic victim of all the horror and suffering of these dark days—her eyes were so sombre, her face so drawn and tired."[27] With all the overwhelming problems around her, Queen Marie could easily have thrown up her hands in defeat. Instead, she chose to tackle them. To have done otherwise would have been to let the enemy win. So Queen Marie took it upon herself to be the driving force that would keep Romania's spirits buoyed. She did so whenever she received the newly injured each morning at the train station at Jassy. Her indefatigable energy and bravery elicited many admirers, among them the French ambassador to Romania, who also had fled to Jassy. He recalled a nurse who said that " 'the Queen is our mascot. . . . Her presence immunizes us better than all the vaccines.' "[28]

The queen's devotion did not go unnoticed or unappreciated among her suffering people. On the contrary, Marie's unflinching dedication to them and to Romania earned her accolades and, above all, love. The wounded and dying soldiers at Jassy greeted their queen reverently and admiringly. Visiting one wounded soldier, Marie was amazed: before her lay a seriously injured man, his bandages soaked in blood. When told that his queen was by his side, the man, who could not see, stretched out his hands toward Marie murmuring something. She moved closer, straining to hear his words: "May the Great God protect you, may he let you live to become Empress—Empress of all the Roumanians!" It was a moment of supreme hope amid unbearable suffering and seemingly inevitable defeat. Marie recalled how "I prayed to God to listen to his wish." She prayed "that the blood of so many humble heroes should not be given in vain, prayed that when the great hour of liberation should sound at last, an echo of the shout of victory that that day would sound all over our land, should reach the heart of this nameless one beyond the Shadow into which he was sinking, so that even beyond the grave he should still have a share in the glory his living eyes were not destined to see."[29]

By December 1916, Romania was in dire straits, prompting Queen Marie to prepare for a personal appeal to the tsar. But the Queen of Romania's appeal was stopped by earth-shattering news concerning the Tsarina of Russia's indispensable favorite, Rasputin.

Nineteen

NEUTRAL NORTH AND SOUTH

ABOUT THE TIME MISSY ASCENDED THE ROMANIAN THRONE, HER cousin, Ena, gave birth to her last child. The guns at Madrid's Campo del Moro fired twenty-one shots in honor of the birth of a son to the King and Queen of Spain. Sadly, the Infante Gonzalo, Ena's seventh child, was afflicted with hemophilia, just like his eldest brother, Alfonsito.

At the time of the Great War, King Alfonso and Queen Victoria Eugenie reigned over a nation that had seen a gradual growth in population. This, coupled with strains in the social structure, slow progress in the educational system, and a growing shift among the left toward radicalism, meant that trouble was brewing within the kingdom, posing a challenge to Alfonso and his successive governments. Both Spain and Russia, with large agrarian populations hampered by illiteracy and poverty, lacked a strong vibrant middle class. Large swaths of land were owned by few landowners, whose property was tilled by landless laborers. Missing were the small landowners who might have helped bridge this deep gap between the extremely wealthy and the dirt-poor peasants. What middle class existed, possessed little political clout. Nevertheless, as time passed, agitations for reform in both countries began to permeate parts of the populace. Socialism and anarchism took root and spread, so that political indifference gave way to activism. The problem for the Spanish and Russian monarchies was that those who were for king and tsar largely remained passive and inert, while those who leaned to the left agitated for drastic change. To make matters worse, as urban centers in both countries grew, so did competition for employment. Crowded cities where jobs were not abundant along with the growing resentment of wealthy landowners proved to be a fatal combination. It became only a matter of time before class conflict erupted. Alexandra and Victoria Eugenie, in fact, graced two of Europe's most tumultuous thrones.

When World War I began, the Spanish royal family left Santander for San Sebastian. Hamstrung by an inadequate navy and an army numbering less than 150,000, of which half had been used for Spain's Moroccan adventure, and with its population divided over which side to take, Spain had no choice but to opt quickly for a policy of neutrality. One historian has summed up the problem: "Neutrality spared Spaniards from the human slaughter of the conflict but its ideological, social and economic impact hastened the erosion of the fragile foundations of the regime. Most dynastic politicians were determined to keep Spain out of the war but it was beyond their power to prevent the war from entering Spain." Though a number of rural Spaniards did not take sides in the conflict because it was beyond their comprehension, in the upper echelons, Spanish society was divided into Germanophiles and Francophiles. The opposing sides took an obsessive interest in the war, which now "was almost perceived as an ideological clash in which each of the warring factions came to symbolize certain transcendent ideas and values: the Allies represented democracy and freedom and the Central Powers, authority and order."[1]

The Spanish royal family was not immune from this ideological divide. Like Queen Elisabeth of Romania, Queen Maria Cristina, born an Austrian archduchess, naturally sympathized with the German Empire, while Ena herself, born and bred in England, easily took to Great Britain's side, as Marie of Romania had done in her adopted country.

Sophie of Greece, Alexandra of Russia, and Maud of Norway were equally in sympathy with England, but the queens of Romania and Spain's experiences during the war were unique. Marie turned out to be the most vociferous supporter of the Allied cause and the most politically influential. Her role in getting King Ferdinand to throw in Romania's lot with the Entente cause cannot be underestimated. Ena, meanwhile, was much more personally affected by the conflict when her brother, Maurice, came in the direct line of enemy fire as he fought the Germans in France.

Not surprisingly, King Alfonso, caught between his Germanophile mother and his Anglophile wife, took to maintaining an elusive stance during the war among his family. There is little doubt, though, that "if his sympathies did from time to time stray towards the Central Powers, it was almost certainly in the direction of Vienna rather than in that of Berlin."[2] This was certainly the conclusion of the American ambassador to Spain, who found Alfonso to have been "anti-German, but pro-Austrian."[3] Nevertheless, his mother and wife were never completely sure whether Alfonso was for the Allies or the Central Powers. Alfonso's cousin, Princess Pilar, wrote that "it is doubtful if even Queen

Ena or Queen Maria Cristina really knew where his personal preferences lay."[4]

The war reopened the chasm that had kept Spain's two queens emotionally apart and prevented them in the early years from enjoying a harmonious relationship. As an Austrian with close relatives fighting on the side of the Central Powers, Queen Maria Cristina openly showed her sympathy for Germany. As queen of a neutral country, Ena was more circumspect in her sympathy toward the Allied cause, but with roots that stretched deep into England, few people doubted which side she was on. Living under the same roof, the two women struggled to keep their relationship on an even keel. One of Ena's ladies-in-waiting recalled how "the Queen was admirable as a neutral Queen but suffered highly on account of her own native country—England. It was remarkable the way both Queens—one English, the other Austrian . . . behaved towards each other."[5] As an Englishwoman surrounded by many pro-Germans at court, Ena found life in Madrid during the war very lonely. And since Maria Cristina lived virtually by Ena's side, there were moments of great strain.

One of the most dramatic, which threatened to explode into an ugly scene, took place during a luncheon that was interrupted by news of the tragic death of Lord Kitchener at sea. Maria Cristina could barely hide her satisfaction at the misfortune that had befallen the Allies. Victoria Eugenie, on the other hand, was shocked. She had known and admired Lord Kitchener for years, ever since she was a child. Since she was deeply disturbed by her mother-in-law's insensitive attitude, and highly distressed at the personal loss, it took a superhuman effort on Ena's part to keep from exploding into anger. But she dug her fingers deep into the white tablecloth and kept quiet—observers were struck by the highly visible marks on the cloth.

Despite the insensitivity displayed here by Queen Maria Cristina, she was not completely without her moments of kindness toward her daughter-in-law. When, early in 1915, Ena received the awful news that her favorite brother, Prince Maurice, had been killed in action in France, the Queen Mother offered her heartfelt sympathies and prayers. Maurice's death and her inability to be at her mother's side in England were particularly hard for Ena. Writing to Queen Mary in February 1915 to thank her for mailing a photograph of Prince Maurice's grave (taken by May's son, Edward, the Prince of Wales), Ena spoke sadly of the war: "What a terrible winter this has been for everyone & I so often think of you all in these sad and anxious times. . . . It is very hard to be away from my old home at such a time as this and especially so since Maurice's death when I know that Mama is so sad and needs me so much. I would give anything to be able to go to her but that I fear will not be possible for a long time to come."[6]

One of the few ways in which Ena could momentarily ease the tensions in her life was to take refuge in music, for which she had a great passion. She excelled at the piano and became an active patron of the performing arts in Madrid. Ena was especially fond of the great pianist Arthur Rubinstein. The two became friends when the young Rubinstein visited the Spanish capital during the war to play a series of concerts. Rubinstein found Ena to be "charming, beautiful, and very musical."[7] Ena, in turn, found in Rubinstein an astonishing talent. She assiduously attended his concerts and even had him play in her private apartments for herself, her daughters, and a lady-in-waiting.

In fact, the queen took a surreptitious role in helping Rubinstein. When the piano he was playing in public performances began to deteriorate, he complained about it to the queen. "I have noticed it myself," replied Ena. Then she added, "If you keep the secret carefully, I shall be pleased to send my own Steinway, which you like, for your concerts in Madrid." A flattered Rubinstein replied, "I hope it will not inconvenience Your Majesty." "Not in the least," answered Ena. "I shall have it brought back to the palace after each concert." In a surprising twist, the queen added, with a smile, "But I do not want to make it known, not even to the King. He might not approve."[8]

All went well until one particular concert, when a worried Rubinstein was set to play but, according to the theater manager, the piano had still not arrived. After a long hour's delay in which the audience grew more impatient by the minute, the coveted piano arrived and the queen appeared at the royal box. Rubinstein later recalled that that concert "turned out to be one of my best." When he asked Queen Ena at intermission what had happened, he found her "flushed with excitement." She proceeded to tell him. "I am sorry about your ordeal waiting for the piano, but something quite unusual happened. At luncheon the Queen Mother and the King entered into a lively political discussion. As a rule, they retire after lunch to rest, but today their differences of opinion led them to continue their quarrel in the very apartment where the piano was ready to be taken out. I was on pins, but I dared not interrupt them. The minute they left the room, my men rushed the piano to the theater, and we rushed here too, didn't we?" Ena then smiled knowingly at her lady-in-waiting, the Duchess of San Carlos.[9]

Moved by the poverty she saw in and around Madrid, Ena sought to alleviate the suffering of her people, and did more than her fair share in assisting her compatriots. Not content to be an adornment at King Alfonso's side, she took it upon herself to push for reform in the sphere of health care. Like her Greek, Russian, and Romanian counterparts, Queen Ena fought ingrained lethargy and prejudices to forge changes. Hospitals and nursing came in for much of her attention.

Spain's war in Morocco, an imbroglio that lasted for years, causing disruption and sadness in many Spanish lives, meant that there was a dire need to help soldiers' families. Ena initiated the Queen's Fund for the Wounded. Like Maud of Norway, who willingly lent her patronage to single mothers, Ena decided to allow charity for children whose mothers did not bear the name of fathers fighting at the front. It was an effort to reach out to as many Spanish families as possible. This liberal approach did not sit well with ultraconservatives, but it was welcomed by many mothers who otherwise might not have received any kind of relief. Ena also saw to it that thousands of vests were sent to the fighting troops in Morocco to help protect them from the wet and cold.

The fighting in Morocco proved fierce. It took fifty thousand Spanish soldiers between 1909 to 1911 to battle their Moroccan adversaries. Not surprisingly, casualties on the Spanish side were high. Queen Ena did her best to mitigate her subjects' suffering. Her efforts were appreciated, prompting the British ambassador to Spain to report that "Her Majesty gained much deserved popularity by initiating and presiding over a committee of Spanish ladies which raised over 80,000 *l*. And collected an immense quantity of medical supplies, clothing, and comforts for the sick and wounded soldiers. Sums of money and other gifts were distributed in the Royal Palace at Madrid by the Queen in person to surviving relatives of the killed."[10]

As World War I dragged on, Ena came into her own as a force in promoting better health care for the Spanish people. She did so by raising the profile of the Spanish Red Cross and reorganizing it. Wishing to include the Queen Mother, Ena chose as her vice president Queen Maria Cristina. In time, Ena's efforts would bear fruit.

Not all of her attention during the war was focused on her own projects, however, for the queen also lent her support to King Alfonso's efforts to help locate and ease the plight of prisoners of war. Ena's husband was spurred into action when a forlorn French washerwoman wrote to the king, trying to ascertain the whereabouts of her husband, missing in action. When he found out her husband was a prisoner in Germany and wrote to tell her so, the French press got wind of it and published Alfonso's benevolent gesture. In no time, similar requests came flooding into the Royal Palace, resulting in the creation of a bureau to tackle this important aspect of the war.

King Haakon had done something similar in Norway, as did the Crown Prince of Denmark; but Alfonso was the most extensive and organized in undertaking this task. The palace bureau, which employed forty people (payment for its cost came out of Alfonso's pocket), was inundated: an estimated minimum "70,000 civilians and 21,000 soldiers were assisted to obtain repatriation; intervention was made in favour of 122,000 French and Belgian, 8,000 British,

6,350 Italians and 400 Portuguese prisoners-of-war," all thanks to King Alfonso's help.[11] An admiring Infanta Eulalia wrote that "anguished mothers of five different countries christened the Madrid Palace the Palace of Pity."[12] One of King Alfonso's biographers has concluded that when it comes to his work on behalf of thousands of prisoners of war, Alfonso "has never received the recognition which is his due."[13]

As if the war, Spain's internal problems, and Alfonso's serial adultery were not enough, Ena was always worried about her sons—the hemophiliac Alfonsito and Gonzalo, and the deaf Jaime. Yet through it all, in public she rarely displayed signs of bitterness or defeat. Instead, trained as she had been at the side of Queen Victoria, Ena continued to present a dignified facade.

Norway's king and queen, like Spain's, were fortunate in that they too escaped the kind of coercion and campaign of vilification that made Constantine and Sophie's life a misery in Greece. Norway fared well during the war, and this naturally boded well for Maud and Haakon VII. Far from being hounded by the Allies as Queen Sophie in Greece experienced to her cost, and far from being at the center of an ideological family argument, as Queen Ena endured, Maud's lot was less contentious. Her only serious immediate concerns (besides a speedy end to the war itself) were worries over German attacks on Norwegian shipping and the fact that she was unable to visit England. Yet Norway did have its share of problems.

Just because her country remained neutral during the war did not mean that Queen Maud was content to sit on the sidelines. Instead, she spearheaded fundraising drives for the relief of those who suffered hardships. In the winter months, the queen chaired a committee meeting every two weeks consisting of ladies from different parishes. The money raised "was distributed annually for many years on her birthday for the purchase of food, fuel, clothing and medicines. It was Maud's wish that special attention should be given to the needs of large families and to single mothers."[14]

In the early stages of the war, Maud was moved to write to Queen Mary about the Germans: "Altogether 'they' behave *too* abominably in every way and are more like mad beasts than ordinary human beings—" Maud, British as ever, could not help but add her pride in England: "How appalling this war is, and how all my thoughts naturally return to 'home' and all you dear ones, I feel *so* far away and lonely, it is terrible being away from one's own beloved country at *such* a ghastly moment—With what pride one reads of the splendid way the dear old country has behaved."[15]

Among Queen Victoria Eugenie's greatest detractors at the Madrid court was the Marquis of Viana. The queen and the marquis crossed swords from the very beginning. As part of King Alfonso's entourage, Viana was with his master during the heady days when Alfonso courted Ena. Back then, Ena received the marquis with characteristic politeness. Viana also was one of a privileged group of invited guests who witnessed Victoria Eugenie officially embrace the Roman Catholic faith at Miramar. Ena's acquaintance with Viana, therefore, predated her marriage. In the early days, she had no inkling that this close friend of Alfonso XIII was to make her life a misery.

Viana's antipathy toward Ena stemmed from an excessive prejudice against foreigners. Scornful as he was, Ena epitomized all that he disliked in non-Spaniards. Sadly for Ena, because Viana was one of King Alfonso's closest and most trusted friends, it was difficult to dislodge the marquis from his favored position at court. Viana's very proximity to the monarch made him all the more of a trial to the long-suffering queen. In time, Ena would be unable to contain her anger, leading to a devastating final confrontation between the two enemies.

Two further friends of King Alfonso also brought their share of mischief and grief into Ena's life. One was Doña Sol, sister of the premier grandee of Spain. The second female confidante and bane of Ena's existence turned out to be none other than her first cousin, Beatrice, who also happened to be Queen Marie of Romania's sister.

Like Doña Sol, Beatrice relished intrigue. Once she had married into the royal family in 1909 by becoming the wife of Alfonso's cousin, the Infante Alfonso ("Ali"), opportunities for wreaking havoc in Ena's life proved too tempting. Ali's marriage to the Protestant Beatrice was frowned upon by many in Spain. King Alfonso had to bow to pressure and express disapproval for the marriage, which meant that Ali and Beatrice lived for a time in exile. When the couple returned to Spain in 1912 and were welcomed into the family fold, Beatrice's intrigues against Ena took off. Though rumor had it that a jealous Beatrice took her revenge on Ena for taking the Spanish crown away from her, it seems more plausible that Beatrice "needed a scapegoat for her husband's discomfitrue, and Ena, who had few friends at the rigid Spanish court, was the perfect victim."[16]

Annoying and hurtful as King Alfonso's numerous cronies and Ena's enemies were, the queen would always view the Marquis de Viana as the most malevolent, for Viana took perverse pleasure in seeing his queen suffer. He never forgave Victoria Eugenie for being an Englishwoman, nor did he forgive the queen for lacking enough charms to keep Alfonso XIII from straying. The marquis cleverly manipulated the king in his quest to bring misery to Ena's life. As one of the king's aristocratic cronies, Pepe Viana had made himself indispensable. He carefully cultivated his friendship with the king, even managing to lay out the royal polo grounds, which were several miles away from the Madrid palace and commanded excellent views of the Guadarrama Mountains.

As the man mainly responsible for seeing to it that Alfonso's insatiable appetite for women was met, the queen deemed the marquis "her principal enemy at Court." Ena saw through Viana, whom she rightly viewed with utter contempt. Not only did he poison minds against the queen, and procure women for Alfonso, but the marquis "did not neglect to cater for his own amusements."[17] Tension between Ena and this implacable enemy continued unabated through the years. Like the bull and the matador facing each other in a dance of death, a showdown between Queen Victoria Eugenie and the Marquis of Viana was imminent.

Whether he indulged himself in Paris incognito or made the nocturnal rounds in Madrid's "high-class" brothels, Spain's playboy king found many women willing to offer their charms to the hot-blooded Alfonso XIII; few of those he set eyes on proved immune to the king's legendary charms. Inevitably, Alfonso ended up siring several illegitimate children. No one knew the exact number, but rumors of numerous offspring abounded. Queen Maria Cristina touched upon this once, telling her sister, the Archduchess Maria Teresa, "If you had to pick out all the grandchildren credited to me, you would not live long enough to be able do so."[18] In spite of King Alfonso's serial adultery, Ena did not give up on her marriage. Their marital relations did not completely break down, as her pregnancy in 1918 attests. This pregnancy, however, ended in a miscarriage.

That King Alfonso had ample opportunity to listen to Queen Ena's advice there is no doubt. For much of their married life, unhappy though they were, Alfonso often set aside time to spend with his long-suffering wife. Both lovers of the outdoors and keen sportspeople, they played tennis and golf together. Sometimes, the king would read out loud to the queen in English, in order to practice the language. Mindful of her husband's military tastes, Ena would find English books for him on army matters and life in India, the jewel in the crown of the British Empire. As for her own reading, it tended toward serious works, especially English authors, but the queen also ventured into Spanish authors. She devoured all the works of Padre Luis Coloma, a Spanish Jesuit whose works, characterized by their defense of the faith, appealed to Spaniards espousing orthodox views of Catholicism. Ena even read one of the most famous authors of twentieth-century

Spain, Vicente Blasco Ibáñez, known for his anti-monarchist and pro-republican leanings. She appeared to have a greater appetite for reading than the king, who gravitated toward physical sports in his spare time.

Among the best times for a tête-à-tête where political matters could be brought up at discretion occurred during that quintessential British habit of tea in the afternoon, which took place in Ena's private sitting room. As the royal children grew older, they were invited to join their parents. Ena ensured that her sons and daughters were brought up along English lines, with plenty of opportunities for exercising outdoors. When asked about her ideas on rearing children, Queen Ena's answer reflected her grandmother, Queen Victoria: "Plenty of fresh air and early to bed." This predilection for fresh air irritated a number of her Spanish ladies, who were accustomed to hermetically sealed homes. They could not understand why the queen wanted her rooms aired or her insistence that the royal children take outdoor exercise no matter what the weather. Nor could some Spaniards understand Ena letting her daughters enjoy such vigorous sports as tennis—which Ena taught the infantas herself. Asked whether tennis might be unladylike, Ena replied: "I hope my girls will be ladies. I do not think tennis will interfere with that, but before all things I want them to be strong young women with healthy minds in healthy bodies."[19]

As the war progressed, Spain's value to the Allied cause diminished. When Italy and Portugal entered the war on the Entente side, the Allies were able to adopt a strategy of "wait and negotiate from a position of strength" toward Spain.[20] This served to ease the pressure on King Alfonso to throw in his lot with the Allied cause and permitted him to devote a good deal of his energy to helping prisoners of war. Queen Ena's husband, and by extension Ena herself, did not feel the kind of intense pressure exerted by the Allies and Eleutherios Venizelos on King Constantine and Queen Sophie. Just how much longer the Greek monarchy could withstand the multi-pronged attack was anyone's guess.

Twenty

BELEAGUERED AND BETRAYED

THE FATE OF NEUTRAL GREECE AND THE ROYAL FAMILY WAS OF GREAT interest to Crown Princess Margaret ("Daisy") of Sweden, another of Queen Victoria's granddaughters. "Here," wrote Daisy from Sweden, "we are anxiously awaiting news from Greece . . . the Balkan question seems as much in a muddled state now as ever it has been in bygone years & that is saying a good deal!"[1] Mossy was equally concerned about Queen Sophie's plight, telling a friend, "you can imagine how much I worry about my sister and the horrible position they are in."[2]

Mossy and Daisy were right to fret about Greece, for the country was split into two irreconcilable camps pitting the followers of Venizelos against those of King Constantine. After the Allied troops poured into the northern Greek city of Salonika and entrenched themselves, Venizelos established a provisional government there, acting as a rival to King Constantine's leadership in Athens. This forced the Greek Army to take sides: either switch over to the Venizelist camp or remain loyal to the royalist side. Heading the Allied forces in Salonika was the heavy-handed anti-monarchist French general M.-P.-E. Sarrail, who thought nothing of interfering in Greek affairs to the detriment of the royalists.

The plight of Queen Sophie resonated with her Russian counterpart, Tsarina Alexandra. Both were in the middle of a vicious campaign to blacken their reputations with allegations of being pro-German. When one of Sophie's brothers-in-law, Prince Christopher, visited Alix in Russia, Greece was the main topic of conversation. Alix then told Nicholas II, in her convoluted English, that Prince Christopher "Says untrue all one said about Sophie [that she was a traitor to Greece], she kept herself very quietly & did not scream out her feelings, never left the country."[3]

The Tsarina of Russia was full of sympathy for the plight of her cousins, Sophie and Tino. In letters to the tsar, Alexandra vented her frustration over Allied policy toward Greece. One letter went: "Why on earth this ultimatum to Greece, for sure England & France are at the bottom of it—to my simple mind, it seems unjust & hard—cannot imagine how Tino will get out of it & it may harm his popularity."[4] In another, the tsarina laments, "what on earth is going on in Greece—looks like a revolution impending, God forbid—the allies [sic] fault then, alas!"[5] How tragic that Alexandra Feodorovna could sense an impending revolution in Greece, but was blind to the revolution brewing within Russia because of her refusal to let go of Rasputin and her incompetent governance of the empire.

When another of King Constantine's brothers, Prince Nicholas, visited Petrograd in the summer of 1916, his talk with Alexandra served to convince her even more that she was correct in her assessment of the Greek situation. The prince had been sent on his mission to Petrograd (When war broke out in August 1914, St. Petersburg was thought to be too German-sounding, so the name was changed to the more Russian-sounding Petrograd.) as a personal emissary of Constantine. The king decided on this move because he saw that his own explanations to the Allied representatives in Greece were getting him nowhere. Since Nicholas was married to a Romanov grand duchess, he seemed a logical choice for the mission. Queen Sophie's brother-in-law met with a sympathetic tsar, who assured the prince, "I have entire confidence in Tino; I know how true and loyal he is. I trust him implicitly. I shall do all I can for him."[6]

King Constantine's other brother, Prince Andrew, meanwhile, was despatched to Paris and London. Nothing came of their visits. Prince Andrew even met with hostility in London. On a visit to the permanent undersecretary at the Foreign Office, Andrew was told point-blank, "what can we expect when your Queen is the sister of the Kaiser?" Andrew replied that "he did not think anybody had the right to ruin a country because of the relationship of its Queen."[7]

Tsarina Alexandra proved more amenable. The Greek predicament struck a sympathetic chord with Alexandra, prompting her to report to the tsar: "I must own that the diplomats of the allies have blundered very often, as usual; in upholding that Veniselos [sic] we may come to grief. Tino thinks that perservering [sic] in this way the allies may force the dynastical question to rise & that might be playing with fire—for no reason."[8] Alexandra was right. King Constantine was thinking the same thing, for he was under no illusions, saying, "I am playing a very dangerous game, but I am convinced that I am right, otherwise I would not act as I am doing."[9]

With passions running high, it was inevitable that attempts would be made on the lives of Queen Sophie and King Constantine. One such incident occurred in

July 1916, at the royal family's summer retreat of Tatoi, not far from Athens. This sprawling estate, with its hilly terrain and forests of pine trees, offered a respite from the dust and heat of the capital. But the summer was a hot one, with temperatures in the shade reaching a scorching 100-plus degrees. Knowing how much the royal family enjoyed Tatoi, a number of their enemies acted on a plan to eliminate them there.

The arsonists set out on a murderous rampage in the early morning of 14 July. In no time, the forests around Tatoi had erupted in a blazing inferno. King Constantine and his party, trapped in the conflagration, found themselves with minutes to spare as they stared at columns of flames and breathed the acrid smoke. Fortunately, the king was able to direct his men to safety. But in the ensuing rush to escape, Constantine fell. The king's life was spared thanks to two aides who carried him off as they fled. Some of those accompanying Constantine were not so lucky. Cut off from the rest of the party, they found themselves trapped. Tragically, these men, eighteen in all, perished in the fire, some burnt beyond recognition.

Queen Sophie, who had accompanied Constantine by car, was separated from the other members of the group and also found herself trapped, the flames heading toward her with great speed. But Sophie was clutching her three-year-old daughter, Princess Katherine, and the instinct for self-preservation drove her to outrun death. She almost fainted from exhaustion; but mother and child survived.

⌒⍣⍣⍣⍜

In Tsarina Alexandra's eyes, what Russia needed was firmness. And if Nicky could not provide that, Alix would see to it that she helped Nicholas rule the way Russia needed to be ruled. Alexandra's pleas for Nicholas to assert himself first came to the fore during World War I. In one letter she pressed her husband on: "You are Autocrat & they dare not forget it."[10] In another: "Play the Emperor! Remember you are the Autocrat. Speak to your Ministers as their Master. . . . Be like Peter the Great. . . . Crush them all. No, don't laugh, you naughty child. I so long to see you treat in this way those who try to govern you, when it is you who should govern them." The tsar did not mind being upbraided by his wife. He wrote back: "My Darling . . . Tender thanks for the severe reprimand in writing. I read it with a smile because you talk to me as to a child." His letter closed: "I . . . remain your 'poor, little, weak husband.' "[11]

Unlike Queen Marie of Romania's steadying and wise influence on King Ferdinand, which was tolerated and even encouraged, Tsarina Alexandra's misguided influence on the tsar was resented and condemned. This was largely due to that arch intriguer, Rasputin. It was he—claimed the chorus of the tsarina's enemies—

along with Alexandra herself, who was responsible for the mess Russia was in. One needed a score card to keep track of who was in and out of power where government ministers were concerned, thanks to that meddlesome duo. In fact, between 1915 and 1917, "Russia had four prime ministers, five ministers of the interior, four ministers of religion, four ministers of justice, three ministers of agriculture, three foreign ministers, and four ministers of war. Twenty-six men held these seven positions over a twenty-month period." Yet out of all these, "only four ministerial positions may have changed hands due to Rasputin."[12]

Alexandra's letters to Nicholas certainly contain numerous references to their "friend" and how the tsar should do what he advised. But a closer examination of the evidence suggests, as one historian has pointed out, that:

> When key political appointments were concerned, however, it is very doubtful whether the absence of Rasputin would have made any significant difference. Given the course which Nicholas was steering, suitable candidates for key government offices were few and far between and it is easy to point to influences other than Rasputin's advice which resulted in the appointment of individuals to top positions. Even in 1915–16 what really mattered about Rasputin was not his actual political influence but the fatal impact he had on the monarchy's prestige.[13]

In a number of instances Rasputin was not so much influencing the tsarina as she was looking to him for confirmation of what she wanted to hear. Rasputin was clever enough to capitalize on this. Alexandra then foolishly thought that every word that came out of Rasputin's mouth was advice he was getting from God; many a time, the *staretz* was telling the tsarina only what he knew she would be receptive to hearing. She then passed his words on the to tsar as orders to be executed without question.

The Alexandra/Rasputin dynamic has some eerie parallels with the Queen Victoria/John Brown episode. From the 1860s to the 1880s, Victoria's Highland servant played a preeminent role in the queen's life, so much so that the queen became known, disparagingly, as "Mrs. Brown." These were bleak years in the queen's personal life, when Victoria purposefully shut herself away from the public's gaze after the death of her beloved Albert. Her self-enforced purdah behind the walls of Balmoral, Windsor, and Osborne House had similar parallels in Alexandra's self-imposed isolation at Tsarskoe Selo, Peterhof, and Livadia.

Like Rasputin, Brown offended many by his loutish behavior, drunkenness, and overfamiliarity with Queen Victoria, who could see no wrong in this man of the lower classes. This view may have stemmed largely from the fact that Brown never profited from his close association with Victoria. It was the same with

Rasputin and Alexandra. Neither Brown nor Rasputin cared for the trappings of personal wealth, and this made their attachment to their sovereigns all the more genuine in each woman's eyes.

The war now took on the tone of a crusade against Germany and all things German. Headlines in Russian papers commonly cited a "Holy War"; and *The Times* maintained that "this war is holy to every one, and its motto is—getting rid of the German spirit in life."[14]

As Russia's fortunes plummeted, the tsarina's close association with Rasputin laid her open to charges of mental instability and treachery. The tsarina from Germany came close to sharing the same fate as the Austrian-born Queen of France, Marie Antoinette, whose portrait hung in Tsarskoe Selo. Of all the calumnies heaped upon the tsarina, the most devastating, and certainly the most unfounded, was the accusation that she was pro-German. In fact, though a German princess by birth, her personal inclinations and her upbringing were thoroughly English. Not for nothing was she a granddaughter of Queen Victoria, and a favored one at that.

Maurice Paléologue, France's ambassador to Russia from 1914 to 1917, was firmly convinced of the tsarina's devotion to Russia, noting in his diary that "Alexandra Feodorovna is German neither in mind nor spirit and has never been so. . . . In her inmost being she has become entirely Russian . . . I have no doubt of her patriotism. . . . Her love for Russia is deep and true. And why should she not be devoted to her adopted country which stands for everything dear to her as woman, wife, sovereign and mother?"[15]

Another of Alexandra's supporters here was the Grand Duke Alexander. He despised Rasputin and decried his association with the tsarina, but Sandro recorded that where Alexandra was concerned, "I must admit that she was far above all her contemporaries in fervent Russian patriotism. Raised by her father, the Duke of Hesse-Darmstadt, to hate the Kaiser, she dreamed all her life to see the day of Prussia's debacle, and next to Russia her admiration lay on the side of Great Britain."[16] And to her husband, the tsarina proclaimed that "yes, I am more Russian than many another," adding that she was motivated to speak her mind, and so "I wont [*sic*] keep quiet."[17]

Even Alexander Kerensky, head of the Provisional Government which came to power later, after the overthrow of Nicholas II, would admit that there was no evidence to back up the assertion that the tsarina was a German spy. The British ambassador to St. Petersburg, Sir George Buchanan, wrote that Kerensky "once told me that not a single compromising document had been found to show that either she or the Emperor had ever contemplated making a separate peace with Germany." And Kerensky recalled Alexandra's spirited defense when she told him after the 1917 Revolution, "I am English and not German, and I have always been true to Russia."[18] But the accusation that Alexandra was a spy and a traitor to Russia was potent, and it had devastating consequences.

The stories of her alleged traitorous actions against Russia were not confined to Petrograd. An English nurse accompanying the Russian forces heard of the rumors swirling about the tsarina, nothing that "in certain cliques she is referred to openly as the *Nemka* [German woman]."[19] Maurice Paléologue recorded that a friend arriving from Moscow reported, "the public there is furious with the Empress. In drawing-rooms, shops and cafés, it is being openly said the *Niemka,* the 'German Woman,' is about to ruin Russia and must be put away as a lunatic."[20]

The abuses hurled at Alexandra were not enough to still her in her quest to get Nicholas II to fight for the throne. On the contrary, the tsarina believed that her own ability to be "strong" was in large part to blame for her unpopularity. She wrote to Nicholas in December 1916:

> Why do people hate me? Because they know I have a strong will, and when convinced that a thing is right do not change my mind. Those who are afraid of me, who don't look me in the eyes, or who are up to some wrong, never like me. . . . But those who are good and devoted to you honestly and purely, they love me—look at the simple people and military. The good and bad clergy, it's all so clear, and that is why it no longer hurts me as when I was younger.[21]

While he was away in *Stavka* at Mogilev, hardly a day went by when the tsar was not greeted by a letter or telegram from his beloved "Wify" or "Sunny" at Tsarskoe Selo. Some may interpret this as nothing short of hectoring. But in plying her husband with comments, opinions, and advice, Alexandra was certainly taking to heart what her grandmother had always advocated: "a good & sensible wife shld. Always tell her Husband what *she* thinks right or wrong & try & be a *real helpmate* to him."[22]

∾∾∾

As Russia hurtled toward implosion, Romania was in pandemonium. The incredible strain placed on the town of Jassy, plus the brutally painful fact that three quarters of Romania lay under German occupation, made it appear as if all was lost. To some, it seemed as if siding with the Entente had brought nothing but misery. Queen Marie recalled years later the anguish of that time: "The remembrance I keep of those days is of a suffering so great that it almost blinded me . . . black waves seemed to be rushing in upon me threatening to drown me, yet I was quite calm and continued living and working as though my heart had not been torn from my breast."[23] Like her beleaguered cousins in Petrograd and Athens, Marie of Romania was trying desperately to keep her head high.

Though Romania seemed all but defeated, the queen was determined not to ease up on her goal of sustaining everyone's morale, including King Ferdinand's. Marie, the warrior queen, was undeterred in her quest to comfort the sick, the dying, and the defeatists, rallying all to Romania's cause. The American ambassador was so impressed with everything Queen Marie accomplished during the country's darkest hours that he wrote, "there is no doubt in my mind that if she could have led the soldiers, the Roumanian army would have been unconquerable."[24]

Unbeknownst to many of her admirers, Queen Marie did actually sometimes feel privately overwhelmed by the immensity of the task before them. But she never let down her guard in public. There were moments when Marie found herself deeply depressed, writing of those dark times, "there is no suffering that my people have not been called upon to endure, no fear, no sorrow, no pain— every misery, both moral and physical, had to be borne at once. . . . And I, their Queen, suffered with them, struggled with them, wept with them, shared and understood their every grief."[25] Marie empathized with her people, consoling them in their grief, but always she put on a brave front, so that when they saw their queen, the Romanians could also see the face of hope.

⚬〰〰⚬

In rallying her husband to fight for autocracy, Tsarina Alexandra was animated by the imprimatur of Rasputin. Reform by way of more power to the people was, in the tsarina's eyes, not something that Russia was prepared to embrace at this point. Autocracy, Orthodoxy, and Nationalism were the principles that needed to be kept intact. As Alexandra pointed out in March 1916, "for Baby's sake we must be firm as otherwise his [Alexei's] inheritance will be awful, as with his [mild?] c[h]aracter [we must see that] he wont [*sic*] bow down to others but be his own master, as *one must* in Russia whilst people are still so uneducated."[26] In an earlier letter to her husband, she wrote, "it is the beginning of the glory of yr. reign, He [Rasputin] said so & I absolutely believe it. Your Sun is rising—& to-day it shines so brightly." "My very own beloved one," she noted optimistically: "I fully believe in our Friend's words that the glory of your reign is coming."[27]

By the fall of 1916, she was writing to the tsar: "I feel cruel worrying you, my sweet, patient Angel—but all my trust lies in our Friend, who *only thinks of you*, Baby & Russia.—And guided by Him we shall get through this heavy time. It

will be hard fighting, but a Man of God's is near to guard yr. boat safely through
the reefs—& little Sunny is standing as a rock behind you, firm & unwavering
with decision, faith & love to fight for her darlings & our country."[28]

In her obsession to uphold the tsar's autocratic powers, Alexandra Feodorovna may have seemed completely out of touch. She was, however, not alone in
her desire to preserve autocracy for the sake of Russia. One of the national
newspapers, *Grazhdanin,* devoted pages to expounding this view:

> [Russian autocracy was] represented as being different from the monarchies
> of Western Europe; it was pointed out that its greatest strength lay in the loyal
> devotion of the Russian people, all of whom believed that the Tsar was the
> sole author of Russia's greatness. This understanding and relationship be-
> tween Tsar and people, it argued, must be preserved in close union, and any
> forces that tended to threaten this union must be destroyed.[29]

Even Sir George Buchanan, the British ambassador at St. Petersburg from
1910 to 1918, conceded that Alexandra may not have been completely incorrect
in thinking this way: "she believed—and in principle, as subsequent events have
shown, she was not altogether wrong—that the autocracy was the only régime
that could hold the Empire together."[30]

Nicholas II shared her views on his role as tsar. For Nicholas, the concept of
preserving autocracy did not stem from any personal desire to hold on to power.
On the contrary, the mild-mannered tsar was always a reluctant emperor, who
held to his prerogatives only because he promised to do so before God at the
coronation.

When one of Nicholas II's generals insisted in 1917 to the tsar that he must
concede more powers to Russia's parliament, Nicholas explained that "this for-
mula was incomprehensible to him and that he would need to have been differently educated, to be born again . . . once more he stressed that he was not
personally hanging on to power but only that he could not take decisions which
were against his conscience and, having shed responsibility for the course of
events before people, he still could not consider that he was not responsible before God."[31]

But a diminution in the tsar's powers had already occurred with the October
Manifesto of 1905, which paved the way for the creation of the Duma. When he
had to address this issue, Nicholas II was tortured by the thought that the armor
of autocracy was being sacrilegiously chipped away. He told his ministers, "The
question still torments me: do I have the right to change the form of that authority which my ancestors bequeathed to me?"[32] Further erosions of the imperial power must be avoided at all costs. To abrogate more powers, especially

because of some subversive elements in society, would be a desecration of his vows at the coronation. In this, Alexandra concurred wholeheartedly.

Alexandra Feodorovna was not by any means an unintelligent woman. She had a curious and able mind and was an avid reader. Her literary tastes were not confined to light novels; besides the numerous foreign newspapers and magazines she subscribed to, and read, the shelves at Tsarskoe Selo were always being replenished with books the tsarina had purchased. Among her favorite topics were the sciences and philosophy. The tsarina once complained to a friend how she wished she had more time to read: "Alas I have not much free time, but when I find a spare moment I sit down to read. I am so fond of 'Boehme' and many of the German & Dutch theosophists of the 15th & 16th cent:—there are such splendours & they help one on in life, & make everything so much easier to bear."[33] "Boehme" was Jakob Boehme (1575–1624), a pious German Lutheran who was moved by his religious visions. He spoke of placing the intellectual world within a person's heart, but also of consciously experiencing everything as connected with the great beyond. Such works struck a deep chord in the tsarina's intellect and soul.

Beyond her beloved world of fifteenth- and sixteenth-century philosophers and religious literature, Nicholas read to her in the evenings from Gogol, Tolstoy, or Turgenev, often in the original Russian. Tolstoy was a favorite, particularly *War and Peace*. So taken was the tsarina by this great work that she came to believe in its portrayals of the Russian people's loyalty to the tsar, commenting, "this indeed is the true Russia."[34] Even at the height of the Great War, with all the anxieties around her, Tsarina Alexandra remained interested in literature and the arts. In March 1916, she wrote to tell her husband, "I had a collection of English ones [books] brought me to-day, but I fear there is nothing very interesting amongst them. No great authors already since a long time & in no other country either, nor celebrated artist, or composer—a strange lack." Alexandra then went on to muse about the future: "One lives too quickly, impressions follow in rapid succession—machinery & money rule the world & crush all art; & those who think themselves gifted, have ill minds.—I do wonder what will be after this great war is over!"[35]

Russia's last empress was therefore someone who possessed some degree of intelligence and whose tastes were certainly not philistine. However, her headstrong personality and propensity to brood served to overshadow her other fine qualities. Ultimately, these flaws prevented the tsarina from breaking free to meet head-on the challenges that had emerged the moment her life in Russia began.

In her defense of autocracy, Alexandra was following Queen Victoria, a monarch who believed firmly that the exercise of monarchical powers at hand was a privilege and a prerogative that needed to be flexed when necessary.

E. F. Benson, son of an Archbishop of Canterbury under Victoria's reign, noted: "One entity . . . was that of Her Majesty the Queen of England, supreme (and determined to exercise her supremacy and to demand the due recognition of it) in all questions that concerned the welfare of her realm." Benson cites an occasion when Victoria opposed moves to make one of her bishops give up his residence, commenting tartly, "If you begin giving up, they will go on grabbing till they get everything."[36]

Tsarina Alexandra had effectively played into the hands of her enemies when she strongly supported government ministers who were notorious for their ineptitude and for their association with Rasputin. Two in particular, Alexander Protopopov, who became minister of the interior in October 1916, and Boris Stürmer, who, to the incredulity of many, became prime minister in February 1916 and foreign minister in July of that year, were particularly hated. Sir George Buchanan had scathing words for Stürmer, whom he described as possessing "a second-rate intelligence." Furthermore, the inexperienced prime minister was "a sycophant, bent solely on the advancement of his own interests."[37] Protopopov was no better. The Duma and its president, Mikhail Rodzianko, a monarchist but a vocal critic of Rasputin, not only disliked Protopopov, they distrusted him. Rodzianko considered Protopopov highly eccentric and quite unsuited to the grave task of helping to govern Russia. One courtier even went so far to say that Protopopov was "a lunatic."[38]

With unpopular and incompetent government leaders championed by the tsar and tsarina at the helm, the clamor for Nicholas and Alexandra to get rid of such ministers was rising. But by this time, Alexandra was impervious to anyone who dared to question her or Rasputin's judgment. Once again, Alexandra refused to heed the warning signs. The embattled Stürmer was eventually removed from power in November 1916, but not without a fight from the tsarina. If people thought Stürmer's removal might ease the situation, they were mistaken. His replacement, the more acceptable Alexander Trepov, was an implacable enemy of Rasputin. Thus, Trepov was in the tsarina's bad books.

Impervious to criticism, Alix exhorted Nicky to fight on:

My own dearest Angel,
    Remember why I am disliked—shows it right to be firm and feared and you be the same . . . believe more in our Friend. . . . He lives for you and Russia.
    And we must give a strong country to Baby, and dare not be weak for his sake, else he will have a yet harder reign. . . . Let our legacy be a lighter one for Alexei. . . .
    Be firm. I your wall, am behind you and won't give way. . . . "Russia loves

to feel the whip"—it's their nature—tender love and then the iron hand to punish and guide.

How I wish I could pour my will into your veins. . . . I love you too deeply and cry over your faults and rejoice over every right step.

Wify[39]

Sandro, the tsar's brother-in-law, tried to talk some sense into both Nicholas and Alexandra. But once the grand duke began to discuss the political instability consuming Petrograd, a look of "mistrust and coldness" came over the tsar's eyes. "You do not seem to trust your friends any more, Nicky," said his old friend. Looking past the grand duke, the Tsar "icily" replied: "I believe no one but my wife."[40]

By the end of 1916, few were immune from the wrath of Alexandra. She had lost all patience with anyone, including close family members, who dared to cross her in areas she conceived as sacrosanct—and this meant the tsar's rule, Rasputin, and her role in governing Russia.

What Alexandra failed to realize was that even after so many years in Russia, she still needed to work at being empress. The symbolic ceremony uniting her to the Russian people which had occurred at the coronation did not mean that Alexandra could ignore learning how to exercise her role as tsarina. It was not enough to be joined by God to the people; she also needed to help herself by earning her subjects' love and respect. This was something Queen Marie of Romania intuitively grasped and it worked to the mutual advantage of the queen and her people.

Marie had revealed her concept of monarchy to Tsarina Alexandra's mistress of the robes: "Things are different with us. In your country, the sovereigns are demigods, who may do anything they please. We have had to work to win the acknowledgment of our people, and I always teach my children: 'Everyone bears the duties of his position. Our duty is to earn the love of our subjects, to be amiable and agreeable.'"[41] With such a level-headed attitude, small wonder that years later, Marie of Romania would have scathing words to say about Alexandra of Russia. In 1929, Marie wrote that "the Emperor Nicolas was lovable, utterly lovable. His wife was a fanatic and had the governess attitude towards all men and things; she was a pharisee."[42]

◦━━━◦

"I cannot help feeling that in this Greek question we have allowed France too much to dictate a policy, and that as a Republic she may be somewhat intolerant of, if not anxious to abolish, the monarchy in Greece,"[43] King George V wrote to the British foreign secretary, Sir Edward Grey, in September 1916. King George would soon find his suspicions confirmed.

Two weeks after receiving this letter, Grey received a dispatch from the British minister at Athens, Sir Francis Elliot, with a similar message: "The King of Greece sent for Russian Minister yesterday and spoke to him more bitterly than ever of conduct of British and French military authorities and diplomatic representatives. His Majesty's anger was greatest against the French. . . . He said he would never be induced to join by pressure; he must choose his own time and opportunity. He had now no army and it would take at least 2 months to form one."[44]

With an intransigent king on its hands, the Allied propaganda machine was cranked up another notch. In October 1916, rumors had it that King Constantine was fortifying Tatoi in readiness for a military engagement. In order to allay British fears and assure them that no such thing was happening, the king invited the British minister in Athens to send his embassy's military attachés to inspect Tatoi for themselves. An embarrassed Sir Francis Elliot replied that "His Majesty's word was enough for me."[45] It seemed almost as if the British were trying to find ways of avoiding chances to confirm that the king was not against the Entente. But proof that the Allies were intent on seeing Sophie and Constantine overthrown is evident in the active efforts on the part of the French to replace the king with their own candidate. In a secret message to London in the summer of 1916, Sir Francis Elliot reported that the French "are concocting a scheme for overthrowing King Constantine and his dynasty and setting up Prince Louis Napoleon! It sounds like lunacy, but it is sober earnest on the part of the conspirators."[46]

Tsarina Alexandra, who was following events in Greece, was especially incensed that Russia was ignoring the Greeks' predicament, even promoting Allied policy against them. She told Nicky what she thought of it all: "I must say our diplomates [sic] behave *shamefully* & if Tino is kicked out, it will be our fault—horrid & unjust. . . . Vile shame!"[47] Three days later, the tsarina was again urging Nicholas II to try to do something about Greece: "we are driving them into a republic [by undermining their king], we, [their fellow] orthodox— its [sic] really shameful . . . we are behaving most unfairly & understand poor Tino going half wild."[48]

Finally, in December 1916, a combination of British and French troops landed in Athens. There, they met with resistance from royalist soldiers, sending tensions in the Greek capital sky-high. The Allies retaliated in the most forceful way possible by bombarding Athens in early December from their ships in Piraeus. Five- to twelve-inch shells pounded the ancient city in a merciless barrage. The Royal Palace itself took a beating. The king and queen were home, as were their two daughters, Helen and Katherine. The palace garden became a battle scene as trees and shrubs were destroyed by large shrapnel. Queen So-phie had sought out the women servants, wishing them to seek shelter from the bombardment. Some hesitated, but the queen insisted, saying, "I have already sent my daughter [three-and-a-half-year-old Princess Katherine] to the cellar. It is better to take no risks."[49] For several terrifying hours, Queen Sophie and her children along with the women of the palace hid in the cellar.

Ten days after the bombardment, King Constantine fired off a lengthy tele-gram to King George V: "You know and have always given me to understand that you believed I have never harboured any plots against you and your Allies. I entreat you do not push us to despair . . . we have been cruelly treated owing to lying and calumnious insinuations of political enemies, acting only for their own interior anti-dynastic party interests."[50]

By this stage, Queen Sophie had already despaired of the royal family's predicament and that of the Greek people. A series of telegrams sent to Berlin at the time, and published by the Greek government in 1919 as the Greek White Book, reveal her agitated state. Among them was one that Queen Sophie sent her brother, the Kaiser, describing her harrowing experience at the Royal Palace:

> By a miracle we are safe after a three-hours' bombardment of the Palace by the French fleet, which fired without warning. The shells exploded very near us. We took refuge in the cellars. Serious engagements also took place next day in the streets; the revolutionaries fired from the houses. The army and the people fought in a magnificent manner . . . and behaved loyally. . . . What will the demands of the Entente be? The health of all is good; great nervous ten-sion. We are prepared for everything. . . . Please inform us when the army in Macedonia will be sufficiently reinforced in order to undertake the definite offensive.[51]

After the Allies imposed a punishing blockade on Greece, the situation be-came intolerable. In another telegram, the queen told her brother in Berlin that "the blockade continues. We have bread enough to last until the end of Decem-ber."[52] And in yet another message said to have been sent by the queen, this time to Nicholas Theotokis, the Greek minister to Berlin, she is quoted as say-ing: "Owing to the continuation of the blockade we have bread for only a few days; other food-supplies too are diminishing. War against the Entente is there-fore now out of the question . . . I consider the game as lost, if the attack does not take place immediately; it will be too late afterwards."[53]

A week later, Queen Sophie found herself and the country in such dire straits that she was forced to send the following message to the Kaiser: "you can real-ize my situation! How much I suffer! . . . May the infamous pigs receive the punishment which they deserve!"[54] It was not so much for herself that Sophie worried but for the harsh circumstances under which the Greeks were barely surviving. In Athens, malnutrition was widespread and many children were dying of starvation. Heartbreaking scenes of people dropping dead in the streets of the capital became a common sight. The poor and the weakest of the population—the elderly and the children—were felled by epidemics of dysentery due to the poor grade of flour used for bread, the main staple of the Greek diet. The French proved merciless in implementing the blockade and even prevented the fishermen from catching anything, oftentimes sinking vessels that dared to venture out. When the fishermen protested, the commanders simply replied, "If you want to be left alone, you have only to drive out your King."[55]

The predicament of the Greek people and Queen Sophie deeply angered Mossy, who wrote to a friend, "You can imagine what I feel like about my sister, it makes ones [sic] hair stand on end. Have people gone quite mad? Oh dear, oh dear, when will they come to their senses again."[56]

The beleaguered Greek people besieged charitable institutions for help, foremost of which was the Patriotic League of Greek Women, which "under the competent management of the Queen, was able to distribute 10,000 meals a day, as well as clothes, blankets, medicine, milk for infants, etc."[57] Yet no matter how hard such institutions tried to combat illness and famine, it was not enough to prevent many unnecessary and dreadful deaths.

In just three weeks, the Allied blockade of Greece had succeeded in inflicting cruel blows on the Greek people. One of the most eloquent defenses on behalf of Queen Sophie came from Prince Nicholas of Greece, who in 1928 vigorously championed the queen by explaining that the documents published by the Greek government of 1919 in the White Book were "only partially authentic" and "others were either faked or . . . falsified for obvious reasons." The government in power at the time was certainly not partial to King Constantine, by then in exile in Switzerland. Prince Nicholas wrote that the essential thing to remember with the messages published in the White Book was that any "compromising messages" were "*not the cause* . . . but the '*the consequence*' of a situation made unbearable by a sequence of measures that were as humiliating as they were inflexible." As for the "several telegrams addressed by the Queen to the Kaiser," which "enquired when his armies would be ready for a decisive offensive in Macedonia," these questions were asked because "the timely interference of the Germans could alone deliver Greece from a frightful situation rendered all the more hopeless by the penury of provisions and munitions and by the pressure of the general blockade." In other words, the so-called "damning" evidence used against the queen was not that she was vehemently pro-German, but that she wanted to know when Greece might be delivered from a brutal blockade imposed by Allies.

As Prince Nicholas rightly pointed out: "The important fact must not be overlooked that the 'sensational and compromising' telegrams are those dated from December 1916 to beginning of February 1917; that is, during the period that the Entente Powers' coercive measures and the suffering and mortification of the King and Queen as well as the people's had reached their limit." In conclusion, Prince Nicholas wrote: "If your house is broken into and plundered and finally set on fire by persons whom you considered to be your best friends, have the latter any right to call you a 'traitor' because, in despair, you opened your window and screamed for help?"[58]

Three hellish months after the blockade started, the Greeks still showed little sign of succumbing to Allied pressure. Incensed, a Greek crowd attacked the French Legation, crying: "Long live the King, and down with the Allies." Later, as the blockade's vise tightened, starving Greeks cried out in their misery, "Long live the King!" and "We are pleased to starve for him!" "There were even cases of mothers snatching the bread from their children's hands, telling them they dare not eat while the King was hungry too."[59] A woman outside a soup kitchen in Piraeus summed it up when she retorted, "Give in? We will eat our children first!" Among the most poignant protestations were inscriptions found over the graves of dead babies: "Here lies my child, starved to death by Venizelos."[60] This accusation had some truth to it. For at the end of December 1916, Venizelos, through the French Legation at Athens, sent off instructions to the French Foreign Office "to let no corn into Greece except by driblets, and to let no money in at all." In the same message, Venizelos also offered "to raise a terrible revolution in Athens and to shatter the King."[61]

Contemporaries allied to the Entente who were familiar with their governments' actions in Greece acknowledged that the tragedy was indeed appalling. One British diplomat wrote that "altogether the proceedings of the Allies in Greece were of an equivocal and inglorious character and were due almost entirely to French initiative."[62] Even Compton Mackenzie, the British adventurer and author, who was not in King Constantine's good books because of his activities with the British Secret Service in Greece, which helped undermine the king's position, had defended Queen Sophie unequivocally: "I will take this opportunity of affirming that I believed none of the fantastic tales about her stratagems and that whenever and wherever I could I suppressed their circulation."[63]

Since Venizelos was openly pro-Entente, many Greeks were bitterly against the politician, whom they viewed with growing suspicion. On Christmas Day, 1916, in a dramatic manifestation of just how much the Greeks despised Venizelos, an anathema against him was carried out, in front of a crowd of thousands.

Sir Francis Elliot reported the event to his superiors in London: "This afternoon a ceremony of Anathema against Venizelos was performed by the Metropolitan of Athens accompanied by the Holy Synod at the Champs de Mars where a grave had been previously dug and filled and piled up with stones thrown by the populace to the cry of Anathema to the traitor. Shops were all shut in principal streets and great concourse attended ceremony."[64] A witness reported watching one old woman take her rock, brought from her farm in Attica, and cry out loudly as she cast the stone and cursed Venizelos: "We made him Premier; but he was not content. He would make himself king. Anathema!"[65]

Of the numerous warnings and pleas directed at the tsar and tsarina over their disastrous association with Rasputin, none was more heart-wrenching than the one made by Alexandra's older sister, the widowed Ella, who visited Tsarskoe Selo in December 1916, Ella did not mince words, telling Alix, "Rasputin is exasperating society. He is compromising the imperial family and will lead the dynasty to ruin." But the tsarina would have none it, replying, "Rasputin is a great man of prayer. All these rumors are slanders."[66] The meeting between the two sisters ended in bitterness. That frosty encounter was the last time the two would meet.

When the much-respected Ella had failed to change Alexandra's mind, there was little hope that anyone else could succeed. After the meeting with her sister, Ella saw Prince Felix Youssopov and related what had happened. This served to strengthen Felix's resolve that something drastic had to be done. A conspiracy to assassinate Rasputin emerged, involving Prince Felix Youssopov, Grand Duke Dmitri, and a member of the Duma, Vladimir Purishkevitch. Felix and Dmitri had close ties to the tsar and tsarina. Felix was married to the tsar's niece, Irina, while Dmitri was a cousin of Nicholas II and a nephew of Queen Sophie of Greece.

Rasputin was lured to Youssopov Palace in Petrograd, where he was plied with poisoned wine and poisoned cake. Incredibly, Rasputin kept on drinking and eating as if nothing was wrong. Finally, Felix shot him with a revolver, and when he saw the victim's immobile body, the *staretz* was taken for dead. But sometime during the early hours of the next day an inexplicable, bizarre event occurred. Youssopov went to the palace basement where Rasputin's lifeless body lay. "According to Felix, he felt for a pulse; there was none. Then, in a burst of rage, he seized the corpse by the shoulders and shook it violently. He threw the body back against the floor, then again knelt down beside it. Suddenly, the left eye twitched and then opened."[67] Rasputin, the miracle man, had done it again. This time, instead of snatching the Tsarevitch Alexei from death, it was the *staretz* himself who seemed to be rising from the dead.

The attacker now found himself attacked. Rasputin, his eyes pierced with fury, decided to lunge after Felix. "With a wild roar, Rasputin stumbled to his feet. Flailing his arms about in the air, he managed to grab Felix and rip one of the epaulets from his tunic. His eyes bulged in their sockets, and a thin stream of blood trickled from his lips. Calling, 'Felix! Felix!' he again reached for his assassin." Purishkevitch finally came to the rescue, but not before Rasputin cried out to Youssopov: "Felix! Felix! I will tell the Tsarina everything!"[68] They were his last words. Purishkevitch shot Rasputin in the back and the head. Their deed done, the murderers threw his body into the Neva River. Poisoned, stabbed, and shot three times, the seemingly indestructible Rasputin finally met his end in the freezing waters of the Neva.

A week after Rasputin's body was found in a tributary of the Neva, Marie of Romania wrote that "something uncanny and dreadful is going on there [in Russia]." Marie added, "how deplorable when a woman has a bad influence over a man! Poor Alix!"[69] But just as Alexandra's world was soon to explode in a wave of a violence, Marie's life was about to undergo tremendous upheaval. The foundations of the dynasty would be shaken to the core, and the cause would prove to be none other than Marie's eldest son, Carol.

Twenty-one

THE ABYSS

"THEY HAVE GOT HIM AT LAST, GENERAL."[1] WITH THOSE WORDS, Major General Hanbury-Williams learned that Russia's most hated man had been eliminated. The deed done, Tsarina Alexandra's final nightmare was set to begin. Only a month before, Alix, whose life was leaden with anxieties, had exhibited signs of renewal. General Hanbury-Williams found her to be "in really good spirits . . . and seemed hopeful about the war."[2] This hopeful mood, however, was shattered by Rasputin's murder.

Rasputin himself had been convinced that his days were numbered and gave out a dire warning:

> If I am killed by common assassins, and especially by my brothers the Russian peasants, you, Tsar of Russia, have nothing to fear . . . if it was your relations who have wrought my death then . . . none of your children or relations, will remain alive for more than two years . . . I shall be killed. I am no longer among the living . . . Gregory.[3]

When news of Rasputin's death came through, according to Pierre Gilliard, it was "like a thunderbolt."[4] Anna Viroubova recalled that Petrograd "burst into a wild orgy of rejoicing"[5]; and according to Sandro, amidst "universal rejoicing," Felix and Dmitri became "national heroes."[6] Lady Sybil Grey, who was living in St. Petersburg, saw how Youssopov had been elevated as a hero by the masses for murdering Rasputin. When rumors circulated that Dmitri and Felix were to be executed, it caused "great agitation among the factory workers." The telephones in the hospital Lady Sybil ran kept "ringing all day to say that they [the workers] had decided to form a body-guard to protect Yousopoff."[7]

Others, such as Dr. Eugene Botkin, viewed the murder with little enthusiasm. "Rasputin dead will be worse than Rasputin alive," he muttered. "Moreover, what Youssoupoff actually has done is to fire the first shot of the revolution. He has showed others the way—when a demand is not granted, take the law into your hands and shoot."[8]

At Tsarskoe Selo, Alexandra was in a state of shock. Gilliard recalled her "agonised features," her "inconsolable" grief.[9] She had lost the only person she deemed indispensable to the survival of her son. Dmitri's sister, Marie, who felt hostile toward the tsarina at the time, nevertheless admitted how "my heart perceived her torture." For Marie envisioned Alexandra hovering anxiously over Alexei, hearing the words Rasputin had endlessly repeated, "So long as I live, the Tsarevitch will live."[10]

The tsarina was also horrified that members of the Romanov dynasty could be behind such a heinous act. Dr. Botkin recounted to his son, Gleb, how the tsarina broke down and said, "I cannot get over it. Dimitriy, whom I have loved as my own son, conspiring against my life! And Youssoupoff—a nobody who owes all he has solely to the mercy of the Emperor! It is terrible."[11] The tsar was equally aghast.

When Prince Felix's father-in-law faced the tsar, begging him to treat Dmitri and Felix as "misguided patriots," Nicholas II retorted, "Nice speech, Sandro. Are you aware, however, that nobody has the right to kill, be it a grand duke or a peasant?"[12]

As punishment, the tsar ordered Dmitri and Felix exiled, the former to the Persian front, the latter to his estate in central Russia. Sixteen members of the Romanov family (including Queen Olga of Greece) wrote to the tsar pleading for him to spare Dmitri severe punishment. Nicholas II scribbled on the margin his answer: "No one has the right to kill, and I am astonished that the family should address itself to me with such requests. *Signed:* Nicholas."[13]

When Dimitri's father begged the tsar to free his son, Nicholas replied, "The Empress cannot allow him to be released."[14] The tsar's rejection of clemency for Dmitri marked a turning point in relations between Nicholas and Alexandra and the rest of the imperial dynasty, for it signaled an open breach between the tsar, tsarina, and the Romanovs. If the gates of Tsarskoe Selo had been left slightly ajar until now to the Romanov clan, Nicholas, with the full approval of his wife, had just slammed them shut. Bereft of much family support and with the masses agitating, Nicholas and Alexandra clung to each other more than ever.

Rasputin was buried at Tsarskoe Selo, along with an icon that had been signed by the tsarina and her daughters and a letter from Alexandra. With his death, anxieties over the future of Russia and the imperial family did not diminish: It was after all a natural extension of what Rasputin had once prophesied to the tsar and tsarina: "If I die or you desert me, you will lose your son and your crown within six months."[15]

⁂

While the political noose around Tsarina Alexandra and her family tightened in the early months of 1917, signaling the imminent fall of the Romanov dynasty, her cousin, Queen Sophie of the Hellenes, watched helplessly as her country was battered by the merciless dictates of the Allied Powers in their campaign to bring Greece to its knees. One historian has said that the Allied blockade amounted to "a more subtle and elegant form of massacre. Instead of the victim's throat being cut he is made to die of starvation."[16]

By the spring of 1917, the Greek people "understood that all the French bullying had but one aim, to deliver over a defenceless Greece to 'the traitor Venizelos.'"[17] The royal family was well aware that most of the unrelenting pressure on Greece emanated from the French. However, the fact that Great Britain supported the French in their perfidious actions proved difficult for this Anglophile family to swallow. Queen Sophie's eldest daughter, Princess Helen, summed up the family's feelings when she said that "it was as though some dear, trusted friend had cold-bloodedly pushed a dagger in one's back."[18]

⁂

Back in Russia, Rasputin's murder did not solve anything. The poisonous cloud of anarchy reappeared. Petrograd descended to being a city on edge, recapturing its reputation as the city of trouble. The people's fury, held in check for so long, was set to erupt. A prominent Russian, Alexander Zvegintsev, once warned his British friend, the historian Sir Bernard Pares: "Do not wish for a Russian Revolution! It will be far more savage than the French."[19]

By the end of February, the tsarist empire was clearly crumbling, thanks to the revolutionary workers and their supporters, who "had in their hands some forty thousand rifles, thirty thousand revolvers, and four hundred machine guns . . . more than sixty-six thousand soldiers went over to the crowd."[20] In a last-ditch effort to save the monarchy, Rodzianko telegraphed Nicholas: "Garrison troops can no longer be relied upon. Reserve battalions of guards in revolt. They are killing their own officers. Sire, do not delay. If the movement reaches the army, it will mean the ruin of Russia. Inevitably, the dynasty will fall with it. Tomorrow may be too late."[21]

Petrograd and its environs were engulfed in a sea of revolutionary fever, red flags fluttering ominously over the city. Atrocities were committed against those who had shown loyalty to the tsar. Even innocent children were not immune.

⟨꙳⟩

Queen Marie of Romania meanwhile was terrified for Romania and for Russia. "What would happen to us if things went wrong in Russia is not to be contemplated. It would mean utter and complete disaster, it would mean the end of everything!"[22] More news of Alix's predicament in Russia reached Queen Marie and she admitted to being "absolutely horrified" at what she heard. "Their [the Russians'] hatred of the Empress," she noted in January 1917, "has reached a terrible pitch; they consider her a misfortune for the country and there is no one to-day who would not gladly get rid of her by any means. How dreadful! I cannot imagine anything more ghastly than to be hated by one's own people, and after all it is not so very difficult to make yourself beloved if you are Queen, in Russia especially where the Tsar and Tsarina are almost sacred figures."[23] Marie was absolutely correct. It was precisely because so many people looked to her for help in Romania's darkest hours that she felt so overwhelmed. Yet she never completely lost hope. "Everything seems too hard, too difficult, too completely dreadful, as though no human strength could stand such pressure and not give way to despair," the queen wrote in her diary. "But I *shall* stand it, I have sworn to stand it to the bitter end, it may even be a glorious end; at the deepest depths of my soul, I still believe it will be a glorious end, though I must admit that nothing at the present time justifies this optimism."[24]

Despite her own crisis, Tsarina Alexandra had not forgotten Marie's predicament at Jassy and sent her supplies for the soldiers and townspeople when possible. The two countries, after all, were formal allies. Even toward Alexandra's dying days of power in February 1917, Marie was grateful to find that five wagons full of goods had arrived for distribution; and just days before the Russian monarchy's downfall, Marie dutifully recorded: "Another beautiful present arrived for me from Empress Alexandra, a quantity of linen, medicines and provisions for the hospitals."[25]

Though the tsarina helped Romania when she could through the donations of medical provisions, the Russian troops so desperately needed by Romania in the war effort were another story. Romania's army had proven no match for the German military machine that charged its way through the country. A lack of well-trained officers and a shortage of artillery marred Romania's efforts. "Artillery and aircraft were in desperately short supply and medical facilities were abysmal. As a result, the suffering of Romanian peasant troops was truly awful, even by the especially dreadful standards of the First World War."[26] The thousands upon thousands of Russian soldiers who were to have been Romania's saviours turned out to be more trouble than they were worth. Feeding them was exceptionally difficult since there was so little food left in Romania.

During the war, the queen was aided in her rounds by one or more of her children, whose formative years were now seared by the firsthand experience of war. All of Marie's children, without exception, were privy to ghastly scenes of suffering: Elisabetta, Nicky, Mignon, Ileana, and Carol. Marie had always looked for signs of growing maturity in Crown Prince Carol. He did not disappoint, exhibiting perseverance, hard work, organization, and a sense of the confidence his father always appeared to lack. Perhaps the experience of war had helped to change Carol for the better.

Writing in 1917, when the war's outcome and Romania's fate were still unknown, Marie refused to be cowed, stating confidently: "I want to declare that in spite of the calamity that has come over her, Roumania does not regret having thrown in her lot with those fighting for a holy cause! . . . Roumania is proud of her Allies, confident in their noble sense of justice." The queen also added that "when the great hour of Victory strikes, those for whom she [Romania] bled so sorely will not forget that she also has won her right to live!"[27] In this, Queen Marie emulated her grandmother, Queen Victoria, who, in the darkest hour of the Boer War and at the end of her life, railed at Arthur Balfour, saying emphatically that no one was depressed and defeat was not in the cards. If the old queen's rallying cry at Windsor was, as one biographer puts it, "the climax of her vocation to 'be of use,'"[28] then Marie of Romania's own battle cry was an exact parallel. It was classic Queen Victoria at her finest.

⌘

While Alexandra exhibited a calm exterior to those living at the Alexander Palace and the soldiers guarding Tsarskoe Selo, her soul burned like a raging volcano. She was worried about Russia, Nicholas, and the Revolution at her gates, and scared for her desperately sick children, Olga, Tatiana and Alexei, now ill with the measles. In one of her last letters to Nicholas as tsarina, Alix, in a tone of mingled anguish, defiance, and sympathy, wrote:

My own beloved, precious Angel, light of my life,
My heart breaks, thinking of you all alone going through all this anguish, anxiety, & we know nothing of you & you neither of us . . . you who are alone, no army behind you, caught like a mouse in a trap, what can you do? Thats [sic] the lowest, meanest thing unknown in history, to stop ones sovereign. . . .

Two currents—*Duma* & revolutionists—two snakes who I hope will eat off each others [*sic*] heads.... Heart aches very much, but I don't heed it.... Only suffer too hideously for you.... God bless & protect you—send His angels to guard & guide you ... this is the climax of the bad. The horror before our Allies!! & the enemies joy!!—Can advise nothing, be only yr. Precious self. If you have to give into things, God will help you to get out of them. Ah my suffering Saint. I am one with you, inseparably one

Old Wify[29]

In early March 1917, at Pskov, where Tsar Nicholas II was sidelined on board a train, the Duma confronted him with two alternatives: Either march on toward Petrograd with loyalist troops and risk civil war or abdicate. Without hesitation the tsar agreed to abdicate, wishing to spare the Russian people further bloodshed.

Thus, with the simple stroke of a pen, Nicholas II put an end to the three-hundred-year Romanov dynasty. With his reign ended, so too ended his wife's position as empress. Alexandra was Tsarina of Russia for twenty-two and a half grueling years. The tsar also decided that his only son would not survive the rigors of being emperor and so was moved to exclude him from the succession. Better to have Alexei with him, Alix, and the girls than to break the close family unit. Besides, if the tsarevitch was separated from his mother at this critical juncture, Nicky knew Alix would be devastated. Nicholas II therefore signed the act of abdication in favor of his younger brother, Grand Duke Michael, rather than Alexei, the son for whom Alexandra had prayed so fervently.

As for Alexandra, the waiting seemed unbearable. Finally, on 3 March 1917, the Grand Duke Paul dropped the bombshell. In an emotional audience, Alexandra heard the dreadful news. After the interview with the grand duke ended, Alix was met by Lili Dehn, who found the tsarina stupefied. Clutching Lili's hands in hers, Alexandra exclaimed: *"Abdiqué!"* In this moment of great tragedy, raw with emotion, she thought solely of the immense sadness of her husband. Barely audible, the words tumbled out: *"le pauvre ... tout seul là bas ... oh, mon Dieu, par quoi il a passé! Et je ne puis pas être près de lui pour le consoler."*[30]

After endless months of plying her husband in her letters with demands that he resolutely hold to the path of autocracy, when it came to reacting to the news that Nicholas had abdicated, Alexandra gave her beloved husband her complete support and understanding. Instead of bemoaning his abdication, Alix thought only of what he must have been going through:

I *fully* understand yr. action [in abdicating], my own heroe [*sic*]! I *know* that [you] could not sign [anything] against what you swore at yr. coronation. We know each other through & through—need no words—as I live, we shall see you back on yr. throne, brought back by your people, to the glory of your reign. You have saved yr. son's reign & the country & yr. saintly purity. . . . I hold you tight, tight in my arms & will never let them touch your shining soul. I kiss, kiss, kiss & bless you & will always understand you.

Wify.[31]

The former tsarina was under no illusions as to what the abdication meant. When she went to see a distraught Anna Viroubova the next morning, she said, "You know, Annia, all is finished for our Russia. But we must not blame the people or the soldiers for what has happened."[32]

Queen Marie of Romania, upon hearing of the abdication, confided to her diary:

What an hour for that woman . . . she who would listen to no one except Rasputin, and separated herself little by little from all the members of the family, then from the whole of society, never showing herself any more, shutting herself up either in Tsarskoe or in the Crimea. . . .

What may her feelings be to-day? How does she bear it, separated, as she is from her husband, he not able to get to her and all her children down with measles. A ghastly situation. I sit and ponder over it and to me it seems tragic and fearful beyond words.

. . . What influence will it have on the War, on our fate? Tragic questions to which I find no answer.[33]

In the days between the tsar's abdication and his anticipated arrival back at the Alexander Palace, Lili Dehn and the ex-tsarina began systematically to destroy numerous letters and diaries to prevent the revolutionaries from seizing them and possibly fabricating all kinds of anti-Romanov propaganda. Alexandra rifled through her correspondence and went on to destroy more after her husband's arrival. The most difficult to part with were the letters from Queen Victoria and Nicholas to Alexandra. When it came time to destroy Nicholas's love letters to her since the days before their marriage, Alix could not stop weeping. Rising from her chair, she took them one by one, placed them in the fire, and watched as her husband's words of love and devotion were consumed by the glowing flames.

Within days of Nicholas II's abdication, the tsarina and her children were placed under house arrest. The tsar's household staff was given an ultimatum:

Either they left the Alexander Palace at once or they could choose house arrest with the tsarina and her family. In what turned out to be "a veritable orgy of cowardice and stupidity, and a sickening display of shabby, contemptible disloyalty," many chose to abandon the tsarina. "People who but a few days previously had paraded their monarchistic convictions were now assuring everybody of their loyalty to the revolution and heaping abuses upon the Emperor and the Empress, referring to His Majesty as 'Colonel Romanov,' or simply 'Nicholas.' "[34] Gleb Botkin's father, the imperial family's physician, could not bring himself to be disloyal. He bravely chose to share the family's uncertain fate, and in so doing, would meet his end with them in a dark cellar in Siberia. Others who chose to stay and share in the uncertainty of captivity included several attendants and retainers and close friends. When Pierre Gilliard told Alexei what had happened and Alix broke the news to her daughters, the children's modesty and deep sense of filial devotion shone forth. Alexei never once expressed regret or even questioned the loss of his position as heir or as tsar. The girls, though seriously ill at the time (Anastasia and Marie had also fallen sick), were only concerned for their father and mother.

One evening, before Nicholas's arrival, Alexandra spent a tense, lonely night in her bedroom; Lili Dehn, keeping her promise to the sick grand duchesses that she would stay with their mother, had made up a bed in the room next to the Mauve Boudoir. All was still and calm—until gunshots crackled and the soldiers in their coarse drunkenness broke the peace with vulgar songs and laughter. Alexandra could hardly sleep that night, nor could Lili, who could hear the former tsarina roaming about her bedroom, coughing. Of all the items in Alexandra's favorite room that night, none was more characteristic than the bunches of lilacs in front of the tall windows. Since fresh supplies from the South of France no longer arrived to grace the Mauve Boudoir, only the old ones were left. "Just before dawn, the dying lilac seemed to expire in a last breath of perfume."[35] Those dead blooms presaged life ahead for Alexandra Feodorovna.

Twenty-two

DEATH AT EKATERINBURG

IN THE DARK DAYS AND MONTHS FOLLOWING THE ABDICATION OF Nicholas II, Alexandra and her family faced a life of captivity at the Alexander Palace. To her credit, Alix remained strong throughout the ordeal. To those who knew her well, there was little doubt as to where Alexandra derived her strength and serenity. "Her faith," noted a friend, "came to her rescue."[1]

When Nicholas returned to Tsarskoe Selo within days of his abdication, an expression of "utter dejection" was etched on the ex-tsar's face, for he was a man whose "spirit seemed completely broken." Only when they were alone in Alix's Mauve Boudoir did Nicky completely lose his self-control, weeping bitter tears. For a moment, Alix was overcome, unable to think how she could comfort her desolate husband. In the end, she rose to the occasion, and though "it was excessively difficult for her to console him," she let her heart speak. In so doing, she assured her beloved Nicky that it was "the husband and father [who were] of more value in her eyes than the Emperor whose throne she had shared."[2]

ᘓᗢᗣᗢᘒ

The tsar's spectacular downfall sent shockwaves throughout Europe. That the once powerful Romanov dynasty should be toppled by the people meant that other thrones were in danger of succumbing to the same fate. Where the King and Queen of the Hellenes were concerned, the tsar's abdication meant more than a tragic turn of events; for the disappearance of Nicholas II from the political scene meant that the Greek king's strongest protector was no more. With the eruption of the Russian Revolution early in 1917, the fates of King Constantine

I and Queen Sophie looked increasingly bleak because the overthrow of the imperial family in Russia emboldened the Greek royal family's enemies—the Venizelists and their Allied partners—to seek the same outcome for Constantine and Sophie.

Sophie's sister, Mossy, was constantly worried and saddened by her sister's predicament. The two sisters had always been close, often meeting in Mossy's home, Friedrichshof, in Germany, which she inherited from their mother. Eastbourne, in England, had also been a favorite rendezvous point for the two sisters. The outbreak of the war, however, put a stop to these vacations together. Writing to a mutual friend of theirs, Mossy lamented the fact that "I get nothing from there [Greece]. Too cruel & so senseless. You can imagine what it means to us both. Soon we shall have been separated 3 years."[3]

In Greece, the king's enemies accused him of acting unconstitutionally, but even Sir Francis Elliot admitted early in April 1917 that "as to the 'unconstitutional behaviour of King Constantine' it is only fair to consider that under present circumstances it is not open to him to behave otherwise."[4] Ten days later, Elliot reported of a desperate Constantine: "He repeated that there is no enmity against us in Greece, that her interests are bound up with ours and that all he wants is to be left alone and to maintain his neutrality. But the French were openly speaking of occupying the country and dethroning him . . . he wanted to know what he could do to satisfy the Entente and he trusted H.M. Government to obtain this information."[5] Constantine I was certainly not exaggerating. In May, Elliot admitted in another confidential despatch to London that "while French Minister is instructed to observe an attitude of reserve French members of military mission openly advocate occupation of Greece and dethronement of king."[6]

By June 1917, the perfidy of the French had reached new lows when a French senator, Charles Jonnart, arrived in Athens and bullied King Constantine and the Greek prime minister, Alexandros Zaïmis, threatening to destroy Athens if the king did not abdicate in favor of his second son, Alexander (the heir, George, was deemed too "pro-German" because of his military training in Germany). Like Tsar Nicholas just months before, King Constantine did not want civil war to erupt on his account and so opted to leave Greece. "I have no choice," he told a shocked Queen Sophie and Princess Helen; "there must be no more blood spilt because of me."[7] Upon meeting with the Crown Council, Constantine announced that he and Prince George would give way, but would not sign an act of abdication, thus leaving the throne to Tino and Sophie's second son, twenty-four-year-old Alexander.

Word of Jonnart's startling ultimatum and the ensuing change of monarchs sent worried Athenians pouring into the streets surrounding Queen Sophie's palace. The crowd, growing in density with each passing hour, became increasingly agitated and shouted its support for the royal family. Cries of "We will never let our Constantine go!" reverberated as church bells "tolled mournfully hour after hour."[8] The fact that this was all happening on 11 June filled the Greeks with trepidation, for Constantine and Sophie were being driven from their throne on a dreaded anniversary. This was the day that Constantine XI Palaeologus, the last Emperor of Byzantium, died while fighting against the Turks, thereby marking the fall of Constantinople. Tino and Sophie could not have suffered their humiliation at a worst time. With the departure of the royal couple imminent, dreams of a new Byzantium under Constantine and Sophie were shattered.

Inside the palace, Sophie's home was thrown into chaos as people filled the place in order to express their disgust at the ultimatum and their support for their sovereigns. The king tried to calm the agitated throng, which consisted of deputations from differing guilds and the military, explaining to them that this sacrifice was necessary. Before leaving, the supplicants kissed Constantine's hand, tears streaming down many faces. As the hours passed, the dense crowds outside the palace sensed that their appeals were not working. Indignation and sorrow changed to fear and determination—fear that the royal family might flee Greece and determination to stop them. All of a sudden, the Greek royal family became captives of their people.

"For more than twenty-four hours," wrote Prince Nicholas, "we were literally besieged in the Palace." It was, in Nicholas's words, a "never-to-be forgotten night . . . there was something infinitely pathetic in the fact that the King was a prisoner in his own house! A prisoner, not guarded by the stern watchfulness of unsympathetic warders, but shielded and protected by his own subjects trembling lest he should desert them."[9]

As darkness descended, the ancient city fell strangely silent. "It was," according to one eyewitness, "as if the people of Athens were visiting a tomb or a lying-in-state."[10] Queen Sophie and the rest of the royal family with her that momentous night could hardly sleep.

At four-thirty the next morning, the king's chauffeur arrived at a side entrance of the palace, and the royal family prepared to leave. They were abruptly stopped when "the guardsmen threw themselves on the ground as much as to say that the vehicle must pass over their bodies. The King and the royal family withdrew, and the car went away empty."[11] When, at six o'clock in the morning, Prince Nicholas, his wife, and Prince Andrew tried again to leave the palace, they were beaten back inside by the vigilant crowds of Athenians. "Go back," they screamed in anger, "we shall not let you pass."[12] Finally, King Constantine issued a proclamation to his people:

Even far from Greece, the Queen and I will always retain the same affection towards the Greek people. I beg you all to accept my decision with serenity, trusting to God, Whose blessing I invoke on the nation. . . . At this moment the greatest solace for the Queen and myself lies in the affection and devotion which you have always shown to us, in the happy days as in the unhappy ones. May God protect Greece.

—Constantine R.[13]

The people answered with mournful wails: "No! No!" "He musn't go!" "We will not let you go." "We want our King!"[14] When Jonnart saw the people's re-action, he grew nervous and ordered French troops to land at Piraeus and ad-vance to Athens. On the same day, Sophie's second son, Alexander, was sworn in and became King of the Hellenes. Between the advancing French troops and the stubborn crowds surrounding the palace, the situation was reaching danger point. It became imperative that Tino and Sophie vacate the palace with their family. Otherwise they risked death either from the French troops or their zeal-ous subjects, for a new cry could now be heard from the crowd: "It would be better to kill the King than let him leave Greece."[15]

The royal family finally bolted into waiting cars, running in an effort to es-cape their devoted but frenzied captors. When the people at the front of the palace saw what was happening, they went wild with grief. Prince Nicholas de-scribed how, "holding each other tightly, and in the midst of cries and protesta-tions, we literally fought our way through to the gate."[16] Prince Christopher also wrote vividly of their harrowing escape:

Queen Sophie, who had been ill, lagged behind and two of us seized her un-der the arms and almost carried her along, spurred on by the yells of the crowd on discovering that it had been tricked. We could hear the wooden railings cracking in the general stampede back to the front of the Palace, but by that time the King, Queen Sophie and their children had hurled them-selves unceremoniously into the cars. The Crown Prince drove off lying on the floor of one, with his legs waving wildly out of the open door . . . and started for Tatoi.[17]

The royal family were not only frightened for themselves but became scared for the very crowds, for suddenly people flung themselves on the ground in an attempt to prevent them from leaving. Even more dramatic were instances of attempted suicide. Prince Nicholas recalled, "I saw one man pull a revolver out of his pocket and try to shoot himself; a guardsman snatched it our of his hand just in time."[18] Once the crowds realized their attempts were in vain, a sudden sense of foreboding hit them. For just as Sophie and her family sped off toward Tatoi, it began to rain, and those who were superstitious saw this as a terrible omen.

From Tatoi, Sophie and her family left for the port of Oropus, an ancient town with a small pier that jutted out into the sea. People had packed the roads leading to Oropus to say good-bye. Once there, the royal family were treated to scenes of more devotion as flowers were thrown onto the pier. Making their way on board the weathered royal yacht *Sphacteria,* Sophie and Constantine were again mobbed by admiring crowds who wanted to touch them, eliciting gentle pleas from the king to be allowed to pass.

Prince Nicholas, still with his brother and sister-in-law, recounted Constantine and Sophie's poignant last minutes on Greek soil:

> The crush became even greater when we advanced along the pier; the nearer the King and Queen drew to the boat the fiercer grew the frenzy of the people, who tried to keep him back by force; many leaped into the sea and held fast to the boat. The King and Queen, after a last handshake right and left, stepped into the boat . . . among lamentations and sobs that rent the air . . . whilst all the people went down on their knees and stretched out their hands towards the King and Queen. It was a heart-rending picture and the King ordered them to put on speed.[19]

A lone voice stood out. Alexander, Sophie's second son, left behind to reign in Constantine's stead, was heard to cry out from the shore at Oropus after his departing father: "You shall come back to us soon."[20]

The French had deposed King Constantine and hounded him and his queen from their country. In the monumental battle that pitted Sophie's husband and the dynasty against Eleutherios Venizelos, Venizelos and the Allies had won. Sir Francis Elliot captured the mood in Athens after Constantine and Sophie's departure: "In practically two days the shops, banks and theatres . . . were closed and the city had the appearance of having been struck dumb."[21]

It has been said that the deposition of the legitimate monarch in Greece in June 1917 was "the end result of a situation which concealed one of the most complicated episodes of inter-allied diplomacy of the whole war."[22] Others have been more blunt. The "martyr King" lost, "persecuted by France and by England and calumnied by the 'Satan of Salonika,' " Venizelos.[23] Of Eleutherios Venizelos, Admiral Kerr concluded that "Constantine and his family were, he considered, a bar to the fulfilment of his great dream [of re-creating the old Greek empire], and so by hook or by crook they must be swept out of his way."[24]

After Constantine and Sophie's deposition, Venizelos began his three-year rule of the country, marked by the imposition of martial law. Concerted efforts to install pro-Venizelists to important positions continued and a purge of pro-royalists within the armed forces was carried out so that over a thousand officers and soldiers were exiled, dismissed, or imprisoned. Instead of seeking to heal a deeply divided country, the Venizelos regime sought instead to consolidate its hold over power, to the detriment of those who had been or continued to be loyal to Constantine I. With Constantine and Sophie in exile and their inexperienced young son, Alexander I, a virtual prisoner in the palace, Venizelos was able to bring Greece into the Allied camp at last.

Sophie was almost forty-seven years old; she had been crown princess for over twenty years and Queen of the Hellenes for just over four. But exile from Greece did not bring tranquility. Worries over the fate of her son would never abate. And Sophie was to find to her great cost that Constantine's sacrifice of his throne had come at an unbearably high personal price.

⚭

Held in captivity at Tsarskoe Selo, Nicholas and Alexandra remained a devoted couple. Physically, the former tsar and tsarina were a study in contrasts. Nicholas continued to carry on with his physical exercise as much as his guards allowed. Shoveling snow in winter, felling trees and preparing and planting a vegetable garden in the warmer months, occupied the outdoor-loving Nicky. Alix, on the other hand, once so beautiful, looked old beyond her years and was a physical wreck. Her weak legs and troubled heart meant that Nicky had to push her about in a wheelchair, a task he did devotedly.

The royal couple's dignified behavior was pronounced in contrast to those who mercilessly hurled taunts at them. The tall iron fencing surrounding the park at Tsarskoe Selo offered no protection from jeering crowds who came to leer and insult their former tsar. And the soldiers guarding the couple were equally impudent. An abusive exchange at the end of March 1917 highlighted this, when some of the soldiers shouted insolently at the ex-tsar: "Well, well, Nicolouchka (Little Nicholas), so you are breaking the ice now, are you? Perhaps you've drunk enough of our blood? . . . And in summer, when there's no more ice—what'll you do then, *Goloubchik nach* (our darling)? Perhaps you'll throw a little sand on the walks with a little shovel?"[25] Only when some of their captors actually spoke to the imperial family did a few minds change in favor of Nicholas and Alexandra. One even conceded to the former tsarina: "Do you know, Alexandra Feodorovna, I had quite a different idea of you? I was mistaken about you."[26]

Alexander Kerensky, as a senior member of the Provisional Government, visited the couple at Tsarskoe Selo. Though he urged them to have confidence in the Provisional Government, Kerensky did not exactly give orders that would endear him to his wards. Lili Dehn and Anna Viroubova were sent off to Petrograd. During one of his visits, Kerensky interrogated Alexandra on her political role. For an hour, a frank exchange took place in which Alexandra told Kerensky that since she and Nicholas were absolutely as one in their marriage, they discussed everything. "It was true that they had discussed the different appointments of ministers, but this could not be otherwise in a marriage which was as united as theirs." Kerensky was satisfied, even "struck by the clarity, the energy and the frankness of her words."[27] He evidently believed in her sincerity, for Kerensky afterwards told Nicholas, "your wife does not lie."[28]

Exile for the family in England came up for discussion. At first the British government, under the prime minister, David Lloyd George, endorsed the idea of granting asylum to Nicholas and Alexandra and their children; but in a curious twist of fate, the couple's cousin, King George V, thought twice about the matter. Owing to domestic opposition, especially from the left, George V instructed his private secretary, Lord Stamfordham, to advise Lloyd George that the granting of asylum to a former autocrat who had been unpopular among the British might not be such a good idea after all.

In all fairness to George V, he did not know that his actions might lead to the imperial family's execution. Anti-German feeling was high at home, prompting the king to change the name of his own house from that of Saxe-Coburg-Gotha to the much more Anglicized House of Windsor; and along with this change came a wholesale shedding of other German titles among the king's numerous English relatives, not least Queen Ena of Spain's two brothers, who lost their title as Princes of Battenberg and became, instead, the Marquis of Carisbrooke and Lord Leopold Mountbatten.

During the family's captivity, Alexandra felt keenly the incessant attacks against her husband in the press. Writing to a Russian Army officer who had been a patient at the hospital at Tsarskoe Selo during the war, the former tsarina poured out her frustration: "They write so much filth about Him [Nicholas II]; a weak mind and so forth. It gets worse and worse, I throw the papers down, it hurts, it hurts all the time. Everything good is forgotten, it is so hard to read curses against the people you love most. . . . When they write filth about Me— let them, they started tormenting me long ago, I don't care now, but that they slander Him, throw dirt on the Sovereign Anointed by God, that is beyond the bearable." Once again, Alexandra's lengthy letter revealed her reliance on God in all her tribulations: "You know that I have nearly lost all faith in people, and yet My whole being is in God, and no matter what happens, this faith cannot be taken away. . . . There is no such adversity that does not pass. God promised us this in His endless mercy, and we know what unimaginable bliss He readies for those who love Him."[29]

In August 1917, Alexandra and her family were ordered to leave Tsarskoe Selo for Tobolsk, seven hundred miles east of Moscow in western Siberia, as the next best alternative. With insolent soldiers and hostile railwaymen making their departure difficult and humiliating, "the scene was as disgraceful as could be."[30]

The family left Tsarskoe Selo forever the day after Alexei's thirteenth birthday. For several days, the train carrying them traveled east, with the window shades pulled down whenever a station was passed. Arriving at Tiumen, on the banks of the Tobol, the family then boarded a steamer that sailed past Pokrovskoie, Rasputin's village. They finally reached their destination, Tobolsk, a town of some twenty thousand people, dotted with onion-domed churches and wooden homes. There Nicholas and Alexandra encamped at the governor's house until the spring of 1918. At first the family's confinement proved less constricting than might have been expected. The town's residents, for one, still felt loyal to the family. When Nicholas and Alexandra went to a nearby church for Mass, they were greeted by people falling on their knees and crossing themselves.

From Tobolsk, Alexandra received some correspondence from a few friends. She was also able to send off messages to the outside world. More and more references to God and the afterlife appeared in the former tsarina's correspondence. In one letter to Anna Viroubova, Alexandra wrote: "Ah God! Still He is merciful and will never forget His own. Great will be their reward in Heaven. The more we suffer here the fairer it will be on that other shore where so many dear ones await us."[31]

At the end of October, Vladimir Lenin and the Bolsheviks seized power and overthrew Kerensky's Provisional Government, marking the beginning of a more radical and dangerous shift to the left. With the withdrawal of the more moderate Kerensky and the appearance of the ruthless Lenin, the lives of the ex-tsar and his family were further endangered.

As the months passed and the outcome of the war and the family's captivity remained unresolved, Alexandra became anxious, especially for her country. "Although we suffer horribly still there is peace in our souls," wrote the ex-tsarina. But above all, "I suffer most for Russia." What pained Alexandra and her family was the tragedy facing the Russian people; as she told Anna, "it is the sufferings of the innocent which nearly kills [sic] us."[32]

As Christmas 1917 approached, Alexandra's melancholy descended into deeper depression, brought on no doubt by the long darkness and intense cold. The notorious Siberian winter made its way into the house with its drafty windows and left in its wake a shivering Alexandra, her fingers nearly frozen, and in pain. With temperatures plunging to near –60 degrees at Christmastime, Gleb Botkin, who was with them, recalled how "the Siberian winter held us, by that time, completely in its icy grip . . . one can only sit in despair and shiver . . . one no longer lives during the Siberian winter but merely vegetates, in a sort of frozen stupor."[33]

Alexandra's conduct during this period touched Dr. Botkin, who told his son, "I was moved to tears. Here are we, come to Tobolsk for the purpose of helping the Imperial family to keep up their courage in exile, but in reality it is they who are helping us." Botkin's son rightly concluded that Alexandra "behaved, throughout, with true heroism, and exhibited a touching kindness for everybody who shared the exile of her family."[34]

As Russia was reeling from the war and Lenin wanted to consolidate power, the Bolsheviks were compelled to make peace with the Central Powers, culminating in the 3 March 1918 Treaty of Brest Litovsk. Lenin ceded huge tracts of land and large swathes of population in a humiliating and harsh agreement imposed by Germany and its allies. Russia gave up Finland, Poland, the Ukraine, the Baltic States, and most of Byelorussia. Not only had Russia lost much land and a good many people to the Central Powers, it had also let down the Entente side by withdrawing from the war. Nicholas was devastated by the news. "Had I known it would come to this," he dejectedly told Dr. Botkin, "I would never have abdicated."[35]

In the former tsarina's eyes, Lenin's actions amounted to nothing short of treachery. "What infamy!" exclaimed Alexandra, "that the Lord God should give peace to Russia, yes, but not by way of treason with the Germans."[36] To Anna Viroubova, she wrote indignantly: "What a nightmare it is that it is Germans who are saving Russia (from Communism). . . . What could be more humiliating for us? With one hand the Germans give, and with the other they take away. Already they have seized an enormous territory. God help and save this unhappy country. Probably He wills us to endure all these insults, but that we must take them from the Germans almost kills me."[37] When Alexandra heard rumors that Germany might actually be asking for the family to be placed in their hands, she recoiled at the thought, saying, "after what they have done to the Tsar, I would rather die in Russia than be saved by the Germans."[38] Within months, Alexandra was to get her wish. The former tsarina most likely had a premonition that the end was drawing near, for in April 1918 she wrote that "though we know that the storm is coming nearer our souls are at peace."[39]

That April, Alexei was felled by another hemophiliac attack. As he slowly improved, a further dilemma befell Alexandra, thanks to the actions of militant Bolsheviks. Three hundred miles to the southeast of Tobolsk stood the industrial city of Ekaterinburg. Among the most fanatically radical of the Bolsheviks, the Ekaterinburg Soviet was intent on getting its hands on Nicholas and Alexandra and their children. In April 1918, the leaders in Moscow ordered Nicholas to leave Tobolsk. Bowing to pressure, Nicholas had no alternative. Alexandra was seized with fear for her husband. Wishing to be by his side, but wracked by the fact that Alexei was still very weak, Alexandra, for once, did not know what to do. Tatiana forced the issue, telling her distraught mother, "You cannot go on tormenting yourself like this." Gathering up her courage, Alexandra chose to accompany Nicholas and leave Alexei in the care of his sisters, Pierre Gilliard, and the few retainers left loyal at Tobolsk. "It is the hardest moment of my life," the distraught mother and wife told her maid. "You know what my son is to me, and I must choose between him and my husband. But I have made up my mind. I must be firm. I must leave my child and share my husband's life or death."[40] Sidney Gibbs, the English tutor, who came to share the family's travails in Tobolsk, recalled that on the evening before the separation, tea was served in Alexandra's room. According to Gibbs, "there was not much talking and no pretence at gaiety. It was solemn and tragic, a fit prelude to an inescapable tragedy."[41] The farewells were heart-wrenching, with Alexandra and her children sobbing. With superhuman effort Alexandra tore herself from the house where her sick son, Alexei, could be heard crying wildly: "Mother, mother."[42]

After several uncertain weeks, the family was reunited at Ekaterinburg. Together, they lived under difficult conditions in the home of the Ipatiev family, commandeered for use by the Bolsheviks as the house of special purpose. Encircled by a high fence, the white brick and stone building housed an increasingly persecuted family. Nearly all the retainers were taken from them, including Nagorny, who had so faithfully helped care for Alexei, carrying him about when the boy could not walk. With the windows whitewashed and simple requests such as opening them during days of stifling heat summarily denied, guarded for the most part by unsympathetic men, the Ekaterinburg experience of captivity descended into nightmare.

As a concerned mother, Alexandra Feodorovna's anxiety for her daughters' safety never abated. After leaving Tsarskoe Selo for Tobolsk, and then Ekaterinburg, the grand duchesses were subjected to varying degrees of humiliation by their captors; but whatever cruelties they suffered, the girls for the most part held up. The children's high moral standards made an impression on some. Describing Alexandra's family earlier in their captivity in March 1917, a Russian Orthodox priest who heard their confessions was struck by the children's innocence, a product no doubt of their mother's upbringing. The priest recorded: "Lord, let all children be morally as upright as the children of the former tsar. Such mildness, restraint, obedience to their parents' wishes, such absolute devotion to God's will . . . and complete ignorance of worldly filth—either passionate or sinful— amazed me."[43]

Though some of the guards could sometimes detect a trace of pride in the ex-tsarina, Alexandra's and her family's comportment in captivity was such that they elicited their share of sympathy. One of the guards at Ekaterinburg, Analoy Yakimov, confessed how his feelings toward the family changed once he took notice of them. "After I had seen them several times I began to feel entirely different towards them," recalled Yakimov. "I began to pity them. I pitied them as human beings . . . I kept on saying to myself, 'Let them escape, or do something to allow them to escape.' "[44]

In their captivity, the family had been comforted by the sporadic visits of priests and the occasional opportunities to hear Mass and partake of confession and holy communion. For this most religious of families, these occasions, precious and sacred as they were, brought the captives closer to God and helped them greatly in coming to terms with their ordeal. On 14 July 1918, a priest came to say Mass at the Ipatiev household, assisted by a deacon; both found the family looking especially worried. A sense of foreboding hung in the room. When the deacon began chanting the prayer, "Rest in peace with the Saints," the whole family fell to their knees, overcome by emotion—one of the girls sobbing. As the deacon left the house, he remarked to the priest: "You know, Father Archpresbyter, I think something must have happened there."[45]

Alexandra and her family had every right to sense imminent danger. The guards watching over them were members of the Cheka, the Bolshevik Secret Police, led by the sinister Jacob Yurovsky. On 16 July, after an uneventful day at the Ipatiev house, the family went to sleep. That evening, Alexandra wrote her final entry in her diary: her last written words were, "Played bezique with Nicholas," and at 10:30 p.m., "To bed. 15 degrees."[46] On the following page Alexandra had already written the date and day, ready for her next entry. It was never filled. Their date with destiny had arrived.

The method of execution chosen was shooting. In order to keep the sound of gunshots to a minimum, handguns and pistols were employed. Awaking his unsuspecting victims around 2 a.m., Yurovsky ordered them to wait in a basement room for cars which were supposedly to whisk them away from the advancing White Army. Nicholas carried a tired Alexei to the room; Alexandra, meanwhile, protested that there were no chairs. Three were brought in. Alexandra sat on one, Nicholas on another, and Alexei took the third. Olga, Tatiana, Marie, and Anastasia stood near their mother. Joining the whole family were the maid, the cook, the footman, and Dr. Eugene Botkin. It was now nearly 3 a.m. Outside the house, a truck was placed strategically, its engine running to drown out the sounds that were about to reverberate. Yurovksky's moment had arrived.

He returned with his execution squad and announced, "Your relations have tried to save you; they have failed, and we must now shoot you."[47] A stupefied Nicholas cried out, "What does this mean?" Yurovsky took his revolver, showed it to Nicholas, and replied viciously, "This! Your race must cease to live."[48] Nicholas was then shot point-blank in the head. His last act was to try to shield his wife.

A hail of bullets followed. Alexandra quickly tried to make the sign of the Cross, then was instantly killed by a single gunshot. Her daughters suffered more. When the startled group of executioners shot at them, they saw that their bullets ricocheted. It turned out that diamonds and other precious jewels were sewn inside the girls' corsets. To dispatch them once and for all, the guards repeatedly stabbed the girls. After some minutes, the shooting stopped. Alexei, still in his father's arms, somehow managed to show signs of life as his hand began to clutch his father's coat. Yurovsky took his gun and fired into the young boy's head. The family's ordeal was ended. Nicholas was fifty years old; Alexandra forty-six; Olga twenty-two; Tatiana twenty-one; Marie nineteen; Anastasia seventeen; and Alexei thirteen.

It had taken twenty minutes to carry out one of history's grisliest political assassinations. So disgusting was the manner in which the family had been killed that Pavel Medvedev, an eyewitness to the murder scene, and a man noted for being "hardened" and "unemotional," recounted that "the sight of the murder and the smell of blood made me sick. I saw that all the members of the Tsar's family were lying on the floor with many wounds in their bodies. The blood was running in streams."[49]

Twenty-three

"MAMMA REGINA"

"SO THEY HAD REALLY DONE IT! I HAD ALWAYS BEEN AFRAID IT would end thus, but had hoped against hope that in some way they could have been saved," wrote Marie of Romania of the ghastly deeds at Ekaterinburg. Romania and its royal family did not escape the effects of the Russian Revolution and the ensuing assassination of the Romanovs. In May 1918, King Ferdinand and Queen Marie, still living in Jassy, were the targets of determined assassins who had orders from Russia. Lenin's seizure of power in Russia also led to pressure on Romania to sue for peace with Germany, angering Romania's fighting queen. She could not believe people around her were prepared to give up. "The 'never-say-die' of my English temperament and upbringing," as Marie put it, "made the struggle unbearable."[1]

Added to this, a battle-weary populace along with battle-scarred troops left large segments of Romanians vulnerable to spreading Bolshevik propaganda that might well have led to the overthrow of the royal family and the emergence of a Communist Romania in its wake. This was made all the more possible by disintegration of the Russian Army fighting in Romania. Redoubling her efforts to comfort everyone, Marie determined to raise the spirits of her fighting regiments, her wounded and dying soldiers, and the long-suffering civilians. The queen often traveled over difficult terrain to reach her destinations, then disembarked from her automobile and tramped through mud, snow, or parched and dusty ground to battle typhus, depression, and death. The stench and mangled bodies she encountered everywhere were enough to turn the stomachs of the hardiest of men.

On one such visit, Queen Marie was moved to tears by the sight of hundreds of emaciated men lying outdoors near a church under a scorching sun. Carefully, she moved among the "parade of skeletons," as she called them, touching them as they cried out for her, bony hands thrust forth to grasp her. Marie was deeply moved when one of these "emaciated phantoms" pulled himself to his feet to thank his queen for "coming down" from her palace "towards their misery, on this Easter Sunday."[2] As she left, grateful villagers ran up to her, pressing cowslips into her hands.

Marie also paid her respects to the many health care workers who died tending the ill. Doctors, nurses, nuns—nearly all of them volunteers—were felled. One contemporary recorded how "Social events in the shape of funerals follow one another with depressing rapidity. To-morrow six victims are to be buried at once. They comprise the best Roumanian typhus expert, the nurse who looked after the last French doctor to die, a sister of charity, a colonel and two young officers."[3]

As her reputation for bravery and generosity spread among her people, Romania's queen became a living symbol of hope and determination. Often dressed in her simple white Red Cross uniform with wimple, Marie became an instantly recognizable icon. "Patriotism is taking the heroic form" in the queen, wrote Maurice Paléologue admiringly. "There is a fiery and warm-hearted ardour about her, an enthusiastic and chivalrous ardour, something of the sacred flame. So she has already become a figure of legend, for her proud and winning loveliness is the very incarnation of the soul of her people."[4]

Queen Marie understood clearly that her role as queen was intertwined with her role as mother of her people—*"Mamma Regina,"* as she was called. Even old men of seventy called Marie mother. Accordingly, she created "Regina Maria" ambulances, "Regina Maria" decorations for those who gave much to the people, and "Regina Maria" hospitals. In one of these hospitals, her portrait, conspicuously displayed, was decorated with flowers; over the men's beds, the words "Regina Maria" were attached to the walls.

Queen Marie was justifiably touched and proud of her popularity. Nevertheless, with her characteristic magnanimity and selflessness, she felt equally proud of King Ferdinand. "We are happy and touched to see the immense popularity Nando has to-day attained, in spite of the ill-success of the War," Marie wrote in her diary in May 1917. "He is now loved and appreciated by his people. They have at last understood how honest, unselfish and loyal he is. The way he has uncomplainingly shared all their misfortunes, has made him dear to their hearts . . . their attitude has undergone a veritable transformation."[5]

Ferdinand and Marie celebrated their twenty-fifth wedding anniversary in January 1918. Marie recorded that "to-day Nando and I, hand in hand, confess to each other that at this hour, in spite of our misfortunes, or should I say because of them, we have become the firmest possible friends, attached to our country in a way not often given to sovereigns."[6] Prince Stirbey made a gallant speech on the anniversary, saying Marie had fulfilled magnificently old King Carol's prediction that she would be the anchor of her country.

Queen Marie's work took on other forms than merely visiting the sick and wounded. The indefatigable queen also made every effort to obtain help for her country from the outside world. Not content with trying to gain sympathy with the various foreign legations still in Jassy, Marie tried her hand at writing, in the hope that help for Romania might pour in. Articles for American magazines were published. She produced *My Country,* a book about Romania, in English; profits from the sales were to be used by the British Red Cross Society for work in Romania. Queen Marie found she enjoyed writing. Characteristically, her style was flamboyant and her efforts paid off, as Marie's work awakened outsiders to Romania's plight. In *My Country,* Marie summed up the evolution she had undergone in her quest to understand Romania: "At first it was an alien country . . . I had to learn to see its beauties—to feel its needs with my heart . . . little by little I learnt to understand this people, and little by little it learned to understand me. Now we trust each other, and so, if God wills, together we shall go towards a greater future!"[7]

Romania's plight was not ignored by the outside world. Volunteers came, some from as far away as America, such as members of the American Red Cross and the YMCA. But despite the help and devotion displayed by Marie and countless others, it was oftentimes not enough, and a feeling of frustration swept over the queen. "Everything is so complicated," she confessed in the latter part of 1917, "as no material is to be found anywhere, no food to be bought in large quantities; in fact nothing is to be had."[8]

With Romania's future at the mercy of both the Central Powers and Bolshevik Russia, Queen Marie went through a maelstrom of emotions, trembling one moment and fired with a desire to fight it out at others. "The situation remains awful," she lamented. "We have simply begun to speculate in which way we are going to die. Whichever way we turn we are sold, we are betrayed . . . there seems no way out."[9] The American ambassador to Romania, in Jassy at the time, pointed out that "the situation in Roumania is hopeless. It should be realized that Roumania is actually between two enemies, and that yielding to one would at least restore peace and order, and permit return to their homes; while acknowledgment of the other, and recognition of its theories, would result in treason, anarchy and famine."[10]

Romanians lived through weeks of uncertainty and fear as plots against the royal family continued to be uncovered. Finally, King Ferdinand personally met with the Austrian minister to Romania about peace terms in the hope of mitigating the Central Powers' wrath. But his efforts were in vain. When the king, resigned to defeat, confronted the Crown Council about what to do next, Marie was beside herself with rage. Though well aware that Romania risked annihilation should it refuse to accept peace on the Central Powers' terms, Marie could not bring herself to have Ferdinand and the government acquiesce. In one of the most violent arguments in their tumultuous twenty-five-year marriage, Marie fired off a tirade against her husband, evoking memories of Carmen Sylva: "If we are to die, let us die with heads high, without soiling our souls by putting our names to our death warrant. Let us die protesting, crying out to the whole world our indignation against the infamy which is expected."[11] Even her own Barbo sided with the king on the matter, eliciting a stinging rebuke from Marie, who cried out that there were "no men in this country," feeling as she did "ashamed of being the Queen of nothing but cowards!"[12] Better to abdicate, implored the queen, than sign the armistice. But no amount of desperate pleading worked. Romania signed a tentative agreement, and a final one—the Treaty of Bucharest in May 1918, to which King Ferdinand refused to affix his signature. Romania acquiesced to the harsh terms imposed upon it, which included turning over the country's oil to the enemy for ninety years, ceding the Dobruja region, and the immediate dismissal of all Allied Military Missions from Romania.

When the time came to say good-bye to the Allied Missions, tears were shed. Still unresigned, Marie cringed at the thought of her country's future. "My English blood refuses to accept disaster," she said defiantely. "If there remains the smallest, most meagre fighting chance, I shall still fight,—a losing battle no doubt, but I would consider myself unworthy of my own ideals were I to give in before I am completely convinced that all is lost."[13] At a farewell dinner on 23 February 1918, the exhausted queen threw herself on a sofa and asked the great Romanian violinist, George Enescu, to play. Listening, the queen heard the death throes of Romania. Among the guests that night was an enigmatic Canadian adventurer by the name of Joe Boyle—"Klondike Boyle," as he was sometimes known. Boyle would become indispensable to Queen Marie and to Romania.

Colonel Boyle's appearance by Marie's side worked as a much-needed tonic on the queen. His devotion to her and Romania, evidenced by his acts of daring and bravery, appealed greatly. The fact that he was middle-aged, of heavy build, and not particularly attractive did not tarnish the glowing light in which Marie saw him. She never forgot Boyle's promise to her. On the night of the farewell dinner for the missions, gripping her hand strongly, Boyle told Marie that he would not forsake her; and true to his word, he delivered on that promise. When a group of Romanian deputies were taken prisoner in Odessa by Bolsheviks, who wanted to kill them, Boyle boarded the ship where they were held, and despite not being able to speak a word of Russian, through sheer force of personality managed to get the Russians to leave the frightened prisoners in a Romanian port after two weeks. In gratitude, the families of the rescued prisoners presented Boyle with an exquisite illuminated address with the inscription: "God bless Canada and her noble son." So incredulous were people that they asked, "are all Canadians like Colonel Boyle?"[14] This feat also earned Boyle Marie's gratitude and admiration, and she awarded him the Cross of the Regina Maria. Here at last, in the chaotic and defeatist atmosphere, was a real man who fought against all odds to do something heroic for Romania.

Boyle's rescue of the Romanian deputies was just one of numerous exploits he undertook in a lifetime that singles him out as one of the most fascinating characters to jump off the pages of history. As a biographer of Queen Marie put it: "An exaggeration of a man, Colonel Boyle reads today like a fictional hero created by his contemporaries to lighten the frustrations of defeat. Were it not for the corroborating memoirs of his partner, Captain George A. Hill of the British Secret Service, we would write Boyle off as the wish fulfillment of a desperate queen looking for a twentieth-century Lancelot." And Captain Hill himself described Boyle as "a man whose equal I have encountered neither before nor since."[15]

This larger-than-life hero was born in Ontario in 1867, of Irish stock. Though his exploits were to take him to the remotest corners of America and Europe, "he was," as one biographer has put it, "as Canadian as is possible."[16] Physically, Colonel Boyle would have impressed any woman. Tall and powerful, blunt and outspoken, Boyle epitomized the rugged, self-made, energetic creature that gave legend to the man of the Wild West. The colonel was also an astute observer and a powerful speaker, who could put his gifts of persuasion to good use in critical times.

Having made his fortune in the Klondike Gold Rush of the late nineteenth century, and having married twice and fathered four children, Boyle turned his energies to Europe. Among many extraordinary exploits, this largely forgotten Canadian aided the Russian cause in 1916 by getting desperately needed men and matériel to the war front and preventing a famine in Moldavia. After discovering and diverting a German plan to murder the Allied Military Missions in *Stavka,* Boyle spirited out of Russia much of the Romanian Foreign Office archives and paper currency worth millions of dollars. It was a difficult feat, as the 1,500-mile journey from Moscow to Jassy involved dodging marauding gangs through Bolshevik territory. But Boyle succeeded.

Far from just an adventurer who took to her cause, Klondike Boyle, like Marie herself, was a person with a strong altruistic streak. He spent his own money to help rebuild the lives of destitute villagers in Romania and became an inspiration to his friend, ten-year-old Princess Ileana. Boyle, in short, possessed all the qualities that a woman like Marie needed in a man. He was, in many ways, the queen's equal.

Marie's frankness and admiration more than flattered Boyle, though he was not easily susceptible to flattery. He came to love her sincerely, harboring a kind of courtly love for the queen. Marie treasured their unique friendship, coming as it did at a time of near hopelessness for her. "I can honestly say," she recorded, "that during that dark period of my life, Joe Boyle often kept me from despairing. . . . This strong, self-reliant man had been as a rock on a stormy sea."[17]

Marie kept an anxious eye on military and political developments, her source for news was the ever devoted Barbo Stirbey. As Stirbey and Boyle both had Romania's fate uppermost in their minds, Marie brought them together. Never far from the action, Marie joined the two men as they saw to it that famine relief was maintained and kept King Ferdinand on the right track. It was a curious trio. Romanians, though suffering under a cruel master in the form of the Germans, nevertheless had much to be thankful for in these champions of their cause. But just as hope appeared with Allied victories on the Western Front, a new and perplexing crisis arose: Crown Prince Carol, Romania's next sovereign, had defied all sense and eloped with a Romanian commoner, "Zizi" Lambrino.

At the time of his marriage, Crown Prince Carol was twenty-four years old, a handsome, mustachioed young man with large blue eyes, straight eyebrows, and blond hair that was clearly inherited from his mother. Carol's bride, the dark-haired, dark-eyed Joana Marie Valentina Lambrino, was nineteen, a native of Moldavia, though in keeping with her society status she had been educated at a convent school in France. Like Helene Vacarescu years before, who had captured the heart of Crown Prince Ferdinand and nearly married him, Zizi moved in court circles, inevitably catching the crown prince's eye. Unlike Ferdinand and Helene, however, Carol and Zizi's budding romance during the war led to the altar.

Carol married Zizi in German-held Odessa in September 1918, after fleeing from Jassy. In defying his country's constitution and deserting his regiment, Marie's son had gravely erred, for "by law the one act could cost him the throne; the other his life."[18] Carol's shocking elopement had in effect caused a "triple crisis"—in the family, dynastic, and national sense.[19] Years afterward, Marie still found it hard to discuss the incident in detail, though the queen did describe Carol's desertion and elopement as "a staggering family tragedy which hit us suddenly, a stunning blow for which we were entirely unprepared."[20] When Marie first heard that Carol had bolted and eloped, she privately confessed: "I felt myself turn very sick. Carol! My honest big boy, at such a moment when the country is in such a state, when all our moral courage is needed, when we, the Royal family, are the only thing that holds it together. I was completely crushed . . . only Boyle and Barbu knew."[21]

Carol's elopement and his abandonment of his military post threatened the dynasty, already buffeted by propaganda and plots, although King Ferdinand and Queen Marie continued to enjoy their people's affection. But in spite of his parents' unimpeachable behavior as sovereigns during the war, Carol's actions had negative repercussions. Aided by Stirbey and Boyle, Marie and Ferdinand sprang into action to limit the damage done by their son. The king punished Carol, imprisoning him for two and a half months at a mountain monastery for deserting his regiment. There, in a painful reunion, King Ferdinand denounced Carol as a traitor while Marie sobbed. Annulment was the only answer to this predicament, the parents determined. Marie visited Carol again, but could not talk him into forsaking Zizi. It was left to Joe Boyle to convince the prince that an annulment of the marriage was the only answer. When Boyle returned to the queen after talking with Carol, Marie recorded that "Boyle was as near tears as a man can be, it was a cruel and sickening victory. . . . Nando and I both thanked Boyle with emotion."[22]

This tragedy in Marie's life played itself out as signs of progress in the war could finally be glimpsed. In the autumn of 1918, the Austro-Hungarian monarchy disintegrated after Bulgaria's capitulation. The tide had sufficiently turned in Romania's favor so that King Ferdinand was confident enough to proclaim war against Germany on 8 November. That same month, Hungary descended into near anarchy, paving the way for Transylvania to join in union with Romania. With Bukovina and Bessarabia also voting for union with Romania, the dreams of a Greater Romania stretching from Transylvania to the Black Sea seemed almost concrete reality.

However promising things looked on the war front, Marie did not let her guard down and break out prematurely into celebration, thanks to the ever astute and loyal Stirbey, who outlined the dangers still facing the nation if hungry peasants were to succumb to Bolshevik propaganda and bullying. Marie related her concerns to Joe Boyle: "The main two dangers and difficulties are, as it seems, the famine danger and a strong Bolshevik propaganda conducted by the Germans in the occupied territories, a ruthless propaganda because they carry with them whatever could be carried, and the empty stomach doesn't reason. The theory is: if they will fall, they want Romania to sink first, to be totally destroyed under all aspects; but we don't want it destroyed, do we?"[23]

King Ferdinand granted land reform for the peasants and universal suffrage, and in the process helped to stop Romania's slide toward revolution and probable anarchy. "I am pleased he has done this without Bratianu or Averescu [both prime ministers] in power," wrote Marie, "so that it should be his name alone which will remain attached to these reforms; the name of the modest, timid, doubting but honest and unselfish Ferdinand I. If he can also realize the unity of the Roumanians, then indeed he will find his recompense for the great sacrifice he made when he declared war."[24] When Marie and Ferdinand met again at the Jassy train station after these momentous reforms were proclaimed, the queen went straight into Nando's welcoming arms.

Jubilant crowds greeted the royal couple that day, for it was a historic one: Armistice Day, 11 November 1918. In recognition of Marie's bravery and loyalty to France, the French minister to Romania presented the queen with the *Croix de Guerre*. Many Romanians felt equally proud of their queen's actions during the war. "I humbly thank God for having allowed our time of humiliation and oppression to have such a marvellous end," noted Marie, "but it will take time before I can consider myself 'the Great Queen' they are so eager to call me." Marie knew that part of the success she and Ferdinand enjoyed as sovereigns was attributable to the indefatigable and wise help offered by Prince Stirbey. "Yes, we owe him a great deal," she recorded. "Much of the good which has come to us to-day is thanks to his fidelity."[25]

In espousing Romania's cause and throwing herself wholeheartedly into the country's struggle to survive during the Great War, Queen Marie identified completely with the Romanians, partaking in their hardships and later sharing in their joys in triumph. An indissoluble bond emerged between the queen and her people, one that would withstand later tragedies to come. Marie had truly turned out to be Romania's *"Mamma Regina,"* the mother queen of her people. Her grandson, King Michael, believes that this was her greatest legacy to her country—and this from a monarch who has dedicated his own life to the service of his country, at great cost.[26]

But for all her devotion to Romania, Queen Marie's attachment to her beloved England never wavered. Nor did her devotion to her old flame, King George V. In November 1918, Marie poured forth her emotions in her first letter to George after years of trial:

Jassy 12/5th Nov. 1918

My Dear George,

Your dear letter . . . you cannot imagine the pleasure it gave me. I never doubted but that you would be a faithful friend and uphold our country and its interests, but to hear it again from you yourself after the awful silence that had fallen upon us for about 9 months was a wonderful moment of happiness.

I can only tell you dear George that I held firm as only a born Englishwoman can. Nothing shook me, neither threats, nor misery, nor humiliation nor isolation. At the darkest hours when no news reached us I clung firmly to my belief in your strength and fidelity. I knew you would win and I kept my people from giving way even at a moment when many had become doubters, luck having been from the beginning so dead set against us. And even if you had not been victorious, I would have stuck to you, for me there are not two forms of fidelity. Forgive me for talking so much of myself, but I have been so insulted and flouted since we were given over into the enemy's hands that really it is my hour now![27]

With the end of the war, Queen Marie and King Ferdinand returned to Bucharest after a two-year absence. The city erupted in celebration as the royal family—including Crown Prince Carol—was welcomed back in a colorful and joyous parade through the main streets, awash in red, yellow, and blue. King Ferdinand, in a moving tribute to his wife, asked her to ride with him at the head of the Allied and Romanian troops for their triumphant entry into the capital. Riding her horse, Jumbo, dressed in military uniform, Marie received the ovation of her people, who jammed the streets and balconies of Bucharest, free at last from subjugation.

Queen Marie, though well aware of the pivotal role she played during the war, was nevertheless keen that her husband's work should also be recognized; she quietly suggested that Ferdinand be given a field marshal's staff. When, upon leaving the cathedral after the service of thanksgiving, a Romanian general approached the unsuspecting king with the offer, Ferdinand was taken aback and deeply moved. Ferdinand and Marie had become a formidable team, who never allowed personal hurts or differences to stand in the way of their mutual desire to serve their country. Some years earlier, Carmen Sylva had written an article about marriage. Though the eccentric poetess-queen was notorious for her high-flown ways, her advice certainly appeared to apply to Marie and Ferdinand's marriage:

Most people fancy they possess the right, especially in the matrimonial state, to bear only themselves in mind, and great is the damage which they cause mankind thereby, for they are here for the sole purpose of giving to the world more perfect, purer, nobler beings than they themselves are. If, then, we could bring ourselves to look upon marriage as a holy sacrifice, an act of perfect self-abnegation, we should make much greater progress. We might not add much or indeed, anything to the sum of our happiness, but that is quite another question; indeed, it is problematical whether we are on the earth at all for the purpose of attaining happiness. . . .

In the service of humanity! That should form the first thought of the bridal couple before the altar, instead of dreams forecasting how happy both may become.[28]

The conference set up in 1919 by the victorious powers to reshape the map of postwar Europe was destined to be mired in conflicting and complex issues that were bound to work against Romania. Dominated by the Big Four—Woodrow Wilson of the United States, David Lloyd George of Great Britain, Vittorio Orlando of Italy, and Georges Clemenceau of France—Romania, their erstwhile ally, having signed a separate peace with Germany, was in trouble. Dreams of a Greater Romania were bound to go unrealized. It did not take long for the Big Four, though at odds with one another over other issues, to act in unison in treating Romania harshly. Romania's prime minister at this time was none other than the wily but heavy-handed Ion Bratianu, who failed to make any headway in Paris with his country's erstwhile allies. Romania's statesmen realized that drastic action was needed. The answer came by way of the country's greatest weapon: its beguiling queen. The idea of sending Queen Marie to the Paris Peace Conference early in 1919 originated in the minds of two of her champions, the French ambassador, the comte de Saint-Aulaire, who had marveled firsthand at her dedication and work during the war, and Colonel Joe Boyle. The offer to appear on the international stage stunned Marie, but she accepted this latest challenge.

Accompanied by her daughters, Queen Marie arrived in Paris in March to a tumultuous welcome. Her reputation for bravery and steadfastness had preceded her, and Paris was at her feet. From her twenty-room suite at the Ritz Hotel, the queen held court. She had come prepared, carefully tutored by Prince Stirbey. Marie, ever the coquette, was also ready to do battle in another way. "There were in all some sixty gowns, thirty-one coats, twenty-two fur pieces, twenty-nine hats, and eighty-three pairs of slippers. 'Perhaps it seems a good many,' piped Marie. 'Still, I feel that this is no time to economize. You see, Roumania simply has to have Transylvania. We want so much Bessarabia too. And what if for the lack of a gown, a concession should be lost?' "[29]

Her choice of French blue over a petticoat of silver brocade obviously worked on the irascible Georges Clemenceau. Though France and Romania shared a common Latin heritage, and though Romanians often looked up to

France culturally, sending their elite to be educated there, Clemenceau had little patience with Romania. When he met Marie, the man known as "the Tiger" bluntly roared, "I don't like your Prime Minister," to which the queen parried with a smile, "Perhaps then you'll find me more agreeable."[30] He did. When the French president, Raymond Poincaré, met with the queen, he confirmed as much, telling her: "Clemenceau's attitude towards Romania has changed since you have represented your country."[31] David Lloyd George, the irascible British prime minister, proved no less difficult to cajole into conversation than Clemenceau. Then, after a week in the French capital, Queen Marie crossed the Channel and stayed as a guest of King George and Queen Mary at Buckingham Palace.

Long accustomed to the chaos and intrigue of Romania, Marie found to her surprise that George and Mary's court was a touch too diffident and conventional for her taste. Nevertheless, she launched into her own whirlwind schedule on behalf of her nation, begging George's indulgence for her unconventional ways. From her Buckingham Palace headquarters, Marie embarked on a frenetic round of socializing, with the goal of acquiring as much goodwill for Romania as she possibly could. From working breakfasts to evening receptions, Marie was on the go. No one was immune from the queen's attentions, from the British king and queen, to Lord Curzon, Winston Churchill, Waldorf and Nancy Astor, business tycoons, diplomats, reporters, and even the confused servants at Buckingham Palace, who did not understand her need to entertain at nine in the morning. She also found time to act as interpreter between King George and Bratianu, and to visit her son, Nicky, then in school at Eton.

Marie was thrilled to be back in England after the long hard years of the war. "It was a tremendous emotion to arrive in London," she remarked, "and to be greeted at the station by George and May, with a crowd of officials and many, many friends. As in a dream I saw familiar faces smiling at me, faces from out of the past and faces belonging to the near present."[32]

Queen Marie's breakfast meetings used to amuse the gruff King of England. At lunches with King George, Marie recorded how "he liked to tease me, endlessly" about them.[33] Yet those breakfast meetings yielded practical help. Around a large round table she assembled politicians, businessmen, military men; anyone who might come to Romania's aid. Two of the most assiduous attendees also happened to be two of the queen's most devoted admirers, Joe Boyle and Waldorf Astor.

After her London visit, Marie returned to Paris, where enthusiasm remained undiminished. Everywhere she went, a crush of people strained to see the exotic Queen of Romania, cheering her every move. One individual, however, was immune to Romania's effervescent queen. President Woodrow Wilson did not succumb to Marie's charm offensive. Edith Wilson, the president's wife, who accompanied him to his audience with the queen, found Marie looking "very becoming" in a "soft grey dress." But the queen set off on the wrong foot when, during this first meeting, she pontificated about Russian laws on sexual relations and their impact on Romania. Seeing she was getting nowhere with Wilson, Marie suddenly stopped to show Mr. Wilson a photograph of Princess Ileana, saying, "This, Mr. President, is a picture of my youngest daughter, Ileana. My love child I call her. Is she not lovely? My other girls are blonde, like me; but she—oh she is dark and passionate." The comment fell spectacularly flat. One of Wilson's aides was shocked by the queen's outspokenness, mumbling after the meeting: "Well, in all the experience I have never heard a lady talk about such things. I honestly did not know where to look, I was so embarrassed."[34]

Though Marie never dented Wilson's armor, she did leave Paris a success. Loaded onto her train were food, medicines, and other supplies for the relief of Romania. Much more was to follow. Just as important, in granting nearly all that the country wanted, the Peace Conference resulted later that year in *Romania Mare*—Greater Romania—in the process doubling Ferdinand and Marie's kingdom, to 295,000 square kilometers. Most of the Banat and Bukovina, southern Dobruja, and Bessarabia were absorbed, as was the coveted Transylvania. It was a complete triumph for Marie and for Romania; as one observer put it, "I know of no one who went away from Paris with more satisfactory annexations than did Marie of Roumania. . . . The Queen arrived at the Peace Conference from a kingdom numbering eight million subjects. She departed the ruler of eighteen million."[35] Grand Duchess Marie, who came to live for a little while in Romania after the war, concluded that Queen Marie, "by her charm, beauty, and ready wit could obtain anything she desired."[36]

As the war dragged on, Queen Maud found the separation from her English relatives difficult. After her birthday on 26 November 1916, Maud wrote: "Oh, I missed you *all* so much on the 26th and felt cheerless thinking of it being the third year in a row where I have not been 'home' to see you *all*. It feels *tougher* for *each* year that passes—And the future seems *so* uncertain, and this terrible war is continuing with all its misery and suffering."[37] A year later, her yearning desire to see her family in England and return to Appleton was still strong, as she told Queen Mary at the end of 1917: "I fear we will all suffer this winter in many ways, but do pray for better & happier times in the spring, there is so much one longs to talk about but daren't write, it is all very hard being separated so long, I am dying to see you all again."[38]

Queen Ena of Spain was equally anxious to return to England, where her mother lived. Not long after the armistice, Ena sent off a letter to King George V.

Thrilled that war had at last ended, Ena's letter was also tinged with pride in being an Englishwoman, which naturally meant a longing for England:

> Though far away from you all, my heart & thoughts have constantly been in
> England. You can understand how trying my position has often been among
> the many conflicting interests of a neutral court & how hard to disguise one's
> true feelings, as the news was good or bad for the Allies. But now in this won-
> derful moment of England's great victory, when your feelings of pride & relief
> must be almost too big for words, I wish by one short line to tell you how truly
> I rejoice with you in this supreme hour & what great pride I feel at having
> been born an Englishwoman with English traditions. The excitement here has
> been intense & the Allied Flags are displayed in most of the streets.[39]

Ena's letter was soon followed by one from Maud, "wild with excitement at the
idea of *at last* coming home and seeing you all again! It seems all like a *dream,* to
me, everything has changed so quickly from the *awful* war into peace."[40] In October 1919, Ena wrote to her English relations, "You can't think how we are both
[Ena and Alfonso] looking forward to seeing you again after all these long sad
years that we have not met."[41] As soon as they possibly could, both cousins were
off to visit relations in England. When it came time to celebrate her fiftieth birthday, in November 1919, Maud preferred to do so in England. An ecstatic Maud
wrote to Queen Mary: "It was a *joy* to spend the day *here* again after six years!"[42]

Although she had been Queen of Norway for nearly fifteen years, Maud remained simple and unaffected. Especially in England, she could forget easily who
she was. When Edith Wilson visited London just prior to the opening of the Paris
Peace talks, she was taken aback by her audience with Maud, Toria, and Queen
Alexandra. Having been introduced simply to "Maud" and "Victoria" by the
queen, Mrs. Wilson was surprised to hear Princess Victoria ask: "Would it be asking too much if I requested you to sign my book?" Queen Maud then clasped her
hands together and added: "Oh, I so wanted the same thing, but alas, my trunks
have not come; so I have no book and must miss this great opportunity." The two
sisters watched Edith Wilson sign Princess Victoria's autograph book: "Edith
Bolling Wilson." Mrs. Wilson then heard them exclaim together: "Oh, you sign
three names." As Maud seemed "even more desolated at the loss of such an autograph," recounted Mrs. Wilson, "I asked if she would like me to sign on a sheet of
the paper bearing the royal crest which was on the desk, and she seemed enchanted by the suggestion."[43]

In the postwar years, energetic as ever, Marie immersed herself in work. Famine relief was a priority. The Americans proved to be generous givers. Herbert Hoover, though no great fan of Romania or Queen Marie, sent provisions, as did the American Red Cross.

Queen Marie's urgent desire to help the Romanian people was based on very human feelings of compassion and pity, but she was also aware that in order to keep communism at bay, her people needed to be fed, and fed quickly. She feared that should the Romanians succumb to Bolshevik propaganda, her countrymen were bound to die by the thousands in an orgy of violence similar to what had taken place in Russia. Among those Marie enlisted for help was her faithful Colonel Boyle. One list the queen gave Boyle was staggering. She asked him to procure 70 farm tractors, 200 threshing machines, 650 hand threshers, 1,000 raking machines, 1,500 mowers, 1,500 seeders, 3,000 reaping machines, 2,375 carloads of Manitoba wheat, 133,000 spades and shovels, 190,000 garden forks, and 600,000 pickaxes. "The quicker we are aided the better for our general peace and the better for the throne," went the attached message, along with a line bound to strike a chord in Joe Boyle's heart: "Marie—The Queen You Are So Faithfully Serving."[44]

Having succeeded in separating Carol and Zizi, Ferdinand and Marie now found themselves reluctantly allowing the couple to get back together. Carol had taken up with a milliner whose ambitions knew no bounds; hence the reappearance of Zizi. In the midst of solving Prince Carol's problems, Queen Marie also had to contend with a new war, against Hungary, led by the Communist Béla Kun. In May 1919, Lenin's Soviet Union, supporting Kun, declared war on Romania. The Romanians, though, defeated Kun's armies in July.

In the meantime, Prince Carol, ordered abroad on an official trip, responded by shooting himself in the leg. When Carol was ordered to join Romanian forces in their push against Kun's army at the end of July, he balked. An infuriated Queen Marie fired off a letter to her son urging him to join his regiment:

> For the last time, in the name of all you hold sacred, I ask you is it possible that you can let your regiment go to the front without you . . . have you lost all sense of honour and duty . . . ? Is it not better to die, a bullet in the head, to be buried in good Roumanian soil than to betray your country. . . . One day, Carol, you will understand all the dreadful things you are doing. . . . Make another effort, become a man again . . . fight like a soldier.[45]

Carol fell in, but insulted his parents and Romania by renouncing his right to the throne in August 1919. In January 1920, Zizi gave birth to a son, named Carol Mircea. To Queen Marie's relief, the child was given his mother's maiden name for a surname. A month later, Carol told Zizi that they could not marry: he wished to be reinstated as crown prince. He was then promptly dispatched on a world tour. Marie arranged through Joe Boyle that Zizi and her child as well as Carol's milliner girlfriend and their child were compensated. The queen hoped her errant son would finally take his duties seriously.

Queen Marie also had to contend with the disappearance of the two men she was closest to, Barbo Stirbey and Joe Boyle. Long looked upon with suspicion as an *éminence grise,* Stirbey finally left his post as head of the Royal Household in the fall of 1919, in order to spare any further assaults on the dynasty. He took his family on an extended visit to Italy to be away for a while from Marie. But Stirbey's departure left them both devastated, after seeing each other daily for so many years.

When Prince Stirbey left his official position with the king's household and temporarily absented himself from Marie's side, Ferdinand and Marie were in a quandary as to who to trust for sage and impartial advice. In one instance in 1919, they both turned to Frank Rattigan, of the British Legation in Bucharest. It was a daring move, which momentarily threw Rattigan off. During his audience with the queen, Rattigan reminded her that though he was "deeply touched and honoured by this proof of Their Majesties' trust, foreign representatives ought in no way to interfere with internal politics." Marie knew how to sidestep that sticky issue. Rattigan reported to his superior, Lord Curzon: "Her Majesty said she quite understood this, but that she was an Englishwoman asking for my help and advice as an Englishman." Rattigan could not resist such an appeal, admitting to Queen Marie that "it was only under the strong pressure of the appeal she made to me as an 'Englishwoman in distress' that I had ventured to give my advice."[46] Rattigan aided the queen in her quest for help in sorting out some issues concerning Romanian politicians.

Not long after Stirbey left, Marie had to accept the fact that Colonel Boyle's presence by her side also had to end. Jealousy from gossips and courtiers over Boyle's closeness to the queen was one factor, but it was the right time for him to leave Romania. "They one and all torture me about faithful old Boyle and my unshakable belief in him," lamented Marie. Many could not or would not bring themselves to empathize with this extraordinary friendship, tinged as it was with strong spiritual undertones. "You and I are man and woman and we have come together at a late period of our lives and come together in a way but few could understand," Marie wrote to Boyle.[47] They remained devoted to each other and stayed in touch for the rest of Boyle's life.

By the end of 1919, Queen Marie of Romania was exhausted. Yet she dug deep within herself to continue the fight for what was right and good for Romania. As she wrote to her friend, the American dancer, Loie Fuller:

The "vision" is what is wanting in my people. They speak of it, but they have not got it. Somewhere in the Bible I found these words: "He that hath no vision perisheth"—I try to keep their "vision" before them, some climb up to my side and try to help me but jealousy like an evil pestilence is always ready to tear from me those that are ready to be my right hand.[48]

PART FOUR

Denouement (1920–1969)

Twenty-four

CAPITULATION AGAIN

THE GREEK ROYAL FAMILY FOUND REFUGE IN SWITZERLAND, TAKING up residence in November 1919 at the Hôtel National in Lucerne. During her stay in Switzerland, Sophie wished to live as normal a life as possible. "I wanted to be just like the other guests—I wanted, as they said I was no longer a Queen, *not* to be a Queen, just to be an ordinary human being." But she was treated as less than a human being by some of her so-called friends. For what was most painful about her exile, aside from being separated from her son, King Alexander, and being away from her home, was the rebuffs she and her husband were subjected to from old friends, especially English friends. Sophie recalled one particularly painful incident:

> Staying in the hotel were several of my old English friends, whom in days gone by I had known quite intimately. They used to be of my party in the opera; I have danced at their houses, dined with them. One and all, they cut me dead. I shouldn't have minded that—for, after all, there are *ways* of cutting people, aren't there? But they did it in the unkindest way possible, publicly—not only to myself but to my husband—leaving any room that I entered, and staring me straight in the face as they went out. Now—it isn't like English people to do that, is it? And yet they did. It was not till I picked up some of the English papers, and learnt what they were saying about us over there, that I realized the reason for it.[1]

Since they were always a tightly knit group, the Greek royal family's exile was especially difficult for Sophie. Unlike his older brother, George, Alexander was not trained to be King of the Hellenes. In fact, he was never happier than when tinkering for hours with motorcars, often in overalls. Leaving her favorite son in Athens in trying circumstances at the mercy of Venizelos meant that Sophie never stopped worrying. Besides the political upheaval, however, there was also the issue of King Alexander's secret engagement to a daughter of one of King Constantine's equerries.

Alexander's fiancée, the nineteen-year-old Aspasia Manos, though descended from an illustrious Greek family, was not deemed worthy to be a queen. As in neighboring Romania, it was felt that having a native of the country marry into the ruling dynasty invited trouble. Aspasia's background did not sit well with many, least of all Queen Sophie, whose letters to her son made this clear, entreating Alexander not to push for the match further lest it lead to a deterioration in King Constantine's health. For the love-struck young man, alone in Greece with little inclination to battle the hotbed of Greek politics, his parent's entreaties proved fruitless. Government spies hovered over him; he missed his family; and the propaganda being perpetrated against them all, deeply saddened Alexander. King Alexander's lonely life only served to increase his yearning to make Aspasia his wife.

By the summer of 1919, Alexander told Venizelos of his determination to marry. Venizelos managed to put off the controversial wedding; but by November an impatient Alexander had taken matters into his own hands. In an echo of Crown Prince Carol's elopement with Zizi Lambrino, Alexander married Aspasia in a secret Orthodox ceremony. The reaction in Greece, when news of the marriage eventually leaked out, was predictably unfavorable, prompting the bride to flee for a while. Eventually, Venizelos allowed Aspasia to accompany Alexander on an official trip to Paris in May 1920, provided she not participate in any formal events where she might be mistaken for a queen. The idyll in Paris would prove to be among the couple's happiest moments.

Though she disapproved of her son's marriage, Alexander's Paris sojourn delighted Queen Sophie. According to Alexander's uncle, Prince Christopher, "Queen Sophie adored her son and fretted out her heart in secret over him." Upon hearing of Alexander's temporary escape from Greece, the queen "shed tears of joy," for days talking of nothing but the chance to speak to Alexander. "At last," she sighed, "I shall be able to telephone him."[2]

But when the queen tried to telephone, it was not Alexander who answered but the Greek minister to Paris. "His Majesty is sorry, but he cannot come to the telephone," was the curt reply. According to Prince Christopher, "Queen Sophie went quietly away from the telephone. She said nothing, but the disappointment in her face wrung one's heart." Alexander was never told that his mother had telephoned. Still, the queen continued to follow news of her son, cutting out "every scanty little notice in the newspapers referring to him . . . [hanging] on to the words of such friends as were able to see him occasionally."[3] Queen Sophie's great-grandson, Crown Prince Alexander of Yugoslavia, familiar with the "striking, emotional letters" exchanged between King Alexander and his parents in exile, has noted that Sophie "was very warm in these letters, extremely concerned."[4] Tragically for Queen Sophie, her anxieties over her son were to grow heavier.

In September 1920, King Alexander was bitten by a gatekeeper's pet monkey at Tatoi. Blood poisoning set in, and in no time, the king lay dying. When word reached Queen Sophie of the incident, she realized that her son was seriously ill. Her request to travel to Greece was cruelly denied by the Greek government, fearful that her appearance might incite royalists to rally round the king and his mother. Prince Christopher recalled that "from the very first moment she had a premonition that her boy would not get better and begged the authorities, almost going on her knees to them, to let her go to him."[5] Frantic with despair, Sophie asked her mother-in-law, Queen Olga, to try to obtain permission to go to Alexander. Queen Olga was allowed to travel to Greece, and Sophie then agonized over each telegram that arrived from there.

Wracked with a high fever, in excruciating pain, the king could be heard screaming by those outside the palace. He fell into fits of delirium, asking for his mother to the very end. Aspasia, who was four months pregnant, nursed him devotedly throughout the ordeal, which lasted for several weeks. After a journey delayed by stormy seas, Queen Olga arrived at Alexander's bedside—but she was too late. He had died just hours before, on 25 October 1920. Alexander was twenty-seven years old.

Recalling that momentous day, Prince Nicholas wrote that "on the day of his death they had already telegraphed from Athens that nothing could be done. Yet, in spite of that, the distracted mother never gave up hope, and bombarded her doctor with questions. She stayed up till late in the night, continually sending to ask if any message had arrived." Though Nicholas and the doctor had seen the telegraph late at night announcing Alexander's death, they kept the news from King Constantine and Sophie to allow them some much-needed rest. It was broken the next morning. "The moments that followed," recorded Nicholas in his memoirs, "are too sacred to speak of."[6]

Queen Olga, Alexander's grandmother, was the only family member present at Alexander's funeral. He was buried at Tatoi, beside his grandfather, the assassinated King George. The ever-devoted Mossy went to her sister's side to comfort a deeply distraught Sophie. Besides being her closest sister, Mossy was well placed to help comfort the grieving mother as Mossy herself had lost her two eldest sons in the early years of the Great War. Writing to an old mutual English friend, Hilda Cochrane, Mossy described her stay at Lucerne: "I spent three weeks with my sister at Lucerne just after the sad news had come. She was heart broken & will never get over this loss, it was all so cruel.—It will be a great thing if they can return & the loyalty of the people is of course a great help, but what it will mean to her to go back & see the empty house & to think of all her poor boy suffered during those lonely years is terrible to imagine."[7] Indeed, Queen Sophie never got over the untimely death of her son and the cruel circumstances leading up to it. The queen's daughter, Lady Katherine, admitted as much.[8]

It would seem that nothing more dramatic could take place in Sophie's life in the remaining months of that year. But no sooner had the young king been buried than a new political crisis emerged in Greece.

Just as Romania continued to feel threatened by the specter of communism in the immediate postwar years, the thought that this revolutionary ideology with its ensuing violence might infect Spain and incite another Russian Revolution unnerved the Spaniards. When industrial troubles plagued the nation in 1920, Ena wrote to Queen Mary of her concerns: "I am sure you must all be anxious about the coal-strike & I do hope that this fearful catastrophe may still be avoided. Really what hateful times we are living in."[9] With the frequent murders of prominent labor and business leaders and the assassination in Madrid of the Conservative prime minister Eduardo Dato, in 1921, the country was once again immersed in political troubles.

In July, Spain suffered a humiliating defeat at the hands of the Moroccans at Anual, when nearly fifteen thousand Spanish soldiers were slaughtered due to the rashness of their commander. Not surprisingly, unrest allowed for the appearance of a strongman, capable of governing with a heavy hand. General Miguel Primo de Rivera's arrival on the political scene marked the death of parliamentary democracy and the birth of a nationalistic, authoritarian regime.

Through the years, Ena proved indefatigable in her efforts to improve health care, and in so doing left a lasting legacy in Spain. The queen's reorganization of the Red Cross in 1918 led to the inauguration of the first Red Cross hospital in the country. Ena also personally paid for a number of nurses to be sent every year to England for training. Ena was active in obtaining help wherever she could. She was particularly grateful when, in 1921, she collected "a large sum of money," as she put it, "from the British Colonies throughout Spain for my Red Cross Fund." She thanked Sir Esme Howard, the British ambassador to Spain, for his efforts in helping her and proceeded to list the most needed items for him to obtain from England, such as "some more air-beds" for the hospitals in

Melilla. Morever, "the Red Cross hospital at Seville is in need of india-rubber hot-water bottles & air-cushions," and so on; Ena added her "renewed grateful thanks" for Howard's "kind help."[10]

The queen also was aware of the Spanish soldiers fighting in Moroccan battles, and spearheaded relief efforts there. Under her auspices, several hospitals with thousands of beds were set up for wounded Spaniards in Morocco. Added to this was Ena's work for the Anti-Tuberculosis League and her own newly founded League Against Cancer.

These endeavors kept Queen Ena busy through the 1920s. Her altruistic work helped to stop her from dwelling too heavily on the volatile state of the nation. Ena's work also helped her cope with Alfonso's infuriating infidelities, which did not abate with the passage of time. If anything, their already rocky marriage became further threatened as the king embarked on his most serious affair: with the Spanish actress Carmen Ruiz Moragas.

⁂

The tragic death of King Alexander I in Greece opened up a Pandora's box for Eleutherios Venizelos. New elections took place in November 1920, resulting in defeat for Venizelos. He fled into exile, paving the way for the dynasty's return to power. As events turned in Constantine and Sophie's favor, reporters besieged the king and queen in Lucerne. During one interview given by Sophie in late November to *The Times,* the reporter noted: "Queen Sophie expressed her joy at the prospect of returning to Greece after an exile 'which had so many dark hours for us,' and insisted that she knew nothing of politics, but in spite of what had been said to the contrary, had always had strong pro-British sympathies, as her mother was English and she had spent so much of her youth in England with Queen Victoria." Sophie, dressed in deepest mourning, made a deep impression on the reporter. "The former Queen," he wrote, "has much changed since I saw her at St. Moritz. She is very pale and obviously greatly upset by King Alexander's death."[11]

In December 1920, a plebiscite was held on the return of King Constantine. The result was a resounding victory for the monarchy and for Constantine. Over 10 million Greeks voted for the monarchy's return and less than 11,000 against.

Excitement gripped Athens at the thought that Constantine was returning. Streets were decorated and illuminated; all through the day of his return there were cries of "*Erchetai! Erchetai!* (He is coming! He is coming!)."[12] Portraits of Venizelos were torn down, replaced by those of Constantine and Sophie. Upon the royal family's arrival on 19 December 1920, the enthusiasm of the Greek people reached fever pitch. Huge crowds pressed ever closer to the royal carriage. Many fainted. There were reports as well of people who "threw themselves down in the street for King Constantine to walk over them." Children sang:

> Arise, O marvellous King!
> And go down into the cellar,
> Where dirty old Venizelos
> Is licking the chamber pot![13]

One soldier was so taken by the sight of the royal couple that he climbed into their carriage headfirst, kissed the knees of his sovereigns, and cried, "We will die for you, Godfather!"[14]

Later in the day, Constantine and Sophie appeared on the balcony of the Royal Palace before a crowd numbering in the hundreds of thousands holding flags and portraits of the king. Athens was truly *en fête*. At the magnificent ruins of the Parthenon an immense illuminated crown burned brightly in the darkness for all to see. The king and queen had come home at last. Queen Sophie's sister-in-law, Marie, was more than pleased to learn that the royal family had returned, telling a friend: "It is indeed a great happiness & triumph to know that the Greek people have called back their lawful King. They were *at last* able to show the whole world what their wish was & that they had remained loyal in spite of the politicians!"[15]

But Prince Christopher observed Sophie at this jubilant homecoming and detected more than a hint of sadness. "I looked at his [Alexander's] mother's grief-stricken face," recalled Christopher, "smiling bravely at the cheering crowds, and knew that her heart bled in secret."[16]

Like their departure from Greece in 1917, King Constantine and Queen Sophie's return in Greece in 1920 was one of the most dramatic events ever to take place in modern Greek history. But just as at their accession in 1913, the king and queen were again saddled with the unenviable responsibility of living up to their historic destiny. In the minds of many, Greece was poised to show the world that here was a country intent on fulfilling its irredentist dreams. It was a potent idea, but one loaded with dangers for Greece, and for Constantine and Sophie.

At this point, the Greek and Romanian royal families, already related by blood, suddenly found themselves bound closer by romance in their midst, not once but twice in the space of weeks.

Crown Prince George of Greece had seen his patience rewarded when, after years of waiting, Princess Elisabetta of Romania agreed to marry him. Unknown to the gentlemanly and kindly George, the princess, like her brother, Prince Carol, was a flawed character. Lazy, self-centered, prone to jealousies, Elisabetta possessed few if any redeeming qualities. Queen Marie was naturally pleased to see that her eldest and most difficult daughter was finally settling down with a man who loved her, warts and all. The fact that Elisabetta was marrying into a royal family plagued by political instability did not bother her mother. Marie knew that the family was as solidly close and loving as they could come in royal circles.

She invited George to accompany her and Elisabetta back to Romania for the engagement announcement. Marie also extended the invitation to George's two younger sisters, Helen and Irene. Before the party left for Romania, Prince Carol arrived back in Switzerland from his world tour, to his mother's delight looking more mature. Once in Romania, at Sinaia, the queen organized excursions where the young people could enjoy themselves. When news came that Helen's brother, King Alexander, had died, Helen needed to return to her parents. Then, the day after Alexander died, word arrived that Queen Marie's mother had died in her sleep in Switzerland, where the duchess had been living in exile. The Duchess of Coburg's last years had been terrible ones. She had seen the collapse of Tsarist Russia, lost numerous Romanov relatives to the Bolsheviks' murderous rampage, and had also witnessed the defeat of her second home, Germany.

Queen Marie accompanied the mourning sisters back to Switzerland, and was surprised that Prince Carol wished to accompany them. On the train ride, the prince treated Helen with much sympathy. In Switzerland, he proposed. Twenty-four at the time, Princess Helen ("Sitta") was a tall, attractive brunette, carefully brought up by her exacting mother. The eldest daughter, elegant and refined, Sitta had all the qualities for a future consort. Queen Marie could not have asked for a better bride for her wayward son. Perhaps this young woman would be his salvation. Already, however, it appeared that the couple's future might not be resting on solid foundations. Sitta, it seems, had accepted Carol's proposal because of Alexander's death. With her favorite brother gone, Helen years later admitted that "I could not face Athens and Tatoi again. To marry Carol and go to Rumania, and not to have to live in the place that would constantly wound me with memories, seemed in these days of sorrow a kind of deliverance." Though King Constantine did not object to the match, Queen Sophie was vehemently opposed to it. Helen noted that "it was my mother who was so upset, chiefly because of the differences of upbringing and background, and also because she was in despair at the idea of losing me so soon after the grievous loss of Alexander. But I insisted and for some time my mother tried pleading with me, and using every argument to induce caution. I little realized then how true were her warning words. Had I listened, I would have been spared years of misery."[17] As for Helen's prospective mother-in-law, Queen Marie, she was thrilled at the engagement. "Carol is saved!" she wrote delightedly. "She is sweet and she is a lady. Besides, she's one of the family, since we're all descended from Grandmamma Queen."[18]

Helen of Greece and Carol of Romania were married in Athens in March 1921, just a week after Elisabetta and George were married in Bucharest. Queen Sophie felt none of Marie's enthusiasm for Helen's marriage to Carol, as Helen's aunt Mossy confided to a friend a week before the wedding. "[Sophie] is so brave fighting down her grief & working for others. It will be terrible for her to give up that daughter she adores & she dreads it."[19]

When the time came for Princess Helen to marry Prince Carol in Athens, Queen Sophie was startled to find herself being snubbed by people she thought were her friends. Unlike the Greeks, who greeted their newly returned king and queen with spontaneous acts of affection, representatives of the Allied Powers in Athens, encouraged by the conspiratorial French, turned their backs on the king and queen in an undignified act of spite. The instruction from Lord Curzon to Lord Granville at Athens was blunt: "You should remain in Athens while avoiding all ceremonial, official or personal relations with King Constantine, his court and family."[20] Lord and Lady Granville took these directives to heart when they ran into the royal couple and family members in Athens for Helen and Carol's wedding. Lord Granville greeted Queen Marie, but he and his wife completely ignored the Greek royals. It was an embarrassing spectacle, a dramatic snub, one that was particularly hurtful to Queen Sophie, who had been on good terms with Lady Granville for years.

Almost immediately after Helen's marriage, Sophie was delighted to find herself becoming a grandmother for the first time when Aspasia gave birth to King Alexander's posthumous child—a daughter, named Alexandra. Sophie may have originally been opposed to her son's marriage, but after his death, she treated his widow with affection and supported Aspasia when she gave birth to Alexandra.

Later that year, Queen Sophie learned that Princess Helen was expecting a child. Having settled in Romania, Helen busied herself with decorating her new home, the Foishor, a charming chalet at Sinaia, not far from King Ferdinand and Queen Marie's home, the Pelishor. At first, Helen was delighted with her new life. She had an attentive, handsome husband and life at Sinaia, located at the foot of the deeply forested Carpathians, was refreshing.

The Greek people were devoted to the royal family and to King Constantine, a fact noted by Queen Marie while she was in Greece for Helen and Carol's wedding: "The love of the Greeks for their King is something magnificent. It is a religion to them, it makes them happy . . . I am talking of what I have seen and heard—I have travelled three days to far-distant corners . . . and it is Constantine, Constantine—with love and adoration it was touching and wondrous to hear."[21] But within months, this unparalleled devotion would crumble. In an incredible turn of events, Queen Sophie was forced to pack her bags, ready again to flee the country. No wonder she once described her position in Greece as being "in a horrible No-Man's Land of distraction!"[22]

Among the most dramatic cries heard on the day of Sophie and Constantine's return to Greece was "Again our King will draw the sword."[23] The hopes for the *megali* idea—Greater Greece—that had consumed Greece at the monarchs' accession in 1913, had never left.

After the couple's exile in 1917, Venizelos had brought Greece onto the Allied side in the war and hence onto the winning side of the conflict. This invigorated Venizelos at home to promote the idea that Greece was set to reclaim its rights over Constantinople and rescue the many Greeks still living under the Turkish yoke. He hammered the point home in impassioned speeches. As Asia Minor contained pockets of Greeks within its borders and as Turkey had been defeated in the war, Venizelos wished to exploit Turkey's weakness and Greece's alliance with the Entente Powers to further his territorial ambitions. At the time, Britain and France accepted this.

Venizelos left the Paris Peace Conference with permission to occupy Smyrna. He ordered Greek troops to do so in May 1919. Smyrna (present-day Izmir) was a flourishing trade center with a thriving Greek population and strong Greek associations in the past; but the port was also a vital economic lifeline to the Turks. Letting go of Smyrna and allowing the Greeks free rein to push farther into Anatolia was therefore unacceptable to Turkey. Within three months, the Greeks had successfully pushed Turkish forces more than two hundred miles farther back inland. Now, after Venizelos's defeat and Constantine's return, Greece was still grappling with the Asia Minor question. The fiery lawyer from Crete had effectively left the contentious issue burning. The king was plunged immediately into an international crisis; and as in World War I, Constantine and Sophie were to find themselves again fighting for their political lives.

Tragically, the unexpected arrival of the king on the scene provided the Allies with a pretext to evade their promises to help Greece. France, in particular, dissatisfied with Allied policy and the mounting costs of maintaining a zone of occupation in Asia Minor, wanted to come to terms with Turkey. The next months showed that "allied policies were confused, inept and risky—and created the ideal conditions for Turkish nationalism to flourish."[24] Into this vacuum stepped a dynamic and determined Turkish leader, set to pick up the pieces of the dying Ottoman Empire and recast it into his vision of a new nation. That man was Mustapha Kemal, who came to be known as Ataturk and as the father of modern-day Turkey. Fiercely nationalistic, a born leader, Ataturk awakened in his followers a rousing desire to fight for the fatherland at whatever cost. If defeat was to be their destiny, then, exhorted Ataturk, they would go down fighting to the bitter end, leaving nothing in their wake for their enemies to exploit. "It was the irony of Fate," wrote one chronicler of the Greek royal family, "that Constantine returned to the throne in time to bear the obloquy that would otherwise have fallen inevitably on the shoulders of Venizelos."[25]

King Constantine was under no illusions as to Greece's predicament. As far back as 1915, he had told Venizelos that a Greek invasion of Asia Minor would mean his country's destruction. "It will bleed Greece to death," warned the king, well aware that his nation was not wealthy or strong enough for such an adventure.[26] But upon Constantine's return, things had gone too far for him to pull back. Faced with little choice but to continue the military campaign, Constantine reluctantly acquiesced.

When Greece carried out an offensive in January 1921, it did so with a shortage of equipment and unprotected supply lines. Moreover, the Allies had withdrawn financial support. And the Turkish forces outnumbered the Greek forces by over 300,000 men.

In order to boost the morale of his troops, Constantine himself went to the battlefields. Living under strenuous conditions did nothing to improve his already delicate health. Intent on helping the soldiers as much as she could, Queen Sophie also spent much of her time at the hospitals. By the summer of 1921, the Greeks had advanced against the Turks and were headed for Ankara. Ataturk, however, wisely chose to retreat, thereby placing incredible strain on the Greeks as their supply lines were weakened and stretched beyond limit. September 1921 saw the Greeks defeated at the Sakarya River. The defeated Greek Army retreated toward Smyrna, already groaning under the weight of thousands of Greek refugees, who feared the advancing Turks. From then on, thanks to Ataturk's superior forces and the Allied failure to aid Greece, it was only a matter of time before Greece faced defeat. Constantine and Sophie had few supporters. Only their aunt, Queen Alexandra of England, raised a concerned voice throughout the Asia Minor campaign.

Always partial to the Greek royal family and to the memory of her brother, King George I, Queen Alexandra was eager to see her nephew, King Constantine, succeed with this second lease on his political life. The queen pleaded emphatically with her son, George V: "Promise me to do all you can for Greece & poor excellent *honest* Tino who has been so infamously treated by the world & France. Don't let England forget that we put my excellent brother on the Greek throne and the only cause of dear *honest* Tino's present awkward position is simply and solely his having married poor dear Sophie the sister of that ass William."[27] But Queen Alexandra's pleas led nowhere.

Throughout the harrowing campaign in Asia Minor, few events pleased Queen Sophie more than a visit from Mossy in the summer of 1922. It was a busy time for Sophie as she also had to entertain Queen Marie of Romania, who, with King Ferdinand, had rushed to Athens to be by their daughter's bedside. Elisabetta, suffering first from typhoid, then pleurisy, was at death's door, but eventually rallied and recuperated slowly.

Sophie implored Mossy to stay as long as possible. It was understandable, for Mossy found her favorite sister utterly careworn. "Alas," Mossy wrote in May 1922, "I do not think my sister well, the heat tries her terribly, & all she has been through tells on her naturally. She ought to have a thorough change, Friedrichshof . . . like in olden times, but there is no possibility of this & she cannot think of going away until peace has been signed & politics are more settled."[28]

Another visitor to Athens during the twilight of King Constantine and Queen Sophie's reign was the gardening expert, Mrs. Philip Martineau, who was moved by the sadness she encountered in Queen Sophie. Far from "the belligerent German," Martineau found a woman who was "gentle and quiet, full of thought and kindness for her guests, and the most feminine and charming lady, ever ready to efface herself and her own views." Expecting "to see a German and masterful lady," Mrs. Martineau admitted her surprise at finding in Queen Sophie "a fragile little lady in deepest mourning, her face itself a tragedy of unhappiness." The queen's first words to her guest, waiting in a room filled with heavy English furniture and piles of English magazines, were by way of an apology: "You will forgive my not being here sooner, but I spend all the mornings in the hospital, where we have many wounded soldiers."[29]

Mrs. Martineau was impressed by Queen Sophie's program to plant the brown Athenian hills with trees in an effort to combat the heat, dust, and drought that often plagued the capital. Already there were rows of shady pepper trees, whose vibrant reddish-pink berries and green leaves broke the monotonous cream and beige hues of the Greek capital. Sophie had great plans to introduce the drought-resistant Maritime pine to the hills and sought Mrs. Martineau's advice about the best trees to improve rainfall in the parched city. Sadly, by the mid-1920s, much of Sophie's hard work in the reforestation of Athens and its vicinity would become a distant memory. As the Infanta Eulalia rightly noted: "The Greeks have forgotten that many of the improvements in Greece were instituted by the Queen, who planted trees in a land where no trees save olives and cypresses grew"[30]

The deliberate destruction of the forests around Tatoi was a bitter blow to Queen Sophie. Mrs. Martineau saw this when, on a drive to Tatoi, she was moved to ask what prompted the French to burn miles and miles of trees around the estate, once "the finest ilex forest in the world." "Why should they do this, ma'am?" said an incredulous Mrs. Martineau. "They said I had a private wire to my brother concealed there." She spoke "as if numb with pain."[31] The scorched land around Tatoi was a brutal symbol of the burden Sophie carried for being Kaiser Wilhelm II's sister.

Amidst the word of Greece's failing campaign in Asia Minor and the Allied Powers' refusal to help, one piece of good news came Queen Sophie's way. Crown Prince Carol and Princess Helen had been blessed with the arrival of a son and heir on 25 October 1921, whom they named Michael. The premature birth, at Sinaia, had been exceptionally difficult and nearly cost mother and baby their lives. Queen Marie was by Sitta's side at the delivery, but Queen Sophie arrived a week after Michael's birth. The fact that this first grandson was born on the first anniversary of the death of her son helped to assuage, somewhat, the memory of that terrible day. Sophie stayed for a while in Romania, helping to nurse her daughter; but as soon as Helen showed signs of recovery, she left to return to Greece. The strong attachment Sitta felt for her Greek family took on new meaning after Michael's birth. Concerned about the never-ending crisis her parents were living through, and anxious to keep away from her new house in Bucharest, which was undergoing renovations, Sitta fled to Greece with Michael within weeks. She did not return to Romania until the following April. To the Greek royal family, long accustomed to relying on one another for support, Helen's long absence from Carol did not strike them as unusual. But the idea of his pretty young wife fleeing the roost did not sit well with Carol, the hot-blooded husband. Much to her surprise, Helen was to find that her prolonged absence proved fatal to her marriage. Upon her return, Sitta found that Carol had sought consolation in the arms of yet another woman who had commanded his attention; a woman by the name of Elena Lupescu.

❦

In the spring of 1922, the Allies brokered a peace that an exhausted Greece could agree to. Ataturk, however, wanted an immediate evacuation of Greek troops from Asia Minor, which he knew was a political impossibility. In a bid to end the stalemate once and for all, the Greeks planned a final attack, but were told by the Allied Powers in Constantinople that it would not be supported. By this time, Ataturk tasted victory. In August, he attacked the Greek Army near Ankara. In two weeks, it was all over. A triumphant Ataturk rode into Smyrna. The Greek tragedy did not end there, however. In an orgy of violence lasting nearly a week, the Turks exacted their revenge on Greeks in Smyrna, plundering and burning the city. The killings were indiscriminate: men, women, and children alike were brutally murdered. Many thousands more died drowning as they fled marauding Turks, trying to escape in overloaded boats. Conservative estimates place the Greek death toll at 30,000 people; some have placed it as high as 300,000.

The Greek rout in Asia Minor and the ensuing massacres shocked Greece and emboldened disgruntled troops and anti-monarchists to go after Constantine, who became a convenient scapegoat. In a swelling chorus of anger, Prince Christopher recalled how "people began to remember all the Venizelist propaganda against him, raked together the still smouldering ashes of the past. Queen Sophie was the ex-Kaiser's sister, they reminded one another, though," added Christopher, "what bearing that could have on the present situation no one exactly knew."[32]

With the army and navy in open revolt, Constantine and Sophie's days as King and Queen of the Hellenes were numbered. On 26 September 1922, some fifteen thousand soldiers made their way toward Athens, demanding that Constantine abdicate. Though his troops were willing to fight the insurgents, the king forbade it, wishing to avoid a civil war. He abdicated, "happy that another opportunity has been given me to sacrifice myself once more for Greece."[33] The *coup d'état,* spearheaded by disgruntled soldiers, officers, and pro-Venizelists had succeeded. It was under these unpromising circumstances that Sophie's thirty-two-year-old son, George, succeeded his father as King of the Hellenes, making Elisabetta Queen of the Hellenes.

For Constantine and Sophie, it was capitulation again. For the second time in five years, the king was compelled to sacrifice himself for the sake of Greece, a victim of disasters wrought by others, disasters he himself had warned against.

Days after the abdication, a subdued Sophie and Tino steeled themselves for what was likely to be their last good-bye to the country for which they had toiled and suffered. On the morning of their departure, Sophie, Constantine, and the former king's brother, Nicholas, visited the tomb of King George I to pay their last respects. Later, the royal family's friend, Ioannis Metaxas, spoke to the couple at Tatoi, just before they left. Telling Constantine that he would not return to his throne, "but will live happily as a private citizen," Metaxas found an exhausted Tino resigned to his fate. As for Sophie, it was noted that "the queen is very dignified." It had all been "a moving farewell."[34] That same evening, without any fanfare, the ex-king and queen left Greece, never to return. Accompanying the couple on their journey into exile was their youngest child, Katherine, and Constantine's brother, Nicholas. They left for Italy from Oropus—the same place where, only five years before, the couple experienced a very different farewell. Back then, crowds had tried to prevent their king and queen from abandoning Greece. This time, only a handful of people saw them off. The Athens of

September 1922 was also a far cry from the Athens of 1917. Now, "complete calm reigned" in the capital, an observer reported, and people seemed almost relieved that all was over.[35] Absent were feelings of regret or sadness at the couple's departure. City life hardly skipped a beat; Athenian restaurants, theaters, and cafés were open, with very little sign that a revolution had taken place.

Sophie and Constantine left on board a bug-infested Greek steamer, the SS *Patris,* disembarking with some relief at Palermo in Sicily a week later. In spite of the uncertainty of what lay in store for them, Sophie and her family conducted themselves on board the *Patris* with restraint. A Royal Naval officer who accompanied them reported that "I was much impressed with the bearing of Their Majesties during the time on board. Though obviously very tired and over-strained they showed great dignity and self-control and made light of the inconveniences with which they had to put up."[36] Dignity and self-control—hallmarks of a British upbringing under the tutelage of Queen Victoria—were to be among the guiding principles to which Sophie adhered in her years of exile.

Twenty-five

"TOO SAD"

NEVER AGAIN HEALTHY AFTER HIS BRUSH WITH DEATH IN 1915, King Constantine following his abdication in 1922 was a broken man, suffering physically from nephritis and arteriosclerosis. He and Queen Sophie, refugees once again, settled in the Sicilian city of Palermo, at the Villa Hygeia. From here, they kept abreast of news on Greece, which was appalling. "Events in Greece are too outrageous and horrible for words," was how Mossy put it. In November, Sophie and Constantine heard the shocking news that five former royalist ministers were labeled as traitors and summarily shot after a mock trial. Mossy noted "the way those unfortunate victims were murdered are [sic] ghastly my sister writes. She feels quite ill from the shock and horror. . . . I knew all those poor martyrs," recalled Mossy, "& saw a good deal of them. They were loyal & devoted to their King & therefore had to disappear."[1] These latest terrible events were more than enough to send Constantine's spirits plummeting.

Princess Helen, in a lengthy letter to her husband, Carol of Romania, in December 1922, poured out her concerns about Queen Sophie:

My darling,
Mama's state simply breaks my heart. I could not possibly leave her just now, I really honestly do not find her well enough, her nerves are in a pitiable state and a mere nothing would cause an absolute breakdown. . . . This suspense is so ghastly, we have meals in Mama's salon, not feeling at all inclined to sit in a room crowded with strangers who stare so . . . it's too too cruel. . . . You can imagine the state we are in and I simply could not leave mama just now, I am so terrified of her getting ill.[2]

Sophie's brother-in-law, Prince Andrew, who had fought in Asia Minor, was accused by the new government of military incompetence.

A flurry of last-minute interventions by representatives of King Alfonso XIII of Spain, King George V of England, and the Pope helped to spare Prince Andrew's life. He went into exile.

Outwardly, the former king tried to put on a brave face on his second exile, but those who knew him well could see that Constantine was but a shell of his old self. In January 1923, Sophie and Constantine were set to move to Florence, but on the morning of 11 January Constantine collapsed on his bed and fell unconscious, a victim of cerebral hemorrhage. He died that day, surrounded by Queen Sophie and most of their children, clutching in his hand a pouch containing Greek soil. Constantine was just fifty-four years old; Sophie, his widow, fifty-two. She sent off a telegram to her son, King George II, in Greece, stating simply: "Father died suddenly heart failure. All my thoughts with you—Mother."[3] Family members were convinced that Constantine had died of a broken heart.

The king's body was ceremoniously taken by gun carriage to a steamer headed for Naples, where a funeral service took place in the city's Greek church. Queen Sophie tried to secure permission to bury her husband in Greece, but the Greek government refused. Sophie eventually had the body taken to the Russian Church of Florence, where it rested in the crypt.

One of the king's friends, the Infanta Eulalia, who admired his honesty and loyalty, recorded that "the late King Constantine was marked for extinction. Some sovereigns are predestined for destruction; he was one of the doomed." As for Queen Sophie, her lot was just as painful. "Poor misjudged Queen Sophie," recorded Eulalia, "is one of the best of women; her patience in adversity was wonderful, and her stoical philosophy enabled her to regard her life entirely as a state of *omnia vanitas*, in which nothing was lasting."[4]

In the space of just fifteen months, Queen Sophie of the Hellenes had experienced exile, the death of a favorite son, the return to reign again in Greece, the abdication, a second exile, and widowhood. Marie of Romania noted Sophie's anguish when Princess Helen returned from Italy with her mother in tow, not long after King Constantine's death. "Yesterday our poor Sitta returned at last, still horribly sad. The death of her father was a terrible and sudden shock, and her poor mother is a sad, penniless, homeless, country-less exile. Too sad."[5]

⟨∞⟩

Queens Marie and Sophie were a study in contrasts. Temperamentally, Marie, the theatrical and expansive one, always overshadowed the more subdued Sophie.

The fates of these two women were also a stark contrast. In the public sphere, Marie emerged from the ashes of the Great War with her reputation greatly enhanced. Sophie, on the other hand, tasted the bitter poison of treachery and exile, and was forever haunted by ugly propaganda painting her as the traitor who tried to deliver Greece into Germany's grasping hands.

In the autumn of 1922, the contrast was even more noticeable. For as Sophie sailed off into exile, ejected from Greece after her husband had been compelled to abdicate, Marie was preparing to be crowned Queen of a Greater Romania alongside her Ferdinand. While Marie was crowned and fêted, Sophie, the refugee, had to bide her time in exile, consumed with anxiety for her sick husband and for her son, George II, at the mercy of intriguing politicians.

Queen Marie and King Ferdinand's coronation took place on 15 October 1922 at Alba Julia, ancient capital of the Roman province of Dacia. Marie had decreed that, far from being simple and current in taste, the ceremony was to be lifted from the pages of the past in a riotous combination of Byzantine and medieval Romanian elements. "I want nothing modern that another Queen might have," she announced emphatically. "Let mine be all medieval."[6]

The highlight of the ceremony was the crowning of the two sovereigns. Ferdinand placed the crown of Carol I, forged from the captured Turkish guns at the Battle of Plevna, on his own head, then crowned Marie as she knelt before him. Marie's crown, made of pure Transylvanian gold and dotted with precious stones, was specially made. It weighed four pounds. Her gown was spectacular, a confection in gold tissue, topped by a cloak of scarlet velvet with an ermine collar. The effect of this theatrical queen evoked comparisons with Byzantine empresses of the past. But far from a mere exercise in triumphalism, the coronation had real meaning for the two sovereigns. Princess Ileana summed it up: "To my parents it emphasized their position as the first servants of the state."[7]

Among the guests who witnessed this spectacle was Crown Princess Helen. The glaring contrast between Marie of Romania's triumph at her coronation and Queen Sophie's pain in exile must have been difficult for Helen to bear. At the first opportunity, she set out for Sicily to be by her parents' side. Sitta's absence from Romania did nothing to improve the deteriorating relationship with her husband.

The breakdown of Carol and Helen's marriage caused intense misery not only to the couple themselves but to the mothers. The marriage did not live up to Queen Marie's expectations but, instead, ended up fulfilling Queen Sophie's worst fears. After Helen's family fled Greece, her companions in Romania were usually female relatives. Prince Carol found a ready excuse in blaming Sitta for their marital woes by drawing attention to these Greek relations who were forever visiting the beleaguered Helen. Carol resented sharing his wife's company with her sister or mother. He attacked what he termed his "crowded" marriage as something insurmountable, and sought diversion elsewhere. Princess Helen may have been preoccupied with her parents' relentless tragedy and had trouble shedding her Greek relations, even while living in Romania; but the fact was that Carol himself was largely to blame for the rapid collapse of the marriage. He simply could not find enough in the refined and elegant Sitta to keep him from straying. Instead, Carol became intoxicated with the exotic, flame-haired, green-eyed Elena Lupescu.

Sadly, Queen Sophie's trepidations over Helen's desire to marry Carol had been proven correct far too soon. Sophie was in the unenviable position of trying to help her daughter through an increasingly unhappy marriage with a man who was turning out to be one of Europe's most notorious womanizers. Nor was the collapsing marriage any easier for Marie of Romania. She, after all, had nudged Carol and Helen toward each other.

In the 1920s, Queen Marie was viewed as having cleverly engineered the marriages of her children so that her immediate descendants would occupy Balkan thrones. After all, her eldest son was married to a Princess of Greece, while Marie's eldest daughter was married to the King of Greece. When, in 1922, Mignon married King Alexander of Yugoslavia in Belgrade, Marie of Romania was the undisputed matriarch of a reigning family that stretched into all major countries of the region barring Bulgaria, earning her the sobriquet "Mother-in-law of the Balkans."

Though the son of an insane father, and hampered by shyness, King Alexander was undoubtedly a fine catch from a dynastic and political point of view. The bespectacled king was also an astute leader, who helped forge a nation from disparate groups consisting of Serbs, Croats, and Slovenes. The fact that he had asked for the hand of the down-to-earth, chubby daughter of Queen Marie was a stroke of good luck for the unassuming Mignon. Eager to be of help to husband, king, and people, a little nudge from her mother was all that Mignon needed to agree to Alexander's proposal in spite of the fact that they were strangers to each other. Her mother was full of praise for her child, saying how "I tremble at her courage, but I cannot help approving, it is worthy of a daughter of mine, brought up to live for others."[8] Critics of the Romanian queen could not resist painting her as a manipulative and overambitious mother, who would willingly sacrifice her children's happiness for the sake of dynastic aggrandizement. But in reality, Marie never forced any of her children to marry without their full consent.

The birth of Marie's Romanian grandson, Prince Michael, in 1921 and that of Prince Peter of Yugoslavia to Mignon two years later, certainly appeared to lend credence to belief in Queen Marie's ambitions, for here were two grandsons destined to rule Romania and Yugoslavia one day. Only the continuing childlessness of George II of Greece and Elisabetta prevented Queen Marie from boasting of a third grandson destined for a throne. But behind the glittering facades, the fact was that two of the three royal couples were already in the throes of marital difficulties. George and Elisabetta found that, like Carol and Helen, their marriage was floundering. Elisabetta's shyness was a great handicap to her and came over as arrogance, making it difficult for her to adjust to life within the Greek royal family. She seemed too aloof for most of the Greek royals; Elisabetta, in her turn, could not find much in the family to endear them to her. This included Queen Sophie, who appeared to keep her distance; nor did Elisabetta seem to give her husband much of a chance to appeal to her. For a short while it appeared hopeful that George and Elisabetta might find happiness in each other's company. But as the situation in Greece deteriorated for the King and Queen of the Hellenes, Elisabetta, already prone to black moods, grew more depressed.

Queen Marie had for years watched anxiously as she tried to encourage her eldest daughter to come out of her propensity for self-pity. When Elisabetta unexpectedly became Queen of Greece in 1922, Queen Marie saw signs that this difficult daughter was not up to the challenges before her. Elisabetta, then still recuperating from her attack of typhoid and pleurisy, used dark makeup to emphasize the shadowy circles under her eyes; her hair was cut short, then dyed red; her face was powdered in white, her eyebrows dyed black. All of which prompted Elisabetta's concerned mother to conclude: "She seems to me in every way utterly unprepared for such an event [becoming Queen of Greece]. She has as yet neither interest nor love for the country. She has studiously refused to have a child, she knows no one, she cares for no one, she trusts no one."9

Sophie, on the other hand, continued to be blessed with children who were a comfort to her and who rarely gave her much grief. True, she had worried when Alexander married Aspasia Manos. But her son's death helped reconcile Sophie to her granddaughter, Alexandra, on whom the queen lavished affection. Sophie was even instrumental in getting Aspasia recognition as a royal widow. According to Prince Christopher of Greece, when Aspasia broached the subject to him, he went to Queen Sophie, who replied, "She could have the title of Princess Alexander, but how in the world I am going to break it to the Court, I don't know. They will never accept it, I am afraid." Christopher said, "They will have to, if you make them." A nervous Queen Sophie did as her brother-in-law suggested. "As she had guessed," recalled the Greek prince, "it was not received with enthusiasm and for some days after there were black looks whenever the subject was mentioned."10 In the end, though, just before King Constantine and Queen Sophie were exiled, Aspasia was recognized as Princess Alexander of Greece. In reporting the event to London, a member of the British Legation in

Athens noted that it was at "the special request of ex-Queen Sophie, who is devoted to her Manos grand-child," that a decree was published on 25 September 1922 "rendering valid the marriage of the late King Alexander with Miss Aspasia Manos."[11]

In 1923, even the Duke of York (the future King George VI of England) could not help noticing a distinct difference between the two royal cousins, Marie and Sophie, whose fates were as opposite as night and day. The duke wrote back his impressions of the two women to his father, King George V. For Queen Marie, the duke noted little change: "Cousin Missy as usual was in great form." But when it came to the former Queen of the Hellenes, it was a different story: "Aunt Sophie was there too. She has aged a great deal, poor lady, after all she has been through."[12]

Less than eight weeks later, misfortune struck again when Sophie's son, George II, fled Greece with Elisabetta. Just fifteen months after ascending the throne, the unhappy king and queen were thrown out by republican elements of the military. Like his father before him, George did not abdicate but left Greece in order to avoid possible civil war. In 1924, the Greek government abolished the monarchy and denied the royal family Greek citizenship.

The couple fled to Romania, where they lived together for a time at the Cotroceni Palace. But an aimless life with a difficult wife in a country to which he felt little affinity prompted George to spend more and more time outside the country. With little to keep them together, the marriage soon crumbled.

Another Englishman, Beverly Nichols, who saw Queens Sophie and Marie in the early 1920s was struck, like the Duke of York, by the differences he found between the two queens. Sophie, who was then reigning, seemed immersed in sorrow. "I shall never forget my first sight of her," wrote Nichols, "for she had the saddest face of any woman I have ever seen. Standing there, dressed entirely in black, a bowl of lilies by her side, her face rose from the shadows like one who has known every suffering." The queen bore herself beautifully, but "the very air which she breathed seemed heavy with sadness." Yet when she greeted Nichols, Sophie disarmed him with her fluent English: "I'm so glad that you don't try to kiss my hand. Some Englishmen seem to think that they must do it, and they always look so embarrassed."[13]

A startled Nichols found that the queen was "absolutely ravenous for information" on the country that was her second home. "And now," Sophie started, "before I tell you about Greece, for Heaven's sake tell me something about England. I haven't been there since the war, and," shrugging her shoulders, "I don't suppose I shall ever be able to go there again." Queen Sophie then bombarded her young visitor with all kinds of questions about the parties being held, the tulips in Hyde Park, the shade of green in Kensington Gardens. As he answered this flood of questions, Nichols noted that he gradually "realized . . . that here was a woman who was sick at heart for the country in which she had played as a child."[14] Sophie then steered the conversation to her current predicament, recounting some of the outrageous stories circulating about her:

> I was supposed, of course, to be in daily touch with my brother in Berlin, by wireless. I never quite gathered where the wireless was, but I believe they said it was in a tree in the garden. I was supposed to concoct elaborate plans for the destruction of the British Army. How, I don't quite know, because my husband always tells me I know nothing whatever about war. I was also reputed to teach all my children nothing but German. I presume that is why I have had nobody to teach them but an English governess who has been here for ten years. . . . In fact—I'm quite impossible. I wonder you dare come to see me.[15]

The queen explained that she loved both England and Germany, and hated the way the war had placed her in an intolerable position. She spoke revealingly of how she had coped: "What was there to do, except to shut my eyes, and to think only of Greece? If I was to follow the struggle—first from this side and then from that—I should have gone mad. And so, as I say, I devoted myself to Greece. I nursed. I did my best in the hospitals. I busied myself in the gardens. I did anything but think."[16] After showing Nichols a fourteen-inch shell from the French bombardment of the Royal Palace in December 1916, and recalling her terrified children huddled in the cellars, Sophie reminded him of her English heritage. "Don't forget that although I may be the sister of the Kaiser, I'm also the daughter of the Princess Royal."[17]

In the six months Nichols stayed in Athens, he determined that "the Queen was utterly sincere and genuine, I do not doubt." He saw her several times more, and she revealed the sparkling side to her character. "But the underlying note of tragedy would always recur."[18] Nichols also met Queen Marie, who struck him as being a different woman from Queen Sophie. Marie of Romania, Nichols concluded, was

> A very remarkable woman. . . . And largely because, of all the Queens in Europe, she is the only one who really dramatizes her position. She is, in the best sense of the word, a *poseuse,* by which I mean that she knows exactly how to present herself to the public imagination. Realizing, as she does, that in these days the Throne has to borrow a great deal of thunder of the stage if it is to

keep its position, and that showmanship is half the craft of sovereignty, she acts accordingly. All her gestures are studied . . . sometimes daring, sometimes startlingly "unconventional." . . . But they remain the gestures of a Queen.[19]

Much as she enjoyed immersing herself in trying to solve the country's problems, Marie was nevertheless exhausted by the experience, as she once admitted to Loie Fuller: "I am a born fighter, I am not afraid, but really I am absolutely *consumed* by others. They eat my life up! . . . But strange to say never perhaps have I looked so well & some say, still extraordinarily young!"[20] Marie was forty-five years old when she wrote those words, far from her luminous beauty decades before. But there must have been more than a grain of truth, for observers like the young Mr. Nichols had certainly found plenty to admire both physically and mentally in Marie of Romania.

Being doubly related through the marriages of four of their children did not lead to a closer relationship between Sophie and Marie. Nor did Sophie's long stays in Romania to be with her daughter, Helen, bring about a closer understanding. Their contrasting personalities created a barrier that the two women found difficult to bridge. They remained outwardly polite but distant as well. In the 1920's, Queen Sophie visited Queen Marie's latest treasure, Bran Castle in Transylvania. Donated to her by the city of Brasov, the medieval fortress is perched on a steep hill. Bran, with its fairy-tale architecture and setting, greatly appealed to Marie. She set about decorating her new home with gusto, creating interiors with a blend of Eastern and Western styles, the overall effect heavily Byzantine. Queen Marie, delighted with her prowess, proudly showed Sophie her Transylvanian retreat. The more down-to-earth Sophie remarked, "Yes, it's very nice, my dear, but at your age?" Unperturbed, Marie replied, laughing, "Yes, my dear, at my age. And I'm not finished yet!"[21]

Marie's decorating and gardening frenzy at Bran, along with her numerous charitable activities, were inspired in large part by a tremendous drive and energy. But they were also a means of keeping her distracted from the tragedies that plagued George and Elisabetta and Carol and Helen. The death of her dear friend, Joe Boyle, in April 1923 was another blow. The news was broken to Marie by Prince Stirbey. Of Boyle, who had done so much for Romania and for her, a distraught queen confided in her diary: "you are still somewhere quite near—and you know it—you know that you cannot die in my heart."[22] At one time, Marie wanted Boyle to be buried at Bran, and her heart to be laid to rest near his tomb. But Boyle was buried in England (and later reburied in Canada).

At the funeral his old friend, George Hill, placed four white lilies, Queen Marie's favorite flowers, on the coffin. In thanks for his selfless service to Romania and the royal family, Queen Marie also sent an ancient Carpathian headstone for Boyle's grave.

As the 1920s progressed, Marie's joy in life became burdened by personal sorrows that developed into one crisis after another. The marital problems of her two eldest children were certainly of great concern, but in no time, they were overshadowed by Crown Prince Carol's outrageous behavior. Boyle had earlier warned Marie about Carol during the Zizi Lambrino affair. "Your son has come around this time. But he'll stray again. He has a yellow streak that cannot be denied."[23] The Lupescu affair proved Boyle right. By 1925, all was over between Carol and Helen—the marriage was in tatters.

Twenty-six

"I WOULD *NEVER* LEAVE ENGLAND"

THE OVERTHROW OF THE ONCE MIGHTY ROMANOV, HOHENZOLLERN, and Habsburg dynasties had shown that even though Queen Maud's family and court lacked the long-standing power and prestige that had set these great dynasties apart like demigods, Maud could take comfort in the fact that she and King Haakon survived the instability that plagued so many countries after the Great War. Visiting the Norwegian royal family after the war, the Infanta Eulalia was struck by the modesty of the court, which she termed "simplicity itself." Here was a kind of monarchical utopia, where "titles and class privileges have disappeared, and a system of absolute equality is in force." Eulalia admired Maud's modest approach to being queen, noting that "her existence is far less pretentious than that of many well-to-do women in other countries." Eulalia even ran into Maud shopping. The queen told a surprised Eulalia, "I always do my own shopping. For one thing, it's easier, and for another, it amuses me. In any case, I've no one to send."[1]

In her fifties, Queen Maud had lost little of her youthful appearance, and her figure remained trim. She may have suffered from chronic pain from her neuralgia and headaches, but unlike her cousin Tsarina Alexandra, who had aged quickly and was relegated to a wheelchair for stretches at a time, Maud did not let her fight with pain keep her from enjoying sports. Winter was for skiing, while spring and summer were reserved for tennis and riding at Appleton and Bygdoy, where Maud still cut a dashing figure in her tailored riding habit.

In 1924, Maud's son, Crown Prince Olav, accompanied his mother to Appleton. From there, he enrolled at Oxford University. It was a natural choice, as Olav had turned out to be practically an English gentleman, who easily took to life in his mother's native land.

The crown prince's stay in England brightened the last year of his maternal grandmother's life. A frail and elderly Queen Alexandra died at Sandringham in November 1925. Maud, dressed in deepest mourning, attended the funeral of the woman who had always been "Motherdear." Their mother's death left a void in the lives of Maud and her siblings and served to bring them closer.

Among the official mourners sent to pay their respects at Queen Alexandra's funeral was Crown Prince Carol of Romania, whose affair with Lupescu flourished. After the funeral, Carol was to have escorted his sister, Ileana, back to Romania from her English boarding school. Instead, he fled to Paris, where Lupescu awaited him with open arms, and the couple then left for Italy.

Concerns over where Spain was headed under General Primo de Rivera came to the fore when, in 1923, King Alfonso XIII and Queen Victoria Eugenie paid an official state visit to Benito Mussolini's Italy. As the couple was accompanied by Primo de Rivera, this gave rise to all sorts of speculation as to whether Spain under the general was set to emulate Mussolini's Fascist Italy. In the end, Spain did not become a clone of Italy. Yet one historian has pointed out that "the dictatorship of Miguel Primo de Rivera constitutes a crossroads in the history of Spain in the twentieth century. Neither fascist nor democratic, Primo de Rivera's regime was anchored in the powerful Liberal tradition of Spain, but in its aimless drift towards nowhere it also looked to Fascism for inspiration."[2]

The Italians entertained King Alfonso and Queen Ena lavishly. Upon their arrival at La Spezia, hundreds of Fascists formed a guard of honor. Once on Italian soil, Alfonso XIII turned the attention to General Primo de Rivera, announcing, "This is my Mussolini."[3] Years later the king admitted that he failed to grasp at the time the full impact of fascism. Nevertheless, his announcement left observers convinced that Spain was headed in the same direction as Italy.

Victoria Eugenie was not in the league of Marie of Romania and Alexandra of Russia when it came to exercising power or influence over her husband. But then neither was Queen Ena a victim of the sort of propaganda launched against Queen Sophie of Greece. Though queen of a neutral country in World War I, Ena was known for her pro-Allied proclivities, and since Spain and Alfonso XIII were never in the cross-hairs of the Allied Powers, Ena never knew what it was like to be persecuted.

Victoria Eugenie herself perpetuated the notion that she was completely uninvolved in Spanish politics—"no; never, never," she replied when asked about whether Alfonso consulted her in such matters.[4] But despite their stormy marriage, Alfonso was not above discussing politics with his wife. Their daughter, the Infanta Beatriz, confirmed this years later: "Queen Ena never discussed politics with anyone except the King. But with him she did discuss the nation's affairs and he often heeded her advice."⁵ Ena did not hesitate to give her opinion of some individuals, citing her "feminine intuition." "I would not trust this one or that one," Ena would say to Alfonso. And she recounted how, "if he had not paid attention, with the passage of time the poor King used to tell me: 'Deep down you were right.' And I would reply: 'I told you so!' "⁶ Ena may not have directly dabbled in politics but was not without some influence in this sphere.

Like her Romanian counterpart, Queen Victoria Eugenie was not averse to discussing political concerns with members of the British Embassy accredited to her country. In a despatch to the British foreign secretary, Sir Austen Chamberlain, marked "Very Confidential," Britain's ambassador to Spain, Sir Horace Rumbold, wrote at length about one meeting with Queen Ena. The conversation began with his congratulations on the "remarkable manifestations of loyalty to the Throne" on the occasion of King Alfonso's name day. Rumbold went on to report that, though Ena noted that this was gratifying, "the attitude of the ex-politicians, however, had been very different, and Her Majesty went on to speak to me, very confidentially and at great length regarding the intrigues of ex-Ministers." She told Rumbold that only one of King Alfonso's ex-ministers had participated in any manifestation of support for the king, but several of them had sent Ena huge baskets of flowers. Ena admitted that a former cabinet minister had spoken to her the past summer (1924). Rumbold continued: "The Queen added that the ex-politicians were clearly trying to involve her in intrigue against the King. One of them had even gone so far as to hint to Her Majesty that the King would have to go, but that the Queen might remain as Regent. Her Majesty did not for a moment intend to lend herself to any such intrigues, and she could only suppose that the ex-politicians were trying to play on the constitutional tradition which they assumed that she had inherited as an English Princess." Ena's loyalty to Alfonso, it seems, was unstinting, for this remarkable attempt to get her to participate in a coup against the king failed. Rumbold concluded:

> The ex-politicians have on their side, as the Queen justly observed, shown a petty feeling of jealousy towards the Directorate, which Her Majesty described as an unfortunate characteristic of Spaniards. There is therefore, a deadlock as between the Directorate and the former political parties. This would not so much matter if the person of the King were not involved . . . the King's responsibility, has, in his recent utterances emphasised the association of His Majesty with the Directorate. This is, to say the least of it, unfortunate.⁷

Time would prove Sir Horace correct. The Queen of Spain was also viewed by the king's political enemies as a possible weapon who could be used against him. But Ena did not have the inclination to play such political games. However much sadness the king may have brought into her life, Ena was not about to betray him.

By the 1920s, Queen Ena's dress sense had reached a high level of sophistication. If Marie of Romania was acknowledged as the most beautiful queen in Europe, Victoria Eugenie was rightly considered the most elegant. Ena, though more subdued than Marie, nevertheless exuded a timeless image of dignity, elegance, and refined taste. Marie's flamboyance tended to spill into her taste in clothes, making her look far too theatrical for some; but Ena's cooler demeanor, reflected in her choice of clothes, rarely rubbed people the wrong way. Always at the height of fashion, Ena wore stylish outfits, usually bought in Paris and London, embellished with the finest jewelry and accessories.

Yet the queen had failed to generate a huge groundswell of love from her compatriots. After many years in Spain, the woman who had been born in England and reared by Queen Victoria could still not shake off the impression that she was in temperament, above all, British. She was admired and respected, yes; but loved by her subjects as Marie of Romania was, no.

In spite of the fact that Ena's two hemophiliac sons, Alfonsito and Gonzalo, were always in danger from the most insignificant cut or fall, there was no Spanish Rasputin. Ena's more distant relationship with her sons, especially Alfonsito, was in stark contrast to the Tsarina Alexandra's—perhaps because Ena had a perfectly healthy son in the Infante Juan; or perhaps because Ena never had to wait for years to give birth to a son, as Alix did. Though she loved her sickly sons, Ena approached their illness very differently. Whereas Alix descended into near hysteria over Alexei, Ena went in the opposite direction, meeting adversity "with an exterior so calm and controlled that she was accused, particularly in relation to the illness of the Prince of the Asturias, of being hard and cold." Because Ena chose to face hemophilia this way, her "manner of combating the agony . . . was misunderstood and made her more unpopular still," according to one of her few very close friends, the Duchess of Lecera.[8]

For all the misery that Ena endured in Spain, not everything in her life was tinged by sorrow. The Queen of Spain had a strong, resilient streak, which allowed her to face the world. Unlike Alexandra of Russia, Victoria Eugenie did not hide from society. Whereas Alix could find nothing redeemable about life outside her palace walls, and kept her circle of intimates to her husband and a few friends, Ena ventured beyond the gates of the Royal Palace for entertainment and recreation. She especially enjoyed attending ballets, concerts, operas, plays, and musicals, and became an appreciative connoisseur of Spanish singers and dancers.

Her group of friends may not have been large, but it certainly was not as restricted as Tsarina Alexandra's had been. And because these groups of aristocrats tended to elicit the jealousies of their other, often older and more staid counterparts, the gulf that arose among Ena's supporters and those of King Alfonso and Queen Maria Cristina widened as the 1920s progressed.

⟨ᴄᴍᴍꝋ⟩

With her children grown and living in various parts of Europe, Sophie and her favorite sister, Mossy, clung to each other for comfort. "All we both wish for," wrote Mossy to their mutual English friend, Hilda Cochrane, "is to see as much as we can of each other. It wrings one's heart to see her sad expression & to hear of all she has been through, but she is wonderfully brave."[9] True to their word, the devoted sisters met whenever they could, whether it be at Sophie's home in Florence, or at Friedrichshof or Panker, Mossy's other home in northern Germany.

Living in exile allowed Queen Sophie time to reflect upon the campaign of vilification pursued by the British press against her and King Constantine, as well as the British government's actions toward her husband, and she might well have become embittered, never wanting to have anything to do with England. Queen Marie of Romania best summed up the close ties the Greek monarchs felt for England and their sense of betrayal at the hands of the English: "They cannot understand how the English nation can believe the horrible lies told of them."[10]

But in fact Queen Sophie lost little of her love for the land that was her second home. Evidence that she had forgiven Britain for its behavior toward her husband during his turbulent reign surfaced as early as 1923, a year after she and King Constantine were forced to leave Greece for the second time. In recounting to his father a visit to Belgrade that year, the Duke of York added: "She [Queen Sophie] sent you & Mama many messages & is longing to come back to England."[11] Queen Sophie's daughter, Lady Katherine, has noted of her mother, "She was very English in her feelings, absolutely."[12]

In 1928, Queen Sophie wrote a letter to King George V that highlights her longing for England and the difficulties she still faced. She did not insist on seeing her British relations, knowing that her presence might offend some:

> You were kind enough to say to my son Georgie last year that you had no objection to my crossing to England, if I kept away from town and remained quietly in a small place. I wanted so much to ask you this once more . . . I am

so homesick and dying to see dear England again. I have absolutely nothing to do with politics—have not seen William since 14 years and hardly ever hear from him—so hope I can give no offence by living quietly—and out of the world in a small place if my means permit.

I am too old and sad and tired to go out in society. . . . If you prefer my not seeing you I would not like to put you to any inconvenience. Else if you could meet me quietly somewhere, it would be a great joy for me to see you dears again after so many long and sad years.[13]

Queen Sophie's longing for England would permeate the rest of her life. Throughout the 1920s, any reference to that country was always couched in terms of great affection:

How I love beloved England I cannot say! God grant we may soon go back again.[14]

I am most dreadfully homesick to dear England & Birchington [in Kent]—If I could, I would *never* leave England.[15]

my beloved London . . . dear England.[16]

I fear this year we shall not be able to come to dear England—the expenses were too great—I hope next year—it may be possible. Its a frightful disappointment.[17]

When Queen Sophie did manage to visit, she dreaded leaving: "It is a great pleasure to be in dear England again. Alas there are only a few days left & then we shall be leaving again."[18] When she wrote those last words, she had but months to live.

෴

"We three [King Ferdinand, Crown Princess Helen, and Queen Marie] sat there as though struck by lightning."[19] That was how Queen Marie described the reaction to Carol's news that he had deserted his wife, child, and Romania to live with Lupescu abroad. Marie's eldest son had done the unthinkable—again. Painting himself as some sort of persecuted victim, Carol announced his intention to give up his family and his position as heir to the throne. A distraught Sitta offered to go to Italy to try and talk some sense into her husband, but King

Ferdinand, livid, put a stop to her offer. "You are going through this for the first time," the princess was told. "For us it is the third time. He escaped the death sentence before only because of the Queen's intervention. Now, nobody must intervene." Rallying round to aid King Ferdinand and Queen Marie in this latest problem with their son were Barbo Stirbey and Ion Bratianu, the Liberal leader and premier whom Prince Carol disliked. Carol believed Bratianu had snubbed him by excluding the prince from leading a regency council while his parents were abroad. Bratianu's close association with his brother-in-law, Prince Stirbey, Carol's other hated nemesis, also added to the crown prince's dislike of the premier. With this latest outrage, it did not take much for Bratianu to announce solemnly, "We can't afford a psychopath as our next ruler, no matter what his intellectual accomplishments."[20]

In the middle of December 1925, Carol wrote to Queen Marie: "Mama dear . . . I've had time to think things over, my decisions have become firm." Carol then made an astounding suggestion. "The best solution I've been able to imagine is that one should find a way of declaring that I've been killed in a motor accident, let's say drowned in the Lago Maggiore, so as to make things pass without any scandal. . . . As I'll be dead for many, let me be dead for everybody. I'll know how to disappear without leaving any trace." Not surprisingly, Queen Marie described this news as "a dreadful letter that tore our lives to pieces."[21]

Helen wrote to her husband, asking him to think again about what he was doing. Queen Marie also wrote an emotional letter:

> What can I say to you, Carol my boy? What can a mother say to a son who is stabbing her in the heart for a second time. . . ? You have everything: a country that needs you, a grand future to make yours, a lovely home, a beautiful and good wife, an adorable child, parents who loved you, whose right hand you ought to have been, parents who are going towards old age, who have given their lives to a mission you were to have completed. All this you give up, tear to pieces, throw away as though it were so much rubbish, and for what?[22]

Marie could not quite fathom how her eldest son, at thirty-two years of age, could have abandoned everything for a woman:

> Love, Carol, does not mean the blind giving-in to all a man wants. . . . As I told you during that sad last interview in Sinaia, what I cannot understand is what is your conception of life? What is your conception of duty? What is your idea of love? Is love for you simply indulgence, simply a letting yourself

go to your animal appetites till you are sick of the one who satisfies you, and then you pass on? Is there no fidelity in your code, no restraint, no accepting of duty, no keeping of promises given, no moral limit, no straight road you want to keep to? Nothing, nothing at all? No ideal, no vision, no dream of the future, only lust, only giving way to each passion which flits across your path?

Then, my boy, you are right to go, then we cannot understand each other, for we speak a different language, then indeed you are not worthy of standing above others, of being chosen as a leader for a people who need a shepherd, who need one capable of sacrifice, one who will love them enough to overcome himself for their sakes. If you recognize no duty, no fidelity, no obligation, then you are indeed unworthy of carrying on the torch.[23]

Queen Marie's outburst failed to sway her wayward son. By the end of 1925, Carol got his wish when King Ferdinand and the Crown Council agreed that he was no longer in line to succeed his father. In the event of the king's death before Prince Michael's majority, a three-man regency would come into being.

To Queen Marie, these incomprehensible actions were like a stab to the heart. In January 1926, she wrote despondently to her son, Nicky:

Nicky boy.

you know the horrible strain we were all living under, how Carol was poisoning our lives with his behaviour. . . . He was reduced to a state of nerves near collapse [*sic*], so was Sitta. . . .

Both Papa and I tried to make him see reason. . . . My interview with him was one of the saddest things I remember in life. . . .

It was a hidious [*sic*] night-mare repetition of the Jassy business but this time still more sordid as he was married . . . finally Papa with bleeding heart, accepts his renunciation & casts him out of his heritage as he had demanded, declaring Michael crown prince—

There is the whole story, fearful, tragic, full of abominable sorrow, pain, grief, humiliation, shame for us all and a real storm of passion of every kind let loose in the country.

Everything around me is burning accutest [*sic*] agony, heart, brain, thoughts, and the fearfulness of the lot he has chosen for himself rises before me in flaming tortures.

How could he, how could he? how could he? Did he imagine that he could eternally play this with us & his country.

Is he mad? or has he gone down morally so completely that nothing real, nothing good, nothing honest, nothing clean touches him any more. . . .

Remember we have only one son left now. . . .

Grief, grief, bitter absolutest, most horrible grief.

Your
Mama[24]

Queen Marie admired the way Helen handled herself when the crisis broke out, telling Carol that Helen had behaved "with a quiet dignity, worthy of her golden heart, forgiving disposition and admirable education."[25] Not surprisingly, Helen visited her mother in Florence as soon as she could. She did so in 1926, and they were by Queen Olga of Greece's side when she died in Rome that year. Queen Olga's body was taken to Florence, where it lay in the crypt of the Russian Church near that of King Constantine, her son.

Princess Helen's father-in-law, exhausted by years of service to Romania, was badly shaken by Carol's abandonment. Queen Marie rightly worried over her husband's health, but was reassured by both the king and his doctors that he was well enough to withstand her absence from Romania. In the fall of 1926, Marie, accompanied by her children, Nicky and Ileana, embarked at last on a prolonged visit to the United States. Long keen on visiting America, Marie—whose wartime exploits were as legendary in America as they were in Europe—was encouraged to do so by the many letters she received from Americans, as well as by her desire to win help for Romania in the form of U.S. loans. Her American friends, the dancer Loie Fuller and the millionaire Sam Hill, also urged her to go.

Loie Fuller had made a name for herself before the Great War as an innovative dancer, whose odd, fluttering butterfly dances captivated European crowds. She and Marie grew friendly, united by their love for art and especially by Loie's stint as a nurse at Jassy during World War I. In the postwar years, Loie introduced Marie to Sam Hill, a one-time gold miner turned millionaire with a penchant for building monuments. Like so many men before him, the North Carolina Quaker succumbed to the charms of Romania's queen and gave Marie much-needed money for her numerous charitable endeavors. Having begun the creation in Washington State of the Maryhill Museum of Fine Arts, which was dedicated to Hill's wife and to Queen Marie, Marie in turn agreed to go to America to open Hill's latest monument. In addition to fifty trunks of clothes she brought crates packed with gifts for the museum.

Marie's trip began with a stop in Paris, where she met with her eldest son, now known simply as Carol Caraiman. He saw her off—without Magda (as she was dubbed by the press) Lupescu—for Cherbourg, where Marie boarded the *Leviathan* along with Craggie, her black spaniel, and nearly two hundred pieces of luggage (for herself and her children). The queen impressed those on board the *Leviathan* with her friendly ways, taking her meals in the main dining room and keeping away from alcohol as a sign of respect for America's Prohibition laws. The press stalked her every move. Hungry for interviews, they were nevertheless politely declined, since the queen had signed a contract with the North American Newspaper Alliance to write about her impressions.

Marie's first glimpse of the United States was fittingly that of New York City: the bustling embodiment of America, where millions of immigrants arrived to pursue the dream of a better life. The city renowned for its vibrant energy welcomed the queen with one of its famed ticker-tape parades, complete with military escort, blazing sirens, and blaring bands. The route from Battery Park to City Hall, lined with over seven hundred policemen, was packed with crowds in the thousands, who failed to let an earlier downpour dampen their enthusiasm for the famous queen. It was all heady stuff, even for this royal accustomed to adulation. "Marie—Marie—I heard my name cried out by thousands of voices." She added that "It was all a little bewildering, very exciting & exceedingly flattering."[26]

Washington, D.C., was next on the itinerary. It was virtually impossible to get a taxi because they were being commandeered by people wishing to follow the celebrated queen. One of the most solemn moments of Marie's trip took place at Arlington National Cemetery. Wearing a tan-colored gown and sable scarf, the queen was driven in an open motorcar on a sunny day past rows of white headstones marking the graves of fallen American soldiers. She proceeded to the Tomb of the Unknown Soldier perched high on a hill. The Queen of Romania stood in silence to pay her respects, made the sign of the Cross, then laid a wreath at the tomb. Touched by the sight of so many war dead, Queen Marie noted in her diary: "The churchyard is one of the most beautiful things I have ever seen. The soldiers and sailors fallen in America's different wars are burried [*sic*] there in a lovely word [world] of beautiful trees upon marvellous emerald green grass small squares stones marking the thousands of graves, all of them in the shade of trees—dignified, beautiful & not melanc[h]oly, I have never seen anything better or more tastefully done anywhere in Europe."[27] After a lightning visit to George Washington's home, Mount Vernon, it was back to Washington and an official dinner at the White House.

Like President Wilson before him, a morose President Calvin Coolidge was not prepared to be enchanted by Marie of Romania. The White House visit, in which Marie sparkled in her diamond tiara and a Jean Patou gown of white velvet, had its awkward moments, thanks to the Coolidges' dour attitude. After lighting up a cigarette together with Alice Longworth, Theodore Roosevelt's daughter, Marie was ushered out of the White House in less than two hours.

The rest of her frenetic journey was awash in fulsome banquets, speeches, and a blaze of publicity. Back in New York City, Marie presided over a ball at the Ritz-Carlton Hotel. According to one eyewitness,

> We had a queen from a medieval legend that night. . . . She was startling. Her gown was black with diamante sequins. From her shoulders hung a brocaded green and gold shawl shifting in iridescent light as she moved in stately splendor under a crown of diamonds studded with sapphires, set above a medieval cap effect of pearls fitted close to the face and finished with hanging bands of pearls. Strings of them hung to her waist. There was a heavy chain of diamonds also, broken at intervals with squares of massive design. From this chain was suspended an unbelievable egg-shaped sapphire, one of the largest, it is said, in the world. This stiff Gothic figure moved with the creak and swing of jewels to an erected throne and received for more than an hour with all the aplomb and finesses that only a modern woman can assemble.[28]

Marie always tried to write to her husband about her experiences. She recorded her first impressions a week after her arrival—"our life has been a whirl, a rush." Ten days later, she wrote from "somewhere west" that "all the time I am making friends & what the Americans call 'putting Roumania on the map.' I would have volumes to write but not time. But I am putting all down in my diary which I shall read to you all on my return. But I keenly feel not being able to write home more & keep you up on all my news, because I never forget any of you at home. . . . The conception of America can only be had by being here."[29]

As she charged through America (with side trips to Canada) on the cross-country tour on board the *Royal Roumania,* the circus really began. The parties

vying for Queen Marie's ear, eyes, touch, nod—anything to show they were at
the center of her attention—multiplied. Ordinary folk, local dignitaries, and
children all beckoned Marie to be with them. And so it went, through West
Point; Toronto and meeting with Joe Boyle's intimates; Ottawa and the hundreds waiting on Parliament Hill. In Canada, Marie thrilled audiences when
she told them that she had always wanted to visit their country ever since, as a
child, she heard stories about it from her grandmother, Queen Victoria.

The list of places visited continued to mount—Philadelphia, Baltimore, Mon-
treal, Utica, Buffalo, Syracuse, Albany, Hamilton, Minneapolis-St. Paul, Winnipeg. Hoping to get a glimpse of American farmers she thought might be the
equivalent of her Romanian peasants, she even chose to visit North Dakota.

The most unusual part of her American trip was Marie's encounter with the
Sioux Indians in that state. The queen's reputation as a wartime leader had
reached this remote area, and it was because of her significant contribution during the war that Marie was welcomed in friendship by Chief Red Tomahawk, famous as the man who killed Sitting Bull. She entered a teepee, where her finger
was pricked for blood and she was welcomed into the Sioux Nation. No fewer
than half a dozen chiefs lifted the buffalo robe on which Marie was sitting and
ceremoniously carried her in. Kneeling on the robe, Marie then graciously accepted the gift of a spectacular feathered war headdress and her adoption into the
tribe as "*Winyan Kipanki Wim*—The Woman Who was Waited For." In a fitting
end to the ceremony, members of the tribe danced round the queen in full cos-
tume, to the beat of a drum. Though long accustomed to theatricality and well
versed in the art of being regal, even the magnificent Marie of Romania could
hardly top such an original event.

When, on 3 November, Queen Marie finally arrived at Maryhill—the climax
of her journey—to dedicate Sam Hill's museum, the site and its surroundings
must have sent her heart sinking. Hundreds of miles from civilization, set in a
stark, treeless landscape marked by volcanic rock, Maryhill looked out over the
mighty and treacherous Columbia River.

The queen, along with other visitors, was in for a shock. Awaiting them was
not some magnificent building, ready to house the many treasures Marie had
brought from Romania (worth an astonishing $500,000 or so). Instead, there was
the mere shell of a dream. Maryhill was nothing but an empty, concrete, win-
dowless edifice, more like an overblown carport. The queen's car drove right inside the main hall and deposited her beside a mounted throne draped in scarlet.
"We drove up to that strange uncouth cement building erected by the just as
strange old Samuel Hill," Marie noted. "I knew when I set out that morning to
consecrate that queer freak of a building that no one would understand why . . .
but a spirit of understanding was strong on me that day & I managed by my own

personality, by my words, by my spirit, to move all hearts beating there this morning."[30]

Rising to the occasion, Marie gave one of the best speeches of her entire trip. "There is much more than concrete in this structure. There is a dream built into this place—a dream for today and especially for tomorrow. There are great dreamers and there are great workers in the world. When a dreamer is also a worker, he is working for today and for tomorrow as well. For he is building for those who come after us."[31] Marie talked of Sam Hill and the gifts she was leaving Maryhill. She ended by saying, "Mr. Hill, I would very much like to shake your hand."[32] The queen had rescued an awkward moment and in the process acquired even more admirers.

Loie Fuller had already annoyed a number of individuals, including Marie. Then an ugly and very public fight broke out between the jolly-looking Sam Hill and the queen's personal aide, Major Stanley Washburn. An alcoholic who suffered from shell shock, Washburn, like so many others connected with Marie on the trip, kept a jealous eye on her, just as Sam Hill did. Things finally came to a head when Hill brandished a pistol at Washburn, who barricaded himself inside the royal train. Loie sided with Hill. In no time, a ravenous press was onto the story. Finally, Hill was booted off the train. But no sooner had that episode ended than some of the Romanians accompanying Marie were up in arms over Washburn. Then followed an altercation between Marie's official host, Colonel John H. Carroll, and Loie. By the time the party made it to Denver, Loie had left the train.

Marie turned fifty-one years old on board the *Royal Roumania* on its way to Winnipeg, lumbering past a desolate Canadian landscape, broken only by the occasional glimpse of lakes and Hudson Bay Company log cabins inhabited by fur trappers. The most touching message she received for her birthday was a telegram from Ferdinand, telling her how proud he was of her success.

But Queen Marie's trip was cut short by word that King Ferdinand was seriously ill. She rushed from Indianapolis to New York, then boarded the *Berengaria* for Europe. In just six weeks, Marie had journeyed over 8,700 miles and had been affectionately mobbed by millions.

Looking back on that exhausting, sometimes exasperating, but always exhilarating journey, she summed up the whole episode for Loie Fuller. The queen's trip, which, "above all . . . was to have been a voyage of love" and which was supposed "to carry a message of love and understanding from the Old World to the New," instead degenerated into a circus. In the end, however, Queen Marie would not let all the criticism mar her memories of the United States and the American people. The "sympathy shown me wherever I passed," she told Fuller, "will live with me to the end of my days." She stressed that she and her children, "in spite of these planned or unplanned contrivances, kept an un-spoiled picture of our visit and our love for the American people who received us with open arms." And she admitted that

> both my children and I have but one dream: to return! To return to that great, stupendous New World which makes you almost guiddy [*sic*] because of its immencity [*sic*], its noise, its striving, its fearful impetuous [*sic*] to get on, to do always more, always bigger, quicker, more astonishingly a restless, flaring great world, where I think everything can be realised. . . .

> I know, as long as I live, breathe and think, the love for America will beautify my life and my thoughts. . . . Perhaps Fate will allow me one day to go back to America.[33]

But Fate had other things in store. For King Ferdinand, exhausted by the dynastic and personal headaches wrought by his eldest son, was dying of cancer.

Back in Romania, the queen was surprised to find Nando a shadow of his former self. Suffering from cancer of the intestines, the king was a victim of blood poisoning. Seeing her husband's pitiful state, Marie prayed fervently that their life together would not yet end. She and Ferdinand had gone through so much, had served their country through thick and thin, and were not ready to relinquish Romania to a five-year-old boy. Leaving the throne to Prince Michael at this stage would surely mean trouble for the child and the volatile nation. Neighboring countries might be tempted to seize their former lands and internal political factions might lead to civil disturbance. But by April 1927, the king's death was so evidently near that he was given the last rites of the Catholic Church. As Marie tried to comfort her husband she was also confronted by Carol's desire to reclaim his place as heir to the throne. Far from being content living abroad with Lupescu, Carol was now itching to play a strong political role.

The queen's generous spirit shone forth as she invited the king's longtime mistress, Aristitza Dissesscu, to his bedside. Marie even lightheartedly encouraged Ferdinand to start listing gifts in his will for his many female conquests, particularly the ever faithful Aristitza.

Even as Ferdinand fought for his life, the political jockeying for power began. The prime minister, General Alexander Averescu, attempted a coup but was thwarted. Ferdinand replaced him with the ever loyal Prince Stirbey, which naturally had people wondering whether the queen had anything to do with the installation of her favorite. Three weeks after Stirbey was nominated, he resigned after the government collapsed. Next came Ion Bratianu. Meanwhile, Ferdinand's condition grew worse. Marie brought her husband to spend his last days in the place they both loved: Sinaia. She hoped that the beauty and cooler air of the mountain resort might do some good. It was an ideal choice, for the botanist king could admire the fir trees, flowers, and mountains around him. He died at Sinaia in July 1927, in the arms of the woman who had been his wife for thirty-five years. Marie wrote: " 'I am so tired' were his last words and when he lay so quiet in my arms about one hour later, I knew that I must thank God for *him* at least. This was rest indeed."[34]

If Queen Sophie's husband had been "one of the doomed," Queen Marie's husband was "a man of sorrows and of self-abnegation."[35] Ferdinand suffered much for Romania: a devout Roman Catholic, he had to raise his children in the Orthodox faith, in return for which he was denied the sacrament of Holy Communion for years; a Hohenzollern to the depths of his being, he threw in his country's lot with the Entente cause against Germany, and as a result was struck off the Hohenzollern roster; and finally, as a father who loved his heir but could not abide his son's conduct toward Romania and the dynasty, as he lay dying, Ferdinand gave up his wish to say good-bye to Carol for fear that his return to Romania might cause untold discord. Throughout all this time, in spite of their differences, Ferdinand was supported by the woman who was always there for him—"my Maddy," as he affectionately called her—without whom the king might not have proved a successful monarch. The queen was well aware of this, admitting: "A great consolation to me is that I was the one he always needed, I was a sort of anchor—till the end *I* was the anchor, and his eyes always searched me even when he hardly spoke anymore . . . I had, all through our long life together, been the one who found solutions, who refused to consider anything beyond one's strength and he had got accustomed to lean, to rely on my unfailing optimism."[36]

Ferdinand was buried at Curtea de Arges, like his uncle, King Carol I. Queen Marie was genuinely saddened by her husband's death. His last months had brought the couple closer than they had ever been. Their partnership had endured and even thrived for the sake of Romania. From then on, Marie would have to fight whatever battles lay ahead without Ferdinand by her side. Before the year was out, old Bratianu had also died, making it seem as if all Marie's old associates were deserting her. Thankfully, she still had the love and loyalty of Barbo Stirbey.

In the summer of 1928, after repeated attempts at bullying his wife for a divorce, Carol finally succeeded. Helen reluctantly conceded, counseled by Stirbey as well as others. The situation had become so intolerable that she felt there really was no other alternative than to go ahead with a divorce. The deteriorating relationship would prompt Queen Marie to record in 1930: "The situation is profoundly tragic."[37]

It is worth mentioning Queen Helen's strength of character at this stage to illustrate the stark contrast in the way the children of Queen Marie and Queen Sophie were raised. However bitter Princess Helen felt about her husband's conduct toward herself and her son, she never let her personal feelings get in the way of raising her only child to place the interests of Romania above all, and to be a decent human being. Helen derived her own values from her mother. Of his maternal grandmother, King Michael of Romania has noted that "she was a very grand lady . . . and a very strong moral person. And at the same time, she was a very sweet person, loving. But there was no nonsense about certain things."[38]

Mother and daughter had always been close and Helen's own troubles caused Queen Sophie unending misery. Sophie's visits to her daughter in Romania were a Godsend to both women. Sophie never took to Romania—"things are very weird & difficult here . . . one feels so far away out of the world." Nevertheless, she went there for her family's sake. In September 1928, she wrote to her friend the Reverend R. W. Cole, "Of course I must not grumble as I am with all my children, happy to be with my dear daughter in her loneliness."[39] Six weeks later, as Sophie prepared to return home to Florence, she confessed: "I dread leaving my daughter—hate to be seperated [*sic*] fr. any of the children—it was a great comfort being together. She is wonderfully brave in all her trouble."[40]

In Sinaia, Sophie found, "one meets no people. Well there is as much to thank for one must not grumble!!! but one feels wicked with others in a difficult atmosphere rather strained circumstances—but then God sends us this—to teach one patience it must be borne and submitted to—and has a good reason. How curious & complicated life is—In England I find the harmony that is missing in these countries."[41]

The accession of the boy-king ushered in a new era in Romania's history, for it marked the beginning of the decline in Queen Marie's influence and power. In a mixture of pomp and poignancy, young Michael, accompanied by his mother, was solemnly proclaimed in Parliament as Romania's new monarch. Sworn in as regents were his uncle, Prince Nicholas; the Patriarch of the Orthodox Church; and the Chief Justice of the High Court. It turned out to be a motley crew. Neither Nicky nor the Patriarch proved particularly keen on taking on their new responsibilities, paving the way for an increasingly bold Carol to plot his comeback. In May 1928, he acted. With the help of a British newspaper owner, Viscount Rothermere (who was intent on seeing Hungary get back Transylvania from Romania), Carol was poised to take off from England for Romania. But he was prevented by English officials from proceeding further, and then expelled from England. Queen Marie was understandably infuriated by her son's actions and sent her apologies to King George V. Unrepentant, Carol needed only to bide his time before another shameful coup attempt. As the 1920s drew to a close, an opportunity arose for Carol to make a second bid for power—this time with serious consequences for Queen Marie.

A fashionable Queen Victoria
Eugenie of Spain, c. 1908.

Windsor Castle, 1907. *Standing, left to right:* King Edward VII, Kaiser Wilhelm II of Germany, and Queen Alexandra. *Seated, left to right:* Queen Ena of Spain, Empress Augusta Victoria of Germany, Queen Amelie of Portugal, King Alfonso XIII of Spain, and Queen Maud of Norway.

King Carol I and Queen Elisabeth, c. 1910, who were responsible for Marie's wretched early years in Romania.

The flamboyant Crown Princess Marie of Romania in her palace at Bucharest, c. 1907.

Queen Maud of Norway and her only child, Crown Prince Olav (the future King Olav V), c. 1907.

Crown Princess Marie with most of her children, c. 1905. *Left to right:* Mignon, the future Queen Marie of Yugoslavia; Elisabetta, the future consort of King George II of Greece; Nicolas, on his mother's lap; and the future King Carol II of Romania. Carol was to cause his mother much anguish in later years.

Queen Ena of Spain surrounded by her children, c. 1918. *Left to right:* Infanta Maria Cristina; Alfonso, the Prince of the Asturias; Infante Gonzalo; Infante Juan; Infante Jaime; and Infanta Beatriz.

The Russian imperial family, 1913. Tsar Nicholas II and Tsarina Alexandra with their five children: the Grand Duchesses Marie, Tatiana, Olga, and Anastasia, and the Tsarevitch Alexei. Alexei's hemophilia caused his mother tremendous anguish, leaving her vulnerable to believing in Rasputin.

Queen Sophie and King Constantine I of Greece with nearly all of their children, c. 1910: the future kings Paul, Alexander, and George II of Greece; the future Queen Helen of Romania, and Irene, the future Duchess of Aosta.

Crown Prince Constantine (Tino), later King
Constantine I of Greece, c. 1912.

Queen Sophie of Greece, c. 1915.

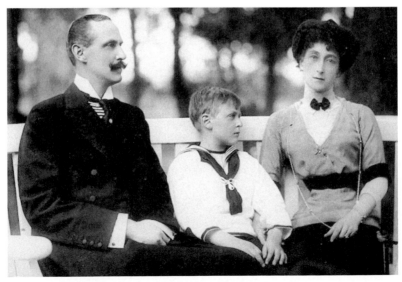

The Norwegian royal family, c. 1912: King Haakon VII, Crown Prince
Olav, and Queen Maud.

Queen Marie as a nurse during World War I.
Her inspiring work for her country earned her
immense admiration from Romanians and foreigners alike.

A majestic-looking
Queen Victoria Eugenie of Spain,
1921.

Princess Helen
and her husband,
Prince Carol, eldest
son of Queen Marie
of Romania, c. early
1920s. Helen's
mother, Queen
Sophie of Greece,
cautioned her
daughter against
marrying the errant
Carol. Sophie
proved prescient.
Helen and Carol's
marriage ended in
divorce.

Queen Sophie of Greece *(third from left)* in her later years, c. mid-1920s. Behind her is her son, Paul. To the far left in the front row is Sophie's youngest child, Princess Katherine (later Lady Katherine Brandram). Between Katherine and Sophie is Princess Frederike of Hanover, who was one day to marry Paul.

Queen Marie of Romania, in a photo inscribed in her own hand in 1924, with her grandson, Michael, who became King of Romania at the age of five. His father later replaced the boy as king in a 1930 coup.

Queen Maud of Norway *(far right)* at the coronation of King George VI and Queen Elizabeth in London, 1937. Also in the photograph are Queen Mary and her two granddaughters, the future Queen Elizabeth II and Princess Margaret.

Queen Victoria Eugenie of Spain with Queen Elizabeth the Queen Mother, Princess Margaret, and the Earl of Snowdon at the wedding of the Duke of Kent at York Minster, 1961.

Twenty-seven

"I THOUGHT I
HAD DONE WELL"

BY THE TIME THE NEW DECADE ARRIVED, ROMANIA WAS ONCE AGAIN in political crisis. The power of the Liberals may have been broken, but the prime minister, Iuliu Maniu, of the National Peasant Party, had nevertheless failed to push through needed reforms. The three-man regency, meanwhile, was to be impotent. When the most competent member, the Chief Justice, died in 1929, Maniu offered Queen Marie the vacant position if Prince Nicholas would resign. She declined, not wishing to become regent by striking a deal. But so well known was Queen Marie's involvement in her country's politics while King Ferdinand was alive that it would not have struck people as strange if Marie had gone after the post. In fact, a report to London by a British Legation member from Bucharest maintained that an "interview," purportedly given by Marie, "cannot fail to strike the average observer as being either most indiscreet or else deliberately intended as a *coup* against the Government." The "interview" had "stirred the political and social circles of Bucharest to their depths." Princess Helen, among others, felt that "Her Majesty was meditating some *coup*." The "efforts of the Liberal party to use the Queen as a political weapon" backfired, however, which meant that the National Peasant Party "must regard Her Majesty as their definite opponent." This would mean that the Peasant Party "should turn henceforth towards Prince Carol."[1]

Amid these turmoils, Marie took solace in her homes, paying avid attention to decorating, gardening, and relaxing as much as she could. Castle Bran in Transylvania and Tenya-Yuvah ("the Nest") on the Black Sea at Balcic were her two favorite hideaways. Also high on her list of interests was her writing. A natural with words, she found comfort in writing fiction (mostly for children) and non-fiction, mainly articles. But in the late 1920s, Marie began an ambitious project: her memoirs, highlighting the ups and downs of her turbulent and colorful life. It was to end up as a three-volume work entitled *The Story of My Life* that met with success and still makes for fascinating reading today.

Queen Marie also took to traveling with her youngest daughter, Princess Ileana. During a visit to Beatrice in Spain, Ileana and Alfonsito, Queen Ena's eldest son, took a serious liking to each other, but Marie was grateful when the romance did not proceed further.

With King Ferdinand dead, Marie removed to the sidelines, and the feckless regency unpopular with the Romanians, more and more people within Romania looked to Carol as a solution to the country's political instability, including the ineffective Iuliu Maniu. Having secured Prince Nicholas's acquiescence to his return, Carol flew into Bucharest on 6 June 1930.

The capital broke out in a rousing welcome as Carol made his way to Parliament. From there, the Act of Succession that King Ferdinand had reluctantly implemented and that Carol himself had engineered was revoked at Carol's instigation. Carol usurped the throne from his son, Michael, becoming King Carol II. At her home, a dumbfounded Princess Helen was coming to grips with the sudden reversal of fortunes and gently trying to explain to her son that he was no longer king. A perplexed Michael gravely asked his mother, "How can Papa be King when I am the King?"[2]

As a condition of Carol's return, Maniu had expected him to take Helen back, if in name only. Princess Helen understandably hesitated to undo her divorce, but eventually agreed. But when Carol insisted that his ex-wife sign a letter stating she was against the reversal of the divorce, Helen refused, knowing that Carol would use that letter against her to show her in a bad light.

When Queen Marie heard of Carol's return, surprisingly enough, she was relieved. She had been anxious at the direction the country was heading as Maniu and the regents proved rudderless leaders. Perhaps with Carol at the helm, an overoptimistic Marie thought, things might finally improve. She viewed Carol's comeback as the return of the Prodigal Son. Unfortunately, Carol was not intent on becoming a repentant son.

When Queen Marie arrived in Romania from abroad, she sensed things would not go well. She became acutely aware of Helen's difficulties and was filled with pity, especially when Carol refused his mother's advice to take Helen back. Marie saw just how poisonous the atmosphere was when the son claimed to his mother: "*She* insisted on divorce. . . . And when it was pronounced, she telegraphed to her mother 'at last liberated from this nightmare!' So why should I chain myself to a woman who loathes me and whom I detest? It would be immoral!"[3] The descent proceeded with a vengeance. Queen Marie had erred in thinking her son might finally be showing some sense; on the contrary, Carol was intent on unleashing a chain of events that would leave Marie and Helen gasping. Having easily succeeded in his coup, and intoxicated at holding power at last, Carol II went out of his way to make life for his mother and his ex-wife unbearable. Marie's household was radically reduced and infiltrated by the king's spies. Her monetary situation worsened as Carol ignored his father's will and confiscated the monies due to her. Marie kept quiet, not wishing to antagonize her son. Whereas before she would likely have fought, she suddenly found herself outmaneuvered by her unfeeling son. As if these injustices were not enough, Carol also exiled his nemesis, Prince Stirbey, from Romania.

When it came to Helen, Carol seemed to take perverse pleasure in seeing to it that she suffered the most. His mother still commanded a degree of respect in Romania, but his ex-wife was a far easier target. Carol's persecution of Helen greatly troubled Queen Sophie, who confessed, "My poor daughter is going through awful times. I am so worried about her."[4]

Carol stripped Helen of her cherished role as Honorary Colonel of the Ninth Hussars, had her house surrounded by police, placed her under surveillance, and soon reduced her visitors to members of the royal family. Helen was in effect under house arrest. Even young Michael became a pawn in his father's quest to make Helen's life a misery. Careful to ensure that he was not seen as unreasonable by removing Michael completely from his mother, Carol nevertheless kept the boy out of his mother's care for most of the day, only sending him back in the evenings. It amounted to an intolerable situation, deeply saddening to Queen Marie. Not long after her son's return, she told the long-suffering Sitta: "You and Carol should never have met. Your characters are poles apart. I am sorry for you. Most people who meet with disaster in their lives are given a second chance, but you have not been free to build up your life again."[5]

Any chance that Helen and Carol could lead a life together vanished completely when Magda Lupescu arrived in Romania. Firmly ensconced at Sinaia, Lupescu's presence by Carol's side was another flagrant violation of his promise to Maniu. Maniu resigned the premiership, unable to serve such an unscrupulous master.

By December 1930, it became apparent that there would be no reconciliation between King Carol and Helen. What was more, according to the British Legation at Bucharest, "every effort is apparently being made to cast the blame for this on Her Royal Highness." Though "there was always a hope that His Majesty and Princess Helen—who, although not exactly a popular figure, commands the esteem of all circles—would be reconciled and that a regulation coronation would be possible," the fact that this had not happened meant that the atmosphere in Romania "has been made worse by the failure of the King to regularise his relations with his former wife." The situation was such that people "are even ready to believe that the King wishes to install his mistress as Queen of Roumania. Others talk, equally wildly, of an approaching Peasant Revolution."[6]

Carol's unwarranted persecution of Princess Helen horrified his mother. Marie instinctively sided with Sitta, choosing not to ostracize her. And Princess Ileana also refused to do Carol's bidding. Ileana was Carol's favorite sibling and it seemed a personal affront to him that she did not support him (unlike the gullible and pliant Nicky and Elisabetta). Carol therefore determined to bring Ileana down, intent on breaking Queen Marie's heart.

ᏬᎶᏯᎵᎾ

Like Queen Marie, Queen Victoria Eugenie took delight in her close relationship with her daughters. Both of Queen Ena's girls had grown to love outdoor life like their mother, and became her golf and tennis companions through the years. In appearance, Beatriz and Maria Cristina shared similarities with their older brothers, the Prince of the Asturias and Infante Jaime. Whereas Jaime and Beatriz, with their dark hair and dark eyes, resembled their father in coloring, Alfonsito and Maria Cristina inherited their mother's fair hair. The infantas were bound to be fine catches for Europe's most eligible bachelors. The question was whether Ena's daughters were hemophilia carriers like their mother.

The Infanta Beatriz, more gregarious than her studious sister, was close to her eldest brother, the sickly Spanish heir. While in England, she chose to learn about the latest farming methods in order to pass them on to Alfonsito. Like the Tsarevitch Alexei before him, the Prince of the Asturias suffered from bouts of painful hemophiliac attacks that kept him incapacitated for long periods. Unlike his Russian cousin, however, Alfonsito grew into manhood. In the 1920s, he was given a separate establishment of his own, La Quinta, on the grounds of a royal estate in the outskirts of Madrid, where the prince, surrounded by nursing staff, devoted himself to his primary interest, poultry farming. Alfonsito's separate life from his family mirrored to some extent that of another sickly cousin, the young Prince John, son of King George V and Queen Mary, who was sent to live away from his family on the Sandringham estate, where he died as a teenager. So for Ena, there had been precedent in her family for this practice of sending off chronically ill children to live outside the family. Nevertheless, once Alfonsito was gone, it would appear that visits from his parents were few. According to Ena's biographer, this might have been largely due to the king's attitude. For "in this, as in many other respects, she was too basically frightened of her husband to take any sturdily independent line of her own."[7]

Ena's other sons continued to thrive, though neither Jaime nor Gonzalo was cured of their physical ailments. Jaime, nevertheless, became adept at lipreading. As for Juan, Ena and Alfonso's only healthy son, he grew into an obedient child and went on to make a career in the navy. Gonzalo, in Ena's view, was the only one of her children who did not inherit anything from either herself or Alfonso—except, of course, for the fatal hemophilia gene.

One of the most difficult episodes Queen Ena had to deal with was the appearance in the 1920s of a certain Carmen Ruiz Moragas. Of all his mistresses, Moragas, an actress, was Alfonso's favorite. She bore him two children, Maria Teresa (b. 1925) and Leandro (b. 1929). Hurt as she was by this betrayal, Ena nevertheless kept her head high. Her highly attuned sense of self-control and training would not have permitted her to do otherwise. Besides, she was finally reaping the rewards of living in Spain for years. Fluent in the language and confident in her role as consort, Ena came to enjoy life as much as was possible. Her circle of friends, such as the Duke and Duchess of Lecera, made up a loyal band of comrades who could stand on their own against Ena's enemies. Life became even less constricting with the removal of the queen's most formidable and despised enemy, the dreaded Marquis of Viana.

Ena saw Viana as an evil genius, urging the gullible Alfonso to pursue his dark side, especially when it came to women. From the beginning, Viana in turn saw Ena as an enemy, and acted to destroy her relationship with the king. He came close to succeeding, but Ena proved stronger in the end. Finally at her wit's end after over two decades of Viana's constant scheming, the queen confronted him in 1927. Summoned to an audience, Viana dutifully arrived at the palace to listen to a powerful indictment from Victoria Eugenie of his transgressions against her. He tried to charm his way out of the accusations, but was cut dead when Ena ended the interview by saying: "It is not in my power to punish you as you deserve. Only God can do that. Your punishment will have to wait for the next world."[8] Viana was so shocked that he literally dropped dead of a heart attack that same evening.

Viana's death may have been a personal loss to Alfonso but it was certainly nowhere near as painful to accept as the death of his mother. In February 1929, Queen Maria Cristina suffered a fatal heart attack in the Royal Palace. For nearly twenty-three years, Ena had hardly known a day without the presence of her formidable mother-in-law. Theirs had been a formally polite but never very close relationship. They had endured rocky patches, especially during World War I. But by the time of Maria Cristina's death, Ena—already in her forties and comfortable in her role as Queen Consort of Spain—had come to appreciate the woman who had been so dominant in Alfonso XIII's life. For Alfonso, the death of his mother was a profound loss. She had always counseled him politically; now Alfonso had one less trusted adviser. Only Ena saw Alfonso's terrible depression when he lost his mother and the great effort it took to overcome it. Fortunately for Maria Cristina, she did not live to see the monarchy's destruction, for less than a year after her death, Alfonso forced the resignation of the one-time saviour of Spain, General Primo de Rivera, signaling the final stages of the monarchy.

The failure of the Military Directory and, later, the Civil Directory (as the generals' governments were called) spelled trouble for Alfonso XIII. A wide array of Spaniards, from Catalan separatists to businessmen to intellectuals, were deeply disappointed by the outcome of the dictatorship. By the end of the decade, the falling peseta, along with a disgruntled military, meant that Primo de Rivera had to go. With the dictator out of the picture, however, the increasingly agitated Spaniards looked at King Alfonso as the cause of their problems. Moreover, in a strange twist of events, when Primo de Rivera died two months after his downfall, the king was conspicuously absent from the funeral in a move designed to disassociate the monarchy from the dictatorship. Ironically, people took to viewing the dictatorship with some nostalgia and Alfonso's absence from the funeral as a sign of cowardice and betrayal.

⟨꩜⟩

Not content with finding easy ways to harass Princess Ileana, as when Carol II curtailed her public duties and patronages, Queen Marie's eldest son sought to get the popular princess out of Romania. Since formal banishment was not so easy, Carol cleverly placed Ileana in the path of Archduke Anton of Habsburg-Lothringen. On her visit to Germany, the couple met again, fell in love, and became engaged. Queen Marie liked Anton well enough and did not even mind the issue of his having to work for a living. What concerned Marie was that the couple might later find they had few interests in common: whereas Anton's tended toward flying and engineering, Ileana's were firmly grounded in the arts and history. Nevertheless, Marie gave her blessing, as did Carol, though with the stipulation that the couple could not live in Romania. This was a blow to Marie, who would have much preferred to have them in the country full time.

To Carol's satisfaction, Ileana married Archduke Anton at Sinaia in July 1931. Ten days earlier, Carol II had scored another victory when he finally succeeded in hounding Helen out of the country. As part of the agreement, Prince Michael was allowed to go to his mother twice a year, while Princess Helen was allowed into Romania once a year for her son's birthday. Ileana's wedding and Sitta's departure helped to bring Queen Marie to the verge of a nervous breakdown. What she could not fathom at that point was that with Helen and Ileana gone, Carol II would be left with more opportunities to focus his campaign of intimidation toward his mother.

Unlike King Carol, Crown Prince Olav—Queen Maud of Norway's son—remained dutiful, the kind of child and heir Queen Marie had always hoped Carol could become. Much of the contrast can be traced to the young men's childhoods. Whereas Carol was removed from his mother by the tyrannical King Carol I and Queen Elisabeth, and grew to resent Marie, Olav was nurtured in a loving environment by both parents. As an only child, Olav predictably became close to his parents. Unlike Carol, who could not abide Marie's decisiveness and popularity, Olav was not only impressed by his mother's strength of character but inspired by her. Olav gave Maud credit for inspiring him to follow in her footsteps and become a keen sportsman. Sailing and ski-jumping were his specialties; in time, he became a champion ski jumper, much to Maud's delight. And when Olav fell in love, he did so with his cousin, Princess Martha of Sweden. From a dynastic point of view, it was an eminently suitable match, as Martha was a royal princess of a reigning house. The fact that Martha was Swedish made the marriage popular, as it seemed to heal the rift between Norway and Sweden that could still be felt over twenty years after the union's separation.

The wedding took place in March 1929 in Oslo (Christiania had become Oslo in 1925). Queen Maud was delighted, writing that. "The young couple are radiantly happy, Martha is really a *very* charming girl, so glad and considerate, pretty and graceful, and she absolute *worships* Olav—For Charles and me it was naturally a *little* sad to lose our Olav, *he* who has *always* lived with us during these 25 years, and who has been a *totally* wonderful son and *never* given us one day of grief. *He* deserves *all* the happiness he can get, and I *really* believe that Martha *truly* is the right one for him and that she will become a great asset to *him*."⁹ Having married off her son to a highly suitable woman, Maud anticipated the arrival of grandchildren and a new generation of royals for Norway.

By the late 1920s, the only reigning consort who came close to experiencing the same kind of intense anxieties over dynastic troubles as Marie of Romania was Victoria Eugenie of Spain. The departure of Primo de Rivera placed more pressure on Alfonso XIII to head off elements of dissent surrounding the monarchy. The intelligentsia and the military were especially unhappy, and calls for a republic grew louder. Not surprisingly, Alfonso's health gave way; in 1930 he suffered a heart attack during a polo game in Madrid. Increasingly out of touch with the pulse of Spain, Alfonso placed his faith in another general, Dámaso

Berenguer. Berenguer, though, was ill suited to the multitude of challenges he faced. The Pact of San Sebastian, formed in August 1930 between Catalans, Socialists, and Republicans, galvanized the monarchy's enemies. Berenguer refused to hold elections. Toward the end of 1930, rumors were rampant throughout Europe that a revolution was in the making in Spain, ready to dethrone Alfonso XIII and Victoria Eugenie.

As 1930 gave way to 1931, the government continued to blunder, gaining enemies as it lurched from one unpopular move to another, dragging Alfonso's reputation in its wake. The national government consisted of second-rate politicians who could not lift Spain out of its problems. In the meantime, José Sánchez Guerra, a former prime minister, approached Ena with a plan to save the monarchy. He proposed that she become regent for one of her sons, most likely the healthy Infante Juan, after King Alfonso relinquished his position. The outcome, had Ena accepted such a proposal, certainly makes for intriguing thought. Nevertheless, the queen declined, unable to bring herself to go against Alfonso XIII. As Ena's biographer has put it, she was "as loyal to Alfonso—to the end—as he was disloyal to her."[10]

In January 1931, Queen Ena's mother, Princess Beatrice, broke her arm and fell seriously ill with bronchitis, prompting Ena to go to London to be at her bedside. Once her mother showed signs of improvement, Ena left England, worried about the deteriorating political situation in Spain. As she arrived by train in Madrid on 17 February, she was astounded to find herself being enthusiastically welcomed home. According to one report, "the poor Queen imagined, upon seeing so many people shouting [at the train station,] that the Republic had already been proclaimed, that was what she later admitted."[11] Never had Ena seen such moving demonstrations of loyalty. Shouts of *"Viva la Reina!"* could be heard everywhere. Caught off guard, Ena was moved to tears. Mobbed at the train station, Ena's tumultuous welcome continued as she made her way back to the Royal Palace. The pace was so slow that her car virtually crawled. Throughout her triumphal journey back to the palace, cheers erupted— "Long live the monarchy!" and "Down with the republic."[12] Once at the palace, the crowds refused to leave, prompting an impromptu appearance by the royal family on the palace balcony. To loud ovations, Queen Ena, joined by King Alfonso and their children, acknowledged the cheers.

As heady as her return to Spain was, this tremendous welcome nevertheless masked deep divisions within Spain. The British ambassador summed this up in a lucid report: "The events of the last few days in Spanish politics have demonstrated once more the extent to which the country is divided. To make a rough generalisation, it appears as split up into two camps—those who desire that things should go on more or less as they have done hitherto, and those who aim at fundamental changes. The ideas and ideals prevalent in these two camps clash in almost every respect." The ambassador pointed out that the country faced a schism between "Young Spain" and "Old Spain."

> Young Spain has behind it the pulsating aspiration of the youth of the country, most of the *intellligentsia* and cultured elements, many of the professional classes and the mass of the organised workers of the country. It is championed by brilliant political speakers, and has, when the censorship is not working, the assistance of numerous and ably-edited organs. Old Spain [on the other hand] has the advantage over its rival of having at its disposal organised strength in the shape of imposing police and military forces. By their aid it can quell and practically silence opposition, at any rate for considerable periods. But the exercise of repression is difficult to sustain perpetually, and there comes a time when it weakens through weariness, faulty direction, or divided counsels, and then the other side has an opportunity of demonstrating the dynamic quality inherent in its ideals of progress and liberty.[13]

Even Ena knew that the end was near. She also could see that the king was taking the wrong advice, saying to one of her ladies, "I cannot understand Spain. Alfonso has as advisors many enemies. In the street, the police detain many university students who shout Viva el Rey! and leave much room to those who cheer Viva la República!"[14]

When nationwide local elections were finally held on 12 April 1931 (the first since 1922), the results were a blow to the monarchy. Though over 22,000 councillors voted in were Monarchists and under 6,000 were Republicans, the Monarchists came overwhelmingly from the rural areas, while Republicans swept all the major urban centers, except for three cities. Events moved quickly as soon as the election results were tallied. Instead of viewing the results "not as a crisis, but as the irreversible finale," Alfonso's ministers, in the next two days, took action that "only contributed further to the worsening of the situation, thereby hastening the premature end of the monarchy."[15] When King Alfonso heard of the election results, he was shocked. Upon learning the extent of the Republican victories in the major cities, the king said dejectedly: "I feel as though I had gone to make a visit to a friend and when I had got to the house I had learnt that he was dead."[16] Nevertheless, he believed the situation was still salvageable if parliamentary elections were held while he was out of the country. But in no time, advisers told Alfonso that the death knell of the monarchy had sounded and civil war was imminent. Emboldened by their victories in the cities and the government's paralysis, the Republicans adeptly pushed their propaganda on the people and demanded that King Alfonso give up his position. When a rumor spread that the king had abdicated, pandemonium broke out in the capital. An eyewitness reported that "crowds of 4,000 and 5,000 persons, mad with joy, swept into the Puerta del Sol, the hub of Madrid." Shouts rang out of "Viva la Republica! and Death to the King!"[17] Even more worrying to Monarchists was the attitude of some members of the Civil Guard, who now switched from pro-Monarchist to anti-Monarchist. Instead of charging a crowd of thousands waving Socialist and Communist flags, as they marched down the Prado, the Civil Guard aided them.

When the king sounded out his supporters, including the military, he found to his dismay that they were abandoning the monarchy and siding with the Republicans. Fearing for the future of Spain, Alfonso finally conceded defeat. He issued a manifesto in which he did not renounce his rights but, instead, suspended his prerogatives. Though he could have fought his enemies, Alfonso announced: "I prefer to stand resolutely aside rather than provoke a conflict which might array my fellow-countrymen against one another in civil and patricidal strife."[18] Not wishing to see blood shed on his behalf, King Alfonso, like King Constantine I of Greece before him, opted to leave his kingdom. And having made that fateful decision, he wasted no time in implementing it.

The king left the Royal Palace just three days after the elections. Since it was imperative that he leave immediately, and since the rest of the family could not do so, the king had no choice but to go without them. He did so reluctantly, and only after he had received assurances that they would be protected from harm.

Not long before the king fled, his director general of security, Emilio Mola Vidal, met with him and Victoria Eugenie. Vidal was convinced that the events of 14 April might have taken the king by surprise. But when it came to the queen, he ventured with "absolute certainty" that she had expected this. When Vidal visited the young Prince of the Asturias, who was seriously ill, Alfonsito rose to greet his visitor but could not get up to say good-bye. Recalling that moment, Vidal said he saw in the prince an expression of "mixed anguish and resignation. . . . The eldest child of the King and Queen in those days, was very scared. I understood then all the intimate tragedy of the royal family and found justification for the sadness in the face of the Queen."[19]

Queen Ena requested that Alfonso dine with her alone on the evening of his departure. Emotion filled the air, but the couple dined mostly in silence. At 8:30 P.M., the family and retainers assembled to bid the king farewell. The atmosphere was highly charged but the send-off was very businesslike. As the crowd outside the palace clamored for a republic, Alfonso said his good-byes, calmly but with clenched fists. To Ena he said simply, "You and the children go to your rooms and stay there tonight. You will leave by a special train in the morning."

A shout from the halberdiers of *"Viva el Rey! Viva el Rey!"* was met by a *"Viva España!"* from the king.[20] The most moving scene of all took place when, just before descending the staircase, Alfonso XIII faced a portrait of his late mother, paused for a moment, and saluted. He then left hurriedly by car for Cartagena and boarded the cruiser *Príncipe Alfonso* for France. He was never to return to Spain.

Queen Sophie's sister, Mossy, commented on the end of the Spanish monarchy: "The events in Spain were indeed terrible. What a shame to treat the King like that, who had been so excellent in every way. That poor country will probably go to rack & ruin now."[21]

On the night that King Alfonso fled Spain, Ena and her children were alone at the Royal Palace, save for a few faithful retainers and family members. Shades of the Russian imperial family's terrible murder at Ekaterinburg haunted the queen. As the family packed what they could to take into exile, shouts could be heard outside calling for blood: *"Muera al Rey! Muera a la Reina!* (Death to the King! Death to the Queen!)" No less audible were shouts of *"Viva la República!"* In the nearby Campo del Moro, where Ena and her children had spent many happy hours, the crowds grew menacing, carrying weapons and shouting obscenities. Those surrounding the palace were massive, surging ever closer to the gates. Incredibly, only twenty-five guards outside and twenty-five inside stood between the agitated populace and the royal family. A tense moment took place when two men broke into the grounds, made for the main balcony, and hoisted the Republican flag. As the night dragged on, tension continued to mount. Ena's children told her they were willing to take up arms in order to defend themselves.

"We did not sleep much that night, as you can imagine!" Ena said later of that petrifying evening.[22] At five in the morning, the queen was advised that plans had to be changed. Because they were in the middle of a revolution, the streets clogged with hostile people anxiously awaiting the return of their republican heroes from exile, the royal family would have to leave for El Escorial by train from Madrid. At seven o'clock on 16 April 1931, Ena, her children, and retainers attended Mass, with the Infante Gonzalo serving as altar boy.

Nerves soon became frayed when a truck began bashing at one of the gates. Then, a group approached and insisted on being let in. Far from enemies, they turned out to be the nuns who had taught Infante Jaime to speak. They came offering to help the deaf Infante understand those terrifying moments; but Jaime understood well what was taking place. Ena, in the meantime, expressed her puzzlement at the land that had been her home for decades. "Spain!" the queen exclaimed when she greeted the nuns, "always does she surprise me! I believe I will never understand her!"[23]

Before leaving, the royal family distributed gifts to their servants. The Prince of the Asturias, seriously ill from a hemophilia attack and unable to walk on his own, gave his valet all his money and asked him to distribute it to those who had served loyally. Alfonsito was then carried by his mechanic into a car for the journey.

Dressed simply in a dark blue traveling suit and small matching hat, Ena and her children left the palace. Missing from the family was the Infante Juan, who was at naval school in Cadiz. He was to make his own way to France. Accompanying Ena on her journey into exile were her cousin, the Princess Beatrice, Marie of Romania's sister; Ena's sister-in-law, the ailing Marchioness of Carisbrooke; and an assortment of aristocrats, among them Ena's ever faithful friends, the Leceras. One of the queen's final thoughts was for the Spanish people when she admonished one of her ladies to "take care of my Red Cross."[24]

During Ena's last hours in Spain, a lady bid the queen a temporary farewell with the words, *"Hasta la vista."* In reply, Victoria Eugenie said, "Those who now leave are not going to return."[25] But Ena's most poignant words were heard not long after Alfonso left for exile. Feeling some responsibility for the monarchy's debacle, an emotional Ena murmured: "I thought I had done well."[26]

On the way to El Escorial, the party stopped at a place called Galápagar while waiting for their train, which was delayed. There, Ena sat on a boulder and chatted with her companions. She was clearly fatigued and anxious, her face betraying all kinds of emotions. According to *The New York Times* account, near the Escorial, at a small town called El Plantillo, they came across a group of peasants, one of whom, a woman, said to the queen, *"Viva la república, Señora."* " 'Long live whatever is best for my people,' the Queen replied, and the little group of onlookers fell respectfully silent."[27]

At El Escorial, the magnificent and imposing monastery built by King Philip II, the royal family went to Queen Maria Cristina's grave to pray. A forbidding place in which to spend last moments on Spanish soil, this was the final resting place of Spain's monarchs. Victoria Eugenie had always found the royal family's crypt too morbid for her tastes. All the onyx, marble, and gold could not make up for the frightening spectacle of so many red marble caskets lining the walls. When Alfonso brought some visitors there and "pointed out his waiting casket with a shrug," Ena was not present. One observer said that "the Queen could not bear the place and always waited in the cathedral."[28]

On her last visit to the Escorial on her way into exile, Victoria Eugenie, her lips trembling and her eyes swollen from weeping, told those around her: "The King has not abdicated; we do not know what is going to happen to us, but I feel sure it will turn out for the best."[29]

Amidst a flood of tears, the family finally boarded the train for France. *The*

New York Times reporter noted: "She has never been very popular with her people, and never was she left more alone than on this day of her final departure. . . . One curtain was raised [on the train] and a lone hand appeared through it. The hand was that of the Queen, her last farewell to a land that never learned affection for her."[30] In time, Victoria Eugenie herself admitted as much when she said, "I have a tranquil conscience of having always stayed outside political divisions, of having treated everyone with the same courtesy and of having dedicated all my efforts to the organization of charitable welfare in Spain. Nevertheless, I have the feeling that I have never really been loved, of having never been popular."[31] One contemporary monarchist comments: "I have always believed that the Spanish people were extremely unjust with Doña Victoria, who was never held in high esteem in spite of her extraordinary personality."[32]

Twenty-eight

"THE GOD WITHIN US!"

KING ALFONSO ARRIVED IN PARIS FROM MARSEILLES TO A HERO'S welcome. Thousands mobbed him at the Gare de Lyon, shouting and waving, as Alfonso made his way to the Hôtel Meurice. Later, Queen Ena and her children arrived by train at the Gare d'Orsay to a similar welcome. Looking haggard and bemused, she bravely smiled and acknowledged the thousands who greeted her with shouts of "Vive la Reine!" No less than ten thousand people, along with French officials, amassed to greet Ena. The family met up with King Alfonso at the Meurice, where they and their entourage took up nearly thirty rooms. The noisy acclamations prompted Alfonso to go to the balcony and acknowledge the crowds. When Ena did the same, the cheers grew even louder.

Ena's life of exile began in the French capital, but within weeks she and her family moved to an annex of the Hôtel Savoie in Fontainebleau, outside Paris. Her eldest son, Alfonsito, still suffering from an attack of hemophilia, left the family to recuperate in a clinic in Switzerland. Never one to keep still for long, the king resented being cooped up with Ena, the children, and the queen's small set of retainers at Fontainebleau.

One visitor to Fontainebleau was none other than Sandro, who had been Tsarina Alexandra's brother-in-law. When he met Ena, Sandro was impressed. "The tragic events she has lived through during the past months have added a certain spiritual halo to her striking blonde handsomeness," he recorded. "Otherwise she is just as friendly and refreshing in the simplicity of her manner as in the old London days . . . I look at her and think: 'The eternal British. . . . Tenacity and loyalty. . . . That's what helps her keep her head up. . . . It takes an English woman to make a proud Queen.' "[1]

Ena proceeded to give Sandro a moving account of the final days of the Spanish monarchy, finding parallels with the Russian Revolution that had destroyed her cousin, Alix::

> I have read and heard many heartbreaking stories about the Russian Revolution, but really, I can not believe it could have been any worse in St. Petersburg. It came so suddenly, so unexpectedly. It seems I returned from London only a day before, not wishing to be absent from Madrid during the political crisis. And the crowds at the station in Madrid that met my train! Oh, Alexander, if you could only have seen those people! Cheering, delighted, throwing flowers at me! I thought I was the most popular human being in Spain! And then! . . . It is unbelievable. . . . How could a nation change its sympathies so abruptly?[2]

Hidden from Sandro during this visit was the tragedy that the couple had virtually decided to separate. With plenty of time on his hands and the burden of kingship stripped from him, Alfonso might have chosen to make amends to his long-suffering wife and begin a fresh start with her in exile. More than likely, with her own capacity for forgiveness, Ena would have given their marriage another chance. But that chance never came. Alfonso was as bitter as he had ever been. The specter of hemophilia in his two sons was still obviously too much for him to bear, and he continued to take out his frustrations on his wife.

Free from the constraints of reigning, Ena had reached her breaking point when it came to Alfonso's cruelty. The last straw came when Alfonso accused her outright of having an affair with her longtime friend, the Duke of Lecera. The duke did harbor romantic feelings for the queen; so too, according to Ena's English biographer, did the Duchess of Lecera. But Ena, as a true byproduct of a proper Victorian upbringing, could not even come to acknowledge this aspect of the duchess's feelings for her. It was out of the question for Ena to be unfaithful in her marital vows. What she did know was that she was unprepared to let go of the Leceras as friends at this stage, since they had supported her through her darkest days, even choosing to go into exile with her. This episode pushed Ena into a fit of hysteria, in which she sent out a venomous reply to Alfonso that was completely uncharacteristic: "I choose them and never want to see your ugly face again."[3] Alfonso was taken aback and appalled. This unsavory incident marked the sad end of the marriage. From then on, they lived separate lives. Ena also eventually dismissed the Leceras from her entourage.

⟨∞⟩

In many ways, Marie too, though still in Romania, was living the life of an exile, thanks to King Carol II's continuing persecution. Intent on preventing her from exercising any kind of power or influence, Carol's jealousy ensured that Marie was kept at arm's length from Bucharest. In a "Very Confidential" report to his superiors in London, Michael Palairet of the British Legation in Bucharest reported that "a weak character like King Carol would always instinctively shrink from a strong and dominating personality like Queen Marie, who is evidently chafing under the necessity of adopting a rôle the inactivity of which is so uncongenial to her tastes and so at variance with her past." The audience, which lasted an hour, touched upon "the present situation in Roumania, which she regards as highly critical."[4]

With Princess Ileana married and making her permanent home outside of Romania, Marie grew increasingly lonely. Of the few retainers left to her, she could at least count on the presence of a certain General Zwiedineck. But loyal retainers could not make up for family; and Marie craved for close family ties. With Ileana gone, who was she to turn to amongst her children? Mignon—"my little Serbian Queen," as Marie liked to call her—was in Belgrade. Elisabetta, the exiled Queen of Greece, had turned out to be a great disappointment to her mother. Carol—well, Carol was just incomprehensible. So what of Nicky?

Queen Marie had placed great hopes in her second son, Prince Nicolas. But like nearly all her children, Nicky failed his mother. Not because of any great omission on Marie's part in raising him; the young man, after all, had escaped the damaging influence of King Carol I and Queen Elisabeth that had so ruined Nicky's two older siblings. It was just that Nicky did not seem to have inherited any of the strengths of either parent and indeed showed some of their weaknesses. His tenure as regent was a failure. Lacking in ambition, ability, and duty, Nicky simply gave in to Carol's desire to return and usurp the throne from Michael. This was a bitter blow to Marie. She had nursed strong hopes that Nicky might help Carol turn his life around. Queen Marie had once admitted to Loie Fuller that she hoped Nicky would be helped by the aid of Dr. Frank Buchman. A well-known American Evangelist, who had been transformed by the power of Christ, Buchman preached that selfishness and pride had to be eliminated so that one could work in the service of Christ. This kind of thinking greatly appealed to Marie, who saw in Buchman a kindred soul. Years later, she was to distance herself from Buchman. But Marie's faith in the 1920s was such that she recommended him to Loie, saying he would be *a healing hand.* Marie also noted that he was "teaching our Nicky to become one day *perhaps* the saviour of his own brother."[5] But Prince Nicolas never became Carol's saviour. And worse was to come when Nicky presented his mother with his choice of a wife.

Queen Marie's interest in the philosophy of men like Buchman reflects her own deep-seated faith in God. It was her faith that helped sustain her through her ordeals. Always transparent in her dealings with others, Marie could never comprehend why they behaved maliciously toward her and chose to misunderstand her motives. Shortly before King Ferdinand died, the queen complained that "life has become a battle, a sad battle against forces working in the dark." She confessed that she might sometimes feel beaten; but she did not despair, thanks to her faith in God:

> On all sides I feel danger, it is all about me like an air that poisons even the strongest lungs, but in spite of that, deep within me my faith, my hope are still green, there is an invincible something which I am built upon, or out of, which cannot, will not, does not despair. . . .

> The God within us! that is what really counts . . . that fundamental something which makes us part of the "beyond," which leads us upwards in spite of ourselves . . . towards a light out of which we came and to which we surely return if we do not allow our spirits to go down in the mine! A light which shines in our souls, a beacon signalling to us from somewhere beyond this quarrelling, hating, doubting, betrayed and betraying, sad suffering world.[6]

It was through Buchman that Queen Marie met Dr. Samuel Shoemaker. Both Buchman and Shoemaker were leading lights in the Oxford Group at Oxford University, which in turn influenced Bill Wilson, co-founder of Alcoholics Anonymous. Marie's interest in Shoemaker's approach to faith led her to include a Sunday visit to the Calvary Church in New York (where Shoemaker was rector) during her hectic American tour. When Shoemaker visited her at Cotroceni Palace earlier, she had promised that she would hear him preach in his church if she ever reached America. Marie fulfilled her promise, arriving at the Calvary Church on a rainy Sunday morning in October 1926. Shoemaker had hoped that the large congregation who had come to honor the queen "would feel themselves drawn closer to The King of Kings before they left the church." According to Marie's American host, "the Queen was much interested and later said that the hour was one of almost heavenly peace and beauty."[7] Marie herself noted in her diary that the "church was a sweet rest. Lovely singing, service neither high nor low, just what I like."[8]

⁍

Queen Sophie of Greece had also found Shoemaker's words uplifting and sent his book of sermons to the British clergyman, the Reverend R. W. Cole. "I think the sermons magnificent," she wrote to Cole, "& hope you will like them."[9] Sophie recommended two other works to the Reverend Cole: "There are two books I should like you to read and think they will interest you—one *In Touch With Christ* by James Reid, M.A. St. Andrews Presbyterian Church Eastbourne. The other, *Twice Born Ministers* by S. M. *Shoemaker*—Rector of Calvary Church New York, the one who wrote *Religion that Works*. I find them very interesting, fine; I think you will enjoy them."[10] Central to the theme of both is the transformative nature of Christianity.

The former Queen of the Hellenes had taken these works to heart and was deeply immersed in her relationship with God. She described herself to the Reverend Cole not as a royal personage but simply as a "poor old sinner—who am just like everybody else."[11]

Like Tsarina Alexandra of Russia, who had felt her own Christian faith intensely, especially in times of pain, Queen Sophie found renewed strength in her close relationship with God. Attending religious services and reading works on Christianity comforted her. Her prayers were also a source of strength. Sophie admitted how she loved "the old prayers of the 17 cent[ury]" which she kept on her table to read so that she might "find strength & comfort."[12]

Sophie came to know Reverend Cole and his family when she visited England in the 1920's. Her youngest daughter, Princess Katherine, was then in school at Broadstairs in Kent. The Reverend Cole preached at an Anglican parish church in the village of Birchington, some seven miles from there. Toward the last years of Queen Sophie's life, she and Cole corresponded, providing her with a link to England. When she received photographs of the church at Birchington, Queen Sophie was thrilled and commented to Cole: "The one of the interior, I love particularly. It makes me so *dreadfully* home sick—when I see the sweet peaceful little church I loved to attend the services there."[13] Though herself a convert to Orthodoxy from Protestantism, Sophie occasionally attended Anglican services while in England and also at the English Church in Florence. She missed the moving services and sermons at Birchington and did not hesitate to tell the Reverend Cole so:

The lovely services I loved so much—Thursdays, Saturday evenings—Sundays at 12:15, Sunday evenings, etc.

How often we speak of you all & like to think back at our delightful time in Birchington.

Love to think back to the happy days in Birchington & we wish we were there again . . . yesterday a year ago we were in Birchington.[14]

Even Margery Bennett, Princess Katherine's governess, wrote to Reverend Cole to let him know of Queen Sophie's affection for his church: "Her Majesty so often speaks of Birchington & everyone she knew there, & only this morning, as I walked back from church with her, she was talking of you & your work, & wishing she could be back at the little church that she loved so much."[15]

Not surprisingly, Queen Sophie believed in the power of faith and prayer. When the depression and turmoil in Europe of the 1930s made for worrying news, Queen Sophie wrote to the Reverend Cole that the world was "still in a great mess." Yet she was convinced that it could change for the better: "Only prayer & Religion can put that right again."[16] She never wavered in her belief. A year later, she repeated the same thoughts, saying: "What a mess the world is in & a lot of prayer is needed to lead people on the right way."[17] This strong faith of Sophie's echoed that of her grandmother, who in 1878 told Sophie's own mother: "The mere abstract idea of goodness will not help people to lead good lives, only belief in God."[18]

⟨⟩

Queen Marie of Romania remained an Anglican, though she had been confirmed in the German Protestant Church. But as the daughter of a Russian Orthodox mother, wife of a Roman Catholic, mother of children and queen of subjects belonging to the Romanian Orthodox Church, it was not surprising that Marie was drawn to other teachings in her quest to reach a deeper relationship with God. She discovered some of her answers in the Baha'i religion, which she encountered in 1926 in the midst of Prince Carol's scandals. Marie found one of its central tenets particularly appealing: surrounded by a diversity in faith among family members, she valued the emphasis on religious unity. Marie admitted that "I really pray better at home with my Baha'u'llah books and teaching which have brought me such a message lately, the message in fact that I have always been waiting for—it has become a joy and comfort to me."[19] She tried to explain the religion's attraction for her and where she stood in the spectrum of faiths: "this dissatisfaction with every religious form made of me a great appreciator of the Baha'i teachings, so that I have even been called a Baha'i! But I am nothing except myself, though officially I am Anglican, but call myself a Protestant. When asked what sort of Protestant, I throw out my hands and smile a smile that might mean anything."[20]

Queen Marie was not prepared to see her second son go down the same route as Carol when it came to choosing a wife. Like his father and brother before him,

Nicolas fell for a Romanian commoner. Again like Ferdinand and Carol, Nicky wanted to marry his Romanian girlfriend; but he could not do so because of the country's constitution. Encouraged by King Carol, Nicky went ahead and eloped with Joana Doletti a day before his mother's fifty-sixth birthday.

Marie was disappointed with Joana. A divorced woman, in the queen's estimation she was nothing but "a hardhearted, painted little hussy whose one idea is money and luxury in every form, and who is eating up his fortune so that soon he will have nothing but debts."[21] Marie was also deeply hurt by Joana's attempts to separate Nicolas from his mother. When Nicky eloped, Carol (although he had supported the move) promptly divested his brother of his military rank and forced the couple out of the country by striking Nicky off the royal family roster and stripping him of his citizenship. Marie had lost another child to exile.

"I have put queer children into the world," Marie once confessed. "I loved them enormously, everything was for them, but they do not recognise this and . . . well I am not going to talk about this because it would be making wounds bleed and I must get along somehow without losing faith & hope and my joy of life which still clings to me astonishingly."[22]

Queen Marie could not understand how her two sons could have betrayed the ideals with which they were raised. For a time, she preferred to lay the blame largely on the women they became entangled with, but she also took responsibility for having failed to raise her children well. Writing in 1934 to a young American friend, Ray Baker Harris, Marie explained:

> I may be rash, sometimes even inconsiderate, but this is out of over-honesty, never with an intention to hurt. My fear of hurting has in fact been a shackle in my life and much of the trouble I have today with my children is that I always respected over-much their personalities and never wanted to tyrannize or oppress. . . . I was the thread upon which they were strung. My will, my faith, my ideal, my love, my sense of duty kept them straight. . . . But at his death they all came into their separate fortune, and they cut the string and each rolled into his own little corner and did his or her worst, except Ileana and Mignon. This is the truth, and, being the truth, it will make the later story of my life difficult to tell.[23]

One person who heard some of this difficult story from Marie herself was her long-lost love, King George V.

> My life has been very difficult & very sad, so sad that it does not bear putting down in writing. . . . If ever we are to meet again in this world, I shall tell you everything . . . I did all I could; I see everything . . . I have struggled for over

two years, swallowing every unkindness, every setback, but all in vain, there is some dark force against which all my good will shatters. . . . Lately I have been living in a world which I no more understand & which has become very lonely; Ileana married, Sitta gone, Nicky banished, but I struggle on, I look beaten, but am I really beaten? I was always a good fighter you remember. But fight against one's flesh & blood?[24]

Deeply moved by the plight of his once-beloved Missy, George replied with a letter referring to the latest cruelty heaped on Marie—Carol's refusal to allow Ileana to give birth to her first child on Romanian soil:

What a terribly sad letter yours is. In reading it the tears came into my eyes, as I fully realise all the misery you have gone through during the last two years. I have seen Sitta and George, and they have both told me of the many insults and unkindnesses that have been heaped upon you; even this last cruel act, that Ileana was forbidden to enter the country to have her baby in your house is cruel and disgraceful. I do hope that some day soon we may meet and then you will be able to pour your heart out to me.[25]

Ileana had her baby, a boy, born in Austria (where she resided), with her mother by her side. Marie was now the grandmother of the former King Michael of Romania, three princes of Yugoslavia, and a baby Archduke of Austria.

King George V's letter was a reminder of those far-off days when he had been among the first young men smitten by her beauty and charm. At nearly sixty years of age, the still luminous Marie had one more conquest to add to her long roster of admirers—her aide-de-camp, General Zwiedineck. Many years her junior, the mustachioed general with the large eyes had taken over Prince Stirbey's old job as head of the Queen's Household. Marie was naturally flattered by Zwiedineck's sudden admission of passion, but she kept him at arm's length.

Ileana's new baby and Zwiedineck's admission of his undying devotion were two of the few happy events that came Queen Marie's way, for life in Romania with the tyrannical King Carol II made his mother increasingly edgy. She was so disgusted with Magda Lupescu that she not only refused to meet her, despite Carol's numerous pleas; Marie also never acknowledged her except to a few intimates. When, not long before she died, the English author Beverly Nichols asked Queen Marie about Lupescu, her reply was characteristically that of a disapproving matriarch against the upstart. "At the mention of the name she became the very *grande dame*; the temperature of the room seemed to drop. 'I have only seen her once,' she said. 'Years ago, at a ball. . . . She seemed quite insignificant, and she was wearing pink, which was hardly the colour to wear with that hair. I suppose she has what they call sex appeal.' " Nichols added: "She made 'sex appeal' sound like some very odious disease."[26]

With Lupescu hated in the country, it was only a matter of time before a strong opposition force against Carol II emerged. It did so in the form of what became known as the Iron Guard, a group backed and encouraged by Mussolini and Hitler under the leadership of Corneliu Codreanu. Marie watched in dismay as Carol tried to battle it out with Codreanu for the heart and soul of Romania, but was not surprised to find that legions flocked to join the Iron Guard. When Carol turned to his mother's old friend, Jean Duca, for help, tragedy ensued: Duca was assassinated in December 1933 by the Iron Guard.

Queen Marie was deeply saddened by the assassination. As for King Carol, Duca's death sent his popularity dropping dramatically. Although Carol encouraged his mother to ride in the annual 10 May parade in order to help his image, he responded to her popularity among Romanians by persecuting the queen even more.

If Carol hoped that this battle of wills might finally push his mother out of the country, he was wrong. Marie refused to concede. For a woman accustomed to fight for what was right to have done so would have been to admit defeat. That was simply not in her nature. Besides, she loved Romania and was prepared to suffer again for her country's sake if there was any way she could help by staying put. Marie, however, had to have breathing space; so she fled to her favorite retreats at Bran and, especially, Balcic—"this peaceful corner I love." There, she had built a simple chapel, the Stella Maris, and filled it with Byzantine decorations. She tended to her flowers, cruised the waters on her motorboat, and enjoyed "my solitude & independence . . . [in] a real Fool's Paradise."[27]

Marie also sought to escape from the scandal and intrigue of Carol's court by visiting Ileana and Anton and their growing brood in Austria. Ileana sometimes obtained permission from Carol to return to Romania, but he kept those visits brief and few. This irritated his mother no end, as she pointed out to a friend: "Ileana adores to be home again, and it is a cowardly cruelty to try and keep her out of the country which adores her and which she so profoundly loves."[28]

The queen also liked to visit Belgrade, where she stayed with Mignon and King Alexander, her moody but intelligent son-in-law, who was a much more astute monarch than Carol. Alexander proved much more attentive to his mother-in-law than the ever jealous Carol back in Bucharest. The only problem for Mignon was that Crown Prince Peter lacked a proper education, a fact the boy's grandmother noticed. At her insistence, Peter was sent to study as a boarder in England, where Marie felt he could be molded into a proper gentleman and become prepared to be Yugoslavia's next king.

In October 1934, Queen Marie was in England to promote her memoirs.

Writing continued to provide an escape, whether it was voluminous letters to friends and relations or working on her autobiography. The queen was flattered to find that her memoirs not only sold well but were critically acclaimed for their lively style. The $50,000 offered by the *Saturday Evening Post* for serialization rights especially thrilled her.

During her October visit to London, a telephone call interrupted Marie's visit to old friends. On the line was the Romanian ambassador to Britain with news that the queen's son-in-law, King Alexander of Yugoslavia, had been assassinated in Marseilles—along with France's foreign minister, Louis Barthou—while on an official visit. Marie wrote: "I was in my beloved home-country, England . . . I was drinking a cup of tea in an old friend's house . . . then the news . . . Sandro killed . . . Mignon a widow . . . little Peter; King!"[29]

She was grateful to be in England at the time, "so that poor little Peter could be brought to me from his school, that I could break the news to him and take him to Paris to meet his mother." Marie was once again the grandmother of a boy-king in the Balkans. The regency of her other grandson, King Michael, had proven ineffective and allowed for Carol's comeback. Would the same kind of political mess be young King Peter's fate? Marie's heart filled with compassion when she saw her newly widowed daughter facing the flag-draped body of King Alexander in France. "She took it standing, like a soldier's wife," wrote the proud mother, "and my heart was crying out all the time—Mignon, Mignon! My child—Mignon."[30]

Upon returning with Mignon to Belgrade, Marie wrote of the tragedy still fresh in their hearts: "We are deeply shaken & the country groans with grief—big & small—the dastardly deed has put an end to a great and good man's life. We bend our heads, we accept but we do not understand."[31]

Queen Marie was compelled to describe herself to her young American friend, Ray Baker Harris, as "one who lately has been living through *too* much—whose heart is sometimes so intolerably heavy that she would like, occasionally, to take it out of her breast and lay it on the table beside her for a rest."[32] But there was to be no respite.

Twenty-nine

"I BLESS YOU WITH MY LAST BREATH"

NOT ONLY HAD KING CAROL BEHAVED WRETCHEDLY TO HIS MOTHER and siblings, he had also embarked upon a program of repression toward Romania's restless peasants. Moreover, Carol surrounded himself with corrupt yesmen whose main qualifications were that they were approved by Lupescu. Nor was he immune from lining his pockets and those of Lupescu's intimates to the tune of tens of millions of dollars.

Marie bemoaned her son's failures—the sordid adventures, the opportunities he had thrown away; there were so many it was hard to enumerate them.

> He wasted & smashed, & tore up by the roots, he worthlessly set aside, changed; persecuted & humiliated those who had worked before him—out of jealousy he set his family aside, hurt their feelings, sacrificed them to a horrible set of low adventurers who had grouped around him & who in his name made havock [*sic*] of his royalty, his honour, his chances, of the hope others had put in him . . . he hurt us all so much that we feel numb, we do not today know how to approach him in his mood . . . today he is master & a jealous one, & worse still, a man who will not shoulder his own mistakes but who tries to throw every fault on others, so there is no health in anything he does.[1]

What was most pitiful was the mother's suffering. "It is abominably difficult," a dejected Marie confessed. "I ought to be with him much more, because when together, the pathetic side of him softens me—when I see him I like him better than when I *think* of him. My brain rejects him, but my heart is still a mother's heart." The queen desperately wanted to help Carol, but he refused all overtures, prompting her to comment warily, "whichever way I turn, there is danger. I always hoped that patience & kindness would win the day; but whilst I remain silent, the danger grows. It is an appalling situation for a woman of my power of action."[2]

Yet she continued to exude good humor and warmth. Ileana remembered how Marie's "presence radiated life and light. . . . Everyone loved her."[3] Whether it was the peasant children near Ileana's Austrian home or the countless friends around the world, Queen Marie had ample space in her aching heart for others. Never—if she could help it—did she let others down. Her dear friend George V saw the old spirited Missy of many years before when she visited him in 1934. "George has always kept an especial affection for me," Marie noted. "I stimulate him, my uncrushable vitality makes the blood course more quickly through his veins. May feels it also. She likes being with me, and then I am never heavy on their hands. I know so perfectly how to look after myself and be happy over everything, finding interests everywhere."[4]

In May 1935, Queen Marie made another trip to England for the Silver Jubilee of King George V's reign. Reminiscing about that visit, she wrote:

> England was a joy, a deep joy. I love it with the love the roots of a tree have for their *own* soil, something deeper than reason, something fundamental, so to say—basic. Something deep down within me responds to England as it does to nothing else. To the soil, the people . . . a sort of delicious, warm pride bubbles up from my depths when I think of England. Everything in me agrees with it, feels at home, at peace. . . . My love for Roumania in no way makes me less proud of being English, of feeling English, with every drop of my blood.[5]

⟨∞⟩

Another royal guest at George V's Silver Jubilee was his youngest sister, Queen Maud of Norway, who was thrilled to have been there. Upon her return to Norway, she scribbled an exuberant letter to Queen Mary:

> I was *very* sad leaving "Home" and you *all,* but I was *so* delighted to have been present at the Jubilee, I *loved* the enthusiasm and devotion which the people have for dear George and you, it is *so* touching—and in no other country I am sure it is like that! One is *proud* to be *British.* I was glad to have been in London for G[eorge]'s birthday and could see you *all* once more.—I do hope both you and George are not *too* tired, with all you have to do. It *is* wonderful, all you have got through.[6]

Age had not taken away the bantering relationship Maud and George V enjoyed since they were children. As neighbors on the Sandringham estate, the place they both loved best, they had had ample opportunity to see each other when Maud was in residence at Appleton. One day during a walk, the King of England kept teasing his sister. When he noticed that Maud had a special handkerchief for her spaniel, he ribbed her with questions: "Where are its galoshes?" "Don't forget its cough drops."[7] Sadly, there would be not much more of that kind of bantering as his health slowly gave way. Maud's brother had almost died in 1928. When he recovered, a relieved Queen Sophie wrote to him:

> It was the greatest joy—to see your picture in the papers again to see you up about & about. It all brought you, if possible, still nearer to your people who showed such touching loyalty. It was splendid.[8]

The Jubilee celebrations were one of the last happy spectacles Maud would attend in England.

⌇⌇⌇

Queen Sophie kept busy in her years of exile, traveling whenever she could afford to. One particularly poignant visit was to Doorn, in the Netherlands, where her brother, the former Kaiser, lived in exile. Sophie visited Wilhelm for his seventieth birthday celebrations there in 1929. The festivities were described by the ex-Kaiser to an old American friend: "a great joy to be surrounded by children & grandchildren of all ages—19 in number!—& my sisters."[9] Here the sisters appear to be almost an afterthought. As it turned out, Sophie's reunion with her brother did not bring them any closer. The ex-Kaiser made no effort to mend bridges, showing neither remorse for his past cruelty toward Sophie nor interest in her future. A photograph taken to commemorate the event shows a sad-faced and veiled Sophie, looking pensive, even melancholy. But Sophie was not always melancholy. When she met with Ferdinand of Bulgaria, who had fought against King Constantine years before, the two had much to discuss. In fact, it was difficult to separate them after lunch. Asked what they had talked about, Sophie replied, "Why old times, of course." Prince Christopher marveled at how Sophie seemed surprised by his question and by the fact that "there was no bitterness in her voice or on her face."[10]

During her years of exile, Queen Sophie also tried to see as much of Mossy as she could. During one visit to Sophie, Mossy wrote, "to be with my sister was joy & I found her much better than last year."[11]

Another relative Sophie delighted in seeing was her only granddaughter,

Princess Alexandra of Greece. As a living link to Sophie's beloved dead son, Alexandra had a special bond with her grandmother. Their meetings were not as frequent as the doting grandmother would have liked, but they did maintain an affectionate relationship. "My little granddaughter Alexandra is in school in England Westfield—Alass [sic], I cannot see her which makes me very sad," Sophie once admitted.[12] And when the princess was scheduled to visit, Sophie could not help but let out her excitement: "My darling little granddaughter Alexandra will come & join us—during her holidays—which is a great joy to look forward to."[13]

In her autobiography, Alexandra left a touching portrait of Queen Sophie as a grandmother—"Amama" to the young girl. Of her time in Florence with the queen, Alexandra recalled: "I had a wonderful time with Amama, who adored me, and spoiled me outrageously." Princess Alexandra had wonderful memories, too, of Queen Marie of Romania. She remembered sitting at Marie's feet and being mesmerized by the fantastic fairy tales Marie created, told in a "melodious" voice with a "bell-like quality" while her maids tended her silver-gold hair. Alexandra remarked that these fairy tales were enhanced as the queen gestured animatedly with "her lovely expressive hands."[14]

Of Sophie of Greece, Alexandra recalled, "She was tall, slim, and very elegant. She always wore mourning colours for King Constantine, and the black, pale mauve, or silver grey of her widow's weeds greatly became her."[15] Like the widowed Queen Marie of Romania, Sophie took to wearing flowing veils, which suited her far better than they did the flamboyant Marie. Sophie's veils framed a soft, melancholy face and gave her an aura of tranquility.

But what made Sophie stand out above all was her goodness. "She never complained," noted her youngest daughter, Lady Katherine. "She always thought about other people: the governesses, the nurses—that they had everything that they wanted, very thoughtful." Being thoughtful of others did not mean that Queen Sophie was devoid of humor. On the contrary, "she was quiet [but] she had a terrific sense of humor."[16] Queen Sophie appears to have passed this on to the next generation. Crown Prince Alexander of Yugoslavia, who knew all of Queen Sophie's children, said that they all admired their sense of humor.

ᦇᨠᩮᦉ

The lives of three queens—Sophie, Marie, and Maud—were drawing to a close. First to succumb was Sophie of Greece. For some years, she had not been well. She brought up her physical ailments to her friend, the Reverend Cole. In 1929, the queen admitted: "I was not well for a long time—nerves—& that painful acidity [sic]—then I saw a French specialist who did me a lot of good & now

I feel much better—& able to eat more." By 1930, her problems were getting
more serious: "I was not very well—& had to go to a clinic in Frankfurt to have
myself thoroughly examined. That lasted a fortnight & now I am back with my
sister—feeling much better."[17] Sophie had grown so weak and tired that it became easier for her to write letters in pencil than in ink—a fact which she con-
tinuously apologized for, just like her mother, who had done the same thing
years before.

But there were also respites in her illness, for which Queen Sophie was always grateful. She wrote the Reverend Cole in October 1928, "I am beginning
to feel much better—the quiet & mountain air did me a lot of good—besides a
strict diet—so the pain is practically gone!! which is a great relief, which I cannot thank God enough for." And in December 1930: "At last I am beginning to
feel much better & stronger after having gone through a cure in a clinic in Germany. I have to keep a strict diet which is the chief thing. I cannot say how
thankful I am to God for allowing me to be better again."[18]

Within a year, however, Sophie was at death's door. Mossy noted that "it all
came so suddenly. She enjoyed herself in England & later in Munich, so much &
seemed so well. Only in Venice in Sept: did she begin to feel less well & said the
heat as usual did not agree with her."[19] In Frankfurt, Sophie was operated on.
The doctors found that cancer had advanced so far she was given only weeks to
live. Sophie was never told of her fatal illness.

That December, Mossy wrote to their friend, Hilda Cochrane:

> You can imagine what I feel like! I try not to think. It is all too, too awful my
> darling sister is growing weaker from day to day, to witness this is almost
> more than I can bear.—She is not in pain, thank God, & some times she is still
> very cheerful, but she cannot understand why she is so weak, a sign that it has
> been possible to keep the truth from her, for wh. we are grateful. It is difficult
> to find the right nourishment as all food disgusts her, & she often suffers from
> sickness. The Drs. give her every sort of injection wh. are a great help & she
> sleeps a great deal. All her children are at Frankfort & to be with them & try
> to help them enables me to fight down my own misery . . . I am afraid there
> can no longer be a question of taking her back to Florence, as the Drs. first
> thought, & she herself said she prefered [sic] to remain where she was as she
> feels so well cared for.[20]

It was only a matter of time. After a slight improvement between Christmas
and New Year's Day, Sophie, unable to eat, grew much weaker. Queen Sophie
of the Hellenes died on 13 January 1932 in Frankfurt, at the age of sixty-one.
The queen's body was taken to Friedrichshof to lie in state, and then brought to

Florence. There, it was placed to rest in the crypt of the Russian Church beside her husband's and that of Queen Olga.

Mossy was shattered by the death of her beloved sister. "You know what *she* was to me," she wrote to Hilda, "& that I shall never get over this loss. Sometimes I try hard not to think, but it is a useless struggle. She is always present wherever I am or whatever I do, as she always was, ever since I exist[ed]. Those terrible two months & all that followed afterwards, still haunt me." Nearly a year after Sophie's death, Mossy still felt the loss keenly: "All the terrible time of last year weighs on me, & I try to get away from the many sad thoughts. Life can never be the same without my dear sister." And when, in 1935, Sophie's son, King George II, was called back to reign once more in Greece, Mossy, though pleased to see the dynasty again on the throne, admitted that their reversal of fortune "makes me so sad to think of all my darling sister & her husband were made to suffer."[21] The Infanta Eulalia had similar views, describing Sophie as a "much-maligned consort"[22]

The death of Queen Sophie may have been hard for Mossy to bear. But for Sophie's children, the loss was even more heartbreaking. "She was so sweet and kind and good," recalled Lady Katherine.[23] And when it came to writing the news, Princess Irene, still raw with grief, confessed that "The loss of our beloved Mother & the agony of the past months was almost more than one could bear & I am still quite stunned from the cruel blow, my heart is a wound that will never heal, only time can ease the pains. Having lost both our beloved parents life doesn't seem worth living any more & one misses them every day more. The only consolation is that at least they are happier on the other side without all the trials & difficulties of this hard life."[24]

In the last years of their lives, Queens Sophie, Maud, and Marie watched in dismay as the world situation deteriorated. The Great Depression had wreaked havoc on millions of lives. Fascist Italy under Benito Mussolini was on the march, as was Nazi Germany under the increasingly belligerent Adolf Hitler. Marie, who had watched in horror as the Bolsheviks plundered Romania years before, was particularly anxious and highly critical of the USSR and the menacing role the Soviet Union played in world affairs. It was an understandable reaction, as Marie lived beneath the shadow of the Communist leviathan. "I resent the ugliness of their conceptions," wrote the queen in 1934, "the murdering of all beauty, personality, initiative. . . . And it is all a vast delusion. Tzarism was also a delusion no doubt, but it had its beautiful and sacred sides . . . horror fills my very soul when I think of their sinister creed, the hideousness of the fear and destruction they have spread around them. To me their creed appears to be the very negation of life and all that makes life worthwhile!"[25] Three years later, she still held to her views. "Bolshevism," she wrote in 1937 when Joseph Stalin, bent on oppressing his people, was sending tens of millions to their deaths, "is the levelling of everything. . . . Every drop of my free blood rises up in protest against such an abominable conception of life."[26]

Of the few joys Queen Marie found in Romania, one was the ever faithful General Zwiedineck, who carefully watched over the queen and read many books to her. Marie's appetite for reading remained high. She even had time to tackle *Gone With the Wind,* and enjoyed it. Then there was her precious Black Sea home of Tenya-Yuvah ("the Nest") in Balcic, where Marie continued to cultivate her gardens with their magnificent lilies and roses. Perhaps most precious of all was the growing understanding with her grandson, Prince Michael. Toward the end of her life, Marie rejoiced in this. "I have made great friends with Michael," she noted; "he wants comprehensive sympathy, senses that I can give it, so has a longing for my company. He is a darling and I anxiously watch his progress."[27]

King Michael later recalled how, in Bucharest, they used to go out together at Cotroceni—"in an old, old park, that's where [we] used to meet. We used to go for a drive. She [Queen Marie] always let me drive her car—a big, big Chrysler, I remember that." These meetings took place on Sundays; "mostly we went there for lunch then for a drive for two or three hours. But when she was in Bran, the same thing. She used to invite me for lunch. And then go [for] local drives around there. She was always very nice, and not at all strict." But King Michael also saw Queen Marie at other times. "I remember, she always used to go to the official ceremonies, the National Day or Easter, all that, she was always with us."[28]

Queen Marie had great hopes for her special grandson, who had been king once and was destined to become so again. When it came to another generation of monarchs, Marie had hopes, too, for England's Edward VIII, who succeeded his father, King George V, when the latter died in 1936. The death of George V in January 1936 was a blow to his cousin and close friend, Queen Marie of Romania, and to his sister, Queen Maud of Norway. Only some six weeks before, George's sister, Toria, had died. For both siblings, long accustomed to chatting to Toria on the telephone, the silence was numbing.

Queen Maud attended George's funeral, but Queen Marie did not. It was a great sacrifice on Marie's part, but she felt she should let Carol represent Romania. In one sense, George V's death marked the end of an era. This year saw the Italo-Abyssinian crisis—which caused much hand-wringing in Europe and marked the death knell of the League of Nations—reach its climax with Mussolini victorious in his disdain of the League and in his conquest of Ethiopia. Adolf Hitler's Germany became more ominous as the country's soldiers marched into the Rhineland in the spring in a blatant violation of the Treaty of Versailles. Spain, meanwhile, continued to descend into civil war. These events boded ill for the future, leaving little doubt that war was once again on the horizon. Queen Marie was certainly anxious, describing the situation just after Hitler's invasion of the Rhineland in no uncertain terms: "The world at present is very explosive. Perhaps this acute crisis will bring about a better atmosphere when nations will look the horrible danger more squarely in the face."[29]

Not long after George V's death, Marie was dealt another blow when her favorite sister, Ducky, died, leaving a huge blank in her life. Like Sophie and Mossy, Marie and Ducky had enjoyed an enviable bond. "The grief of seeing my most beloved sister die," wrote a disconsolate Marie, "is one of those griefs which seem to cut into the very roots of life."[30]

When, in December 1936, the once promising and glamorous King Edward VIII abdicated the throne because of his romance with the twice divorced Wallis Simpson, there was little sympathy from the older generation such as his aunt, Queen Maud of Norway, and his cousin, Queen Marie of Romania, whose own conceptions of duty were far stronger than those of the ex-king. Maud could not bring herself to mention Mrs. Simpson by name in a letter to Queen Mary soon after the abdication: "Where is She? *Do* wish something *could* happen and prevent them from marrying. *How* sad it all is, that he has ruined his life, fear later he will be sorry what he has done and given up."[31]

Queen Marie had even harsher words for the former Edward VIII, whom the family affectionately called David. "Personally, I am too royal not to look upon David as a deserter. There is too much poetry in my heart and soul to be touched by this love story. She is an uninteresting heroine." Then, as if seeing the parallels between Carol and Lupescu and Edward and Mrs. Simpson, Marie lamented: "The whole world was open to him . . . it seemed so unnecessary to stand the whole British Empire on its head, to compromise the throne, and shake the foundations of monarchy." Of England's golden-haired king and great hope, Marie bemoaned: "I could weep over him."[32]

Among her own children, Marie could feel at ease only with her two youngest, Mignon, the widowed Queen of Yugoslavia, and Ileana, a Habsburg archduchess. It was ironic that the two children who had a grasp of duty and honor were the ones who had little to do with ruling Romania—Mignon out of circumstance as mother of King Peter and Ileana as a result of Carol II's direct orders to stay away. Marie's three eldest children, Carol, Elisabetta, and Nicky, on the other hand, were in Romania (Nicky returned in 1935) and continued to disappoint their mother. Nicky was an embittered man, still attached to his grasping wife. Elisabetta, who embarked on an affair with a Greek businessman, divorced the affable King George of Greece. Moreover, Elisabetta did not hesitate to ally herself with Carol in order to keep in her brother's good books. It was an exercise in self-preservation and self-aggrandizement that left her mother shaking her head in disbelief.

Queen Marie's relations with her son, King Carol II, never improved. She wrote that "He denies his mother, alas and wishes her to be forgotten, hoping thus to become himself a brighter light by treading hers underfoot."[33] The whole distasteful way in which Carol II had treated his mother through the years was the more painful because Marie always hoped he would redeem himself and was prepared to pardon him. Princess Ileana herself admitted that where Marie was concerned, "Mama had the most forgiving heart in the world"[34]

The great tragedy in Marie's life was not only that Carol had treated her so badly but that the two were never completely reconciled. And the ever-perceptive queen knew exactly why: "there is a sort of unreasoned jealousy against my past, against what I have been to the country . . . I am a sort of living reproach. I cannot admire all he does; I know his *métier*, I alone in the country know it, and he knows that I know it and this, for some reason, infuriates him."[35] In 1936 she admitted for the first time: "I am obliged to make a mighty effort to preserve my optimism . . . I am continually hit in the back and subjected to ugly and unnecessary humiliations by those surrounding the master . . . I will not bow down to what I consider wrong and harmful. . . . It has become the reign of evil . . . I never thought it would come to this!"[36]

As she faced her twilight years, Queen Marie, once so beautiful, did not resent aging or losing some of her characteristic vitality and brilliance. Instead, a mature Marie reflected: "It is not in vain that, on decline, so much is taken from us. It is so as to prepare us for the end. To sow the seed of longing for another life in our tired souls."[37]

In March 1937, she collapsed from internal bleeding. Carol II, in the meantime, callously threw his brother, Nicky, out of Romania along with Joana. Marie was greatly hurt by the bitter feuding between her two sons and feared that she had lost Nicky forever. Marie's daughters, along with her sister, Beatrice, urged the king to get better help than the one Romanian doctor assigned. Carol, as it turned out, was not particularly eager to move quickly, but he acquiesced after much insistence.

The specialists who examined Queen Marie announced that her liver was the culprit and that nearby blood vessels were affected, resulting in severe bleeding, though one of the doctors disagreed with this diagnosis. Dr. Aldo Castellani, a specialist in tropical medicine, who was physician to a number of senior European royals, met with King Carol, along with the other specialists at Sinaia. Castellani recalled Marie's Romanian doctor insisting that "none of us will ever think the disease is cancer." "Unfortunately," wrote Castellani years later, "it was the correct diagnosis—the Queen was suffering from cancer of the pancreas." Dr. Castellani did not budge from his conclusion, writing in his memoirs, "I never had any doubts that it was cancer. The official diagnosis given was cirrhosis of the liver." Castellani recalled how "Queen Marie, who had a keen sense of humour," when she heard the official diagnosis, "smiled and said: 'Then there must be a non-alcoholic cirrhosis of the liver, because I have never in my life tasted alcohol.' "[38]

A diet of cold foods, injections, and complete bed rest was ordered for the suffering queen. Marie, who had been healthy all her life, felt helpless. Nevertheless, she did not complain, nor was she bad-tempered throughout her debilitating illness. For weeks on end, she lay in her floridly decorated golden bedroom at Cotroceni, surrounded by her icons and the large crucifix, so weak she could hardly take up a pen. In February 1938, she was sent to a sanatorium in Merano, Italy, to recuperate. She stayed there for two months.

In Merano, Queen Marie was visited by Nicky and Joana. Joana left the meeting impressed by her mother-in-law, who forgave Joana for her transgressions. Then came a visit from Helen. She had bought a lovely old villa outside of Florence, which her mother, Queen Sophie, had admired. Renamed the Villa Sparta, Helen made a life for herself there amidst the cypress-covered hills of Tuscany. Seven years had passed since Helen and Marie last met. Whereas Marie had forgiven Joana for her harsh treatment, it was now Marie's turn to ask Helen to accept her apologies for sometimes having not sided more with Helen in her painful battles with Carol. Marie was also touched by a visit from her old friend Waldorf Astor, who flew to her side.

Marie's final months were further bleakened by the deteriorating situation in Romania. More trouble broke out for Carol from the Iron Guard, and the king's Fascist prime minister, Octavian Goga, who was persecuting the Jews. Carol also trampled on the constitution, banned political parties, threw out the parliamentary system of government, and made himself dictator.

In March 1938, Hitler marched into Austria. Queen Marie, in Merano still, became anxious for Ileana and her family. Ileana had just returned home to her castle in Austria, and found Nazi storm troopers swarming. Marie told Ray Baker Harris that "the *anschluss* of Austria with Germany . . . meant the final annihilation of her adopted country." When Ileana telephoned to tell Marie she was all right, she had to conduct the conversation with her mother in German, instead of the customary English. "Hitler's deadly efficiency," as Marie put it, infuriated her. "I, fervent lover of freedom, felt my blood boiling, but was obliged to keep my emotions to myself, knowing that at the other side of the wire she was doing the same."[39]

Marie's last letter to Harris was posted from the Wiesser-Hirsch Sanatorium in Dresden, where she was transferred upon orders of a new German specialist, Dr. Störmer. Marie's weakness is evident as she admits, "I am gradually crawling up hill again after a very bad two months of complete exhaustion . . . I have undergone strenuous treatments which left me no strength to hold a pen." Ileana followed this up with a brief message: "I think she has suffered overmuch sorrow. She is of a patience and endurance which in anyone so active as her is truly wonderful to behold. Her thoughts are always for others. For instance, when an injection into her veins (they are almost inaccessible) does not succeed, she is sorry for the doctor and not for her pain!"[40]

Dr. Störmer and another able colleague, Professor Wanerkroze, were deeply suspicious. Störmer told Princess Ileana: "But it's not natural for a woman who has lived the kind of life the Queen has lived—no alcohol, fixed hours, daily riding, nutritious foods—to have cirrhosis." He thought the queen's dilated blood vessels stemmed "only from complications secondary to alcoholic poisoning of longstanding duration." Warnerkroze added: "Even if the illness itself had a natural beginning, which we don't know, she has been neglected and mistreated all along in a way that's absolutely criminal. . . . She's had this disease for years, and she's been given the wrong treatment from the beginning. I can only say that the doctor who did that had to have done it purposely. He can't have been that stupid."[41]

Toward the end of her life, Marie wrote to Prince Barbo Stirbey, still exiled in Switzerland. Barbo replied: "I am inconsolable at being so far, incapable of being any help whatsoever to you, living in the memory of the past with no hope for the future. . . . Remember my longing, my nostalgia, the prayers which I constantly offer up for your health and never doubt the boundlessness of my devotion. Ilymmily [I love you my Marie, I love you?]"[42]

Just before she left on her last journey, to die in Romania, Marie wrote to Stirbey of "all my longing, my sadness, all the dear memories which flood back into my heart. The woods with the little yellow crocuses, the smell of the oaks when we rode through those same woods in early summer—and oh! so many, many things which are gone. . . . God bless you and keep you safe. . . ."[43]

King Carol denied Queen Marie a more comfortable journey by airplane, as her doctors recommended; instead, she had to make her way to Sinaia by train. The lurching and jostling induced more bleeding, and since it was summer, the heat became intense. As the train carrying their queen made its way to its destination, Romanians watched in disbelief, murmuring the unbelievable fact, "Regina is dying."[44]

Marie was taken to her home, the Pelishor, at Sinaia. Present by her bedside were Carol, Elisabetta, and Michael. Marie wanted to say good-bye to Zwiedineck, but Carol, true to form, refused his mother's request. Even more cruel was

Carol's deliberate plan to bar his mother from saying good-bye to Nicky and Ileana. The insensitive son telephoned his siblings only when he knew they would arrive too late. Marie had held out as long as she could and kept her eyes fixed on the door, but to no avail.

Aware that she was a step away from eternal life, a joy she was prepared to embrace fully, the queen asked for the Lord's Prayer to be said in English. As no one knew it in English, Marie, the lifelong Protestant, was given the last rites of the Orthodox Church. Then, with thoughts for Romania still uppermost in her mind, Marie implored Carol, in a whisper, to be a strong and just monarch. At that, she lapsed into a coma and died peacefully in the late afternoon of 18 July 1938, aged sixty-two.

Queen Marie's youngest daughter and close confidante, Princess Ileana, wrote to Ray Baker Harris not long after her mother passed away: "she is not dead of that I am sure, she has only found a new freedom & can at last unfold her wings."[45]

As if to make up for all his wrongdoings, Carol gave his mother a fitting funeral. Marie wanted mauve—her favorite color, just as it had been for Tsarina Alexandra—to be her mourning color instead of black. Romanians responded by draping Bucharest in shades of mauve and purple, along with the Romanian tricolor. The queen's body was placed on a gun carriage. As bells tolled mournfully, a quarter of a million people watched the slow-moving procession wind its way to the train station. King Carol allowed Ileana and Nicolas to attend their mother's funeral, but denied permission to Prince Stirbey.

Queen Marie's coffin was taken from the capital by train to Curtea de Arges. So many people lined the route to kneel and throw flowers that the train arrived four hours late. Marie's body was buried beside her husband, King Ferdinand. Her heart, as she had instructed, was buried at the Stella Maris chapel she had built at Balcic.

After Queen Marie's death, a Romanian, Constantin Argetoianu, who was a "cynic . . . far from kind in his appreciation of the queen," nevertheless acknowledged her worth and wrote a moving tribute of her that would have made the queen proud:

Whatever Queen Marie's errors before and after the war, the war remains her page, the page of which she may boast, the page that will seat her in history's place of honor. . . . We find her in the trenches among the combatants, in forward positions; we find her in the hospitals and all the medical units among the wounded, among the sick; we find her present wherever people met to try to do some good. She knew no fear of bullets and bombs, just as she knew no fear or disgust at disease, or impatience with the often useless efforts provoked by her desire for something better. Queen Marie fulfilled her duty on all the multiple fronts of her activity, but above all in encouraging and raising the morale of those who lived around her and who had to decide, in the most tragic moments, the fate of the country and the people.[46]

In a final good-bye to the subjects among whom she had lived for nearly half a century, Queen Marie had composed an emotional letter entitled "To My People," touching on the long and often difficult journey she had embarked upon to be a part of Romania:

I was only 17 years old, when I came to you; I was young and ignorant, but very proud of my country of origin, and today still, I am proud of being born English; but when I embraced a new nationality, I had to try hard at becoming a good Romanian.

At the beginning it was not easy. I was a stranger, in a strange country, alone amongst strangers . . . that a foreign princess has to travel to become one with the new country where she was called.

I became yours through joy and sorrow . . . I bless you, my dear Romania, land of my joys and of my sorrows, beautiful country which lived in my heart. . . . Beautiful country which I saw unified and that I shared the lot for thirty years, that I also dreamed the ancestral dream, that it gave me. . . . Be always . . . grand and full of integrity. . . .

And now, I bid you farewell forever . . . remember, my people, that I loved you and that I bless you with my last breath.

Marie[47]

Of that special group of five women who were the reigning granddaughters of Queen Victoria, Queen Marie of Romania's death in July 1938 left only Queen Victoria Eugenie of Spain and Queen Maud of Norway.

At sixty years of age, there were few indications that Maud was near the end of her life. She continued to remain active despite a lifetime of health problems, never losing her love for the outdoors, still as enthusiastic about sports as she had been as a girl. When Maud went skiing with Haakon in Nordmarka, she could cut a good form. Once, when she skied down a steep slope, a couple, who did not recognize the king, remarked, "look at that girl go." "Yes," answered Haakon, "when the girl is sixty it's pretty well done." "Is she really sixty? Do you know her?" "Yes," replied the king, "I know her pretty well, she's my wife!"[48]

Maud's obsession with England had not abated through the years. At Christmas 1932, the queen lamented to her sister-in-law, May, her homesickness for England and her longing to be at Appleton:

> The "flu" caught me badly and I got *acute* bronchitis which I have had *only* once before *years* ago, and I felt *very* bad and an *awful* cough and aches in all my limbs. . . . It was *very* sad about poor Sophie, and *dreadful* for the three children, without any home or money—Also poor Mossy wrote she was heartbroken, *adored* Sophie—What a lot of troubles and worries there are, and the new year has not begun well.[49]

She continued to be blessed with an uncomplicated family life. Olav found marital contentment with Martha, and Queen Maud became a doting grandmother to the couple's three children, including their only son, the future King Harald.

Where possible, she still participated fully in the great family and dynastic dramas that absorbed the British royal family during the 1930s. She was present at the impressive celebrations for the Silver Jubilee of her brother, George V, in 1935. Standing on the balcony of Buckingham Palace after the service at St. Paul's Cathedral, Maud witnessed the mass of humanity cheering her brother. Also on the balcony that day and at St. Paul's were two little princesses in pink—Elizabeth and Margaret—who were soon to become the center of the British Empire's attention when their parents became King George VI and Queen Elizabeth at the end of 1936.

At George V's death in January 1936, Queen Maud of Norway became the last surviving child of King Edward VII and Queen Alexandra. Having just lost her sister, Toria, six weeks before, George's death made those last weeks of 1935 and early weeks of 1936 especially trying. Maud attended her brother's funeral heavily draped in a black veil and dress.

Like Queen Marie of Romania, Maud of Norway had been charmed by George's successor, Edward VIII. Also like Marie, Maud was taken aback by David's unexpected abdication. He had always been a favorite; she found in her carefree nephew something of the same irrepressible high spirits that she herself possessed. Maud never accepted Wallis Simpson and told her sister-in-law, Mary, just what she really thought of Wallis: "It makes me *quite* low to think of *him* banished out there and that he has given up everything of his own free will all on account of one *bad* woman who has hypnotized him—I hear that *every* English and French person gets up at Monte Carlo whenever *she* comes in to a

place. *Hope* she will *feel* it."[50] To Maud and Marie, there was nothing "romantic" about David and Carol's affairs with what they viewed as fast and loose
women. In both Maud's and Marie's eyes, these women brought nothing but
shame to their royal paramours.

Maud was in London again for another spectacular event: the coronation of
her other nephew, George VI, and his wife, Queen Elizabeth. Dressed in a simple gold gown with an ermine-lined purple robe about her shoulders and a diamond tiara, the Queen of Norway watched intently as the couple was crowned.
Maud was well disposed toward the new monarchs, whose family life and concept of monarchy were so grounded on tradition: "Thank goodness dear Bertie
and Elizabeth are so devoted to each other, and great help to each other, and
they are *so* popular, and so are the darling little children"[51]

Maud had also never forgotten her Russian cousins who suffered so much
during the Russian Revolution. Her first cousin, the Grand Duchess Xenia (Tsarina Alexandra's sister-in-law), was one of the fortunate ones who escaped from
Russia. Xenia settled in England with her family and was never far from Maud's
thoughts. In an undated reply to an Easter greeting from Xenia, Maud wrote:

> Beloved Xenia. *My* thoughts *so* constantly with you . . . God bless you. . . .
> Heaps of love fr. yr. loving Harry.[52]

And another undated card:

> Darling Xenia,
>
> Glad we met. . . . Here frightfully cold & I feel it & have aches. . . . Dreadful
> about dear Sophie, & Mossy *miserable*. I miss darling Louise.
>
> Ever yr. devoted Maud.[53]

This second message to Xenia was most likely written during the Christmas season of 1931. Maud's mention of Mossy's misery seems to allude to Queen Sophie's illness. The reference to missing "darling Louise" most likely alludes to
the fact that Princess Louise, Maud's eldest sister, was no longer alive.

Queen Maud set out for England as usual for a prolonged stay in October
1938. In November, she felt unwell and checked into a nursing home. An X ray
prompted doctors to operate on an abdominal obstruction. King Haakon made
his way to London to be by his wife's side. Queen Mary, who had always found
Maud to be her favorite sister-in-law, sat with the Queen of Norway before her
operation. Afterwards, Maud appeared to be recovering. But she died suddenly

in the middle of the night of a heart attack on 20 November, attended only by a nurse. Maud was just shy of her sixty-ninth birthday.

A grieving King Haakon issued a message that was read out in the Norwegian Church at Rotherhithe in London: "God has taken the Queen from me this night and it is a heavy loss for me to bear, though I well understand it is His will. He has taken her because her work on earth is finished, and He has, I know, spared her thus much suffering."[54] Back in Norway, the prime minister, Johann Nygaardsvold, announced:

We who had been more closely connected with the royal family knew what a warm, generous personality she was. The government and myself personally had learned to appreciate her burning interest for the Norwegian people and Norway.

We all share the sorrow of the royal family. I know that the whole Norwegian nation also feels the Queen's death as a great loss.[55]

The tributes in England were equally heartfelt. In the House of Lords, Lord Snell said: "People treasured her friendships and her life was rich both in service and in example." And from Lord Gainsford: "She was a person who was extraordinarily fond of the country of her birth."[56]

Queen Maud's body was taken to lie in state at the chapel in Marlborough House and then placed on board the battleship HMS *Royal Oak* for the journey back to Norway. Though she had expressed a desire to be buried in England, as Queen of Norway, it was only natural that Maud should be laid to rest in the country of which she had been queen. Her body lay in state at the medieval fort and castle of Akershus, where she was laid to rest.

That first Christmas without his wife was a somber one for King Haakon. The void left in his life was difficult to overcome. Haakon was grateful for the company of his grandchildren, who helped keep him from dwelling too much on his grief. In January 1939, he wrote to Grand Duchess Xenia, in reply to her message of sympathy on the death of his wife: "You can imagine what it meant to me, when we all got Xmas presents from darling Maud." Haakon added that he was grateful to have taken the opportunity to stay with Olav and Martha, for it would have been difficult to be by himself at Christmas. Haakon also told Xenia how hard it was to reconcile himself to the fact that "darling Maud who was always full of life" had died. Then, he mentioned something surprising: "I found the enclosed money in Maud's safe and I divided it between you and Olga [Xenia's sister] guessing that she at times helped you in one way or another, so don't thank me for it, but thank Maud as I feel I am only carrying out her wish by passing on to you two . . . Olga will get hers when I get a chance of sending it in a safe way."[57]

Even in death, Maud's kindness and generosity toward her Romanov cousins, the sisters of the late Tsar Nicholas II, was evident. In a fitting act of remembrance, King Haakon distributed the money Maud had been keeping for the Grand Duchesses Xenia and Olga; and in keeping with his own modest manner, Haakon asked that if thanks needed to be expressed, they must certainly be directed not at him but at Maud.

In death, Queens Maud, Sophie, and Marie were spared the horrors of having to live through the World War II. Unlike her four cousins, Queen Victoria Eugenie was to live much longer. Only Ena survived to see the conflagration that engulfed the world for six long years. Though exiled from Spain, she would never escape Spanish politics completely. They were to encroach upon her world as she watched a conflict over the Spanish monarchy erupt, pitting her son, the Infante Don Juan, against Spain's Generalissimo Francisco Franco in a duel that would last for years. The question was, would Queen Ena be content to sit on the sidelines? And would she live long enough to see the outcome?

Thirty

FROM EXILE TO "*VIVA LA REINA!*"

QUEEN ENA'S SEPARATION FROM KING ALFONSO MEANT THAT SHE had to try to carve a life for herself independently from her husband, who led a peripatetic life, traveling frequently, partly to alleviate boredom, partly to stay away from his wife. Increasingly, Alfonso found himself gravitating toward Rome. Ena, meanwhile, was drawn to England. As her children grew older, Ena naturally followed their marital prospects. Alfonsito was the first to marry. Back in 1918, Ena had written to Queen Mary of her eldest son: "I think you would approve of him as he looks absolutely English & English characteristics come out in him more & more."[1] But in time, Alfonsito ended up being far more of a hot-blooded Bourbon like his father than a cool-headed Briton like his mother.

Alfonsito fell in love with a Cuban commoner, Edelmira Sampedro-Ocejo y Robato. The prince went against his father's wishes and married, renouncing his claim to the throne and becoming the Count of Covadonga. Ena had asked her husband to show his support by going to their son's wedding ceremony: "Alfonso is our eldest child and you should attend his wedding." Alfonso ignored his wife's plea, saying, "Ena, I have lost this son forever."[2]

Victoria Eugenie's other hemophiliac son, Gonzalo, was less hampered by his chronic illness than Alfonsito, and appeared headed for a promising life, enrolling at the University of Louvain in Belgium to study engineering. But tragedy struck in the summer of 1934, when Gonzalo died after a minor car accident. Ena rushed to her son's side, but arrived too late, only to embrace her dead son's body. She and King Alfonso watched disconsolately as they buried their son in the village cemetery. After the funeral, they went their separate ways.

In London, Ena found an elegant home to use as a base at 34 Porchester

Terrace, just north of Bayswater Road, not far from Hyde Park. This afforded her the opportunity of being near her aged mother, Princess Beatrice, at Kensington Palace. When she was in London, Ena maintained a close friendship with the British royal family. Queen Mary and King George V counted her as a favorite among their many relatives. In late 1934, Ena faced a dilemma when she realized she might have to pay all the expenses of shipping her belongings from her palace in Santander. Ena said "she would prefer to do without the things." But George V ordered his private secretary to continue with efforts "on her behalf," saying that he "would himself pay the expenses."[3]

Sometime after she and Alfonso were separated, Ena approached Sir Esme Howard, who had been British ambassador to Madrid, to obtain help in settling the separation. As a well-known English convert to Catholicism, whose wife was a prominent Italian, Howard appeared to be an ideal intermediary. Since Alfonso was proving uncooperative, Ena thought she might seek the help of Cardinal Pacelli. The Howards drafted a letter in Italian on Ena's behalf to the cardinal, which stated:

> H[er] M[ajesty] spoke with pain and sadness about her private relations with King Alphonso. In fact, from the time we were at the British Embassy in Madrid, from 1920 to 24—there was open talk of the abandonment of the Queen by the King. . . . She told us that it has been fifteen years since the King left her. . . . It is our duty to add that having spent about five years at the British Embassy in Madrid, having been very close to many Spaniards we heard nothing but eulogies concerning the private life of Queen Vittoria in abandoned, very difficult and painful circumstances.
>
> While the monarchy was still in Spain, HM told us, that she endured it all in order not to make the position of the King and of his sons more difficult, however now that the political rationale was not there, and the King . . . had openly demonstrated his indifference to her . . . the Queen in order to maintain the dignity due to her requests that she live separately with an amiable agreement between the two parties that guarantees her peace and independence.[4]

They added that "we have dared to report all of this . . . in the hope that" the Pope might take an interest "in the sad situation" and influence King Alfonso to "regularize in an amicable manner the separation 'de jure' that which already exists 'de facto.' "[5]

In thanking Lord Howard for writing the draft letter, Ena said she found it "perfect." She did, however, wish Lord Howard to add two points. The first was "that my children are being bribed by Alfonso to remain with him & threatened to be left without maintenance if they came to me." The second was "that the Duke & Duchess of Lecera have nothing to do whatever in my demand for a separation & that with or without them I shall never go back to my husband. Already in Madrid on the day of the revolution I said to the Duke of Miranda, that I would separate rather than to put up in exile with what I had gone through during the monarchy."[6] Ena had obviously endured much pain in her marriage and had put loyalty to Spain, the monarchy, and her family before her own interests for some time.

Two family marriages took place in 1935. Ena's son, the Infante Jaime—who had renounced his rights and those of his heirs not long after his eldest brother's wedding—married, as did the Infante Juan.

In July 1936, hostilities broke out and what became the Spanish Civil War began. The Nationalists, under the military leadership of General Franco, revolted against the Spanish government, known as the Republicans. For decades, Spanish society had been torn by rising enmity between factions determined to uphold traditional views and institutions versus those who viewed the old guard traditionalists as oppressive influences. Often seen as a kind of dress rehearsal for World War II, the Spanish Civil War attracted support for both sides from abroad. Many flocked to Spain to fight on either side. Hitler's Germany and Mussolini's Italy lent a hand to Franco's side, while an assortment of left-leaning individuals, organizations, and countries sided with the Republicans. In three brutal years, which saw mass executions and atrocities committed by both sides, some 400,000 people were killed. By the time the war ended in 1939, Franco was victorious. He became Spain's leader until his death in 1975. Even the Spanish royal family was touched by the tragedy of the Spanish Civil War when Ali and Beatrice's son, Alonzo, was killed—his airplane shot down.

During her years in exile, Queen Ena never completely lost faith that the monarchy would someday be restored in Spain, though she believed that Juan would take on the mantle of king. When Ena went to visit her ailing son Alfonsito in New York City, who was suffering a hemophilia attack and recuperating at the Presbyterian Hospital, Ena expressed her views through her spokesman, the Count of Mora. Mora spoke to reporters as Ena boarded the *Queen Mary* for her journey back to England. Asked if Ena thought that she might get back the throne, the count replied: "No, it is expected that the Duchess of Toledo [Ena] would not return, but that Prince Juan, who is now heir to King Alfonso, would become King of Spain."[7]

In April 1938, when it appeared the Nationalists were getting the upper hand in Spain, concerns arose over security at Queen Victoria Eugenie's home in London. King George VI's private secretary wrote a confidential letter to New Scotland Yard:

> The King thinks that at this moment when feeling is naturally running very high over the Civil War in Spain, it would not be very wise to remove all police protection from Queen Ena. If Franco does succeed as looks inevitable now, he might quite easily restore the Monarchy in the person of the third son of the Queen of Spain and Her Majesty might thus be still further involved.[8]

Evidently restoration of the Spanish monarchy was a real possibility in George VI's mind and Ena's third son, Juan, was increasingly seen as the next King of Spain. The birth in 1938 of Ena's grandson Juan Carlos to Infante Juan meant the continuation of the Bourbon dynasty. Ena and Alfonso were briefly reunited when they appeared together at Juan Carlos's baptism. Looking the height of fashion in her fur-edged ensemble and a fine set of pearls, Ena stood as godmother to the baby, who was baptized by Cardinal Eugenio Pacelli (soon to become Pope Pius XII). Within eight months of the baptism, a new tragedy struck. Alfonsito died after crashing his car in Miami. Alfonsito's marriage with Edelmira had ended in divorce in 1937. He then married another Cuban woman, but that marriage was dissolved after six months. Alfonsito was considering a third marriage with a nightclub girl when he died. Just as King Alexander of Greece had called for his mother before he died, the Count of Covandonga on his deathbed asked for Queen Ena. Sadly, like Sophie before her, Ena never saw her son alive. By the time she arrived in Miami, it was too late. "My dear son's tragic death is a terrible blow," wrote Victoria Eugenie, "& all the sad circumstances make my grief all the harder to bear."[9]

As the 1930s came to an end, Ena became preoccupied with Alfonso's deteriorating health. She lived for a time in Rome in order to be near her husband, though the couple were still separated. In January 1941, a critically ill Alfonso renounced his right to the throne in favor of his third son, Juan. When, in February 1941, it became evident that King Alfonso was dying, Ena and their children went to him. Alfonso may have tried to keep Ena at bay since they separated in 1931, but this time, he agreed to her coming. The family kept vigil at the Grand Hotel in a room next to the king's. Alfonso's death throes were prolonged as he suffered multiple heart attacks, but he faced his torment bravely.

As death drew closer, Alfonso was given the last rites by his Jesuit confessor. When the priest ended the prayers commending Alfonso's soul to God, the dying king answered resoundingly, "Amen!" Ena and the children, fighting back tears, fell to their knees and kissed Alfonso's hand in a gesture of love and farewell. The king lingered a few days longer, slowly asphixiating, but as dawn broke in the Eternal City on 28 February, he was ready to let go of his earthly life. At one point he managed to murmur: "My God! My God!" And to his wife, sobbing by his side, he muttered: "It is over, Ena!"[10] When the priest presented Alfonso with a crucifix, he kissed it, whispering the word *"España."* Shortly afterwards, Alfonso XIII of Spain died. Ena, on her knees, cried for the man who had been her husband for forty-four tumultuous years. Alfonso was buried in the Eternal City.

Within a year of his death, Ena was forced to move again, since members of Mussolini's government implied that as a British princess, the queen was capable of spying. To which a miffed Ena retorted: "I am not a Mata Hari."[11] There was also the issue of money. According to a "secret" despatch from the British Embassy in Madrid to the Foreign Office in London, "it might be necessary for the Queen to leave Italy . . . because her income which was in sterling and dollars was inaccessible in Italy."[12] Ena chose to live in Lausanne, Switzerland, in 1942, at the Hotel Royal.

The queen next visited an England at war in 1944 to be with her dying mother. Princess Beatrice's funeral was held at St. George's Chapel, Windsor. In reply to one sympathy letter, the queen expressed her feelings: "You can imagine how sad & broken I feel at losing that best & dearest of mothers & she leaves such a great blank in my life."[13] Ena's hemophiliac brother, Leopold, had died in 1922, leaving only her brother, Drino, as her closest relative in England.

As World War II raged, Ena returned to Lausanne. There, she was joined by her son, Don Juan, and his growing family. Besides Prince Juan Carlos ("Juanito"), Ena's grandchildren from Juan included Pilar, Margarita, and Alfonso, who brightened their grandmother's life. The Bourbon family and Queen Ena were very visible residents in Lausanne—the queen in an elegant suite at the Hotel Royal and the Bourbons at a nearby house. Together, they regularly attended eleven o'clock Mass at the Church of Sacré-Coeur in Ouchy each Sunday.

The queen took a special interest in Margarita and Juan Carlos. Ena tried to help Margarita who was blind. Ena tried to teach her various ways of overcoming her handicap. Like any grandmother, Ena also loved to let her grandchildren get away with harmless infractions that helped endear her to them. Not surprisingly, Ena chose to be called "Gangan" as she herself had called Queen Victoria years before.

As for Juan Carlos, Ena made a special point of teaching him how to pronounce the Spanish "r." Recalling the embarrassments she suffered as a foreigner for being unable to speak Spanish with a pure accent, she tried to ensure Juanito would not be saddled with the same problems. In a curious twist, this very English Queen of Spain was instrumental in helping a future King of Spain speak the country's native tongue. When Juanito studied as a boarder at Fribourg after his parents went to Portugal, the lonely prince was grateful for the weekends spent in the company of Queen Ena, who lived not far away. Years later, King Juan Carlos remembered how lonely he was, but "happily, my grandmother, Queen Victoria, was there to look after me, although I suspect that they told her not to spoil me too much."[14]

Another set of grandchildren on whom Ena doted were Alfonso and Gonzalo, sons of Infante Jaime, who was divorced in 1947. These grandsons spent prolonged periods in Queen Ena's company. Aldo Corbani, the queen's majordomo during Ena's years in exile, recalled that "these boys were very alone [in relation to their parents] and Victoria Eugenie had them almost always with her. She felt a real passion for them . . . the Queen lived for her grandchildren and the grandchildren adored her." But when it came to Jaime's sons, "more than loving them, she felt sorry for them and protected them." Corbani served Ena loyally for years; he admired her for her humanity and ability to remain a dignified queen. Years later, Corbani noted that "the Queen was a great lady, a great lady."[15]

But however much Ena adored these grandchildren, there was always a void. Toward the end of her life, Ena permitted a glimpse of this inner agony when she admitted candidly: "The burdens of State, the difficulty of living with a King whose faults were as extreme as his duties were little compared with my grief in losing two sons, the eldest and the youngest. Love rarely dies a sudden death, especially when it is maternal love. And today I am obliged to close my eyes sometimes and try not to remember."[16] In expressing the greatest heartache that could befall a mother, Ena echoed tragedies shared with Sophie of Greece and Marie of Romania.

In 1948, Ena purchased a small villa in Lausanne called Vieille Fontaine, roomy enough to house Ena and her small entourage of servants. The design both outside and inside was in keeping with her elegant taste. Visitors were greeted by double front doors decorated with two bronze fleurs-de-lys, symbol of the royal House of Bourbon. Inside, a splendid solid oak staircase dominated the hall. Two magnificent paintings hung as reminders of the two most influential persons in Queen Ena's long life: in the foyer was a beautiful and detailed painting of her wedding to King Alfonso XIII; and in the library was a portrait of Queen Victoria, the beloved grandmother with whom Ena had spent her childhood years. Surprisingly, there were numerous reminders of Alfonso XIII, from photographs to paintings to miniatures, amounting to more than fifty items. Ena once referred to Alfonso affectionately in these years of exile with the words, "poor, poor King, Always such a gentleman and so good!"[17] The passage of time seemed to dim the pain.

Some of the items Ena had at Vieille Fontaine came back to her years after her exile, thanks to the laborious efforts of British officials in Spain. For it turned out that a mini-battle between Spanish and British officials had taken place, culminating in 1934. As Sir George Grahame, the British ambassador to Spain, admitted, "we have been making [efforts] for over two years to induce the Spanish Government to give up the personal belongings of Queen Victoria Eugenia."[18] So exasperated had Grahame become over the failure of Spanish authorities to act that he made some "astringent remarks" to one senior Spanish official, saying: "You and I are anxious that they should not think in London that, because there is a Republic in Spain, Spaniards have ceased to be 'caballeros' and you are running the risk that this impression should get abroad on account of a few chairs, a couple of clocks and a sofa or two." Grahame admitted that "I showed a good deal of impatience and said that I was inclined to speak and complain of the delays to the President of the Republic."[19] Numerous items were eventually rescued, not just from the palace in Madrid but also from Santander, thanks to the diligent efforts of Grahame and his staff. The queen wrote to Sir George, telling him of her "grateful thanks . . . I know only too well how difficult the negotiations must have been with the very trying people now in power."[20]

Ena was always attuned to the political machinations surrounding General Franco and Don Juan and eventually Juan Carlos over the touchy issue of restoration. A concerned Ena watched as Franco and Don Juan continued to remain wary of each other over the years. Both men did, however, agree to having Juan Carlos educated in Spain. The ten-year-old prince was duly shipped off.

Juanito's departure meant that his grandmother was deprived of the presence of her favorite grandson. His blond good looks and impish disposition endeared him to nearly all who came into contact with the prince, most of all his doting grandmother. When the time came for Juan Carlos to leave for a new life in Spain, she wrote: "Indeed, it makes me sad to be separated from this grandson who I love so much, but since the moment my son had taken the decision to send him to Spain, I accepted his will without reservation."[21]

Juanito was eventually joined in Spain by his younger brother, Alfonso. In an interesting link with the past, and with their grandmother, the two princes found themselves being schooled in the former palace at Miramar. These two grandsons wrote their Gangan with regularity, much to Ena's joy. But on 29 March 1956, while on holiday at their parents' home in Estoril, Portugal, eighteen-year-old Juan Carlos was playing with a revolver: it went off, killing the fourteen-year-old Alfonso. The official version had it that Alfonso accidentally shot himself while cleaning the revolver. Yet another tragedy in the long list that continued to haunt Ena.

Time did not ease the long-standing fractious relationship between General Franco and the Count of Barcelona, which meant that the issue of the Spanish succession to the throne remained unresolved. Once Prince Juan Carlos came of marriageable age, it became more and more evident that this prince might well have an even greater chance at getting Franco's nod to be his successor than Don Juan. Queen Victoria Eugenie certainly thought so. She had misgivings about her son, whom she felt "did not demonstrate the willpower necessary for the difficult task of the Restoration. Numerous signs made it seem probable that Doña Victoria Eugenia felt that her grandson Juan Carlos would end up having more possibilities to reign than her son Juan."[22]

In 1962, Juan Carlos married Princess Sofía of Greece. A daughter of King Paul I of the Hellenes, Sofía had been named after her grandmother, Queen Sophie. Victoria Eugenie was more than pleased with this granddaughter of Queen Sophie as Juan Carlos's choice for a wife and possible future queen. She was full of advice for Sofía and full of stories of her days as Queen of Spain. "She told me," recounted Queen Sofía years later, "in spite of the difficulties she had with the illnesses of her sons, and with such shifting and revolutionary politics, she had been very happy, *very, very happy!*, in Spain."[23]

As Ena entered her twilight years, the unending guessing game as to when Franco would name his successor was still unresolved. Nor was anyone certain who that successor would be. There was Don Juan, and his son, Juan Carlos. There was also the very real possibility that Franco might even choose a Carlist to be the next king. When Ena's second son, Jaime, suddenly reversed his decades-old renunciation of the throne in 1964, Ena was highly displeased by this development, which threatened to complicate the chances of Juan or Juan Carlos succeeding. She was aware that the crafty Franco might well use this latest turn of events to continue his games. The wily general kept his cards close to his chest and conceded nothing.

During the 1960s, Ena continued to be generally in good health, despite a lifetime of smoking, a habit she had to let go of in old age. When she celebrated her eightieth birthday in October 1967, the elderly queen was still managing to look as regal as ever. In January 1968 came the exciting news that Princess Sofía had given birth to a baby boy, Felipe. Since Queen Ena was chosen as godmother, the question was, would Franco allow the queen to go to Madrid for the baptism? He did, provided it was to be a private visit. Ena received the news of Felipe's birth while staying in Monte Carlo. She had become friends with Prince Rainier and particularly with Princess Grace, who sought out Ena for useful advice when she first married into the ranks of royalty. They remained good friends, and Ena often visited the Rainiers in Monaco to escape Switzerland's cold winters. But on 7 February 1968, Queen Victoria Eugenie of Spain interrupted her stay on the Côte d' Azur and headed for a special place. She was driven to Nice airport, where the eighty-year-old queen boarded an Air France jet to Spain to attend the baptism of the Infante Felipe.

Don Juan wanted to accompany his mother on her historic arrival in Spain. But Ena, whose political antennae had sharpened through the years, thought this move much too political for her taste. She rejected her son's suggestion, saying firmly, "If I go to Spain, I wish to go alone."[24]

Once on board the plane, Ena could hardly contain her excitement. She asked: "Are we flying yet over Spain?" The Duke of Alba told her they were still over France. Ena asked one of her ladies, "When do I visit the Red Cross?" On Friday, came the answer.[25] As the plane flew over Barcelona, champagne was passed round and everyone toasted the moment, not least Queen Ena. When the plane landed at Madrid's Barajas airport on a cold February day, Queen Ena stepped out to an amazing sight. Thousands of people had come to greet the queen who was stepping onto Spanish soil for the first time in thirty-seven long years of exile. The elderly queen, dressed in a fur coat and matching fur hat, smiled delightedly and waved, then gingerly stepped down the gangway to her awaiting son, Don Juan.

The exit from the airport in a convoy of cars was reminiscent of her return in April 1931. The queen was mobbed by admiring Spaniards. Even the roof of the airport was brimming with people. Ena could not have anticipated a more rapturous welcome. In many parts of Madrid as she made her way around the capital, crowds of people greeted her. She was impressed by the many changes she saw in Madrid. She asked to travel along the same route that she took on her wedding day. At the Church of San Jerónimo, where she was married, the queen prayed for her husband, and then proceeded to relive that unforgettable day as she passed through Madrid's streets, including the Calle Mayor where she nearly lost her life when the infamous Mateo Morral threw his bomb.

Ena visited her beloved Red Cross in Madrid. There the queen saw a large portrait of her dressed as a nurse. People had not forgotten Victoria Eugenie's significant contribution to the welfare of Spain, and they showed their appreciation by turning up to greet the queen in large numbers.

The highlight of the visit was the baptism itself. Looking especially elegant in a gold dress, Ena arrived at Juan Carlos and Sofía's home, the Zarzuela Palace, on the outskirts of the capital. Everyone was riveted by the sight of Queen Ena, who stood proudly carrying her great-grandson, Felipe, as he was baptized. Also present was General Franco. Felipe's mother, Sofía, remembered how Ena impressed the Generalissimo: "Franco was emotional seeing Queen Victoria Eugenia: he was a sentimental [person]. I was very near him and I saw how his eyes shone."[26] After the ceremony, Queen Ena met with General Franco. Stories have circulated that Victoria Eugenie took the opportunity to confront Franco about the future of the dynasty and said: "You've got all three Borbóns in front of you. Decide!"[27] But Franco refused to reply. During a particularly emotional cabinet meeting the next year, Franco insisted on naming a successor. Time, after all, was not on his side, as he was already seventy-seven years old. It would be far better for Spain's future stability to forge on with the law of succession while he was still alive. "Additionally, he claimed that during her visit to Madrid the previous year, Victoria Eugenia had implicitly acknowledged the need to sacrifice Don Juan for the sake of the dynasty."[28] This, of course, meant that Queen Ena was paving the way for her grandson, Juan Carlos, to ascend the throne.

This was not the first time Victoria Eugenie acknowledged that the Count of Barcelona needed to be sacrificed in order to forward the monarchy's cause. She was said to have passed on a message to Franco that stated: "Though for me the king is Don Juan, we are all old and no one knows what will happen if things are not resolved. The first is Spain, the second the Monarchy, the third the dynasty and the fourth the person. And the prince [Don Juan Carlos] is mature."[29]

Another version of Queen Ena and General Franco's brief talk at the Zarzuela Palace after the Infante Felipe's baptism has the two discussing the succession in slightly more detail, though the main points still centered on Ena urging Franco to make a decision soon, to which he reportedly replied: "The wishes of your majesty will be carried out." This meeting between two historical figures of twentieth-century Spain illustrates that at the end of her life, Ena did not hesitate to intervene politically when it came to the nation's future. One chronicler of Alfonso and Victoria Eugenie has concluded that "the intervention of the queen on the 8th of February 1968 was significant. Don Juan Carlos was king of Spain because of the steps taken by his grandmother with General Franco. She knew it and said after her visit: 'Now I can die in peace.' "[30]

When the time came after her four-day visit for Victoria Eugenie to leave Madrid, she was accompanied to the airport by her son, the Count of Barcelona, Prince Juan Carlos, and Princess Sofía. Admiring Spaniards also flocked to the airport by the tens of thousands to say good-bye. It marked a fitting tribute to the woman who had endured so much as their queen. The emotion on Ena's face the day she left Madrid was evident to all. Barely able to contain her tears, knowing that she would never set foot again in Spain, Ena bravely made her way on board the Iberia jet and left for Nice. It had been an emotional journey from exile to "Viva la Reina!"—a triumphant return at the end of Ena's life.

In the spring of 1969, the eighty-one-year-old queen's health gave cause for concern. Her liver was failing her. Queen Sofía of Spain recalled those days: "My husband loved her madly. I did also. She was Gangan. She was a grandmother. We went frequently to Lausanne, to be near her in the last stage of her illness. She fell into a coma three times. And surprisingly recovered. Up to [the point when] she got up to attend Mass on the Sunday, the last week."[31]

On a spring evening in April 1969, Queen Ena lay dying in her pink and white bedroom at Vieille Fontaine, surrounded by her family. She had already been given the last rites by the priest assigned to the Spanish Mission in Lausanne. As he commended her soul to God, Ena died peacefully just before midnight. It was 15 April 1969, thirty-eight years to the day since Victoria Eugenie fled Spain. In a surprise move, General Franco ordered three days of national mourning and sent his minister of foreign affairs to the queen's funeral. Three days after her death, Ena's funeral took place at the Church of the Sacre Coeur at Ouchy where she had spent so many Sundays worshipping at Sunday Mass. Her body was buried at the cemetery of Boix-de-Vaux near Lausanne.

Queen Ena's death and funeral in Lausanne in 1969 marks the closing chapter in the stories of five very special granddaughters of Queen Victoria, all of whom had reigned as consorts in the four corners of Europe. They embraced their new lives, adapted, and came to love their new countries and peoples. Condemned and praised, forgotten and famous, these five women can be seen as special legacies of Queen Victoria.

Raised in an era where responsibility, commitment, sacrifice, and duty before self were elevated as the highest ideals and embodied admirably by their grandmother, Queen Victoria, these royal women approached their roles as consorts for the most part embodying those ideals. It was an ethos best articulated by the indefatigable Queen Marie of Romania, who once wrote: "We are hardly ever arbiters of our own Fate. We must move, do, live, according to our several duties and our own desires and wishes have to be fitted in with what we *can* do more often than what we desire to do—"[32]

Maud of Norway, Sophie of Greece, Alexandra of Russia, Marie of Romania, and Victoria Eugenie of Spain may have been marked out by their illustrious positions and glittering marriages. But it is ultimately their dignity, devotion to duty, strong sense of responsibility, and steadfastness in the face of adversity that distinguishes them and makes their stories both compelling and timeless.

EPILOGUE

QUEEN VICTORIA EUGENIE DID NOT LIVE TO SEE HER DEAREST wish come true. But a mere three months after her death, General Franco proclaimed Prince Juan Carlos his successor, paving the way for the monarchy's restoration. In an interesting twist, a link between Victoria Eugenie of Spain and Francisco Franco took place when Queen Ena's grandson, Alfonso, elder son of the Infante Jaime, married Franco's granddaughter, Maria del Carmen, in 1972. When Franco died in November 1975, Juan Carlos ascended the throne as King Juan Carlos I, just as his grandmother had surmised. Juan Carlos has generally been credited with helping to steer Spain successfully from decades of dictatorship under Franco to a democracy. Today, King Juan Carlos and Queen Sofía enjoy the respect and affection of the Spanish people. The remains of King Alfonso XIII and Queen Victoria Eugenie were returned to Spain in 1980 and 1985, respectively, and placed in the resting place of Spain's kings, El Escorial.

In Norway, King Haakon VII went on to reign until his death in 1957. He was succeeded by his only son, King Olav V of Norway. His wife, Princess Martha, never became queen, having died in 1954. Olav never remarried. When he died in 1991, he was succeeded by Queen Maud's only grandson, Harald. King Harald V's daughter, Princess Martha Louise, brought the queen's memory to the fore when the princess named her daughter (born in 2003) Maud Angelica.

For the rest of the twentieth century, Greece alternated between a monarchy and a republic. Queen Sophie's eldest son, King George II, returned to reign in 1935. In 1936, George's brother, Crown Prince Paul, escorted the coffins containing the remains of King Constantine I, Queen Sophie, and Queen Olga from Italy to Greece. After an impressive funeral ceremony in Athens, the coffins were taken to Tatoi for burial. In 1938, Prince Paul married Princess Frederike of Hanover, a granddaughter of Kaiser Wilhelm II. Their eldest child, Princess Sofía, married Queen Ena's grandson, Juan Carlos, in 1962. When King George II died in 1947, Paul and Frederike became King and Queen of the Hellenes. Their only son, Constantine II, succeeded his father upon King Paul's death in 1964. In September 1964, the king married Princess Anne-Marie of Denmark, making her then, at eighteen years of age, the youngest queen in the world. In 1967, a coup instigated by army officers took place. When a countercoup failed later in the year, King Constantine, Queen Anne-Marie, and their two children fled Greece. In 1973, the Greek government deposed King Constantine II. In a plebiscite weeks later, the result of the voting went in favor of a republic.

Queen Sophie of Greece's daughter, Irene, married Aimone, the Duke of Aosta, in 1939; Katherine married an Englishman, Major Richard Brandram, in 1947 at Athens. They settled in England. King George VI issued a royal warrant which granted Princess Katherine the style, title, and precedence of a British duke's daughter, thereby allowing her to become Lady Katherine Brandram.

Queen Sophie of Greece and Queen Marie of Romania were already doubly connected when their children married—Helen of Greece (d. 1982) to Carol of Romania (d. 1953) and George (d. 1947) of Greece to Elisabetta of Romania (d. 1956). In the next generation, Queen Marie and Queen Sophie's descendants were again united when Sophie's granddaughter, Princess Alexandra of Greece (d. 1993), married Queen Marie's grandson, King Peter II of Yugoslavia (d. 1970). Their son, Crown Prince Alexander of Yugoslavia (b. 1945), currently resides in Belgrade with his second wife, Princess Katherine.

Queen Marie's grandson, Michael of Romania, became king again when his father, King Carol II, fled the country in 1940. King Michael's mother, Helen, eventually returned to Romania and was given the courtesy title of Queen Mother. Queen Helen gave her son as much support as possible as she watched Michael battle Nazism and Communism almost single-handedly while only in his early twenties. Queen Marie would have been proud of her grandson's actions during his turbulent reign. Only a young man during World War II, King Michael bravely dismissed Romania's General Ion Antonescu in 1944. The pro-Nazi Antonescu had placed Romania on the Axis side. After his dismissal, Romania fought on the side of the Allies. The Communists then gained power in 1946 with help from Moscow, eventually forcing King Michael to abdicate in 1947. He fled the country in 1948. King Michael married Princess Anne of Bourbon-Parma in 1948, and they have five daughters. The king eventually returned to Romania in 1997. King Michael and Queen Anne now divide their time between Romania and Versoix, outside Geneva, where they have resided for many years.

In exile, the former King Carol II and Magda Lupescu stayed together. They eventually married: in 1947 at a civil ceremony in Rio de Janeiro and in 1949 at a religious one in Lisbon. Carol died in Estoril, Portugal, in 1953, and Magda, also in Estoril, in 1977. Carol's sister, Mignon (d. 1961), settled in England after her son, Peter II of Yugoslavia, was ousted by the Germans. Queen Marie of Romania's second son, Nicolas, lived outside Romania and died in Spain in 1978. Queen Marie's youngest daughter, Ileana, went to the United States with her family. She became a nun later (Mother Alexandra) and lived in a monastery in Pennsylvania. Ileana died in Ohio in 1991.

In Russia, after the fall of Communism in 1989, a shift of seismic proportions has taken place. When the bones of Tsar Nicholas II, Tsarina Alexandra, and their children were found and later exhumed (1991) from a forest outside Ekaterinburg, DNA testing linked the skeletons to the imperial family. Two bodies, however, were missing: those of Alexei and one sister, most likely Marie. Boris Yeltsin agreed to a state funeral and burial in St. Petersburg in spite of disagreement from the Patriarch of the Russian Orthodox Church in Russia, who disputed the authenticity of the bones. At the funeral, held eighty years after the murders, vast numbers of Russians paid their last respects. The family's canonization by the Russian Orthodox Church has paved the way for their veneration as saints of the Orthodox Church.

A huge cathedral, the Cathedral on the Blood, has been built on the site where the Ipatiev house stood in Ekaterinburg. Moreover, the Monastery of the Royal Passion Sufferers, consisting of seven churches are being built at the site where the family's remains were buried after their murders—one church for each family member killed. The largest, that of St. Nicholas, has seventeen onion domes in honor of 17 July, the day of their deaths. In a country now rediscovering and openly celebrating its religious heritage, many Russians are increasingly drawn to this family, whose piety in the face of adversity appears to be touching many hearts. Time, therefore, has not diminished people's fascination with Queen Victoria's five special granddaughters, who were born to rule.

NOTES

INTRODUCTION

1. Elizabeth Longford, *Queen Victoria: Born to Succeed* (New York: Harper & Row, 1964), p. 341.
2. Diana Fotescu, ed., *Americans and Queen Marie of Roumania: A Selection of Documents* (Iași: The Center for Romanian Studies, 1998), p. 137.

PART I

ONE: MORE MOTHER THAN GRANDMOTHER

1. Crown Princess Victoria to Queen Victoria, 25 July 1870, in Sir Frederick Ponsonby, ed., *Letters of the Empress Frederick* (London: Macmillan and Co., 1929), p. 80.
2. Celia Clear, *Royal Children, 1840–1980* (New York: Stein & Day, 1981), p. 58.
3. George Plumptre, *Edward VII* (London: Pavilion Books, 1995), p. 97.
4. David Duff, *Hessian Tapestry* (London: Frederick Muller, 1967), p. 121.
5. Gerard Noel, *Princess Alice: Queen Victoria's Forgotten Daughter* (London: Constable, 1974), p. 216.
6. Alfred, Duke of Edinburgh, to Countess Alexandrine Tolstoy, 9 November 1875, Mountbatten Papers, MB1/U24, Hartley Library, University of Southampton.
7. Marie, Duchess of Edinburgh, to Countess Alexandrine Tolstoy, 3 November 1875, *ibid.* ("The gentle little one I produced, with the big eyes and a large nose, and small mouth, and plenty of hair, has the appetite of a monster. In a word, I am very proud of my production and a daughter, after all and above all these predictions. She is making a frightful noise and puts her ten fingers in her mouth because she is already hungry. I was stupefied and did not want to believe my ears.")
8. Noel, *Princess Alice,* p. 227.
9. Tor Bomman-Larsen, *Kongstanken: Haakon & Maud—I* (Oslo: J. W. Cappelen, 2002), p. 119.

10. Richard Hough, *Edward & Alexandra: Their Private and Public Lives* (London: Hodder & Stoughton, 1992), p. 153; Clear, *Royal Children,* p. 60.
11. Georgina Battiscombe, *Queen Alexandra* (Boston: Houghton Mifflin, 1969), p. 139.
12. Arvid Møller, *Dronning Maud: Et Portrett* (Oslo: J. W. Cappelen, 1992), p. 13.
13. Battiscombe, *Queen Alexandra,* p. 122.
14. Bomann-Larsen, *Kongstanken,* p. 118.
15. *Ibid.,* p. 145.
16. Emperor Wilhelm II of Germany, *My Early Life* (New York: George H. Doran Co., 1926; AMS edition, 1971), p. 74.
17. Princess Victoria of Prussia, *My Memoirs* (London: Eveleigh Nash & Grayson, 1929), p. 15.
18. Victoria, Crown Princess of Germany, to Queen Victoria, 25 August 1881, in Roger Fulford, ed., *Beloved Mama: Private Correspondence of Queen Victoria and the German Crown Princess 1878–1885* (London: Evans Brothers, 1981), p. 106.
19. Meriel Buchanan, *Queen Victoria's Relations* (London: Cassell & Co., 1954), p. 7.
20. Theo Aronson, *Grandmama of Europe: The Crowned Descendants of Queen Victoria* (Indianapolis: Bobbs-Merrill Co., 1973), p. 64.
21. Queen Marie of Romania, *The Story of My Life.* Vol. I (London: Cassell & Co., 1934), p. 15.
22. *Ibid.,* p. 19.
23. Marie, Duchess of Edinburgh, to Countess Alexandrine Tolstoy, undated, 1879, Mountbatten Papers, MB 1/U24, Hartley Library, University of Southampton ("her character is always delicious").
24. Duff, *Hessian Tapestry,* p. 189.
25. Prince Christopher of Greece, *Memoirs of H.R.H. Prince Christopher of Greece* (London: The Right Book Club, 1938), p. 56.
26. Queen Victoria to Princess Victoria of Hesse, 12 September 1879, in Richard Hough, ed., *Advice to My Grand-Daughter: Letters from Queen Victoria to Princess Victoria of Hesse* (New York: Simon & Schuster, 1975), p. 18.
27. Queen Victoria to Princess Victoria of Hesse, 26 April 1884, in *ibid.,* p. 65.

TWO: "MAD. NEVER MIND."

1. Katherine Hudson, *A Royal Conflict: Sir John Conroy and the Young Victoria* (London: Hodder & Stoughton, 1994), p. xvii.
2. Longford, *Queen Victoria,* p. 50.
3. Queen Marie, *My Life,* p. 157.
4. *Ibid.,* pp. 156–57.
5. Arthur Christopher Benson and Viscount Esher, eds., *The Letters of Queen Victoria: A Selection from Her Majesty's Correspondence Between the Years 1837 and 1861.* Vol. III (London: J. Murray, 1907), p. 321.
6. Queen Marie, *My Life,* p. 180.
7. Giles St. Aubyn, *Queen Victoria: A Portrait* (London: Sinclair-Stevenson, 1991), p. 60.
8. Queen Marie, *My Life,* p. 43.
9. Queen Victoria to Victoria, Crown Princess of Prussia, 17 July 1878 and 21 August 1878, in Fulford, ed., *Beloved Mama,* pp. 23 and 24.
10. Tsarevitch Nicholas, diary entry, 31 May 1884, in Andrei Maylunas and Sergei Mironenko, eds., *A Lifelong Passion: Nicholas and Alexandra: Their Own Story* (London: Weidenfeld & Nicolson, 1996), p. 10.

11. Duff, *Hessian Tapestry*, p. 186.
12. Marie, Duchess of Edinburgh, to Countess Alexandrine Tolstoy, undated, May 1885, MB 1/U24, Hartley Library, University of Southampton.
13. Marie, Duchess of Edinburgh, to Countess Alexandrine Tolstoy, 13 January 1885, *ibid.*
14. Queen Victoria to the Empress Frederick, 17 July 1888, in Agatha Ramm, ed., *Beloved and Darling Child: Last Letters Between Queen Victoria and Her Eldest Daughter, 1886–1901* (Stroud, Glos.: Alan Sutton, 1990), p. 74.
15. Gerard Noel, *Ena: Spain's English Queen* (London: Constable & Co., 1984), p. 3.
16. Evelyn Graham (pseud. Netley Lucas), *The Queen of Spain: An Authorized Life Story* (London: Hutchinson & Co., 1929), p. 26.
17. Egon Caesar Corti, *The English Empress: A Study in the Relations Between Queen Victoria and Her Eldest Daughter, Empress Frederick of Germany* (London: Cassell & Co., 1957), p. 301.
18. *Ibid.,* p. 302.
19. Empress Frederick to Queen Victoria, 15 June 1888, in Ponsonby, ed., *Empress Frederick,* p. 316.
20. Interview with Lady Katherine Brandram, 2 May 2001, Marlow, Bucks.
21. Princess Victoria, *My Memoirs,* p. 4.
22. Lord Howard of Penrith, *Theatre of Life: Life Seen from the Pit, 1863–1905* (London: Hodder & Stoughton, 1935), pp. 93–94.
23. Empress Frederick to Queen Victoria, 25 October 1889, in Ramm, ed., *Beloved and Darling Child,* p. 77.
24. Bomann-Larsen, *Kongstanken,* p. 188.
25. *Ibid.*
26. Sir James Rennell Rodd, *Social and Diplomatic Memories, 1884–1893* (London: Edward Arnold & Co., 1922), pp. 187–88.
27. Tsarevitch Nicholas to Empress Marie, 20 October 1889, in Edward J. Bing, ed., *The Letters of Tsar Nicholas and Empress Marie: Being the Confidential Correspondence Between Nicholas II, Last of the Tsars, and His Mother, Dowager Empress Marie Feodorovna* (London: Ivor Nicholson & Watson, 1937), p. 39.
28. Prince Nicholas of Greece, *My Fifty Years* (London: Hutchinson & Co., 1926), p. 96.
29. G. Nicholas Tantzos and Marlene A. Eilers, eds., *A Romanov Diary: The Autobiography of H.I. & R.H. Grand Duchess George* (New York: Atlantic International Publications, 1988), p. 41.
30. *Ibid.,* p. 42.
31. Ponsonby, ed., *Empress Frederick,* pp. 393–94.
32. Arthur Gould Lee, ed., *The Empress Frederick Writes to Sophie, Crown Princess and Later Queen of the Hellenes* (London: Faber & Faber, 1955), pp. 52–53.
33. Bomann-Larsen, *Kongstanken,* p. 314.
34. Queen Victoria to Victoria of Hesse, 25 May 1894, in Hough, ed., *Advice to My Grand-Daughter,* p. 123. The "Uncle" referred to here is the Prince of Wales.
35. James Pope-Hennessy, *Queen Mary, 1867–1953* (New York: Alfred A. Knopf, 1960), pp. 314–15.
36. Battiscombe, *Queen Alexandra,* p. 200.
37. Pope-Hennessy, *Queen Mary,* p. 315.
38. Empress Frederick to Princess Sophie, 1894, in Lee, ed., *Empress Frederick Writes to Sophie,* p. 162.
39. Bomann-Larsen, *Kongstanken,* p. 332.
40. Plumptre, *Edward VII,* p. 97.

41. Prince Maximilian of Baden (1867–1929) was the last chancellor of Imperial Germany. In an effort to salvage the monarchy, Max had asked Kaiser Wilhelm II to abdicate during World War I. When the Kaiser refused, Max himself announced the abdication, thus putting an end to the rule of the Hohenzollern dynasty in Germany in November 1918.

42. Pope-Hennessy, *Queen Mary,* p.296.

43. Bomann-Larsen, *Kongstangken,* p. 349.

44. Lee, ed., *Empress Frederick Writes to Sophie,* p. 59.

45. Queen Victoria to the Empress Frederick, 20 July 1890, in Ramm, ed., *Beloved and Darling Child,* p. 113.

46. Anonymous, *The Royal Family of Greece: King Constantine, Queen Sophie, Their Royal Relatives and Some Events* (Toronto: Warwick Brothers & Rutter, 1914), p. 4.

47. Také Jonescu, *Some Personal Impressions* (New York: Frederick A. Stokes, 1920), p. 286.

48. Hannah Pakula, *An Uncommon Woman: The Empress Frederick, Daughter of Queen Victoria, Wife of the Crown Prince of Prussia, Mother of Kaiser Wilhelm* (New York: Simon & Schuster, 1995), p. 562.

49. Corti, *English Empress,* p. 337.

50. *Ibid.,* p. 338.

51. Count Robert Zedlitz-Trützschler, *Twelve Years at the Imperial German Court* (London: Nisbet & Co., 1951), p. 82.

52. Lee, ed., *Empress Frederick Writes to Sophie,* p. 74.

53. *Ibid.,* pp. 85–86.

54. *Ibid.,* p. 86.

55. *Ibid.*

56. Corti, *English Empress,* p. 339.

57. Interview with Lady Katherine Brandram, 2 May 2001, Marlow, Bucks.

THREE: "GANGAN"

1. David Duff, *The Shy Princess: The Life of Her Royal Highness Princess Beatrice* (London: Evans Brothers, 1958), p. 154.

2. Queen Victoria to Princess Victoria of Hesse, 12 October 1889, in Hough, ed., *Advice to My Grand-Daughter,* p. 105.

3. Graham, *Queen of Spain,* p. 21.

4. Genevieve de Vilmorin, "The Queen of Spain's Own Story," *Chatelaine* (May 1962), p. 92.

5. Queen Victoria's journal, 10 February 1894, in George Earle Buckle, ed., *The Letters of Queen Victoria, Third Series: A Selection from Her Majesty's Correspondence Between the Years 1862 and 1885 and Between the Years 1886 and 1901.* Vol. II: *1891–1895* (London: John Murray, 1931), p. 359.

6. Michaela Reid, *Ask Sir James: Sir James Reid, Personal Physician to Queen Victoria and Physician-in-Ordinary to Three Monarchs* (New York: Viking, 1987), p. 105.

7. Lee, ed., *Empress Frederick Writes to Sophie,* pp. 162–63.

8. Queen Victoria to Princess Victoria of Hesse, 15 February 1894, in Hough, ed., *Advice to My Grand-Daughter,* p. 122.

9. Emperor William II to Queen Victoria, telegram, 25 February 1894, in Buckle, ed., *Letters of Queen Victoria,* p. 363.

10. Queen Victoria's journal, 3 March 1894, in *ibid.,* p. 371.

11. Queen Victoria's journal, 10 March 1894, in *ibid.,* p. 380.

12. Sir Charles Petrie, *King Alfonso XIII and His Age* (London: Chapman & Hall, 1963), p. 46.

13. The Carlists were supporters of Don Carlos, brother of King Ferdinand IV of Spain (r. 1814–33), who did not recognize the king's promulgation of the pragmatic sanction, which allowed for female succession to the throne, at the expense of a close male relative to the king. In so doing, Ferdinand IV paved the way for his daughter, Isabella II, to reign (1833–68). Such a move by Ferdinand, which cost Don Carlos the throne, was unacceptable not only to Carlos but to his followers, precipitating this dynastic crisis. Three wars were fought throughout the nineteenth century over this very dispute.

14. Petrie, *King Alfonso XIII,* p. 49.

15. Robert Sencourt (pseud. Robert Esmonde Gordon George), *King Alfonso: A Biography* (London: Faber & Faber, 1942), p. 64.

16. Petrie, *King Alfonso XIII,* p. 43.

17. John D. Bergamini, *The Spanish Bourbons: The History of a Tenacious Dynasty* (New York: G. P. Putnam's Sons, 1974), p. 307.

18. Queen Marie, *My Life,* p. 140.

19. Hannah Pakula, *The Last Romantic: A Biography of Queen Marie of Roumania* (New York: Simon & Schuster, 1985), p. 57.

20. Queen Marie, *My Life,* p. 137.

21. Pakula, *Last Romantic,* p. 127.

22. Queen Victoria to Victoria of Hesse, 24 September 1893, in Hough, ed., *Advice to My Grand-Daughter,* p.120. Missy also had another cousinly admirer, the Grand Duke George Michaelovitch, from the Russian side of her family. Though just as unlucky as Prince George of Wales in failing to secure Missy as a wife, Grand Duke George never seemed to come close to being remembered as fondly by Missy as was her cousin George of Wales.

23. Queen Marie, *My Life,* pp. 226, 223.

24. Queen Victoria to Empress Frederick, 14 June 1892, in Ramm, ed., *Beloved and Darling Child,* p. 142.

25. Queen Marie, *My Life,* p. 226.

26. Pope-Hennessy, *Queen Mary,* p. 242.

27. Pakula, *Last Romantic,* p. 60.

28. Queen Victoria to Victoria of Hesse, 2 June 1892, in Hough, ed., *Advice to My Grand-Daughter,* p. 117.

29. Pope-Hennessy, *Queen Mary,* p. 242.

30. Lee, ed., *Empress Frederick Writes to Sophie,* p. 119.

31. Letter of Lord Rosebery on the Romanian Marriage Treaty, 11 September 1892, P.R.O., F.O. 104/110/No. 5, The National Archives.

32. Foreign Office Memorandum of 20 September 1892 on the Roumanian Marriage Treaty, P.R.O., F.O. 104/110/No. 7, The National Archives.

33. Memorandum of Lord Rosebery on the Roumanian Marriage Treaty, 27 September 1892, P.R.O., F.O. 104/110/No. 18, The National Archives.

34. Sir Henry Ponsonby to Lord Rosebery, 7 November 1892, P.R.O., F.O. 104/110/No. 43, The National Archives.

35. P.R.O., F.O. 104/110/No. 47, The National Archives.

36. Foreign Office to Charles Hardinge, 11 December 1892, P.R.O., F.O. 104/110/No. 152, The National Archives.

37. *The Times,* 11 January 1893.
38. Lord Edward Malet to the Earl of Rosebery, 13 January 1893, P.R.O., F.O. 184, No. 2, The National Archives.
39. *The Times,* 12 January 1893.
40. Lee, ed., *Empress Frederick Writes to Sophie,* p. 135.
41. Queen Marie, *My Life,* p. 288.
42. Pope-Hennessy, *Queen Mary,* p. 241.
43. Queen Victoria to the Empress Frederick, 11 January 1893, in Ramm, ed., *Beloved and Darling Child,* pp. 153–54.
44. Queen Victoria to Princess Frederick William of Prussia, 16 May 1860, in Christopher Hibbert, ed., *Queen Victoria in Her Letters and Journals* (Stroud, Glos.: Sutton Publishing, 2000), p. 104.

FOUR: IN PURSUIT OF ALIX

1. Diary entry of Tsarevitch Nicholas, 21 December 1891, in Maylunas and Mironenko, eds., *Lifelong Passion,* p. 20.
2. Marie, Duchess of Edinburgh, to Countess Alexandrine Tolstoy, 13 January 1885, MB 1/24, Hartley Library, University of Southampton.
3. Queen Victoria to Princess Victoria of Hesse, 31 March 1889, in Hough, ed., *Advice to My Grand-Daughter,* p. 100.
4. Pope-Hennessy, *Queen Mary,* p. 183.
5. Queen Victoria to Princess Victoria of Hesse, 21 October 1883, in Hough, ed., *Advice to My Grand-Daughter,* p. 56.
6. Queen Victoria to Princess Victoria of Hesse, 29 December 1890, in *ibid.,* p. 110.
7. E. M. Almedingen, *The Empress Alexandra, 1872–1918* (London: Hutchinson & Co., 1961), p. 21.
8. Lamar Cecil, "William II and His Russian 'Colleagues,'" in Carole Fink, Isabel V. Hull, and MacGregor Knox, eds., *German Nationalism and the European Response, 1890–1945* (Norman, OK: University of Oklahoma Press, 1985), p. 26.
9. Almedingen, *Empress Alexandra,* p. 20.
10. *Ibid.,* p. 22.
11. E. P. P. Tisdall, *Marie Feodorovna: Empress of Russia* (New York: John Day Co., 1957), p. 178
12. Lee, ed., *Empress Frederick Writes to Sophie,* p. 163.
13. Diary entry of Tsarevitch Nicholas, 1 April 1892, in Maylunas and Mironenko, eds., *Lifelong Passion,* p. 22.
14. Almedingen, *Empress Alexandra,* p. 20.
15. Princess Alix to Grand Duchess Xenia, 8 November 1893, in Maylunas and Mironenko, eds., *Lifelong Passion,* p. 32.
16. Princess Alix to Tsarevitch Nicholas, 8 November 1893, in *ibid.,* p. 32.
17. *Ibid.,* pp. 32–33.
18. Diary entry of Tsarevitch Nicholas, 18 November 1893, in *ibid.,* p. 33.
19. Tsarevitch Nicholas to Princess Alix, 17 December 1893, in *ibid.,* p. 34.
20. Tsarevitch Nicholas to Empress Marie, 10 April 1894, in *ibid.,* pp. 48–49.
21. Cecil, "William II and His Russian 'Colleagues,'" in Fink, Hull, and Knox, eds., *German Nationalism and the European Response,* pp. 105, 104.

22. Wolfgang J. Mommsen, "Kaiser Wilhelm II and German Politics," *Journal of Contemporary History* 25 (1990), p. 297.

23. Lee, ed., *Empress Frederick Writes to Sophie,* p. 170.

24. Christine Sutherland, *Enchantress: Marthe Bibesco and Her World* (New York: Farrar, Straus & Giroux, 1996), p. x.

25. Queen Marie of Romania, *The Story of My Life.* Vol. II (London: Cassell & Co., 1934), pp. 14–15.

26. Charles Hardinge, *Old Diplomacy* (London: Jonathan Cape, 1947), p. 51.

27. Queen Marie, *My Life,* vol. II, p. 16.

28. Princess Marie of Edinburgh to Queen Victoria, 21 November 1891, RA Z84/107, Royal Archives, Windsor Castle, copy deposited at the Hoover Institution, Stanford University.

29. Queen Marie, *My Life,* vol. II, p. 25.

30. Pakula, *Last Romantic,* p. 96.

31. Queen Victoria to the Empress Frederick, 14 October 1894, in Ramm, ed., *Beloved and Darling Child,* p. 170.

32. Tsarevitch Nicholas to Empress Marie, 10 April 1894, in Maylunas and Mironenko, eds., *Lifelong Passion,* p. 49.

33. Diary entry of Tsarevitch Nicholas, 8 April 1894, in *ibid.,* p. 47.

34. Princess Marie Louise of Schleswig-Holstein, *My Memories of Six Reigns* (London: Evans Brothers, 1956), p. 50.

35. Baroness Sophie Buxhoeveden, *The Life and Tragedy of Alexandra Feodorovna: Empress of Russia* (London: Longmans, Green & Co., 1928), p. 34.

36. Mathilde Kschessinska, *Dancing in St. Petersburg: The Memoirs of Kschessinska* (Garden City, NY: Doubleday & Co., 1961), p. 51.

37. Theodore H. Von Laue, *Sergei Witte and the Industrialization of Russia* (New York: Columbia University Press, 1963), pp. 122–23.

38. Almedingen, *Empress Alexandra,* p. 24.

39. Lee, ed., *Empress Frederick Writes to Sophie,* p. 170.

40. Queen Victoria's journal, 20 April 1894, in Buckle, ed., *Letters of Queen Victoria,* vol. II, pp. 394–95.

41. Tsarevitch Nicholas to Princess Alix, 23 April 1894, in Maylunas and Mironenko, eds., *Lifelong Passion,* p. 60.

42. Charles Lowe, *Alexander III of Russia* (New York: Macmillan and Co., 1895), p. 353.

43. Princess Alix to Tsarevitch Nicholas, 22 April 1894, in Maylunas and Mironenko, ed., *Lifelong Passion,* p. 60.

44. Princess Alix to Tsarevitch Nicholas, 26 April 1894, in *ibid.,* p. 63.

45. Princess Alix to Tsarevitch Nicholas, 22 April 1894, in *ibid.,* p. 59.

46. Tsarevitch Nicholas to Princess Alix, 22 July 1894, in *ibid.,* p. 86.

47. Princess Alix to Tsarevitch Nicholas, 22 April 1894, in *ibid.,* p. 60.

48. Princess Alix to Queen Victoria, 28 May 1894, in *ibid.,* p. 71.

49. Diary of Tsarevitch Nicholas, 15 October 1894, in *ibid.,* p. 98.

50. Almedingen, *Empress Alexandra,* p. 39.

51. Vladimir Poliakoff, *The Tragic Bride: The Story of the Empress Alexandra of Russia* (New York: D. Appleton & Co., 1928), p. 62.

52. Grand Duke Alexander, *Once a Grand Duke* (Garden City, NY: Garden City Publishing Co., 1932), p. 168.

53. Tsar Nicholas II to Queen Victoria, 30 October 1894, in Maylunas and Mironenko, eds., *Lifelong Passion,* p. 102.
54. Bomann-Larsen, *Kongstangken,* p. 352.
55. Grand Duchess Elizabeth to Queen Victoria, 24 October/ 5 November 1894, in Lubov Millar, *Grand Duchess Elizabeth of Russia* (Redding, CA: Nikodemos Orthodox Publication Society, 1991), p. 81.
56. Queen Victoria's journal, 1 November 1894, in Buckle, ed., *Letters of Queen Victoria,* vol. II, p. 438.
57. Queen Victoria to the Empress Frederick, 5 November 1894, in Ramm, ed., *Beloved and Darling Child,* p. 172.
58. Queen Victoria to the Empress Frederick, 2 November 1894, in *ibid.,* p. 173.
59. Charlotte Knollys to Mrs. Archibald Knollys, 25 November 1894, MSS 21/M69/25/2, Knollys Papers, Hampshire Record Office.
60. Lee, ed., *The Empress Frederick Writes to Sophie,* p. 181.
61. Queen Victoria to Princess Victoria of Hesse, 7 November 1894, in Hough, ed., *Advice to My Grand-Daughter,* p. 128.
62. Queen Victoria's journal, 26 November 1894, in Buckle, ed., *Letters of Queen Victoria,* vol. II, p. 454.
63. *Ibid.*
64. Bomann-Larsen, *Kongstangken,* pp. 356–57.
65. Queen Victoria's journal, 26 November 1894, in Buckle, ed., *Letters of Queen Victoria,* vol. II, p. 454.
66. Charlotte Knollys to Mrs. Archibald Knollys, 25 November 1894, MSS 21M69/25/2, Knollys Papers, Hampshire Record Office.
67. Tsar Nicholas II to Grand Duke George, 19 November 1894, in Maylunas and Mironenko, eds., *Lifelong Passion,* p. 114.
68. Grand Duchess Elizabeth to Queen Victoria, 19 November/1 December 1894, in Millar, *Grand Duchess Elizabeth,* p. 85.
69. Poliakoff, *Tragic Bride,* p. 82.
70. Tsarina Alexandra to Queen Victoria, 24 November 1894, in Maylunas and Mironenko, eds., *Lifelong Passion,* p. 115.
71. Princess Catherine Radziwill, *Nicholas II: The Last of the Tsars* (London: Cassell & Co. Ltd., 1931), p. 89.
72. Diary entry of Tsar Nicholas II, 31 December 1894, in Maylunas and Mironenko, eds., *Lifelong Passion,* p. 118.
73. Tsarina Alexandra to the Rev. William Boyd Carpenter, Bishop of Ripon, 15 February 1895, Add. MSS 46721/231, The British Library.
74. Tsarina Alexandra to Prince Louis of Battenberg, 10 January 1895, in MSS MB1/T95, Broadlands Archives, Hartley Library, University of Southampton.
75. Bomann-Larsen, *Kongstanken,* p. 336.

FIVE: "MAUD COULD NOT HAVE DONE BETTER"

1. The Duchess of Edinburgh from this point will be referred to as the Duchess of Coburg since she had become the reigning Duchess of Saxe-Coburg-Gotha.
2. Pakula, *Last Romantic,* p. 103.
3. Queen Marie, *My Life,* vol. II, p. 85.

4. *Ibid.,* p. 86.

5. Hardinge, *Old Diplomacy,* p. 51.

6. Queen Marie, *My Life,* vol. II, p. 47.

7. Pakula, *Last Romantic,* p. 103.

8. Buxhoeveden, *Alexandra Feodorovna,* p. 56.

9. Queen Victoria to Princess Victoria of Hesse, 8 December 1895, in Hough, ed., *Advice to My Grand-Daughter,* p. 133.

10. Bomann-Larsen, *Kongstangken,* p. 400.

11. *Ibid.,* p. 374.

12. Pope-Hennessy, *Queen Mary,* p. 315 ("Poor little one, she loved him a lot." "His conduct towards this little one was cruel; he did not respond to her letters, and you know one should not ever play with a woman's heart").

13. Sir Sidney Lee, *King Edward VII.* Vol. I: *From Birth to Accession, 1841–1901* (London: Macmillan & Co., 1925), p. 607.

14. Pope-Hennessy, *Queen Mary,* p. 316.

15. Bomann-Larsen, *Kongstangken,* pp. 378, 380.

16. *Ibid.,* p. 381.

17. *Ibid.,* p. 381.

18. *Ibid.,* p. 389.

19. John Van der Kiste, *Edward VII's Children* (Stroud, Glos.: Alan Sutton Publishing, 1989), pp. 81–82.

20. Queen Victoria's journal, 28 October 1895, in Buckle, ed., *Letters of Queen Victoria,* vol. II, p. 569.

21. Møller, *Dronning Maud,* p. 39.

22. Ian Vorres, *The Last Grand Duchess: Her Imperial Highness Grand Duchess Olga Alexandrovna* (New York: Charles Scribner's Sons, 1965), p. 60.

23. Patricia Phenix, *Olga Romanov: Russia's Last Grand Duchess* (Toronto: Viking, 1999), p. 6.

24. Grand Duchess George, *Romanov Diary,* p. 81.

25. Diary entry of 7 May 1884 in Norman Rich and M. H. Fisher, eds., *The Holstein Papers: The Memoirs, Diaries and Correspondence of Friedrich von Holstein, 1837–1909.* Vol. II: *Diaries* (Cambridge: Cambridge University Press, 1957), p. 139.

26. Mabel Potter Daggett, *Queen Marie of Romania: The Intimate Story of the Radiant Queen* (New York: George H. Doran Co., 1926), p. 113.

27. When Queen Victoria was asked by the Marquis of Salisbury in 1887 whether men who had been divorced because of their adultery should not be given "social recognition of any kind," the queen instructed her private secretary to reply that she "entirely agrees about the gentlemen. It would have the best effect. Society is too bad *now*; some stop should be put to it." Letter of March 1887 from Queen Victoria to Henry Ponsonby in George Earle Buckle, ed., *The Letters of Queen Victoria: Third Series, A Selection from Her Majesty's Correspondence and Journal Between the Years 1886 and 1901.* Vol. I (London: John Murray, 1930), p. 288.

28. Almedingen, *Empress Alexandra,* p. 44.

29. Lili Dehn, *The Real Tsaritsa* (London: Thornton Butterworth, 1922), p. 59.

30. *Ibid.,* p. 61.

31. Dominic Lieven, *Nicholas II: Twilight of the Empire* (New York: St. Martin's Press, 1993), p. 57.

32. Vorres, *Last Grand Duchess,* p. 55.

33. Robert K. Massie, *Nicholas and Alexandra* (New York: Atheneum, 1967), p. 117.

34. Lord Frederic Hamilton, *The Vanished World of Yesterday* (London: Hodder & Stoughton, 1950), p. 475.

35. Massie, *Nicholas and Alexandra,* p. 117.

36. Greg King, *The Last Empress: The Life and Times of Alexandra Feodorovna, Tsarina of Russia* (New York: Birch Lane Press, 1994), p. 105.

37. W. Bruce Lincoln, *Sunlight at Midnight: St. Petersburg and the Rise of Modern Russia* (New York: Basic Books, 2000), p. 29.

38. *The Times,* 27 May 1896.

39. Queen Marie, *My Life,* vol. II, pp. 67–68.

40. The Widow of an American Diplomat, *Intimacies of Court and Society: An Unconventional Narrative of Unofficial Days* (New York: Dodd, Mead & Co., 1912), p. 122.

41. Queen Marie, *My Life,* vol. II, p. 73.

42. Massie, *Nicholas and Alexandra,* p. 59.

43. Queen Marie, *My Life,* vol. II, p. 72.

44. Statement of Colonel Sir Henry Knollys, undated, MSS 21M69/33/92, Knollys Papers, Hampshire Record Office.

45. Anne Kjellberg, *Dronning Maud: Et Liv—en Motehistorie* (Oslo: Grøndahl og Dreyers, 1995), pp. 20–21.

46. Pope-Hennessy, *Queen Mary,* p. 270.

47. Van der Kiste, *Edward VII's Children,* p. 84.

48. E. C. F. Collier, ed., *A Victorian Diarist: Later Extracts from the Journals of Mary, Lady Monkswell, 1895–1909* (London: John Murray, 1946), p. 16.

49. Queen Victoria to the Empress Frederick, 26 September 1896, in Ramm, ed., *Beloved and Darling Child,* p. 195.

50. Tsar Nicholas II to Empress Marie, 2 October 1896, in Bing, ed., *Tsar Nicholas and Empress Marie,* p. 120.

51. Queen Victoria's journal, 3 October 1896, in George Earle Buckle, ed., *The Letters of Queen Victoria: Third Series, A Selection from Her Majesty's Correspondence and Journal Between the Years 1886 and 1901.* Vol. III (London: John Murray, 1932), p. 88.

52. Tsarina Alexandra to Madge Jackson, 3 October 1896, in Buxhoeveden, *Alexandra Feodorovna,* p. 73.

53. Marie, Duchess of Edinburgh, to Countess Alexandrine Tolstoy, 20 November (2 December) 1896, MB 1/U24, Hartley Library, University of Southampton.

SIX: "TOO PAINFUL TO BEAR"

1. William Le Quex, *Things I Know About Kings, Celebrities, and Crooks* (London: Eveleigh Nash & Grayson, 1923), p. 96.

2. Queen Elisabeth, letter of 13 December 1901, in Queen Elisabeth (and Henry Howard Harper), *Letters and Poems of Queen Elisabeth (Carmen Sylva)* (Boston: Bibliophile Society, 1920), p. 127.

3. Queen Marie, *My Life,* vol. II, p. 82.

4. Kjellberg, *Dronning Maud,* p. 27.

5. Maud, Princess Carl of Denmark, to Lady Charles Scott, 6 December 1898, Add. MSS 52307/153, The British Library.

6. Battiscombe, *Queen Alexandra,* p. 200.

7. Maud, Princess Carl of Denmark, to Lady Charles Scott, 27 January 1897, Add. MSS 52307/145, The British Library.

8. Maud, Princess Carl of Denmark, to Lady Charles Scott, 1 May 1898, Add. MSS 52307/147, The British Library.

9. Van der Kiste, *Edward VII's Children*, p. 85.

10. Queen Marie, *My Life*, vol. II, p. 125.

11. Crown Princess Sophie to Empress Frederick, 16 January 1897, in Buckle, ed., *Letters of Queen Victoria*, vol. III, p. 121.

12. *Ibid.*

13. Marquis of Salisbury to Queen Victoria, 12 February 1897, in *ibid.*, pp. 130–31.

14. Queen Victoria to Marquis of Salisbury, 15 February 1897, in *ibid.*, p. 133.

15. Extract of letter from Crown Princess Sophie to Empress Frederick, 18 February 1897, in *ibid.*, p. 136.

16. Empress Frederick to Queen Victoria, 19 February 1897, in *ibid.*, p. 135.

17. Queen Victoria to Marquess of Salisbury, 21 February 1897, in *ibid.*, p. 138.

18. Queen Victoria to Empress Frederick, 31 March 1897, in Ramm, ed., *Beloved and Darling Child*, p. 201.

19. Collier, ed., *Victorian Diarist*, p. 25.

20. *The Times*, 2 April 1897.

21. *The Times*, 8 April 1897.

22. Empress Frederick to Queen Victoria, 18 April 1897, in ed., Buckle, *Letters of Queen Victoria*, vol. III, p. 150.

23. Stephen Gwynne, ed., *The Letters and Friendships of Sir Cecil Spring Rice: A Record*. Vol. I (London: Constable & Co., 1929), p. 221.

24. Lee, ed., *Empress Frederick Writes to Sophie*, p. 245.

25. Prince Nicholas, *My Fifty Years*, p. 159.

26. Theodore George Tatsios, *The Megali Idea and the Greek-Turkish War of 1897: The Impact of the Cretan Problem on Greek Irredentism, 1866–1897* (New York: Columbia University Press, 1984), p. 115.

27. *Ibid.*, p. 215, note 56.

28. Lee, ed., *Empress Frederick Writes to Sophie*, p. 250.

29. Queen Victoria to Empress Frederick, 24 April 1897, in Ramm, ed., *Beloved and Darling Child*, p. 203.

30. Edward Egerton to Queen Victoria, 25 April 1897, in Buckle, ed., *Letters of Queen Victoria*, vol. III, p. 154.

31. Lee, ed., *Empress Frederick Writes to Sophie*, pp. 251–52.

32. Queen Victoria's journal, 9 May 1897, in Buckle, ed., *Letters of Queen Victoria*, vol. III, p. 160.

33. Queen Victoria to Sir Edward Egerton, 9 May 1897, in *ibid.*, p. 161.

34. Emperor Wilhelm II to Queen Victoria, 13 May 1897, in *ibid.*, pp. 162–63.

35. John Van der Kiste, *Kings of the Hellenes: The Greek Kings, 1863–1914* (Stroud, Glos.: Sutton Publishing, 1994), p. 59.

36. Interview with Lady Katherine Brandram, 2 May 2001, Marlow, Bucks.

37. Van der Kiste, *Kings of the Hellenes*, p. 82.

38. Mary Allsebrook, *Born to Rebel: The Life of Harriet Boyd Harris* (Oxford: Oxbow Books, 1992), p. 34.

39. Grand Duchess George, *Romanov Diary*, p. 57.

40. Allsebrook, *Born to Rebel*, p. 70.

41. *Ibid.*, p. 74.

42. Queen Victoria to Empress Frederick, 5 August 1897, in Ramm, ed., *Beloved and Darling Child*, p. 206.

43. Queen Victoria to Empress Frederick, 9 October 1897, in *ibid.,* pp. 207–08.

44. Sir Arthur Bigge to the Marquis of Lansdowne, 29 October 1897, P.R.O., W.O. 32/6276, The National Archives.

45. Sir Arthur Bigge to the Marquis of Lansdowne, 7 November 1897, P.R.O., W.O. 32/6276, The National Archives.

46. Empress Frederick to the Reverend William Boyd Carpenter, Bishop of Ripon, 28 December 1897, Add. MSS. 46721/99, The British Library.

47. Queen Olga to Harriet Boyd Hawes, 22 December/2 January 1898/99 in Allsebrook, *Born to Rebel,* p. 79.

48. Princess Alice of Albany, *For My Grandchildren: Some Reminiscences of H.R.H. Princess Alice, Countess of Athlone* (London: Evans Brothers, 1966), p. 74.

49. Marfa Mouchanow, *My Empress* (New York: John Lane Co., 1928), p. 91.

50. Edgar T. S. Dugdale, *Maurice de Bunsen: Diplomat and Friend* (London: John Murray, 1934), p. 164.

51. Empress Frederick to Queen Victoria, 9 July 1897, in Ramm, ed., *Beloved and Darling Child,* p. 217.

52. Diary entry of Grand Duchess Xenia, 14 June 1899, in Maylunas and Mironenko, eds., *Lifelong Passion,* p. 185.

53. Queen Victoria to Tsar Nicholas II, 2–14 July 1899, in Alia Barkovets and Valentina Tenikhina, *Nicholas II: The Imperial Family* (St. Petersburg: Abris Publishers, 1999), p. 14.

54. Tsar Nicholas II to Tsarina Alexandra, 10 July 1899, in Maylunas and Mironenko, eds., *Lifelong Passion,* p. 188.

55. Longford, *Queen Victoria,* p. 554.

56. Empress Frederick to Queen Victoria, 10 February 1900, in Ramm, ed., *Beloved and Darling Child,* p. 246.

57. Queen Victoria to the Empress Frederick, [20 December 1899], in *ibid.,* p. 241.

58. Lee, ed., *Empress Frederick Writes to Sophie,* p. 308.

59. Pakula, *Last Romantic,* pp. 108, 123.

60. Paul D. Quinlan, *The Playboy King: Carol II of Romania* (Westport, CT: Greenwood Press, 1995), p. 17.

61. *Ibid.*

62. *Ibid.*

63. *Ibid.*

64. Queen Marie of Romania, *My Life,* vol. I, p. 19.

65. Marino Gómez Santos, *La Reina Victoria Eugenia, de Cerca* (Madrid: Afrodisio Aguado, 1969), p. 21.

66. Jerrold M. Packard, *Farewell in Splendour: The Passing of Queen Victoria and Her Age* (New York: E. P. Dutton, 1995), p. 206.

67. de Vilmorin, "The Queen of Spain's Own Story," *Chatelaine,* p. 94.

68. Tony Rennell, *Last Days of Glory: The Death of Queen Victoria* (London: Viking, 2000), p. 263.

69. Vilmorin, "The Queen of Spain's Own Story," *Chatelaine,* p. 94.

70. *The Times,* 3 February 1901.

71. *The Times,* 26 January 1901.

72. Buxhoeveden, *Alexandra Feodorovna,* p. 90.

73. Queen Marie, *My Life,* vol. I, pp. 74–75.

74. Dehn, *Real Tsaritsa,* p. 59.

75. Møller, *Dronning Maud,* p. 42.
76. Vilmorin, "The Queen of Spain's Own Story," *Chatelaine,* p. 93.
77. Queen Marie, *My Life,* vol. I, p. 19.

PART II

SEVEN: SPLENDID ISOLATION

1. Pope-Hennessy, *Queen Mary,* p. 271.
2. Queen Victoria to Princess Victoria of Hesse, 2 February 1887, in Hough, ed., *Advice to My Grand-Daughter,* p. 86.
3. Count Paul Vassili (a.k.a. Princess Catherine Radziwill), *Confessions of the Czarina* (New York: Harper & Brothers, 1918), p. 52.
4. Diary entry of Grand Duchess Xenia, 5 June 1901, in Maylunas and Mironenko, eds., *Lifelong Passion,* p. 206.
5. *Daily Mail,* 19 June 1901.
6. Tsarina Alexandra to the Reverend William Boyd Carpenter, Bishop of Ripon, 29 December 1902/11 January 1903, Add. MSS 46721/239, The British Library.
7. Count Sergei Witte, *The Memoirs of Count Witte,* ed. Sidney Harcave (Armonk, NY: M. E. Sharpe, 1990), p. 360.
8. Lee, ed., *Empress Frederick Writes to Sophie,* p. 337.
9. *Ibid.,* pp. 309–10.
10. Interview with Lady Katharine Brandram, 2 May 2001, Marlow, Bucks.
11. Letter of Crown Princess Sophie of Greece, 26 August 1901, private collection.
12. Ponsonby, ed., *Letters of the Empress Frederick,* pp. 468–69.
13. Almedingen, *Empress Alexandra,* p. 74.
14. Queen Marie of Romania, *My Life,* vol. I, p. 15.
15. Tsarina Alexandra to the Reverend William Boyd Carpenter, Bishop of Ripon, 29 December 1902/11 January 1903, Add. MSS 46721/239, The British Library.
16. *Ibid.*
17. Maurice Paléologue, *Ambassador's Memoirs.* Vol. I (London: Hutchinson, 1927), p. 321.
18. Massie, *Nicholas and Alexandra,* p. 243.
19. Lieven, *Nicholas II,* p. 163.
20. Longford, *Queen Victoria,* p. 313.
21. Queen Victoria to the Crown Princess of Prussia, 16 July 1867, in Hibbert, ed., *Queen Victoria in Her Letters and Journals,* p. 199.

EIGHT: EMBATTLED BUT NOT DEFEATED

1. Queen Marie of Romania, *My Life,* vol. II, p. 177.
2. *Ibid.,* p. 178.
3. Harper, *Letters and Poems of Queen Elisabeth,* p. 157.
4. Queen Marie, *My Life,* vol. II, p. 179.
5. The acerbic Nancy Astor (1879–1964) met her match in Winston Churchill. During a famous exchange of words at Blenheim Palace, Nancy shouted, "If I were your wife I would put poison in your coffee." To which, the equally blistering Churchill shot back, "And if I were your husband, I would drink it." See Consuelo Vanderbilt Balsan, *The Glitter and the Gold* (New York: Harper & Brothers, 1952), pp. 204–05.

6. Crown Princess Marie of Romania to Nancy Shaw, 27 February 1906, Astor Papers, University of Reading.

7. Crown Princess Marie of Romania to Nancy Shaw, 8 April 1906, Astor Papers, University of Reading.

8. Maurice Collis, *Nancy Astor* (London: Faber & Faber, 1960), p. 42.

9. James Fox, *The Langhorne Sisters* (London: Granta Books, 1999), p. 96.

10. Queen Marie, "Is Royal Blood a Blessing?" (1926) in Queen Marie of Romania Papers, Kent State University.

11. Tsarina Alexandra to Grand Duke Ernst Ludwig of Hesse, 17 March 1904, in Roderick R. McLean, "Kaiser Wilhelm II and His Hessian Cousins: Intra-state Relations in the German Empire and International Dynastic Politics, 1890–1918," *German History,* vol. 19, no. 1 (2001), p. 43.

12. Buxhoeveden, *Alexandra Feodorovna,* p. 109.

13. *Ibid.,* pp. 108–09.

14. *Daily Mail,* 25 January 1901.

15. Hardinge, *Old Diplomacy,* p. 51.

16. Princess Anne-Marie Callimachi, *Yesterday Was Mine* (London: Falcon Press, 1952), p. 49.

17. Rosemary and Donald Crawford, *Michael and Natasha: The Life and Love of the Last Tsar of Russia* (London: Weidenfeld & Nicolson, 1997), p. 43.

18. Callimachi, *Yesterday Was Mine,* p. 51.

19. Gordon Brooks-Shepherd, *Royal Sunset: The European Dynasties and the Great War* (Garden City, NY: Doubleday & Co., 1987), p. 235.

20. Roger Fulford, *Hanover to Windsor* (London: Collins, 1970), p. 155.

21. Barbara Tuchman, *The Proud Tower: A Portrait of the World Before the War, 1890–1914* (New York: The Macmillan Company, 1966), pp. 19, 49.

22. *Ibid.,* p. 19.

23. See Maria Teresa Puga Eusebio Ferrer, *Victoria Eugenia: Esposa de Alfonso XIII* (Barcelona: Editorial Juventud, 1999), p. 32; and Fernando Gonzalez-Doria, *Las Reinas de España* (Madrid: Editorial Bitacora, 1989), p. 577.

24. David Chavchavadze, *The Grand Dukes* (New York: Atlantic International Publications, 1990), p. 235.

NINE: THE FACADE CRUMBLES

1. Edward Crankshaw, *Shadow of the Winter Palace: Russia's Drift to Revolution, 1825–1917* (New York: Viking Press, 1976), p. 329.

2. Mouchanow, *My Empress,* p. 155.

3. Diary entry of Tsar Nicholas II, 8 September 1904, in Harrison E. Salisbury, *Black Night, White Snow: Russia's Revolutions, 1905–1917* (New York: Doubleday & Co., 1977), p. 110.

4. Vorres, *Last Grand Duchess,* p. 113.

5. W. Bruce Lincoln, *In War's Dark Shadow: The Russians Before the Great War* (New York: Dial Press, 1983), p. 295.

6. *Ibid.,* p. 297.

7. Witte, *Memoirs,* p. 480.

8. *Ibid.*

9. McLean, "Kaiser Wilhelm," *German History* (2001), p. 44.

10. Salisbury, *Black Night,* p. 160.

11. Witte, *Memoirs,* p. 604.

12. Grand Duke Alexander, *Once a Grand Duke,* p. 225.
13. Tsar Nicholas II to Empress Marie, 19 October 1905, in Bing, ed., *Tsar Nicholas and Empress Marie,* pp. 188–89.
14. Salisbury, *Black Night,* p. 162.
15. Tuchman, *Proud Tower,* p. 50.
16. Salisbury, *Black Night,* p. 161.
17. Anna Viroubova, *Memories of the Russian Court* (New York: The Macmillan Company, 1923), p. 17.
18. Elizabeth Narishkin-Kurakin, *Under Three Tsars: The Memoirs of the Lady-in-Waiting Elizabeth Narishkin-Kurakin,* ed. René Fülöp-Miller (New York: E.P. Dutton, 1931, p. 190.
19. Count V. N. Kokovtsov, *Out of My Past: The Memoirs of Count Kokovtsov,* trans. Laura Matveev, ed. H. H. Fisher (Stanford: Stanford University Press, 1935), pp. 130–31.
20. Grand Duke Alexander, *Once a Grand Duke,* p. 227.
21. Diary entry of Grand Duchess Xenia, 30 April 1906, in Maylunas and Mironenko, eds., *Lifelong Passion,* p. 293.
22. Cecil Spring Rice to Sir Edward Grey, 9 May 1906, in D. C. B. Lieven, Kenneth Bourne, and D. C. Watt, eds., *British Documents on Foreign Affairs: Reports and Papers from the Foreign Office Confidential Print, Part I, from the Mid-Nineteenth Century to the First World War. Series A, Russia 1859–1914.* Vol. 4: *1906–1907,* ed. Dominic Lieven (Frederick, MD: University Publications of America, 1983), Document 38.
23. *Ibid.*
24. Tim Greve, *Haakon VII of Norway: Founder of a New Monarchy* (London: Hurst, 1983), p. 24.
25. Salisbury, *Black Night,* p. 180.
26. Narishkin-Kurakin: *Under Three Tsars,* p. 192.
27. Buxhoeveden, *Alexandra Feodorovna,* p. 126.
28. Pierre Gilliard, *Thirteen Years at the Russian Court* (London: Hutchinson & Co., 1921), p. 26.
29. From Anna Viroubova's *Unpublished Memoirs,* quoted in Yuri Shclayev, Elizabeth Shelayeva, and Nicholas Semenov, *Nicholas Romanov: Life and Death* (St. Petersburg: Liki Rossii, 1998), p. 43.

TEN: DESTINY BECKONS

1. Robert Sencourt, *The Spanish Crown, 1808–1931: An Intimate Chronicle of a Hundred Years* (New York: Charles Scribner's Sons, 1932), p. 275.
2. Vicente R. Pilapil, *Alfonso XIII* (New York: Twayne Publishers, 1969), p. 94.
3. Noel, *Ena,* p. 43.
4. *Ibid.,* p. 53.
5. Pilapil, *Alfonso XIII,* p. 33.
6. Princess Victoria Eugenie of Battenberg to King Alfonso XIII of Spain, 26 June 1905, no. 54 in Ministerio de Obras Publicas, Transportes y Medio Ambiente, Secretaria General de Comunicacion Organismo Autonomo Correos y Telegrafos y Patrimonio Nacional, eds., *Correspondencia Epistolar de la Princesa Victoria Eugenia de Battemberg al Rey Alfonso XIII, 1905–1906* (Madrid: Patrimonio Nacional, 1993), p. 21.
7. Princess Victoria Eugenie of Battenberg to King Alfonso XIII of Spain, undated, no. 12 in *ibid.,* p. 26.

8. Princess Victoria Eugenie of Battenberg to King Alfonso XIII of Spain, undated, no. 45 in *ibid.,* p. 35.

9. Princess Victoria Eugenie of Battenberg to King Alfonso XIII of Spain, undated, no. 10 in *ibid.,* p. 26.

10. Princess Victoria Eugenie of Battenberg to King Alfonso XIII of Spain, 5 December 1905, no. 11 in *ibid.,* p. 24.

11. Princess Victoria Eugenie of Battenberg to King Alfonso XIII, 31 December 1905, no. 48 in *ibid.,* p. 36.

12. Princess Victoria Eugenie of Battenberg to King Alfonso XIII, 10 January 1906, no. 78 in *ibid.,* p. 38.

13. Angeles Hijano, *Victoria Eugenia de Battenberg: Una Reina Exiliada (1887–1969)* (Madrid: Alderabán Ediciones, 2000), p. 69.

14. Kellogg Durland, *Royal Romances To-day* (London: T. Werner Laurie, 1912), p. 18.

15. Ferrer, *Victoria Eugenia,* p. 75.

16. Sir Sidney Lee, *King Edward VII: A Biography.* Vol. II (New York: The Macmillan Company, 1927), p. 513.

17. E. R. Norman, *Anti-Catholicism in Victorian England* (New York: Barnes & Noble, 1968), p. 20.

18. Longford, *Queen Victoria,* p. 204.

19. Ricardo de la Cierva, *Alfonso y Victoria: Las Tramas Íntimas, Secretas y Europeas de Un Reinado Desconocido* (Madrid: Editorial Fénix, 2001), p. 189.

20. Princess Victoria Eugenie of Battenberg to King Alfonso XIII, 20 February 1906, in *ibid.,* p. 190.

21. Princess Victoria Eugenie of Battenberg to King Alfonso XIII, 21 February 1906, in *ibid.*

22. Princess Victoria Eugenie of Battenberg to King Alfonso XIII, 22 February 1906, in *ibid.*

23. Hijano, *Victoria Eugenia,* pp. 61–62.

24. de la Cierva, *Alfonso y Victoria,* p. 193.

25. Hijano, *Victoria Eugenia,* p. 62.

26. *Ibid.*

27. Ferrer, *Victoria Eugenia,* p. 78.

28. Noel, *Ena,* pp. 71, 75.

29. Santos, *Victoria Eugenia,* pp. 71–72.

30. Princess Beatrice to Louisa, Lady Antrim, 16 February 1906, MSS D/4091/B/3/1/5, Public Record Office of Northern Ireland.

31. Princess Victoria Eugenie of Battenberg to Mrs. Oglander, 11 April 1906, MSS OG/CC/2208 (103/177), Oglander Papers, Isle of Wight County Record Office.

32. Møller, *Dronning Maud,* pp. 59–60.

33. Lee, *Edward VII,* vol. II, p. 317.

34. Roderick R. Mclean, *Royalty and Diplomacy in Europe, 1890–1914* (Cambridge: Cambridge University Press, 2001), p. 118.

35. Lee, *Edward VII,* vol. II, p. 318.

36. *The Family Herald* (May 1903), p. 777.

37. John Van der Kiste, *Northern Crowns: The Kings of Modern Scandinavia* (Stroud, Glos.: Sutton Publishing, 1996), p. 38.

38. Lee, *Edward VII,* vol. II, p. 321.

39. Kjellberg, *Dronning Maud,* p. 31.

40. Pope-Hennessy, *Queen Mary,* p. 403.

41. Empress Marie to Tsar Nicholas II, 1 November 1905, in Bing, ed., *Tsar Nicholas and Empress Marie,* p. 194.
42. *The Times,* 20 November 1905.
43. *The Times,* 22 November 1905.
44. Massie, *Nicholas and Alexandra,* p. 193.
45. Salisbury, *Black Night,* p. 208.
46. Dostoevsky quoted in Gilliard, *Thirteen Years,* p. 54. See also Salisbury, *Black Night,* p. 208, and Massie, *Nicholas and Alexandra,* p. 194.
47. Vorres, *Last Grand Duchess,* pp. 130–31.
48. Dehn, *Real Tsaritsa,* p. 100.
49. Paléologue, *Ambassador's Memoirs,* p. 292.

ELEVEN: BAPTISM OF FIRE

1. Pope-Hennessy, *Queen Mary,* p. 398.
2. Durland, *Royal Romances,* p. 21.
3. Albert Frederick Calvert, *The Spanish Royal Wedding* (Taunton, Devon: Privately printed, 1906), p. 86.
4. Dugdale, *Maurice de Bunsen,* pp. 218–19.
5. Calvert, *Royal Wedding,* pp. 26–27.
6. William Miller Collier, *At the Court of His Catholic Majesty* (Chicago: A. C. McClurg & Co., 1912), pp. 138, 151.
7. Petrie, *King Alfonso XIII,* p. 88.
8. Pope-Hennessy, *Queen Mary,* p. 400.
9. H.R.H. Princess Pilar of Bavaria and Major Desmond Chapman-Houston, *Don Alfonso XIII: A Study of Monarchy* (London: John Murray, 1931), p. 128.
10. Calvert, *Royal Wedding,* p. 260.
11. Noel, *Ena,* p. 95.
12. E. Thornton Cook and Catherine Moran, *Royal Daughters* (London: Heath Cranton, 1935), p. 171.
13. Collier, ed., *Victorian Diarist,* pp. 168–69.
14. Calvert, *Royal Wedding,* p. 266.
15. Collier, ed., *Victorian Diarist,* p. 167.
16. Pope-Hennessy, *Queen Mary,* p. 401.
17. Noel, *Ena,* p. 101.
18. Pope-Hennessy, *Queen Mary,* p. 401.
19. Paul Cambon, letter of 2 June 1906, in *Correspondance 1870–1924.* Vol. II (Paris: Grasset, 1940), p. 218.
20. Queen Victoria Eugenie to the Rev. William Boyd Carpenter, Bishop of Ripon, 2 June 1906, Add. MSS 46722/71, The British Library.
21. Pope-Hennessy, *Queen Mary,* p. 401 ("As for me, I am so much accustomed to this sort of thing").
22. Noel, *Ena,* p. 104.
23. Princess Beatrice to the Rev. William Boyd Carpenter, Bishop of Ripon, 14 June 1906, Add. MSS 46721/161, The British Library.
24. Noel, *Ena,* p. 101.
25. Durland, *Royal Romances,* p. 39.

26. Princess Beatrice to Louisa, Lady Antrim, 9 June 1906, MSS D/4091/B/3/1, Public Record Office of Northern Ireland.

27. Queen Victoria Eugenie to Mrs. Paget, 22 June 1906, Paget Papers, Add. MSS 43830, The British Library.

TWELVE: NORWAY'S ENGLISH QUEEN

1. Mary Bronson Hartt, "Haakon VII, The New King of Norway," *The Outlook,* 23 June 1906, pp. 464–65.

2. *The Times,* 27 November 1905.

3. Battiscombe, *Queen Alexandra,* p. 256.

4. Van der Kiste, *Edward VII's Children,* p. 108.

5. Hartt, "Haakon VII," *The Outlook,* p. 470.

6. Van der Kiste, *Edward VII's Children,* p. 109.

7. *The Times,* 23 June 1906.

8. Pope-Hennessy, *Queen Mary,* p. 403.

9. Van der Kiste, *Northern Crowns,* p. 56.

10. Hartt, "Haakon VII," *The Outlook,* p. 464.

11. Sir Frederick Ponsonby, *Recollections of Three Reigns* (New York: E. P. Dutton & Co., 1952), p. 276.

12. Hartt, "Haakon VII," *The Outlook,* p. 468.

13. *Ibid.,* p. 469.

14. Queen Victoria Eugenie to the Rev. William Boyd Carpenter, Bishop of Ripon, 13 January 1907, Add. MSS 46722/73, The British Library.

15. Joan Kennard to John H. Oglander, 6 April 1907, MSS OG/CC/2258 (103/228), Oglander Papers, Isle of Wight Record Office.

16. John H. Oglander to Florence Oglander, 17 March 1907, MSS OG/CC/2255A (107/57), Oglander Papers, Isle of Wight Record Office.

17. Noel, *Ena,* p. 135.

18. Collier, *His Catholic Majesty,* p. 231.

19. *Illustrated London News,* 1 June 1907.

20. Collier, *His Catholic Majesty,* p. 234.

21. *Ibid.,* pp. 235, 241.

22. Princess Henry of Battenberg to the Rev. William Boyd Carpenter, Bishop of Ripon, 14 May 1907, Add. MSS 46721/168, The British Library.

THIRTEEN: REVOLUTIONARY FEVER

1. General Report on Roumania for the Year 1907 in Kenneth Bourne, D. Cameron Watt, and John F. V. Keiger, eds., *British Documents on Foreign Affairs* (cited hereafter as *BDFA*), Part I, Series F: *Europe, 1848–1914.* Vol. 16: *Montenegro, 1914; Romania, 1878–1914,* ed. John F. V. Keiger (Frederick, MD: University Publications of America, 1987), Document 28.

2. Pakula, *Last Romantic,* p. 149.

3. Callimachi, *Yesterday Was Mine,* p. 138.

4. Pakula, *Last Romantic,* p. 161.

5. Callimachi, *Yesterday Was Mine,* p. 139.

6. Terence Elsberry, *Marie of Romania: The Intimate Life of a Twentieth-Century Queen* (New York: St. Martin's Press, 1972), p. 86.

7. Sir Conynham Greene to Sir Edward Grey, Inclosure, Annual Report on Roumania for the Year 1906, in *BDFA,* Part I, Series F, vol. 16, Document 26.

8. R. W. Seton-Watson, *A History of Roumanians: From Roman Times to the Completion of Unity* (New York: Archon Books, 1963), pp. 469–70.

9. Anthony Di Iorio, "Italy and Rumania in 1914: The Italian Assessment of the Rumanian Situation, 1907 to 1914," in *Rumanian Studies: An International Annual of the Humanities and Social Sciences.* Vol. IV: *1976–1979* (Leiden: E. J. Brill, 1979), p. 130.

10. Crown Princess Marie of Romania to Nancy Astor, 6 April 1907 (though inadvertently dated 1906 by Marie), Astor Papers, University of Reading.

11. Sir Francis Elliot and A. Young to Sir Edward Grey, Annual Report on Greece for 1909, 14 February, 1910, in Kenneth Bourne, D. Cameron Watt, and John F. V. Keiger, eds., *BDFA,* Part I, Series F: *Europe, 1848–1914.* Vol. 14: *Greece, 1847–1914,* ed. David Stevenson and John F. V. Keiger (Frederick, MD: University Publications of America, 1987), Document 55.

12. *Ibid.*

13. Minute to a confidential despatch by Sir Francis Elliot to Sir Edward Grey, 21 December 1909, P.R.O., F.O. 371/679/No. 98, The National Archives.

14. S. Victor Papacosma, *The Military in Greek Politics: The 1909 Coup d'Etat* (Kent, OH: Kent State University Press, 1977) p. 85.

15. *Ibid.,* pp. 170–71.

16. *Ibid.,* p. 172.

17. Margrete, Landgravine of Hesse, to Hilda Chichester, 19 August 1910, MSS 364/38, Bodleian Library, University of Oxford.

18. Margrete, Landgravine of Hesse, to Hilda Chichester, 8 November 1910, MSS 364/40, Bodleian Library, University of Oxford.

19. Sir Francis Elliot and H. Beaumont to Sir Edward Grey, 8 February 1911, Annual Report on Greece for 1910, in *BDFA,* Part I, Series F, vol. 14, Document 58.

20. Sir Francis Elliot to Sir Edward Grey, 12 February 1912, Inclosure in Document 59, Annual Report on Greece for the Year 1911, in *BDFA,* Part I, Series F, vol. 14, Document 60.

21. Max Nord, "Sisters of the German Kaiser," *The Scrap Book,* 8 (August 1908).

22. Sir Francis Elliot to Sir Edward Grey, 26 February 1913, Inclosure in Document 61, Annual Report on Greece for 1912, in *BDFA,* Series F, vol. 14, Document 62.

23. Petrie, *King Alfonso XIII,* p. 102.

24. Sir Maurice de Bunsen to Sir Edward Grey, 7 August 1909, in Kenneth Bourne, D. Cameron Watt and John F. V. Keiger, eds., *BDFA,* Part I, Series F: *Europe, 1848–1914.* Vol. 28: *Spain, 1908–1914,* ed. David Stevenson and John F. V. Keiger (Frederick, MD: University Publications of America, 1987), Document 25.

25. *The Times,* 2 August 1909.

26. Ferrer, *Victoria Eugenia,* p. 138.

27. Sir Maurice de Bunsen to Sir Edward Grey, 19 December 1909, in *BDFA,* Part I, Series F, vol. 28, Document 44.

FOURTEEN: *"LA REINA HERMOSA"*

1. Princess Henry of Battenberg to the Rev. William Boyd Carpenter, Bishop of Ripon, 23 December 1907, Add. MSS 46721/178, The British Library.

2. Ricardo de la Cierva, *Alfonso y Victoria: Las Tramas Íntimas, Secretas y Europeas de Un Reinado Desconocido* (Madrid: Editorial Fénix, 2001), p. 225.

3. *Ibid.*

4. *Ibid.,* p. 226.

5. Durland, *Royal Romances,* p. 11.

6. Santos, *Victoria Eugenia,* p. 214.

7. Infanta Eulalia, *Memoirs of a Spanish Princess* (London: Hutchinson & Co., 1936), p. 159.

8. Juan Balansó, *Por Razón de Estado: Las Bodas Reales en España* (Barcelona: Plaza y Janés, 2002), p. 226.

9. Graham, *Queen of Spain,* p. 189.

10. *Ibid.,* p. 200.

11. Queen Victoria Eugenie to Lady Llangattock, 14 January 1907, private collection.

12. Ferrer, *Victoria Eugenia,* pp. 112–13.

13. H. R. H Princess Pilar of Bavaria and Major Desmond Chapman-Houston, *Don Alfonso: XIII: A Study of Monarchy* (London: John Murray, 1931), p. 346.

14. *Ibid.,* p. 347.

15. Marqués de Villavieja, *Life Has Been Good: Memoirs of the Marqués de Villavieja* (London: Chatto & Windus, 1938), p. 213.

16. *The Times,* 4 August 1909.

17. John van der Kiste, *Crowns in a Changing World: The British and European Monarchies, 1901–36* (London: Grange Books, 1993), pp. 71–73.

18. Barbara Tuchman, *The Guns of August* (New York: The Macmillan Company, 1962), p. 1.

19. Theo Aronson, *Crowns in Conflict: The Triumph and the Tragedy of European Monarchy, 1910–1918* (London: John Murray, 1986), p. 11.

20. Hijano, *Victoria Eugenia,* p. 121.

21. Pakula, *Last Romantic,* p. 158.

22. Buxhoeveden, *Alexandra Feodorovna,* p. 150.

23. Dehn, *Real Tsartitsa,* p. 81.

24. Buxhoeveden, *Alexandra Feodorovna,* p. 150.

25. *Ibid.,* p. 168.

FIFTEEN: "MAMMA, HELP ME!"

1. Gilliard, *Thirteen Years,* p. 43.

2. *Ibid.,* p. 40.

3. Buxhoeveden, *Alexandra Feodorovna,* p. 173.

4. Gleb Botkin, *The Real Romanovs* (New York: Fleming H. Revell Co., 1931), p. 123.

5. M. V. Rodzianko, *The Reign of Rasputin: An Empire's Collapse* (London: A. M. Philpot, 1927), p. 24.

6. W. Bruce Lincoln, *The Romanovs: Autocrats of All the Russias* (New York: Dial Press, 1981), p. 681.

7. King, *Last Empress,* p. 185.

8. Count V. N. Kokovtsov, *Out of My Past: The Memoirs of Count Kokovtsov,* trans. Laura Matveev, ed. H. H. Fisher (Stanford: Stanford University Press, 1935), pp. 295–96.

9. Viroubova, *Memories,* p. 93.

10. Tsar Nicholas II to Empress Marie, 20 October 1912, in Bing, ed., *Tsar Nicholas and Empress Marie,* pp. 276–77.

11. Viroubova, *Memories,* pp. 92–93.

12. Gilliard, *Thirteen Years,* p. 29.

13. Buxhoeveden, *Alexandra Feodorovna,* p. 132.

14. Greg King, *The Man Who Killed Rasputin: Prince Felix Youssoupov and the Murder That Helped Bring Down the Russian Empire* (Secaucus, NJ: Citadel Press, 1995), p. 32.

15. Paléologue, *Ambassador's Memoirs,* p. 148.

16. Viroubova, *Memories,* p. 94.

17. Vorres, *Last Grand Duchess,* p. 140.

18. A. A. Mossolov, *At the Court of the Last Tsar: Being the Memoirs of A. A. Mossolov, Head of the Court Chancellery, 1900–1916,* trans. E. W. Dickes, ed. A. A. Pilenco (London: Methuen & Co., 1935), p. 151.

19. Vorres, *Last Grand Duchess,* p. 140.

20. Alex De Jonge, *The Life and Times of Grigorri Rasputin* (New York: Coward, McCann & Geoghegan, 1982), p. 152.

21. Vorres, *Last Grand Duchess,* p. 140.

22. King, *Man Who Killed Rasputin,* p. 36.

23. De Jonge, *Grigorri Rasputin,* p. 343.

24. Mossolov, *Court of the Last Tsar,* p. 152.

25. Tsarina Alexandra to the Rev. William Boyd Carpenter, Bishop of Ripon, 24 January/ 7 February 1913, Add. MSS 46721/244, The British Library.

26. *Ibid.*

27. Prince Christopher of Greece, *Memoirs of H. R. H. Prince Christopher of Greece* (London: The Right Book Club, 1938), p 113.

28. Walter Christmas, *King George of Greece* (London: Eveleigh Nash, 1914), p. 359.

29. Crown Prince Constantine to Paola, Princess of Saxe-Weimar, 11 November 1912, in Paola, Princess of Saxe-Weimar, *A King's Private Letters: Being Letters Written by King Constantine of Greece to Paola, Princess of Saxe-Weimar During the Years 1912–1923* (London: Eveleigh Nash & Grayson, 1925), p. 88.

30. Christmas, *King George,* p. 363.

31. *Ibid.,* p. 368.

32. *The Times,* 31 October 1912.

33. Hugo Vickers, *Alice: Princess Andrew of Greece* (London: Hamish Hamilton, 2000), p. 101.

34. *Ibid.,* p. 103.

35. Prince Christopher, *Memoirs,* p. 118.

36. G. Nicholas Tantzos, *The Inheritors of Alexander the Great: An Illustrated History* (New York: Atlantic International Publications, 1986), p. 43.

37. Van der Kiste, *Kings of the Hellenes,* p. 80.

38. *Ibid.,* p. 76.

39. *The Times,* 20 March 1913.

40. Sir Francis Elliot, et al., to Sir Edward Grey, 20 May 1914, Annual Report on Greece for 1913, in *BDFA,* Series F, vol. 14, Document 64.

41. Margrete, Landgravine of Hesse, to Hilda Chichester, 3 April 1913, MSS 364, Bodleian Library, University of Oxford.

42. Doros Alastos, *Venizelos: Patriot, Statesman, Revolutionary* (Gulf Breeze, FL: Academic International Press, 1978), p. 125.

43. E. P. P. Tisdall, *Royal Destiny: The Royal Hellenic Cousins* (London: Stanley Paul & Co., 1955), p. 113.

44. Alastos, *Venizelos,* p. 128.
45. Queen Marie, *My Life,* vol. II, p. 305.
46. *Ibid.,* p. 309.
47. Pakula, *Last Romantic,* p. 167.

SIXTEEN: BEFORE THE STORM

1. Kokovtsov, *Out of My Past,* p. 361.
2. Viroubova, *Memories,* p. 100.
3. Buxhoeveden, *Alexandra Feodorovna,* p. 166.
4. *Ibid.,* p. 173.
5. Mossolov, *Court of the Last Tsar,* p. 63.
6. Buxhoeveden, *Alexandra Feodorovna,* p. 153.
7. Dehn, *Real Tsaritsa,* p. 75.
8. Paul and Beatrice Grabbe, eds., *The Private World of the Last Tsar: In the Photographs and Notes of General Count Alexander Grabbe* (Boston: Little, Brown, 1984), p. 60.
9. *Ibid.,* p. 63.
10. Mossolov, *Court of the Last Tsar,* p. 64.
11. Buxhoeveden, *Alexandra Feodorovna,* p. 155.
12. Mossolov, *Court of the Last Tsar,* p. 64.
13. Grabbe, eds., *Private World,* p. 69.
14. Dehn, *Real Tsaritsa,* p. 82.
15. *Ibid.,* p. 83.
16. Tsarina Alexandra to the Rev. William Boyd Carpenter, Bishop of Ripon, 24 January/ 7 February 1913, Add. MSS 46721/244, The British Library.
17. Elseberry, *Marie of Romania,* p. 92.
18. *Ibid.,* p. 95.
19. Queen Marie, *My Life,* vol. II, p. 327.
20. *Ibid.,* p. 326.
21. *Ibid.,* p. 330.
22. *Ibid.,* p. 332.
23. Grabbe, eds., *Private World,* p. 75.
24. N. N. Ralinin, *The Romanovs and the Crimea,* trans. Yekaterina Tabidze (Moscow: Kruk, 1993), p. 160.
25. Interview with Dmitri Likhachev in *The Last of the Czars: Part Two—The Shadow of Rasputin,* The Discovery Channel, 1996.
26. Gilliard, *Thirteen Years,* p. 94.
27. Queen Marie, *My Life,* vol. II, p. 337.
28. *Ibid.*
29. Eugene de Schelking, *Suicide of Monarchy: Recollections of a Diplomat* (Toronto: Macmillan Company of Canada, 1918), p. 309.
30. Gilliard, *Thirteen Years,* p. 95.
31. *Ibid.* p. 96.
32. Lieven, *Nicholas II,* p. 198.
33. Serge Sazanov, *Fateful Years: The Reminiscences of Serge Sazanov, Russian Minister for Foreign Affairs, 1914* (London: Jonathan Cape, 1928), p. 110.
34. *Ibid.*

35. Edvard Radzinsky, *The Last Tsar: The Life and Death of Nicholas II* (New York: Double-day, 1992), p. 117.

36. Sazanov, *Fateful Years,* p. 110.

37. Interview with Lady Katherine Brandram, 2 May 2001, Marlow, Bucks.

38. Vickers, *Alice,* p. 108.

39. Interview with Lady Katherine Brandram, 2 May 2001.

40. Copy of a copy, unsigned and undated but written by King Haakon VII from Christiana about 2 May 1907 to Francis Knollys, MSS 21M69/32/13, Knollys Papers, Hampshire Record Office.

41. Colonel Sir Henry Knollys to King Haakon VII, 8 May 1907, MSS 21M69/32/14, Knollys Papers, Hampshire Record Office.

42. Colonel Sir Henry Knollys to King Haakon VII, 10 May 1907, MSS 21/M65/32/15, Knollys Papers, Hampshire Record Office.

43. Colonel Sir Henry Knollys to King Haakon VII, 27 September 1911, MSS 21M69/32/48, Knollys Papers, Hampshire Record Office.

44. *Ibid.*

45. Precis of Draught of Letter from King Haakon to King George, 17 September 1911, MSS 21M69/32/45, Knollys Papers, Hampshire Record Office.

46. Pope-Hennessy, *Queen Mary,* p. 483.

47. Arthur Gould Lee, *Helen: Queen Mother of Rumania* (London: Faber & Faber, 1956), p. 34.

PART III

SEVENTEEN: BALKAN CAULDRON

1. Tsar Nicholas II to King George V, 2 August 1914, in Van der Kiste, *Crowns in a Changing World,* p. 103.

2. Nicolson, *King George V: His Life and Reign* (London: Constable & Co., 1952), p.247.

3. Gilliard, *Thirteen Years,* p. 105.

4. *Ibid.,* p. 106.

5. Viroubova, *Memories,* p. 107.

6. Anonymous, *Russian Court Memoirs 1914–1916* (Cambridge: Ian Faulkner Publishing, 1992), p. 46.

7. Diary entry of 1 August 1914 in Paléologue, *Ambassador's Memoirs,* p. 52.

8. *The Times,* 3 August 1914.

9. Buxhoeveden, *Alexandra Feodorovna,* p. 189.

10. Gilliard, *Thirteen Years,* pp. 107–10.

11. Viroubova, *Memories,* p. 105.

12. Kaiser Wilhelm II to King Constantine I, 31 July 1914, in S. P. P. Cosmetatos, *The Tragedy of Greece* (London: Kegan Paul, Trench, Trubner & Co., 1928), p. 4.

13. King Constantine I to Kaiser Wilhelm II, 2 August 1914, in *ibid.,* p. 5.

14. G. F. Abbott, *Greece and the Allies, 1914–1922* (London: Methuen & Co., 1922), p. 9.

15. Prince Nicholas, *Fifty Years,* pp. 259–60.

16. Queen Marie, *My Life,* vol. II, p. 341.

17. *Ibid.*

18. *Ibid.,* p. 349.

19. *Ibid.,* p. 353.

20. Lincoln, *Romanovs,* p. 685.

21. Bernard Pares, *My Russian Memoirs* (New York: AMS Press, 1969 [1931]), p. 355.

22. Salisbury, *Black Night,* p. 269.

23. De Schelking, *Suicide of Monarchy,* p. 118.

24. Diary entry of 24 July 1915 in Maurice Paléologue, *An Ambassador's Memoirs,* vol. II (London: Hutchinson & Co., 1927) pp. 35–36.

25. De Schelking, *Suicide of Monarchy,* p. 312.

26. Elsberry, *Marie of Romania,* p. 116.

27. *Ibid.,* p. 113.

28. Prince Nicholas of Greece, *Political Memoirs, 1914–1917: Pages from My Diary* (Freeport, NY: Books for Libraries Press, 1972 [1928]), p. 98.

29. Cosmetatos, *Tragedy of Greece,* pp. 118–19.

30. Aronson, *Crowns in Conflict,* p. 135.

31. Alexander S. Mitrakos, *France in Greece During World War I: A Study in the Politics of Power* (Boulder, CO: East European Monographs, 1982), p. ix.

32. Cosmetatos, *Tragedy of Greece,* p. 108.

33. Christos Theodolou, *Greece and the Entente: August 1, 1914–September 25, 1916* (Thessaloniki: Institute for Balkan Studies, 1971), p. 218.

34. Admiral Mark Kerr, *Land, Sea, and Air: The Reminiscences of Mark Kerr* (London: Longmans, Green & Co., 1927), p. 194.

35. *Ibid.,* pp. 194–95.

36. Prince Nicholas, *Political Memoirs,* p. 96.

37. Van der Kiste, *Kings of the Hellenes,* p. 99.

38. Daggett, *Marie of Roumania,* p. 221.

39. Queen Marie of Romania, *The Story of My Life.* Vol. III (London: Cassell & Co., 1935), p. 39.

40. Aronson, *Crowns in Conflict,* p. 131.

41. Elsberry, *Marie of Romania,* p. 118.

42. Queen Marie, *My Life,* vol. III, pp. 8, 10, and 11.

43. Daggett, *Marie of Roumania,* p. 224.

44. Van der Kiste, *Crowns in a Changing World,* pp. 118, 120.

45. Princess Marthe Bibesco, *Royal Portraits* (New York: D. Appleton & Co., 1928), p. 70.

EIGHTEEN: "HOLD MY HAND THAT I MAY HAVE COURAGE"

1. Tsarina Alexandra to the Rev. William Boyd Carpenter, Bishop of Ripon, 20 January/ 2 February 1915, Add. MSS 46721/246, The British Library.

2. Diary entry of 15 August 1915 in Paléologue, *Ambassador's Memoirs,* vol. II, p. 52.

3. Diary entry, 25 December 1915 in *ibid.,* p. 135.

4. Ethel Greening Pantazzi, *Roumania in Light and Shadow* (Toronto: The Ryerson Press, n.d.), p. 150.

5. Comte de Saint-Aulaire, *Confession d'un Vieux Diplomate* (Paris: Flammarion, 1953), p. 339.

6. Charles J. Vopicka, *Secrets of the Balkans: Seven Years of a Diplomatist's Life in the Storm Centre of Europe* (Chicago: Rand McNally & Co., 1921), p. 100.

7. Queen Marie, *My Life,* vol. III, p. 67.

8. Pakula, *Last Romantic,* p. 205.

9. Patanzzi, *Roumania,* p. 167.

10. Mrs. Will Gordon, *Roumania: Yesterday and To-Day* (London: John Lane Co., 1919), p. xxii.

11. Pantazzi, *Roumania,* p. 167.

12. R. Bruce Lockhart, *Giants Cast Long Shadows* (London: Putnam, 1960), p. 106.

13. Gordon, *Roumania,* pp. 179–81.

14. Viroubova, *Memories,* pp. 109–10.

15. *Ibid.,* p. 109.

16. *Ibid.,* p. 110.

17. Tsarina Alexandra to Tsar Nicholas II, 1 October 1915, in Joseph T. Fuhrmann, ed., *The Complete Wartime Correspondence of Tsar Nicholas II and the Empress Alexandra, April 1914–March 1917* (Westport, CT: Greenwood Press, 1999), no. 504, p. 257.

18. Tsarina Alexandra to Tsar Nicholas II, 17 November 1914, in *ibid.,* no. 57, p. 41.

19. Sir John Hanbury-Williams, *The Emperor Nicholas as I Knew Him* (London: Arthur L. Humphreys, 1922), p. 145.

20. Lieven, *Nicholas II,* p. 208.

21. Tsarina Alexandra to the Rev. William Boyd Carpenter, Bishop of Ripon, 20 January/ 2 February 1915, Add. MSS 46721/248, The British Library.

22. Tsarina Alexandra to Tsar Nicholas II, 15 September 1915, in Furhmann, ed., *Complete Wartime Correspondence,* no. 460, p. 228.

23. Note 219 in *ibid.,* no. 811, p. 384.

24. Tsar Nicholas II to Tsarina Alexandra, 6 February 1916, in *ibid.,* no. 811, p. 384.

25. Queen Marie, *My Life,* vol. III, p. 98.

26. Elsberry, *Marie of Romania,* p. 134.

27. Pantazzi, *Roumania,* p. 169.

28. Comte de Saint-Aulaire, *Confession,* p. 360.

29. Gordon, *Roumania,* pp. 152–53.

NINETEEN: NEUTRAL NORTH AND SOUTH

1. Francisco Romero, "Spain and the First World War," in Sebastian Balfour and Paul Preston, eds., *Spain and the Great Powers in the Twentieth Century* (New York: Routledge, 1999), pp. 32, 54.

2. Petrie, *King Alfonso XIII,* p. 122.

3. Charles Seymour, ed., *The Intimate Papers of Colonel House.* Vol. I: *Behind the Political Curtain, 1912–1915* (London: Ernest Benn, 1926), p. 417.

4. Princess Pilar and Chapman-Huston, *Don Alfonso XIII,* p. 160.

5. Sencourt, *Queen of Spain,* p. 243.

6. Van der Kiste, *Crowns in a Changing World,* pp. 111.

7. Arthur Rubinstein, *My Young Years* (New York: Alfred A. Knopf, 1973), p. 463.

8. *Ibid.,* p. 472.

9. *Ibid.,* p. 473.

10. Sir Maurice de Bunsen to Sir Edward Grey, 25 January 1910, Inclosure, Document 46 in Annual Report on Spain for the Year 1909, in *BDFA,* Part I, Series F, vol. 28, Document 45, p. 111. (80,000 L is the old way of writing £ 80,000.)

11. Princess Pilar and Chapman-Huston, *Don Alfonso XIII,* p. 190.

12. Infanta Eulalia, *Memoirs,* p. 220.

13. Petrie, *King Alfonso XIII,* p. 125.

14. Van der Kiste, *Edward VII's Children,* p. 142.

15. *Ibid.,* p. 140.

16. Marlene A. Eilers, *Queen Victoria's Descendants* (Falköping, Sweden: Rosvall Books, 1997), p. 87.

17. Noel, *Ena,* p. 167.
18. Ferrer, *Victoria Eugenia,* p. 164.
19. Graham, *Queen of Spain,* pp. 231, 245.
20. Romero, "Spain and the First World War," in Balfour and Preston, eds., *Spain and the Great Powers,* p. 39.

TWENTY: BELEAGUERED AND BETRAYED

1. Crown Princess Margrethe of Sweden to Lady Edward Cecil, 23 November 1915, MSS C630/4, Bodleian Library, University of Oxford.
2. Margrete, Landgravine of Hesse, to Hilda Cochrane, 30 December 1915, MSS 364/145, Bodleian Library, University of Oxford.
3. Tsarina Alexandra to Tsar Nicholas II, 3 April 1916, in Fuhrmann, ed., *Complete Wartime Correspondence,* no. 928, p. 434.
4. Tsarina Alexandra to Tsar Nicholas II, 9 June 1916, in *ibid.,* no. 1119, p. 498.
5. Tsarina Alexandra to Tsar Nicholas II, 22 September 1916, in *ibid.,* no. 1439, p. 600.
6. Prince Nicholas, *Political Memoirs,* p. 136.
7. Grand Duchess George, *Romanov Diary,* p. 198.
8. Tsarina Alexandra to Tsar Nicholas II, 15 July 1916, in Fuhrmann, ed., *Complete Wartime Correspondence,* no. 1242, p. 535.
9. King Constantine II to Paola, Princess of Saxe-Weimar, 17 February 1916, in Paola, *A King's Private Letters,* p. 173.
10. Tsarina Alexandra to Tsar Nicholas II, 28 August 1915, in Fuhrmann, ed., *Complete Wartime Correspondence,* no. 409, pp. 189–90.
11. Edmund A. Walsh, *The Fall of the Russian Empire* (Boston: Little, Brown, 1928), p. 117.
12. King, *Last Empress,* p. 245.
13. Lieven, *Nicholas II,* p. 228.
14. *The Times,* 13 October 1914.
15. Diary entry of 7 January 1915 in Paléologue, *Ambassador's Memoirs,* vol. I, pp. 238–39.
16. Grand Duke Alexander, *Once a Grand Duke,* p. 271.
17. Tsarina Alexandra to Tsar Nicholas II, 20 September 1916, in Fuhrmann, ed., *Complete Wartime Correspondence,* no. 1430, p. 592.
18. Sir George Buchanan, *My Mission to Russia and Other Diplomatic Memories.* Vol. II (Boston: Little, Brown, 1923), p. 77.
19. Florence Farmborough, *With the Armies of the Tsar: A Nurse at the Russian Front, 1914–18* (New York: Stein & Day, 1975), p. 233.
20. Diary entry of 22 December 1916 in Maurice Paléologue, *An Ambassador's Memoirs.* Vol. III (London: Hutchinson & Co., 1927), p. 121.
21. Tsarina Alexandra to Tsar Nicholas II, 4 December 1916, in Radziwill, *Nicholas,* p. 182.
22. Queen Victoria to Princess Victoria of Hesse, 26 April 1884, in Hough, ed., *Advice to My Grand-Daughter,* p. 65.
23. Gordon, *Roumania,* p. xx.
24. Vopicka, *Secret of the Balkans,* p. 317.
25. Gordon, *Roumania,* p. xix.
26. Tsarina Alexandra to Tsar Nicholas II, 17 March 1916 in Fuhrmann, ed., *Complete Wartime Correspondence,* no. 892, p. 421.

27. Tsarina Alexandra to Tsar Nicholas II, 22 August 1915 in Fuhrmann, ed., *Complete Wartime Correspondence,* no. 383, p. 171.

28. Tsarina Alexandra to Tsar Nicholas II, 31 October 1916, in *ibid.,* no. 1538, p. 634.

29. Quoted in Kokovtsov, *Out of My Past,* pp. 434–35.

30. Buchanan, *My Mission,* vol. II, p. 31.

31. Lieven, *Nicholas II,* p. 232.

32. Lincoln, *Romanovs,* p. 664.

33. Tsarina Alexandra to the Rev. William Boyd Carpenter, Bishop of Ripon, 29 December 1902/11 January 1903, Add. MSS 46721/236, The British Library.

34. Almedingen, *Empress Alexandra,* p. 73.

35. Tsarina Alexandra to Tsar Nicholas II, 5 March 1916, in Fuhrmann, ed., *Complete Wartime Correspondence,* no. 849, p. 398.

36. E. F. Benson, *As We Were: A Victorian Peep-Show* (London: Longmans, Green & Co., 1932), pp. 27–28.

37. Buchanan, *My Mission,* vol. II, p. 3.

38. Mossolov, *Court of the Last Tsar,* p. 174.

39. Tsarina Alexandra to Tsar Nicholas II, 13 December 1916, in Maylunas and Mironenko, eds., *Lifelong Passion,* p. 490.

40. Grand Duke Alexander, *Once a Grand Duke,* p. 275.

41. Narishkin-Kurakin, *Under Three Tsars,* pp. 201–02.

42. Queen Marie to Mr. Barron, 8 September 1929, George Duca Papers, Hoover Institution, Stanford University.

43. King George V to Sir Edward Grey, 4 September 1916, in Nicolson, *King George,* p. 282.

44. Sir Francis Elliot to Sir Edward Grey, 17 September 1916, P.R.O., F.O. 286/586/No. 1384, The National Archives.

45. Sir Francis Elliot to Sir Edward Grey, British Foreign Secretary, 1 October 1916, P.R.O., F.O. 286/586/No. 1467, The National Archives.

46. Christos Theodolu, *Greece and the Entente: August 1, 1914–September 25, 1916* (Thessaloniki: Institute for Balkan Studies, 1971), p. 270.

47. Tsarina Alexandra to Tsar Nicholas II, 24 September 1916, in Fuhrmann, ed., *Complete Wartime Correspondence,* no. 1447, p. 603.

48. Tsarina Alexandra to Tsar Nicholas II, 27 September 1916, in *ibid.,* no. 1461, p. 610.

49. Paxton Hibben, *Constantine I and the Greek People* (New York: The Century Co., 1920), pp. 470–71.

50. King Constantine I to King George V, private telegram, 11 December 1916, P.R.O., F.O. 286/587/No. 1477, The National Archives.

51. Queen Sophie to Kaiser Wilhelm II, 23 November/6 December 1916 in *The Greek White Book: Supplementary Diplomatic Documents 1913–1917* (New York: Oxford University Press, 1919), no. 62.

52. Queen Sophie to Kaiser Wilhelm II, 18/31 December 1916, in *ibid.,* no. 73.

53. Queen Sophie to Nicholas Theotokis, 20 December 1916/2 January 1917, in *ibid.,* no. 75.

54. Queen Sophie to Kaiser Wilhelm II, 27 December/9 January 1917, in *ibid.,* no. 77.

55. Abbott, *Greece and the Allies,* p. 174.

56. Margrete, Landgravine of Hesse, to Hilda Cochrane, 2 December 1916, MSS 364/151, Bodleian Library, University of Oxford.

57. Abbott, *Greece and the Allies,* p. 173.

58. Prince Nicholas, *Political Memoirs,* pp. 263–64.

59. Grand Duchess George, *Romanov Diary,* pp. 199, 201.
60. Abbott, *Greece and the Allies,* p. 176.
61. Cosmetatos, *Tragedy of Greece,* p. 128.
62. Hardinge, *Old Diplomacy,* p. 204.
63. Compton Mackenzie, *First Athenian Memories* (London: Cassell & Co., 1931), p. 261.
64. Sir Francis Elliot to Arthur Balfour, British Foreign Office, 25 December 1916, P.R.O., F.O. 286/587/No. 2120, The National Archives.
65. Hibben, *Constantine I,* p. 521.
66. Hugo Mager, *Elizabeth, Grand Duchess of Russia* (New York: Carroll & Graf, 1998), pp. 302–03.
67. King, *Man Who Killed Rasputin,* p. 157.
68. *Ibid.,* p. 158.
69. Queen Marie, *My Life,* vol. III, p. 117.

TWENTY-ONE: THE ABYSS

1. Sir John Hanbury-Williams, *The Emperor Nicholas II as I Knew Him* (London: Arthur L. Humphreys, 1922), p. 139.
2. *Ibid.,* p. 133.
3. Sir Bernard Pares, *Fall of the Russian Monarchy: A Study of the Evidence* (New York: Random House, 1961), p. 399.
4. Gilliard, *Thirteen Years,* p. 182.
5. Viroubova, *Memories,* p. 182.
6. Grand Duke Alexander, *Once a Grand Duke,* p. 278.
7. Michael Harmer, *The Forgotten Hospital: An Essay* (Chichester, Sussex: Chichester Press, 1982), p. 117.
8. Botkin, *Real Romanovs,* p. 127.
9. Gilliard, *Thirteen Years,* p. 183.
10. Grand Duchess Marie, *Education of a Princess: A Memoir* (New York: Blue Ribbon Books, Inc., 1930), p. 271.
11. Botkin, *Real Romanovs,* pp. 127–28.
12. Grand Duke Alexander, *Once a Grand Duke,* p. 279.
13. Princess Paley, *Memories of Russia, 1916–1919* (London: Herbert Jenkins, 1924), p. 38.
14. Meriel Buchanan, *The City of Trouble* (New York: Charles Scribner's Sons, 1918), p. 79.
15. Diary entry of 11 February 1917 in Paléologue, *Ambassador's Memoirs,* vol. III, p. 191.
16. Cosmetatos, *Tragedy of Greece,* p. 262.
17. *Ibid.*
18. Lee, *Helen,* p. 54.
19. Pares, *My Russian Memoirs,* p. 361.
20. Lincoln, *The Romanovs,* pp. 722–23.
21. *Ibid.,* p. 723.
22. Diary entry of 1–14 March 1917, in Queen Marie, *My Life,* vol. III, pp. 150–51.
23. Diary entry of 17/30 January 1917, in *ibid.,* p. 129.
24. Diary entry of 23 January/5 February 1917, in *ibid.,* pp. 134–35.
25. Diary entry of 16 February/1 March 1917, in *ibid.,* p. 147.
26. Mark Axworthy, "Through British Eyes: Romanian Military Performance in World War I," in Kurt W. Treptow, ed., *Romania During the World War I Era* (Iaşi: The Center for Romanian Studies, 1999), p. 123.

27. Gordon, *Roumania,* pp. xxxi–ii.
28. Longford, *Queen Victoria,* p. 554.
29. Tsarina Alexandra to Tsar Nicholas II, 2 March 1917, in Mark D. Steinberg and Vladimir M. Khrustalëv, eds., *The Fall of the Romanovs: Political Dreams and Personal Struggles in a Time of Revolution* (New Haven, CT: Yale University Press, 1995), pp. 93–95. Alexandra's punctuation here, as in many of her letters, is littered with mistakes.
30. Dehn, *Real Tsaritsa,* p. 165 ("The poor one . . . all by himself . . . oh my God, why has it happened! And I was not there to console him").
31. Ex-Tsarina Alexandra to ex-Tsar Nicholas II, 3 March 1917 in Fuhrmann, ed., *Complete Wartime Correspondence,* no. 1688, pp. 701–02.
32. Viroubova, *Memories,* p. 210.
33. Queen Marie, *My Life,* vol. III, pp. 151–52.
34. Botkin, *Real Romanovs,* p. 141.
35. Dehn, *Real Tsaritsa,* p. 186.

TWENTY-TWO: DEATH AT EKATERINBURG

1. Buxhoeveden, *Alexandra Feodorovna,* p. 263.
2. Dehn, *Real Tsaritsa,* pp. 190–91.
3. Margrete, Landgravine of Hesse, to Hilda Cochrane, 29 May 1917, MSS 364/155, Bodleian Library, University of Oxford.
4. Sir Francis Elliot to Mr. Balfour, 8 April 1917, P.R.O., F.O. 286/602/783, The National Archives.
5. Sir Francis Elliot to Mr. Balfour, 18 April 1917, P.R.O., F.O. 286/602/862, The National Archives.
6. Sir Francis Elliot to Mr. Balfour, 7 May 1917, P.R.O., F.O. 286/602/No. 1013, The National Archives.
7. Lee, *Helen,* p. 56.
8. *Ibid.,* p. 58.
9. Prince Nicholas, *Fifty Years,* p. 271.
10. Abbott, *Greece and the Allies,* p. 196.
11. *Ibid.*
12. Prince Nicholas, *Fifty Years,* p. 272.
13. *Ibid.,* pp. 272–73.
14. Abbott, *Greece and the Allies,* p. 197.
15. Prince Christopher, *Memoirs,* p. 144.
16. Prince Nicholas, *Fifty Years,* p. 275.
17. Prince Christopher, *Memoirs,* p. 144.
18. Prince Nicholas, *Fifty Years,* p. 275.
19. *Ibid.,* p. 277.
20. Abbott, *Greece and the Allies,* p. 220.
21. Sir Francis Elliot to Arthur Balfour, 16 June 1917, P.R.O., F.O. 286/670/31099, The National Archives.
22. David Dutton, "The Deposition of King Constantine of Greece, June 1917: An Episode in Anglo-French Diplomacy," *Canadian Journal of History,* vol. 12, no. 4 (1977), p. 411.
23. Léon Maccas, *Constantin Ier, Roi des Hellènes* (Paris: Editions Bossard, 1917), p. 79.
24. Kerr, *Land, Sea, and Air,* p. 196.

25. Princess Paley, *Memories,* p. 87.
26. Buxhoeveden, *Alexandra Feodorvna,* p. 301.
27. Count Paul Benckendorff, *Last Days at Tsarskoe Selo: Being the Personal Notes and Memories of Count Paul Benckendorff,* trans. Maurice Baring (London: William Heinemann, 1927), p. 76.
28. Buxhoeveden, *Alexandra Feodorovna,* p. 282.
29. Alexandra Feodorovna to Aleksandr Syroboiarsky, 29 May 1917, in Steinberg and Khrustalëv, eds., *Fall of the Romanovs,* pp. 150–52.
30. Benckendorff, *Last Days,* p. 108.
31. Viroubova, *Memories,* p. 298.
32. *Ibid.,* pp. 305, 318.
33. Botkin, *Real Romanovs,* p. 165.
34. *Ibid.,* p. 166.
35. *Ibid.,* p. 173.
36. Bergamini, *Tragic Dynasty,* p. 455.
37. Viroubova, *Memories,* pp. 334–35.
38. Gilliard, *Thirteen Years,* p. 257.
39. Buxhoeveden, *Alexandra Feodorovna,* p. 327.
40. *Ibid.,* p. 329.
41. Frances Welch, *The Romanovs & Mr. Gibbes: The Story of the Englishman Who Taught the Children of the Last Tsar* (London: Short Books, 2002), p. 69.
42. Poliakoff, *Tragic Bride,* p. 278.
43. Diary of Archpriest Afanasy Beliaev, 2–31 March 1917, in Steinberg and Khrustalëv, eds., *Fall of the Romanovs,* p. 144.
44. The Examination of Anatoly Yakimov in Robert Wilton, *The Last Days of the Romanovs: From 15th March, 1917, Part I—The Narrative; Part II—The Depositions of Eye-Witnesses* (London: Thornton Butterworth, 1920), p. 275.
45. Paul Bulygin, "The Sorrowful Quest," in Bulygin, *The Murder of the Romanovs: The Authentic Account.* Including *The Road to the Tragedy* by Alexander Kerensky (Westport, CT: Hyperion Press, 1975 [1935]), p. 236.
46. Diary entry of Alexandra Feodorovna, 3/16 July 1918 in Vladimir A. Kozlov and Vladimir M. Khrustalëv, eds., *Last Diary of Tsaritsa Alexandra,* trans. Laura E. Wolfson (New Haven, CT: Yale University Press, 1997), p. 198.
47. Bulygin, "The Sorrowful Quest," in Bulygin, *Murder of the Romanovs,* p. 238.
48. Deposition of Philip Proskuriakov in Wilton, *Last Days,* p. 305.
49. Deposition of Pavel Medvedev in *ibid.,* p. 290.

TWENTY-THREE: *"MAMMA REGINA"*

1. Queen Marie, *My Life,* vol. III, pp. 394, 286.
2. *Ibid.,* p. 169.
3. Lady Kennard, *A Roumanian Diary 1915, 1916, 1917* (New York: Dodd, Mead & Co., 1918), p. 170.
4. Diary entry of 26 February 1917, in Paléologue, *Ambassador's Memoirs,* vol. III, p. 208.
5. Queen Marie, *My Life,* vol. III, p. 190.
6. *Ibid.,* p. 311.
7. Queen Marie, *My Country* (London: Hodder & Stoughton, 1916), p. 6.

8. Queen Marie, *My Life,* vol. III, p. 252.

9. *Ibid.,* p. 289.

10. Vopicka, *Secrets,* p. 152.

11. Queen Marie, *My Life,* vol. III, p. 336.

12. Pakula, *Last Romantic,* p. 235.

13. Queen Marie, *My Life,* vol. III, p. 341.

14. Pantazzi, *Roumania,* p. 264.

15. Pakula, *Last Romantic,* pp. 240, 242.

16. William Rodney, *Joe Boyle: King of the Klondike* (Toronto: McGraw-Hill Ryerson, 1974), p. 3.

17. Queen Marie, *My Life,* vol. III, pp. 369, 386.

18. Elseberry, *Marie of Romania,* p. 149.

19. Comte de Sainte-Aulaire, *Confession,* p. 451.

20. Queen Marie, *My Life,* vol. III, p. 414.

21. Rodney, *Joe Boyle,* p. 206.

22. *Ibid.,* p. 207.

23. Appendix 6: Queen Marie to Colonel Joseph Boyle, 29 October 1918, in Treptow, ed., *Romania,* p. 75.

24. Queen Marie, *My Life,* vol. III, p. 429.

25. *Ibid.,* pp. 433–34.

26. Interview with King Michael I of Romania, 26 September 2000, Versoix, Switzerland.

27. Nicolson, *King George,* p. 335.

28. *The Family Herald,* 2 March 1903, p. 471.

29. Dagget, *Marie,* pp. 268–69.

30. *Ibid.,* p. 270.

31. Diana Fotescu, "Regina Maria şi războiul de întregire naţională," in Treptow, ed., *Romania,* p. 62.

32. Rodney, *Joe Boyle,* 233.

33. *Ibid.,* p. 234.

34. Edith Bolling Wilson, *My Memoir* (Indianapolis: Bobbs Merrill Co., 1939), p. 298.

35. Dagget, *Marie,* pp. 264, 275.

36. Grand Duchess Marie, *Princess in Exile* (New York: Viking Press, 1932), p. 16.

37. Kjellberg, *Dronning Maud,* p. 65.

38. Van der Kiste, *Crowns in a Changing World,* p. 134.

39. *Ibid.,* p. 139.

40. Van der Kiste, *Edward VII's Children,* p. 145.

41. Van der Kiste, *Crowns in a Changing World,* p. 142.

42. Van der Kiste, *Edward VII's Children,* p. 147.

43. Wilson, *My Memoir,* pp. 194–95.

44. Leonard W. Taylor, *The Sourdough and the Queen: The Many Lives of Klondike Joe Boyle* (Toronto: Methuen, 1983), p. 320.

45. Prince Paul of Hohenzollern-Roumania, *King Carol II: A Life of My Grandfather* (London: Methuen, 1988), p. 50.

46. Frank Rattigan to Earl Curzon, August 15, 1919, Document No. 110 in E. L. Woodward and Rohan Butler, eds., *Documents on British Foreign Policy, First Series.* Vol. VI: *1919* (London: HMSO, 1956), pp. 149, 151.

47. Rodney, *Joe Boyle,* pp. 264, 261.

48. Queen Marie to Loie Fuller, 15 December 1919, MSS 1982-04-40, Maryhill Museum of Art, Goldendale, Washington.

PART IV

TWENTY-FOUR: CAPITULATION AGAIN

1. Beverley Nichols, *25: Being a Young Man's Candid Recollections of His Elders and Betters* (London: Jonathan Cape, 1926), p. 137.
2. Prince Christopher, *Memoirs,* p. 153.
3. *Ibid.*
4. Interview with Crown Prince Alexander of Yugoslavia, 1 May 2001, London.
5. Prince Christopher, *Memoirs,* p. 154.
6. Prince Nicholas, *Fifty Years,* p. 287.
7. Margrete, Landgravine of Hesse, to Hilda Cochrane, 6 December 1920, MSS 364/164, Bodleian Library, University of Oxford.
8. Interview with Lady Katherine Brandram, 2 May 2001, Marlow, Bucks.
9. Van Der Kiste, *Crowns in a Changing World,* p. 143.
10. Queen Victoria Eugenie to Sir Esme Howard, 8 November 1921, DHW8/11, Sir Esme Howard Papers, Cumbria Record Office, Carlisle.
11. *The Times,* 22 November 1920.
12. Prince Nicholas, *Fifty Years,* p. 291.
13. Bert Birtles, *Exiles in the Aegean: A Personal Narrative of Greek Politics and Travel* (London: Victor Gollancz, 1938), p. 67.
14. Abbott, *Greece and the Allies,* p. 228.
15. Grand Duchess George of Russia (née Princess Marie of Greece) to Miss Barratt, undated, private collection.
16. Prince Christopher, *Memoirs,* p. 172.
17. Lee, *Helen,* p. 74.
18. Elsberry, *Marie of Romania,* p. 169.
19. Margrete, Landgravine of Hesse, to Hilda Cochrane, 3 March 1921, MSS 364/167, Bodleian Library, University of Oxford.
20. Earl Curzon to Earl Granville, 18 December 1920, in Rohan Butler and J. P. T. Bury, eds., *Documents on British Foreign Policy, 1919–1939,* First Series, Vol. XII (London: HMSO, 1962), no. 482, p. 546.
21. Queen Marie to Loie Fuller, 23 March 1921, MSS 1982.04.43, Maryhill Museum of Art, Goldendale, Washington.
22. Nicholas, *25,* p. 116.
23. Abbott, *Greece and the Allies,* p. 228.
24. Margaret Macmillan, *Paris 1919: Six Months That Changed the World* (New York: Random House, 2002), p. 434.
25. Arthur Gould Lee, *The Royal House of Greece* (London: Ward Lock, 1948), p. 54.
26. Kerr, *Land, Sea, and Air,* p. 196.
27. Van der Kiste, *Crowns in a Changing World,* p. 151.
28. Margrete, Landgravine of Hesse, to Hilda Cochrane, 28 May 1922, MSS 364/188, Bodleian Library, University of Oxford.
29. Mrs. Philip Martineau, *Roumania and Her Rulers* (London: Stanley Paul & Co., 1927), pp. 188–89.

30. Infanta Eulalia, *Courts and Countries After the War* (New York: Dodd, Mead & Co., 1925), p. 237.
31. Martineau, *Roumania,* pp. 190–91.
32. Prince Christopher, *Memoirs,* p. 173.
33. Abbott, *Greece and the Allies,* p. 285.
34. Michael Llewellyn Smith, *Ionian Vision: Greece in Asia Minor, 1919–1922* (New York: St. Martin's Press, 1973), p. 316, n. 7.
35. *The Times,* 30 September 1922.
36. Stella King, *Princess Marina: Her Life and Times* (London: Cassell, 1969), pp. 87–88.

TWENTY-FIVE: "TOO SAD"

1. Margrete, Landgravine of Hesse, to Hilda Cochrane, 19 December 1922, MSS 364/196, Bodleian Library, University of Oxford.
2. Paul of Hohenzollern-Roumania, *King Carol II,* p. 80.
3. *The Times,* 15 January 1923.
4. Infanta Eulalia, *Courts and Countries,* p. 236.
5. Elseberry, *Marie of Romania,* p. 183.
6. Daggett, *Marie of Romania,* pp. 294–95.
7. Princess Ileana, *I Live Again* (New York: Rinehart & Co., 1951), p. 24.
8. Queen Marie to Loie Fuller, 16 January 1922, MSS 1982.04.48, Maryhill Museum of Art, Goldendale, Washington.
9. Pakula, *Last Romantic,* p. 317.
10. Prince Christopher, *Memoirs,* p. 192.
11. C. H. Bentinck to Marquess Curzon of Kedleston, 5 December 1923, P.R.O., F.O. 286/862/ No. 962, The National Archives.
12. Sir John W. Wheeler-Bennett, *King George VI: His Life and Reign* (London: Macmillan, 1965), p. 194.
13. Nichols, *25,* p. 114.
14. *Ibid.,* p. 115.
15. *Ibid.,* p. 116.
16. *Ibid.,* p. 117.
17. *Ibid.,* p. 118.
18. *Ibid.,* p. 135.
19. *Ibid.,* pp. 118, 114.
20. Queen Marie to Loie Fuller, 24 May 1921, MSS 1982.04.44, Maryhill Museum of Art, Goldendale, Washington.
21. Elsberry, *Marie of Romania,* p. 174.
22. Rodney, *Joe Boyle,* p. 305.
23. Elsberry, *Marie of Romania,* p. 187.

TWENTY-SIX: "I WOULD *NEVER* LEAVE ENGLAND"

1. Infanta Eulalia, *Memoirs,* p. 231.
2. Ismael Saz, "Foreign Policy Under the Dictatorship of Primo de Rivera," in Balfour and Paul Preston, eds., *Spain and the Great Powers,* p. 53.
3. Santos, *Victoria Eugenia,* p. 269.
4. *Ibid.,* p. 298.

5. Noel, *Ena,* p. 195.

6. Santos, *Victoria Eugenia,* p. 298.

7. Sir Horace Rumbold to Sir Austen Chamberlain, 30 January 1925, in Christopher Seton-Watson, Kenneth Bourne, and Donald Cameron Watt, eds., *British Documents on Foreign Affairs,* Part II, Series F, *Europe, 1919–1939.* Vol. 25: *Spain, March 1919–June 1931,* ed. Antony Adamthwaite (Frederick, MD: University Publications of America, 1990), Document 76, pp. 149–50.

8. Noel, *Ena,* p. 172.

9. Margrete, Landgravine of Hesse, to Hilda Cochrane, 11 October 1924, MSS 364/215, Bodleian Library, University of Oxford.

10. Martineau, *Roumania,* p. 196.

11. Wheeler-Bennett, *King George VI,* p. 194.

12. Interview with Lady Katherine Brandram, 2 May 2001, Marlow, Bucks.

13. Van der Kiste, *Crowns in a Changing World,* p. 173.

14. Queen Sophie to the Rev. R. W. Cole, 14 August 1928, MSS 8783/1, University of Cambridge.

15. Queen Sophie to the Rev. R. W. Cole, 1 September 1928, MSS 8783/2, University of Cambridge.

16. Queen Sophie to the Rev. R. W. Cole, 12 October 1928, MSS 8783/3, University of Cambridge.

17. Queen Sophie to the Rev. R. W. Cole, 22 March 1929, MSS 8783/5, University of Cambridge.

18. Queen Sophie to the Rev. R. W. Cole, 1 August 1931, MSS 8783/16, University of Cambridge.

19. Pakula, *Last Romantic,* p. 334.

20. Elsberry, *Marie of Romania,* p. 190.

21. Paul of Hohenzollern-Roumania, *King Carol II,* pp. 94, 93.

22. *Ibid.,* p. 97.

23. *Ibid.,* pp. 97–98.

24. Queen Marie to Prince Nicholas of Romania, 4 January 1926, Queen Marie of Romania Papers, Kent State University.

25. Paul of Hohenzollern-Roumania, *King Carol II,* p. 104.

26. Adrian-Silvan Ionescu, ed., *America Seen by a Queen: Queen Marie's Diary of Her 1926 Voyage to the United States of America* (Bucharest: Romanian Cultural Foundation, 1999), pp. 35, 37.

27. *Ibid.,* p. 40.

28. Constance Lily Morris, *On Tour with Queen Marie* (New York: Robert M. McBride & Co., 1927), pp. 43–44.

29. Ionescu, ed., *America Seen by a Queen,* pp. 169, 177.

30. *Ibid.,* pp. 95–96.

31. John E. Tuhy, *Sam Hill: The Prince of Castle Nowhere* (Goldendale, WA: Maryhill Museum of Art, 1992), p. 244.

32. *Ibid.,* p. 245.

33. Queen Marie to Loie Fuller, 3 July 1927, MSS 1982-04-60, Maryhill Museum of Art.

34. Queen Marie to Mr. Barron, 20 October 1927, George Duca Papers, Hoover Institution, Stanford University.

35. Martineau, *Roumania,* p. 201.

36. Queen Marie to Mr. Barron, 20 October 1927, George Duca Papers, Hoover Institution, Stanford University.
37. Elsberry, *Marie of Romania,* p. 234.
38. Interview with King Michael I of Romania, 26 September 2000, Versoix, Switzerland.
39. Queen Sophie to the Rev. R. W. Cole, 1 September 1928, MSS 8783/3, University of Cambridge.
40. Queen Sophie to the Rev. R. W. Cole, 12 October 1928, MSS 8783/3, University of Cambridge.
41. Queen Sophie to the Rev. R. W. Cole, 1 September 1928, MSS 8783/2, University of Cambridge.

TWENTY-SEVEN: "I THOUGHT I HAD DONE WELL"

1. R. G. Howe to Sir Arthur Henderson, 21 October 1929, *British Documents on Foreign Affairs,* Part II, Series F, *Europe, 1919–1939.* Vol. 8: *Italy and South-Eastern Europe, January 1929–June 1931,* Document 84, pp. 118–19.
2. Lee, *Helen,* p. 135.
3. Elsberry, *Marie,* p. 232.
4. Queen Sophie to the Rev. R. W. Cole, 15 July 1930, MSS 8783/12, University of Cambridge.
5. Lee, *Helen,* p. 145.
6. Michael Palairet to Arthur Henderson, 3 December 1930, *BDFA,* Part II, Series F, vol. 8, Document 231, p. 325.
7. Noel, *Ena,* p. 198.
8. *Ibid.,* p. 205.
9. Kjellberg, *Dronning Maud,* p. 54.
10. Noel, *Ena,* p. 216. According to Noel, the king "knew nothing" of Sánchez Guerra's plan. *Ibid.*
11. Rafael Borràs Betriu, *Cambio de Régimen: Caída de lea Monarquía y Proclamación de la República* (Barcelona: Flor del Viento Ediciones, 2001), p. 169.
12. Pilapil, *Alfonso XIII,* p. 179.
13. Sir George Grahame to Arthur Henderson, 19 February 1931, *BDFA,* Part II, Series F, vol. 25, Document 105, p. 205.
14. María Teresa Puga, *La Vida y la Época de Alfonso XIII* (Barcelona: Editorial Planeta, 1999), p. 160.
15. Pilapil, *Alfonso XIII,* p. 187.
16. *Daily Mail,* 13 April 1931.
17. *New York Times,* 14 April 1931.
18. *The Times,* 16 April 1931.
19. Emilio Mola Vidal, *Memorias* (Barcelona: Editorial Planeta, 1977), p. 25.
20. *New York Times,* 16 April 1931.
21. Margrete, Landgravine of Hesse, to Hilda Cochrane, 10 May 1931, MSS 365/76, Bodleian Library, University of Oxford.
22. Santos, *Victoria Eugenia,* p. 281.
23. Ferer, *Victoria Eugenia,* p. 196.
24. Santos, *Victoria Eugenia,* p. 285.
25. Pilapil, *Alfonso XIII,* pp. 195–96.
26. Sencourt, *Spanish Crown,* p. 369.

27. *New York Times,* 16 April 1931.
28. Claude G. Bowers, *My Mission to Spain: Watching the Rehearsal for World War II* (New York: Simon & Schuster, 1954), p. 220.
29. *New York Times,* 16 April 1931.
30. *Ibid.*
31. Pedro Sainz Rodríguez, *Testimonio y Recuerdos* (Barcelona: Editorial Planeta, 1978), p. 12.
32. Eugenio Vegas Latapie, *Memorias Políticas: El Suicidio de la Monarquía y la Segunda República* (Barcelona: Editorial Planeta, 1983), p. 265.

TWENTY-EIGHT: "THE GOD WITHIN US"

1. Grand Duke Alexander, *Twilight of Royalty* (New York: Ray Long & Richard R. Smith, 1932), p. 21.
2. *Ibid.,* p. 23.
3. Noel, *Ena,* p. 240.
4. Michael Palairet to Sir John Simon, 16 November 1931, in *BDFA,* vol. 8, Document 43.
5. Queen Marie to Loie Fuller, 8 March 1926, MSS 1982-04-54, Maryhill Museum of Art, Goldendale, Washington.
6. Queen Marie to Loie Fuller, 15 March 1927, MSS 1982-04-59, Maryhill Museum of Art, Goldendale, Washington.
7. Morris, *On Tour,* p. 71.
8. Diary entry of Queen Marie, 24 October 1926, in Ionescu, ed., *America Seen by a Queen,* p. 69.
9. Queen Sophie to the Rev. R. W. Cole, undated, 1929, MSS 8783/6, University of Cambridge.
10. Queen Sophie to the Rev. R. W. Cole, 3 January 1930, MSS 8783/10, University of Cambridge.
11. Queen Sophie to the Rev. R. W. Cole, 1 September 1928, Add. MSS 8783/2, University of Cambridge.
12. Queen Sophie to the Rev. R. W. Cole, 3 January 1930, MSS 8783/10, University of Cambridge.
13. Queen Sophie to the Rev. R. W. Cole, 12 October 1928, MSS 8783/3, University of Cambridge.
14. Queen Sophie to the Rev. R. W. Cole, 1 September 1928, MSS 8783/2; 22 March 1929, MSS 8783/5; and undated, 1929, MSS 8783/6, University of Cambridge.
15. Margery Bennett to the Rev. R. W. Cole, undated, MSS 8783/13, University of Cambridge.
16. Queen Sophie to the Rev. R. W. Cole, 13 April 1930, MSS 8783/11, University of Cambridge.
17. Queen Sophie to the Rev. R. W. Cole, 31 March 1931, MSS 8783/15, University of Cambridge.
18. Longford, *Queen Victoria,* p. 419.
19. Della L. Marcus, *Her Eternal Crown: Queen Marie of Romania and the Bahá'í Faith* (Oxford: George Ronald, 2000), p. 54.
20. Fotescu, ed., *Americans and Queen Marie,* p. 92.
21. Elsberry, *Marie of Romania,* p. 241.
22. Queen Marie to Lavinia Small, 24 August 1933, Hoover Institution, Stanford University.
23. Fotescu, ed., *Americans and Queen Marie,* p. 92.
24. Van der Kiste, *Crowns in a Changing World,* pp. 177–78.

25. *Ibid.,* p. 178.
26. Beverly Nichols, *All I Could Ever Be: Some Recollections* (London: Jonathan Cape, 1949), p. 259.
27. Queen Marie to Georges Duca, 25 October 1933, Hoover Institution, Stanford University.
28. Queen Marie to Lavinia Small, 19 June 1933, Hoover Institution, Stanford University.
29. Fotescu, ed., *Americans and Queen Marie,* p. 104.
30. *Ibid.,* p. 105.
31. Marcus, *Her Eternal Crown,* p. 233.
32. Fotescu, ed., *Americans and Queen Marie,* p. 108.

TWENTY-NINE: "I BLESS YOU WITH MY LAST BREATH"

1. Queen Marie to Lavinia Small, 2 April 1934, Hoover Institution, Stanford University.
2. *Ibid.*
3. Princess Ileana, *I Live Again,* p. 41.
4. Fotescu, ed., *Americans and Queen Marie,* p. 109.
5. *Ibid.,* pp. 111–13.
6. Van der Kiste, *Edward VII's Children,* p. 171.
7. Rose, *George V,* p. 293.
8. Van der Kiste, *Crowns in a Changing World,* p. 174.
9. Kaiser Wilhelm II to Poultney Bigelow, Poultney Bigelow Papers, New York Public Library.
10. Prince Christopher, *Memoirs,* p. 260.
11. Margrete, Landgravine of Hesse, to Hilda Cochrane, 24 May 1926, MSS 365/23, University of Cambridge.
12. Queen Sophie to the Rev. R. W. Cole, 22 March 1929, MSS 8783/5, University of Cambridge.
13. Queen Sophie to the Rev. R. W. Cole, 15 July 1930, MSS 8783/12, University of Cambridge.
14. Queen Alexandra of Yugoslavia, *For Love of a King* (Garden City, NY: Doubleday & Co., 1956), pp. 21, 27.
15. *Ibid.,* p. 21.
16. Interview with Lady Katherine Brandram, 2 May 2001, Marlow, Bucks.
17. Queen Sophie to the Rev. R. W. Cole, 28 December 1929, MSS 8783/8; 15 July 1930, MSS 8783/12, University of Cambridge.
18. Queen Sophie to the Rev. R. W. Cole, 12 October 1928, MSS 8783/3; 16 December 1930, MSS 8783/14, University of Cambridge.
19. Margrete, Landgravine of Hesse, to Hilda Cochrane, 17 December 1931, MSS 365/82, Bodleian Library, University of Oxford.
20. *Ibid.*
21. Margrete, Landgravine of Hesse, to Hilda Cochrane, 23 February 1932, MSS 365/88; 20 December 1932, MSS 365/94–95; and 17 November 1935, MSS 365/140, Bodleian Library, University of Oxford.
22. Eulalia, *Courts and Countries,* p. 240.
23. Interview with Lady Katherine Brandram, 2 May 2001, Marlow, Bucks.
24. Princess Irene of Greece to Irina Procopiu, 21 March 1932, Hoover Institution, Stanford University.
25. Fotescu, ed., *Americans and Queen Marie,* pp. 96–97.
26. *Ibid.,* p. 130.
27. *Ibid.,* pp. 117–18.

28. Interview with King Michael I of Romania, 26 September 2000, Versoix, Switzerland.

29. Queen Marie to Baroness Ines Taxis Damenstofft, 20 March 1936, Folder 70017-10.V, Hoover Institution, Stanford University.

30. *Ibid.*

31. Van der Kiste, *Edward VII's Children,* p. 175.

32. Fotescu, ed., *Americans and Queen Marie,* pp. 128, 130.

33. Queen Marie to Baroness Ines Taxis Damesnstofft, 20 March 1936, Folder 70017-10.V, Hoover Institution, Stanford University.

34. Princess Ileana of Romania to Ray Baker Harris, 9 September 1938, Queen Marie of Romania Papers, Kent State University.

35. Fotescu, ed., *Americans and Queen Marie,* p. 125.

36. *Ibid.*

37. *Ibid.,* p. 122.

38. Aldo Castellani, *Of Microbes, Men and Monarchs: A Doctor's Life in Many Lands* (London: Victor Gollancz, 1960), pp. 122–23.

39. Fotescu, ed., *Americans and Queen Marie,* pp. 139–40.

40. *Ibid.,* p. 141.

41. Elsberry, *Marie,* p. 279.

42. Pakula, *Last Romantic,* p. 416. Pakula understands these letters written by Stirbey to mean "I love you my Marie, I love you."

43. *Ibid.*

44. Elsberry, *Marie of Romania,* p. 280.

45. Princess Ileana to Ray Baker Harris, 6 August 1938, Queen Marie of Romania Papers, Kent State University.

46. Lucian Boia, *History and Myth in Romanian Consciousness* (Budapest: Central European University Press, 2001), p. 208.

47. Queen Marie, "A Mon Pays et à Mon Peuple," Collections of the Manuscript Division, Library of Congress.

48. Møller, *Dronning Maud,* p. 130.

49. Van der Kiste, *Edward VII's Children,* p. 167.

50. *Ibid.,* p. 176.

51. *Ibid.*

52. Queen Maud to Grand Duchess Xenia, undated, private collection.

53. Queen Maud to Grand Duchess Xenia, undated, private collection.

54. *New York Times,* 21 November 1938.

55. *Ibid.*

56. Extracts from the House of Lords Debates, 22 November 1938, P.R.O., F.O. 372/3301, The National Archives.

57. King Haakon VII to Grand Duchess Xenia, 16 January 1939, private collection.

THIRTY: FROM EXILE TO *"VIVE LA REINA!"*

1. Van der Kiste, *Crowns in a Changing World,* p. 172.

2. Ferrer, *Victoria Eugenia,* p. 205.

3. Sir George Grahame to Sir Robert Vansittart, 4 October 1934, P.R.O., F.O. 120/61/34, The National Archives.

4. Draft Letter to His Eminence Cardinal Pacelli by Lord Howard of Penrith and Lady

Howard, 3 December 1934, DHW9/23/3, Sir Esme Howard Papers, Cumbria Record Office, Carlisle.

5. *Ibid.*

6. Queen Victoria Eugenie to Lord Howard of Penrith, 3 December 1934, DHW9/23/3, Sir Esme Howard Papers, Cumbria Record Office, Carlisle.

7. *New York Times,* 22 October 1936.

8. Alexander Hardinge to Air Vice-Marshall Sir Philip Game, Metropolitan Police Office, New Scotland Yard, 5 April 1938, P.R.O., MEPO 2/3290, The National Archives.

9. Queen Victoria Eugenie to Mr. Paget Cooke, 5 October 1938, private collection.

10. Julián Cortés-Cavanillas, *Alfonso XIII: Vida, Confesiones y Muerte* (Barcelona: Editorial Juventud, 1966), p. 361.

11. de la Cierva, *Alfonso y Victoria,* p. 377.

12. Arthur Yencken to R. A. Butler, 28 March 1941, P.R.O., F.O. 371/26974/13/18/41, The National Archives.

13. Queen Victoria Eugenie to Lord Mottistone, 3 November 1944, MSS 6/144, Mottistone Papers, Nuffield College, University of Oxford.

14. José Luis de Vilallonga, *El Rey: Conversaciones con D. Juan Carlos I de España* (Barcelona: Salvat Editores, 1995), p. 54.

15. José Antonio Gurriarán, *El Rey en Estoril: Don Juan Carlos y su Familia en el Exilio Portugués* (Barcelona: Editorial Planeta, 2000), pp. 134, 133.

16. Noel, *Ena,* p. 268.

17. Gonzalez-Doria, *Las Reinas de España,* p. 604.

18. Sir George Grahame to Mr. Bates, 7 March 1934, P.R.O., F.O. 185/1753/120/8/34, The National Archives.

19. Sir George Grahame to Sir Robert Vansittart, 14 February 1934, P.R.O., F.O. 185/1753/120/4/34, The National Archives.

20. Queen Victoria Eugenie to Sir George Grahame, 14 July 1934, P.R.O., F.O. 120/46e/34v, The National Archives.

21. Juan Antonio Pérez Mateos, *El Rey Que Vino del Exilio* (Barcelona: Editorial Planeta, 1981), p. 31.

22. de la Cierva, *Alfonso y Victoria,* pp. 383–84.

23. Pilar Urbano, *La Reina* (Barcelona: Plaza y Janés, 2001), p. 139.

24. de la Cierva, *Alfonso y Victoria,* p. 388.

25. Santos, *Victoria Eugenia,* p. 307.

26. Urbano, *La Reina,* p. 217.

27. Gabrielle Ashford Hodges, *Franco: A Concise Biography* (London: Weidenfeld & Nicolson, 2000), p. 243.

28. Charles Powell, *Juan Carlos of Spain: Self-Made Monarch* (London: Macmillan Press, 1996), p. 41.

29. Juan Balansó, *La Corona Vacilante: Historia Vida de los Borbones en España* (Barcelona: Plaza y Janés, 1996), p. 285.

30. de la Cierva, *Alfonso y Victoria,* pp. 389–90.

31. Urbano, *La Reina,* p. 222.

32. Queen Marie to Loie Fuller, 3 July 1927, MSS 1982-04-60, Maryhill Museum of Art, Goldendale, Washington.

BIBLIOGRAPHY

PRIMARY SOURCES

Interviews

H.R.H. Crown Prince Alexander of Yugoslavia
Lady Katherine Brandram (née H.R.H. Princess Katherine of Greece)
H.M. King Michael I of Romania

Unpublished Letters

United Kingdom
The British Library
William Boyd Carpenter Papers
Paget Papers
Lord Charles and Lady Scott Papers

Cumbria Record Office, Carlisle
Sir Esme Howard Papers, Cumbria Record Office, Carlisle

Hampshire Record Office
Knollis Papers

The Isle of Wight County Record Office
Oglander Papers

The National Archives—The Public Record Office, Kew
Foreign Office Files: 104, 120, 184, 185, 286, 371, 372
Metropolitan Police Office: 2
War Office Files: 32

The Public Record Office of Northern Ireland
Letters of Princess Beatrice to Louisa, Lady Antrim

The University of Cambridge
Letters of Queen Sophie to the Rev. R. W. Cole

The University of Oxford
Bodleian Library
Crown Princess Margrethe of Sweden to Lady Edward Cecil
Letters of Margrete, Landgravine of Hesse, to Hilda (Chichester) Cochrane

Nuffield College
Letter of Queen Victoria Eugenie to Lord Mottistone, Mottistone Papers

The University of Reading
Astor Papers

The University of Southampton
Correspondence of Alfred, Duke of Edinburgh to Countess Alexandrine Tolstoy, Mountbatten Papers, Hartley Library
Correspondence of Tsarina Alexandra to Prince Louis of Battenberg, Broadlands Archives, Hartley Library
Correspondence of Marie, Duchess of Edinburgh to Countess Alexandrine Tolstoy, Mountbatten Papers, Hartley Library

United States of America
Kent State University
Queen Marie of Romania Papers

Library of Congress
Collections of the Manuscript Division
Queen Marie, "A Mon Pays et à Mon Peuple"

Maryhill Museum of Art
Correspondence of Queen Marie to Loie Fuller

New York Public Library
Poultney Bigelow Papers

Stanford University
Correspondence of Princess Irene of Greece to Irina Procopiu
Correspondence of Princess Marie of Edinburgh to Queen Victoria, Royal Archives, Windsor Castle, copy deposited at the Hoover Institution, Stanford University
Correspondence of Queen Marie of Romania from the Queen Marie/Lavinia Small Collection in the George Duca Papers, Hoover Institution, Stanford University
Correspondence of Queen Marie to Baroness Ines Taxis Damenstofft

Private Collection
Letter of Crown Princess Sophie of Greece, 26 August 1901
Queen Maud to Grand Duchess Xenia Correspondence, undated
Queen Victoria Eugenie of Spain to Lady Llangattock, 14 January 1907
Queen Victoria Eugenie to Mr. Paget Cooke, 5 October 1938
King Haakon VII to Grand Duchess Xenia, 16 January 1939
Letter of Grand Duchess George of Russia (née Princess Marie of Greece) to Miss Barratt, undated

Published Diplomatic and Political Documents

Bourne, Kenneth, D. Cameron Watt, and John F. V. Keigers, eds. *British Documents on Foreign Affairs,* Part I, Series F: *Europe 1848–1914.* Vol. 1: *The Scandinavian Peninsula and Baltic I, 1855–1907;* Vol. 14: *Greece, 1847–1914;* Vol. 16: *Montenegro, 1914; Romania, 1878–1914;* Vol. 28: *Spain, 1908–1914,* all ed. David Stevenson and John K. V. Keiger. Frederick. MD: University Publications of America, 1987.

Butler, Rohan, and J. P. T. Bury, eds. *Documents on British Foreign Policy, 1919–1939,* First Series, Vol. XII. London: HMSO, 1962.

Lieven, D. C. B., Kenneth Bourne, and D. C. Watts, eds. *British Documents on Foreign Affairs: Reports and Papers from the Foreign Office Confidential Print,* Part I: *From the Mid-Nineteenth Century to the First World War.* Series A: *Russia, 1859–1914;* Vol. 3: *1905–1906;* Vol. 4: *1906–1907,* both ed. Dominic Lieven. Frederick, MD: University Publications of America, 1983.

Seton, Christopher, Kenneth Bourne, and D. C. Watts, eds. *British Documents on Foreign Affairs,* Part II. Series F: *Europe, 1919–1939.* Vol. 5: *Italy and South-Eastern Europe, July 1921–December 1923;* Vol. 8: *Italy and South-Eastern Europe, January 1929–June 1931;* Vol. 25: *Spain, March 1919–June 1931;* all ed. Antony Adamthwaite. Frederick, MD: University Publications of America, 1990.

The Greek White Book: Supplementary Diplomatic Documents, 1913–1917. New York: Oxford University Press, 1919.

Parliamentary Debates, Fourth Series. Vol. LXXXIX. *Edward VII.* London: Wyman & Sons, 1901.

Woodward, E. L., and Rohan Butler, eds. *Documents on British Foreign Policy,* First Series. Vol. VI: *1919.* London: HMSO, 1956.

Periodicals

The Daily Mail
The Family Herald
Illustrated London News
The New York Times
The Times

Published Letters and Memoirs

Albany, Princess Alice of. *For My Grandchildren: Some Reminiscences of H.R.H. Princess Alice, Countess of Athlone.* London: Evans Brothers, 1966.

Alexander, Grand Duke. *Once a Grand Duke.* Garden City, NY: Garden City Publishing Co., 1932.

———. *Twilight of Royalty.* New York: Ray Long & Richard R. Smith, 1932.

Alexandra, Queen of Yugoslavia, *For Love of a King.* Garden City, NY: Doubleday & Co., 1956.

Anonymous. *The Royal Family of Greece: King Constantine, Queen Sophie, Their Royal Relatives and Some Events.* Toronto: Warwick Brothers & Rutter, 1914.

———. *Russian Court Memoirs 1914–1916.* Cambridge: Ian Faulkner Publishing, 1992.

Balsan, Consuelo Vanderbilt. *The Glitter and the Gold.* New York: Harper & Brothers, 1952.

Benckendorff, Count Paul. *Last Days at Tsarskoe Selo: Being the Personal Notes and Memories of Count Paul Benckendorff,* trans. Maurice Baring. London: William Heinemann, 1927.

Benson, Arthur Christopher, and Viscount Esher, eds. *The Letters of Queen Victoria: A Selection from Her Majesty's Correspondence Between the Years 1837 and 1861.* Vol. III. London: John Murray, 1907.

Benson, E. F. *As We Were: A Victorian Peep-Show.* London: Longmans, Green & Co., 1932.

Bing, Edward J., ed. *The Letters of Tsar Nicholas and Empress Marie: Being the Confidential Correspondence Between Nicholas II, Last of the Tsars, and His Mother, Dowager Empress Marie Feodorovna.* London: Ivor Nicholson & Watson, 1937.

Birtles, Bert. *Exiles in the Aegean: A Personal Narrative of Greek Politics and Travel.* London: Victor Gollancz, 1938.

Botkin, Gleb. *The Real Romanovs.* New York: Fleming H. Revell Co., 1931.

Bowers, Claude G. *My Mission to Spain: Watching the Rehearsal for World War II.* New York: Simon & Schuster, 1954.

Boyd, Rt. Rev. W. Carpenter. *Further Pages of My Life.* London: Williams & Norgate, 1916.

———. *Some Pages of My Life.* London: Williams & Norgate, 1911.

Buchanan, Sir George. *My Mission to Russia and Other Diplomatic Memories.* Vol. I. Boston: Little, Brown, 1923.

———. *My Mission to Russia and Other Diplomatic Memories.* Vol. II. Boston: Little, Brown, 1923.

Buckle, George Earle, ed. *The Letters of Queen Victoria, Third Series: A Selection from Her Majesty's Correspondence and Journal Between the Years 1886 and 1901.* Vol. I. London: John Murray, 1930.

———. *The Letters of Queen Victoria, Third Series: A Selection from Her Majesty's Correspondence Between the Years 1862 and 1885 and Between the Years 1886 and 1901.* Vol. II: *1891–1895.* London: John Murray, 1931.

Bulygin, Paul. *The Murder of the Romanovs: The Authentic Account,* including *The Road to the Tragedy* by Alexander Kerensky. Westport, CT: Hyperion Press, 1975 [1935].

Buxhoeveden, Baroness Sophie. *The Life and Tragedy of Alexandra Feodorovna, Empress of Russia.* London: Longmans, Green & Co., 1928.

Callimachi, Princess Anne-Marie. *Yesterday Was Mine.* London: Falcon Press, 1952.

Cambon, Paul. *Correspondence 1870–1924.* Vol. II. Paris: Grasset, 1940.

Cantacuzène, Princess Juliana. *Revolutionary Days: Recollections of Romanoffs and Bolsheviki, 1914–1917.* Boston: Small, Maynard & Co., 1919.

Castellani, Aldo. *Of Microbes, Men and Monarchs: A Doctor's Life in Many Lands.* London: Victor Gollancz, 1960.

Christopher, Prince of Greece. *Memoirs of H.R.H. Prince Christopher of Greece.* London: The Right Book Club, 1938.

Collier, E. C. F., ed. *A Victorian Diarist: Later Extracts from the Journals of Mary, Lady Monkswell, 1895–1909.* London: John Murray, 1946.

Collier, William Miller. *At the Court of His Catholic Majesty.* Chicago: A. C. McClurg & Co., 1912.

Dehn, Lili. *The Real Tsaritsa.* London: Thornton Butterworth, 1922.

De Schelking, Eugene. *Suicide of Monarchy: Recollections of a Diplomat.* Toronto: The Macmillan Company of Canada, 1918.

De Vilallonga, José Luis. *El Rey: Conversaciones con D. Juan Carlos I de España.* Barcelona: Salvat Editores, 1995.

Duff, David, ed. *Queen Victoria's Highland Journal.* Exeter: Webb & Bower, 1980.

Elisabeth, Queen (and Henry Howard Harper). *Letters and Poems of Queen Elisabeth (Carmen Sylva).* Vol. I. Boston: Bibliophile Society, 1920.

Eulalia, Infanta. *Courts and Countries After the War.* New York: Dodd, Mead & Co., 1925.

———. *Memoirs of a Spanish Princess.* London: Hutchinson & Co., 1936.

Farmborough, Florence. *With the Armies of the Tsar: A Nurse at the Russian Front, 1914–18.* New York: Stein & Day, 1975.

Fotescu, Diana, ed. *Americans and Queen Marie of Romania: A Selection of Documents.* Iaşi: The Center for Romanian Studies, 1998.

Fulford, Roger, ed. *Beloved Mama: Private Correspondence of Queen Victoria and the German Crown Princess, 1878–1885.* London: Evans Brothers, 1981.

———. *Dearest Child: Letters Between Queen Victoria and the Princess Royal, 1858–1861.* New York: Holt, Rinehart & Winston, 1964.

———. *Dearest Mama: Letters Between Queen Victoria and the Crown Princess of Prussia, 1861–1864.* New York: Holt, Rinehart & Winston, 1969.

Fuhrmann, Joseph T., ed. *The Complete Wartime Correspondence of Tsar Nicholas II and the Empress Alexandra, April 1914–March 1917.* Westport, CT: Greenwood Press, 1999.

Gilliard, Pierre. *Thirteen Years at the Russian Court.* London: Hutchinson & Co., 1921.

Gwynne, Stephen, ed. *The Letters and Friendships of Sir Cecil Spring Rice: A Record.* Vol. I. London: Constable & Co., 1929.

Hamilton, Lord Frederic. *The Vanished World of Yesterday.* London: Hodder & Stoughton, 1950.

Hanbury-Williams, Sir John. *The Emperor Nicholas II as I Knew Him.* London: Arthur L. Humphreys, 1922.

Hardinge, Sir Charles. *Old Diplomacy.* London: Jonathan Cape, 1947.

Hibben, Paxton. *Constantine I and the Greek People.* New York: The Century Co., 1920.

Hibbert, Christopher, ed. *Queen Victoria in Her Letters and Journals.* Stroud, Glos.: Sutton Publishing, 2000.

Hough, Richard, ed. *Advice to My Grand-Daughter: Letters from Queen Victoria to Princess Victoria of Hesse.* New York: Simon & Schuster, 1975.

Howard of Penrith, Lord. *Theatre of Life: Life Seen from the Pit, 1863–1905.* London: Hodder & Stoughton, 1935.

———. *Theatre of Life: Life Seen from the Stalls, 1905–1936.* London: Hodder & Stoughton, 1935.

Ileana, Princess of Romania. *I Live Again.* New York: Rinehart & Co., 1951.

Ionescu, Adrian-Silvan, ed. *America Seen by a Queen: Queen Marie's Diary of Her 1926 Voyage to the United States of America.* Bucharest: Romanian Cultural Foundation, 1999.

Jonescu, Také. *Some Personal Impressions.* New York: Frederick A. Stokes Co., 1920.

Kennard, Lady. *A Roumanian Diary, 1915, 1916, 1917.* New York: Dodd, Mead & Co., 1918.

Kerr, Admiral Mark. *Land, Sea, and Air: The Reminiscences of Mark Kerr.* London: Longmans, Green & Co., 1927.

Kokovtsov, Count V. N. *Out of My Past: The Memoirs of Count Kokovtsov,* trans. Laura Matveev, ed. H. H. Fisher. Stanford: Stanford University Press, 1935.

Kozlov, Vladimir A., and Vladimir M. Khrustalëv, eds., *Last Diary of Tsaritsa Alexandra,* trans. Laura E. Wolfson. New Haven, CT: Yale University Press, 1997.

Kschessinksa, Mathilde. *Dancing in St. Petersburg: The Memoirs of Kschessinksa.* Garden City, NY: Doubleday & Co., 1961.

Latapie, Eugenio Vegas. *Memorias Politicas: El Suicidio de la Monarquía y la Segunda República.* Barcelona: Editorial Planeta, 1983.

Lee, Arthur Gould, ed. *The Empress Frederick Writes to Sophie, Letters 1889–1901.* London: Faber & Faber, 1955.

Le Quex, William. *Things I Know About Kings, Celebrities, and Crooks.* London: Eveleigh Nash & Grayson, 1923.

Lockhart, R. Bruce. *Giants Cast Long Shadows.* London: G. P. Putnam, 1960.

Mackenzie, Compton. *First Athenian Memories.* London: Cassell & Co., 1931.

Mallet, Victor, ed. *Life with Queen Victoria: Marie Mallet's Letters from Court, 1887–1901.* Boston: Houghton Mifflin, 1968.

Marie, Grand Duchess of Russia. *Education of a Princess: A Memoir.* New York: Viking Press, 1931.

———. *A Princess in Exile.* New York: Viking Press, 1932.

Marie, Queen of Romania. *My Country.* London: Hodder & Stoughton, 1916.

———. *The Story of My Life.* London: Cassell & Co., Vol. I, 1934; Vol. II, 1934; Vol. III, 1935.

Marie Louise, Princess. *My Memories of Six Reigns.* London: Evans Brothers, 1956.

Martineau, Mrs. Philip. *Roumania and Her Rulers.* London: Stanley Paul & Co., 1927.

Maylunas, Andrei, and Sergei Mironenko, eds. *A Lifelong Passion: Nicholas and Alexandra Their Own Story.* London: Weidenfeld & Nicolson, 1996.

Ministerio de Obras Publicas, Transportes y Medio Ambiente, Secretaria General de Comunicacion Organismo Autonomo Correos y Telegrafos y Patrimonio Nacional, eds. *Correspondencia Epistolar de la Princesa Victoria Eugenia de Battemberg al Rey Alfonso XIII, 1905–1906.* Madrid: Patrimonio Nacional, 1993.

Morris, Constance Lily. *On Tour with Queen Marie.* New York: Robert M. McBride & Co., 1927.

Mossolov, A. A. *At the Court of the Last Tsar: Being the Memoirs of A. A. Mossolov Head of the Court Chancellery, 1900–1916,* trans. E. W. Dickes, ed. A. A. Pilenco. London: Methuen & Co., 1935.

Mouchanow, Marfa. *My Empress: Twenty-Three Years of Intimate Life with the Empress of All the Russias from Her Marriage to the Day of Her Exile.* New York: John Lane Co., 1928.

Narishkin-Kurakin, Elizabeth. *Under Three Tsars: The Memoirs of the Lady-in-Waiting Elizabeth Narishkin-Kurakin,* ed. René Fülöp-Miller. New York: E. P. Dutton, 1931.

Nicholas, Prince of Greece. *My Fifty Years.* London: Hutchinson & Co., 1926.

———. *Political Memoirs 1914–1917: Pages from My Diary.* Freeport, NY: Books for Libraries Press, 1972 [1928].

Nichols, Beverley. *All I Could Ever Be: Some Recollections.* London: Jonathan Cape, 1949.

———. *25: Being a Young Man's Candid Recollections of His Elders and Betters.* London: Jonathan Cape, 1926.

Paléologue, Maurice. *An Ambassador's Memoirs.* Vols. I, II, and III. London: Hutchinson & Co., 1927.

Paley, Princess. *Memories of Russia, 1916–1919.* London: Herbert Jenkins, 1924.

Pantazzi, Ethel Greening. *Roumania in Light and Shadow.* Toronto: Ryerson Press, 1920.

Paola, Princess of Saxe-Weimar. *A King's Private Letters: Being Letters Written by King Constantine of Greece to Paola, Princess of Saxe-Weimar During the Years 1912–1923.* London: Eveleigh Nash & Grayson, 1925.

Pares, Bernard. *My Russian Memoirs.* New York: AMS Press, 1969 [1931].

Ponsonby, Sir Frederick, ed. *Letters of the Empress Frederick.* London: Macmillan and Co., 1929.

———. *Recollections of Three Reigns.* New York: E. P. Dutton, 1952.

Pope-Hennessy, James, ed. *Queen Victoria at Windsor and Balmoral: Letters from Her Grand-Daughter Princess Victoria of Prussia.* London: Allen & Unwin, 1959.

Ramm, Agatha, ed. *Beloved and Darling Child: Last Letters Between Queen Victoria and Her Eldest Daughter 1886–1901.* Stroud, Glos.: Alan Sutton, 1990.

Rich, Norman, and M. H. Fisher, eds. *The Holstein Papers: The Memoirs, Diaries and Correspondence of Friedrich von Holstein, 1837–1909. Diaries.* Cambridge: Cambridge University Press, Vol. I, 1957; Vol. II, 1961.

Rodd, Sir James Rennell. *Social and Diplomatic Memories, 1884–1893.* London: Edward Arnold & Co., 1922.

Rodríguez, Pedro Sainz. *Testimonio y Recuerdos.* Barcelona: Editorial Planeta, 1978.

Rubinstein, Arthur. *My Young Years.* New York: Alfred A. Knopf, 1973.

Saint-Aulaire, Comte de. *Confession d'un Vieux Diplomate.* Paris: Flammarion, 1953.

Sazanov, Serge. *Fateful Years: The Reminiscences of Serge Sazanov, Russian Minister for Foreign Affairs, 1914.* London: Jonathan Cape, 1928.

Seymour, Charles, ed. *The Intimate Papers of Colonel House.* Vol. I: *Behind the Political Curtain, 1912–1915.* London: Ernest Benn, 1926.

Steinberg, Mark D., and Vladimir M. Khrustalëv, eds. *The Fall of the Romanovs: Political Dreams and Personal Struggles in a Time of Revolution.* New Haven, CT: Yale University Press, 1995.

Sylva, Carmen. *From Memory's Shrine: The Reminiscences of Carmen Sylva,* trans. Edith Hopkir. London: Sampson, Low, Marston & Co., 1920.

Tantzos, G. Nicholas, and Marlene A. Eilers, eds. *A Romanov Diary: The Autobiography of H.I. & R.H. Grand Duchess George.* New York: Atlantic International Publications, 1988.

Victoria, Princess of Prussia. *My Memoirs.* London: Eveleigh Nash & Grayson, 1929.

Vidal, Emilio Mola. *Memorias.* Barcelona: Editorial Planeta, 1977.

Villavieja, Marqués de. *Life Has Been Good: Memoirs of the Marqués de Villavieja.* London: Chatto & Windus, 1938.

Viroubova, Anna. *Memories of the Russian Court.* New York: The Macmillan Company, 1923.

Vopicka, Charles J. *Secrets of the Balkans: Seven Years of a Diplomatist's Life in the Storm Centre of Europe.* Chicago: Rand McNally & Co., 1921.

The Widow of an American Diplomat. *Intimacies of Court and Society: An Unconventional Narrative of Unofficial Days.* New York: Dodd, Mead & Co., 1912.

William II, Kaiser. *My Early Life.* New York: AMS Edition, 1971 [1926].

Wilson, Edith Bolling. *My Memoir.* Indianapolis: Bobbs-Merrill Company, 1939.

Wilton, Robert. *The Last Days of the Romanovs: From 15th March, 1917, Part I—The Narrative, Part II—The Depositions of Eye-Witnesses.* London: Thornton Butterworth, 1920.

Witte, Count Sergei. *The Memoirs of Count Witte,* ed. Sidney Harcave. Armonk, NY: M. E. Sharpe, 1990.

Yousoupoff, Prince Felix. *Lost Splendour.* London: Jonathan Cape, 1953.

Zedlitz-Trützschler, Count Robert. *Twelve Years at the Imperial German Court.* London: Nisbet & Co., 1951.

Secondary Sources

Books

Abbott, G. F. *Greece and the Allies, 1914–1922.* London: Methuen & Co., 1922.

Alastos, Doros. *Venizelos: Patriot, Statesman, Revolutionary.* Gulf Breeze, FL: Academic International Press, 1978.

Allsebrook, Mary. *Born to Rebel: The Life of Harriet Boyd Harris.* Oxford: Oxbow Books, 1992.

Almedingen, E. M. *The Empress Alexandra, 1872–1918: A Study.* London: Hutchinson & Co., 1961.

Aronson, Theo. *Crowns in Conflict: The Triumph and the Tragedy of European Monarchy, 1910–1918.* London: John Murray, 1986.

———. *A Family of Kings: The Descendants of Christian IX of Denmark.* London: Cassell & Co., 1976.

———. *Grandmama of Europe: The Crowned Descendants of Queen Victoria.* Indianapolis: Bobbs-Merrill Company, 1973.

———. *Queen Victoria and the Bonapartes.* London: Cassell & Co., 1972.

Balansó, Juan. *La Corona Vacilante: Historia Vida de los Borbones en España.* Barcelona: Plaza y Janés, 1996.

———. *Por Razón de Estado: Las Bodas Reales en España.* Barcelona: Plaza y Janés, 2002.

Barkovets, Alia, and Valentina Tenikhina. *Nicholas II: The Imperial Family.* St. Petersburg: Abris Publishers, 1999.

Battiscombe, Georgina. *Queen Alexandra.* Boston: Houghton Mifflin, 1969.

Beavan, Arthur H. *Marlborough House and Its Occupants Present and Past.* London: White, 1896.

Bennett, Daphne. *Vicky: Princess Royal of England and German Empress.* New York: St. Martin's Press, 1971.

Bergamini, John D. *The Spanish Bourbons: The History of a Tenacious Dynasty.* New York: G. P. Putnam's Sons, 1974.

Betriu, Rafael Borràs. *Cambio de Régimen: Caída de lea Monarquía y Proclamación de la República.* Barcelona: Flor del Viento Ediciones, 2001.

Bibesco, Princess Marthe. *Royal Portraits.* New York: D. Appleton & Co., 1928.

Boia, Lucian. *History and Myth in Romanian Consciousness.* Budapest: Central European University Press, 2001.

Bomann-Larsen, Tor. *Kongstanken: Haakon & Maud—I.* Oslo: J. W. Cappelen, 2002.

Brooks-Shepherd, Gordon. *Royal Sunset: The European Dynasties and the Great War.* Garden City, NY: Doubleday & Co., 1987.

Buchanan, Meriel. *The City of Trouble.* New York: Charles Scribner's Sons, 1918.

———. *Queen Victoria's Relations.* London: Cassell & Co., 1954.

Buxhoeveden, Baroness Sophie. *The Life and Tragedy of Alexandra Feodorovna.* London: Longmans, Green & Co., 1930.

Calvert, Albert Frederick. *The Spanish Royal Wedding.* Taunton, Devon: Privately printed, 1906.

Carey, Agnes. *Empress Eugenie in Exile.* New York: The Century Co., 1920.

Charques, Richard. *The Twilight of Imperial Russia.* London: Oxford University Press, 1965.

Chavchavadze, David. *The Grand Dukes.* New York: Atlantic International Publications, 1990.

Christmas, Walter. *King George of Greece.* London: Eveleigh Nash, 1914.

Clear, Celia. *Royal Children, 1840–1980.* New York: Stein & Day, 1981.

Collis, Maurice. *Nancy Astor.* London: Faber & Faber, 1960.

Cook, E. Thornton, and Catherine Moran. *Royal Daughters.* London: Heath Cranton, 1935.

Cortés-Cavanillas, Julián. *Alfonso XIII: Vida, Confesiones y Muerte.* Barcelona: Editorial Juventud, 1966.

Corti, Egon Caesar. *The English Empress: A Study in the Relations Between Queen Victoria and Her Eldest Daughter, Empress Frederick of Germany.* London: Cassell & Co., 1957.

Cosmetatos, S. P. P. *The Tragedy of Greece.* London: Kegan Paul, Trench, Trubner & Co., 1928.

Cowles, Virginia. *The Romanovs.* New York: Harper & Row, 1971.

Crankshaw, Edward. *The Shadow of the Winter Palace: Russia's Drift to Revolution, 1825–1917.* New York: Viking Press, 1976.

Crawford, Rosemary and Donald. *Michael and Natasha: The Life and Love of the Last Tsar of Russia.* London: Weidenfeld & Nicolson, 1997.

Daggett, Mabel Potter. *Queen Marie of Romania: The Intimate Story of the Radiant Queen.* New York: George H. Doran Co., 1926.

De Jonge, Alex. *The Life and Times of Grigorii Rasputin.* New York: Coward, McCann & Geoghegan, 1982.

De la Cierva, Ricardo. *Alfonso y Victoria: Las Tramas Íntimas, Secretas y Europeas de Un Reinado Desconocido.* Madrid: Editorial Fénix, 2001.

De Vilallonga, José Luis. *El Rey: Conversaciones con D. Juan Carlos I de España.* Barcelona: Salvat Editores, 1995.

Derry, T. K. *A History of Modern Norway, 1814–1972.* Oxford: Clarendon Press, 1973.

Duff, David. *Eugenie and Napoleon III.* New York: William Morrow, 1978.

———. *Hessian Tapestry.* London: Frederick Muller, 1967.

———. *The Shy Princess: The Life of Her Royal Highness Princess Beatrice.* London: Evans Brothers, 1958.

Dugdale, Edgar T. S. *Maurice de Bunsen: Diplomat and Friend.* London: John Murray, 1934.

Durland, Kellogg. *Royal Romances To-day.* London: T. Werner Laurie, 1912.

Eilers, Marlene A. *Queen Victoria's Descendants.* Falköping, Sweden: Rosvall Books, 1997.

Elsberry, Terence. *Marie of Romania: The Intimate Life of a Twentieth Century Queen.* New York: St. Martin's Press, 1972.

Epton, Nina. *Victoria and Her Daughters.* London: Weidenfeld & Nicolson, 1971.

Erskine, Mrs. Steuart. *Twenty-Nine Years: The Reign of King Alfonso XIII of Spain: An Intimate and Authorised Life Story.* London: Hutchinson & Co., 1931.

Ferrer, Maria Teresa Puga Eusebio. *Victoria Eugenia: Esposa de Alfonso XIII.* Barcelona: Editorial Juventud, 1999.

Fox, James. *The Langhorne Sisters.* London: Granta Books, 1999.

Fulford, Roger. *Hanover to Windsor.* London: Collins, 1970.

Gonzalez-Doria, Fernando. *Las Reinas de España.* Madrid: Editorial Bitacora, 1989.

Gordon, Mrs. Will. *Roumania: Yesterday and To-Day.* London: John Lane Co., 1919.

Grabbe, Paul and Beatrice, eds. *The Private World of the Last Tsar: In the Photographs and Notes of General Count Alexander Grabbe.* Boston: Little, Brown, 1984.

Graham, Evelyn (pseud. Netley Lucas). *The Queen of Spain: An Authorized Life Story.* London: Hutchinson & Co., 1929.

Graham, Stephen. *Russia in 1916.* London: Cassell & Co., 1917.

Greve, Tim. *Haakon VII of Norway: Founder of a New Monarchy.* London: Hurst Publications, 1983.

Gurriarán, José Antonio. *El Rey en Estoril: Don Juan Carlos y su Familia en el Exilio Portugués.* Barcelona: Editorial Planeta, 2000.

Halstead, Mural, and A. J. Munson. *Life and Reign of Queen Victoria.* Chicago: H. L. Barber, 1901.

Hamilton, Lord Frederic. *The Vanished World of Yesterday.* London: Hodder & Stoughton, 1950.

Harcave, Sidney. *Years of the Golden Cockerel: The Last Romanov Tsars, 1814–1917.* New York: The Macmillan Company, 1968.

Harmer, Michael. *The Forgotten Hospital: An Essay.* Chichester, Sussex: Chichester Press, 1982.

Hijano, Angeles. *Victoria Eugenia de Battenberg: Una Reina Exiliada (1887–1969).* Madrid: Alderabán Ediciones, 2000.

Hodges, Gabrielle Ashford. *Franco: A Concise Biography.* London: Weidenfeld & Nicolson, 2000.

Hopkins, J. Castell. *The Life of King Edward VII.* London: W. E. Scull, 1910.

Hough, Richard. *Edward and Alexandra: Their Private and Public Lives.* London: Hodder & Stoughton, 1992.

Hudson, Katherine. *A Royal Conflict: Sir John Conroy and the Young Victoria.* London: Hodder & Stoughton, 1994.

Kalinin, N. N. *The Romanovs and the Crimea,* trans. Yekaterina Tabidze. Moscow: Kruk, 1993.

Kerr, Admiral Mark. *Prince Louis of Battenberg: Admiral of the Fleet.* London: Longmans, Green & Co., 1934.

King, Greg. *The Last Empress: The Life and Times of Alexandra Feodorovna, Tsarina of Russia.* New York: Birch Lane Press, 1994.

———. *The Man Who Killed Rasputin: Prince Felix Youssoupov and the Murder That Helped Bring Down the Russian Empire.* Secaucus, NJ: Citadel Press, 1995.

King, Stella. *Princess Marina: Her Life and Times.* London: Cassell & Co., 1969.

Kjellberg, Anne. *Dronning Maud: Et Liv—en Motehistorie.* Olso: Grøndahl og Dreyers Forlag, 1995.

Lee, Arthur Gould. *Helen: Queen Mother of Rumania.* London: Faber & Faber, 1956.

———. *The Royal House of Greece.* London: Ward Lock, 1948.

Lee, Sir Sidney. *King Edward VII.* Vol. I: *From Birth to Accession, 1841–1901.* London: Macmillan & Co., 1925.

———. *King Edward VII.* Vol. II: *The Reign, 22nd January 1901 to 6th May 1910.* New York: The Macmillan Company, 1927.

Lieven, Dominic. *Nicholas II: Twilight of the Empire.* New York: St. Martin's Press, 1993.

Lincoln, W. Bruce. *In War's Dark Shadow: The Russians Before the Great War.* New York: Dial Press, 1983.

———. *The Romanovs: Autocrats of All The Russias.* New York: Dial Press, 1981.

———. *Sunlight at Midnight: St. Petersburg and the Rise of Modern Russia.* New York: Basic Books, 2000.

Longford, Elizabeth. *Queen Victoria: Born to Succeed.* New York: Harper & Row, 1964.

Lowe, Charles, *Alexander III of Russia.* New York: Macmillan & Co., 1895.

Maccas, Léon. *Constantin Ier, Roi des Hellènes.* Paris: Editions Bossard, 1917.

Macmillan, Margaret. *Paris 1919: Six Months That Changed the World.* New York: Random House, 2002.

Madol, Hans R. *The Private Life of Queen Alexandra.* London: Hutchinson & Co., 1940.

Mager, Hugo. *Elizabeth: Grand Duchess of Russia.* New York: Carroll & Graf, 1998.

Magnus, Philip. *King Edward the Seventh.* London: John Murray, 1964.

Marcus, Della L. *Her Eternal Crown: Queen Marie of Romania and the Bahá'í Faith.* Oxford: George Ronald, 2000.

Massie, Robert K. *Nicholas and Alexandra.* New York: Atheneum, 1967.

Mateos, Juan Antonio Pérez. *El Rey Que Vino del Exilio.* Barcelona: Editorial Planeta, 1981.

Mclean, Roderick R. *Royalty and Diplomacy in Europe, 1890–1914.* Cambridge: Cambridge University Press, 2001.

Michael, Maurice. *Haakon: King of Norway.* London: Allen & Unwin, 1958.

Millar, Lubov. *Grand Duchess Elizabeth of Russia.* Redding, CA: Nikodemos Orthodox Publication Society, 1991.

Minney, R. J. *Rasputin.* London: Cassell & Co., 1972.

Mitrakos, Alexander S. *France in Greece During World War I: A Study in the Politics of Power.* Boulder, CO: East European Monographs, 1982.

Møller, Arvid. *Dronning Maud: Et Portrett.* Oslo: J. W. Cappelens Forlag, 1992.

Mullen, Richard, and James Munson. *Victoria: Portrait of a Queen.* London: BBC Books, 1987.

Nelson, Michael. *Queen Victoria and the Discovery of the Riviera.* London: I. B. Tauris & Co., 2001.

Nicolson, Harold. *King George V: His Life and Reign.* London: Constable & Co., 1952.

Nisbet, J. *The Empress Frederick: A Memoir.* London: James Nisbet & Co., 1913.

Noel, Gerard. *Ena: Spain's English Queen.* London: Constable, 1984.

———. *Princess Alice: Queen Victoria's Forgotten Daughter.* London: Constable, 1974.

Norman, E. R. *Anti-Catholicism in Victorian England.* New York: Barnes & Noble, 1968.

Packard, Jerrold M. *Farewell in Splendour: The Passing of Queen Victoria and Her Age.* New York: E. P. Dutton, 1995.

Pakula, Hannah. *The Last Romantic: A Biography of Queen Marie of Roumania.* New York: Simon & Schuster, 1985.

———. *An Uncommon Woman: The Empress Frederick, Daughter of Queen Victoria, Wife of the Crown Prince of Prussia, Mother of Kaiser Wilhelm.* New York: Simon & Schuster, 1995.

Paléologue, Maurice. *The Tragic Empress: A Record of Intimate Talks with the Empress Eugénie, 1901–1919,* trans. Hamish Miles. New York: Harper & Brothers, 1928.

Papacosma, S. Victor. *The Military in Greek Politics: The 1909 Coup d'Etat.* Kent, OH: Kent State University Press, 1977.

Pares, Sir Bernard. *The Fall of the Russian Monarchy: A Study of the Evidence.* New York: Random House, 1961.

Paul, Prince of Hohenzollern-Roumania. *King Carol II: A Life of My Grandfather.* London: Methuen & Co., 1988.

Petrie, Sir Charles. *King Alfonso XIII and His Age.* London: Chapman & Hall, 1963.

Phenix, Patricia. *Olga Romanov: Russia's Last Grand Duchess.* Toronto: Viking, 1999.

Pilapil, Vicente R. *Alfonso XIII.* New York: Twayne Publishers, 1969.

Pilar, H. R. H. Princess of Bavaria, and Major Desmond Chapman-Houston. *Don Alfonso XIII: A Study of Monarchy.* London: John Murray, 1931.

Plumptree, George. *Edward VII.* London: Pavilion Books, 1995.

Poliakoff, Vladimir. *The Tragic Bride: The Story of the Empress Alexandra of Russia.* New York: D. Appleton & Co., 1928.

Pope-Hennessy, James. *Queen Mary, 1867–1953.* New York: Alfred A. Knopf, 1960.

Powell, Charles. *Juan Carlos of Spain: Self-Made Monarch.* London: Macmillan Press, 1996.

Puga, María Teresa. *La Vida y la Época de Alfonso XIII.* Barcelona: Editorial Planeta, 1999.

Quinlan, Paul D. *The Playboy King: Carol II of Romania.* Westport, CT: Greenwood Press, 1995.

Radzinsky, Edvard. *The Last Tsar: The Life and Death of Nicholas II.* New York: Doubleday & Co., 1992.

Radziwill, Princess Catherine. *The Intimate Life of the Last Tsarina.* London: Cassell & Co., 1929.

————. *Nicholas II: The Last of the Tsars.* London: Cassell & Co., 1931.

Reid, Michaela. *As Sir James: Sir James Reid, Personal Physician to Queen Victoria and Physician-in-Ordinary to Three Monarchs.* New York: Viking Press, 1987.

Rennell, Tony. *Last Days of Glory: The Death of Queen Victoria.* London: Viking Press, 2000.

Rodney, William. *Joe Boyle: King of the Klondike.* Toronto: McGraw-Hill Ryerson, 1974.

Rodzianko, M. V. *The Reign of Rasputin: An Empire's Collapse.* London: A. M. Philpot, 1927.

Röhl, John. *Young Wilhelm: The Kaiser's Early Life, 1859–1888.* Cambridge: Cambridge University Press, 1998.

Rose, Kenneth. *King George V.* New York: Alfred A. Knopf, 1984.

St. Aubyn, Giles. *Queen Victoria: A Portrait.* London: Sinclair-Stevenson, 1991.

St. John Nevill, Barry, ed. *Life at the Court of Queen Victoria, 1861–1901.* Agincourt, ON: Methuen Publications, 1984.

Salisbury, Harrison E. *Black Night, White Snow: Russia's Revolutions, 1905–1917.* New York: Doubleday & Co., 1977.

Santos, Marino Gómez. *La Reina Victoria Eugenia, de Cerca.* Madrid: Afrodisio Aguado, 1969.

Sencourt, Robert (pseudo. Robert Esmonde Gordon George). *King Alfonso: A Biography.* London: Faber & Faber, 1942.

————. *The Spanish Crown, 1808–1931: An Intimate Chronicle of a Hundred Years.* New York: Charles Scribner's Sons, 1932.

Serrano, Matilde Lopez. *Royal Palace of Madrid.* Madrid: Editorial Patrimonio Nacional, 1977.

Seton-Watson, R. W. *A History of Roumanians: From Roman Times to the Completion of Unity.* New York: Archon Books, 1963.

Shelayev, Yuri, Elizabeth Shelayeva, and Nicholas Semenov. *Nicholas Romanov: Life and Death.* St. Petersburg: Liki Rossii, 1998.

Smith, Michael Llewellyn. *Ionian Vision: Greece in Asia Minor, 1919–1922.* New York: St. Martin's Press. 1973.

Sullivan, Michael John. *A Fatal Passion: The Story of the Uncrowned Last Empress of Russia.* New York: Random House, 1997.

Sulzberger, C. L. *The Fall of Eagles.* New York: Crown Publishers, 1977.

Sutherland, Christine. *Enchantress: Marthe Bibesco and Her World.* New York: Farrar, Straus & Giroux, 1996.

Tantzos, G. Nicholas. *The Inheritors of Alexander the Great: An Illustrated History.* New York: Atlantic International Publications, 1986.

Tatsios, Theodore George. *The Megali Idea and the Greek-Turkish War of 1897: The Impact of the Cretan Problem on Greek Irredentism, 1866–1897.* New York: Columbia University Press, 1984.

Taylor, Edmond. *The Fall of the Dynasties: The Collapse of the Old Order, 1905–1922.* Garden City, NY: Doubleday & Co., 1963.

Taylor, Leonard W. *The Sourdough and the Queen: The Many Lives of Klondike Joe Boyle.* Toronto: Methuen, 1983.

Theodolou, Christos. *Greece and the Entente: August 1, 1914–September 25, 1916.* Thessaloniki: Institute for Balkan Studies, 1971.

Tisdall, E. E. P. *Marie Feodorovna: Empress of Russia.* New York: John Day Co., 1957.

————. *Royal Destiny: The Royal Hellenic Cousins.* London: Stanley Paul & Co., 1955.

Treptow, Kurt W., ed. *Romania During the World War I Era.* Iaşi: The Center for Romanian Studies, 1999.

Tuchman, Barbara. *The Guns of August*. New York: The Macmillan Company, 1962.
———. *The Proud Tower: A Portrait of the World Before the War, 1890–1914*. New York: The Macmillan Company, 1966.
Tuhy, John E. *Sam Hill: The Prince of Castle Nowhere*. Goldendale, WA: Maryhill Museum of Art, 1992.
Urbano, Pilar. *La Reina*. Barcelona: Plaza y Janés, 2001.
Van der Kiste, John. *Childhood at Court, 1819–1914*. Stroud, Glos.: Alan Sutton Publishing, 1995.
———. *Crowns in a Changing World: The British and European Monarchies, 1901–36*. London: Grange Books, 1993.
———. *Edward VII's Children*. Stroud, Glos.: Alan Sutton Publishing, 1989.
———. *Kings of the Hellenes: The Greek Kings, 1863–1914*. Stroud, Glos.: Sutton Publishing, 1994.
———. *Northern Crowns: The Kings of Modern Scandinavia*. Stroud, Glos.: Sutton Publishing, 1996.
———. *Princess Victoria Melita: Grand Duchess Cyril of Russia, 1876–1936*. Stroud, Glos.: Alan Sutton Publishing, 1991.
———. *The Romanovs, 1818–1959: Alexander II of Russia and His Family*. Stroud, Glos.: Sutton Publishing, 1998.
Vassili, Count Paul (a.k.a. Princess Catherine Radziwill). *Behind the Veil of the Russian Court*. London: Cassell & Co., 1913.
———. *Confessions of the Czarina*. New York: Harper & Brothers, 1918.
Vickers, Hugo. *Alice: Princess Andrew of Greece*. London: Hamish Hamilton, 2000.
Volkhonsky, Felix. *Russia Under Alexander III1,* trans. J. Morrison. New York: Macmillan and Co., 1893.
Von Laue, Theodore H. *Sergei Witte and the Industrialization of Russia*. New York: Columbia University Press, 1963.
Vorres, Ian. *The Last Grand Duchess: Her Imperial Highness Grand Duchess Olga Alexandrovna*. New York: Charles Scribner's Sons, 1965.
Walsh, Edmund A. *The Fall of the Russian Empire*. Boston: Little, Brown, 1928.
Welch, Frances. *The Romanovs & Mr. Gibbes: The Story of the Englishman Who Taught the Children of the Last Tsar*. London: Short Books, 2002.
Wheeler-Bennett, Sir John W. *King George VI: His Life and Reign*. London: Macmillan, 1965.
Ziegler, Philip. *King Edward VIII*. New York: Alfred A. Knopf, 1991.

Articles and Essays

Axworthy, Mark. "Through British Eyes: Romanian Military Performance in World War I," in Kurt W. Treptow, ed., *Romania During the World War I Era*. Iaşi: The Center for Romanian Studies, 1999.
Cecil, Lamar. "William II and His Russian 'Colleagues,'" in Carole Fink, Isabel V. Hull, and MacGregor Knox, eds., *German Nationalism and the European Response, 1890–1945*. Norman, OK: University of Oklahoma Press, 1985.
De Vilmorin, Genevieve. "The Queen of Spain's Own Story," *Chatelaine* (May 1962).
Di Iorio, Anthony. "Italy and Rumania in 1914: The Italian Assessment of the Rumanian Situation, 1907 to 1914," in *Rumanian Studies: An International Annual of the Humanities and Social Sciences*. Vol. IV: *1976–1979*. Leiden: E. J. Brill, 1979.
Dutton, David. "The Deposition of King Constantine of Greece, June 1917: An Episode in Anglo-French Diplomacy," *Canadian Journal of History*, vol. 12, no. 4 (1977).

Fotescu, Diana. "Regina Maria şi războiul de întregire naţională," in Treptow, ed., *Romania During the World War I Era.*

Hartt, Mary Bronson. "Haakon VII, The New King of Norway," *The Outlook,* 23 June 1906.

McLean, Roderick R. "Kaiser Wilhelm II and his Hessian Cousin: Intra-state Relations in the German Empire and International Dynastic Politics, 1890–1918," *German History,* vol. 19, no. 1 (2001).

Mommsen, Wolfgang J. "Kaiser Wilhelm II and German Politics," *Journal of Contemporary History,* 25 (1990).

Nord, Max. "Sisters of the German Kaiser," *The Scrap Book,* August 1908.

Romero, Francisco. "Spain and the First World War," in Sebastian Balfour and Paul Preston, eds., *Spain and the Great Powers in the Twentieth Century.* New York: Routledge, 1999.

Saz, Ismael. "Foreign Policy Under the Dictatorship of Primo de Rivera," in Sebastian Balfour and Paul Preston, eds., *Spain and the Great Powers in the Twentieth Century.* New York: Routledge, 1999.

Documentary

Interview with Dmitri Likhachev in *The Last of the Czars: Part Two—The Shadow of Rasputin,* The Discovery Channel, 1996.

INDEX

X, Dr., 14–15
Xenia Alexandrovna, Grand Duchess, 44,
    85, 93, 119, 368, 369–70

Yakimov, Analoy, 270
Yeltsin, Boris, 385
Young, Mrs. George, 141
Youssopov, Felix, assassination of
    Rasputin, 250–53

Youssopov, Marie, 253
Youssopov Palace, 250
Yurovsky, Jacob, 270–71

Zaïmis, Alexandros, 261
Zarzuela Palace, 380
Zedlitz-Trützchler, Count Robert, 26
Zvegintsev, Alexander, 254
Zwiedineck, General, 346, 351, 360, 364